WRISTWATCH ANNUAL

2026

THE CATALOG

of

PRODUCERS, PRICES, MODELS,

and

SPECIFICATIONS

BY PETER BRAUN

WITH MARTON RADKAI

ABBEVILLE PRESS

New York London

CONTENTS

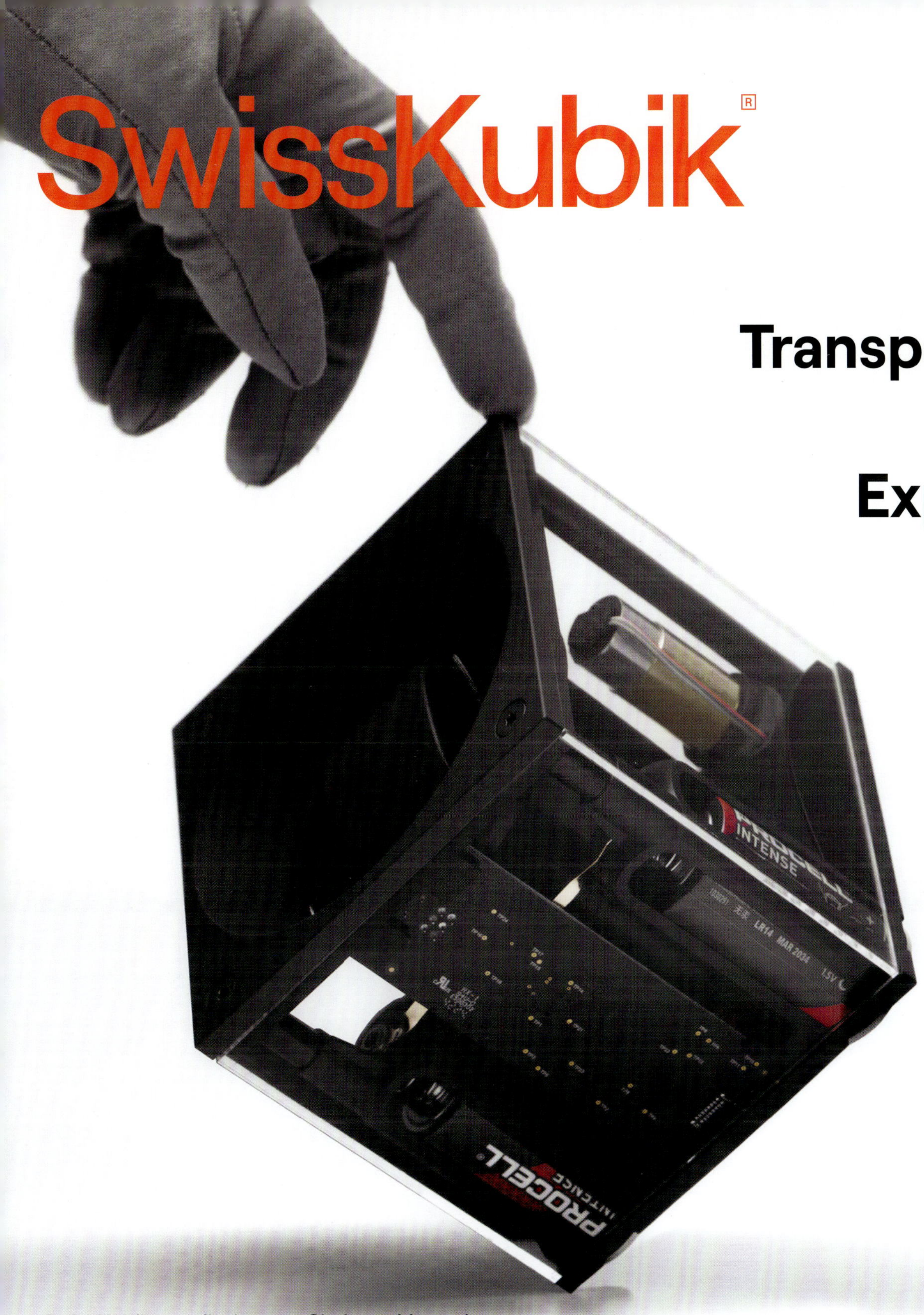

CONTENTS

Advertisers

Alexander Shorokhoff
Aristo
Azimuth
Curtis Australia
Detroit Watch Company
Edouard Koehn
Hong Kong Watch & Clock Fair
Itay Noy
JS Watch Co.
Kobold
Louis Moinet
Ming
Nivada Grenchen
Orbita
Parmigiani Fleurier
Pilo & Co. Genève
Porsche Design
Scatola del Tempo
Stollenwurm
SwissKubik
Tourby Watches
Tutima
Vario
Wempe Glashütte
Zeitwinkel
ZRC

Dear Reader,

If you are here with a copy of *Wristwatch Annual*, it's because you know, appreciate, and want to explore mechanical watches and their universe. By their very nature, they are symbols of stability, rationality, and self-control. Just think of all the power in a coiled spring being released in tiny bursts by a complicated braking mechanism. And many are beautiful, intriguing, funny, inspiring, practical, historic.

Unlike these products, the invisible hand behind markets does not function like clockwork. Markets are driven more by whims and ideologies, or "animal spirits," to quote John Maynard Keynes. Booms and busts are the rule. And the past year has been one of those periods when the animal spirits were running wild. 2026 is not looking much better.

As 2024 came to a close, the watch industry appeared to have regained a bit of bounce after some heavy weather—over-production, it seems. Then came the new US administration with its constant distractions, but above all its on-again, off-again tariffs.

Ironically, Switzerland received its punishment in the midst of the Watches & Wonders fair in Geneva in April. "Why us?" was a question I heard often. It's not the Swiss people's fault that they manufacture extremely high-quality products, especially watches. "Doesn't Donald Trump know that his own watches are made in Switzerland?" one Swiss journalist asked me, deep consternation in his eyes. Plus, American brands use Swiss movements and parts.

And yet, despite the disruptions, 2025 turned out a fairly good watch year, though according to experts, this was largely due to inventory liquidation. You might remember that before the tariffs struck, many brands shipped as many watches as possible to the United States. At any rate, the Big Three (Rolex, Patek, Audemars Piguet) maintained their grip, while the mid-level brands (up to about $20,000) had a dynamic year, including, interestingly, some independents—which may signal the emergence of a new generation of buyers seeking something different. One CEO, whose watches fetch upward of $20,000, told me sales were quite steady because the buyers had the income to absorb higher prices. Signs of an infamous K-shaped economy? "Yes," he said.

Speaking of independents: agility pays off. These small brands, who often must fight hard for recognition, have adaptability as a secret weapon. This year, I joined Elizabeth Doerr (see page 10) in examining the history of this movement and its rich

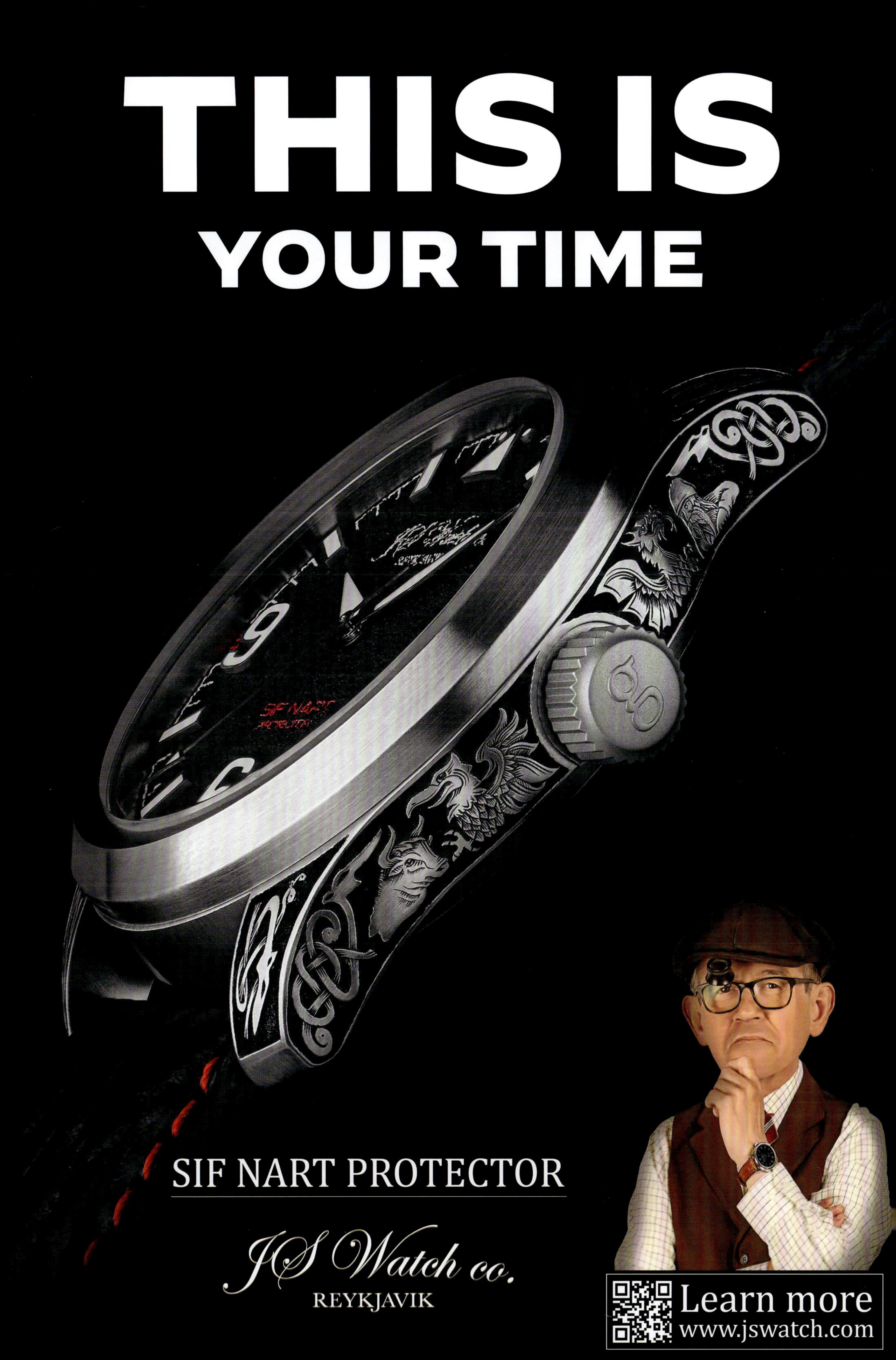

THIS IS
YOUR TIME

SIF NART PROTECTOR

JS Watch co.
REYKJAVIK

community of brilliant artists and engineers. One of the protagonists, Stéphane von Gunten, is given a place of honor in the Masters and Mavericks chapter (see page 20) alongside other individuals who contribute their personal art to the industry.

GET A GRIP

Uncertain times? Perhaps the solution lies on the cover of this book and in one of its main chapters. The Fool, the first figure of the Major Arcana in the Tarot, is an invitation to move through life with a light, inquisitive, humorous disposition, especially toward things we cannot change—see Magic Watches (page 26) for more on this watch and other horological nods to faith and mysticism. In that chapter you will find watches as touchstones for your beliefs, your faith, your spirituality, your intellectual puzzlement. Go with ease, the Taoists would say.

COTTAGE INDUSTRY

Watchmaking is a craft that needs constant nourishment. The British watch industry (see page 34) was by far number one in the world until the mid-nineteenth century, when it succumbed to Swiss and American competition. But it's coming back, and the cottage industry approach that contributed to its decay is now a strength, according to Roger W. Smith. The independent watchmaker, a leading actor in the revival, praised the "independence, honesty, originality, and a willingness to challenge expectations" of the recovering British watch industry.

KNOW THINE WATCH!

Wristwatch Annual is for collectors and enthusiasts. So, on page 44 you will find a selection of watchmakers and companies offering the experience of building your own timepiece. It is well worth the time and money, if only to step away from the permanent stress of living online.

As for this year's choice of brands, it ranges from the entry level to highest end. Among the new faces are the vintage specialist Nivada Grenchen; the ur-Swiss brand Favre Leuba; and Yellowstone, sister of Detroit Watch, joining its American brethren (RGM, Towson, Kobold, and Hager).

An important note: The pricing you find in the book are always subject to change. This year, however, they could be subject to veritable mood swings.

Finally, a word of thanks: Cindi Barton, Stephanie Sarkany, Erin Morris, and others helped review the text, managed the workflow in difficult times, laid out the chapters, and remained calm under pressure. Many thanks also to the brands that advertise with *Wristwatch Annual* and trust in the power of a real book filled

with images and original copy. Errors do occur—if you find one, please note it gently so we can correct it. And if you don't see your favorite watch or brand here, maybe next year. Have a great read.

Marton Radkai

WRISTWATCH ANNUAL
2026

The Catalog of Producers, Prices, Models & Specifications

This year's *Wristwatch Annual* cover features Stollenwurm's Series 2 "The Fool," the first card in the Major Arcana of the Tarot. The image, which symbolizes a new journey in life, was painted by artist Hannah Perry Saucier and then reproduced by the specialist enamellers Donzé Cadrans in Grand Feu enamel using champlevé and cloisonné techniques. The 42-millimeter case is crafted of platinum and tantalum and is just 8.65 millimeters high. It is water-resistant to 5 atm. The two parallel spring barrels of the automatic caliber, which was developed in collaboration with the Swiss company Télôs delivers 80 hours of power reserve. The movement's special architecture visible through the sapphire back showcases the signature Stollenwurm, a dragon with a cat's face, sliding through the gears. The Fool is made in a limited edition of five pieces.

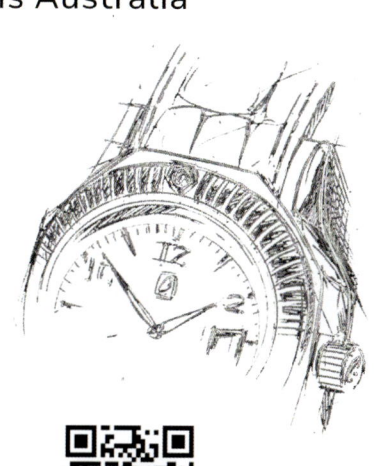

THE INDEPENDENT SCENE
PAST & PRESENT

BY ELIZABETH DOERR
WITH MARTON RADKAI

The indie watch scene is having a midlife crisis and, in spite of its serious challenges, seems to be loving every minute of it. Once born out of a kind of defiance, the movement has evolved into a full-fledged horological phenomenon, earning much admiration on the part of the industry and the collector alike.

The origins of modern independent watchmaking trace back to 1985, when Svend Andersen and Vincent Calabrese founded the AHCI (Académie Horlogère des Créateurs Indépendants / Horological Academy of Independent Creators). These brave idealists were choosing to work as individuals off the beaten paths in an industry that was dominated by big names—and to a great extent still is—and required some serious financial risks.

Nevertheless, this early international group of creative watchmakers proved pivotal, sparking a movement that revitalized a watch world still reeling from the notorious Quartz Crisis in Switzerland and demonstrating that watchmaking was alive and well outside of all the brand constraints that tend to hobble larger companies.

Over the years, the AHCI has included some of watchmaking's most illustrious and famous modern names, such as George Daniels,

1. Konstantin Chaykin meets Boticelli for a cheeky new "Wristmon" model.

2. and 3. Svend Andersen (l.), co-founder of the AHCI, and his slim Mundus world timer (r.).

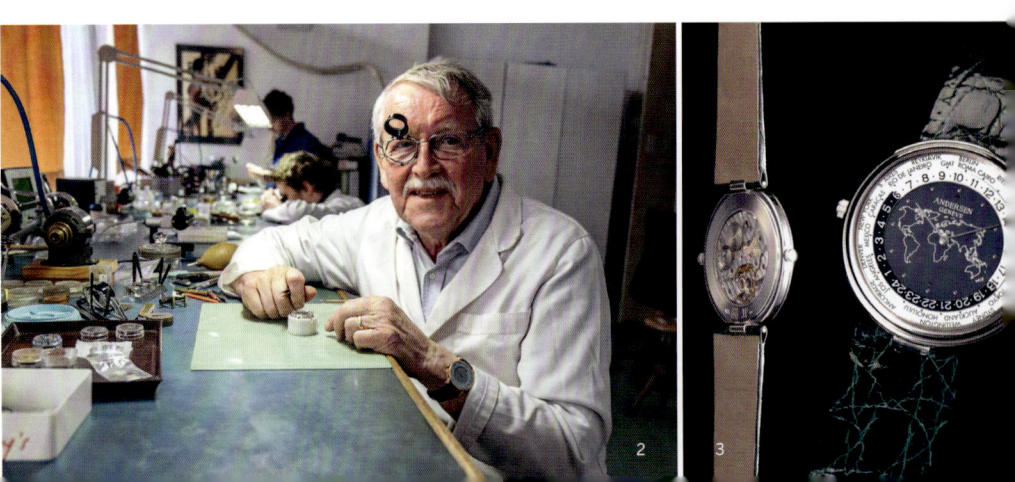

Philippe Dufour, François-Paul Journe, Franck Muller, Kari Voutilainen, Christiaan van der Klaauw, Konstantin Chaykin, and Vianney Halter. They are "all strong, independent characters," as "the godfather of independent watchmaking" Philippe Dufour said in an interview with Elizabeth Doerr in 2008. "The group has lasted so long because it provides young watchmakers the opportunity to exhibit."

Over the subsequent decades, more passionate watchmakers have taken the plunge into independence, some joining the AHCI and remaining "lone wolves" and some founding their own boutique brands instead. It is always a gamble. Some have managed to survive, others not.

SPREADING THE GOSPEL

The advent and development of the Internet changed everything. With time, printed watch media has largely given way to online opportunities and new business models. Crucially, social media—Facebook, Instagram, Snapchat, and TikTok—allows independent watchmakers to personally and directly interact with clients and prospective customers, opening new avenues and possibilities and expanding scope. This, in turn, has encouraged a greater number of watchmakers, designers, and enthusiasts, to fulfill their dreams and thus boosted the industry.

In the 2010s, a new term was coined for a slightly different type of independent watch company: micro brand. The hundreds of micro brands now in existence are typically small and independently owned, manufacturing on scales of a few hundred watches at a time. A great deal of these are design-led rather than led by mechanics and are therefore founded by a designer and/or someone who passionately loves watches.

An outstanding example of this is Ming, launched by Ming Thein, an ardent watch enthusiast and photographer who knew exactly what he wanted in a watch but just couldn't find it anywhere on the market. So he created it. Another example, of course, Gautier Massonneau, founder of Trilobe.

Price ranges vary greatly with micro brands, from a few hundred per watch to the very highest end. Their distribution models are usually direct, so many avoid all middleman mark-ups. One huge advantage of the micro brand community is a larger amount of transparency concerning origins of components; this is often even worn as a badge of honor. CODE41 is a great example with its policy of transparency of origin. The same can be said for now 20-year-old high-end boutique brand MB&F, who lists suppliers on its press releases and website.

1. and 2. Philippe Dufour, the excellence is in the detail.

3. Kari Voutilainen: the 28 Kohan features Japanese lacquer art to depict Finland's Lake Saimaa in autumn

4. Ming Thein plays with light and shadows and invents a unique high-tech polymesh titanium hybrid strap.

5. Ludovic Ballouard makes time disappear when it's not "now."

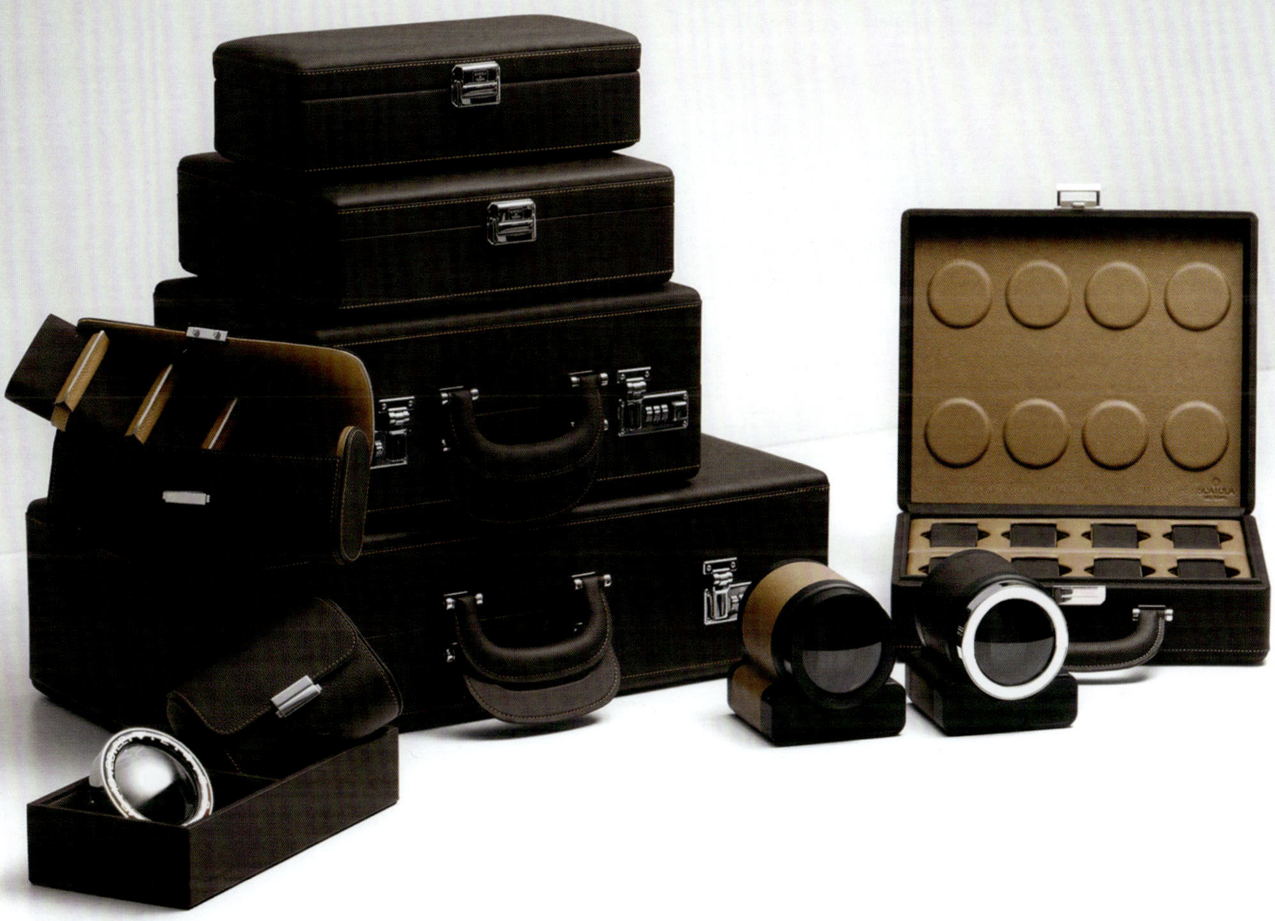

1

2

Some micro brand founders come from within the industry, like Octavio Garcia of Gorilla Watches, previously the head designer at Audemars Piguet. Two other excellent examples of higher end boutique brands led by previous employees of big brands include the stunning Artime, created and run by a handful of previous employees of Greubel Forsey; and Haute-Rive, founded by Stéphane von Gunten, an engineer and third-generation watchmaker who previously worked at Patek Philippe and Ulysse Nardin. Haute-Rive's first effort is a mechanical watch with an impressive thousand-hour power reserve. But you don't have to be wealthy to have a well-made, solid Swiss mechanical. Hakim El-Kadiri (see page XXX) revived Elka and now has a small showroom in Neuchâtel where he sells watches and locally made whisky along with clocks by Utinam, a brand from Besançon, France.

To increase their scope and spark intriguing new aesthetic ideas, many of these small brands and individual watchmakers have launched collaborations with other brands. Vianney Halter and Behrens or Louis Erard come to mind, or Studio UnderD0g and H. Moser & Cie. There is power in numbers of course, and who should know this better than the twenty-five or so brands that joined the Swiss Independent Watchmakers Pavilion (SIWP).

These valiant representatives of Swiss watchmaking show up in varying constellations at trade fairs far and wide, from the Hong Kong Watch and Clock Fair to the SIAR in Mexico City, from Singapore to Dubai, where they enjoy, in the words of Amarildo Pilo, "direct encounters between creators and enthusiasts."

5

MODERN TIMES

When the pandemic hit Europe and everything closed down, for about three months there was a distinct lull in business worldwide as manufacturers and consumers alike figured out how to deal with sheltering in place . . . in front of a computer screen. The situation was new, and at first shopping was the furthest thing from anyone's mind. But in the summer of 2020—a moment in time when things briefly opened again and people had gotten used to the new situation—things changed. Xavier de Roquemaurel, CEO of Czapek (see page XXX), remembers that strange moment well. The company was in its fifth year and moving forward at a snail's pace, when he suddenly found himself driving frantically around Switzerland's Jura Mountains transporting various components for final assembly. "We feared everything

1. Gorilla Watches: Swiss-made, innovative materials, affordable prices.

2. Hakim El-Kadiri keeps it simple with his Elka brand.

3. The traveling horologists of the Swiss Independent Watch Pavilion (SIWP) led by Amarildo Pilo.

4. and 5. An electric meter inspired the KWH, a collaboration between Behrens' Lin Binggiang (l.) and Vianney Halter (r.)

6. and 7. Explosive growth: Xavier de Roquemaurel and the 2025 Antarctique Plique-à-Jour

This loose group was founded in 2012 by Amarildo Pilo (page XXX) and Stéphane Gréco, who run their own independent brands in Geneva. Their mission, says Pilo, is "to promote exclusively independent watchmaking based in Switzerland and offer the public 'another side of watchmaking,' as a complementary alternative to the industrial brands." Besides the two founders, the SIWP includes such names as Adriatica, David Candaux, H992, Vianney Halter, and more.

would collapse at first, and exactly the opposite happened," he recalls. "Suddenly, orders for our new Antarctique were flooding in so fast we could hardly keep up."

Little did de Roquemaurel know, he was experiencing a perfect storm created by "pandemic spending." A ramping up of sales was a phenomenon noted by practically all the independent watchmakers with their own e-boutiques and online sales outlets. MB&F founder and owner Maximilian Büsser told Elizabeth then that he, too, had expected to see at least a 50% drop in sales that year. "[B]ut then something happened that nobody expected," he told her. "Our retailers were selling even though they were *closed.* And then May and June were incredible."

The sharp upswing was aided by MB&F's own e-shop, and 2020 ended up being a surprisingly great year for the brand—and practically every other independent maker with stock to sell. The thirst for new and unexplored horological creations was driving a boom among independents, especially since stocks of blue-chip companies like Rolex and Patek Philippe had sold out. In addition, online shoppers had the money to spend, and they found independent watchmakers.

Simultaneously, Geneva Watch Days was created. In the vacuum created by the absence of Baselworld, this easygoing, outdoor "fair" has become a meeting place for independent brands and creators. And other such venues have also been established with a focus on independent and micro brands and the ability to purchase watches on the spot. These include (but are not limited to) Windup Watch Fair in a variety of US cities, the Toronto Timepiece Show, and Timezones in Dubai.

All these factors lead to the reason that the general public is hearing more and more about independent watchmakers, boutique brands, and micro brands—particularly since some micro brands are quite affordable and easily accessible through the Internet. Some of today's hottest micro and boutique brands

include SpaceOne, Studio Underd0g, ID Genève, Benrus, Fears, Brew, AnOrdain/Paulin, Massena Lab, Ming, Furlan Marri, Unimatic, Atelier Wen, Baltic, Christopher Ward, De Bethune, MB&F (also with its affordable sub-brand M.A.D.Editions), and Urwerk (the latter at the very high end).

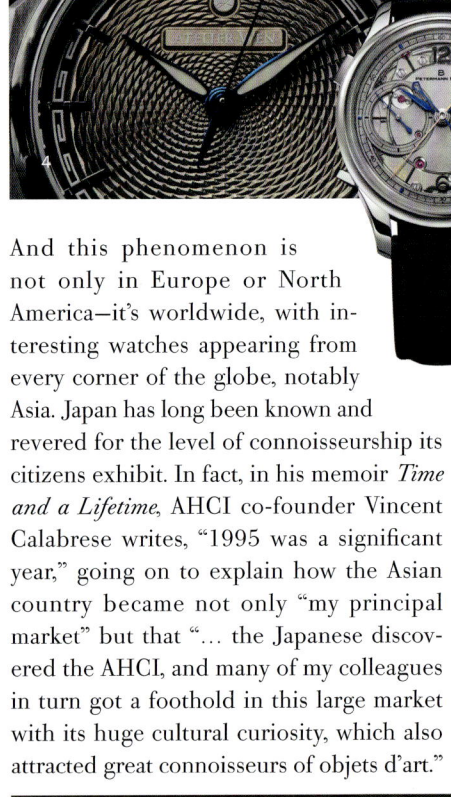

And this phenomenon is not only in Europe or North America—it's worldwide, with interesting watches appearing from every corner of the globe, notably Asia. Japan has long been known and revered for the level of connoisseurship its citizens exhibit. In fact, in his memoir *Time and a Lifetime,* AHCI co-founder Vincent Calabrese writes, "1995 was a significant year," going on to explain how the Asian country became not only "my principal market" but that "… the Japanese discovered the AHCI, and many of my colleagues in turn got a foothold in this large market with its huge cultural curiosity, which also attracted great connoisseurs of objets d'art."

While Casio and Seiko have dominated Japanese production for decades, it is safe to say that the country is now producing its own notable creators in indie spaces. These include (but are not limited to) micro brand Kuoe, for example, or Minase; AHCI members Hajime Asaoka with his very popular side micro brand Kurono Tokyo, Masahiro Kikuno, and Daizoh Makihara; and independents Norifumi Seki of Quiet Club and Masa & Co.

1. and 2. Max Büsser, the man who made independence edgy with series like the Legacy Machines.

3. The chiming watch by Alexandre Hazemann and Victor Monnin, winners of the 2023 F.P. Journe Young Talent Competition.

4. The Perception line by Atelier Wen European mechanics, hand-guilloché by Master Cheng in China.

5. Gaël Petermann and Florian Bédat: Reference 2941: a monopusher, split-seconds chronograph all made in-house.

6. Vincent Calabrese, co-founder of the AHCI and still going strong.

7. Kurono Tokyo's first GMT by AHCI member Hajime Asaoka, technology with a Art-Deco style.

While China still suffers from its image of "the world's forge" and the place to find cheap labor and cheap items, it has actually quietly developed a very strong and very determined fashion industry seeking authenticity, that is, a national expression. Watches, long on the sidelines, have also made it into the mix now, and are gradually being noticed. The Hong Kong Watch and Clock Fair is therefore evolving into an exciting meeting place for independents in search of an entry into markets in the East and a place to see what is happening in the Middle Kingdom. Indeed, visitors will find a remarkable number of Chinese brands there, some of which fall in the boutique category, like Hedone, Angles Watch, or Vario —not to speak of the larger brands like Behrens, CIGA Design, and Shanghai. And the next market might well be India. . . .

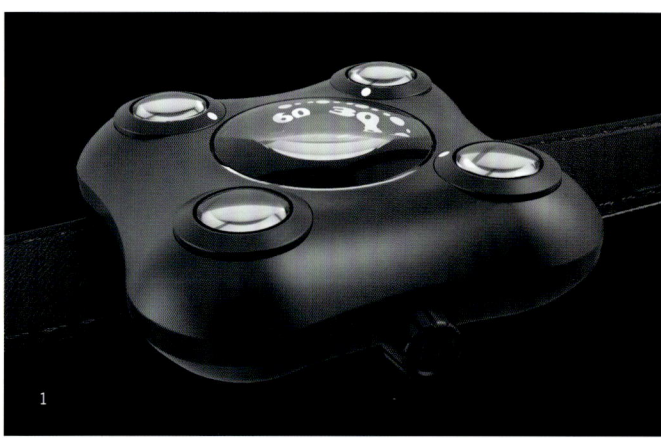

REACHING MATURITY

Today, the independent scene is wildly different from when many of us got into watches, a fact that Vianney Halter talked to Elizabeth about during Geneva Watch Days 2025. "We are dinosaurs in this world," the horological master of steampunk observed with a laugh. "And it's quite difficult for me to put myself into the mind and hearts of the new generation of watchmakers, who have experienced so much success so quickly—it took me 20 years to get where I am. Because the market is so different today, prospective clients focus so much more attention on them in a much stronger way. Covid was a huge factor; it allowed them to discover unique independent watchmaking.

"But we are still very few," he pointed out. "The quantity of watches produced by independent watchmakers is still next to nothing."

With prices ranging from the very affordable to the highest of high end imaginable, this segment of watchmaking is populated by creators who love what they're doing. More and more of these brands are appearing, so keeping up with them all could almost be a full-time job.

But was Halter deploring the low output? Market thinking would say that fewer watches produced would maintain exclusivity. And the disproportionately low volume of watches as compared to the "big" established brands means the customer investing time and money into this segment certainly will never see anyone sitting next to them on an airplane wearing the same watch.

Elizabeth Doerr is a freelance journalist specialized in watches and was senior editor of *Wristwatch Annual* until the 2010 edition.

1. Angles Watch's Bastion by Roy Chan, a watch to conquer.

2. Fam Al Hut (Xinyan Dai and Lukas Young) clinch the Audacity Prize of the GPHG for their Mark I: highest-level steampunk.

3. Casquette redux by Amida (Matthieu Allègre) covered in a sapphire crystal.

MASTERS & MAVERICKS

BY MARTON RADKAI

It takes genuine passion to devote years to an art as intricate as watchmaking, and the industry really benefits from gifted individuals who translate some of the most highfalutin' ideas into reality. Three are portrayed below.

THE STRETCHER OF TIME

Some people radiate intensity without saying a word, like unexploded ordnance. That was my first impression of Stéphane von Gunten when he presented his Honoris I in a small room at the Beau-Rivage hotel in Geneva in 2023.

The Honoris I is, at first glance, a strange watch. Parts of the movement seem to have broken through the dial. A wagon-wheel grid at twelve o'clock hides what appear to be a tight agglomeration of gear wheels. A flying tourbillon at six o'clock makes the watch seem very much alive. The time-setting mechanism is visible through a crack extending from the crown toward the center, secured by an X-shaped bridge. The thin hands indicate the time almost as an afterthought, stretching from the exposed setting mechanism to a narrow minute track tucked discreetly along the edge of the sprawling dial.

What is not immediately visible is the extraordinary 1000-hour reserve of power hidden behind the dial. The indicator on the movement side takes up the entire surface of the 42.5-millimeter timepiece, which is also quite thin at 11.95 millimeters.

In a measured French accent tinged with the lilt of his native La Chaux-de-Fonds, Stèphane von Gunten recounted the story of his firstborn watch: how it got its name and how it was conceived.

Von Gunten was born into a family whose ties to watchmaking go back generations. He might have become an optician, he told me later, "because in our family we either made watches or glasses." But he chose the world of watches, possibly because his paternal grandfather, a watchmaker, would often come home for lunch and talk about his work at the *établi*.

After completing his engineering studies, von Gunten found employment in Geneva, notably at Patek Philippe. Ultimately, though, he returned with his wife and young family (they now have three children and two dogs) to La Chaux-de-Fonds. There he joined Ulysse Nardin, where his skill and creativity were quickly recognized, especially in the conception of iconic models, like the Freak and the Free Wheel, both of which display movement components prominently on the dial.

It was during the pandemic that he began reflecting on the story of his great-great-grandfather, Irénée Aubry, who originally came from the Jura but later opened a small workshop called the *Fabrique d'horlogerie* in the lakeside village of Haute-Rive. "It was really small, he may have had one employee," von Gunten told me. "A little like me now; I'm also all alone."

Aubry had made a name for himself with an eight-day pocket watch known as the *Hebdomas*. In 1887, he was asked—probably

1. Stéphane von Gunten, founder of Haute-Rive

2. Honoris 1 *Lagoverde*, 1,000 hours of power, dial inspired by Lake Neuchâtel

3. The power reserve indicator occupies the whole back

4. Carving the enamel dial to make the wavelets

5. Irénée Aubry's *Hebdomas* with eight days of power

by the local bishopric—to create a special watch to be presented to Pope Leo XIII on the occasion of his sacerdotal jubilee on April 1, 1888. Aubry conceived and built a unique piece with a staggering forty-day power reserve, which was then carried to Rome by pilgrims from the Jura Mountains.

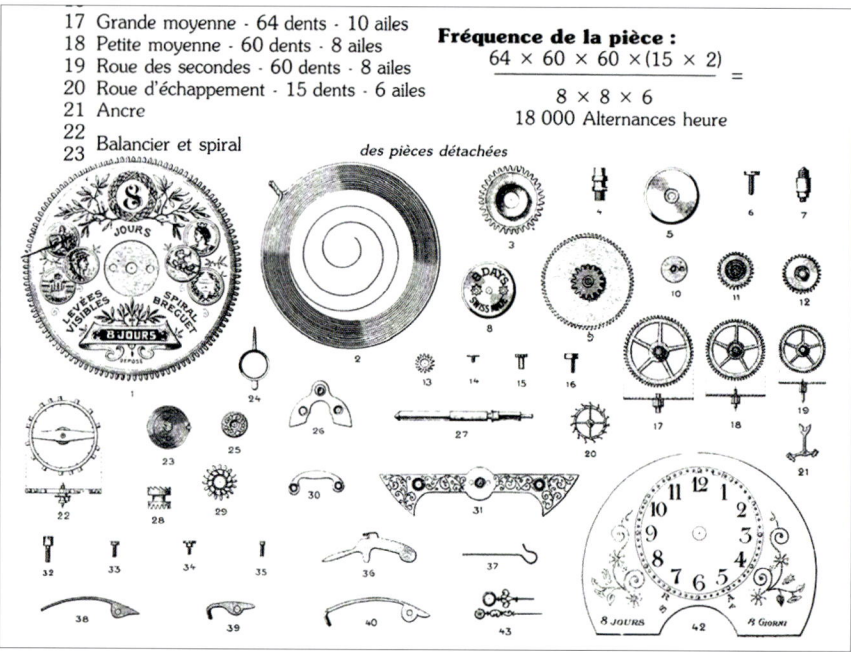

17 Grande moyenne · 64 dents · 10 ailes
18 Petite moyenne · 60 dents · 8 ailes
19 Roue des secondes · 60 dents · 8 ailes
20 Roue d'échappement · 15 dents · 6 ailes
21 Ancre
22
23 Balancier et spiral

Fréquence de la pièce :

$$\frac{64 \times 60 \times 60 \times (15 \times 2)}{8 \times 8 \times 6} =$$

18 000 Alternances heure

des pièces détachées

1

The original watch has disappeared from the public eye. The Vatican auctioned it off in 1982, and the buyer remains unknown. Determined to revive that spirit of ingenuity, however, von Gunten found his ancestor's hand-drawn plans and then sought out suppliers and investors who believed in his vision. The big challenge was translating the concept into a smaller wristwatch. In the end, the Honoris I's power reserve is, in fact, closer to forty-two days. Achieving this required a single three-meter-long mainspring, coiled between the dial and mainplate. This, in turn, created a separate set of technical challenges. Chief among them was how to wind the watch. A selector at 2 o'clock connected to a column wheel lets the user select time-setting via the crown or winding by turning the slightly fluted bezel counterclockwise.

The Honoris I is a deepfelt tribute to a family legacy. Von Gunten has since produced the watch in several limited iterations, including the Lagoverde, whose deep-green tones echo the rippling waters of Lake Neuchâtel, where he frequently goes for inspiration. And since creativity is a never-ending process, we can safely look forward to an Honoris II.

1. The hand-drawn plans for the *Hebdomas* pocket watch

2. The "Woman with a Flower" drawn precisely before being "wired."

3. and 4. Sylvie Villa and Marc Miehlbradt, founders of Wire Art

2

GOLDILOCKS

No one has to be stuck in a job once they hear the call for change. Sylvie Villa and Marc Miehlbradt began their careers in the world of science and electronics. She first learned how to draw and make printed circuits before studying physics at EPFL Lausanne, one of Europe's top technical universities; he studied microtechnology and has worked with several watch brands.

One process in making printed circuits involves using very fine gold wire to bond semiconductor devices to printed circuit boards. The process is done by machines that have been steadily improved to work much faster. This might sound like a banal

industrial step, but Sylvie Villa had heard from two Canadian chemists that the same machines could actually be used to create beautiful designs and drawings. "We proposed to develop the idea in Switzerland for use in watchmaking, but their company was not interested," she wrote to me. So, Villa and Miehlbradt founded Wire Art Switzerland in January 2017.

The drawings can depict figures, such as "Woman with a Flower," or various hypnotic geometric shapes. The weave of gold wire gives them real texture, depth, and even a shimmering movement. Wire Art collaborates with individuals who want to personalize a watch or ornament but also works with established brands. "I am the one who translates the designs," Villa said, "but now design teams deliver their desired models with their own wiring ideas." Wire Art recently collaborated with Louis Erard, for example.

Besides producing striking decoration, the company also makes use of bonding machines that would otherwise be scrapped because they can no longer keep up with modern industrial speeds. "Because we have to check each weld under binoculars, we do not seek speed," she explained. "On the contrary, we slow them down, and thus these machines end their careers with an artistic purpose."

3

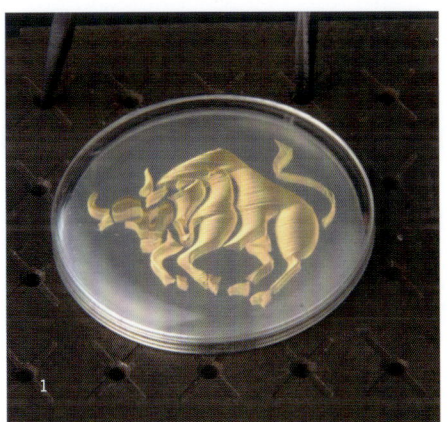

1

2

MAN IN THE MAKING

Grant Fryburger was bitten by the horology bug while still in high school. It all began when he bought an automatic watch from the Chinese brand Heimdallr. As he tells it, he then went down "the rabbit hole of YouTube" while doing his own research—proof that collectors and watchmakers alike can start simply, even serendipitously. "As I was learning more about watches," he wrote to me, "I discovered that a family friend, a horse-and-buggy Mennonite formerly in the furniture business, was a full-time watchmaker!" Perhaps living in Dundee, New York, a few miles south of Geneva, New York, had something to do with it.

He has since visited fairs and completed an internship with Christopher Ward in England. "I was given a desk and some tools, and over my time there I did dial, hand, date-wheel, and case-back swaps—and even serviced one of the watches, which was pretty cool." In the meantime, he applied for and was accepted to the Rolex Watchmaking Training Center in Dallas, Texas.

Fryburger is multitalented. In 2025, he began drawing horologically inspired comics—a niche in a field that often takes itself quite seriously. His takes on the industry are cool, deadpan, and gently ironic. One drawing shows a Cartier Tank-style watch asking a more baroque Gerald Charles-type piece, "Does this strap make me look fat?" Good ideas travel fast: Fryburger soon saw his cartoons enliven the pages of *Horological Times.* It's a niche he now hopes to expand into other industries as well.

4

Audemars Piguet R & D

Regal Elm
Imperial Oak
Noble Birch
Royal Spruce
King Cedar
Sovereign Pine

We're close Johnson... I can feel it

5

1. and 2. Swiss icons as decor for watches or jewelry: a bull (top) and the Matterhorn in a frame with an Edelweiss

3. and 4. Grant Fryburger of New York, watchmaker in the making and cartoon observer of the industry

MAGIC WATCHES

BY MARTON RADKAI

Watches both tell time and represent it and are, as such, symbols of a metaphysical, one could even say spiritual, dimension of existence. And some modern watchmakers boldly imbue their creations with references to those mysteries.

1

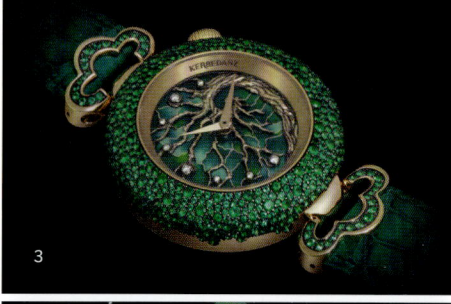

1. The Year of the Fire Horse: Symbolizing energy, power, passion, and visibility—especially for those born in 1966, the last such year—celebrated here by Shanghai Watch. (source: Erin Morris, Evergreen Design Studio)

2. – 6. Amulets on the wrist: Jewels and watches evoking the spiritual dimension of life. (2) The Egyptian *Eye of Horus* offers protection and wisdom (source: Siren-Com, CC BY-SA 4.0), also reimagined (5) in a model by CIGA Design. (3) *Tree of Life* by Kerbedanz—symbol of death, rebirth, and connection between sky, earth, and underworld. (4 and 5) Ity Now's *Hebrew Identity* with a Star of David made of two interlocking isosceles triangles, uniting heaven and earth. (6) *Elka x Ace Jewelers* celebrates Eastern Arabic culture.

Throughout history, jewelry has served many purposes besides embellishment of the self and expressing social and economic status. Necklaces, bracelets, and rings made of precious stones and metals, along with other accessories, have also been used to remind the wearer of a deeper meaning to life, whether real or imagined, like touchstones to a spiritual and invisible realm. They have also been worn to ward off illness, misfortune, or evil. One thinks of the Eye of Horus or the scarab from ancient Egypt, or the myriad religious symbols people wear around their necks to connect with the divine: Christian crosses, the Throne Verse (Āyat al-Kursī) from the Quran, the Star of David, the ankh cross, or the Tree of Life.

In this ornamental lineage, the watch occupies a special place. On the one hand, it is an instrument to keep us in sync with social and professional rhythms, practical intentions that would label it as particularly unspiritual. But time itself is an invisible dimension that can only be tracked with the transformation of material, and it has puzzled philosophers, scientists, and other thinkers for millennia. Unfathomably, it flows just as our life does, through joys and sorrows, success and failures, and may be as finite as human consciousness. As far as we know.

Not surprisingly, watches—and clocks in particular—are frequently used as a medium to express a personal belief or a religious affiliation. One thinks of the extraordinary

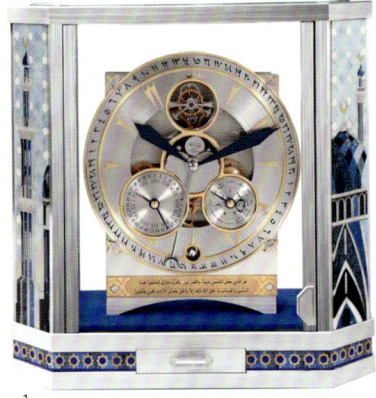

1

Hijra by Konstantin Chaykin or of Vacheron Constantin with their multiple calendars that directly connect to the history of major religions. Watches, due to their small size, make this relationship far more intimate. Itay Noy, for example, created the 42-millimeter Hebrew Identity, which features Hebrew letters as hour markers and a pattern of stars of David in the middle of the dial. The Eastern Arabic numerals of Arabic Identity, much like those found on a limited edition X series of Elka, immediately recall the world of Islam as well. A little company in Geneva, Switzerland, called Etoile came out with the Calendrier Hijri with a tri-retrograde day and Islamic month, a Gregorian calendar, and a moon phase, all made by Agenhor.

2

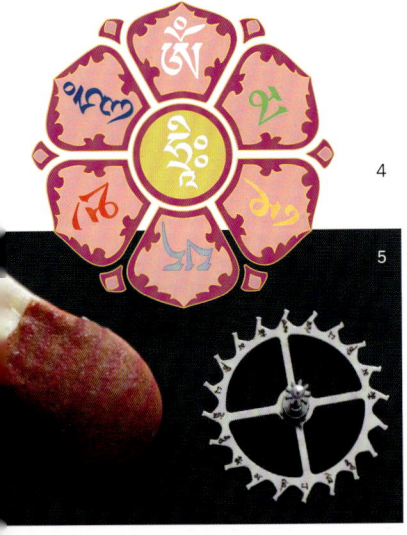

3

INNER PEACE

Eastern religions, philosophies, and their practices have long been a source of amazement and inspiration to people around the world. More than half a billion people today practice Buddhism in one form or another, often alongside other faiths. In Japan, for instance, many perform both Shinto and Buddhist rituals; in the West, it is not uncommon for Christians to embrace Buddhist meditation or philosophy as a complementary path.

4

5

6

This intersection of ideas found an unexpected echo in the work of Martin Klocke, founder of the watch brand Sherpa, launched in 2019. Klocke was first drawn to the design of an Enicar collection that originally gained fame in 1956, when the Seapearl model accompanied a Swiss expedition to the summits of Everest and Lhotse. Enicar, which today is in Chinese hands, capitalized on that triumph by developing its Sherpa line. For Klocke, an engineer by training, the appeal was both technical and aesthetic in equal measure. The cases of the original models were produced by Ervin Piquerez (EPSA), whose design ingeniously used the pressure of the water itself to reinforce the seal as the diver descended. The crowns featured gaskets made from a brand new thermoplastic material. EPSA went on to supply similar cases to brands such as IWC, Fortis, and Jaeger-LeCoultre, particularly for dual-crown dive watches with internal bezels.

As Sherpa began to gain traction, Klocke, who has been practicing Tibetan Buddhism for more than two decades, felt an increasing sense of connection to the Himalayan guides after whom his brand is named. He had never been to Nepal, but he knew about the omnipresent prayer wheels that are believed to spread positive energy through their motion. So, with his teacher's blessing, he created the Mantramatic movement based on a Sellita SW 200-1 for his OPS and Ultradives. Using femtosecond laser technology and a specially designed font, he had the sacred phrase *Om mani padme hum* engraved onto the seconds wheel. "The wheels inside the movement rotate constantly, sending out vibes of love, wisdom, and compassion from your wrist straight into the world 30 million times per year," he told me. His customers can ask for other prayers of good wishes to be inscribed in or on the watch. Needless to say, Klocke has made sure that a portion of proceeds from his Sherpas support charitable initiatives in Nepal, from education and school programs to environmental clean-up projects in the mountains his watches quietly celebrate.

7

1. and 2. Astronomy meets spirit: Konstantin Chaykin's *Lunar Hijra* clock follows the Islamic lunar calendar, while Étoile's triretrograde watch unites Gregorian and Islamic time.

3. – 7. Sending out prayers: *The Mantramatic* movement in Martin Klocke's Sherpa Watches (3) draws from Tibetan Buddhist prayer wheels (6 Source: ISivakumar, CC BY-SA 3.0). The mantra Om *Mani Padme Hum*—a call for compassion (4)—is femto-laser-inscribed on the seconds wheel (5 and 6).

THE WAY

China's intellectual and spiritual roots are ancient and complex, mixing Confucianism and Taoism as two ways of life and philosophies, with an older religion, the Five Deities, and then Buddhism, which began spreading in China as of the first century AD. Altogether, they have shaped Chinese society and customs and have created a veritable encyclopedia of symbols and irrepressible aesthetic traditions. I explored the movement known as *guochao*, or "national trend" in *Wristwatch Annual 2024*, noting some of the more visible symbols, from dragons to special numbers, but also elements that the Western eye might not pick up so easily. A case in point: the round case and square movement of CIGA Design's Fang Yuan, meaning squares and circles, or Earth and Sky respectively, the dual nature of existence, which in turn is perfectly represented by the wristwatch: the heavens (the aesthetic) are spiritual and expansive, representing eternal time, while earth (the mechanism) embodies the physical (i.e., finite, perishable) and grounded elements. The Yin and the Yang.

Present watches, a Chinese brand, has tapped into much of Chinese philosophical lore for its inspiration. The Loto's dial for example, features a lotus made of natural jadeite and mother-of-pearl. As a flower of great beauty that is found in muddy, murky waters, the lotus often appears in Chinese creation myths, where it represents the emergence of life from chaos. It also reminds the wearer to always remain dignified when facing the slings and arrows of the ambient world.

In a more philosophical vein is the Dejavu with its three butterflies recalling the dream

1. Wisdom of the East: Philosopher Zhuangzi and the waterfall embody wu-wei (無爲) suggesting: "in turbulent times, go with the flow."

2. The Way: Early representation of the Tao (道).

3. – 6. Spirit on the wrist: Modern creations honor the Buddha (3) and Zhuangzi's dream of butterflies (4). CIGA Design's *Jade* (5) reminds us we stand between Earth (square) and Sky (circle). Present's *Loto* (6) teaches dignity, even in muddy waters.

7. Mahakali (महाकाली): The all-powerful Hindu goddess of time and death, revered as the Goddess of Great Wisdom, with her ten heads symbolizing transcendence.

of the philosopher Zhuangzi, who woke up and wondered if he was a butterfly dreaming of Zhuangzi, or vice-versa, a universal and enduring comment on the nature of reality and identity. "The worldview of Zhuangzi, the idea of spiritual freedom and ease, is something many Chinese people aspire to, especially in midlife," shared Noelle Chow, who handles Present's communication. "This is also why tea drinking holds such a special place in Chinese culture. With a simple cup of tea, it's as if your consciousness has traveled to a place free from constraints." Achieving such calm is probably for all ages, especially in the frenetic energy of our twenty-first existence.

THE POWER OF TIME

Much like gravitation, time is an invisible and intangible fabric of our lives. Not surprisingly, myths and religions abound with very dramatic visual expressions of time. It is frequently depicted as an old man with a child, or a skeleton. The ancient Greeks had Chronos. Hinduism has entrusted time to the goddess Kali, the "Black One," who represents death, change, and creation. Her name is directly related to two Sanskrit terms that became mixed up in the popular ear: *kālà*, meaning time, and *kāla*, meaning black.

As Shakti, she embodies the dynamic energy that gives power to her husband Shiva, who is pure consciousness. And yet, while her appearance is fearsome, she is revered as a compassionate mother who destroys the ego to liberate her devotees.

People may well have been less stressed before the advent of clocks, when time was simply tracked by the sun's reliable rising and setting. Clocks, however, chop time up into discrete segments that tell us about quantity of time, but very little about its quality. So we can live as if it did not quite exist, an illusion Sylvia Plath captured so poignantly in her sonnet "To Time," which speaks of "ticking jeweled clocks that mark / our years," concluding later "we vaunt our days in neon and scorn the dark."

Honing consciousness of time and its passing was Emmanuel Bouchet's focus when he created his Complication One. It has two escapements: one to drive the seconds at normal speed on the movement side, real time; the other powers the large balance wheel that oscillates over the dial every fifteen seconds thanks to a Releaux triangle, whose three bulging sides drive the pallet fork. The minutes appear on a subdial but are read digitally: when one hand is on 5 and the other passes the 9, the hands go back to 0.

Bouchet's latest creation, the Source Aleph, repeats the topic of "decomposing time," as he puts it. Three cones made of various materials poke strangely out of the southeast quadrant of the dial. Bouchet compares them to mountain peaks or fir trees, which

is appropriate since they are made in the Jura Mountains famous for its pine woodlands. They each turn at different speeds: the one at 3 o'clock takes 12 hours, the one at 4 o'clock takes 24 hours, and the one at 5 o'clock takes a second, reflecting the idea that time flows subjectively.

Emmanuel Bouchet demands that we really consider time and its movement—an entity to be observed, felt, and mulled over. Meanwhile, life goes on. It's a silly quotidian platitude so frequently thrown out there . . . until life actually happens—with its myriad challenges, ups and downs, heartache and joys, dilemmas, and insufferably boring moments as well. French philosopher Henri Bergson, who also considered time as a state of consciousness, once wrote: "The road we travel through time is strewn with the remains of all that we once began to be, of all that we might have become." This is when that intangible dimension becomes real. This is the deeper message behind the Tarot series by the brand Stollenwurm, featured on this year's cover of *Wristwatch Annual*.

The name of the brand refers to a mythical dragon-like creature with the face of a cat and short legs, said to live in the Swiss mountains. This is precisely why founder Ed Tourtellotte chose to name his brand after a dragon-like creature from nineteenth-century Swiss lore—one that crawls among ores, the treasures deep inside mountains. "Besides the Swissness, it is the guardian of hidden

1. – 5. Does time pass quickly—or slowly? At his workbench (1 and 2), Emmanuel Bouchet created the *Complication One* with a slow-moving balance wheel (4). His *Source Ribbon* (3) and *Source Aleph* (5) feature rotating pyramids to show time's shifting pace. But does it really?

6. The Stollenwurm: Appears on the eponymous movement.

or lost treasures," he wrote to me. "It can be a ferocious predator or a benevolent creature depending on your intent and purity of heart."

The term *Wurm* ("worm") is actually an older German word for dragon. As for *Stollen,* they are the short, thick posts supporting mineshafts and allude to the creature's stubby legs. In southern Germany and Austria, the Stollenwurm is called Tatzelwurm—*Tatze* meaning a large feline paw.

The brand was launched in 2024. Tourtellotte, a Connecticut native with a thirty-year career in pharmaceutical technology, had been intent on launching a handful of new ventures, among them Stollenwurm. To make sure he could achieve his goal, he teamed up with renowned players in the Jura Mountains of Switzerland, like designer Antoine Tschumi, the case-maker AB Concept, and Donzé Cadrans for the Grand Feu enamel dials. Télôs was put in charge of the intricate, bespoke movements.

Stollenwurm watches plunge us into the world of mysticism, esotericism, and symbolism. The Series 1 features a day-date complication with the days represented by their seven ancient symbols for the Sun, the Moon, and the five planets (Mars, Mercury, Jupiter, Venus, and Saturn). In Roman times, each day of the week was imbued with a certain quality based on its patron deity: Luna for the soul, Mars for conflicts made visible, Jupiter for abundance, and so forth. In fact, Christianity's Holy Week is based on this symbolism, but let us not go into those more Jungian weeds.

For the second collection, Tourtellotte chose the Tarot, that series of cards developed in Renaissance Italy as a game that later became used for divination. The images of the 22 Major Arcana cards, each of which has a name, are striking and hold a certain fascination for anyone interested in symbolism: "I had the idea of combining métiers d'art, inspired by Vacheron Constantin, and the Tarot, inspired by the Fergus Hall deck from the 1974 James Bond movie," Tourtellotte told me. But even though he is a friend of Hall's, he was unable to secure the rights to the deck, and so, he asked his niece, Hannah Perry Saucier—a painter living in Barcelona—if she would be willing to paint the card designs for the watch dials.

1. – 5. The Alpine dragon reimagined: Depictions of the mythical *Stollenwurm*—a cat-faced Alpine dragon (1 and 2)—as it appears on *The Fool* movement (4), a watch drawing inspiration from the Tarot (5).

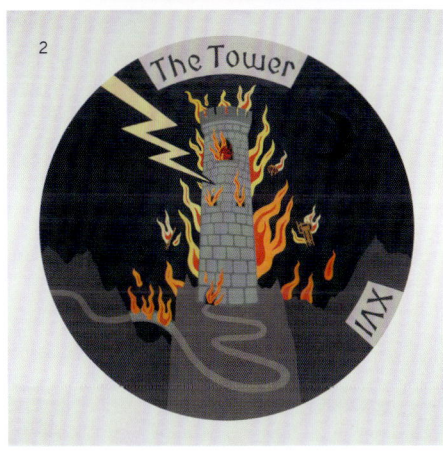

The Tarot tends to conjure images of crystal balls and palms needing to be crossed with silver to reveal the future of the querant. A more subtle reading of the Major Arcana, the "picture cards" reveals a path of initiation. The first card, numbered zero, hence the first model in the Stollenwurm collection, is the Fool. It is the archetype of that carefree wanderer ready to move through life with ease and confidence, very much in the spirit of an adept of Taoism. On his way, he—or she—will encounter twenty-one challenges or learning moments. The dramatic Tower, for example, casts us out of a comfort zone to seek a new beginning. The Hanged Man suggests looking at the world from a different perspective. There are also cards for the Lovers, the Hermit, the Hierophant, the High Priestess, and so on.

Saucier has her work cut out for her: "We aim to stay true to the original meanings while adding our own symbolism based on watches, time, Switzerland, and the Stollenwurm. This is why you see mountains in almost every card, for example."

CONNECTIONS

When we choose our accessories, and in this case our watches, we often do so in the spur of the moment. Something clicks and we engage in an unspoken dialogue with the object as if with an intimate friend, and sometimes with ourselves and our history. And how many people inherit a piece of jewelry, or even an old, sometimes broken watch, and will pass it down the family line. . . .

Many brands understand this human need for connection with an object as if it were a living being, and because a watch ticks and the balance wheel moves, it does seem possessed of life at times. Itay Noy's watches often play on this idea, like the City Squares, one of his first ever. When you look at it, you can see a familiar map. With his Fractal models, he went a step further. Time and space are infinite and the unpredictability can feel unsettling, so garnishing the dial with fractals, those infinitely repeating patterns, is a way of suggesting order in the chaos.

Of course, the "magic watches" mentioned above—and many more that I cannot mention due to space—don't really change anything empirically speaking. That is to say the change cannot be measured in pounds and ounces. What they will do, though, is tweak the wearers' consciousness each time they consult or otherwise view their watches. And that might well have an impact on the choices make in their daily lives, moment by moment.

1. and 2. Tarot in the making: Artist Hannah Perry Saucier painting the cards that will become enameled dials.

3. and 4. Order in chaos: Itay Noy's *Fractals*—a wrist-borne reminder that harmony exists even when unseen.

5. Good vibes: Elka's watch carries a message of peace.

6. Fuego Nuevo: Louis Moinet's celebration of the rebirth of the sun—a message of hope.

THE BRITISH ARE COMING!

BY MARTON RADKAI

No industry is safe from competition. Once dominant throughout the world, British watchmaking suddenly vanished. But lately, it has staged a real comeback.

Real innovation is not just a buzzword. Rather, it's the key to maintaining an edge in the face of competition. And for almost two centuries, from the 1670s to the 1850s, England dominated the world of watches thanks to several drivers working in perfect harmony.

In the seventeenth century, the scientific pioneers of the Royal Society, which included men such as Isaac Newton and Robert Hooke, laid the foundations for modern timekeeping through their studies of motion and mechanics. Their discoveries inspired a generation of skilled artisans and inventors, including Daniel Quare, Thomas Tompion,

Thomas Mudge, George Graham, and John Harrison. These craftsmen turned theory into precision instruments: Quare co-developed the repeater mechanism; Tompion refined the balance spring; Graham perfected the pallet fork and introduced mercury compensation; and Harrison, a cabinetmaker, created the revolutionary H4 marine chronometer that made accurate navigation at sea possible. His achievement secured Britain's mastery of global navigation and established Greenwich as the Prime Meridian—the reference point for time throughout the world.

In turn, these wizards thrived because watchmakers could rely on parts that met high quality standards set by the guilds and the Clockmakers' Livery Company. And during this time period, owning a watch and being on time became fashionable, even a bit obsessive. One of the early collectors known of, thanks to his diaries, was Member of Parliament Samuel Pepys (1633-1703), who noted in 1666: "The King hath yesterday in Council declared his resolution of setting a fashion for clothes, which he will never alter. It will be a vest…" And that new garment would have a pocket for holding . . . a pocket watch!

1. The Struthers: Seeking authentic Great British watchmaking

2. and 3. The "Father of British Watchmaking" Thomas Tompion and one of his repeater watches

GEORGE GRAHAM.   1

PRIDE AND FALL

By the mid-nineteenth century, Britain was manufacturing about half the watches and clocks sold in the known world. In fact, the industry was doing so well that some companies had even started outsourcing work to Holland and Switzerland where labor was cheaper.

But then the market moved to Switzerland and the USA, where interchangeable parts enabled mass production. The reason, according to Alistair Audsley, CEO and co-founder of the Alliance of British Watch and Clock Makers (ABWC): "Logic would suggest that, during the Industrial Revolution, Great Britain's watch sector would have grown exponentially at a time when the new working classes needed an accurate, cheap timekeeper for managing their work days," he wrote me. "As such it seems incredible that, instead of embracing the paradigm shift that was happening both in the market opportunity and in manufacturing, that Britain tried to remain a 'cottage' industry." Also worth noting: British watchmakers were using the English lever escapement, which was not as efficient and stable as the new Swiss lever escapement.

THE COMEBACK

British watchmaking did not entirely die out. Rather, it sort of paused—and when it resumed, it did so with in the same creative spirit as British engineering. Think of the World War I tank—immortalized on wrists worldwide by Cartier, no less—or Sir Malcolm Campbell's Blue Bird setting land speed records in the 1930s. Even Britain's iconic fleet and legendary aircraft, such as the Spitfire, reflect this continuous inventiveness.

Some watch brands enjoyed commercial success, like Sekonda, which began producing watches in the USSR in the 1960s using foreign parts and expertise. These were good, reliable timepieces, but they lacked that special identity that reflects a truly national horological culture. British watchmaking today evokes a distinct aesthetic style, a uniquely British sensibility that shapes both design and philosophy. This spirit, visible in the works of British émigré watchmakers such as Peter Speake-Marin and Stephen Forsey, formerly of Greubel Forsey, is best described as understatement.

Then, a small revolution occurred when, in 1974, George Daniels (1926–2011) came out with the genuinely innovative co-axial escapement: a refinement of the traditional lever escapement that reduced friction and improved precision through the use of two impulse wheels. He patented the mechanism in 1980, and it was then snapped up and developed by Omega.

1. and 2. George Graham (1674-1751), scientist and clockmaker: improved his teacher Tompion's cylinder escapement, invented the mercurial pendulum on clocks

3. Thomas Mudge (1715-1794), Graham apprentice, invented the more accurate lever escapement and a marine chronometer

4. The H3 marine chronometer by John Harrison (1693-1776), who spent a lifetime building chasing accurate timekeeping at sea.

5. British basic: a 1970s Sekonda running on a Slawa movement from the USSR.

6. and 7. In the tradition of great watchmakers: George Daniels, inventor of the co-axial escapement.

BACK TO THE ROOTS

Roger W. Smith is one of those towering figures in watchmaking who nevertheless remains modest, as is natural when you are working on capturing time. He apprenticed with Daniels and may be one of his most important successors. In his atelier on the Isle of Man, a small band of craftsmen build no more than fifteen timepieces a year around Smith's single-wheel co-axial escapement. The inspiration, he says frankly, comes from nineteenth-century British pocket watches, "tools where clarity and precision mattered more than decoration." It's the construction itself that creates the visual vibe, "particularly the three-dimensional aesthetic strength of those movements, with their three-quarter plates, raised barrel bridges, and screwed gold chatons."

When asked about some aesthetic value common to British watches these days, he pointed out that modern British brands were not bound by a shared visual code. "Instead, they're deliberately different from one another. What unites them isn't how they look, but why they're made: independence, honesty, originality, and a willingness to challenge expectations." What follows is just a sampling of the many wristwatches made on the British Isles.

5. – 8. Bremont: well-crafted timepieces with an air of adventure; under CEO Davide Cerrato, the brand has evolved with pieces like the Terra Nova Jumping Hour and the Skeletonised Altitude Perpetual Calendar GMT Monopusher.

1. – 4. The small Roger W. Smith atelier on the Isle of Man: small series of outstanding pieces using Smith's own single-wheel co-axial evolution.

ACTION TIME

Founded in 2002 by two brothers with a 1930s biplane, Nick and Giles English, the brand **Bremont** (see page 89) burst onto the scene with watches inspired by aviation and the military, two recurring themes in British watchmaking. The company's rugged, no-nonsense timepieces quickly found a fan base and so the company grew. It naturally branched out into sports watches, like the divers of the Supermarine collection, and began addressing women in search of something more feminine to wear. Strong growth allowed the company to open a large manufacturing facility in quaint Henley-on-Thames, some 40 miles west of London, where it could expand its portfolio. In 2023, Davide Cerrato of Tudor fame, came on as CEO. The newest collection, Terra Nova, is, unsurprisingly, more urban and geared towards buyers with a taste for cultured watches with sophisticated complications.

THE PURIST

"The typical aesthetic of a truly British watch is the large gear-train bridge, namely the three-quarter plate common in British pocket watches," says David Brailsford, who founded **Garrick** in 2014 (see page 137). His goal was to return as much as possible to artisanal watchmaking, with much of the finishing, like beveling, black polishing, frosting, and engine-turning done by hand. This slow, painstaking approach ultimately produces timepieces with a distinctively modern look that still incorporate traditional elements. The company makes many parts at its Norwich workshop, including in-house calibers such as the UT-G01 for the Regulator, S1, S2, and S3 models. "What makes the 16-line (36.09 mm) calibers special is the extremely large free-sprung balance with high inertia," he points out. "Once adjusted, the movement achieves a daily variance of no more than +3 seconds." Garrick produces only around 50 watches a year, some with a more technical appearance, others more aesthetic, with a central guilloché section. And the brand has been attracting attention beyond the British Isles: the S3 MK2, for example, was nominated for a prize at the Grand Prix d'Horlogerie de Genève in 2024.

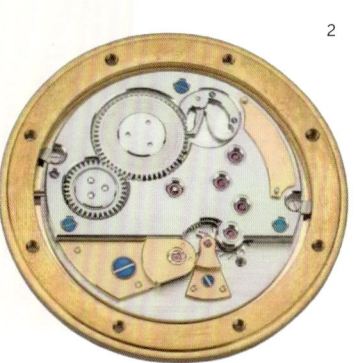

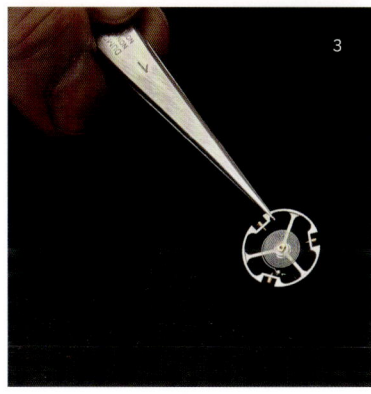

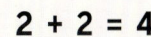

2 + 2 = 4

Christopher Ward has long defined itself as a proudly British-led watchmaker even though it merged with Synergies Horlogères in Switzerland in order to ensure a safe supply of calibers. The brand's first collection, the Malvern, drew inspiration from the Malvern Hills—an early signal of its homegrown sensibility. "Some of the greatest advances in precision timekeeping came from British minds," Patrick Gilbertson, PR manager, emailed me. "That spirit—pragmatic, empirical, quietly inventive—still informs how we approach watchmaking today." Christopher Ward has indeed challenged convention. It launched a direct-to-consumer model before it became the norm, developed the first in-house British movement in over half a century, and earned a coveted GPHG award for its affordable repeater with a *sonnerie au passage,* the C1 Bel Canto.

1. – 3. Garrick Watches: own calibers with a large free-sprung balance, handmade guilloche and bold colors.

4. – 6. Christopher Ward, fun and affordable: The chiming Bel Canto, the hyper-pure Jump Hour MKII with sapphire minute hand, and the very cute Celestial Moonphase.

DIAL POWER

For the Glasgow-based **anOrdain**, founded in 2015, the movements must be reliable machines, such as the La Joux-Perret G101 and the Sellita SW210. It lets the company focus all the attention on the dials, which shine thanks to vitreous enamel coatings. Its style combines streamlined Bauhaus-inspired design with the strong, deep colors created by numerous layers of enamel baked at high temperatures.

What makes anOrdain special is the texturing of a silver substrate using a die, hand-engraving, or even lasers to create distinctive patterns. Models 1 and 2 introduced a *fumé* gradient effect thanks to enamel layers accumulating along the periphery of the slightly vaulted dial. More recently, responding to customer demand, the company has started experimenting with black porcelain on a brass back plate, which produces a dial with a sleek, modern look and lasting visual appeal.

In 2023, anOrdain took over another Glaswegian watch brand that also made dials a priority. **Paulin** is like a playful little sister. Its watches, in three collections named Mara, Modul, and Neo, sport unabashedly modern and brightly colored dials. The Neo line uses anodized aluminum processed in a local factory. These affordable timepieces come in quartz and mechanical versions. Whatever one thinks about them, they are bound to attract attention and maybe start younger people on a career of collecting.

1. – 6. Scottish brand anOrdain finds special processes to create dynamic enamel and porcelain dials.

7. – 8. anOrdain sister brand Paulin's Modul: a collaboration with San Jose type foundry OH no (l.) and in a more formal version (r.)

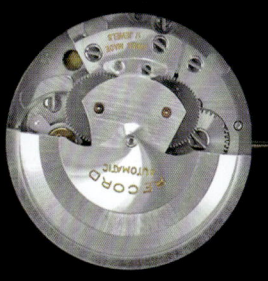

WRINKLES IN TIME

Human beings are pattern-seeking and pattern-loving creatures. It may have been the driving force in watch-lover Jamie Boyd's mind in 2015 when he launched **Wessex Watch**. Indeed, this small brand located in Harrogate, north of Leeds, has reinvented guilloché and taken it to new heights by applying it to two silver plates soldered together, which allows for deeper cuts—using in part a laser and in part other techniques that the company does not divulge. The stark relief gives the illusion of movement much like observing an ancient Roman mosaic or one of Victor Vasarely's hypnotic tableaux. The rest is all about finding new patterns and arranging these on the dial. The watches run on Swiss movements. The heat-blued hands complete the tableau, two shiny strips of color moving silently over the ridges and valleys below.

FAMILY AFFAIR

Bristol, 1846: Edwin Fear founds a watch company that will thrive for around 130 years before going dormant in the 1970s. In 2016, his great-great-great-grandson Nicholas Bowman-Scargill relaunched the brand and added an "s" to the name: **Fears**.

Besides several collaborations, notably with Garrick, Studio Underd0g, and Ace Jewelers in Holland, Fears offers three sober collections that pay tribute to the original brand and, by extension, to its home city in southwestern England. One is a classic round watch named after Redcliff Street, where the original workshop once stood. The Brunswick models were named after Brunswick Square, where the company's dispatch office was located. They come in a comfortable, vintage-inspired cushion case. The third collection, called Arnos, is a long rectangular watch in Art-Deco style with a discreet round dial set against a clous de Paris backdrop.

Fears carefully balances past and present, as designer Lee Yuen-Rapati told me: "We are influenced by our heritage but not constrained by it. The forms are classical, but with more color and more texture to make them contemporary."

1. Wessex Watch's Velocity model, deepdial guilloche on a specially prepared dial.

2. – 4. Fears of Bristol with elegant watches, and a collaboration with Ace Jewelers in Holland to celebrate artist Mondrian in the Brunswick case.

5. – 6. A personal story created the Edward Christopher brand; Manta-skin dial pattern, and the Ripples.

TIME AND MEMORY

The story behind **Edward Christopher** transcends the usual notion of a watch brand and reads more like the working-out of a personal destiny. Seán Edward Brickell, a former journalist and serial entrepreneur, says he always wanted to be a father, a role denied him by life. So, he instead directed his energy towards helping children and young people in need. In 2023, he launched Edward Christopher, a brand dedicated to two men in his family. Christopher Brickell, his father, once saved a girl who was suffocating during an asthma attack, while Edward, his great-uncle, shortly after returning from the Great War, rescued a boy from drowning by jumping into an icy river. The first collection is a diver's watch, the Manta, featuring a scaly guilloché pattern on colorful dials. The second is a dress watch, aptly named Ripple for the deep, off-center circular furrows that seem to ripple across its dial. Ten percent of the profits from sales go to organizations that support children and young people.

LOUIS MOINET
1806

1816

AN ICON REBORN
louismoinet.com

PLAYING WITH FIRE

Another personal story: If you are traveling to Newcastle, and you happen to stay at the Gotham Hotel, you will be right where **William Wood**, a firefighter of the Newcastle & Gateshead Fire Brigade, once did his duty. Among his feats of courage during his 25-year stint, was saving five children's lives in 1962 along with four fellow firefighters. They were all given a Certificate of Merit. Wood's grandson, Jonny Garrett, pays tribute to his grandfather through this boutique brand, which also supports firefighting organizations around the world. The collections make use of upcycled materials, such as brass from 1920's British firefighter's helmets or decommissioned fire hoses (for the straps). History buffs will no doubt appreciate the Dunkirk collection. It honors the Massey Shaw London fireboat, which saved over 600 soldiers from the beaches of Dunkirk in World War II. William Wood watches run on ETA and TMI (Seiko) movements (NH35s).

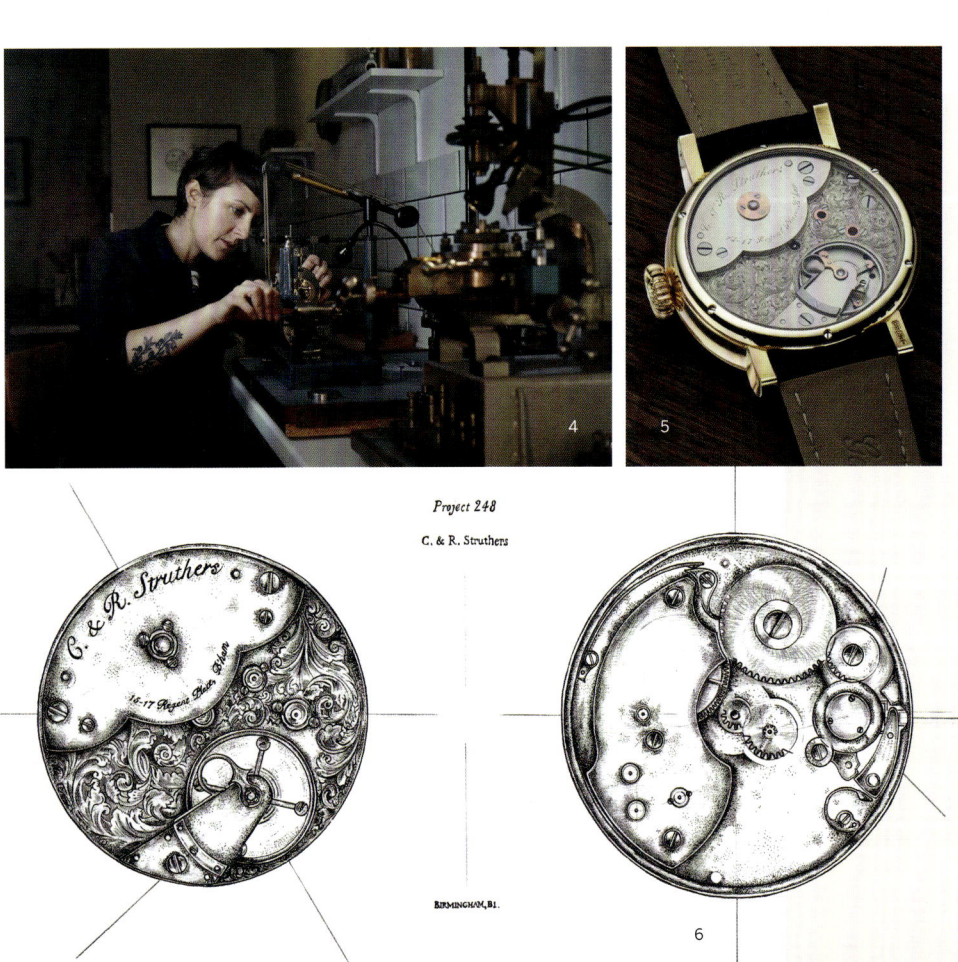

Project 248

C. & R. Struthers

BIRMINGHAM, B1.

THE REAL THING

In the world of classical music, there is a niche of performers who play on period instruments, either rebuilt or restored. The equivalent in watchmaking is work on antique pieces using traditional tools. Several specialists I have spoken to say unequivocally that this approach genuinely hones both mechanical and aesthetic skills. The husband and wife team of Craig and Rebecca **Struthers** have taken this path, building simple, limited edition timepieces with extreme care on restored equipment, including two East German lathes, curiously named Helga and Heidi. Craig is a fully fledged watchmaker, while Rebecca, who also plays a major role at the bench, is an "antiquarian horologist" and the first person in Britain to have earned a PhD in horology. She has written passionately about watches and time. Their minimal output includes the prize winning Stella pocket watch, which helped launch their business in 2013; the Kelso, an octagonal Art Deco inspired piece; and the sober Carter. Their current project, called simply 248, involves building a movement with a traditional English lever escapement, thus picking up the thread of the great British watch industry where it was dropped in the mid-nineteenth century.

1. – 3. Jonny Garrett created firefighter-themed watches to honor his fireman grandfather, William Wood.

4. – 6. Craig and Rebecca Struthers carefully and willfully reconnect with the past; Project 248 will revive the English lever escapement.

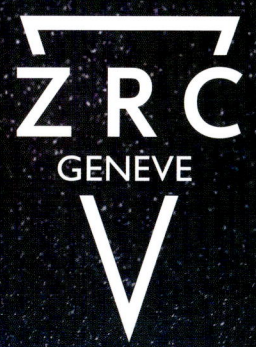

THE PAST IS PRESENT

London is, scientifically speaking, at the center of the world. So is the ten-year-old brand named **Zero West** (see page 299), a reference to the Prime Meridian that runs through Greenwich. Design engineer Graham Collins and graphic designer Andrew Brabyn have extracted inspiring pieces from Great Britain's past, its heroics, resilience, and technological inventiveness, or sometimes all at once, as in the models recalling the famous "Dambusters." The endless parade of inventions and culture from the British Isles all have a place at Zero West: from Spitfires and Lancaster bombers to the Turing machine, the Flying Scotsman locomotive and the "café racers," rebellious kids who raced around on motorbikes in the 1950s and 1960s. The brand often incorporates fragments of these celebrated icons into some of its watches, which are powered by Swiss movements. They have proudly added dial-printing to their in-house capacities and the HO1 BWD in the hiOctane line is the first project. It will be auctioned off at the British Watch Days (March 7, 2026) with proceeds going to the British Watch and Clock Alliance.

NOW AND LATER?

The number of British watch companies has grown significantly over the past decade, many being fairly small. Shortly before printing, I came across **Nomadic**, a Belfast-based brand popular for its sports watches, and a newcomer called **Milek**, which at this point has only plans and a website. Altogether, it's a lively and economically viable scene. According to the Alliance Bellwether Survey 2025, the sector has achieved a compound annual growth rate of 18.6% since 2021, reaching £200 million ($275 million) in revenue, with employment up by around 300% over the same period.

However, Alistair Audsley remarks that this progress has occurred despite strong headwinds, notably Brexit. "Growth has happened despite economic challenges such as losing frictionless EU trade," he notes. "The resulting bureaucracy and duties have hit micro-brands particularly hard."

Looking ahead, Audsley says the next steps are to strengthen awareness both domestically and internationally. In addition, the British Watch and Clock Alliance is preparing to launch an online Careers Hub, "to attract new talent, while encouraging re-shoring through in-house production and targeted acquisitions," he says, but adds a note of caution: "We're in luxury products people cherish but don't need. Turbulent geopolitics and living costs hit indulgence hard."

1. – 3. Graham Collins and Andrew Babyn highlight British tech achievements with Zero West; their latest, the unique HO1 BWD Heritage Special with in-house dial.

4. and 5. Nomadic's special St. Patrick's Day: The Black Shamrock Céad 126, front and back.

6. Studio UnderdOg celebrating the creative diversity of British Watchmaking at the British Watch Day 2025

TIME TONE

GET REAL: DIY WATCHES

BY MARTON RADKAI

You can learn a lot about watches from consulting books and visiting ateliers, museums, and trade fairs. But if you want to experience a great leap in your knowledge, Switzerland has a solution that will let you acquire a very personal watch in the process.

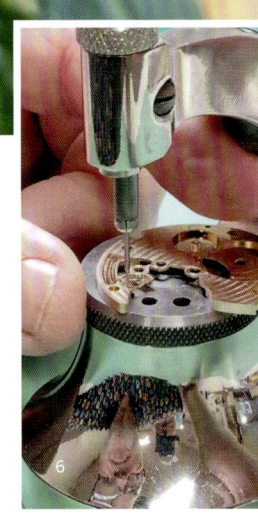

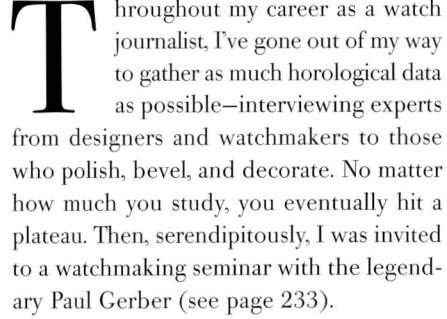

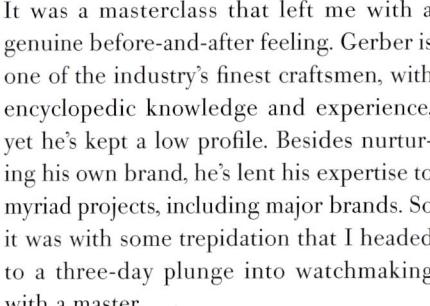

Throughout my career as a watch journalist, I've gone out of my way to gather as much horological data as possible—interviewing experts from designers and watchmakers to those who polish, bevel, and decorate. No matter how much you study, you eventually hit a plateau. Then, serendipitously, I was invited to a watchmaking seminar with the legendary Paul Gerber (see page 233).

It was a masterclass that left me with a genuine before-and-after feeling. Gerber is one of the industry's finest craftsmen, with encyclopedic knowledge and experience, yet he's kept a low profile. Besides nurturing his own brand, he's lent his expertise to myriad projects, including major brands. So it was with some trepidation that I headed to a three-day plunge into watchmaking with a master.

The seminar was a revelation, creating an "after" in a life of "befores." Gerber's wife, Ruth, assisted and essentially chaperoned our group of three. I'd expected an ostentatiously orderly space. Instead, we worked in the basement of the family home in Zurich: a watchmaker's "cave" with mysterious tools and gadgets everywhere. There were drawers full of sketches and blueprints of watches and clocks Gerber had made or collected. One room functioned as the office. The room that served as our work space for three days housed the workbenches, a lathe, and other machines; the rhodium-plating station was in the restroom, if memory serves; and a sanding apparatus stood in the garage.

Gerber calmly explained the dense program for the coming days. Our task: disassemble a simple Unitas caliber, decorate it (including rhodium-plating a pre-cut three-quarter plate), bevel the parts, polish and heat-blue the screws, lathe-cut the dial's minuscule feet, reassemble everything, oil the movement, and pass it over the Witschi to test it for accuracy. It sounds straightforward, but engineering is perhaps the easy part—at least with a basic movement. Mirror-polishing tiny screw heads demands steady, even finger-pressure; beveling isn't a simple 45° but closer to 30° to reflect light outward from the case back. Bluing screws means fixating on a glowing speck until it hits the perfect hue (my notes say 285°C; beyond that temperature and the screw head will have a different color). You end with a watch that's truly yours, with your name engraved on a plaque visible through the transparent case back, a strap of your choice, and a feeling of exhilaration at having done something unimaginable a few days earlier. Above all, you learn that watchmaking rewards patience: haste truly makes waste, making it an antidote to our frenetic daily grind.

Paul Gerber
www.gerber-uhren.ch
info@gerber-uhren.ch
Tel.: +41 44 401 45 69

1. Learning with Paul Gerber

2. The rhodium-plated mainplate

3. The author lathing the dial feet

4. The proud result

5. The precise skill of blueing screws

6. Delicate drilling into the mainplate

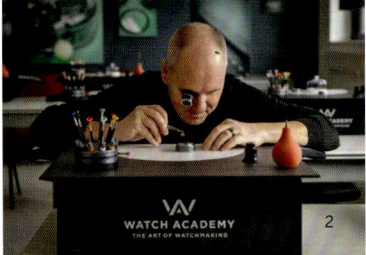
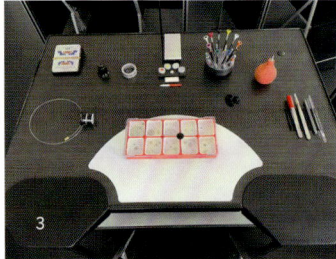

Wa – Watch Academy
wa-watchacademy.ch
info@wa-watchacademy.com
+41 (0) 76 630 11 60

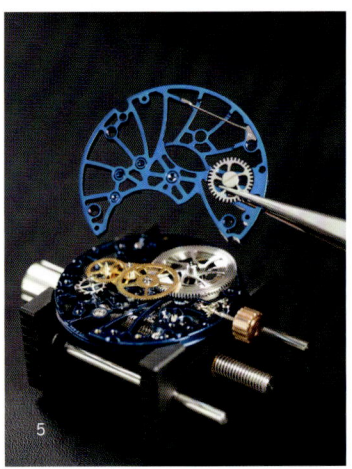

Montres Cimier SA
watch-academy.com
info@watch-academy.com
+41 (0) 41 720 29 29

1. – 3. At the Watch Academy run by Boris
Kuijper you can have your old watch restored
and also learn to take apart and reassemble
a watch.

4. – 5. At Montres Cimier you can buy a
watch, or make your own, or both.

Should you be visiting Zurich and have a little time for a
horological outing, you might to try the Watch Academy in
Egnach on the shores of Lake Constance (near St. Gallen).
It's where another independent master, Boris Kuijper, offers
hands-on watchmaking, only in a shorter period. After years
of working with big brands he decided to open a repair and
restoration workshop selling lovingly refurbished vintage
watches. In 2012, he launched the Watch Academy, where
enthusiasts build their own timepiece from a smorgasbord of
parts such as multicolored dials, an assortment of hands and
so forth. The movements are Swiss ones, like the ST3600 (an
ETA 6497 clone).

Among the programs offered, there is the five-hour "Custom
Made Watch," which dives straight into assembly, echoing
Gerber's ethos of tactile mastery in a personal setting. In
addition to the courses, Kuijper also offers "mobile" watchmaking seminars throughout Europe.

THE HEARTLAND

This chapter began in the German-speaking part of Switzerland.
But the country's horological heart beats more in the French-
speaking regions tucked inside and around the Jura Mountains
that saddle the Franco-Swiss border. The Vallée de Joux is
there, as are the UNESCO-certified towns of Le Locle and
La Chaux-de-Fonds, and the Franches-Montagnes (Free
Mountains), where, for centuries, the farmer-watchmakers
plied their trade, often in large houses that served as home
to more than one family.

Not surprisingly, a number of courses are held in the region.
Some are short, like the next "academy," offered by Cimier
in the bilingual town of Biel/Bienne—technically in the
Canton of Bern, but it really snuggles up to the Jura. They
offer a full-day or half-day workshop under the guidance of
experienced watchmakers. The longer seminar starts with the
obligatory *viennoiseries* with coffee or tea. Participants then
create their own watch from a wide selection parts, cases,
dials, hands, straps, and buckles or clasps. The next step is to
get into a white smock and assemble the movement, which
will be the trusty Unitas 6497-1, either openworked, which is
a little more expensive, or with a small second. Those short
on time can attend half-day courses or pay CHF 350 (about
$450) to attend an introduction to watchmaking.

IN THE VALLEY OF THE WATCHES

Nineteen years ago, Olivier Piguet (no direct relation to the Audemars Piguet clan) turned a personal setback into a mission. An armed robbery at his parents' shop, coupled with insufficient insurance, prompted him to restore a sprawling farmhouse in Le Sentier, the diminutive Vallée de Joux village that's home to Audemars Piguet, Jaeger-LeCoultre, and Romain Gauthier, among other big names. There, he began inviting individuals and small groups to immerse themselves in the life of the watchmakers of yore.

His two-day seminars are capped at three participants, open to watch enthusiasts and industry pros alike. They begin with some history of watchmaking in the Jura, peppered with personal anecdotes. He covers some technical teachings on the evolution of movements and how the chase for complications and precision sparked waves of technical ingenuity.

Hands-on instruction follows on a watch's anatomy, culminating in the signature thrill: disassembling and reassembling a skeleton movement. Over two full days, in a wood-paneled room guarded by a tall grandfather clock, "apprentices" get a real feeling for the complexities of building a watch before departing proudly with their handmade timepiece and a certificate in hand.

With Olivier Piguet, you will learn that Geneva was the source of watchmaking in Switzerland and the knowledge spread from there to the Jura. This knowledge was often spread by farmers, who would travel from the Jura to the city for supplies during the warmer months. Then during the harsh *jurassien* winters, they would spend months snow-locked in their farmsteads and pass the time by making watch parts.

The company **Initium** bridges this gap by holding courses in both Geneva *and* in the village of Le Noirmont in the Free Mountains, a region that got its name because in 1384, the Prince-Bishop of Basel freed people settling above 1000 meters from paying taxes.

None of the Initium courses last more than a day. As with the other ones mentioned in this chapter, the participants have a wide range of styles and dials available before setting down to take apart the caliber: a choice between a manually-wound Unitas 6497 or the automatic ETA 2892 in this case. To diversify the portfolio, the company has partnered with Furlan Marri to assemble one of their sector watches. Another option for the courageous amateur watchmaker with steady fingers and around $20,000 to spare is the tourbillon course. And if your partner does not share your enthusiasm for horology, Initium has created courses in making a Swiss Army knife or, for romantic souls, a wedding ring.

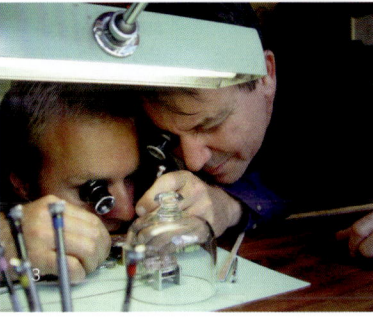

Centre d'Initiation à l'Horlogerie
www.olivierpiguet.ch
mywatch@olivierpiguet.ch
+41 (0) 21 845 71 24

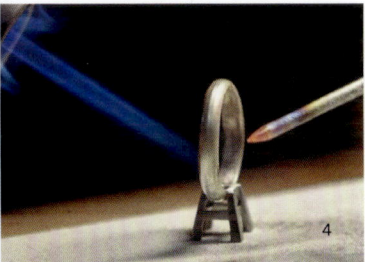

Initium Noirmont
+41(0)32 953 10 87
noirmont@
initium.swiss

Initium Geneva
+41(0)22 810 85 13
geneva@initium.swiss
www.initium.swiss/en/

1. – 3. Olivier Piguet 's old farmhouse in the Joux Valley offers total immersion watchmaking, with a skeleton at the end of your course.

4. – 6. With Initium, you can choose to make a watch, a Swiss knife, or a wedding ring.

TOUCHING METAL

Anecdotal evidence seems to indicate that most watch collectors have the soul of tinkerers. The mysteries of springs and gearwheels and strange cams draw many to take things apart and at least try to put everything back together again. The invisible hand of the market has naturally found this niche and many companies sell kits that provide a genuinely immersive experience of watchmaking in your own home without—ironically—time pressure.

One of these companies was founded by Initium's COO, Lucas Weber. **Bewatchmaker** lets the buyer select a watch from categories similar to those of "regular" brands: Vintage, Pilot, Heritage, and Initium. From there, the buyer chooses special options, including a skeleton version, a GMT, a watch with a classic guilloché dial, and so on. The base movements used are Sellita or ETA, and tools are included. Kits cost upward of $2,100 (at current exchange rates), but if you order further kits, the cost of the tools (around $800) is subtracted. The customer receives instructions by way of videos or email.

There are other DIY companies that operate in the same manner and offer even more affordable kits, notably the **DIY Watch Club** (www.diywatch.club), which uses Japanese movements, or **Horologic** (www.horologic. shop). Those most hesitant about trying out their skills might find these to be a safer bet for a first course.

Of all the do-it-yourself kits, though, none, perhaps, has made more of a splash than the Persée table clock created by **Maison Alcée** (www.maison-alcee.com). The first release in 2023 clinched the Audacity Prize at the Grand Prix d'Horlogerie de Genève that year. The company was launched by Alcée Montfort, who hails from Belfort, France, but now lives in Reims. As an engineer, she worked, among others, for brands such as Hermès, Cartier, and TAG Heuer, where she met and came to admire the artisans

behind the scenes: "On my first day there [at TAG], I had no idea what they were talking about," she remembers of her first real encounters with watchmaking. "But I really enjoyed these experiences because I discovered the pride they feel when they work with their hands."

Some of these crafters were secretive, but one named Christian was more open. He told her that his greatest fear was that the knowledge would some day die out. That triggered the idea of spreading the Gospel of the Watch to everyone by letting people physically feel the craft. "In my view, the culture of beauty elevates us and does a lot of good," she told me. "We need to reconnect with reality through manual labor."

Before starting, Alcée Monfort gathered an excellent team to support her. Besides two professors of horology and her husband Benoît, she brought Antoine Tschumi, a renowned Swiss designer, and Thierry Ducret on board. In 2007, Ducret, a watchmaker, became the 55th person in a century to win the coveted "Best Worker of France" accolade.

1. – 3. Kits for watches at home are also widely available.

4. – 5. Engineer Alcée Monfort (top), who created the Persée clock, and husband Benoit Monfort (bottom).

6. Living the watchmaker's life at a personal *établi*

And excellence is crucial with a clock since the parts are usually larger than in a watch and errors are more easily noticed.

The Persée is a table clock weighing about two pounds. The name refers to a constellation and a famous meteor shower, the Perseids. In Greek mythology, Perseus slew Medusa, married Andromeda, and had a son, Alcaeus, or Alcée in French.

The clock's movement is sandwiched between two circular elements that are four inches in diameter and allow the clock to stand at over six inches, or be laid down, which makes it look like the chassis of an old cannon. The mechanism is wound with a big key and will deliver fourteen days of power in addition to ringing each hour. There are now four models, with prices ranging from $8,000 to $13,500: the plain steel Douce, the Azur (with blue parts), the Nuit (with black DLC coated parts), and the Or, which has Galvano-plated segments with 24-carat gold. The customer can add on an optional watchmaker's workbench of French walnut (around $1,800). Inside is a detailed book explaining each of the 233 parts (including the preassembled escapement) and the workings of the clock. The 17 tools needed for the job include beryllium copper screw drivers made especially for Maison Alcée to prevent scratching any parts if the tool should slip.

HANDS ON

This listing is just a sample of some of the ways you can begin a deeper journey into the world of watches. There are many more such courses and kits available, maybe in your own country as well. By taking a course in watchmaking or building a watch or a clock, we who take pleasure in all things horological can deepen our knowledge of these extraordinary objects that keep everything running on time . . . or not. In a world that occasionally seems chaotic, these mechanisms are reminders that there is some form of order in the cosmos, even if we cannot see it. They are also fun objects, and, as Alcée Monfort once found out, they can have a genuinely positive impact on family life. One customer wrote that the most exciting aspect of building the Persée was working on it together with his son. As she told me that, I thought I heard a voice in her head saying, "Mission accomplished."

1. – 3. The many benefits of assembling a Maison Alcée clock: family life, all parts finished by a master watchmaker, and a clock that reminds you of your acquired skills.

A. LANGE & SÖHNE

A. Lange & Söhne exemplifies the steady, deliberate, and effective approach that characterizes many German businesses, especially family-run ones. Walter Lange, who passed away in January 2017, re-registered the brand A. Lange & Söhne in its original hometown of Glashütte. He did so on December 7, 1990, exactly 145 years after the company was originally founded by his great-grandfather, Ferdinand Adolph Lange. Ferdinand Adolph had originally launched the firm to create employment for the local population, and soon after German reunification in 1990, that was precisely what Glashütte once again needed.

Lange is renowned for its distinctive aesthetic and mechanical principles, both integral to the Glashütte watchmaking tradition. Notable elements include the three-quarter plate made of German silver—an alloy that resembles silver but is harder and more durable—and the hand-engraved balance cock. The company's expanding portfolio now comprises sixty-nine exceptional calibers, all developed and produced in-house. Each is decorated and assembled by hand, with the fine adjustment performed in five positions. Patented innovations include the signature Lange large date, the automatic "zero-reset" seconds mechanism, and three distinct constant-force escapements, one of which powers the Lange 31, providing an extraordinary 744-hour power reserve. The range of case materials has also grown to include platinum, various golds (including the proprietary "Honeygold"), stainless steel, and titanium.

The entry-level collection is the classically proportioned two-hand Saxonia, while the Lange 1, introduced in 1994, remains the brand's defining flagship. Innovation continues to drive the company forward, from the introduction of "Honeygold" cases in 2020 to fitting the Zeitwerk with a minute repeater. In 2019, Lange created a stir among watch collectors by venturing into the competitive field of blue-dialed sports watches with the Odysseus, featuring a custom automatic movement and day-date display. The original stainless-steel version has since been joined by a white gold model with an integrated leather or rubber strap, elevating everyday sportiness to *haute horlogerie* levels. The Odysseus line has since evolved further with a chronograph edition offered in a limited series.

LANGE UHREN GMBH
Ferdinand-A.-Lange-Platz 1
D-01768 Glashütte
Germany

TEL.:
+49-35053-44-0

E-MAIL:
info@lange-soehne.com

WEBSITE:
www.alange-soehne.com

FOUNDED:
1990

NUMBER OF EMPLOYEES:
750 employees, almost half of whom are watchmakers

U.S. DISTRIBUTOR:
A. Lange & Söhne
645 Fifth Avenue
New York, NY 10022
800-408-8147

MOST IMPORTANT COLLECTIONS/ PRICE RANGE:
Lange 1 / $40,300 to $359,400; Saxonia / $19,700 to $287,800; 1815 / $27,300 to $253,500; Richard Lange / $36,800 to $247,800; Zeitwerk / $89,200 to $141,300; Odysseus / $34,900 to $56,500

Odysseus

Reference number: 363.179
Movement: automatic, Lange caliber L155.1 Datomatic; ø 32.9 mm, height 6.2 mm; 31 jewels; 28,800 vph; swan-neck fine adjustment, hand-engraved escapement bridge, 1 screw-mounted gold chaton, parts finished and assembled by hand; 50-hour power reserve
Functions: hours, minutes, subsidiary seconds; date and weekday
Case: stainless steel, ø 40.5 mm, height 11.1 mm; sapphire crystal; transparent case back; water-resistant to 12 atm
Band: stainless steel, folding clasp
Price: $34,900
Variations: in titanium ($56,500; limited to 250 pieces)

Odysseus Honeygold

Reference number: 363.150
Movement: automatic, Lange caliber L155.1 Datomatic; ø 32.9 mm, height 6.2 mm; 31 jewels; 28,800 vph; swan-neck fine adjustment, hand-engraved escapement bridge, 1 screw-mounted gold chaton, parts finished and assembled by hand; 50-hour power reserve
Functions: hours, minutes, subsidiary seconds; date and weekday
Case: yellow gold "Honeygold", ø 40.5 mm, height 11.1 mm; sapphire crystal; transparent case back; water-resistant to 12 atm
Band: yellow gold "Honeygold", folding clasp
Price: $118,000
Variations: in stainless steel, in white gold

Odysseus Chronograph

Reference number: 463.178
Movement: automatic, Lange caliber L156.1 Datomatic; ø 34.9 mm, height 8.4 mm; 52 jewels; 28,800 vph; swan-neck fine adjustment, hand-engraved escapement bridge, 4 screw-mounted gold chatons, parts finished and assembled by hand; rapid rotation reset of the seconds and minute chronograph counters; 50-hour power reserve
Functions: hours, minutes, subsidiary seconds; chronograph; date and weekday
Case: stainless steel, ø 42.5 mm, height 14.2 mm; sapphire crystal; transparent case back; water-resistant to 12 atm
Band: stainless steel, folding clasp
Remarks: limited to 100 pieces
Price: $145,000

Grand Lange 1

Reference number: 137.033
Movement: hand-wound, Lange caliber L095.1;
ø 34.1 mm, height 4.7 mm; 42 jewels; 21,600 vph;
7 screw-mounted gold chatons, swan-neck fine
adjustment, hand-engraved balance cock, parts finished
and assembled by hand; 72-hour power reserve
Functions: hours, minutes, subsidiary seconds; power
reserve indicator; large date
Case: red gold, ø 41 mm, height 8.2 mm; sapphire
crystal; transparent case back; water-resistant to 3 atm
Band: reptile skin, pin buckle
Price: $48,100
Variations: in white gold ($48,100)

Lange 1 Moon Phase

Reference number: 192.032
Movement: hand-wound, Lange caliber L121.3;
ø 30.6 mm, height 6.3 mm; 47 jewels; 21,600 vph;
8 screw-mounted gold chatons, swan-neck fine
adjustment, hand-engraved balance cock, parts finished
and assembled by hand; 72-hour power reserve
Functions: hours, minutes, subsidiary seconds; power
reserve indicator; large date, moon phase
Case: red gold, ø 38.5 mm, height 10.2 mm; sapphire
crystal; transparent case back; water-resistant to 3 atm
Band: reptile skin, pin buckle
Price: $57,600
Variations: in white gold; in platinum

Lange 1 Time Zone

Reference number: 136.025
Movement: hand-wound, Lange caliber L141.1;
ø 34.1 mm, height 6.7 mm; 38 jewels; 21,600 vph;
3 screw-mounted gold chatons; hand-assembled and
-finished movement; 72-hour power reserve
Functions: hours, minutes, subsidiary seconds;
additional 12-hour display (second time zone), double
day/night indication; power reserve indicator; daylight
savings indication; large date
Case: platinum, ø 41.9 mm, height 10.9 mm; crown-
activated ring with city references; sapphire crystal;
transparent case back; water-resistant to 3 atm
Band: reptile skin, pin buckle
Price: $74,000
Variations: in red or white gold

Lange 1 Perpetual Calendar

Reference number: 345.036
Movement: automatic, Lange caliber L021.3;
ø 35.8 mm, height 8.8 mm; 63 jewels; 21,600 vph; off-
center escapement, 5 screw-mounted gold chatons,
hand-engraved balance cock, gold rotor platinum
oscillating mass; 50-hour power reserve
Functions: hours, minutes, subsidiary seconds; day/
night indication; perpetual calendar with large date,
weekday, month, moon phase, leap year
Case: platinum, ø 41.9 mm, height 12,1 mm; sapphire
crystal; transparent case back; water-resistant to 3 atm
Band: reptile skin, pin buckle
Price: $139,800
Variations: in red or white gold

Datograph Perpetual

Reference number: 410.038
Movement: hand-wound, Lange caliber L952.1;
ø 32 mm, height 8 mm; 45 jewels; 18,000 vph; off-
center balance; in-house balance wheel, column wheel
control of chronograph functions; 4 screw-mounted
gold chatons; 36-hour power reserve
Functions: hours, minutes, subsidiary seconds; day/
night indication; flyback chronograph with precisely
jumping minute counter; perpetual calendar with large
date, weekday, month, moon phase, leap year
Case: white gold, ø 41 mm, height 13.5 mm; sapphire
crystal; transparent case back; water-resistant to 3 atm
Band: reptile skin, pin buckle
Price: on request

Minute Repeater Perpetual Calendar

Reference number: 607.091
Movement: hand-wound, Lange caliber L122.2;
ø 30 mm, height 7.6 mm; 54 jewels; 21,600 vph;
4 screw-mounted gold chatons; hand-engraved balance
cock; 72-hour power reserve
Functions: hours, minutes, subsidiary seconds; minute
repeater; perpetual calendar with large date, weekday,
month, moon phase, leap year
Case: platinum, ø 40.5 mm, height 12.1 mm; sapphire
crystal; transparent case back
Band: reptile skin, folding clasp
Remarks: enameled gold dial; limited to 50 pieces
(boutique edition)
Price: on request

Zeitwerk

Reference number: 142.031
Movement: hand-wound, Lange caliber L043.6; ø 33.6 mm, height 8.9 mm; 61 jewels; 18,000 vph; swan-neck fine adjustment, 2 screw-mounted gold chatons, constant force mechanism (remontoir), hand-engraved balance cock; parts finished and assembled by hand; 72-hour power reserve
Functions: hours and minutes (digital, jumping), subsidiary seconds; power reserve indicator
Case: pink gold, ø 41.9 mm, height 12.2 mm; sapphire crystal; transparent case back; water-resistant to 3 atm
Band: reptile skin, pin buckle
Price: $121,100
Variations: in platinum

1815 Up/Down

Reference number: 234.032
Movement: hand-wound, Lange caliber L051.2; ø 30.6 mm, height 4.6 mm; 29 jewels; 21,600 vph; 7 screw-mounted gold chatons, three-quarter plate, screw balance, hand-engraved normal type, no par, cock, balance cock , parts finished and assembled by hand; 55-hour power reserve
Functions: hours, minutes, subsidiary seconds; power reserve indicator
Case: pink gold, ø 39 mm, height 8.7 mm; sapphire crystal; transparent case back; water-resistant to 3 atm
Band: reptile skin, pin buckle
Price: $38,300
Variations: in white gold ($38,300)

1815 Chronograph

Reference number: 414.028
Movement: hand-wound, Lange caliber L951.5; ø 30.6 mm, height 6.1 mm; 34 jewels; 21,600 vph; 4 screw-mounted gold chatons, hand-engraved balance cock, parts finished and assembled by hand; 60-hour power reserve
Functions: hours, minutes, subsidiary seconds; flyback chronograph
Case: white gold, ø 39.5 mm, height 11 mm; sapphire crystal; transparent case back; water-resistant to 3 atm
Band: reptile skin, pin buckle
Price: on request
Variations: in red gold

1815 Rattrapante Perpetual Calendar

Reference number: 421.056
Movement: hand-wound, Lange caliber L101.1; ø 32.6 mm, height 9.1 mm; 43 jewels; 21,600 vph; 4 screw-mounted gold chatons; 42-hour power reserve
Functions: hours, minutes, subsidiary seconds; power reserve indicator; split-seconds chronograph; perpetual calendar with date, weekday, month, moon phase, leap year
Case: white gold, ø 41.9 mm, height 14.7 mm; sapphire crystal; transparent case back; water-resistant to 3 atm
Band: reptile skin, folding clasp
Remarks: red-gold dial
Price: $319,000; limited to 100 pieces

Richard Lange Jumping Seconds

Reference number: 252.029
Movement: manually wound, Lange Caliber L094.1; ø 33.6 mm, height 6 mm; 50 jewels; 21,600 vph; zero-reset mechanism, constant force escapement (remontoir); 42-hour power reserve
Functions: off-center hours and minutes, large seconds (jumping); winding reminder
Case: white gold, ø 39.9 mm, height 10.6 mm; sapphire crystal; transparent case back; water-resistant to 3 atm
Band: reptile skin, buckle
Price: $97,800

Richard Lange Minute Repeater

Reference number: 606.079
Movement: manually wound, Lange Caliber L122.1; ø 30 mm, height 5.4 mm; 40 jewels; 21,600 vph; 4 screw-mounted gold chatons, hand-engraved balance cock, parts finished and assembled by hand; 72-hour power reserve
Functions: hours, minutes, subsidiary seconds; minute Repeater
Case: platinum, ø 39 mm, height 9.7 mm; sapphire crystal; transparent case back; water-resistant to 2 atm
Band: reptile skin, folding clasp
Price: $400,000; limited to 50 pieces (boutique edition)

Caliber L155.1 Datomatic

Automatic; swan-neck fine adjustment, stop-seconds mechanism, oscillating mass in platinum; single mainspring barrel; 50-hour power reserve

Functions: hours, minutes, subsidiary seconds; date and weekday
Diameter: 32.9 mm
Height: 6.2 mm
Jewels: 31, including 1 in a screw-mounted gold chaton
Balance: glucydur with regulating screws
Frequency: 28,800 vph
Hairspring: in-house manufacture
Remarks: parts finished and assembled by hand; 312 parts

Caliber L021.3

Automatic; unidirectional gold rotor with platinum oscillating mass; single mainspring barrel, 50-hour power reserve

Functions: hours, minutes, subsidiary seconds; day/night indicator; perpetual calendar with large date, weekday, month, moon phase, leap year
Diameter: 35.8 mm
Height: 8.8 mm
Jewels: 63, including 5 in screw-mounted gold chatons
Balance: glucydur with eccentric adjustment cams
Frequency: 21,600 vph
Hairspring: in-house manufacture
Remarks: hand-engraved and -decorated, hand-engraved balance cock; 621 parts

Caliber L951.6

Hand-wound; second-stop system, jumping minute totalizer; single mainspring barrel, 60-hour power reserve

Functions: hours, minutes, subsidiary seconds; power reserve indicator; flyback chronograph; large date
Diameter: 30.6 mm
Height: 7.9 mm
Jewels: 46
Balance: glucydur screw balance
Frequency: 18,000 vph
Hairspring: in-house manufacture
Shock protection: Incabloc
Remarks: untreated German-silver three-quarter plate, mostly hand-engraved and -decorated according to top quality criteria, hand-engraved balance cock; 451 parts

Caliber L043.6

Hand-wound; jumping minute display; constant-force mechanism (remontoir); patented barrel mechanism; stop-seconds device; single mainspring barrel; 72-hour power reserve

Functions: jumping hours and minutes (digital display), subsidiary seconds; power reserve indicator
Diameter: 33.6 mm
Height: 8.9 mm
Jewels: 61, including 2 in screw-mounted gold chatons
Balance: glucydur with eccentric poising weights
Frequency: 18,000 vph
Hairspring: in-house manufacture with patented clamping system
Shock protection: Incabloc
Remarks: parts finished and assembled by hand, hand-engraved balance cock; 451 parts

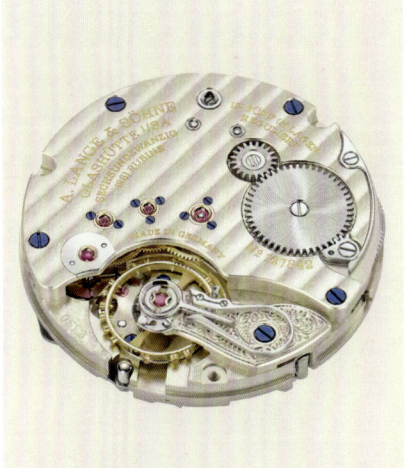

Caliber L051.3

Hand-wound; swan-neck fine adjustment, stop-seconds mechanism; mainplate and bridges in German silver; single mainspring barrel; 72-hour power reserve

Functions: hours, minutes, subsidiary seconds; annual calendar with date, weekday, month, moon phase
Diameter: 30.6 mm
Height: 5.7 mm
Jewels: 26, including 3 in screw-mounted gold chatons
Balance: glucydur with regulating screws
Frequency: 21,600 vph
Hairspring: in-house manufacture
Remarks: parts finished and assembled by hand, hand-engraved balance cock; 345 parts

Caliber L101.1

Hand-wound; stop-seconds mechanism; single mainspring barrel; 42-hour power reserve

Functions: hours, minutes, subsidiary seconds; power reserve indicator; split-seconds chronograph; perpetual calendar with date, weekday, month, moon phase, leap year
Diameter: 32.6 mm
Height: 9.1 mm
Jewels: 43, including 4 in screw-mounted gold chatons
Balance: glucydur with regulating screws
Frequency: 21,600 vph
Hairspring: in-house manufacture
Shock protection: Kif
Remarks: parts finished and assembled by hand, hand-engraved balance cock; 528 parts

ALEXANDER SHOROKHOFF

The goal for the watch connoisseur may be realizing one's own ideas for timepieces. In the first stages of his life, Alexander Shorokhoff, born in Moscow in 1960, was a civil engineer and then an architect with his own construction company. This turned out to be an excellent platform to begin expanding into the field of fine timepieces. In 1992, shortly after the break-up of the Soviet Union, Shorokhoff founded a distribution company in Germany to market Russia's own Poljot watches. This gave him the insight and practice needed to launch phase two of his plan: establishing his own manufacturing facilities for an independent watch brand under his own name.

At Shorokhoff Watches, three main creative lines are bundled under the general concept "Art on the Wrist": Heritage, Avantgarde, and Vintage. The three families share a design with a distinctly artistic orientation. They all focus on technical quality, sophisticated hand-engraving, and culture. "We consider watches not only as timekeepers, but also as works of art," says Alexander Shorokhoff. It's a statement that is clearly expressed by the product. The brand is at home in the world of international and Russian art and culture, with some watches named after, or inspired by, Russian artists like Leo Tolstoy and Fyodor Dostoevsky, or figures like the Austrian architect Friedensreich Hundertwasser, like in the Home 2. Each dial is designed down to the smallest detail. The engraving and finishing of the movements are unique as well. These timepieces are bold, innovative, and visually striking, which explains numerous and illustrious design awards.

The movements are mostly Swiss-made, with some Russian movements thrown in. They are taken apart in Alzenau, reworked, decorated, and then reassembled with great care, which is why the brand has stamped each watch with "Handmade in Germany." Some of the modules used in these timepieces were developed by the company itself. Before a watch leaves the *manufacture*, it is subjected to strict quality control. The timepiece's functionality must be given the cleanest bill of health before it can be sent out to jewelers around the world.

ALEXANDER SHOROKHOFF UHRENMANUFAKTUR
Hanauer Strasse 25
63755 Alzenau
Germany

TEL.:
+49-6023-919-93

E-MAIL:
info@alexander-shorokhoff.de

WEBSITE:
alexander-shorokhoff.com/en

FOUNDED:
2003

NUMBER OF EMPLOYEES:
17

ANNUAL PRODUCTION:
approx. 1,500-2,000 watches

DISTRIBUTOR:
About Time Luxury Group
210 Bellevue Avenue
Newport, RI 02840
401-846-0598

**MOST IMPORTANT COLLECTIONS/
PRICE RANGE**
Heritage / starting at approx. $4,500; Avantgarde / starting at approx. $1,500; Vintage / starting at approx. $800

Avantgarde Full Calendar "Cadamomo"

Reference number: AS.VK-CDMM4
Movement: automatic, Dubois Dépraz Caliber 9000; ø 28 mm, height 5.2 mm; 25 jewels; 28,800 vph; hand-engraved oscillating mass, blued screws; 42-hour power reserve
Functions: hours, minutes, sweep seconds; full calendar with date, weekday, month, moon phase
Case: stainless steel, ø 43.5 mm, height 11.55 mm; sapphire crystal; transparent case back; water-resistant to 5 atm
Band: leather, pin buckle
Remarks: "Cadamomo" comes from calendar, date, month, moon phase
Price: $5,200; limited to 50 pieces

Avantgarde "Flensi"

Reference number: AS.DD06-TG
Movement: automatic, MLJP Caliber G100; ø 25.6 mm, height 4.45 mm; 24 jewels; 28,800 vph; hand-engraved oscillating mass, blued screws; 68-hour power reserve
Functions: hours, minutes, sweep seconds; date
Case: stainless steel, ø 45 mm, height 13.75 mm; titanium bezel; sapphire crystal; water-resistant to 10 atm
Band: rubber, folding clasp
Price: $3,700; limited to 60 pieces

Avantgarde "Home 2"

Reference number: AS.KD02-HOME2
Movement: automatic, ETA Caliber 2892-A2; ø 25.6 mm, height 3.6 mm; 21 jewels; 28,800 vph; hand-engraved and finished rotor, blued screws; 47-hour power reserve
Functions: hours, minutes, sweep seconds; date
Case: stainless steel with enamel coating on the case flanks, 41 mm x 41 mm, height 9 mm; sapphire crystal; transparent case back; water-resistant to 3 atm
Band: rubber, folding clasp
Price: $5,300; limited to 10 pieces

Avantgarde "Big Date Chrono"

Reference number: AS.BD01-4
Movement: automatic, Dubois Dépraz Caliber 4500; ø 30 mm, height 7.4 mm; 49 jewels; 28,800 vph; 42-hour power reserve
Functions: hours, minutes, subsidiary seconds; chronograph; large date
Case: stainless steel, ø 43.5 mm, height 14.4 mm; sapphire crystal; transparent case back; water-resistant to 5 atm
Band: leather, pin buckle
Remarks: limited to 30 pieces
Price: $4,950

Avantgarde "Neva Color"

Reference number: AS.NEV-COL1
Movement: hand-wound, Caliber 3105.AS (Poljot 3105 base); ø 31 mm, height 5.38 mm; 17 jewels; 21,600 vph; finely finished movement; 42-hour power reserve
Functions: hours, minutes, subsidiary seconds; date
Case: stainless steel with brown IP coating, ø 43.5 mm, height 11.5 mm; sapphire crystal; transparent case back; water-resistant to 5 atm
Band: leather, pin buckle
Price: $2,700; limited to 98 pieces

Avantgarde "Emotio Due"

Reference number: AS.EMO2-5
Movement: automatic, Caliber STP12-1; ø 25.6 mm, 36 jewels; 28,800 vph; hand-engraved oscillating mass, blued screws; 42-hour power reserve
Functions: hours, minutes, subsidiary seconds; power reserve indicator; date
Case: stainless steel, ø 42 mm, height 10.6 mm; sapphire crystal; transparent case back; water-resistant to 5 atm
Band: reptile skin, pin buckle
Price: $3,550; limited to 50 pieces

Avantgarde "Bella & Alla"

Reference number: AS.KD02-B&A
Movement: automatic, ETA Caliber 2892-A2; ø 25.6 mm, height 3.6 mm; 21 jewels; 28,800 vph; hand-engraved and finished rotor, blued screws; 47-hour power reserve
Functions: hours, minutes, sweep seconds
Case: stainless steel with black PVD, 41 mm x 41 mm, height 9 mm; sapphire crystal; water-resistant to 3 atm
Band: reptile skin, folding clasp
Price: $6,500; limited to 25 pieces

Avantgarde "Square & Round"

Reference number: AS.SR02-5
Movement: automatic, ETA Caliber 7753; ø 30 mm, height 7.9 mm; 27 jewels; 28,800 vph; hand-engraved oscillating mass, blued screws; 42-hour power reserve
Functions: hours, minutes, subsidiary seconds; chronograph; date
Case: stainless steel, 44.5 mm x 44.5 mm, height 14.75 mm; sapphire crystal; transparent case back; water-resistant to 3 atm
Band: reptile skin, pin buckle
Price: $4,800; limited to 30 pieces

Avantgarde "Summer"

Reference number: AS.AP.SOM1
Movement: automatic, ETA Caliber 2000-1; ø 20 mm, height 3.6 mm; 20 jewels; 28,800 vph; hand-engraved oscillating mass, blued screws; 40-hour power reserve
Functions: hours, minutes, sweep seconds
Case: stainless steel, 36 mm x 36 mm, height 8.55 mm; sapphire crystal; transparent case back; water-resistant to 3 atm
Band: ostrich leather, pin buckle
Price: $3,950; limited to 31 pieces

ALPINA

Alpina essentially grew out of a confederation of watchmakers known as the Alpina Union Horlogère, founded by Gottlieb Hauser. The group expanded quickly to reach beyond Swiss borders into Germany, where it opened a factory in Glashütte. For a while in the 1930s, it even merged with Gruen, one of the most important watch companies in the United States at the time.

After World War II, the Allied Forces decreed that the name Alpina could no longer be used in Germany, and so that brand was renamed "Dugena" for Deutsche Uhrmacher-Genossenschaft Alpina, or the German Watchmaker Cooperative Alpina.

Today, Geneva-based Alpina is no longer associated with that watchmaker cooperative of yore. Now a sister brand of Frédérique Constant, it has a decidedly modern collection enhanced with a series of movements designed, built, and assembled in-house: the Tourbillon AL-980, the World Timer AL-718, the Automatic Regulator AL-950, the Small Date Automatic AL-710, and, more recently, the Flyback Chronograph Automatic AL-760, which features the patented Direct Flyback technology. Owners Peter and Aletta Stas sold it to Citizen Group in 2016.

Alpina has a history of pioneering advances in watchmaking. Its iconic Block Uhr of 1933 and the Alpina 4 of 1938, with an in-house automatic movement, set the pace for all sports watches, with a waterproof stainless-steel case and an antimagnetic movement. In 2015, Alpina together with its sister company Frédérique Constant introduced its first Swiss-made Horological Smartwatch. The company again caught the attention of the public when it came out in 2022 with the Seastrong Diver 300 Automatic Calanda, which featured a case of recycled marine steel called PuReSteel®, made by ThyssenKrupp, and a strap of recycled plastic. This line remains one of the brand's leading collections and has now been combined with the Extreme line to create a sports watch with dressier touches in a cushion case.

ALPINA WATCH INTERNATIONAL SA
Route de la Galaise, 8
CH-1228 Plan-les-Ouates, Geneva
Switzerland

TEL.:
+41-0-22-860-87-40

E-MAIL:
info@alpina-watches.com

WEBSITE:
www.alpinawatches.com

FOUNDED:
1883

NUMBER OF EMPLOYEES:
100

U.S. SUBSIDIARY:
Alpina Frederique Constant USA
customercare@alpinawatches.com

MOST IMPORTANT COLLECTIONS/PRICE RANGE:
Alpiner Extreme / from approx. $1,695 to $2,595;
Seastrong / from approx. $1,595 to $1,895;
Startimer Pilot / from approx. $695 to $2,995

Alpiner Extreme Automatic

Reference number: AL-525BG3AE6B
Movement: automatic, Caliber AL-525 (Sellita SW200-1 base); ø 25.6 mm, height 4.6 mm; 26 jewels; 28.800 vph; 38-hour power reserve
Functions: hours, minutes, sweep seconds; date
Case: stainless steel, 39 mm x 40.5 mm, height 11.5 mm; sapphire crystal; transparent case back; screw-down crown; water-resistant to 20 atm
Band: stainless steel, folding clasp
Price: $2,295
Variations: various cases, straps, and dials

Seastrong Diver Extreme GMT

Reference number: AL-560B3VE6
Movement: automatic, Caliber AL-560 (Sellita SW330 base); ø 25.6 mm, height 3.6 mm; 25 jewels; 28.800 vph; 50-hour power reserve
Functions: hours, minutes, sweep seconds; additional 24-hour display (second time zone); date Case: stainless steel, 39 mm x 40.5 mm, height 12 mm; bidirectional bezel with ceramic insert and 0-24 scale; sapphire crystal; screw-down crown; water-resistant to 30 atm
Band: rubber, folding clasp
Price: $2,795
Variations: with white dial

Alpiner Extreme Quartz

Reference number: AL-220S2AE2B
Movement: quartz
Functions: hours, minutes, sweep seconds; date
Case: stainless steel, 34 mm x 35.2 mm, height 8.35 mm; bezel with rose-gold PVD; sapphire crystal; crown with rose-gold PVD; water-resistant to 10 atm
Band: stainless steel with rose-gold middle links, folding clasp
Price: $1,595
Variations: various cases, straps, and dials

ANGELUS

The watch landscape in Switzerland has always been rich in small, vital brands. Many are no longer active, but their names still make for weepy eyes with connoisseurs and collectors. And every now and then, an older company is revived with varying degrees of success. In its day, Angelus, founded by Gustave and Albert Stolz in Le Locle in 1891, quickly forged a reputation for complicated watches, notably repeaters and chronographs. The brothers, Catholics, named the brand after the first word of a standard Catholic prayer and the midday church bells.

One of the brand's claims to fame was a two-handed chronograph, which became a hit in the thirties, culminating in a contract with the Hungarian air force in 1940. The company then built a chronograph with a date, and later one of the first digital dates. Meanwhile, it was creating excellent movements, one of which drove Panerai's Mare Nostrum in the fifties. Among its most iconic models was the waterproof repeater/alarm called the Tinkler, and, in the seventies, a five-minute repeater that never really got off the ground due to the quartz crisis, which brought Angelus to its knees…

In 2011, La Joux-Perret, a company known for movements and modules and which was already behind Arnold & Son, relaunched the brand and returned to its chronographic roots. The chronograph actually looked like a three-hand watch with a retro style. Only the push-button embedded in the crown and the tachymeter scale printed on the outer edge of the dial revealed to the trained eye that the watch must be a measuring device for short time intervals. The new Chronographe Télémètre has a more conventional design, with a small seconds dial and half-hour counter. Fortunately, nothing has changed when viewed through the transparent case back. Connoisseurs can delight in the architecture of the A5000 hand-wound movement and its very obvious ratchet wheel.

ANGELUS
Manufacture La Joux-Perret SA
Boulevard des Éplatures 38
2300 La Chaux-de-Fonds
Switzerland

TEL:
+41-032-967-97-97

E-MAIL:
info@angelus-watches.com

WEBSITE:
www.angelus-watches.com

FOUNDED:
1891; relaunched 2011

NUMBER OF EMPLOYEES:
about 100, including at the La Joux-Perret manufacture

DISTRIBUTOR:
Exquisite Timepieces INC.
4380 Gulfshore Blvd., N. Suite 800
Naples, Fl 34103
team@exquisitetimepieces.com
239-227-2932

MOST IMPORTANT COLLECTIONS/ PRICE RANGE
U23 / U30 / U41 / U50 / U51 / U53 / La Fabrique $32,000; Chronographe Télémètre; various tourbillons / $28,000 to $110,000

Chronodate Titanium Storm Blue

Reference number: 0CDZF.U03A.M009T
Movement: automatic, Angelus Caliber A-500 (on MLJP base L100); ø 30 mm, height 7.9 mm; 26 jewels; 28,800 vph; column-wheel control of chronograph functions; 60-hour power reserve
Functions: hours, minutes, small seconds; chronograph; date
Case: titanium, ø 42.5 mm, height 14.25 mm; sapphire crystal; transparent case back; carbon-fiber pushers; water-resistant to 3 atm
Band: reptile skin, folding clasp
Price: $28,500
Variations: with rubber strap; with titanium bracelet

Flying Tourbillon Titanium Blue Alligator

Reference number: 0TSZF.U02A.C009A
Movement: automatic, Angelus Caliber A-310 (on MLJP base T100); ø 32.8 mm, height 4.3 mm; 23 jewels; 28,800 vph; flying one-minute tourbillon; skeletonized movement; 60-hour power reserve
Functions: hours, minutes, small seconds
Case: titanium and carbon fiber, ø 42.5 mm, height 13.4 mm; sapphire crystal; transparent case back; water-resistant to 3 atm
Band: reptile skin, folding clasp
Remarks: comes with additional rubber strap; limited to 25 pieces
Price: $53,400

Chronographe Télémètre

Reference number: 0CHCQ.I01A.V010Q
Movement: hand-winding, Angelus Caliber A5000 (on MLJP base); ø 29.4 mm, height 4.2 mm; 23 jewels; 21,600 vph; column wheel; crown pusher control of the chronograph functions; 42-hour power reserve
Functions: hours, minutes, small seconds; chronograph
Case: yellow gold, ø 37 mm, height 11 mm; sapphire crystal; transparent case back; water-resistant to 3 atm
Band: leather, pin buckle
Price: $36,700
Variations: various dial colors and case materials

ARISTO

"If you lie down with dogs,..." goes the old saying. And if you work closely with watchmakers . . . you may catch their more beneficial bug and become one yourself. That at any rate is what happened to the watch case and metal bracelet manufacturer Vollmer, Ltd., established in Pforzheim, Germany, by Ernst Vollmer in 1922. Is it any wonder, then, that the third-generation president Hansjörg Vollmer decided he was interested in producing watches as well?

Vollmer, who studied business in Stuttgart, had the experience but also the connections with manufacturers in Switzerland. He speaks French fluently, another asset. He acquired Aristo and in 1998 launched a series of pilot watches housed in sturdy titanium cases with bold onion crowns and secured with Vollmer's own light and comfortable titanium bracelets. Bit by bit, thanks to affordable prices and no-nonsense design—reviving some classic dials from World War II—Vollmer's watches caught hold. The collection grew with limited editions and a few chronographs.

In 2005, Vollmer GmbH and Aristo Watches consolidated for a bigger impact. Besides their own lines, they produce quartz watches, automatics, and chronographs under various names. The Aristo brand has been trademarked worldwide and is sold mainly in Europe, North America, and Asia. The collection is divided up into Classic, Design, and Sports with the mechanical segment further split based on the elements Land, Water, and Air. The classic pilot's watches are still the mainstay of the brand, whereby anyone seeking a more upscale watch will find satisfaction with the "Erbprinz" series, named after the street where the company also has a workshop for manufacturing metal bracelets. Finally, Aristo has a special section devoted to historical movements. In 2024, the company launched a limited edition of watches running on NOS (new old stock) Swiss Record movements from the late 1950s and encased in equally NOS cases made by Reister & Nittel in the 1970s.

ARISTO VOLLMER GMBH
Erbprinzenstr. 36
D-75175 Pforzheim
Germany

TEL.:
+49-7231-17031

FAX:
+49-7231-17033

E-MAIL:
info@aristo-uhren.de

WEBSITE:
www.aristo-uhren.de

FOUNDED:
1907/1998

NUMBER OF EMPLOYEES:
12

ANNUAL PRODUCTION:
4,000 watches and 4,000 bracelets

DISTRIBUTION:
Retail

U.S. DISTRIBUTOR:
Long Island Watch, Marc Frankel
273 Walt Whitman Road, Suite 217
Huntington Station, NY 11746
631-470-0762; 888-673-1129 (fax)
www.longislandwatch.com

MOST IMPORTANT COLLECTIONS:
Flieger, U-Boot, Vintage

Chrono Retro Design "Flieger"

Reference number: 3H242-M
Movement: automatic, Sellita Caliber SW500; ø 30 mm, height 7.9 mm; 25 jewels; 28,800 vph; 48-hour power reserve
Functions: hours, minutes, small seconds; chronograph; date and weekday
Case: stainless steel, ø 40.5 mm, height 14 mm; unidirectional bezel, with 0-60 scale; sapphire crystal; water-resistant to 5 atm
Band: stainless steel Milanese mesh, sliding clasp
Price: $1,650
Variations: with leather strap

U-Boot Watch Burnished

Reference number: 7H174-M
Movement: automatic, Sellita Caliber SW200-1; ø 25.6 mm, height 4.6 mm; 26 jewels; 28,800 vph; 38-hour power reserve
Functions: hours, minutes, sweep seconds; date
Case: burnished stainless steel, ø 38.5 mm, height 11 mm; sapphire crystal; screw-down crown; water-resistant to 10 atm
Band: burnished stainless steel Milanese mesh, sliding clasp
Remarks: full-lume dial
Price: $745

Blue Pilot Aristomatic Plus

Reference number: 7H171-M
Movement: automatic, Aristomatic Plus (modified Sellita SW200-1); ø 25.6 mm, height 4.6 mm; 26 jewels; 28,800 vph; XL tungsten rotor; 48-hour power reserve
Functions: hours, minutes, sweep seconds; date
Case: burnished stainless steel, ø 47 mm, height 12 mm; sapphire crystal; water-resistant to 5 atm
Band: burnished stainless steel Milanese mesh, folding clasp
Price: $995

Flieger 39 Gold PVD

Reference number: 0H31-L
Movement: automatic, Sellita Caliber SW200-1;
ø 25.6 mm, height 4.6 mm; 26 jewels; 28,800 vph;
38-hour power reserve
Functions: hours, minutes, sweep seconds
Case: stainless steel with matte-gold PVD, ø 38.5 mm,
height 10 mm; sapphire crystal; water-resistant to 5 atm
Band: leather, pin buckle
Price: $725

Flieger 42 Gold PVD Automatic

Reference number: 0H32-L
Movement: automatic, Sellita Caliber SW200-1;
ø 25.6 mm, height 4.6 mm; 26 jewels; 28,800 vph;
38-hour power reserve
Functions: hours, minutes, sweep seconds; date
Case: stainless steel with matte-gold PVD, ø 42 mm,
height 10.5 mm; sapphire crystal; water-resistant to
5 atm
Band: leather, pin buckle
Price: $790

Flieger 42 Black PVD

Reference number: 0H30-L
Movement: automatic, Sellita Caliber SW200-1;
ø 25.6 mm, height 4.6 mm; 26 jewels; 28,800 vph;
38-hour power reserve
Functions: hours, minutes, sweep seconds; date
Case: stainless steel with black PVD, ø 42 mm, height
10.5 mm; sapphire crystal; water-resistant to 5 atm
Band: leather, pin buckle
Price: $660

Vintage 38 Beo RECORD

Reference number: 7H173
Movement: automatic, Record Caliber 1959-2;
ø 25.6 mm, height 4.8 mm; 17 jewels; 21,600 vph;
historic Record automatic movement from the 1970s,
like the ones used by Longines; revised new old stock;
40-hour power reserve
Functions: hours, minutes, sweep seconds
Case: burnished stainless steel, ø 38.5 mm, height
11 mm; sapphire crystal; water-resistant to 5 atm
Band: leather, pin buckle
Price: $790; limited to 50 pieces

Vintage 42 Pilot RECORD

Reference number: 7H166
Movement: automatic, Record Caliber 1959-2;
ø 25.6 mm, height 4.8 mm; 17 jewels; 21,600 vph;
historic Record automatic movement from the 1970s,
like the ones used by Longines; revised new old stock
updated; 40-hour power reserve
Functions: hours, minutes, sweep seconds
Case: burnished stainless steel, ø 42 mm, height 11 mm;
sapphire crystal; water-resistant to 5 atm
Band: leather, pin buckle
Remarks: limited to 50 pieces
Price: $790

Titanium Flieger Beo

Reference number: 5H101Ti-VIN
Movement: automatic, Sellita Caliber SW200-1;
ø 25.6 mm, height 4.6 mm; 26 jewels; 28,800 vph;
38-hour power reserve
Functions: hours, minutes, sweep seconds; date
Case: matte titanium, ø 41 mm, height 10.5 mm;
sapphire crystal; water-resistant to 5 atm
Band: leather, pin buckle
Price: $750

ARMIN STROM

For more than thirty years, Armin Strom's name was associated mainly with the art of skeletonizing. But this "grandmaster of skeletonizers" then decided to entrust his life's work to the next generation, which turned out to be the Swiss industrialist and art patron Willy Michel.

Michel had the wherewithal to expand the one-man show into a full-blown *manufacture* able to conceive, design, and produce its own mechanical movements. The endeavor attracted Claude Geisler, a very skilled designer, and Michel's own son, Serge, who became business manager. When this triumvirate joined forces, it came up with a technically impressive movement that drove the One Week model, which, as the name suggests, only requires winding once a week.

The state-of-the-art manufacture, which opened in 2009 in Bözingen, a suburb of Biel/Bienne, operates with a completely vertical structure and employs around 30 craftspeople across all specialized disciplines. The portfolio of movements has grown to over twenty calibers, a testament to the company's strategic success, all developed and produced in-house, including intricate tourbillons.

The ARF15 caliber of the Mirrored Force Resonance, for example, features two balance wheels placed close enough to influence each other (resonance) and give the movement greater stability. The two oscillating systems are coupled via a spiral spring with two counter-rotating coils, which was developed completely in-house. The company has innovated in many other directions, notably in its System 78 line with a clever stop-work mechanism for an automatic movement and development of a motor barrel, whereby the barrel's arbor drives the movement.

The advantages of vertical integration are rapid decision-making, comprehensive expertise, and quick response times. It lets the *manufacture* conceive extraordinary, even experimental expressions of *haute horlogerie*.

ARMIN STROM AG
Bözingenstrasse 46
CH-2502 Biel/Bienne
Switzerland

TEL.:
+41-32-343-3344

E-MAIL:
info@arminstrom.com

WEBSITE:
www.arminstrom.com

FOUNDED:
2006 (first company 1967)

NUMBER OF EMPLOYEES:
22

ANNUAL PRODUCTION:
approx. 1000 watches

U.S. REPRESENTATIVE:
Jean-Marc Bories
Head of North America
929-353-5395
Jean-marc@arminstrom.com

**MOST IMPORTANT COLLECTIONS/
PRICE RANGE:**
Masterpiece Collection, Resonance Collection, Skeleton Collection, System 78 Collection / $9,900 to $100,000 plus

Gravity Equal Force Ultimate Sapphire Rose Gold

Reference number: RG24-GEF.SA
Movement: automatic, Armin Strom Caliber ASB19; ø 35.52 mm, height 11.67 mm; 28 jewels; 25,200 vph; micro-rotor; spring barrel with constant and limited driving force thanks to Maltese cross escapement; finely finished movement; 72-hour power reserve
Functions: hours and minutes (off-center), subsidiary seconds; power reserve indicator
Case: rose gold, ø 41 mm, height 12.65 mm; sapphire crystal; transparent case back; water-resistant to 3 atm
Band: leather, folding clasp
Price: $45,500

Gravity Equal Force Ultimate Sapphire Blue

Reference number: ST24-GEF.BLU
Movement: automatic, Armin Strom Caliber ASB19; ø 35.52 mm, height 11.67 mm; 28 jewels; 25,200 vph; micro-rotor; spring barrel with constant and limited driving force thanks to Maltese cross escapement; finely finished movement; 72-hour power reserve
Functions: hours and minutes(off-center), subsidiary seconds; power reserve indicator
Case: stainless steel, ø 41 mm, height 12.65 mm; sapphire crystal; transparent case back; water-resistant to 3 atm
Band: leather, folding clasp
Price: $40,900

Mirrored Force Resonance Ice Blue

Reference number: ST25-RF.05
Movement: hand-wound, Caliber ARF21; ø 37.2 mm, height 6.7 mm; 39 jewels; 25,200 vph; two independent regulating systems that mutually stabilize each other; finely finished movement; 48-hour power reserve
Functions: hours and minutes (off-center), two subsidiary seconds
Case: stainless steel, ø 43 mm, height 11.55 mm; sapphire crystal; transparent case back; water-resistant to 3 atm
Band: leather, double folding clasp
Price: $90,000; limited to 15 pieces

Dual Time GMT Resonance Manufacture Edition

Reference number: ST25-DT.90
Movement: hand-wound, Caliber ARF22; ø 34.15 mm, height 4.92 mm; 70 jewels; 25,200 vph; two independent regulation systems connected by a resonance clutch spring; two mainsprings; hand-decorated mainplate and bridges; 42-hour power reserve
Functions: hours, minutes (double); additional 24-hour display (second time zone), power reserve indicator (double)
Case: stainless steel, ø 39 mm, height 9.05 mm; sapphire crystal; transparent case back; water-resistant to 5 atm
Band: reptile skin, pin buckle
Price: $99,700; limited to 50 pieces

One Week Titanium Skeleton

Reference number: TI25-OW.75
Movement: hand-wound, Armin Strom Caliber ARM21; ø 36.6 mm, height 6 mm; 35 jewels; 25,200 vph; 2 spring barrels, escapement with variable inertia; mainplate with anthracite PVD; finely finished movement; 168-hour power reserve
Functions: hours, minutes, subsidiary seconds
Case: titanium, ø 41 mm, height 10.6 mm; sapphire crystal; transparent case back; water-resistant to 10 atm
Band: titanium, double folding clasp
Price: $45,000; limited to 100 pieces

Orbit Purple

Reference number: ST25-OR.01
Movement: automatic, Armin Strom Caliber ASS20; ø 35.52 mm, height 8.42 mm; 30 jewels; 25,200 vph; micro-rotor; spring barrel with constant and limited driving force thanks to Maltese cross escapement; finely finished movement; 72-hour power reserve
Functions: hours and minutes (off-center), subsidiary seconds; date
Case: stainless steel with black DLC, ø 43.4 mm, height 12.6 mm; sapphire crystal; transparent case back; water-resistant to 5 atm
Band: textile, pin buckle
Price: $42,000; limited to 20 pieces

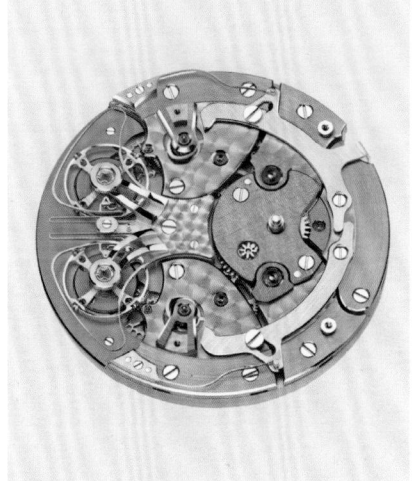

Caliber ASB19

Automatic; micro-rotor; mainspring drive with constant force escapement (Maltese cross); simple spring barrel, 72-hour power reserve
Functions: hours, minutes, subsidiary seconds; power reserve indicator
Diameter: 35.52 mm
Height: 11.67 mm
Jewels: 28
Balance: screw balance with variable inertia
Frequency: 25,200 vph
Remarks: movement finely decorated by hand; 202 parts

Caliber ARF21

Hand-wound; two independent regulating systems connected with a clutch spring; single spring barrel; 48-hour power reserve
Functions: hours, minutes (off-center), subsidiary seconds
Diameter: 37.2 mm
Height: 6.7 mm
Jewels: 39
Balance: with variable inertia
Frequency: 25,200 vph
Hairspring: flat hairspring
Remarks: movement finely decorated by hand; 276 parts

Caliber ARF22

Hand-wound; two spring barrels, 42-hour power reserve
Functions: hours, minutes (double); additional 24-hour display (second time zone), power reserve indicator (double)
Diameter: 34.15 mm
Height: 4.92 mm
Jewels: 70
Balance: two independent regulating systems connected by a resonance clutch spring
Frequency: 25,200 vph
Remarks: hand-decorated mainplate and bridges

ARNOLD & SON

John Arnold holds a special place among British watchmakers of the eighteenth and nineteenth centuries as the first to organize chronometer production along industrial lines. He developed his own standards and employed numerous watchmakers. During his lifetime, he is said to have manufactured around 5,000 marine chronometers, which he sold at reasonable prices to the Royal Navy and the West Indies merchant fleet. Arnold chronometers accompanied some of the greatest explorers, from John Franklin and Ernest Shackleton to Captain James Cook and Dr. David Livingstone.

Just as Arnold & Son was once synonymous with precision timekeeping on the high seas, the modern brand logically focuses its designs on the interplay of time and geography, alongside the basic functions of navigation. Now independent from The British Masters Group, the venerable English chronometer maker is reorienting itself toward classic, elegant watchmaking. With the expertise of watch manufacturer La Joux-Perret behind it, including the technical knowledge housed in its facility on the main road between La Chaux-de-Fonds and Le Locle, the brand has been able to implement several new ideas.

Remaining modern is perhaps the biggest challenge for any heritage brand, and here Arnold & Son shows remarkable skill by uniting three key aspects: astronomy, chronometry, and universal time. Like an echo of John Arnold's own inventions and interests, these three pillars form the foundation of its collections. The Globetrotter, for example, features a bold split bridge over the dial. The Luna Magna presents a sculptural moon that closely resembles what we see in the night sky. And the Longitude's simplicity is a direct link to Arnold's glorious maritime past.

A more subtle update for connoisseurs: the movements have been reworked to fit into slightly smaller cases, a change that aligns perfectly with the trend of the past few years.

ARNOLD & SON
38, boulevard des Eplatures
CH-2300 La Chaux-de-Fonds
Switzerland

TEL.:
+41-32-967-9797

E-MAIL:
info@arnoldandson.com

WEBSITE:
www.arnoldandson.com

FOUNDED:
1995

NUMBER OF EMPLOYEES:
approx. 30

U.S. DISTRIBUTOR:
Arnold & Son USA
510 West 6th Street, Suite 309
Los Angeles, CA 90014
213-622-1133

**MOST IMPORTANT COLLECTIONS/
PRICE RANGE:**
Eight-Day / Globetrotter / Longitude / Nebula /
TB88, TBR, TE8 (Tourbillon), Time Pyramid, UTTE /
from approx. $10,000 to $325,000

Longitude

Reference number: 1LTAT.F01A.N001U
Movement: automatic, Arnold & Son Caliber 6302 (base MLJP); ø 33 mm, height 6.65 mm; 36 jewels; 28,800 vph; COSC-certified chronometer; 60-hour power reserve
Functions: hours, minutes, small seconds; power reserve indicator
Case: titanium, ø 42.5 mm, height 12.25 mm; sapphire crystal; transparent case back; water-resistant to 10 atm
Band: textile, pin buckle
Remarks: comes with an additional titanium bracelet
Price: $24,400

Ultrathin Tourbillon Skeleton

Reference number: 1UTBR.Z01A.C246R
Movement: hand-wound, Arnold & Son Caliber 8320 (on MLJP base); ø 32 mm, height 3.3 mm; 29 jewels; 21,600 vph; flying 1-minute tourbillon; skeletonized movement; 100-hour power reserve
Functions: hours, minutes
Case: red gold, ø 41.5 mm, height 8.4 mm; sapphire crystal; transparent case back; water-resistant to 3 atm
Band: reptile skin, folding clasp
Remarks: limited to 28 pieces
Price: $84,600

Perpetual Moon 38

Reference number: 1GLBR.U02A.C283A
Movement: hand-wound, Arnold & Son Caliber 1612 (on MLJP base); ø 29.4 mm, height 4.95 mm; 24 jewels; 21,600 vph; moon phase astronomically precise for 122 years; 90-hour power reserve
Functions: hours, minutes; moon phase
Case: red gold, ø 38 mm, height 10.44 mm; sapphire crystal; transparent case back; water-resistant to 3 atm
Band: reptile skin, pin buckle
Price: $36,700

ARTYA

The business gurus like to use or create buzzwords for their processes like "agility," and "disruptive," and even "innovative," to describe more of the same with a few small changes. . . . In watchmaking, the approach often involves small engineering advances and a noisy campaign. Yvan Arpa, founder of ArtyA watches, does it differently.

This refreshingly candid personality who spent his *Wanderjahre* crossing Papua New Guinea on foot and practicing Thai boxing in its native land, lives, breathes, and garrulously posts his lived horology online, be it the diving trip to test his divers' watches, or some trek up a mountain.

After various trials and tribulations in the industry, Arpa founded ArtyA, where he could get his "monster" off the slab as it were, with a divine spark. "I had worked with water, rust, dust, and other elements, and then I really caught fire," says Arpa. Indeed, among his first creations were steel cases struck by artificial lightning from a Tesla generator.

One of Arpa's not-so-secret weapons in the fight for market share is his artist wife, Dominique Arpa-Cirpka, who delivers dreamier dials that carefully mix textures and pigments or use real butterfly wings and collages of earth, shells, pigments, or fish scales. And now one of his sons, Jérémie, has joined the team by designing a very "wavy" sapphire crystal case.

Artya's watches hit nerves and draw a gamut of emotional responses. His dials shake up the owner and are often unique in the real sense of the word. No two are alike.

Thinking outside of the box is not enough for Arpa. He thinks out of the dial. An "ordinary" chronograph can become a byzantine riot of subdials and visible parts. He will personally go and test watches like the Depth Gauge, whose arched colored bands on the dial disappear as the watch reaches depths at which certain color frequencies fail. He continues to explore artificial sapphire that changes color. The recent Tiny Purity Tourbillon took a full 7 mm off compared to its bigger sister (it's la montre in French) thanks to some serious reorganizing of the movement that included keeping the double barrel for the full 72-hour power reserve.

LUXURY ARTPIECES ARTYA SA
Route de Gy, 27
1252 Meinier
Switzerland

TEL.:
+41-22-752-4940

WEBSITE:
www.artya.com

FOUNDED:
2010

NUMBER OF EMPLOYEES:
12

U.S. DISTRIBUTOR:
BeauGeste Luxury Brands
www.beaugesteluxury.com

MOST IMPORTANT COLLECTIONS/PRICE RANGE:
Purity, Liminity, Aqua, Art, Complications / $3,800 to $190,000; more for individual complications

Dôme Boréale
Movement: hand-wound, exclusive ArtyOn caliber; ø 25.6 mm, height 3.6 mm; 25 jewels; 28,800 vph; movement fully skeletonized; COSC-certified chronometer; 42-hour power reserve
Functions: hours, minutes, sweep seconds
Case: stainless steel, ø 41 mm, height 15 mm; domed sapphire crystal; screw-mounted transparent case back; water-resistant to 10 atm
Band: leather, pin buckle
Remarks: malachite dial
Price: $16,100; unique piece

Dôme Mars
Movement: hand-wound, exclusive ArtyOn caliber; ø 25.6 mm, height 3.6 mm; 25 jewels; 28,800 vph; movement fully skeletonized; COSC-certified chronometer; 42-hour power reserve
Functions: hours, minutes, sweep seconds
Case: stainless steel, ø 41 mm, height 15 mm; domed sapphire crystal; screw-mounted transparent case back; water-resistant to 10 atm
Band: leather, pin buckle
Remarks: domed dial engraved and galvanized, then given a special coloring to replicate planet Mars
Price: $12,300; unique piece

Butterfly Farfalla
Movement: automatic, exclusive ArtyOn caliber; ø 25.6 mm, height 3.6 mm; 25 jewels; 28,800 vph; skeletonized; COSC-certified chronometer; 42-hour power reserve
Functions: hours, minutes, sweep seconds
Case: stainless steel with carbon inserts in the barrel, ø 40 mm, height 10.8 mm; engraved and screwed-down transparent case back; water-resistant to 5 atm
Band: rubber, pin buckle
Remarks: butterfly wings on the dial
Price: $11,900; unique piece

Luminity AMR-01 Titanium & Amazonite

Movement: automatic, ArtyA AMR-01 Caliber; ø 25.6 mm, height 3.6 mm; 30 jewels; 28,800 vph; micro-rotor; two barrels with extra-long and thin mainspring for 82-hour power reserve
Functions: hours, minutes, subsidiary seconds
Case: titanium matt finishing with transparent DLC, ø 35 mm, height 11.45 mm; transparent case back; water-resistant to 5 atm
Band: leather, pin buckle
Remarks: dial with amazonite in the center and under the subsidiary seconds
Price: $22,400; limited to 99 pieces
Variations: rubber strap; titanium "wavy" case; sapphire crystal with sapphire dial ($43,600), with stone dial ($47,300)

Purity Curvy HMS Mirror

Movement: hand-wound, ArtyA "Stairway to Heaven"; ø 32.4 mm x 27.8 mm, height 5.43 mm; 28,800 vph; 22 jewels; fully skeletonized movement; 2 parallel-mounted spring barrels, with special design; centrally positioned, suspended screw balance; hand-finished parts; 72-hour power reserve
Functions: hours, minutes, subsidiary seconds
Case: brushed titanium with a polished section on the middle section; ø 39.5 mm x 43 mm, height 12 mm; wavy sapphire crystal dome; screwed-down transparent case back; water-resistant to 5 atm
Band: leather, pin buckle
Price: $35,900; limited to 99 pieces
Variations: titanium with black DLC in sapphire crystal; sapphire crystal case ($60,900); NanoSaphir with changing colors ($98,900)

Purity Wavy Central Tourbillon (Purple)

Movement: automatic, ArtyA PUR-T4 Caliber; ø 30.4 mm, height 9.35 mm; 28,800 vph; 36 jewels; 2 parallel-mounted spring barrels; 1-minute, 20-millimeter central flying tourbillon; fully skeletonized movement; hand-finished parts; 72-hour power reserve
Functions: peripheral hours, minutes, seconds on tourbillon cage
Case: sapphire crystal; 43 mm, height 18 mm; screwed-down transparent case back; water-resistant to 3 atm
Band: black nubuck, pin buckle
Remarks: violet-tinted sapphire crystal dial; ArtyA in-house tourbillon
Price: $154,000; unique piece

Luminity Wavy AMR-02

Movement: automatic, ArtyA AMR-02 Caliber; ø 32.4 mm, height 3.6 mm; 30 jewels; 28,800 vph; tungsten micro-rotor; with côtes de Genève; two barrels with extra-long and thin mainspring for 82-hour power reserve
Functions: hours, minutes, sweep seconds
Case: titanium matt finishing with transparent DLC, ø 40 mm, height 13 mm; transparent case back; water-resistant to 5 atm
Band: nubuck leather, pin buckle
Remarks: dial with amazonite in the center and under the subsidiary seconds
Price: $21,300; limited to 99 pieces
Variations: titanium with black DLC; sapphire crystal with sapphire dial ($45,000), with stone dial ($47,400)

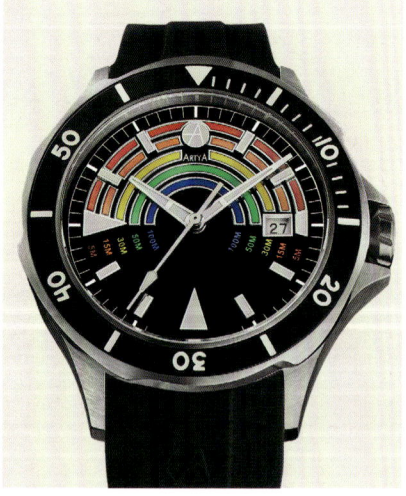

Aqua Steel Depth Gauge

Movement: automatic, La Joux-Perret G100 modified by ArtyA; ø 25.60 mm, height 4.45 mm; 24 jewels; 28,800 vph; with côtes de Genève; 68-hour power reserve
Functions: hours, minutes, sweep seconds; date
Case: stainless steel, ø 43 mm, height 14 mm; unidirectional rotating bezel in steel with ceramic insert; transparent case back; water-resistant to 30 atm
Band: rubber, pin buckle
Remarks: depth gauge on dial with colored arches that disappear one by one the deeper the diver goes due to light wavelengths no longer reaching the dial.
Price: $9,900; limited to 99 pieces

Aqua Carbon Diver

Movement: automatic, exclusive ArtyOn caliber (also with La Joux-Perret G100); ø 25.6 mm, height 3.6 mm; 25 jewels; 28,800 vph; COSC-certified movement; 42-hour power reserve (68 hours with the La Joux-Perret caliber)
Functions: hours, minutes, sweep seconds; date
Case: forged carbon, ø 41 mm, height 14 mm; engraved and screwed-down transparent case back; water-resistant to 30 atm
Band: rubber, pin buckle
Remarks: forged-carbon dial
Price: $12,300; unique piece

AUDEMARS PIGUET

Jules-Louis Audemars (b. 1851) and Edward-Auguste Piguet (b. 1853) knew they would follow in the footsteps of their fathers and grandfathers and become watchmakers. They were members of the same sports association, sang in the same choir, attended the same vocational school—and both became outstandingly talented watchmakers. The *manufacture*, founded 150 years ago by these two, is still in family hands, and it has become one of the leading names in the industry.

In the history of watchmaking, only a handful of watches have really achieved cult status. One of them is the Royal Oak, which in the mean 1970s, disrupted the idea that the quartz watch was the end-all in horology. Audemars Piguet contacted the designer Gérald Genta to create a watch for a new generation of customers, a sportive luxury timepiece with a modern look, which could be worn every day. The result was a luxurious watch of stainless steel. The octagonal bezel held down with boldly "industrial" hexagonal bolts onto a 39-millimeter case was provocatively big and was nicknamed "Jumbo." It ran on what was then the thinnest automatic movement, a slice 3.05 millimeters high.

The iconic Royal Oak is still delivering. To mark the 150th anniversary of the brand in 2025, a new perpetual calendar was mounted into a Royal Oak case, available in stainless steel or the special alloy called "sand gold." It was also added to a CODE 11.59 case. The movement driving these timepieces has been completely redesigned and equipped with an all-in-one crown that controls all functions and simplifies adjustments, a technical feat that is not only of interest to collectors but also proves its worth in everyday use. It eliminates correctors on the case side and underscores the sophistication of the three models. Finally, to close off 2025, Audemars Piguet presented the Royal Oak Concept Tourbillon Companion, a creative collaboration with New York artist KAWS.

What has also contributed to the brand's enduring success is no doubt the acquisition of the atelier Renaud et Papi in 1992. APRP, as it is known, specializes in creating and executing complex complications, a skill it lets other brands share in as well.

MANUFACTURE D'HORLOGERIE
Audemars Piguet
Route de France 16
CH- 1348 Le Brassus
Switzerland

TEL.:
+41-21-642-3900

E-MAIL:
info@audemarspiguet.com

WEBSITE:
www.audemarspiguet.com

FOUNDED:
1875

NUMBER OF EMPLOYEES:
approx. 1,300

ANNUAL PRODUCTION:
50,000 watches

U.S. DISTRIBUTOR:
Audemars Piguet (North America) Inc.
Service Center of the Americas
3040 Gulf to Bay Boulevard
Clearwater, FL 33759

MOST IMPORTANT COLLECTIONS/PRICE RANGE:
CODE 11.59 / from approx. $26,000; Millenary / from approx. $28,400; Royal Oak / from approx. $17,800; special concept watches
Note: Some prices given in Swiss francs (CHF) with a daily exchange in dollars

Royal Oak Doppelte Balance Squelette

Reference number: 15416CD.OO.1225CD.01
Movement: automatic, AP Caliber 3132; ø 26.6 mm, height 4.4 mm; 38 jewels; 21,600 vph; double balance, skeletonized movement, skeletonized rotor in rose gold; 45-hour power reserve
Functions: hours, minutes, sweep seconds
Case: ceramic, ø 41 mm, height 9.7 mm; bezel mounted to case back with 8 white-gold screws; sapphire crystal; transparent case back; screw-down crown; water-resistant to 5 atm
Band: ceramic, titanium folding clasp
Price: $106,200

Royal Oak Offshore Chronograph

Reference number: 26420SO.OO.A029VE.01
Movement: automatic, AP Caliber 4401; ø 32 mm, height 6.8 mm; 40 jewels; 28,800 vph; fully hand-decorated movement; 70-hour power reserve
Functions: hours, minutes, subsidiary seconds; flyback-chronograph; date
Case: stainless steel, ø 43 mm, height 14.4 mm; ceramic bezel mounted to case back with 8 white-gold screws; sapphire crystal; transparent case back; ceramic crown and pusher; water-resistant to 10 atm
Band: leather, pin buckle
Remarks: comes with rubber strap
Price: $45,000

CODE 11.59 Perpetual Calendar Automatic

Reference number: 26494BC.OO.D350KB.01
Movement: automatic, AP Caliber 7138; ø 29.6 mm, height 4.1 mm; 41 jewels; 28,800 vph; finely finished movement; 55-hour power reserve
Functions: hours, minutes; perpetual calendar with date, weekday, month, moon phase, leap year
Case: white gold, ø 41 mm, height 10.6 mm; sapphire crystal; transparent case back; water-resistant to 3 atm
Band: rubber, folding clasp
Price: $114,800; limited to 150 pieces

Royal Oak Perpetual Calendar Automatic

Reference number: 26674SG.OO.1320SG.01
Movement: automatic, AP Caliber 5134; ø 29 mm, height 4.5 mm; 38 jewels; 19,800 vph; skeletonized rose-gold rotor, finely finished movement; 40-hour power reserve
Functions: hours, minutes; perpetual calendar with date, weekday, week number, month, moon phase, leap year
Case: sand gold, ø 41 mm, height 9.5 mm; bezel mounted to case back with 8 white-gold screws; sapphire crystal; transparent case back; water-resistant to 5 atm
Band: rose gold ("sand gold"), folding clasp
Price: $159,000

CODE 11.59 Flying Tourbillon Automatic

Reference number: 26665SG.ZZ.D209CR.01
Movement: automatic, AP Caliber 2968; ø 29.6 mm, height 3.4 mm; 33 jewels; 21,600 vph; flying one-minute tourbillon; skeletonized rotor; 50-hour power reserve
Functions: hours, minutes
Case: sand gold, set with 235 brilliant-cut diamonds, ø 38 mm, height 9.6 mm; sapphire crystal; transparent case back; water-resistant to 3 atm
Band: reptile skin, folding clasp set with 42 brilliant-cut diamonds
Price: on request

Royal Oak Offshore Chronograph

Reference number: 26420CE.OO.A063VE.01
Movement: automatic, AP Caliber 4401; ø 32 mm, height 6.8 mm; 40 jewels; 28,800 vph; fully hand-decorated movement; 70-hour power reserve
Functions: hours, minutes, subsidiary seconds; flyback-chronograph; date
Case: ceramic, ø 43 mm, height 14.4 mm; bezel mounted to case back with 8 white-gold screws; sapphire crystal; water-resistant to 10 atm
Band: textile with rubber coating, pin buckle
Price: $61,300

CODE 11.59 Automatic

Reference number: 15210ST.OO.A009KB.01
Movement: automatic, AP Caliber 4302; ø 32 mm, height 4.9 mm; 32 jewels; 28,800 vph; gold rotor, finely finished movement; 70-hour power reserve
Functions: hours, minutes, sweep seconds; date
Case: stainless steel, ø 41 mm, height 10.7 mm; sapphire crystal; transparent case back; water-resistant to 3 atm
Band: textile with rubber coating, pin buckle
Price: $27,400
Variations: various cases, straps, and dials

CODE 11.59 Chronograph

Reference number: 26393ST.OO.A009KB.01
Movement: automatic, AP Caliber 4401; ø 32 mm, height 6.8 mm; 40 jewels; 28,800 vph; skeletonized gold rotor, finely finished movement; 70-hour power reserve
Functions: hours, minutes, subsidiary seconds; flyback chronograph; date
Case: stainless steel, ø 41 mm, height 12.6 mm; sapphire crystal; transparent case back; water-resistant to 3 atm
Band: textile with rubber coating, pin buckle
Price: $37,900
Variations: various cases, straps, and dials

Royal Oak Concept Tourbillon "Companion"

Reference number: 26656TI.GG.D019VE.01
Movement: hand-wound, AP Caliber 2979; ø 32.3 mm, height 10.4 mm; 39 jewels; 21,600 vph; 1-minute tourbillon, titanium bridges with black PVD, finely finished movement; 72-hour power reserve
Functions: hours and minutes ("mysterious")
Case: titanium, ø 43 mm, height 17.4 mm; bezel with 8 white gold screws; sapphire crystal; transparent case back; ceramic crown; water-resistant to 10 atm
Band: leather, triple folding clasp
Remarks: special edition made in collaboration with the New York artist KAWS, creator of the character "Companion"
Price: on request; limited to 250 pieces

Royal Oak Frosted Gold automatic

Reference number: 77450BC.GG.1361BC.01
Movement: automatic, AP Caliber 5800; ø 23.9 mm, height 4 mm; 28 jewels; 28,800 vph; finely finished movement; 50-hour power reserve
Functions: hours, minutes, sweep seconds; date
Case: white gold, with structured surface, ø 34 mm, height 8.8 mm; bezel mounted to case back with 8 white-gold screws; sapphire crystal; transparent case back; water-resistant to 5 atm
Band: white gold, folding clasp
Remarks: micro-structured white gold-dial ("Crystalsand")
Price: $68,500

CODE 11.59 automatic

Reference number: 77410BC.ZZ.D132CR.01
Movement: automatic, AP Caliber 5900; ø 26.2 mm, height 3.9 mm; 29 jewels; 28,800 vph; gold rotor, finely finished movement; 60-hour power reserve
Functions: hours, minutes, sweep seconds
Case: white gold, set with diamonds, ø 38 mm, height 9.6 mm; sapphire crystal; transparent case back; water-resistant to 3 atm
Band: reptile skin, pin buckle
Remarks: dial fully set with various colored diamonds
Price: $108,900

CODE 11.59 automatic

Reference number: 77410OR.OO.A623CR.01
Movement: automatic, AP Caliber 5900; ø 26,2 mm, height 3.9 mm; 29 jewels; 28,800 vph; gold rotor, finely finished movement; 60-hour power reserve
Functions: hours, minutes, sweep seconds; date
Case: rose gold, ø 38 mm, height 9.6 mm; sapphire crystal; transparent case back; water-resistant to 3 atm
Band: reptile skin, pin buckle
Price: $35,900
Variations: various cases, straps, and dials

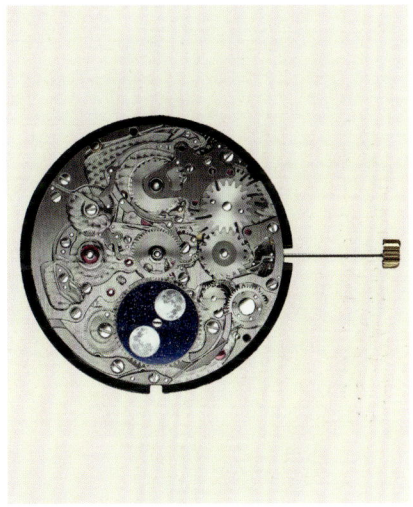

Caliber 7138

Automatic; control of all settings via the winding crown; simple spring barrel, 55-hour power reserve
Functions: hours, minutes; perpetual calendar with date, weekday, calendar week, month, moon phase, leap year
Diameter: 29.6 mm
Height: 4.1 mm
Jewels: 41
Frequency: 28,800 vph
Shock protection: Kif
Remarks: finely finished movement; 423 parts

Caliber 4404

Automatic; column-wheel control of chronograph functions; skeletonized rotor; single barrel spring; 70-hour power reserve
Functions: hours, minutes, subsidiary seconds; flyback chronograph; date
Diameter: 32 mm
Height: 8 mm
Jewels: 40
Balance: with variable inertia
Frequency: 28,800 vph
Remarks: fully skeletonized movement; 433 parts

Caliber 2968

Automatic; flying one-minute tourbillon; skeletonized rotor; simple barrel spring, 50-hour power reserve
Functions: hours, minutes
Diameter: 29.6 mm
Height: 3.4 mm
Jewels: 33
Frequency: 21,600 vph
Remarks: 226 parts

AZIMUTH

Creativity can take on all forms and accept all forms. This appears to be the philosophy behind Azimuth, an independent watch brand that has sprouted an eclectic and surprising bouquet of watch designs. For the company, the path is by no means well-beaten: Azimuth always guarantees a raised eyebrow with its avant-garde designs for luxury timepieces, with several iconic models like the Mr. Roboto, the Spaceship series, and the automobile series enjoying cult status.

The creation of the Land Cruiser is yet another testament to Azimuth's enduring love affair between imagination and science fiction, fused into the realm of horology. The Land Cruiser carries the DNA of its predecessor, the SP-1 Landship created in 2010, which was inspired by the World War I military tank. The Land Cruiser comes stacked with interesting functions reflecting the original designs of the Landship. Time is told by the domed wondering hour at the 12 o'clock position and the slanted retrograde minute aperture at the 6 o'clock position. The Land Cruiser has now taken on a sleeker design with chiseled sides and smooth curves, creating a whole new dimension of stealth-look. To mimic the effect of a supersonic aircraft's afterburner, the winding crown has also been repositioned to 12 o'clock. The result is an ergonomically designed spacecraft that sits snugly on your wrist.

This year, Azimuth introduces a new Back in Time Series 2 (BIT S2) in turquoise stone dial, a timepiece that celebrates the relentless pursuit of excellence in craftsmanship and innovation. Azimuth's original Back in Time captivated the horology world with its debut at Baselworld 2009. As the first single-hand, counterclockwise timepiece, it broke new grounds in watchmaking, enchanting collectors and enthusiasts alike. Over this period, Azimuth has dedicated itself to refining its designs and enhancing the technical performance of this timepiece, ensuring that the BIT S2 is not just a continuation but a significant evolution of the original.

2025 welcomes an unusual collaboration—The Billionaire's Watch by Azimuth X Bobby Saputra; a watch that is not merely crafted but ordained. Created with a private vision where dragon and phoenix converge, the dragon embodies power and command, and the phoenix symbolizes renewal and destiny. "Inspired by Indo-Chinese traditions and Bobby Saputra's personal legacy," this stunning timepiece results from a forward-thinking partnership that imbues modern *haute horlogerie* with rich cultural symbolism.

AZIMUTH WATCH CO. SÀRL
Rue des Draizes n° 5
CH-2000 Neuchâtel
Switzerland

TEL.:
+41-79-765-1466

E-MAIL:
gpi@azimuthwatch.com
chrislong@azimuthwatch.com

WEBSITE:
www.azimuthwatch.com

FOUNDED:
2003

NUMBER OF EMPLOYEES:
4

U.S. DISTRIBUTOR:
Grenon's of Newport
210 Bellevue Avenue
Newport RI 02840
401-846-0598

MOST IMPORTANT COLLECTIONS/PRICE RANGE:
SP-1 collections / from $4,800

SP-1 Mr. Roboto Titanium
Reference number: SP.TI.MRT.L001
Movement: automatic, in-house modified ETA 2836-2 caliber; ø 32.5 mm, height 6.7 mm; 28,800 vph; 36-hour power reserve
Functions: regulator hours, retrograde minutes, second time zone (GMT)
Case: crystalized titanium, 43 mm x 50 mm, height 18.6 mm, sapphire crystal, water-resistant to 3 atm
Band: rubber strap, pin buckle
Price: $6,400

SP-1 Mr. Roboto Sapphire
Reference number: SP.TI.MRS.L003
Movement: automatic, in-house modified ETA 2836-2 caliber; ø 32.5 mm, height 6.7 mm; 28,800 vph; 36-hour power reserve
Functions: regulator hours, retrograde minutes, second time zone (GMT)
Case: sapphire crystal, 43 mm x 50 mm, height 19 mm, water-resistant to 3 atm
Band: calf strap, bronze pin buckle
Remarks: Damascus steel dial
Price: $23,000; limited to 20 pieces

SP-1 Mr. Roboto Bronzo Artist Series
Reference number: SP.BR.MRB.L002
Movement: automatic, in-house modified ETA 2836-2 caliber; ø 32.5 mm, height 6.7 mm; 28,800 vph; 36-hour power reserve
Functions: regulator hours, retrograde minutes, second time zone (GMT)
Case: bronze, 43 mm x 50 mm, height 18.6 mm, sapphire crystal, water-resistant to 3 atm
Band: calf strap, bronze pin buckle
Remarks: unique piece with bespoke hand-engraved bezel
Price: $10,450

SP-1 Mr. Roboto R2

Reference number: SP.SS.ROT.N001
Movement: automatic, in-house modified ETA 2836-2 caliber; ø 32.50 mm, height 6.7 mm; 28,800 vph; 36-hour power reserve
Functions: regulator hours, retrograde minutes, second time zone (GMT)
Case: stainless steel, 47 mm x 55 mm, height 18.3 mm, sapphire crystal, water-resistant to 3 atm
Band: calf strap, folding clasp
Price: $6,600
Variations: mid-case in titanium with blue PVD treatment

SP-1 Land Cruiser Black PVD

Reference number: SP.SS.LC.L002
Movement: automatic, in-house modified SW 200-1 caliber; 28,800 vph, ø 32.5 mm, height 6.7 mm; 36-hour power reserve
Functions: regulator hours, retrograde minutes
Case: stainless steel in black PVD, 50 mm x 45 mm, body height 15 mm, water-resistant to 3 atm
Band: rubber strap, folding clasp
Price: $7,500; limited to 30 pieces

SP-1 Spaceship Predator Ti Lava OverLand

Reference number: SP.TI.PR.N004
Movement: hand-wound, ETA 6497-1 caliber; ø 36.6 mm, height 4.5 mm; 18,800 vph; rhodium finishing with côtes de Genève and blued screws, 40-hour power reserve
Functions: jumping hours, minutes
Case: titanium and stainless steel, ø 44 mm, height 20 mm, domed sapphire crystal, water-resistant to 3 atm
Band: rubber strap, folding clasp
Price: $4,800

Azimuth X Bobby Saputra The Billionaire's Watch

Reference number: RN.SS.BS.N001
Movement: automatic, in-house modified ETA 2892-A2 caliber; ø 25.6 mm, height 3.7 mm; 28,800 vph; 40-hour power reserve
Functions: hour, minute, sweep seconds, date, moonphase
Case: stainless steel, ø 41.3 mm, height 12.50 mm, sapphire crystal, water-resistant to 3 atm
Band: calf strap, folding clasp
Price: $3,000; limited to 99 pieces

Back-In-Time Series 2

Reference number: RN.BT.SS.S203
Movement: automatic, in-house modified Sellita SW 200-1; ø 32.9 mm, height 4.5 mm; 28,800 vph; 38-hour power reserve
Functions: hour and minute hands in counterclockwise motion
Case: stainless steel, ø 41.3 mm, height 13.35 mm, sapphire crystal, water-resistant to 3 atm
Band: calf strap, folding clasp
Price: $2,850
Remarks: dial styled with turquoise stone and ceramic hour ring with luminous numerals

Back-In-Time Series 2

Reference number: RN.BT.SS.S201
Movement: automatic, in-house modified Sellita SW 200-1; ø 32.9 mm, height 4.5 mm; 28,800 vph; 38-hour power reserve
Functions: single hand in counterclockwise motion
Case: stainless steel, ø 41.3 mm, height 13.35 mm, sapphire crystal, water-resistant to 3 atm
Band: calf strap, folding clasp
Price: $2,850
Variations: various dial colours and straps combination

BA111OD

While much of the watch industry is focused primarily on great engineering and maintaining a brand image, Thomas Baillod originally set out to persuade the watch industry to adopt a new, customer-centric sales model. The brands he approached dismissed the idea out of hand: "That will never work!" So the marketing specialist took matters into his own hands. He founded his own watch brand with a clear mission of doing everything differently—or doing it right, in other words.

The first step was to create a watch that would become "chapter" 1. Boldly, Baillod commissioned designers and manufacturers to produce one in China, which is not exactly appreciated in Switzerland. But for the next "chapter," he turned to Swiss suppliers. Case, base movement, movement components and finishing, hands, crystals, straps were all produced by renowned Swiss specialists who also supply the major names in the industry. The result was a modern, sporty three-hand watch with a skeletonized automatic movement, priced at under 600 euros. Baillod had intended only to prove that he could come up with affordable watches of excellent quality by tapping into top-drawer suppliers. He ended up creating a watch brand.

The difference was his cost-saving distribution concept—"user-generated commerce," a hybrid of Tupperware party and pyramid scheme—quickly reached its limits as growth accelerated. In the meantime, a sophisticated online shop has become increasingly important, and the first specialist retailers have begun adding the brand, despite its hard-to-decipher logo (*Ba111od—how do you even pronounce that?*), to their portfolios.

Since its founding six years ago, Thomas Baillod's watch brand has expanded at remarkable speed, relocating to larger premises several times and progressing to the eighth "chapter" of its model history. The collection now spans straightforward three-hand models and chronometers, contemporary skeleton designs, elegant ladies' pieces, and complications ranging from tourbillons to curved-hand displays. Only one thing remains constant: an almost unbeatable price-to-performance ratio.

BA111OD SÀRL
Place des Halles 8
CH-2000 Neuchâtel
Switzerland

TEL.:
+41 79 316 94 28

E-MAIL:
contact@ba111od.com

WEBSITE:
www.ba111od.com

FOUNDED:
2019

DISTRIBUTION:
Community of owners through "we-commerce," online, retailers

Chapter 8 Sand
Movement: automatic, Soprod P024 caliber; ø 25.6 mm, height 4.6 mm; 25 jewels; 28,800 vph; 38-hour power reserve
Functions: hours, minutes, sweep seconds; date
Case: stainless steel, ø 41 mm, height 12.75 mm; sapphire crystal; transparent case back; water-resistant to 5 atm
Band: leather, folding clasp
Price: $750
Variations: with Milanese-mesh bracelet

Chapter 4 GMT Tourbillon
Movement: hand-wound, Ba111od BA.01 caliber; ø 31 mm, height 31 mm; 19 jewels; 21,600 vph; tourbillon at 7 o'clock; 100-hour power reserve
Functions: hours, minutes, seconds on tourbillon cage; additional 12-hour display (2nd time zone)
Case: titanium with gold PVD, ø 44 mm, height 12.75 mm; sapphire crystal; transparent case back; water-resistant to 5 atm
Band: leather, folding clasp
Price: $10,900; limited to 30 pieces
Variations: stainless steel Milanese mesh with gold PVD,

Chapter 8 Moonphase Grey
Movement: automatic, Soprod C105 caliber; ø 25.6 mm, height 5.1 mm; 33 jewels; 28,800 vph; 42-hour power reserve
Functions: hours, minutes, subsidiary seconds; date; moon phase
Case: stainless steel, ø 41 mm, height 12.75 mm; sapphire crystal; transparent case back; water-resistant to 5 atm
Band: leather, folding clasp
Price: $1,380
Variations: with Milanese-mesh bracelet

Chapter 7 Chronometer Forest Green

Movement: automatic, Soprod P024 caliber; ø 25.6 mm, height 4.6 mm; 25 jewels; 28,800 vph; TIMELAB-certified chronometer; 38-hour power reserve
Functions: hours, minutes, sweep seconds; date
Case: stainless steel, ø 40 mm, height 10.5 mm; sapphire crystal; transparent case back; water-resistant to 10 atm
Band: stainless steel, folding clasp with fine adjustment
Price: $950
Variations: with rubber strap ($899)

Chapter 7 Chronometer Frost Blue

Movement: automatic, Soprod P024 caliber; ø 25.6 mm, height 4.6 mm; 25 jewels; 28,800 vph; TIMELAB-certified chronometer; 38-hour power reserve
Functions: hours, minutes, sweep seconds; date
Case: stainless steel, ø 40 mm, height 10.5 mm; sapphire crystal; transparent case back; water-resistant to 10 atm
Band: rubber, double folding clasp
Price: $899
Variations: with stainless steel bracelet ($950)

Chapter 6.6 Laura

Movement: automatic, Soprod P024 caliber; ø 25.6 mm, height 4.6 mm; 25 jewels; 28,800 vph; skeletonized mainplate; 38-hour power reserve
Functions: hours, minutes, sweep seconds
Case: stainless steel, ø 36.5 mm, height 11 mm; fluted bezel; sapphire crystal; transparent case back; water-resistant to 5 atm
Band: satin, folding clasp
Remarks: aventurine dial
Price: $1,150

Chapter 4 Flying Tourbillon Onyx

Movement: hand-wound, Ba111od BA.02 caliber (modified BCP); ø 31 mm, 19 jewels; 21,600 vph; flying one-minute tourbillon; blackened movement finishing; 120-hour power reserve
Functions: hours, minutes
Case: stainless steel, ø 41 mm, height 9.75 mm; sapphire crystal; transparent case back; water-resistant to 5 atm
Band: leather, pin buckle
Remarks: onyx dial
Price: $11,990

Chapter 4.1 Tourbillon "The Veblen Dilemma"

Movement: hand-wound, Ba111od BA.01 caliber (modified BCP); ø 31 mm, 19 jewels; 21,600 vph; flying one-minute tourbillon; skeletonized movement; 120-hour power reserve
Functions: hours, minutes, subsidiary seconds
Case: titanium with DLC coating, ø 44 mm, height 12.9 mm; sapphire crystal; transparent case back; water-resistant to 5 atm
Band: leather, folding clasp
Remarks: The playful model name refers to sociologist Thorstein Veblen's observation that a low price can make a product appear less desirable.
Price: $9,200

Chapter Delta.3

Movement: automatic, Ba111od 09310 caliber (modified Soprod M100); ø 25.6 mm; 25 jewels plus module; 28,800 vph; hypocycloid hour display with rolling drive; hand tip traces a triangular path; 42-hour power reserve
Functions: hours (hypocycloid), minutes
Case: stainless steel, ø 44 mm, height 12.9 mm; sapphire crystal; transparent case back; water-resistant to 5 atm
Band: rubber, folding clasp
Price: $3,490

BALL

Ball's collections trace back to the company's origins and evoke the romantic age when trains blowing smoke and steam crisscrossed America, driving the country into an economic boom. The General Railroads Timepiece Standards back then included such norms as regulation in at least five positions, precision to within thirty seconds per week, Breguet hairsprings, and so on. One of the chief players in developing the standards was a man named Webster Clay Ball, a farm boy-turned-watchmaker from Fredericktown, Ohio. He decided to leave the homestead and apprentice as a watchmaker.

Ball worked as a sales representative for Dueber watch cases and finally opened the Webb C. Ball Company in Cleveland. In 1891, he added the position of chief inspector of the Lake Shore Lines to his CV. His defining moment came when a hogshead's watch stopped for a few minutes on April 18 that year, resulting in a crash between a fast mail train and the Toledo Express near Kipton, Ohio.

The Lake Shore and Michigan Southern Railroad appointed Ball to investigate the tragedy, which killed nine people. After a two-year investigation, Ball decided to establish quality benchmarks for watch manufacturing that included antimagnetic technology. He also set up a standardized timekeeping tool that gave rise to an expression in the American vernacular, to be "on the Ball." It also inspired the future Swiss Society of Chronometry (COSC), which governs the highest watch timing certification standards today.

Sticking to its origins, Ball still produces tool-like watches, including divers, although now the manufacturing is done in Switzerland. These rugged, durable watches aim to be "accurate in adverse conditions," so says the company tagline—and at a very decent price. Since functionality is a top priority, Ball has developed several mechanisms like the patented SpringLOCK anti-shock system that prevents the balance spring from unfurling when jostled. Ball has also developed special oils for cold temperatures, and it is one of few brands to use tritium gas tubes to light up dials, hands, and markers. For those who need to read the time accurately in dark places—divers, pilots, commandos, hunters, and so forth—this is essential.

BALL WATCH COMPANY SA
Rue du Châtelot 21
CH-2300 La Chaux-de-Fonds
Switzerland

TEL.:
+41-32-724-53-00

E-MAIL:
info@ballwatch.ch

WEBSITE:
www.ballwatch.com

FOUNDED:
1891

U.S. DISTRIBUTION:
888-660-0691

MOST IMPORTANT COLLECTIONS/PRICE RANGE:
Engineer, Fireman, Roadmaster, Trainmaster /
$1,200 to $6,600

Engineer III Bright Path

Reference number: NM9028C-S46CJ-YTE
Movement: automatic, BALL Caliber RR1103-C; ø 25.6 mm, height 4.6 mm; 25 or 26 jewels; 28,800 vph; anti-magnetic mu-metal shield; COSC-certified chronometer; Amortiser anti-shock system; 38-hour power reserve
Functions: hours, minutes, sweep seconds; magnified date
Case: stainless steel, ø 43 mm, height 12.75 mm; Mu-metal shield; sapphire crystal; screwed-in crown; water-resistant to 10 atm
Band: stainless steel, folding buckle
Remarks: micro gas tube illumination; shock-resistant; anti-magnetic
Price: $2,549
Variations: ø 36 mm, height 11.5 mm or ø 40 mm, height 13.15 mm

Engineer III Outlier

Reference number: DG9002B-S2C-BE
Movement: automatic, BALL Manufacture Caliber RRM7337-C; ø 26.2 mm, height 4.5 mm; 25 jewels; 28,800 vph; anti-magnetic mu-metal shield; COSC-certified chronometer; Amortiser anti-shock system; 42-hour power reserve
Functions: hours, minutes, sweep second; magnified date; quick-set local 12-hour hand; second time zone indication
Case: stainless steel, ø 40 mm, height 13.8 mm; ceramic bidirectional bezel; sapphire crystal; screwed-in crown; water-resistant to 20 atm
Band: stainless steel, folding buckle
Remarks: micro gas tube illumination; shock-resistant; anti-magnetic
Price: $4,099
Variations: steel bezel; black, turquoise, or white dial

Engineer M Marvelight Amazing Grace

Reference number: NM9032C-S7CJ-MALR
Movement: automatic, BALL Manufacture Caliber RRM7309-C; ø 34.24 mm, height 5.16 mm; 25 jewels; 28,800 vph; COSC-certified chronometer; 80-hour power reserve
Functions: hours, minutes, sweep seconds; magnified date
Case: stainless steel, ø 40 mm, height 12.05 mm; sapphire crystal; transparent case back; screw-down crown; water-resistant to 10 atm
Strap: stainless, folding buckle
Remarks: micro gas tube illumination; shock-resistant; anti-magnetic
Price: $3,099
Variations: classic tubes colors; ø 43 mm stainless steel, height 13.4 mm; ø 43-mm bronze case, height 13.5 mm

Engineer Hydrocarbon AeroGMT II Meteorite

Reference number: DG2018C-S20C-MSL
Movement: automatic, Ball caliber RR1201-C;
ø 25.6 mm, height 4.1mm; 21 jewels; 28,800 vph; COSC-certified chronometer; 42-hour power reserve
Functions: hours, minutes, sweep seconds; date; three time zone indication
Case: stainless steel, ø 42 mm, height 13.85 mm; sapphire bidirectional bezel with micro gas tubes; dome-shaped anti-reflective sapphire crystal; crown protection system; water-resistant to 10 atm
Band: stainless steel, folding clasp and extension
Remarks: micro gas tube illumination; shock-resistant; anti-magnetic
Price: $4,699
Variations: rubber strap; comes in smaller size, ø 40 mm, height 14.5 mm

Engineer Hydrocarbon EOD

Reference number: DM3200A-S1C-BK
Movement: automatic, Ball caliber RR1101-CSL; ø 25.6 mm, height 3.6 mm; 25 jewels; 28,800 vph; COSC-certified chronometer; SpringLOCK antishock system; SpringSEAL patented regulator anti-shock system; special movement oil to endure -45°C to 80°C / -49°F to 176°F; 42-hour power reserve
Functions: hours, minutes, sweep seconds; magnified date
Case: titanium, ø 42 mm, height 13.7 mm; stainless steel unidirectional bezel with micro gas tube inset; mu-metal shield; sapphire crystal; special screwed-in crown protection cap; push-in crown; water-resistant to 30 atm; patented shock absorption ring
Band: titanium and stainless steel, folding clasp with extension link
Remarks: micro gas tube illumination; shock-resistant; anti-magnetic
Price: $3,699
Variations: ceramic bezel

Engineer Hydrocarbon NEDU

Reference number: DC3226A-S3C-BE
Movement: automatic, Ball caliber RR1402-C; ø 30 mm, height 7.9 mm; 25 jewels; 28,800 vph; COSC-certified chronometer; 48-hour power reserve
Functions: hours, minutes, subsidiary seconds; day, date; 12-hour chronograph operable underwater
Case: stainless steel, ø 42 mm, height 17.3 mm; patented helium system; ceramic unidirectional bezel; sapphire crystal; crown protection system; water-resistant to 60 atm
Band: titanium and stainless steel, folding clasp with extension link
Remarks: micro gas tube illumination; shock-resistant; anti-magnetic
Price: $5,049
Variations: black dial; rubber strap

Engineer III Marvelight Chronometer Meteorite

Reference number: NM9026C-S46C-MSLR
Movement: automatic, Ball caliber RR1103; ø 25.6 mm, height 4.6 mm; 25 or 26 jewels; 28,800 vph; anti-magnetic mu-metal shield; COSC-certified chronometer; 38-hour power reserve
Functions: hours, minutes, sweep seconds; magnified date
Case: stainless steel, ø 40 mm, height 13.15 mm; sapphire crystal; screw-down crown; water-resistant to 10 atm
Band: stainless steel, folding clasp
Remarks: micro gas tube illumination; shock-resistant; anti-magnetic
Price: $2,899
Variations: classic tube colors

Engineer III Marvelight Chronometer (36mm)

Reference number: NL9616C-S1C-PK
Movement: automatic, Ball caliber RR1101-C; ø 25.6 mm, height 3.6 mm; 25 jewels; 28,800 vph; COSC-certified chronometer; Amortiser anti-shock system; 42-hour power reserve
Functions: hours, minutes, sweep seconds; magnified date
Case: stainless steel, ø 36 mm, height 11.5 mm; mu-metal shield; sapphire crystal; screw-in crown; water-resistant to 10 atm
Band: stainless steel, folding clasp
Remarks: micro gas tube illumination; shock-resistant; anti-magnetic
Price: $2,999
Variations: black dial; ice blue dial; green dial; rainbow tubes colors

Engineer III Marvelight Chronometer Day/Date

Reference number: NM9036C-S1C-IBE
Movement: automatic, Ball caliber RR1102-C; ø 25.6 mm, height 5.05 mm; 25 or 26 jewels; 28,800 vph; COSC-certified chronometer; Amortiser anti-shock system; 38-hour power reserve
Functions: hours, minutes, sweep seconds; day, magnified date
Case: stainless steel, ø 40 mm, height 13 mm; mu-metal shield; sapphire crystal; screwed-in crown; water-resistant to 10 atm
Band: stainless steel, folding buckle
Remarks: micro gas tube illumination; shock-resistant; anti-magnetic
Price: $2,699
Variations: black dial; blue dial; green dial; grey dial; rainbow tubes colors

Roadmaster M Model A

Reference number: DA9100C-S1-BKR
Movement: automatic, Ball caliber RRM7379;
ø 30.4 mm, height 7.6 mm; 31 jewels; Amortiser anti-shock system; 28,800 vph; 40-hour power reserve
Functions: hours, minutes, sweep seconds; magnified date; AlarmMATIC 12-hour automatic mechanical alarm; triple time zone
Case: titanium, ø 41 mm, height 15.2 mm; bidirectional ceramic bezel; sapphire crystal; screw-down crown; transparent case back; water-resistant to 10 atm
Band: stainless-steel, folding clasp
Remarks: micro gas tube illumination; shock-resistant; anti-magnetic
Price: $6,599
Variations: classic tube colors

Roadmaster Marine GMT

Reference number: DG3000A-S4C-BK
Movement: automatic, Ball Caliber RR1203-C;
ø 31.4 mm, height 5.75 mm; 25 or 26 jewels; 28,800 vph; COSC-certified chronometer; 38-hour power reserve
Functions: hours, minutes, sweep seconds; day and date
Case: titanium, ø 40 mm, height 14 mm; bidirectional bezel; sapphire crystal; screwed-in crown; transparent case back; water-resistant to 20 atm
Band: titanium and stainless steel, folding clasp
Remarks: micro gas tube illumination; shock-resistant; anti-magnetic
Price: $3,349

Roadmaster Perseverer

Reference number: NM9050C-S1-IBE
Movement: automatic, Ball caliber RR1103; ø 25.6 mm, height 4.6 mm; 25 or 26 jewels; 28,800 vph; 38-hour power reserve
Functions: hours, minutes, sweep seconds; magnified date
Case: stainless steel, ø 40 mm, height 12 mm; bidirectional bezel; sapphire crystal; screwed-down crown; transparent case back; water-resistant to 10 atm
Band: stainless steel bracelet with folding clasp
Remarks: micro gas tube illumination; shock-resistant; anti-magnetic
Price: $1,949
Variation: with black dial

Roadmaster Rescue Chronograph

Reference number: DC3030C-S-BK
Movement: automatic, Ball caliber RR1402; ø 30 mm, height 7.9 mm; 25 or 26 jewels; 28,800 vph; special movement oil to endure -45°C / -49°F; 48-hour power reserve
Functions: hours, minutes, subsidiary seconds; day and date; chronograph; pulsometer
Case: titanium, ø 41 mm, height 14.8 mm; unidirectional ceramic bezel; sapphire crystal; screw-down crown; transparent case back; water-resistant to 10 atm
Band: titanium and stainless steel, folding clasp
Remarks: micro gas tube illumination; shock-resistant; anti-magnetic
Price: $3,899
Variation: with blue, green, or white dial

Engineer Hydrocarbon DeepQUEST Protector

Reference number: NM2080D-S2J-IBE
Movement: automatic, BALL caliber RR1102; ø 25.6 mm, height 5.05 mm; 25 or 26 jewels; 28,800 vph; 38-hour power reserve
Functions: hours, minutes, sweep seconds; date
Case: stainless steel, ø 39.5 mm, height 11.8 mm; sapphire crystal; transparent case back; screw-down crown; water-resistant to 3 atm
Band: stainless steel, folding buckle
Remarks: micro gas tube illumination; shock-resistant; anti-magnetic
Price: $2,099
Variations: black dial; silver dial; reptile skin

Fireman Victory

Reference number: NM2098C-S28J-IBER
Movement: automatic, BALL Caliber RR1103; ø 25.6 mm, height 4.6 mm; 25 or 26 jewels; 28,800 vph; 38-hour power reserve
Functions: hours, minutes, sweep seconds; date
Case: stainless steel, ø 40 mm, height 11.3 mm; sapphire crystal; screw-down crown; water-resistant to 10 atm
Band: stainless steel, folding buckle
Remarks: micro gas tube illumination; shock-resistant; anti-magnetic
Price: $1,499
Variations: classic tubes colors

BALTIC WATCHES

In 2005, Etienne Malec found a treasure: a suitcase once belonging to his photographer father, who had died when he was just a boy and who had been an avid watch collector. Inside, he found a diary filled with notes on purchases, trades, and sales of various watches. The discovery ignited Malec's fascination with horology and set him on a very unexpected path.

Armed with an MBA, Etienne Malec founded Baltic Watches in 2016 using Kickstarter. The name is a tribute to his father, who came from northeastern Poland, a region with a rich history and culture and a stunning landscape that includes a coastline on the Baltic Sea. Another acknowledgement of his father's collection and heritage is a vintage spirit that governs many of the brand's models without being overwhelming.

This aesthetic mission means that the collections often have modern touches, like the off-center subsidiary seconds dial on the MR series, which has a diameter of 36 millimeters. The Prismic series, for its part, features a combination of guilloché and a sandy surface on the dial.

Malec's idea, when founding his brand, was to make affordable timepieces, which is one reason why they distributed by direct sales. They are equipped with Miyota and Sea-Gull movements, which have improved their quality over the past decade and are becoming competitive. Parts are made in Hong Kong, and all assembly and adjustments are done in Besançon, France, which is a hub of watchmaking in the country and has the expertise. Accessories, like bracelets and straps of rubber, Perlon, and leather, or rolls for traveling are made in Italy.

Among Baltic's other collections are the Aquascaphe diving watches, which have full functionality for underwater exploration (water-resistant to 20 atm) and a very retro look reminiscent of 1950s dive watches. Chronographs, which are always popular, are also part of the portfolio, including the "panda" Tricompax and the Bicompax, which has a typical stepped case from the 1940s. And for its part, MR collection is dressy watch with a cleverly attractive small seconds dial at 7 and 8 o'clock. It comes in a variety of colors to fit any sartorial fashion, including beach garb.

BALTIC WATCHES
29, rue du Château Landon
F-75010 Paris
France

TEL.:
+33-1-40-16-07-17

E-MAIL:
support@baltic-watches.com

WEBSITE:
www.baltic-watches.com

FOUNDED:
2016

DISTRIBUTION:
Direct sales

MOST IMPORTANT COLLECTIONS/PRICE RANGE:
Aquascaphe, Bicompax, Hermétique, HMS, Tricompax / $500 to $1000

MR Classic Gold PVD Black

Movement: automatic, Hangzhou CAL5000a caliber; ø 30 mm, height 3.95 mm; 24 jewels; 28,800 vph; bidirectional micro-rotor; machined côtes de Genèves decoration; 42-hour power reserve
Functions: hours, minutes, subsidiary seconds
Case: stainless steel with gold PVD coating, ø 36 mm, height 9.9 mm; hesalite crystal; transparent case back; water-resistant to 3 atm
Band: leather, pin buckle
Price: $638
Variations: with black dial

Prismic Stone Bloodstone

Movement: hand-wound, La Joux-Perret caliber D100; ø 23.3 mm, height 2.5 mm; 18 jewels; 21,600 vph; mainplate with côtes de Genève; 50-hour power reserve
Functions: hours, minutes, subsidiary seconds
Case: stainless steel, ø 36 mm, height 9.2 mm; sapphire crystal ; transparent case back; water-resistant to 3 atm
Band: stainless steel Milanese mesh, folding clasp or leather strap, pin buckle
Price: $1,767
Variations: comes with Pietersite, Pink Albite and Dumortierite stone dials or Salmon, Purple, Grey-blue or Green metal dials

Scalegraph Transat Café L'Or Limited Edition

Movement: hand-wound, SW511 BH; ø 30 mm, height 7.6 mm; 27 jewels; 28,800 vph; column wheel control chronograph; 63-hour power reserve
Functions: hours, minutes, subsidiary seconds; chronograph with 15-minute regatta totalizer; tachymeter bezel with 1/10th nautical mile scale graduated in knots; date
Case: stainless steel, ø 39.5 mm, height 14.1 mm; sapphire crystal; aluminum bezel; screw down pushers; water-resistant to 10 atm
Band: rubber, pin buckle or stainless steel, folding clasp
Remarks: limited edition for Baltic's first participation as timekeeper in the Transat Café L'Or regatta
Price: $2,047
Variations: metallic champagne dial

BAUME & MERCIER

Baume & Mercier, a company founded in 1830, has staked a claim on the market by its ability to keep a finger on the pulse of stylish, urban fashionistas, who are looking for affordable yet remarkable timepieces. Since the early 2000s, it has created a number of noteworthy—and often copied—classics, like the Riviera and the Catwalk.

Joining the Richemont Group has boosted the brand's technical value. In 2018, after four years of development with ValFleurier, the Group's movement manufacturer, and the RIMS research and innovation team, Baume & Mercier released its first in-house *manufacture* movement, the Baumatic Caliber BM12-1975A. In 2020, it added two new complications to the in-house caliber. Models using the caliber boast a five-day power reserve and accuracy of just −4/+6 seconds per day and antimagnetism that is about twenty-five times higher than the current ISO norm.

The 1970s have left a big mark on Baume & Mercier's current collection. In 1973, the brand introduced the Riviera model, which has been a key part of their lineup ever since. What makes it stand out is the sporty stainless-steel case and the angular, twelve-sided bezel with four screws. The fifth generation of the Riviera came out in 2021 and has been the brand's best seller ever since.

In 2025, Baume & Mercier expanded the Riviera collection with chronographs in a new 41mm size, including a limited edition of just 73 pieces. They're also adding a 42-millimeter version to the main collection, plus two 39-millimeter models with the Baumatic, a powerful movement combining a 120-hour power reserve with magnetic field protection. It appears in the Riviera under a tinted sapphire crystal dial.

The women's 33-millimeter models are getting four additional timepieces with quartz movements. The Clifton collection has been updated and now shows off its slimmer design in 39-millimeter. The Hampton collection is being expanded with a smaller size option.

BAUME & MERCIER
Rue André de Garrini 4
CH-1217 Meyrin
Switzerland

TEL.:
+41 22 580 29 48

WEBSITE:
www.baume-et-mercier.com

FOUNDED:
1830

ANNUAL PRODUCTION:
100,000 (estimated)

U.S. DISTRIBUTOR:
Baume & Mercier
Richemont North America
New York, NY 10022
800-637-2437

MOST IMPORTANT COLLECTIONS/ PRICE RANGE:
Clifton (men) / $3,250 to $26,800;
Riviera (men and women) / $1,900 to $6,400 /
Classima (men and women) / $1,050 to $4,700;
Hampton (men and women) / $1,600 to $4,450

Riviera Baumatic
Reference number: M0A10822
Movement: automatic, caliber Baumatic BM13.1975A; ø 28.2 mm, height 4.2 mm; 21 jewels; 28,800 vph; silicon anchor and escape wheel; balance wheel with variable inertia; skeletonized rotor; 120-hour power reserve
Functions: hours, minutes, sweep seconds; date
Case: stainless steel with blue PVD, ø 39 mm, height 10.31 mm; sand-blasted titanium bezel screwed to case with 4 screws; sapphire crystal; transparent case back; water-resistant to 10 atm
Band: stainless steel, triple folding clasp
Price: $3,900

Riviera chronograph
Reference number: M0A10827
Movement: automatic, ETA Caliber 7753; ø 30 mm, height 7.9 mm; 27 jewels; 28,800 vph; 48-hour power reserve
Functions: hours, minutes, small seconds; chronograph; date
Case: stainless steel, ø 41 mm, height 13.94 mm; bezel screwed to case with 4 screws; sapphire crystal; transparent case back; water-resistant to 10 atm
Band: stainless steel, double folding clasp
Price: $4,100

Riviera chronograph
Reference number: M0A10828
Movement: automatic, MLJP Caliber 8147; ø 30 mm, height 8.4 mm; 27 jewels; 28,800 vph; 42-hour power reserve
Functions: hours, minutes, small seconds; chronograph; date
Case: stainless steel, ø 41 mm, height 14.34 mm; bezel screwed to case with 4 screws; sapphire crystal; transparent case back; water-resistant to 10 atm
Band: stainless steel, double folding clasp
Price: $8,100; limited to 73 pieces

Riviera Baumatic

Reference number: M0A10815
Movement: automatic, Caliber Baumatic BM13.1975A;
ø 28.2 mm, height 4.2 mm; 21 jewels; 28,800 vph;
silicon anchor and escape wheel; escapement with
variable inertia; skeletonized rotor; 120-hour power
reserve
Functions: hours, minutes, sweep seconds; date
Case: rose gold, ø 39 mm, height 9.6 mm; bezel screwed
to case with 4 screws; sapphire crystal; transparent
case back; water-resistant to 5 atm
Band: leather, pin buckle
Remarks: transparent blue sapphire dial
Price: $20,500

Riviera

Reference number: M0A10829
Movement: automatic, Sellita Caliber SW200-1;
ø 25.2 mm, height 4.6 mm; 26 jewels; 28,800 vph;
38-hour power reserve
Functions: hours, minutes, sweep seconds; date
Case: stainless steel, ø 42 mm, height 10.66 mm;
bezel screwed to case with 4 screws; sapphire crystal;
transparent case back; water-resistant to 10 atm
Band: stainless steel, double folding clasp
Price: $2,900

Clifton Baumatic

Reference number: M0A10771
Movement: automatic, Caliber Baumatic BM13.1975A;
ø 28.2 mm, height 4.2 mm; 21 jewels; 28,800 vph;
silicon anchor and escape wheel; escapement with
variable inertia; skeletonized rotor; 120-hour power
reserve
Functions: hours, minutes, sweep seconds; date
Case: stainless steel, ø 39 mm, height 11.22 mm;
sapphire crystal; transparent case back; water-resistant
to 5 atm
Band: reptile skin, double folding clasp
Price: $3,450; limited to 350 pieces

Clifton Baumatic

Reference number: M0A10802
Movement: automatic, Caliber Baumatic BM13.1975A;
ø 28.2 mm, height 4.2 mm; 21 jewels; 28,800 vph;
silicon anchor and escape wheel; escapement with
variable inertia; skeletonized rotor; 120-hour power
reserve
Functions: hours, minutes, sweep seconds; date
Case: rose gold, ø 39 mm, height 11.54 mm; sapphire
crystal; transparent case back; water-resistant to 5 atm
Band: reptile skin, pin buckle
Price: $8,500

Clifton Baumatic

Reference number: M0A10793
Movement: automatic, Caliber Baumatic BM13.1975A;
ø 28.2 mm, height 4.2 mm; 21 jewels; 28,800 vph;
silicon anchor and escape wheel; escapement with
variable inertia; skeletonized rotor; 120-hour power
reserve
Functions: hours, minutes, sweep seconds; date
Case: stainless steel, ø 39 mm, height 11.22 mm;
sapphire crystal; transparent case back; water-resistant
to 5 atm
Band: stainless steel, double folding clasp
Price: $3,600

Clifton Baumatic

Reference number: M0A10778
Movement: automatic, Caliber Baumatic BM13.1975A;
ø 28.2 mm, height 4.2 mm; 21 jewels; 28,800 vph;
silicon anchor and escape wheel; escapement with
variable inertia; skeletonized rotor; 120-hour power
reserve
Functions: hours, minutes, sweep seconds; date
Case: stainless steel, ø 39 mm, height 11.22 mm;
sapphire crystal; transparent case back; water-resistant
to 5 atm
Band: leather, double folding clasp
Price: $3,450; limited to 350 pieces

BELL & ROSS

If there is such a class as "military chic," Bell & Ross is undoubtedly one of the leaders. The Paris-headquartered brand develops, manufactures, assembles, and regulates its timepieces in a modern factory in La Chaux-de-Fonds in the Jura mountains of Switzerland. The early models had a certain stringency that one might associate with soldierly life, but in the past years, working with outside specialists, the company has ventured into even more complicated watches such as tourbillons and wristwatches with uncommon shapes. This kind of ambitious innovation has only been possible since perfume and fashion specialist Chanel—which also maintains a successful watch line in its own right—became a significant Bell & Ross shareholder and brought the watchmaker access to the production facilities where designer Bruno Belamich and team can create more complicated, more interesting designs for their aesthetically unusual "instrument" watches.

What sets Bell & Ross timepieces apart from those of other, more traditional professional luxury makers is their special, roguish look: a delicate balance between striking, martial, and poetic—think Lawrence of Arabia, the gallivanting warrior. And it is this beauty for the eye to behold that makes the company's wares popular with style-conscious "civilians" as well as with the pilots, divers, astronauts, sappers, and other hard-riding professionals drawn to Bell & Ross timepieces for their superior functionality. The plane-cockpit gauge look is especially strong in recent models, like the Radiocompass and the one paying tribute to France's air ace troop, Patrouille de France.

The latest line, the BR-05, forms a bridge between the square instrument watches and the round vintage ones. And it's not only about the geometrical patterns, but rather about aesthetics.

BELL & ROSS LTD.
8 rue Copernic
F-75116 Paris
France

TEL.:
+33 1 73 73 93 00

E-MAIL:
sav@bellross.com

WEBSITE:
www.bellross.com

FOUNDED:
1992

U.S. DISTRIBUTOR:
Exquisite Timepieces Inc.
4380 Gulfshore Blvd., N. Suite 800
Naples, Fl 34103
team@exquisitetimepieces.com
239-227-2932

**MOST IMPORTANT COLLECTIONS/
PRICE RANGE:**
Instrument BR-X1, BR-01, BR-03, and BR-05 /
approx. $3,100 to $450,000

BR-03 Astro
Reference number: BR03A-EMM-CE/SRB
Movement: automatic, Caliber BR-CAL.327 (modified Sellita SW300-1); ø 25.6 mm, height 3.6 mm; 21 jewels; 28,800 vph; 54-hour power reserve
Functions: celestial bodies as "mysterious" hands: hours (Mars), minutes (moon), sweep seconds (satellite)
Case: ceramic, 41 mm x 41 mm, height 11.5 mm; bezel fixed to monocoque case with 4 screws; sapphire crystal; transparent case back; water-resistant to 10 atm
Band: rubber, pin buckle
Remarks: comes with additional textile strap
Price: $4,990; limited to 999 pieces

BR-05 36 MM Black Steel
Reference number: BR05A-S-BL-ST/SST
Movement: automatic, Caliber BR-CAL.329 (modified Sellita SW300-1); ø 25.6 mm, height 3.6 mm; 21 jewels; 28,800 vph; 54-hour power reserve
Functions: hours, minutes, sweep seconds
Case: stainless steel, 36 mm x 36 mm, height 8.5 mm; bezel fixed to monocoque case with 4 screws; sapphire crystal; screw-down crown; water-resistant to 10 atm
Band: stainless steel, folding clasp
Price: $4,500
Variations: various dial colors

BR-05 Skeleton Arctic Blue
Reference number: BR05A-AB-SKST
Movement: automatic, Caliber BR-CAL.322-1 (modified Sellita SW300-1); ø 25.6 mm, height 3.6 mm; 21 jewels; 28,800 vph; 54-hour power reserve
Functions: hours, minutes, sweep seconds
Case: stainless steel, 40 mm x 40 mm, height 10.33 mm; bezel fixed to monocoque case with 4 screws; sapphire crystal; transparent case back; screw-down crown; water-resistant to 10 atm
Band: rubber, folding clasp
Remarks: skeletonized dial
Price: $8,100; limited to 250 pieces
Variations: with stainless-steel strap ($8,600)

BR-X5 Blue Lum

Reference number: BRX5R-BLUM-TC/SRB
Movement: automatic, Caliber BR-CAL.323; ø 31 mm;
28 jewels; 28,800 vph; 70-hour power reserve
Functions: hours, minutes, sweep seconds; power
reserve indicator; date
Case: titanium with luminescent coating (LM3D),
41 mm x 41 mm, height 12.8 mm; bezel fixed to
monocoque case with 4 screws; sapphire crystal;
transparent case back; screw-down crown; water-
resistant to 10 atm
Band: rubber, folding clasp
Price: $13,900; limited to 500 pieces

BR-03 Skeleton Black Ceramic

Reference number: BR03A-BL-SKCE/SRB
Movement: automatic, Caliber BR-CAL.328 (modified
Sellita SW300-1); ø 25.6 mm, height 3.6 mm; 25 jewels;
28,800 vph; skeletonized mainplate and bridges, with
black coating; 54-hour power reserve
Functions: hours, minutes, sweep seconds
Case: ceramic, 41 mm x 41 mm, height 10.6 mm;
sapphire crystal; screw-down crown; water-resistant
to 10 atm
Band: rubber, pin buckle
Price: $6,300
Variations: stainless steel ($5,900)

BR-03 Skeleton Grey Steel

Reference number: BR03A-GR-SKST/SRB
Movement: automatic, Caliber BR-CAL.328 (modified
Sellita SW300-1); ø 25.6 mm, height 3.6 mm; 25 jewels;
28,800 vph; skeletonized mainplate and bridges, with
black coating; 54-hour power reserve
Functions: hours, minutes, sweep seconds
Case: stainless steel, 41 mm x 41 mm, height 10.6 mm;
sapphire crystal; screw-down crown; water-resistant
to 10 atm
Band: rubber, pin buckle
Price: $5,900
Variations: ceramic ($6,300)

BR-03 Skeleton Lum

Reference number: BR03A-LM-SKCE/SRB
Movement: automatic, Caliber BR-CAL.328 (modified
Sellita SW300-1); ø 25.6 mm, height 3.6 mm; 25 jewels;
28,800 vph; skeletonized mainplate and bridges, with
black coating; 54-hour power reserve
Functions: hours, minutes, sweep seconds
Case: ceramic, 41 mm x 41 mm, height 11.25 mm;
sapphire crystal; screw-down crown; water-resistant
to 10 atm
Band: textile, pin buckle
Remarks: skeletonized dial with Super-LumiNova;
comes with additional rubber strap
Price: $6,900; limited to 250 pieces

BR-05 Chrono "Patrouille de France"

Reference number: BR05C-PAF-ST
Movement: automatic, Caliber BR-CAL.326 (modified
Sellita SW510-1); ø 30 mm, height 7.9 mm; 25 jewels;
28,800 vph; 60-hour power reserve
Functions: hours, minutes, small seconds;
chronograph; date
Case: stainless steel, 42 mm x 42 mm, height 14.25 mm;
bezel fixed with 4 screws; sapphire crystal; transparent
case back; screw-down crown; water-resistant to 10 atm
Band: stainless steel, folding clasp
Price: $7,700; limited to 500 pieces
Variations: with leather strap ($7,200)

BR-03 Diver Lum Outline

Reference number: BR03A-D-OL-CE/SRB
Movement: automatic, Caliber BR-CAL.302-1 (modified
Sellita SW300-1); ø 25.6 mm, height 3.6 mm; 25 jewels;
28,800 vph; 54-hour power reserve
Functions: hours, minutes, sweep seconds; date
Case: ceramic, 42 mm x 42 mm, height 12.05 mm;
unidirectional bezel, with 0-60 scale; sapphire crystal;
screw-down crown; water-resistant to 30 atm
Band: synthetic, pin buckle
Price: $5,600
Variations: various dial colors

BLANCPAIN

Founded in 1735, Blancpain is Switzerland's oldest watch brand and it proudly remains a company that has never produced a quartz watch. In the 1970s, Blancpain was part of the renowned conglomerate Société Suisse pour l'Industrie Horlogère (SSIH), but after the "Quartz Crisis" devastated the watch industry, its name was sold to Jacques Piguet and Jean-Claude Biver. The company then focused on crafting exceptional mechanical timepieces, including one with six grand complications that sold for an impressive one million Swiss francs. This achievement made Blancpain one of the key spearheads in the global revival of the mechanical wristwatch.

Blancpain's success soon caught the attention of the Swatch Group—then known as SMH—which acquired both companies in 1992. By mid-2010, the integration of movement production and watchmaking resulted in the creation of the Blancpain Manufacture.

Yet, avoiding quartz has never meant being outdated. Under the leadership of President Marc A. Hayek, Blancpain has devoted significant energy to technical innovation and creativity. The brand's watches have long stood apart for their complex complications and distinctive craftsmanship. Today, Blancpain's collections are organized into four main families: Villeret; the legendary Fifty Fathoms diver's line; Ladybird, an elegant women's series; and Métier's d'art, a range of unique masterpieces showcasing artistic and horological expertise.

For nearly two decades, Blancpain has also been a leading advocate for ocean preservation. As a passionate diver, Hayek has championed projects supporting marine protected areas (MPAs)—regions where human activity is banned or strictly limited to allow coral and fish populations to recover. In 2022, Blancpain expanded these efforts through a new initiative to restore marine and coastal ecosystems around the island of Pangatalan in the Philippines.

The iconic Fifty Fathoms celebrated its seventieth anniversary in 2023, marking a wave of new interpretations of this classic diver's watch. The latest models, now offered in refined 42-millimeter stainless-steel cases, come in various sizes and colors—from a feminine 38-millimeter titanium edition with pink accents to the bold Tech Ocean Commitment IV. The latter represents the next generation of the Gombessa line, designed for rebreather divers, and features a three-hour hand with a matching rotating bezel—reflecting the extended dive times made possible by modern rebreathing technology.

Having established itself in the world of diving, Blancpain has also made the preservation of the oceans and marine life a lasting pillar of its sustainability philosophy.

BLANCPAIN SA
Le Rocher 12
CH-1348 Le Brassus
Switzerland

TEL.:
+41-21-796-3636

WEBSITE:
www.blancpain.com

FOUNDED:
1735

U.S. DISTRIBUTOR:
Blancpain
The Swatch Group (U.S.), Inc.
1200 Harbor Boulevard
Weehawken, NJ 07086
201-271-4680

MOST IMPORTANT COLLECTIONS/PRICE RANGE:
Villeret, Fifty Fathoms, Ladybird, Air Command,
Métiers d'Art / $9,800 to $420,000

Fifty Fathoms Automatique

Reference number: 5010-1130-71S
Movement: automatic, Blancpain Caliber 1315;
ø 30.6 mm, height 5.65 mm; 35 jewels; 28,800 vph;
silicon hairspring; 120-hour power reserve
Functions: hours, minutes, sweep seconds; date
Case: stainless steel, ø 42.3 mm, height 14.3 mm;
unidirectional bezel with sapphire crystal insert and
0-60 scale; sapphire crystal; transparent case back;
screw-down crown; water-resistant to 30 atm
Band: stainless steel, folding clasp
Price: $22,000
Variations: various cases, straps, and dials

Fifty Fathoms Tech Ocean Commitment IV

Reference number: 5029A-12B30-64A
Movement: automatic, Blancpain Caliber 1315A;
ø 30.6 mm, height 5.65 mm; 35 jewels; 28,800 vph;
silicon hairspring; 120-hour power reserve
Functions: hours, minutes, sweep seconds; date
Case: titanium, ø 45 mm, height 14.1 mm; unidirectional
bezel with sapphire-crystal insert, with 0-60 scale;
sapphire crystal; transparent case back; screw-down
crown; decompression valve; water-resistant to 30 atm
Band: rubber, pin buckle
Price: $26,000; limited to 100 pieces

Fifty Fathoms Automatique

Reference number: 5007-3644A-B64B
Movement: automatic, Blancpain Caliber 1153;
ø 26.2 mm, height 3.25 mm; 28 jewels; 28,800 vph;
silicon hairspring; 100-hour power reserve
Functions: hours, minutes, sweep seconds
Case: red gold, ø 38.2 mm, height 12 mm; unidirectional
bezel with sapphire-crystal insert, with 0-60 scale;
sapphire crystal; screw-down crown; water-resistant
to 30 atm
Band: rubber, folding clasp
Remarks: mother-of-pearl dial
Price: $38,400
Variations: various cases, straps, and dials

Fifty Fathoms Automatique

Reference number: 5007-12B44R-NAFA
Movement: automatic, Blancpain Caliber 1153;
ø 26.2 mm, height 3.25 mm; 28 jewels; 28,800 vph;
silicon hairspring; 100-hour power reserve
Functions: hours, minutes, sweep seconds
Case: titanium, ø 38.2 mm, height 12 mm; unidirectional
bezel with sapphire-crystal insert, with 0-60 scale;
sapphire crystal; screw-down crown; water-resistant
to 30 atm
Band: textile, pin buckle
Remarks: mother-of-pearl dial
Price: $20,500
Variations: various cases, straps, and dials

Fifty Fathoms Bathyscaphe Quantième Complet Phases de Lune

Reference number: 5054-0140-01S
Movement: automatic, Blancpain Caliber 6654.P;
ø 32 mm, height 5.48 mm; 28 jewels; 28,800 vph;
2 spring barrels, 72-hour power reserve
Functions: hours, minutes, sweep seconds; full calendar
with date, weekday, month, moon phase
Case: ceramic, ø 43.6 mm, height 14.1 mm;
unidirectional bezel, with 0-60 scale; sapphire crystal;
transparent case back; screw-down crown; water-
resistant to 30 atm
Band: ceramic, folding clasp
Price: $31,700

Fifty Fathoms Automatique

Reference number: 5010-36B30-B64B
Movement: automatic, Blancpain Caliber 1315;
ø 30.6 mm, height 5.65 mm; 35 jewels; 28,800 vph;
silicon hairspring; 120-hour power reserve
Functions: hours, minutes, sweep seconds; date
Case: red gold, ø 42.3 mm, height 14.3 mm;
unidirectional bezel with sapphire-crystal insert, with
0-60 scale; sapphire crystal; transparent case back;
screw-down crown; water-resistant to 30 atm
Band: rubber, folding clasp
Price: $41,800

Fifty Fathoms Bathyscaphe Chronograph Flyback

Reference number: 5200-3640-52A
Movement: automatic, Blancpain Caliber F385;
ø 31.8 mm, height 6.65 mm; 37 jewels; 36,000 vph;
silicon hairspring; 50-hour power reserve
Functions: hours, minutes, subsidiary seconds; flyback
chronograph; date
Case: red gold, ø 43 mm, height 14.9 mm; unidirectional
bezel with ceramic insert and 0-60 scale; sapphire
crystal; transparent case back; water-resistant to
30 atm
Band: rubber, folding clasp
Price: $37,700

Chronograph Air Command

Reference number: AC02-36B40-63B
Movement: automatic, Blancpain Caliber F388B;
ø 31.8 mm, height 6.65 mm; 35 jewels; 28,800 vph;
50-hour power reserve
Functions: hours, minutes; flyback chronograph
Case: red gold, ø 42.5 mm, height 13.77 mm;
bidirectional bezel with ceramic insert, with 0-60 scale;
sapphire crystal; transparent case back; water-resistant
to 3 atm
Band: leather, folding clasp
Price: $40,300
Variations: in titanium ($23,500)

Chronograph Air Command

Reference number: AC03-12B40-98S
Movement: automatic, Blancpain Caliber F388B;
ø 31.8 mm, height 6.65 mm; 35 jewels; 28,800 vph;
50-hour power reserve
Functions: hours, minutes; flyback chronograph
Case: titanium, ø 42.5 mm, height 13.77 mm;
bidirectional bezel with ceramic insert, with 0-60 scale;
sapphire crystal; transparent case back; water-resistant
to 3 atm
Band: titanium, folding clasp
Price: $23,500

Villeret Calendrier Chinois Traditionnel

Reference number: 0888-3432C-55B
Movement: automatic, Blancpain Caliber 3638;
ø 32 mm, height 8.3 mm; 39 jewels; 28,800 vph; silicon
hairspring; 168-hour power reserve
Functions: hours, minutes; traditional Chinese calendar
with date, weekday, month, moon phases
Case: platinum, ø 45.2 mm, height 15.1 mm; sapphire
crystal; transparent case back; water-resistant to 3 atm
Band: reptile skin, folding clasp
Price: $94,450; limited to 50 pieces

Villeret Ultraplate

Reference number: 6605-1127-55B
Movement: hand-wound, Blancpain Caliber 11A4B;
ø 27.4 mm, height 2.8 mm; 21 jewels; 21,600 vph; 100-
hour power reserve
Functions: hours, minutes; power reserve indicator (on
the rear)
Case: stainless steel, ø 39.7 mm, height 7.45 mm;
sapphire crystal; transparent case back; water-resistant
to 3 atm
Band: reptile skin, folding clasp
Price: $13,300

Villeret Quantième Complet

Reference number: 6654-3653A-55B
Movement: automatic, Blancpain Caliber 6654.4;
ø 27 mm, height 6 mm; 28 jewels; 28,800 vph; 2 spring
barrels, silicon hairspring; 72-hour power reserve
Functions: hours, minutes, sweep seconds; full calendar
with date, weekday, month, moon phase
Case: red gold, ø 40.5 mm, height 10.94 mm; sapphire
crystal; transparent case back; water-resistant to 3 atm
Band: reptile skin, folding clasp
Price: $35,200

Villeret Tourbillon Carrousel

Reference number: 2322-3631-55B
Movement: hand-wound, Blancpain Caliber 2322;
ø 35.3 mm, height 5.85 mm; 70 jewels; 21,600 vph;
escapement with flying 1-minute tourbillon and
differential compensation; 3 spring barrels, 168-hour
power reserve
Functions: hours, minutes; power reserve indicator (on
the back); date
Case: red gold, ø 44.6 mm, height 11.94 mm; sapphire
crystal; transparent case back; water-resistant to 3 atm
Band: reptile skin, folding clasp
Remarks: enamel dial
Price: $436,300

Ladybird Colors Phases de Lune

Reference number: 3662E-2954-55B
Movement: automatic, Blancpain Caliber 1163L;
ø 26.2 mm, height 4.58 mm; 30 jewels; 28,800 vph;
100-hour power reserve
Functions: hours, minutes, subsidiary seconds; moon
phase
Case: red gold, ø 34.9 mm, height 10.43 mm; bezel and
lugs set with diamonds; sapphire crystal; transparent
case back; water-resistant to 3 atm
Band: reptile skin, folding clasp
Remarks: mother-of-pearl dial set with diamonds
Price: $42,500

Ladybird Colors

Reference number: 3661A-1954-95A
Movement: automatic, Blancpain Caliber 1163;
ø 26.2 mm, height 3.25 mm; 30 jewels; 28,800 vph;
100-hour power reserve
Functions: hours, minutes, subsidiary seconds
Case: white gold, ø 34.9 mm, height 9.2 mm; bezel and
lugs set with diamonds; sapphire crystal; transparent
case back; water-resistant to 3 atm
Band: reptile skin, pin buckle
Remarks: mother-of-pearl dial set with diamonds
Price: $47,400

BOVET

If any brand can claim real connections to China, it is Bovet, founded by Swiss businessman Edouard Bovet. Bovet emigrated to Canton, China, in 1818 and sold four watches of his own design there. On his return to Switzerland in 1822, he set up a company for shipping his Fleurier-made watches to China. The company, pronounced "Bo Wei" in Mandarin, became a synonym for "watch" in Asia and at one point had offices in Canton. For more than eighty years, Bovet and his successors supplied the Chinese ruling class with valuable timepieces.

In 2001, the brand was bought by entrepreneur Pascal Raffy. He ensured the company's industrial independence by acquiring several other companies as well, notably the high-end watchmaker Swiss Time Technology (STT) in Tramelan, which he renamed Dimier 1738. In addition to creating its own line of watches, this *manufacture* produces complex technical components such as tourbillons for Bovet watches. Assembly of Bovet creations takes place at the headquarters in the thirteenth-century Castle of Môtiers in Val-de-Travers not far from Fleurier.

These high-end timekeepers, with appeal to men and women, do have several distinctive features. The first is intricate dial work, featuring not only complex architecture, but also intricate guilloché patterns and very fine enameling techniques. Bovet has collaborated with car manufacturers like Pininfarina and Rolls-Royce, for which it manufactured a bespoke dashboard clock that can be used as a table clock or wristwatch thanks to the Amadéo conversion system. This allows the wristband to be easily attached or removed from the watch. Some models convert to table clocks, and the Amadeo Fleurier Miss Audrey series can even be worn on a necklace.

Bovet always pushes the envelope, and it has earned them several "Oscars" at the Grand Prix d'Horlogerie in Geneva, as well as a lifetime achievement award for Pascal Raffy at the 2019 Watches & Jewellery of the Year Awards. The 2024 Récital 28 Prowess 1 featured a genuine first in terms of complications, a world timer mechanism on twenty-four cylinders that can be corrected for Daylight Savings Time in the USA and Europe. The complication reappeared in 2025 in the more wearable Récital 30.

BOVET FLEURIER S.A.
Le Château, CP20
CH-2112 Môtiers
Switzerland

TEL.:
+41-32-862-0808

E-MAIL:
info@bovet.com

WEBSITE:
www.bovet.com

FOUNDED:
1822

ANNUAL PRODUCTION:
around 1,000 timepieces

U.S. DISTRIBUTOR:
Bovet LLC North America
305-974-4826

MOST IMPORTANT COLLECTIONS/PRICE RANGE:
Dimier, Fleurier, Pininfarina / $18,500 to $1,000,000

Miss Audrey Bris de Verre
Reference number: AS36069-SD12
Movement: automatic, Bovet Caliber 11BA13; ø 26.20 mm, height 5.09 mm; 25 jewels; 28,800 vph; 42-hour power reserve
Functions: hours, minutes
Case: stainless steel, ø 36 mm, height 11.30 mm; sapphire crystal; bezel and necklace bow set with 103 brilliant-cut round diamonds; water-resistant to 3 atm
Band: reptile skin, pin buckle
Remarks: hand-engraved dial with "shattered glass" look; 4 pear-shaped sapphire indices
Price: $42,000
Variations: red or blue sapphire indices

Recital 30
Movement: automatic, caliber R30-70-001, ø 33.50 mm, height 8.7 mm; 38 jewels; 28,800 vph; fully skeletonized; finely finished movement; 62-hour power reserve
Functions: hours, minutes, additional minute hand; central world timer for 25 time zones on rollers with adjustment for daylight saving time in different parts of the globe
Case: titanium, ø 42 mm, height 12.90 mm; crown set with sapphire cabochon; water-resistant to 3 atm
Band: rubber, folding clasp
Remarks: with Delhi time (off-set by 30 minutes) on the dial; customization options for collectors requiring different cities
Price: $73,500; limited to about 30 pieces per year
Variations: red gold case ($104,200)

Recital 21
Movement: hand-wound, caliber 13DM05-QPR, ø 30.44 mm (36 mm with module), height 6.75 mm; 37 jewels; 21,600 vph; 5-day power reserve
Functions: hours, minutes, subsidiary coaxial seconds; day, retrograde date, month, leap year; power reserve indicator
Case : polished titanium, ø 44.4 mm, height 10.25 to 15.4 mm; crown set with sapphire cabochon; water-resistant to 3 atm;
Band: reptile skin, pin buckle
Remarks: slant-top case; transparent, tinged sapphire dial
Price: $110,000; limited to 60 pieces
Variations: brown (smoked) or green dial

BREGUET

Abraham-Louis Breguet (1747–1823), a native of Switzerland, brought his craft to Paris in the late eighteenth century. It was fertile ground for one of the most inventive watchmakers in the history of horology, and his creations soon won favor at the highest levels of society.

In 1999, after a period of drifting, Breguet became a prized acquisition of the Swatch Group and came under the personal management of Nicolas G. Hayek. He worked tirelessly to restore the brand's roots, going so far as to rebuild the legendary Marie Antoinette pocket watch and contribute to the restoration of the Petit Trianon at Versailles.

To mark its 250th anniversary in 2025, Breguet returned to its origins with a series of so-called *Souscription* watches. Echoing the brand's beginnings, these classically designed models, including a single-hand watch, can be ordered with a deposit, with the balance due upon delivery. This principle, first introduced centuries ago, was designed to make the dream of owning a fine timepiece attainable for a wider audience.

Breguet today is a full-fledged manufacture, enabling it to forge ahead uncompromisingly with both *haute horlogerie* and jewelry. In its modern facilities on the shores of Lake Joux, traditional craftsmanship remains central to production, even as the brand pioneers modern materials for its movements.

After years focusing on the Reine de Naples, Tradition, Classique, and Marine collections, Breguet has turned its attention once more to pilot chronographs. In the post-war years, the company supplied the French Air Force with standard pilot's chronographs and on-board instruments. Today, the model family expands with two new designs combining historic inspiration and a newly developed self-winding chronograph movement.

The two new watches reinterpret Breguet's celebrated Type XX line, which has delighted watch lovers for seventy years: a "military" bicompax version featuring horizontally aligned small-seconds and half-hour subdials, and a "civilian" tricompax version with three total-izers, including a 15-minute counter—a nod to the days when long-distance calls had to be timed. The "military" chronograph (reference 2057) bears the designation "Type 20," written in Arabic numerals as in the 1950s originals, while the "civilian" version (reference 2067) is labeled "Type XX" in Roman numerals.

MONTRES BREGUET SA
CH-1344 L'Abbaye
Switzerland

TEL.:
+41-21-841-9090

WEBSITE:
www.breguet.com

FOUNDED:
1775 (Swatch Group since 1999)

NUMBER OF EMPLOYEES:
1,000

U.S. DISTRIBUTOR:
Breguet
The Swatch Group (U.S.), Inc.
1200 Harbor Boulevard, 7th Floor
Weehawken, NJ 07086
201-271-1400

MOST IMPORTANT COLLECTIONS:
Classique, Tradition, Héritage, Marine, Reine de
Naples, Type XX, Type XXI, Type XXII

Classique Souscription 2025

Reference number: 2025BH289W6
Movement: hand-wound, Breguet Caliber VS00;
ø 35.9 mm, height 5.96 mm; 21 jewels; 21,600 vph;
Nivachron hairspring with Breguet end curve; 96-hour
power reserve
Functions: hours (five-minute interval markers)
Case: rose gold ("Breguet-Gold"), ø 40 mm, height
10.8 mm; sapphire crystal; transparent case back;
water-resistant to 3 atm
Band: reptile skin, pin buckle
Remarks: enamel dial
Price: $59,400

Tradition Seconde Rétrograde

Reference number: 7035BHH29V6
Movement: automatic, Breguet Caliber 505 SR;
ø 33 mm, height 6.3 mm; 38 jewels; 21,600 vph; silicon
Breguet hairspring and anchor pallet; 50-hour power
reserve
Functions: hours and minutes (off-center), subsidiary
seconds (retrograde)
Case: rose gold, ø 38 mm, height 12.6 mm; sapphire
crystal; transparent case back; water-resistant to 3 atm
Band: reptile skin, pin buckle
Remarks: hand-guilloché enamel dial
Price: $56,800; limited to 250 pieces

Type XX

Reference number: 2075BH99398
Movement: hand-wound, Breguet Caliber 7279;
ø 32.7 mm, height 6 mm; 38 jewels; 36,000 vph; silicon
Breguet hairspring and escapement; 60-hour power
reserve
Functions: hours, minutes, subsidiary seconds; flyback
chronograph
Case: rose gold, ø 38.3 mm, height 13.2 mm;
bidirectional bezel, with 0-12 scale; sapphire crystal;
transparent case back; water-resistant to 5 atm
Band: leather, pin buckle
Remarks: silver dial
Price: $48,200

Type 20

Reference number: 2057ST92SW0
Movement: automatic, Breguet Caliber 7281;
ø 32.7 mm, height 6.6 mm; 34 jewels; 28,800 vph;
silicon Breguet hairspring and escapement, gold
oscillating mass; 60-hour power reserve
Functions: hours, minutes, subsidiary seconds; flyback
chronograph; date
Case: stainless steel, ø 42 mm, height 14.1 mm;
bidirectional bezel with reference markings; sapphire
crystal; transparent case back; water-resistant to
10 atm
Band: stainless steel, folding clasp
Remarks: comes with additional textile strap
Price: $27,200

Classique 5177

Reference number: 5177PT2N9V601
Movement: automatic, Breguet Caliber 777Q;
ø 27.1 mm, height 3.8 mm; 26 jewels; 28,800 vph; silicon
anchor, anchor wheel and hairspring; 55-hour power
reserve
Functions: hours, minutes, sweep seconds; date
Case: platinum, ø 38 mm, height 8.8 mm; sapphire
crystal; transparent case back; water-resistant to 3 atm
Band: reptile skin, pin buckle
Remarks: enamel dial
Price: $48,600
Variations: with white or blue dial; in white gold or rose
gold

Classique 7787

Reference number: 7787PT2N9VU
Movement: automatic, Breguet Caliber 591 DRL;
ø 25.6 mm, height 4.2 mm; 25 jewels; 28,800 vph;
silicon Breguet hairspring and escapement; 38-hour
power reserve
Functions: hours, minutes, sweep seconds; power
reserve display; moon phase
Case: platinum, ø 39 mm, height 10.3 mm; sapphire
crystal; transparent case back; water-resistant to 3 atm
Band: reptile skin, folding clasp
Remarks: enamel dial
Price: $49,300
Variations: with white dial; in rose gold

Type XX

Reference number: 2067RKY99WU
Movement: automatic, Breguet Caliber 728; ø 32.7 mm;
39 jewels; 28,800 vph; silicon Breguet hairspring and
escapement, gold oscillating mass; 60-hour power
reserve
Functions: hours, minutes, subsidiary seconds; flyback
chronograph; date
Case: rose gold, ø 42 mm, height 14.1 mm; bidirectional
bezel with ceramic insert and 0-12 scale; sapphire
crystal; transparent case back; water-resistant to
10 atm
Band: reptile skin, pin buckle
Remarks: comes with additional textile strap
Price: $46,200
Variations: in stainless steel

Marine Tourbillon Équation Marchante

Reference number: 5887PT925WY
Movement: automatic, Breguet Caliber 581DPE;
ø 37.2 mm, height 5 mm; 57 jewels; 28,800 vph;
1-minute tourbillon; silicon anchor, escape wheel and
hairspring; 80-hour power reserve
Functions: hours, minutes, subsidiary seconds (on the
tourbillon cage), running equation of time; perpetual
calendar with date (retrograde), weekday, month
Case: platinum, ø 43.9 mm, height 11.8 mm; sapphire
crystal; transparent case back; water-resistant to
10 atm
Band: rubber, folding clasp
Price: $329,800
Variations: with blue dial; in rose gold

Classique Tourbillon 3358

Reference number: 3358BB8D986D0
Movement: hand-wound, Breguet Caliber 187D;
21 jewels; 18,000 vph; 1-minute tourbillon; 50-hour
power reserve
Functions: hours and minutes (off-center)
Case: white gold, ø 35 mm, height 9.4 mm; bezel and
lugs set with 69 diamonds; sapphire crystal; transparent
case back; water-resistant to 3 atm
Band: reptile skin, folding clasp set with 42 diamonds
Remarks: dial set with 281 diamonds
Price: $210,800
Variations: in rose gold

Marine Dame

Reference number: 9518STYDS80D001
Movement: automatic, Breguet Caliber 591A;
ø 25.6 mm, height 7.5 mm5; 25 jewels; 28,800 vph;
silicon Breguet hairspring and escapement, gold
oscillating mass and set with 31 diamonds; 38-hour
power reserve
Functions: hours, minutes, sweep seconds; date
Case: stainless steel, ø 33.8 mm, height 9.9 mm; bezel
set with 50 diamonds; sapphire crystal; transparent
case back; water-resistant to 5 atm
Band: stainless steel, folding clasp
Remarks: dial set with 8 diamonds
Price: $33,000
Variations: various dials; in rose gold

Marine Chronograph

Reference number: 5527BBY25WV
Movement: automatic, Breguet Caliber 582QA;
ø 32.7 mm; 28 jewels; 28,800 vph; silicon pallet lever
and hairspring; 48-hour power reserve
Functions: hours, minutes, subsidiary seconds;
chronograph; date
Case: white gold, ø 42.3 mm, height 13.85 mm; sapphire
crystal; transparent case back; screw-down crown;
water-resistant to 10 atm
Band: rubber, folding clasp
Price: $39,750
Variations: in rose gold

Tradition Grande Complication

Reference number: 7047PT1Y9ZU
Movement: hand-wound, Breguet Caliber 569;
ø 35.7 mm, height 10.82 mm; 43 jewels; 18,000 vph;
silicon Breguet hairspring, torque regulation by fusée
and chain; 1-minute tourbillon; 50-hour power reserve
Functions: hours, minutes; power reserve indicator
Case: platinum, ø 41 mm, height 15.95 mm; sapphire
crystal; transparent case back; water-resistant to 3 atm
Band: reptile skin, folding clasp
Price: $271,300
Variations: in rose gold ($247,680)

Reine de Naples

Reference number: 8918BB5D964D0
Movement: automatic, Breguet Caliber 537/3;
ø 19.7 mm, 26 jewels; 21,600 vph; silicon Breguet
hairspring and escapement; 45-hour power reserve
Functions: hours, minutes
Case: white gold, 28.45 mm x 36.5 mm, height
10.05 mm; bezel and flange set with 117 diamonds;
sapphire crystal; transparent case back; crown with
diamond; water-resistant to 3 atm
Band: reptile skin, folding clasp set with 26 diamonds
Remarks: mother-of-pearl dial with drop-shaped
diamonds and a central diamond pavé
Price: $60,600
Variations: various cases, straps, and dials

Reine de Naples

Reference number: 8918BR2C364D00D
Movement: automatic, Breguet Caliber 537/3;
ø 19.7 mm; 26 jewels; 21,600 vph; silicon hairspring and
escapement; 45-hour power reserve
Functions: hours, minutes
Case: rose gold, 28.45 mm x 36.5 mm, height 10.05 mm;
bezel and flange set with 117 diamonds; sapphire
crystal; transparent case back; crown with diamond;
water-resistant to 3 atm
Band: reptile skin, folding clasp set with 26 diamonds
Remarks: mother-of-pearl dial with drop-shaped
diamond
Price: $52,100
Variations: various cases, straps, and dials

Reine de Naples

Reference number: 8928BR5W944DD0D3L
Movement: automatic, Breguet Caliber 586/1;
ø 19.7 mm; 29 jewels; 21,600 vph; silicon hairspring and
pallet horns; 38-hour power reserve
Functions: hours, minutes
Case: rose gold, 24.95 mm x 33 mm, height 10.05 mm;
bezel, flange, and lugs set with 139 diamonds; sapphire
crystal; transparent case back; crown with diamond
cabochon; water-resistant to 3 atm
Band: reptile skin, folding clasp set with 26 diamonds
Remarks: mother-of-pearl dial
Price: $50,200
Variations: in white gold ($53,600)

BREITLING

When Léon Breitling opened his workshop in St. Imier in the Jura Mountains in 1884, he set a course focusing consistently on instrument watches with a distinctive design. High quality standards and the rise of aviation completed the picture.

Today, Breitling's relationship with air sports and commercial and military aviation is clear from its brand identity. The unveiling of its own modern chronograph movement at Basel in 2009 was a major milestone in the company's history and also a return to its roots. The new design was to be "100 percent Breitling" and industrially produced in large numbers at a reasonable cost. Although Breitling's operations in Grenchen and in La Chaux-de-Fonds both boast state-of-the-art equipment, the contract for the new chronograph was awarded to a small team in Geneva. In 2006, the brand-new Caliber B01 made the COSC grade and has enjoyed great popularity ever since. For the team of designers, the innovative centering system on the reset mechanism that requires no manual adjustment was one of the great achievements.

Under CEO Georges Kern, Breitling expanded beyond the pilot watch niche and tapped markets in the Far East. The new collections were streamlined and given more defined profiles, a recipe Kern brought in from his IWC days. The winged logo was replaced mostly with a coquettish "B."

The brand has also introduced a new hypoallergenic material called Breitlight and is boldly using bright colors, like bright red straps. For its seventieth birthday in 2022, the Navitimer was equipped with the in-house Caliber B01, housed in an entirely redesigned case. Because the slide rule function was indispensable, water resistance remained a modest 3 atmospheres (30 meters/100 feet).

In recent years, the company has focused on expanding its popular lines, introducing new models for the Chronomat family such as the Chronomat GMT and the Super Chronomat 38. In 2024, to celebrate its 140th anniversary, Breitling unveiled the iconic pilot's chronograph, the Navitimer, featuring a slide rule bezel in a 43-millimeter case. Alongside the anniversary models for the 140th jubilee last year, a limited edition of the Navitimer with a platinum bezel and an ice-blue dial was launched in 2025.

BREITLING
Léon Breitling-Strasse 2
2540 Grenchen
Switzerland

TEL.:
+41-32-654-5454

E-MAIL:
info.US@Breitling.com

WEBSITE:
www.breitling.com

FOUNDED:
1884

ANNUAL PRODUCTION:
700,000 (estimated)

U.S. DISTRIBUTOR:
Breitling U.S.A. Inc.
206 Danbury Road
Wilton, CT 06897
203-762-1180
www.breitling.com

MOST IMPORTANT COLLECTIONS:
Navitimer, Avenger, Premier, Chronomat, Top Time, Superocean Heritage, Superocean, Professional, Classic Avi

Top Time B31
Reference number: AB3113281A1X1
Movement: automatic, Breitling Caliber B31; ø 28 mm, height 4.8 mm; 26 jewels; 28,800 vph; 78-hour power reserve; COSC-certified chronometer
Functions: hours, minutes, sweep seconds; date
Case: stainless steel, ø 38 mm, height 10.5 mm; sapphire crystal; transparent case back; water-resistant to 10 atm
Band: leather, pin buckle
Price: $5,850
Variations: various strap and dial variants

Top Time B31
Reference number: AB3113A71C1A1
Movement: automatic, Breitling Caliber B31; ø 28 mm, height 4.8 mm; 26 jewels; 28,800 vph; 78-hour power reserve; COSC-certified chronometer
Functions: hours, minutes, sweep seconds; date
Case: stainless steel, ø 38 mm, height 10.5 mm; sapphire crystal; transparent case back; water-resistant to 10 atm
Band: stainless steel, folding clasp
Price: $6,150
Variations: various strap and dial variants

Top Time B31
Reference number: AB3113171L1A1
Movement: automatic, Breitling Caliber B31; ø 28 mm, height 4.8 mm; 26 jewels; 28,800 vph; 78-hour power reserve; COSC-certified chronometer
Functions: hours, minutes, sweep seconds; date
Case: stainless steel, ø 38 mm, height 10.5 mm; sapphire crystal; transparent case back; water-resistant to 10 atm
Band: stainless steel, folding clasp
Price: $6,150
Variations: various strap and dial variants

Superocean Heritage B31 Automatic 40

Reference number: AB3110361L1S1
Movement: automatic, Breitling Caliber B31; ø 28 mm, height 4.8 mm; 26 jewels; 28,800 vph; 78-hour power reserve
Functions: hours, minutes, sweep seconds; date
Case: stainless steel, ø 40 mm, height 12.8 mm; unidirectional bezel with ceramic insert; sapphire crystal; screw-down crown; water-resistant to 20 atm
Band: rubber, folding clasp
Price: $6,500
Variations: various cases, straps, and dials

Superocean Heritage B01 chronograph 42

Reference number: AB0156161C1A1
Movement: automatic, Breitling Caliber B01; ø 30 mm, height 7.2 mm; 47 jewels; 28,800 vph; column-wheel control of chronograph functions; COSC-certified chronometer; 70-hour power reserve
Functions: hours, minutes, subsidiary seconds; chronograph; date
Case: stainless steel, ø 42 mm, height 14.2 mm; unidirectional bezel with ceramic insert and with 0-60 scale; sapphire crystal; screw-down crown; water-resistant to 20 atm
Band: stainless steel Milanaise mesh, folding clasp
Price: $9,600

Superocean Heritage B31 Automatic 42

Reference number: UB3111241B1A1
Movement: automatic, Breitling Caliber B31; ø 28 mm, height 4.8 mm; 26 jewels; 28,800 vph; 78-hour power reserve
Functions: hours, minutes, sweep seconds; date
Case: stainless steel, ø 42 mm, height 12.8 mm; unidirectional red-gold bezel with ceramic insert; sapphire crystal; screw-down crown; water-resistant to 20 atm
Band: stainless steel Milanaise mesh, folding clasp
Price: $8,350
Variations: various cases, straps, and dials

Superocean Heritage 36

Reference number: A10390361L1S1
Movement: automatic, Breitling Caliber 10 (modified Sellita SW300-1); ø 25.6 mm, height 3.6 mm; 25 jewels; 28,800 vph; 42-hour power reserve
Functions: hours, minutes, sweep seconds; date
Case: stainless steel, ø 36 mm, height 12.2 mm; unidirectional bezel, with 0-60 scale; sapphire crystal; screw-down crown; water-resistant to 20 atm
Band: rubber, folding clasp
Price: $5,500
Variations: various cases, straps, and dials

Chronomat Automatic GMT 40

Reference number: P32398101C1S2
Movement: automatic, Breitling Caliber 32 (modified Sellita SW330-2); ø 25.6 mm, height 4.1 mm; 21 jewels; 28,800 vph; COSC-certified chronometer; 42-hour power reserve
Functions: hours, minutes, sweep seconds; additional 24-hour display (second time zone); date
Case: stainless steel, ø 40 mm, height 11.77 mm; unidirectional platinum bezel with 0-60 scale; sapphire crystal; screw-down crown; water-resistant to 20 atm
Band: rubber, folding clasp
Price: $8,750

Chronomat Automatic GMT 40

Reference number: A32398101A1A1
Movement: automatic, Breitling Caliber 32 (modified Sellita SW330-2); ø 25.6 mm, height 4.1 mm; 21 jewels; 28,800 vph; COSC-certified chronometer; 42-hour power reserve
Functions: hours, minutes, sweep seconds; additional 24-hour display (second time zone); date
Case: stainless steel, ø 40 mm, height 11.77 mm; unidirectional bezel, with 0-60 scale; sapphire crystal; screw-down crown; water-resistant to 20 atm
Band: stainless steel, folding clasp
Price: $6,700

Chronomat B01 42

Reference number: AB0134101G1A1
Movement: automatic, Breitling Caliber B01; ø 30 mm, height 7.2 mm; 47 jewels; 28,800 vph; column-wheel control of chronograph functions; COSC-certified chronometer; 70-hour power reserve
Functions: hours, minutes, subsidiary seconds; chronograph; date
Case: stainless steel, ø 42 mm, height 15.1 mm; unidirectional bezel, with 0-60 scale; sapphire crystal; transparent case back; screw-down crown; water-resistant to 20 atm
Band: stainless steel, folding clasp
Price: $9,650

Super Chronomat B01 44

Reference number: EB0136251M1S1
Movement: automatic, Breitling Caliber B01; ø 30 mm, height 7.2 mm; 47 jewels; 28,800 vph; column-wheel control of chronograph functions; COSC-certified chronometer; 70-hour power reserve
Functions: hours, minutes, subsidiary seconds; chronograph; date
Case: titanium, ø 44 mm, height 14.4 mm; unidirectional bezel, with 0-60 scale; sapphire crystal; transparent case back; screw-down crown; water-resistant to 20 atm
Band: rubber, folding clasp
Price: $11,900

Navitimer B01 chronograph 46

Reference number: RB0137241L1R1
Movement: automatic, Breitling Caliber B01; ø 30 mm, height 7.2 mm; 47 jewels; 28,800 vph; column-wheel control of chronograph functions; COSC-certified chronometer; 70-hour power reserve
Functions: hours, minutes, subsidiary seconds; chronograph; date
Case: red gold, ø 46 mm, height 13.9 mm; bidirectional bezel, with integrated slide rule and tachymeter scale; sapphire crystal; transparent case back; water-resistant to 3 atm
Band: red gold, folding clasp
Price: $46,300
Variations: various cases, straps, and dials

Navitimer B01 chronograph 43

Reference number: AB0138211B1P1
Movement: automatic, Breitling Caliber B01; ø 30 mm, height 7.2 mm; 47 jewels; 28,800 vph; column-wheel control of chronograph functions; COSC-certified chronometer; 70-hour power reserve
Functions: hours, minutes, subsidiary seconds; chronograph; date
Case: stainless steel, ø 43 mm, height 13.6 mm; bidirectional bezel, with integrated slide rule and tachymeter scale; sapphire crystal; transparent case back; water-resistant to 3 atm
Band: reptile skin, folding clasp
Price: $10,300
Variations: various cases, straps, and dials

Navitimer Automatic GMT 41

Reference number: A32310211G1P1
Movement: automatic, Breitling Caliber 32 (modified Sellita SW330-2); ø 25.6 mm, height 4.1 mm; 21 jewels; 28,800 vph; COSC-certified chronometer; 42-hour power reserve
Functions: hours, minutes, sweep seconds; additional 24-hour display (second time zone); date
Case: stainless steel, ø 41 mm, height 11.6 mm; bidirectional bezel, with integrated slide rule and tachymeter scale; sapphire crystal; water-resistant to 3 atm
Band: reptile skin, pin buckle
Price: $6,450
Variations: various cases, straps, and dials

Navitimer Automatic 41

Reference number: A17329171C1A1
Movement: automatic, Breitling Caliber 17 (modified Sellita SW200-1); ø 25.6 mm, height 4.6 mm; 26 jewels; 28,800 vph; COSC-certified chronometer; 38-hour power reserve
Functions: hours, minutes, sweep seconds
Case: stainless steel, ø 41 mm, height 11.6 mm; bidirectional bezel, with integrated slide rule and tachymeter scale; sapphire crystal; water-resistant to 3 atm
Band: stainless steel, folding clasp
Price: $6,150
Variations: various cases, straps, and dials

Navitimer Automatic 36

Reference number: A17327381B1P1
Movement: automatic, Breitling Caliber 17 (modified Sellita SW200-1); ø 25.6 mm, height 4.6 mm; 26 jewels; 28,800 vph; COSC-certified chronometer; 38-hour power reserve
Functions: hours, minutes, sweep seconds
Case: stainless steel, ø 36 mm, height 11.4 mm; bidirectional bezel, with integrated slide rule and tachymeter scale; sapphire crystal; water-resistant to 3 atm
Band: reptile skin, folding clasp
Price: $5,700

Navitimer 32

Reference number: R77320E61A1R1
Movement: quartz, Breitling Caliber 77; COSC-certified chronometer
Functions: hours, minutes, sweep seconds
Case: red gold, ø 32 mm, height 8 mm; sapphire crystal; water-resistant to 5 atm
Band: red gold, folding clasp
Remarks: mother-of-pearl dial set with 12 diamonds
Price: $25,800
Variations: various cases, straps, and dials

Chronomat 32

Reference number: U77310101A2U1
Movement: quartz, Breitling Caliber 77; COSC-certified chronometer
Functions: hours, minutes, sweep seconds; date
Case: stainless steel, ø 32 mm, height 8.54 mm; red gold bezel; sapphire crystal; red-gold crown; water-resistant to 10 atm
Band: stainless steel with red-gold elements, folding clasp
Price: $9,200
Variations: various cases, straps, and dials

Caliber B01

Automatic; column-wheel control of the chronograph functions; vertical clutch; single mainspring barrel; COSC-certified chronometer; 70-hour power reserve
Functions: hours, minutes, subsidiary seconds; chronograph; date
Diameter: 30 mm
Height: 7.2 mm
Jewels: 47
Balance: glucydur
Frequency: 28,800 vph
Remarks: 346 parts

Caliber B31

Automatic; simple barrel spring; COSC-certified chronometer; 78-hour power reserve
Functions: hours, minutes, sweep seconds; date
Diameter: 28 mm
Height: 4.8 mm
Jewels: 26
Balance: glucydur
Frequency: 28,800 vph
Remarks: skeletonized rotor

Caliber B04

Automatic; column-wheel control of the chronograph functions; vertical clutch; single mainspring barrel; COSC-certified chronometer; 70-hour power reserve
Functions: hours, minutes, subsidiary seconds; additional 24-hour display (second time zone); chronograph; date
Diameter: 30 mm
Height: 7.4 mm
Jewels: 47
Balance: glucydur
Frequency: 28,800 vph

BREMONT

Bremont watches have adventure in their DNA. But it's the kind of adventure tempered by a touch of Anglo-Saxon understatement. They have accompanied a number of individuals with a taste for derring-do, such as polar explorer Ben Saunders or Levison Wood, the first recorded person to walk the length of the Nile. Small wonder, given that the brand was founded by brothers Nick and Giles English, both dyed-in-the-wool pilots and restorers of vintage aircraft. Even the brand name has its own remarkable backstory: while forced to land their vintage biplane in a field in southern France to avoid a storm, the brothers were welcomed by a hospitable farmer and former World War II pilot named Antoine Bremont.

British-made and launched in 2007, Bremont timepieces quickly struck a chord with those who wanted a watch that not only told the time but also expressed a quiet fascination with danger. They feature robust COSC- or ISO-3159-certified automatic movements, extensively modified calibers housed in specially hardened steel cases with a patented shock-absorbing system. The rotor design evokes an aircraft formation.

Since its founding, the brand has expanded both production and creative scope, drawing inspiration from quintessentially British icons such as the Spitfire, Bletchley Park (where German codes were deciphered during World War II), Jaguar sports cars, and even Boeing. Bremont has also ventured into the world of water sports, with models inspired by the legendary J-Class yachts, including the ladies' AC I 32, and a collection dedicated to the America's Cup.

Among the standout releases of 2024 is the Supermarine 300m GMT diver's watch, presented in a classically proportioned 40-millimeter case crafted from 904L stainless steel, known for its superior resistance to corrosion and ideally suited to saltwater environments. The Terra Nova models employ the same steel and feature bold Super-LumiNova hands and numerals, conceived as rugged companions for explorers. In 2025, Bremont introduced the Jumping Hour within this collection, a striking, retro model that displays the time through small apertures, paying homage to vintage watches of a past era.

BREMONT WATCH COMPANY
P.O. Box 4741
Henley-on-Thames
RG9 9BZ Oxfordshire
United Kingdom

TEL.:
+44-800-817-4281

E-MAIL:
info@bremont.com

WEBSITE:
www.bremont.com

FOUNDED:
2002

NUMBER OF EMPLOYEES:
100+

ANNUAL PRODUCTION:
several thousand watches

U.S. DISTRIBUTOR:
Michael Pearson
Michael.Pearson@bremont.com
Anthony Kozlowsky
Anthony.Kozlowsky@bremont.com
Bremont Inc.
501 Madison Avenue
New York, NY 10022
855-273-6668

MOST IMPORTANT COLLECTIONS/PRICE RANGE:
ALT1, Armed Forces collection, Bremont Boeing, Bremont Jaguar, MB, SOLO, Supermarine, U-2, and limited editions / $3,600 to $42,500

Terra Nova Jumping Hour

Reference number: TN38-JH-BZ-CC
Movement: automatic, Bremont Caliber BC634AH (modified Sellita SW300-1); ø 25.6 mm, height 4.1 mm; 29 jewels; 28,800 vph; 56-hour power reserve
Functions: hours (jumping), minutes (trailing), sweep seconds (compass)
Case: aluminum bronze, ø 38 mm, height 9.1 mm; sapphire crystal; water-resistant to 3 atm
Band: aluminum bronze, double folding clasp
Price: $5,650; limited to 100 pieces
Variations: with leather strap ($5,220); in stainless steel (unlimited)

Supermarine 500M Full Ceramic

Reference number: SM43-DT-BKCER-WH-N-S
Movement: automatic, Bremont Caliber BB64AH (modified Sellita SW300-1); ø 25.6 mm, height 3.6 mm; 25 jewels; 28,800 vph; 56-hour power reserve
Functions: hours, minutes, sweep seconds
Case: black ceramic, ø 43 mm, height 13 mm; unidirectional ceramic bezel with 0-60 scale; sapphire crystal; screw-down crown, automatic helium valve; water-resistant to 50 atm
Band: textile, Velcro fastener
Remarks: white ceramic dial
Price: $6,950
Variations: with rubber strap

Altitude MB Meteor

Reference number: ALT42-MT-GRTI-GR
Movement: automatic, Bremont Caliber BB14-AH (on MLJP base G100); ø 26 mm, height 4.45 mm; 24 jewels; 28,800 vph; anti-magnetic soft-iron protection ring; elastic movement mount for shock absorption; 68-hour power reserve
Functions: hours, minutes, sweep seconds; date
Case: titanium with black PVD, ø 49.3 mm, height 12.23 mm; crown-operated inner bi-directional bezel with 0-60 scale; sapphire crystal; transparent case back; water-resistant to 10 atm
Band: titanium, double folding clasp
Price: $6,840; limited to 400 pieces

BULGARI

Bulgari, one of the world's largest jewelry manufacturers, has always treated watchmaking as a central part of its identity. The acquisitions of Daniel Roth and Gérald Genta in the Vallée de Joux marked a turning point, bringing cutting-edge facilities and the region's deep horological know-how, especially in the art of complications, into the brand's fold.

In March 2011, Louis Vuitton Moët Hennessy (LVMH) acquired all Bulgari family shares, exchanging them for 16.5 million LVMH shares and offering the family a voice within the group's leadership. Backed by the strength of LVMH, Bulgari accelerated its drive toward full autonomy. Under the bold direction of Guido Terrini, the watch division pursued a daring course, producing an exceptional series of ever thinner and more complex automatic timepieces.

Following the 2014 tourbillon, Bulgari introduced the 2016 minute repeater—just 3.12 millimeters thick, with slotted indices designed to optimize sound transmission. This was succeeded by the 5.15-millimeter Octo Finissimo Automatic, powered by the Caliber BVL 138. The 2019 Chronograph GMT set yet another record at only 6.9 millimeters in height, driven by the BVL 318 with its peripheral rotor and quick-set GMT function.

In 2020, the Octo Finissimo Tourbillon Chronograph Skeleton Automatic combined multiple major complications in a case of unprecedented thinness, securing Bulgari's sixth world record. The brand crowned this legacy in 2021 when the Octo Finissimo Perpetual Calendar—measuring 5.8 millimeters—won the Aiguille d'Or at the Grand Prix d'Horlogerie de Genève (GPHG).

Then came the Octo Finissimo Ultra in 2023, an engineering feat measuring just 1.8 millimeters and setting a new global standard for slimness. A year later, Bulgari refined the formula once more: the Octo Finissimo Ultra Mk II shed another tenth of a millimeter to reach a total height of 1.7 millimeters. Today, the latest Octo Finissimo Ultra Tourbillon not only establishes a new record as the thinnest tourbillon ever made (1.85 millimeters) but stands as a bold manifesto of contemporary watchmaking mastery.

BULGARI HORLOGERIE SA
Rue de Monruz 34
CH-2000 Neuchâtel
Switzerland

TEL.:
+41-32-722-7878

E-MAIL:
info@bulgari.com

WEBSITE:
www.bulgari.com

FOUNDED:
1884 (Bulgari Horlogerie was founded in the early 1980s as Bulgari Time)

U.S. DISTRIBUTOR:
Bulgari Corporation of America
555 Madison Avenue
New York, NY 10022
212-315-9700

MOST IMPORTANT COLLECTIONS/PRICE RANGE:
Bulgari-Bulgari / from approx. $4,700 to $30,300; Diagono / from approx. $3,200; Octo Roma or Finissimo / from approx. $7,700 to $690,000 and above; Daniel Roth and Gérald Genta collections

Octo Finissimo Automatic

Reference number: 102713
Movement: automatic, Bulgari caliber BVL 138 Finissimo; ø 36 mm, height 2.23 mm; 23 jewels; 21,600 vph; platinum micro-rotor; finely finished with côtes de Genève; 60-hour power reserve
Functions: hours, minutes, subsidiary seconds
Case: titanium, ø 40 mm, height 6.9 mm; sapphire crystal; transparent case back; screw-down crown; water-resistant to 10 atm
Band: titanium, folding clasp
Price: $18,800

Octo Finissimo Automatic

Reference number: 103856
Movement: automatic, Bulgari caliber BVL 138 Finissimo; ø 36 mm, height 2.23 mm; 23 jewels; 21,600 vph; platinum micro-rotor; finely finished with côtes de Genève; 60-hour power reserve
Functions: hours, minutes, subsidiary seconds
Case: stainless steel, ø 40 mm, height 6.9 mm; sapphire crystal; transparent case back; screw-down crown; water-resistant to 10 atm
Band: stainless steel, folding clasp
Price: $13,500

Octo Finissimo Automatic

Reference number: 103812
Movement: automatic, Bulgari caliber BVL 138 Finissimo; ø 36 mm, height 2.23 mm; 23 jewels; 21,600 vph; platinum micro-rotor; finely finished with côtes de Genève; 60-hour power reserve
Functions: hours, minutes, subsidiary seconds
Case: yellow gold, ø 40 mm, height 6.9 mm; sapphire crystal; transparent case back; screw-down crown; water-resistant to 10 atm
Band: yellow gold, folding clasp
Price: $45,500

Octo Finissimo Automatic

Reference number: 103286
Movement: automatic, Bulgari caliber BVL
138 Finissimo; ø 36 mm, height 2.23 mm; 23 jewels;
21,600 vph; platinum micro-rotor; finely finished with
côtes de Genève; 60-hour power reserve
Functions: hours, minutes, subsidiary seconds
Case: rose gold, ø 40 mm, height 6.4 mm; sapphire
crystal; transparent case back; screw-down crown;
water-resistant to 10 atm
Band: reptile skin, pin buckle
Price: $26,800

Octo Finissimo Tourbillon Skeleton

Reference number: 103981
Movement: hand-wound, Bulgari caliber BVL 268SK;
ø 36 mm, height 1.95 mm; 24 jewels; 21,600 vph; flying
1-minute tourbillon; skeletonized movement; 52-hour
power reserve
Functions: hours, minutes
Case: rose gold, ø 40 mm, height 4.85 mm; sapphire
crystal; transparent case back; water-resistant to 3 atm
Band: reptile skin, pin buckle
Price: on request

Octo Finissimo Skeleton 8 Days

Reference number: 103667
Movement: hand-wound, Bulgari caliber BVL 199 SK;
ø 33.9 mm, height 2.5 mm; 33 jewels; 21,600 vph;
skeletonized movement; 192-hour power reserve
Functions: hours, minutes, subsidiary seconds; power
reserve indicator
Case: rose gold, ø 40 mm, height 5.95 mm; sapphire
crystal; transparent case back; water-resistant to 3 atm
Band: reptile skin, pin buckle
Remarks: skeletonized dial
Price: $39,200

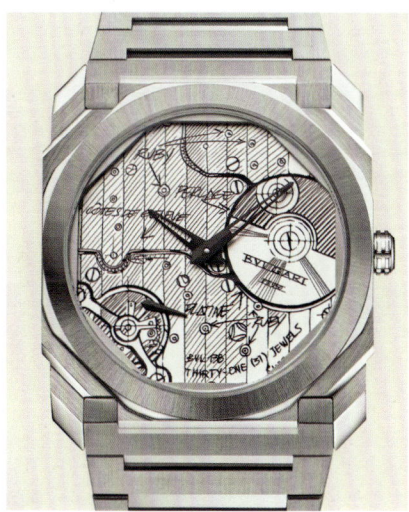

Octo Finissimo Sketch

Reference number: 104163
Movement: automatic, Bulgari caliber BVL
138 Finissimo; ø 36 mm, height 2.23 mm; 23 jewels;
21,600 vph; platinum micro-rotor; finely finished with
côtes de Genève; 60-hour power reserve
Functions: hours, minutes, subsidiary seconds
Case: stainless steel, ø 40 mm, height 6.4 mm; sapphire
crystal; transparent case back; screw-down crown;
water-resistant to 10 atm
Band: stainless steel, folding clasp
Remarks: dial with sketch of the movement
Price: $16,200; limited to 280 pieces

Bulgari Bulgari

Reference number: 103968
Movement: automatic, Bulgari caliber BVL 191;
ø 26.2 mm, height 3.8 mm; 26 jewels; 28,800 vph; with
côtes de Genève; 42-hour power reserve
Functions: hours, minutes, sweep seconds; date
Case: rose gold, ø 38 mm, height 8.7 mm; sapphire
crystal; water-resistant to 5 atm
Band: reptile skin, pin buckle
Price: $13,200

Bulgari Bulgari

Reference number: 103897
Movement: quartz
Functions: hours, minutes
Case: yellow gold, ø 26 mm, height 7 mm; sapphire
crystal; water-resistant to 3 atm
Band: reptile skin, pin buckle
Price: $8,250

Octo Roma Precious Naturalia

Reference number: 103675
Movement: hand-wound, Bulgari caliber BVL 206; ø 34 mm, height 5 mm; 21,600 vph; flying 1-minute tourbillon; skeletonized movement, bridges with brown DLC; 64-hour power reserve
Functions: hours, minutes
Case: rose gold, ø 44 mm, height 11.35 mm; sapphire crystal; water-resistant to 5 atm
Band: reptile skin, folding clasp
Price: $167,070

Octo Roma Tourbillon Sapphire Carbon

Reference number: 103316
Movement: hand-wound, Bulgari caliber BVL 206; ø 34 mm, height 5 mm; 21,600 vph; flying 1-minute tourbillon; skeletonized movement, 11 bridges as hour markers with green DLC; 64-hour power reserve
Functions: hours, minutes
Case: carbon fiber with sapphire crystal barrel, ø 44 mm, height 11.02 mm; sapphire crystal; transparent case back; crown in titanium; water-resistant to 5 atm
Band: reptile skin with rubber coating, folding clasp
Price: on request

Octo Roma Chronograph

Reference number: 103829
Movement: automatic, Bulgari caliber BVL 399 (Bulgari BVL 191 base with Dubois Dépraz module); 28,800 vph; 48-hour power reserve
Functions: hours, minutes, subsidiary seconds; chronograph; date
Case: stainless steel, ø 42 mm, height 12.4 mm; sapphire crystal; water-resistant to 10 atm
Band: stainless steel, folding clasp
Price: $9,150

Aluminum Smeraldo Chronograph

Reference number: 104076
Movement: automatic, ETA caliber 2894; ø 28.6 mm, height 6.1 mm; 37 jewels; 28,800 vph; 42-hour power reserve
Functions: hours, minutes, subsidiary seconds; chronograph; date
Case: aluminum, ø 40 mm, height 11.1 mm; bezel in titanium with rubber coating; sapphire crystal; water-resistant to 10 atm
Band: rubber, pin buckle
Price: $5,000; limited to 1,000 pieces

Aluminum GMT

Reference number: 103554
Movement: automatic, Bulgari caliber B192 (ETA 2893-2 base); ø 25.6 mm, height 4.1 mm; 21 jewels; 28,800 vph; 50-hour power reserve
Functions: hours, minutes, sweep seconds; additional 24-hour display (second time zone); date
Case: aluminum, ø 40 mm, height 9.4 mm; bezel in titanium with rubber coating; sapphire crystal; water-resistant to 10 atm
Band: rubber, pin buckle
Price: $3,700
Variations: various straps and dials

Aluminum

Reference number: 103382
Movement: automatic, ETA caliber 2892-A2; ø 25.6 mm, height 3.6 mm; 21 jewels; 28,800 vph; 42-hour power reserve
Functions: hours, minutes, sweep seconds; date
Case: aluminum, ø 40 mm, height 9.4 mm; bezel in titanium with rubber coating; sapphire crystal; water-resistant to 10 atm
Band: rubber, pin buckle
Price: $3,150
Variations: with black dial

Serpenti Tubogas Infiniti

Reference number: 103924
Movement: quartz
Functions: hours, minutes
Case: rose gold, ø 35 mm; bezel set with diamonds; sapphire crystal; crown with rubellite cabochon
Band: rose gold (Tubogas clasp), set with diamonds
Remarks: dial set with diamonds (full pavé)
Price: $67,000

Serpenti Tubogas

Reference number: 103434
Movement: quartz
Functions: hours, minutes
Case: stainless steel, ø 35 mm; bezel set with diamonds; sapphire crystal; crown with rubellite cabochon
Band: stainless steel (Tubogas clasp)
Price: $9,900

Serpenti Tubogas

Reference number: 101815
Movement: quartz
Functions: hours, minutes
Case: rose gold, ø 35 mm; bezel set with diamonds; sapphire crystal; crown with rubellite cabochon
Band: rose gold (Tubogas clasp)
Price: $31,700

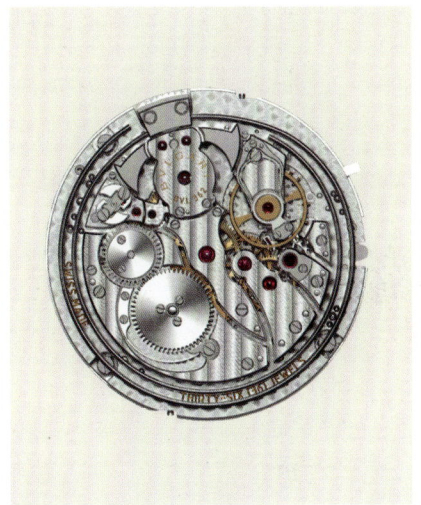

Caliber BVL 362

Hand-wound; single mainspring barrel, 42-hour power reserve
Functions: hours, minutes, subsidiary seconds; minute repeater
Diameter: 28.5 mm
Jewels: 36
Height: 3.12 mm
Frequency: 21,600 vph
Hairspring: flat hairspring
Remarks: hand-decorated, côtes de Genève; 362 parts

Caliber BVL 305

Automatic; platinum micro-rotor; single flying mainspring barrel, 60-hour power reserve
Functions: hours, minutes; perpetual calendar with date (retrograde), weekday, month, leap year display (retrograde)
Diameter: 36 mm
Height: 2.75 mm
Jewels: 30
Balance: glucydur
Frequency: 21,600 vph
Hairspring: flat hairspring with index fine adjustment
Shock protection: Incabloc
Remarks: finely finished with côtes de Genève; currently the thinnest perpetual calendar

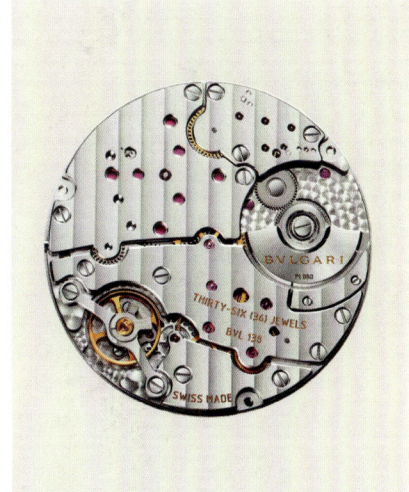

Caliber BVL 138 "Finissimo"

Automatic; flying platinum micro-rotor; single flying mainspring barrel, 60-hour power reserve
Functions: hours, minutes, subsidiary seconds; date
Diameter: 36 mm
Height: 2.23 mm
Jewels: 23
Balance: glucydur
Frequency: 21,600 vph
Hairspring: flat hairspring with index fine adjustment
Shock protection: Incabloc
Remarks: finely finished with côtes de Genève

CARL SUCHY & SÖHNE

Reviving an old and venerable brand is always a risky enterprise. Carl Suchy & Söhne, founded in 1822, was a clock and pocket-watch maker with a presence in Vienna and Prague. Its workshops were located in La Chaux-de-Fonds, creating products in the ultimately fashionable, if somewhat restrained, bourgeois Biedermeier style, which found favor well beyond Vienna's borders.

In 2016, a Viennese businessman with experience in "curating art" decided it was time for Vienna to have a watch brand again. The new Carl Suchy, however, would be an ode to the city, which was once at the center of a huge empire.

The story begins with a modern timepiece reflecting the streamlined aesthetic concepts of architect Adolf Loos. His main idea was encapsulated in a 1910 essay entitled "Ornament and Crime," in which he formulated his basic tenet: "Cultural evolution is equivalent to the removal of ornament from articles in daily use."

The Waltz N°1 was designed in a dialogue between CEO Robert Punkenhofer and a young graduate from the ECAL in Lausanne, Miloš Ristin, with the final product supervised by Swiss watchmaker Marc Jenni. This calm, thin model features a simple geometrical pattern with horizontal guilloché on one half and vertical guilloché on the other. At 6 o'clock, a small seconds disk turns, breaking up the pattern but "clicking in place" twice each minute—much like a waltzing couple. The Waltz N°1 was skeletonized for the second version, giving the dial a peculiar look, as if the movement, a Vaucher 5401/180, was covered by a shutter.

In the meantime, the brand has come up with different styles and colors. The latest iteration is a special design, Vienna Night, by Eric Giroux.

After devoting time and energy to a table clock, Carl Suchy & Söhne released a second collection, the Belvedere. This watch is a homage to the eponymous palace in Vienna, which appears as an engraving on the gold-plated rotor. The watch runs on a Dubois Dépraz movement. The hands, resembling spires with a porthole attic window, point to indices clearly inspired by the great arched entrance of the Belvedere Palace.

CARL SUCHY & SÖHNE
Prinz-Eugen-Strasse 48/Top 3
A-1010 Wien
Austria

TEL.:
+43-660-75-24-331

E-MAIL:
office@carlsuchy.com

WEBSITE:
www.carlsuchy.com

FOUNDED:
1822/2017

DISTRIBUTION:
Retail

MOST IMPORTANT COLLECTIONS:
Waltz Nº1, Waltz Nº1 Skeleton, Belvedere

Vienna

Movement: automatic, Carl Suchy Caliber CSS-V1 (modified Vaucher VMF 5401); ø 30 mm, height 2.6 mm; 29 jewels; 21,600 vph; micro-rotor; finely finished movement; 48-hour power reserve
Functions: hours, minutes, subsidiary seconds (as a rotating disc)
Case: stainless steel, ø 39 mm, height 7.9 mm; sapphire crystal; transparent case back; water-resistant to 3 atm
Band: leather, folding clasp
Remarks: dial with horizontal and vertical guilloché pattern (design by Eric Giroud); micro-engraved details from the roof of St. Stephen's Cathedral, Vienna, on the inside of the strap
Price: $22,500
Variations: various dial colors (Blue Danube, Day)

Belvedere Titanium

Movement: automatic, Caliber CSS201 (modified Dubois Dépraz DD90010); ø 25.6 mm, height 3.8 mm; 21 jewels; 28,800 vph; gold-plated oscillating mass with micro-engraving of Belvedere Palace in Vienna; 42-hour power reserve
Functions: hours, minutes, sweep seconds; date aperture on a rotating disc
Case: titanium, ø 40.8 mm, height 12.2 mm; sapphire crystal; transparent case back; water-resistant to 3 atm
Band: rubber, folding clasp
Price: $11,900
Variations: various dial colors (Champagne, Day, Night, Danube) with black DLC on case

Belvedere Bordeaux

Movement: automatic, Caliber CSS201 (modified Dubois Dépraz DD90010); ø 25.6 mm, height 3.8 mm; 21 jewels; 28,800 vph; gold-plated oscillating mass with micro-engraving of Belvedere Palace in Vienna; 42-hour power reserve
Functions: hours, minutes, sweep seconds; date aperture on a rotating disc
Case: stainless steel, ø 40.8 mm, height 12.2 mm; sapphire crystal; transparent case back; water-resistant to 3 atm
Band: rubber, folding clasp
Price: $9,900
Variations: various dial colors (Champagne, Day, Night, Danube) with black DLC on case

CARTIER

Cartier, founded as a jeweler in 1847, is one of the main drivers of the Richemont Group these days, which acquired a controlling stake in the company in 1993. It was Carole Forestier-Kasapi—now at TAG Heuer—who, as head of watchmaking, managed the vertical integration of Cartier. The brand then launched a host of outstanding calibers, beginning with the 1904 MC, a reference to the year in which Louis Cartier developed the first wristwatch made for men, a pilot's watch custom designed for his friend and early pioneer of aviation, Alberto Santos-Dumont. The automatic movement is powered by twin barrels and is available for chronographs or diver's watches. It is also now just one of a family of outstanding calibers that continue to push Cartier to the top rung of *haute horlogerie*.

In a period that values vintage, the Cartier brand has an advantage. More than a century of watchmaking has provided it with a steady stream of models to revive and modernize. The Pasha, Santos, Tank, Rotonde, Drive, and Calibre de Cartier are among the best-known and most successful watches in the world. And there is the series of "mystérieuse" watches, which in fine watchmaking stands for the invisible drive of an indicator or function.

Skeletonization has been on the menu recently, with a new version of the Santos-Dumont featuring a newly developed movement that provides some animation on the dial. The micro-rotor of the automatic caliber 9629 MC bears a miniature of the Demoiselle (damselfly) air-planes designed by pilot Alberto Santos-Dumont, for whom Cartier once developed the watch.

At Watches and Wonders 2025, Cartier presented mostly new Tank models. This iconic watch is now available in a larger rose gold case measuring 38 mm x 28 mm. There were also some special creations, which are traditionally found in the Cartier Privé line, but in 2025, the new models came in the rectangular Tank case. The Tank à Guichets (meaning "with apertures") doesn't use hands to show the time. Instead, it features rotating discs that display the hours and minutes on the otherwise flat, polished top of the case. There are several variations, which, one should note, are based on designs from 1928.

CARTIER
1201 Geneva
Switzerland

E-MAIL:
contact.na@cartier.com

WEBSITE:
https://www.cartier.com

FOUNDED:
1847

NUMBER OF EMPLOYEES:
approx. 1,300 (watch manufacturing)

U.S. DISTRIBUTOR:
Cartier North America
645 Fifth Avenue
New York, NY 10022
1-800-CARTIER
www.cartier.us

MOST IMPORTANT COLLECTIONS:
Santos de Cartier, Panthère de Cartier, Baignoire, Tank, Ballon Bleu de Cartier, Drive de Cartier, Calibre de Cartier, Clé de Cartier, Ronde de Cartier, Pasha de Cartier, Mystérieuse

Santos-Dumont XL
Reference number: WGSA0108
Movement: hand-wound, Cartier caliber 430 MC; ø 20.55 mm, height 2.1 mm; 18 jewels; 21,600 vph; 38-hour power reserve
Functions: hours, minutes
Case: yellow gold, 33.9 mm x 46.6 mm, height 7.5 mm; sapphire crystal; crown with sapphire cabochon; water-resistant to 3 atm
Band: reptile skin, pin buckle
Price: $19,100

Santos-Dumont XL
Reference number: WGSA0111
Movement: hand-wound, Cartier caliber 430 MC; ø 20.55 mm, height 2.1 mm; 18 jewels; 21,600 vph; 38-hour power reserve
Functions: hours, minutes
Case: yellow gold, 33.9 mm x 46.6 mm, height 7.5 mm; sapphire crystal; crown with sapphire cabochon; water-resistant to 3 atm
Band: reptile skin, pin buckle
Price: $19,700

Santos-Dumont XL
Reference number: WGSA0112
Movement: hand-wound, Cartier caliber 430 MC; ø 20.55 mm, height 2.1 mm; 18 jewels; 21,600 vph; 38-hour power reserve
Functions: hours, minutes
Case: rose gold, 33.9 mm x 46.6 mm, height 7.5 mm; sapphire crystal; crown with sapphire cabochon; water-resistant to 3 atm
Band: reptile skin, pin buckle
Price: $19,700

Tank Louis Cartier XL

Reference number: WGTA0346
Movement: automatic, Cartier caliber 1899 MC;
12.9 mm x 16.4 mm, height 3.63 mm; 24 jewels;
28,800 vph; 40-hour power reserve
Functions: hours, minutes
Case: rose gold, 25.5 mm x 33.7 mm, height 6.6 mm;
sapphire crystal; crown with sapphire cabochon; water-
resistant to 3 atm
Band: reptile skin, pin buckle
Price: $16,400

Tank Louis Cartier XL

Reference number: WGTA0211
Movement: hand-wound, Cartier caliber
1917 MC; 12.9 mm x 16.4 mm, height 2.9 mm; 19 jewels;
21,600 vph; 38-hour power reserve
Functions: hours, minutes
Case: yellow gold, 25.5 mm x 33.7 mm, height 6.6 mm;
mineral glass; crown with sapphire cabochon; water-
resistant to 3 atm
Band: reptile skin, pin buckle
Price: $15,100

Ballon Bleu de Cartier

Reference number: WGBB0062
Movement: automatic, Cartier caliber 1847 MC;
ø 25.6 mm, height 3.77 mm; 23 jewels; 28,800 vph;
40-hour power reserve
Functions: hours, minutes, sweep seconds; date
Case: yellow gold, ø 42 mm, height 13 mm; sapphire
crystal; crown with spinel cabochon; water-resistant
to 3 atm
Band: reptile skin, pin buckle
Price: $18,100

Tank Américaine

Reference number: WGTA0367
Movement: automatic, Cartier caliber 1899 MC;
ø 25.6 mm, height 3.63 mm; 24 jewels; 28,800 vph;
40-hour power reserve
Functions: hours, minutes
Case: platinum, 24.4 mm x 44.4 mm, height 8.6 mm;
sapphire crystal; crown with ruby cabochon; water-
resistant to 3 atm
Band: reptile skin, folding clasp
Price: $32,000

Santos de Cartier

Reference number: W2SA0030
Movement: automatic, Cartier caliber 1847 MC;
ø 25.6 mm, height 3.77 mm; 23 jewels; 28,800 vph;
40-hour power reserve
Functions: hours, minutes, sweep seconds; date
Case: stainless steel, 39.8 mm x 47.5 mm, height
9.38 mm; yellow-gold bezel; sapphire crystal; crown with
spinel cabochon; water-resistant to 10 atm
Band: stainless steel, double folding clasp
Remarks: comes with additional reptile skin band with
QuickSwitch rapid-change system
Price: $13,250

Santos de Cartier Dual Time

Reference number: WSSA0076
Movement: automatic, Cartier-modified Sellita SW330-
2; ø 25.6 mm, height 4.5 mm; 25 jewels; 28,800 vph;
56-hour power reserve
Functions: hours, minutes, sweep seconds; additional
12-hour indicator; day/night indication; date
Case: stainless steel, 40.2 mm x 47.5 mm, height
10.1 mm; sapphire crystal; crown with spinel cabochon;
water-resistant to 10 atm
Band: stainless steel, double folding clasp
Remarks: comes with additional reptile skin band with
QuickSwitch rapid-change system
Price: $10,700

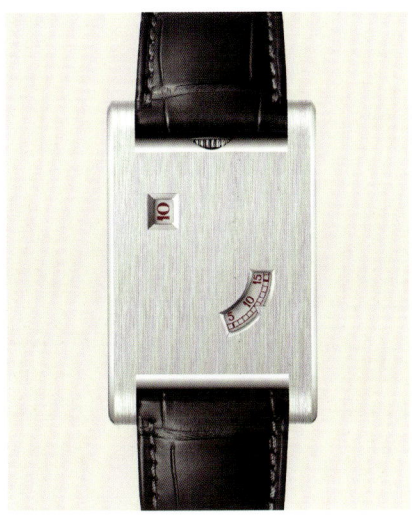

Tank à Guichets

Reference number: WGTA0237
Movement: hand-wound, Cartier caliber 9755 MC;
ø 22.55 mm, height 2.1 mm; 17 jewels; 21,600 vph;
43-hour power reserve
Functions: hours (jumping), minutes (digital)
Case: platinum, 24.8 mm x 37.6 mm, height 6 mm;
sapphire crystal; water-resistant to 3 atm
Band: reptile skin, pin buckle
Price: $55,500; limited to 200 pieces
Variations: with burgundy reptile skin strap; in yellow or
rose gold ($47,700)

Tank à Guichets

Reference number: WGTA0234
Movement: hand-wound, Cartier caliber 9755 MC;
ø 22.55 mm, height 2.1 mm; 17 jewels; 21,600 vph;
43-hour power reserve
Functions: hours (jumping), minutes (digital)
Case: yellow gold, 24.8 mm x 37.6 mm, height 6 mm;
sapphire crystal; water-resistant to 3 atm
Band: reptile skin, pin buckle
Price: $47,700
Variations: in rose gold ($47,700); in platinum
($55,500)

Santos-Dumont Micro-Rotor

Reference number: WHSA0044
Movement: automatic, Cartier caliber 9629 MC;
23.2 mm x 23.2 mm, height 4.4 mm; 33 jewels;
25,200 vph; skeletonized movement with integrated
jewel elements; bridges coated with blue lacquer; off-
center micro-rotor; 44-hour power reserve
Functions: hours, minutes
Case: stainless steel with black lacquer, 31.4 mm x
43.5 mm, height 8 mm; sapphire crystal; transparent
case back; crown with sapphire cabochon; water-
resistant to 3 atm
Band: reptile skin, pin buckle
Price: $35,300

Tank Louis Cartier

Reference number: WGTA0303
Movement: hand-wound, Cartier caliber
1917 MC; 12.9 mm x 16.4 mm, height 2.9 mm; 19 jewels;
21,600 vph; 38-hour power reserve
Functions: hours, minutes
Case: platinum, 25.5 mm x 33.7 mm, height 6.6 mm;
sapphire crystal; crown with ruby cabochon; water-
resistant to 3 atm
Band: reptile skin, pin buckle
Price: $33,300

Tank Française Squelette

Reference number: WHTA0025
Movement: hand-wound, Cartier caliber 9630 MC;
28.6 mm x 28.6 mm, height 3.9 mm; 28 jewels;
28,800 vph; skeletonized movement with integrated
hour numerals; 2 spring barrels; 72-hour power reserve
Functions: hours, minutes, subsidiary seconds
Case: stainless steel, 30.5 mm x 36.7 mm, height
10.11 mm; sapphire crystal; transparent case back;
crown with sapphire cabochon; water-resistant to 3 atm
Band: stainless steel, double folding clasp
Price: $30,800

Santos de Cartier

Reference number: HPI01687
Movement: automatic, Cartier caliber 1847 MC;
ø 25.6 mm, height 3.77 mm; 23 jewels; 28,800 vph;
40-hour power reserve
Functions: hours, minutes, sweep seconds; date
Case: white gold, set with 126 baguette-cut diamonds,
40 mm x 47.5 mm, height 9.1 mm; sapphire crystal;
crown with brilliant-cut diamond; water-resistant to
3 atm
Band: reptile skin, double folding clasp with
28 baguette-cut diamonds
Price: $184,000

CERTINA

In 1888, brothers Adolf and Alfred Kurth founded Kurth Frères in Grenchen, one of Switzerland's watchmaking hubs. At first, they did finishing for other firms, but then they developed their own portfolio based on reliable calibers. Thus, early on, the company built itself a reputation for sporty watches, which became quite fashionable as the wristwatch industry progressed. By 1938, the brand had a name, Certina, from the Latin for "secure."

In 1959, the company launched a new shock protection system. The concept was called DS (for "double security") and utilized a rubber ring as a bumper between the movement holder ring and the case. The new Certina DS proved its reliability in 1960 when it survived the 8,167-meter-high climb of Dhaulagiri in the Himalayas with a Swiss expedition.

The spectacular tests continued. One DS was put into a hockey puck, where it withstood the extreme shock of play without the movement being damaged. The DS 2 was used by the crew of the undersea project Sealab II, while the DS 3 was even secured to a submarine tower to prove that it was water-resistant even at great depths.

The brand's path took a corporate turn in 1971 with its integration into ASUAG Holding GWC, which became part of the Swatch Group after the quartz crisis. Though its independent manufacture faded, Certina carved a solid niche in the Group as a maker of rugged watches, keeping the DS concept alive.

The focus on tool watches remains foundational to Certina's lineup today, with a number of dressy models to round out the collections. Fans of the brand prize the re-editions of 1960s and 1970s classics, which are all polished nods to the brand's heritage. In 2025, Certina went all in on this tradition, expanding the DS system with three new components: one for secure movement mounting, another for enhanced dial stability, and a third to strengthen the crystal. These upgrades deliver superior shock resistance, especially in the DS Action Diver models.

CERTINA SA
Länggasse 85
CH-2503 Biel / Bienne
Switzerland

TEL.:
+41-32-343-3838

E-MAIL:
sales@certina.com

WEBSITE:
www.certina.com

FOUNDED:
1888

ANNUAL PRODUCTION:
over 600,000 watches (estimated)

DISTRIBUTION:
Retail, sales and service through authorized watch dealers;
contact sales@certina.com for information

MOST IMPORTANT COLLECTIONS/PRICE RANGE
DS Action, DS PH, DS-1, and DS-2 / $ 500 to $3,500

DS Action 40 mm

Reference: C048.410.11.091.00
Movement: quartz
Functions: hours, minutes, sweep seconds; date
Case: stainless steel, ø 40 mm, height 11.2 mm; bezel in titanium with aluminum insert, unidirectional rotating, with 60-minute scale; sapphire crystal; screw-down crown; water-resistant to 30 atm
Band: stainless steel, folding clasp
Price: $580
Variations: with black dial; in titanium with light blue dial ($680)

DS Action Diver

Reference: C048.407.18.051.01
Movement: automatic, ETA caliber 80.611 Powermatic; ø 25.6 mm, height 4.74 mm; 25 jewels; 21,600 vph; 80-hour power reserve
Functions: hours, minutes, sweep seconds; date
Case: stainless steel, ø 40.5 mm, height 14.1 mm; bezel with ceramic insert, unidirectional rotating, with 60-minute scale; sapphire crystal; screw-down crown; water-resistant to 30 atm
Band: textile, pin buckle
Price: $1,180
Variations: with stainless steel bracelet and black or white dial ($1,230); in titanium with blue dial ($1,310)

DS Action Diver Chrono

Reference: C032.827.11.051.00
Movement: automatic, ETA caliber A05.231; ø 30 mm, height 7.9 mm; 27 jewels; 28,800 vph; silicon balance spring; 60-hour power reserve
Functions: hours, minutes, subsidiary seconds; chronograph; date
Case: stainless steel, ø 44.5 mm, height 16.2 mm; bezel with ceramic insert, unidirectional rotating, with 60-minute scale; sapphire crystal; screw-down crown; water-resistant to 30 atm
Band: stainless steel, folding clasp, with extension link
Price: $2,040
Variations: with blue dial; with textile strap and champagne-colored dial ($2,080)

CHANEL

After putting the occasional jewelry watch onto the market, family-owned Chanel decided to launch its own horology division in 1987, a move that gave the brand instant access to the world of watchmaking art. While the brand's first collections were directed exclusively at its female clientele, it was actually with the rather simple and masculine J12 that Chanel finally achieved a breakthrough. That was in 1999, over twenty years ago. The brand's artistic director at the time was still Jacques Hélleu. The J12 collection showpiece, the Rétrograde Mystérieuse, was a stroke of genius—courtesy of the innovative think tank Renaud et Papi. Its sleek ceramic case and complex mechanics instantly propelled Chanel into the world of *haute horlogerie*.

It was Arnaud Chastaingt, formerly at Cartier, who actually designed the iconic J12. It still comes in a shiny ceramic case. As part of a rejuvenation move, a new caliber was added to the roster. It was built by Kenissi, a joint venture Chanel shares with Tudor and Breitling. It no longer uses a silicon hairspring and has returned to the soft iron cage to protect it from magnetic fields.

The J12 is still going strong a quarter century after its original launch. In 2025, the company came out with several versions in an assertive matte blue ceramic that would fit any wrist, male or female. At the end of 2024, Chanel also acquired a 25 percent stake in the independent high-end watch brand MB&F. Through numerous acquisitions, Chanel is securing access to watchmaking expertise and a partner network of brands and component suppliers.

CHANEL
135, avenue Charles de Gaulle
F-92521 Neuilly-sur-Seine Cedex
France

TEL.:
+33-1-41-92-08-33

WEBSITE:
www.chanel.com

FOUNDED:
1914

DISTRIBUTION:
retail and 200 Chanel boutiques worldwide

U.S. DISTRIBUTOR:
Chanel Fine Jewelry and Watches
733 Madison Avenue
New York, NY 10022
212-535-5828
www.chanel.com

MOST IMPORTANT COLLECTIONS:
J12, Première, Boy.Friend, Monsieur de Chanel

J12 Bleu Caliber 12.1
Reference number: H9632
Movement: automatic, Chanel Caliber 12.1; ø 26 mm, height 4.99 mm; 28 jewels; 28,800 vph; COSC-certified chronometer; 70-hour power reserve
Functions: hours, minutes, sweep seconds; date
Case: ceramic, ø 38 mm, height 12 mm; stainless-steel bezel with ceramic insert; sapphire crystal; screw-down crown, with ceramic cabochon; water-resistant to 20 atm
Band: ceramic, double folding clasp in blackened stainless steel
Price: $10,500

Monsieur de Chanel Superleggera Bleu Edition
Reference number: H10336
Movement: hand-winding, Chanel Caliber I; ø 32.6 mm, height 5.5 mm; 30 jewels; 28,800 vph; 2 spring barrels; skeletonized blackened mainplate and bridges; 72-hour power reserve
Functions: hours (digital, jumping), minutes (retrograde), subsidiary seconds
Case: ceramic with stainless-steel elements, ø 42 mm, height 12 mm; sapphire crystal; transparent case back; water-resistant to 3 atm
Band: textile with leather lining, folding clasp
Remarks: guilloché on the dial
Price: $45,600; limited to 100 pieces

J12 Bleu Diamond Tourbillon
Reference number: H10334
Movement: hand-winding, Chanel Caliber 5; ø 28.4 mm, height 6.25 mm; 29 jewels; 28,800 vph; flying 1-minute tourbillon with large diamond capstone; 42-hour power reserve
Functions: hours and minutes (off-center)
Case: ceramic, ø 38 mm; bezel in blackened stainless steel with 34 baguette-cut sapphires; sapphire crystal; transparent case back; crown in blackened stainless steel with diamond cabochon; water-resistant to 5 atm
Band: ceramic, double folding clasp in blackened stainless steel
Remarks: skeletonized dial
Price: on request; limited to 55 pieces

CHOPARD

The Chopard *manufacture* was founded by Louis-Ulysse Chopard in 1860 in the tiny village of Sonvillier in the Jura mountains of Switzerland. In 1963, it was purchased by Karl Scheufele, a goldsmith from Pforzheim, Germany, and revived as a producer of fine watches and jewelry.

In the 1990s, Karl Scheufele's son, Karl-Friedrich, and his sister, Caroline, decided to create watches with in-house movements, thus restoring the old business launched by Louis-UIysse back in the nineteenth century.

In 1996, Chopard opened up its watchmaking *manufacture* in the sleepy town of Fleurier in the Val-de-Travers, which had not yet experienced the revival of the mechanical watch. Focus on vertical integration drove the opening of a second building, Fleurier Ebauches SA, a hub of caliber kits, including the L.U.C series. Chopard now has a line-up of eleven calibers, ranging from simple three-hander automatics to a tourbillon; a perpetual calendar; chronographs; an ultra-high-frequency chronometer; and a minute repeater, now with sapphire chimes that produce a very clear sound.

The sportive bestseller at the Geneva-based company is the Alpine Eagle series. It was visibly inspired by the Chopard classic of the 1980s, the St. Moritz. In keeping with the times, the new model has been given a modern facelift, and the inner workings have also been updated. In 2023, Chopard presented the 41 XPS, a version with small seconds and a particularly thin movement, the L.U.C 96.40-L caliber, which measures just 3.3 millimeters. The cases, by the way, use the very shiny, sustainable "Lucent" steel, which is composed mostly of recycled steel.

To mark the 20th anniversary of the "Qualité Fleurier" (QF) seal, Chopard launched a limited L.U.C special edition with a micro-rotor, referencing the very first model to be certified under these rigorous, self-imposed quality standards. The certification process takes into account aesthetic excellence as much as precision, manufacturing depth, and shock resistance.

CHOPARD & CIE. SA
8, rue de Veyrot
CH-1217 Meyrin (Geneva)
Switzerland

TEL.:
+41-22-719-3131

E-MAIL:
info@chopard.ch

WEBSITE:
www.chopard.ch

FOUNDED:
1860

DISTRIBUTION:
149 boutiques

U.S. DISTRIBUTOR:
Chopard USA
75 Valencia Ave, Suite 1200
Coral Gables, FL 33134
1-800-CHOPARD
www.chopard.com/en-us

MOST IMPORTANT COLLECTIONS/PRICE RANGE:
L.U.C / from $8,110; Happy Sport / from $4,420; Imperiale / from $5,780; Classic Racing / from $5,910; Alpine Eagle / from $9,810

L.U.C Quattro Spirit 25 Straw Marquetry Edition

Reference number: 161977-5009
Movement: hand-wound, L.U.C Caliber 98.06-L; ø 28.6 mm, height 4.85 mm; 42 jewels; 28,800 vph; 4 spring barrels, hairspring with Phillips end curve; Geneva Seal; 192-hour power reserve
Functions: hours (digital, jumping), minutes; power reserve indicator (on the rear)
Case: rose gold, ø 40 mm, height 10.3 mm; sapphire crystal; transparent case back; water-resistant to 5 atm
Band: reptile skin, pin buckle
Remarks: rose-gold dial with straw marquetry; case of certified Fair mined gold
Price: $78,700; limited to 8 pieces

L.U.C Quattro Mark IV

Reference number: 161954-9001
Movement: hand-wound, L.U.C Caliber 98.09-L; ø 28.6 mm, height 3.75 mm; 38 jewels; 28,800 vph; 4 spring barrels, swan-neck fine regulator, gold rotor; Geneva Seal, COSC-certified chronometer; 216-hour power reserve
Functions: hours, minutes, subsidiary seconds; power reserve indicator (on the rear); date
Case: platinum, ø 39 mm, height 10.4 mm; sapphire crystal; transparent case back; water-resistant to 3 atm
Band: reptile skin, pin buckle
Price: $55,100
Variations: in rose gold ($44,200)

L.U.C Quattro Mark IV

Reference number: 161954-5001
Movement: hand-wound, L.U.C Caliber 98.09-L; ø 28.6 mm, height 3.75 mm; 38 jewels; 28,800 vph; 4 spring barrels, Swan-neck fine regulator, Gold rotor; Geneva Seal, COSC-certified chronometer; 216-hour power reserve
Functions: hours, minutes, subsidiary seconds; power reserve indicator (on the rear); date
Case: rose gold, ø 39 mm, height 10.4 mm; sapphire crystal; transparent case back; water-resistant to 3 atm
Band: reptile skin, pin buckle
Remarks: case of certified Fair mined gold
Price: $44,200
Variations: in platinum ($55,100)

L.U.C Full Strike Revelation

Reference number: 161947-0002
Movement: hand-wound, L.U.C Caliber 08.01-L; ø 37.2 mm, height 7.97 mm; 63 jewels; 28,800 vph; sapphire-crystal gongs; Geneva Seal, COSC-certified chronometer; 60-hour power reserve
Functions: hours, minutes, subsidiary seconds; power reserve indicator, minute repeater
Case: yellow gold, ø 42.5 mm, height 11.55 mm; sapphire crystal; transparent case back
Band: reptile skin, folding clasp
Remarks: case of certified Fair mined gold; limited to 20 pieces; exclusively available in Chopard boutiques
Price: on request

L.U.C Flying T Twin Perpetual

Reference number: 161989-0001
Movement: hand-wound, L.U.C Caliber 96.36-L; ø 33 mm, height 6 mm; 25 jewels; 28,800 vph; 1-minute flying tourbillon, 2 spring barrels; Geneva Seal, COSC-certified chronometer; 65-hour power reserve
Functions: hours, minutes, subsidiary seconds (on tourbillon cage); additional 24-hour display; perpetual calendar with large date, weekday, month, leap year
Case: yellow gold, ø 40.5 mm, height 11.63 mm; sapphire crystal; transparent case back; water-resistant to 3 atm
Band: reptile skin, folding clasp
Remarks: exclusively available in Chopard boutiques
Price: on request

L.U.C Lunar One

Reference number: 161951-1001
Movement: automatic, L.U.C Caliber 96.13-L; ø 33 mm, height 6 mm; 32 jewels; 28,800 vph; Geneva Seal, COSC-certified chronometer; 65-hour power reserve
Functions: hours, minutes, subsidiary seconds; additional 24-hour display (second time zone); perpetual calendar with large date, weekday, month, orbital moon phase display, leap year
Case: white gold, ø 40.5 mm, height 11.63 mm; sapphire crystal; transparent case back; water-resistant to 5 atm
Band: reptile skin, folding clasp
Price: $98,800
Variations: in rose gold ($98,800)

L.U.C XPS

Reference number: 168629-3001
Movement: automatic, L.U.C Caliber 96.12-L; ø 27.4 mm, height 3.3 mm; 29 jewels; 28,800 vph; COSC-certified chronometer; 65-hour power reserve
Functions: hours, minutes, subsidiary seconds
Case: stainless steel ("Lucent Steel"), ø 40 mm, height 7.2 mm; sapphire crystal; transparent case back; water-resistant to 3 atm
Band: leather, pin buckle
Remarks: "Lucent Steel" has a bright shimmer and is composed mostly of recycled steel
Price: $13,600

L.U.C Quattro Spirit 25

Reference number: 161977-1001
Movement: hand-wound, L.U.C Caliber 98.06-L; ø 28.6 mm, height 4.85 mm; 42 jewels; 28,800 vph; 4 spring barrels, hairspring with Phillips end curve; Geneva Seal; 192-hour power reserve
Functions: hours (digital, jumping), minutes; power reserve display (on the rear)
Case: white gold, ø 40 mm, height 10.3 mm; sapphire crystal; transparent case back
Band: reptile skin, pin buckle
Remarks: enamel dial; case of certified Fair mined gold; limited to 100 pieces
Price: $59,600

Mille Miglia Classic Chronograph "La Gara"

Reference number: 168619-3005
Movement: automatic, ETA Caliber A32.211; ø 28.6 mm, height 6.1 mm; 37 jewels; 28,800 vph; COSC-certified chronometer; 54-hour power reserve
Functions: hours, minutes, subsidiary seconds; chronograph; date
Case: stainless steel ("Lucent Steel"), ø 40.5 mm, height 12.9 mm; sapphire crystal; transparent case back; crown; water-resistant to 5 atm
Band: perforated leather, pin buckle
Remarks: "Lucent Steel" has a bright shimmer and is composed mostly of recycled steel
Price: $10,800

Alpine Eagle 41 SL Cadence 8HF

Reference number: 298600-3028
Movement: automatic, Chopard Caliber 01.14-C; ø 28.8 mm, height 4.95 mm; 28 jewels; 57.600 vph; high-frequency escapement (8Hz) with silicon anchor and escape wheel; ceramicized titanium and bridges; tungsten rotor; COSC-certified chronometer; 60-hour power reserve
Functions: hours, minutes, sweep seconds; date
Case: titanium, ø 41 mm, height 9.75 mm; bezel mounted to case with 8 screws; sapphire crystal; transparent case back; screw-down crown; water-resistant to 10 atm
Band: rubber, pin buckle
Remarks: limited to 250 pieces
Price: $28,700

Alpine Eagle 41 XP CS Platinum

Reference number: 295393-9001
Movement: automatic, Chopard Caliber 96.42-L; ø 27.4 mm, height 3.3 mm; 29 jewels; 28,800 vph; 2 spring barrels, Swan-neck fine regulator, hairspring with Phillips end curve; platinum micro-rotor; Geneva Seal, COSC-certified chronometer; 65-hour power reserve
Functions: hours, minutes, sweep seconds
Case: platinum, ø 41 mm, height 8 mm; bezel mounted to case with 8 screws; sapphire crystal; transparent case back; water-resistant to 10 atm
Band: platinum, triple folding clasp
Remarks: exclusively available in Chopard boutiques
Price: $110.500

Alpine Eagle 41 XP TT

Reference number: 298630-3001
Movement: automatic, L.U.C caliber 96.17-S; ø 27.4 mm, height 3.3 mm; 29 jewels; 28,800 vph; 2 mainsprings; yellow-gold micro-rotor; skeletonized mainplate; Geneva Seal; 65-hour power reserve
Functions: hours, minutes
Case: titanium, ø 41 mm, height 8 mm; sapphire crystal; transparent case back; water-resistant to 10 atm
Band: titanium, triple folding clasp
Price: $30,500

Alpine Eagle Chronograph

Reference number: 295393-5002
Movement: automatic, Chopard caliber 03.05-C; ø 28.8 mm, height 7.6 mm; 45 jewels; 28,800 vph; COSC-certified chronometer; 60-hour power reserve
Functions: hours, minutes, subsidiary seconds; flyback chronograph; date
Case: rose gold, ø 44 mm, height 13.15 mm; bezel mounted to case with 8 screws; sapphire crystal; transparent case back; screw-down crown; water-resistant to 10 atm
Band: rose gold, folding clasp
Price: $91,600
Variations: various cases, straps, and dials

Alpine Eagle Chronograph

Reference number: 295387-9001
Movement: automatic, Chopard caliber 03.05-C; ø 28.8 mm, height 7.6 mm; 45 jewels; 28,800 vph; COSC-certified chronometer; 60-hour power reserve
Functions: hours, minutes, subsidiary seconds; flyback chronograph; date
Case: titanium and rose gold, ø 44 mm, height 13.15 mm; bezel mounted to case with 8 screws; sapphire crystal; transparent case back; screw-down crown; water-resistant to 10 atm
Band: calfskin, folding clasp
Price: $47,700
Variations: various cases, straps, and dials

Alpine Eagle Chronograph

Reference number: 298609-3001
Movement: automatic, Chopard Caliber 03.05-C; ø 28.8 mm, height 7.6 mm; 45 jewels; 28,800 vph; COSC-certified chronometer; 60-hour power reserve
Functions: hours, minutes, subsidiary seconds; flyback chronograph; date
Case: stainless steel, ø 44 mm, height 13.15 mm; bezel mounted to case with 8 screws; screw-down crown; sapphire crystal; transparent case back; water-resistant to 10 atm
Band: stainless steel, folding clasp
Price: $24,900
Variations: various cases, straps, and dials

Alpine Eagle Large

Reference number: 298600-3014
Movement: automatic, Chopard Caliber 01.01-C;
ø 28.8 mm, height 4.95 mm; 31 jewels; 28,800 vph;
COSC-certified chronometer; 60-hour power reserve
Functions: hours, minutes, sweep seconds; date
Case: stainless steel ("Lucent Steel"), ø 41 mm, height
9.7 mm; bezel mounted to case with 8 screws; sapphire
crystal; transparent case back; water-resistant to
10 atm
Band: stainless steel, folding clasp
Remarks: "Lucent Steel" has a bright shimmer and is
composed mostly of recycled steel
Price: $18,700
Variations: various dials

Alpine Eagle Large

Reference number: 298600-3001
Movement: automatic, Chopard Caliber 01.01-C;
ø 28.8 mm, height 4.95 mm; 31 jewels; 28,800 vph;
COSC-certified chronometer; 60-hour power reserve
Functions: hours, minutes, sweep seconds; date
Case: stainless steel ("Lucent Steel"), ø 41 mm, height
9.7 mm; bezel mounted to case with 8 screws; sapphire
crystal; transparent case back; water-resistant to
10 atm
Band: stainless steel, folding clasp
Remarks: "Lucent Steel" has a bright shimmer and is
composed mostly of recycled steel
Price: $17,000
Variations: various dials

Alpine Eagle Large

Reference number: 295363-5007
Movement: automatic, Chopard Caliber 01.01-C;
ø 28.8 mm, height 4.95 mm; 31 jewels; 28,800 vph;
COSC-certified chronometer; 60-hour power reserve
Functions: hours, minutes, sweep seconds; date
Case: rose gold, ø 41 mm, height 9.7 mm; bezel
mounted to case with 8 screws; sapphire crystal;
transparent case back; water-resistant to 10 atm
Band: rose gold, folding clasp
Price: $71,000
Variations: in stainless steel ($18,700)

Alpine Eagle Flying Tourbillon

Reference number: 298616-3003
Movement: automatic, L.U.C Caliber 96.24-L;
ø 27.4 mm, height 3.3 mm; 25 jewels; 25,200 vph; flying
one-minute tourbillon, 2 spring barrels, micro-rotor;
Geneva Seal, COSC-certified chronometer; 65-hour
power reserve
Functions: hours, minutes, subsidiary seconds (on the
tourbillon cage)
Case: stainless steel ("Lucent Steel"), ø 41 mm, height
8 mm; bezel mounted to case with 8 screws; sapphire
crystal; transparent case back; water-resistant to
10 atm
Band: stainless steel, folding clasp
Remarks: "Lucent Steel" has a bright shimmer and is
composed mostly of recycled steel
Price: $126,500

Alpine Eagle 33

Reference number: 298617-4001
Movement: automatic, L.U.C Caliber 09.01-C;
ø 20,4 mm, height 3,65 mm; 27 jewels; 25.200 vph;
2 spring barrels, hairspring with Phillips end curve, gold
oscillating mass; COSC-certified chronometer; 42-hour
power reserve
Functions: hours, minutes, sweep seconds
Case: stainless steel ("Lucent Steel"), ø 33 mm, height
7.95 mm; yellow gold bezel with diamonds; sapphire
crystal; transparent case back; crown in yellow gold;
water-resistant to 5 atm
Band: stainless steel with yellow gold elements, folding
clasp
Remarks: "Lucent Steel" has a bright shimmer and
is composed mostly of recycled steel; dial set with
8 diamonds
Price: $25,900

Alpine Eagle Large

Reference number: 295363-5013
Movement: automatic, Chopard caliber 01.01-C;
ø 28.8 mm, height 4.95 mm; 31 jewels; 28,800 vph;
COSC-certified chronometer; 60-hour power reserve
Functions: hours, minutes, sweep seconds
Case: rose gold, ø 41 mm, height 9.7 mm; bezel
mounted to case with 8 screws, set with baguette-cut
diamonds; sapphire crystal; transparent case back;
water-resistant to 10 atm
Band: rose gold, folding clasp
Price: $106,000

Caliber L.U.C 01.01-C

Automatic; single mainspring barrel; COSC-certified chronometer; 60-hour power reserve
Functions: hours, minutes, sweep seconds; date
Diameter: 28.8 mm
Height: 4.95 mm
Jewels: 31
Balance: glucydur
Frequency: 28,800 vph
Hairspring: flat hairspring, Nivarox
Remarks: 207 parts

Caliber L.U.C 03.05-C

Automatic; column-wheel control of chronograph functions, vertical clutch; single spring barrel; COSC-certified chronometer; 60-hour power reserve
Functions: hours, minutes, subsidiary seconds; flyback chronograph; date
Diameter: 28.8 mm
Height: 7.6 mm
Jewels: 45
Balance: glucydur
Frequency: 28,800 vph
Hairspring: flat hairspring
Remarks: slotted bridges; skeletonized rose-gold winding rotor

Caliber L.U.C 98.06-L

Hand-wound; swan-neck fine adjustment; four spring barrels, arranged serially in pairs; Geneva Seal; 192-hour power reserve
Functions: hours (digital, jumping), minutes; power reserve indicator (on the movement side) Diameter: 28.6 mm
Height: 4.85 mm
Jewels: 42
Frequency: 28,800 vph
Hairspring: Breguet hairspring with Phillips end curve
Remarks: 240 parts

Caliber L.U.C 01.14-C

Automatic; high-frequency escapement; silicon roller jewel, anchor and escape wheel; single spring barrel; COSC-certified chronometer; 60-hour power reserve
Functions: hours, minutes, sweep seconds; date
Diameter: 28.8 mm
Height: 4.95 mm
Jewels: 28
Balance: glucydur
Frequency: 57,600 vph
Hairspring: flat hairspring, Nivarox 1
Remarks: mainplate and bridges in ceramicized titanium; 210 parts

Caliber L.U.C 96.42-L

Automatic; swan-neck fine regulator, platinum micro-rotor; double spring barrel; Geneva Seal; COSC-certified chronometer; 65-hour power reserve
Functions: hours, minutes, sweep seconds
Diameter: 27.4 mm
Height: 3.3 mm
Jewels: 29
Balance: glucydur
Frequency: 28,800 vph
Hairspring: with Phillips end curve
Remarks: 181 parts

Caliber L.U.C 09.01-C

Automatic; single spring barrel; COSC-certified chronometer; 42-hour power reserve
Functions: hours, minutes, sweep seconds
Diameter: 20.4 mm
Height: 3.65 mm
Jewels: 27
Frequency: 25,200 vph
Remarks: 159 parts

CHRONOSWISS

Gerd-Rüdiger Lang, the Chronoswiss founder who died in 2023, used to joke about having "the only Swiss watch factory in Germany." Indeed, the brand combined Swiss technology with concepts and designs "made in Germany," specifically in Karlsfeld, near Munich.

Lang was a pioneer who created regulator watches in the 1980s, an idea that found many fans of new ways to tell the time. Whether in a rectangular or round case, with a tourbillon or without, the off-center dial became the absolute identity of Chronoswiss watches and remains so to this day.

Chronoswiss has always been a little on the edge of the industry in terms of style and technical developments. It created the enduring *manufacture* caliber C.122—based on an old Enicar automatic movement with a patented rattrapante mechanism—and its Chronoscope chronograph has earned a solid reputation for technical prowess.

In March 2012, a Swiss couple, Oliver and Eva Ebstein, purchased Chronoswiss and moved the company headquarters to Lucerne, Switzerland. They decided to remain faithful to the brand's codes. In-house calibers beat inside, and the design became edgier, with daring skeletonizing feats and bold colors. The new tagline, "Modern Mechanical," suggests the brand's direction. The geometrically cut bridges and deep black of the case and parts further underline the contemporary design.

Among today's leading collections is the Delphis, with jumping hour and retrograde minute. The dial of the Delphis Oracle is in "curved-hand guilloché" with Grand Feu enamel lines winding mellifluously under the hands of the minute and small seconds. The movement that powers this timepiece was developed by movement specialist La Joux-Perret in exclusivity.

Another remarkable model is the Pulse One, which is equipped with the automatic caliber C.6001, also the product of a collaboration with La Joux-Perret. After the successful reincarnation of the Régulateur as Pulse One, Pulse Two had to follow. And with new interpretations of great classics such as the Opus chronograph, Chronoswiss manages to maintain its leading position in the field of modern watchmaking—or "Modern Mechanical," as the brand tagline promises.

CHRONOSWISS AG
Löwenstrasse 16b
CH-6004 Lucerne
Switzerland

TEL.:
+41-041-552-21-00

E-MAIL:
luzern@chronoswiss.com

WEBSITE:
www.chronoswiss.com

FOUNDED:
1983

NUMBER OF EMPLOYEES:
approx. 20

ANNUAL PRODUCTION:
About 3,000 wristwatches

U.S. DISTRIBUTOR:
Chronoswiss US Service Office
Shami Fine Watchmaking
372 Fairfield Road
Fairfield, NJ 07004
973-785-0004

MOST IMPORTANT COLLECTIONS/PRICE RANGE:
Approx. 30 models, including Space Timer, Flying Regulator, Open Gear, ReSec, Lunar Chronograph, Opus Chronograph, SkelTec, Sirius Artist, (no current collection) / approx. $5,800 to $47,000

Delphis Firestarter

Reference number: CH-1429RE.1E-BKRE
Movement: automatic, Chronoswiss Caliber C.6004; ø 33 mm; 37 jewels; 28,800 vph; finely finished movement; 55-hour power reserve
Functions: hours (off-center, jumping), minutes (retrograde), small seconds
Case: titanium with colored composite covering, ø 42.6 mm, height 14.5 mm; sapphire crystal; transparent case back; water-resistant to 10 atm
Band: rubber, folding clasp
Remarks: hand-guilloched enamel dial
Price: $45,900; limited to 50 pieces

Strike Two Terra

Reference number: CH-5023-BRSI
Movement: automatic, Chronoswiss Caliber C.6000; ø 33 mm; 25 jewels; 28,800 vph; skeletonized tungsten rotor; finely finished movement; 55-hour power reserve
Functions: hours (off-center), minutes, small seconds
Case: stainless steel, ø 40 mm, height 12.7 mm; sapphire crystal; transparent case back; water-resistant to 3 atm
Band: leather, pin buckle
Price: $11,800; limited to 100 pieces

Space Timer Supernova

Reference number: CH-9343M.2-SIBK
Movement: automatic, Chronoswiss Caliber C.308; ø 32.8 mm; 33 jewels; 28,800 vph; hands mechanism (transmission wheel) visible on dial side; finely finished movement; 42-hour power reserve
Functions: hours (off-center), minutes, sweep seconds; date
Case: stainless steel, ø 44 mm, height 15.2 mm; sapphire crystal; transparent case back; water-resistant to 10 atm
Band: leather, pin buckle
Price: $25,700; limited to 50 pieces

Strike Two Highland

Reference number: CH-5023-GRSI
Movement: automatic, Chronoswiss Caliber C.6000;
ø 33 mm; 25 jewels; 28,800 vph; skeletonized tungsten
rotor; finely finished movement; 55-hour power reserve
Functions: hours (off-center), minutes, small seconds
Case: stainless steel, ø 40 mm, height 12.7 mm;
sapphire crystal; transparent case back; water-resistant
to 3 atm
Band: leather, pin buckle
Price: $11,880

ReSec Vertical Red Manufacture

Reference number: CH-6923T.1-ARDB
Movement: automatic, Chronoswiss Caliber C.6005;
ø 33 mm; 31 jewels; 28,800 vph; hands mechanism
(transmission wheel) visible on dial side; skeletonized
tungsten rotor; finely finished movement; 55-hour
power reserve
Functions: hours (off-center), minutes, small seconds
(retrograde)
Case: titanium, ø 42 mm, height 14.2 mm; sapphire
crystal; transparent case back; water-resistant to
10 atm
Band: rubber, folding clasp
Price: $16,200; limited to 100 pieces

Pulse One Sand

Reference number: CH-6823-BRSI
Movement: automatic, Chronoswiss Caliber C.6001;
ø 33.4 mm; 31 jewels; 28,800 vph; skeletonized
tungsten rotor; finely finished movement; 55-hour
power reserve
Functions: hours (off-center), minutes, small seconds
(retrograde)
Case: titanium (matte), ø 41 mm, height 12.75 mm;
sapphire crystal; transparent case back; water-resistant
to 10 atm
Band: titanium (matte), folding clasp
Price: $14,300; limited to 100 pieces
Variations: with blue dial

ReSec "Beast" Manufacture

Reference number: CH-6926T.1-ARBL
Movement: automatic, Chronoswiss Caliber C.6005;
ø 33 mm; 31 jewels; 28,800 vph; hands mechanism
(transmission wheel) visible on dial side; skeletonized
tungsten rotor; finely finished movement; 55-hour
power reserve
Functions: hours (off-center), minutes, small seconds
(retrograde)
Case: titanium with blue CVD, ø 42 mm, height 14.2 mm;
sapphire crystal; transparent case back; water-resistant
to 10 atm
Band: rubber, folding clasp
Price: $18,000; limited to 100 pieces

Flying Regulator Night and Day "Midnight"

Reference number: CH-8763.1-BLSI2
Movement: automatic, Chronoswiss caliber C.296;
ø 26.2 mm, height 4.35 mm; 27 jewels; 28,800 vph;
skeletonized rotor; finely finished movement; 42-hour
power reserve
Functions: hours (off-center), minutes, subsidiary
seconds; day/night indicator; date
Case: stainless steel, ø 41 mm, height 13.85 mm;
sapphire crystal; transparent case back; water-resistant
to 10 atm
Band: bamboo, folding clasp
Remarks: hand guilloché on dial; as "Whiteout" model
with white dial
Price: $11,700; limited to 50 pieces

Opus Chronograph Titanium

Reference number: CH-7543T.1S-BL2
Movement: automatic, Chronoswiss caliber C.741 S
(Valjoux 7750 base); ø 30 mm, height 7.9 mm; 25 jewels;
28,800 vph; fully skeletonized movement and with
decorative ribbing, skeletonized rotor; 46-hour power
reserve
Functions: hours, minutes, small seconds;
chronograph; date
Case: titanium, ø 41 mm, height 14.8 mm; sapphire
crystal; transparent case back; water-resistant to
10 atm
Band: textile, folding clasp
Remarks: skeletonized dial
Price: $16,830

CIGA DESIGN

Jianmin Zhang hails from China's northwestern province of Qinghai and is considered one of the country's top industrial designers. He built a reputation for creating guidance systems for large architectural projects, like the Shanghai Expo and the Beijing Olympics. It may sound like a long way from designing watches, but showing the way in physical space is not that far from showing the way in time.

In 2016, he founded CIGA Design (named from a Chinese word meaning amazing) with a mission to make high-quality, eye-catching watches at an affordable price for the young generation. China's very efficient and low-cost production opportunities made this possible: all he needed was good design. And so, CIGA began manufacturing a range of watches, from sleek Bauhaus-inspired one-handers to edgily futuristic and minimalist pieces, like the J Series Zen, to more complex pieces with skeletonized or open-worked dials.

Several models have won awards in Europe, but in 2021, the Blue Planet clinched the Challenge Prize at the Grand Prix d'Horlogerie in Geneva. The watch features a detailed view of Earth from the sky, with engraved silver land masses. The time-telling mechanism is complex, with a static hour ring and a rotating minute ring that coordinate with the little compass on the globe that acts as a single hand. The watch is a general statement for ecology, but there are many Chinese references as well, like the compass, a Chinese invention. Another is the duality of Earth and Sky so firmly anchored in Chinese culture and Daoism.

CIGA Design has used the Blue Planet as a kind of flagship watch, letting it evolve naturally. The recent Moon Walker, for instance, accurately displays the surface of the moon as seen on NASA maps. Using a magnifying glass, you can even see Neil Armstrong's famous footprint. Another tribute to human achievement, but closer to home, is the Mount Everest Central Tourbillon, with its dial made of Everest rock. It turns two ice axes into an hour and minute hand. Another recent addition to the portfolio is the more abstract Hunter, a three-hander skeleton with CIGA's hallmark X-bridge. It also showcases the company's readiness to create complicated cases.

CIGA DESIGN
43F, Block A, Tanglang Square Office Bldg
Liuxian Blvd, Nanshan District
Shenzhen, Guangdong 518000
China

TEL.:
+86-755-827-951-80

E-MAIL:
waterman@cigadesign.com

WEBSITE:
www.cigadesign.com

FOUNDED:
2016

NUMBER OF EMPLOYEES:
109

DISTRIBUTION:
Online sales
www.cigadesign.com

MOST IMPORTANT COLLECTIONS:
Chinese Astrology watches, Blue Planet, Magician, Edge, Zen, Denmark Rose

Hunter

Movement: automatic, in-house CD-07 caliber; 28,800 vph; 24 jewels fully skeletonized movement, finely finished with beveled bridges; 40-hour power reserve
Functions: hours, minutes, sweep seconds
Case: stainless steel with DLC, 48 mm x 43 mm, height 12.1 mm; sapphire crystal; sterling silver case back with personalization option; water-resistant to 3 atm
Band: stainless steel, folding clasp
Price: $499

Moonwalker

Movement: automatic, unique CB-09 caliber (based on Sellita SW200 with CIGA Design's Asynchronous Follow Technology to allow for a single hand); ø 25.6 mm, height 4.6 mm; 26 jewels; 28,800 vph; 41-hour power reserve
Functions: hours, minutes
Case: ceramic, silver plating; ø 46 mm, height 17.05 mm; sapphire crystal; partly open case back; water-resistant to 5 atm
Band: fluororubber; folding clasp
Remarks: real moon surface with the Sea of Tranquility, the Montes Apenninus, Tycho Copernicus Crater, and a miniature footprint of Armstrong; single hand as astronaut
Price: $1,699
Variations: Blue Planet, Ice Age, Black Star

Central Tourbillon Mount Everest Homage

Movement: automatic, CD-05 caliber; in-house customized movement; ø 35.6 mm; 33 jewels; 21,600 vph; openworked center; 120-hour power reserve
Functions: hours (part of the bezel), minutes
Case: titanium, ø 45 mm, height 11.65 mm; lugless case; sapphire crystal; water-resistant to 3 atm
Band: rubber, pin buckle
Remarks: dial made of hand-selected and processed rock from Mount Everest; ice axe-shaped hands with green luminous mass for night viewing; "It is not the mountain we conquer but ourselves" engraved on the case back
Price: $3,999

CLAUDE MEYLAN

The Swiss brand Claude Meylan, located in L'Abbaye near Joux Lake in the heart of watch country, specializes in skeletonization, which is the art of removing as much material as possible from bridges, plates, the dial, even the hands. It transforms a watch, making it transparent and allowing a view of the movement. Further, it allows for imaginative designs using what's left of the material.

Skeletonization has become popular in recent years, but it's not as simple as it might sound. As the various metal components are hollowed out and properly finished with chamfering and sanding, the tensions within the material change. This can then have a deleterious effect on the functioning of the mechanism, since the bridges and plates are in fact used to hold and stabilize the movement.

In 1988, Claude Meylan founded his company. It was taken over soon after by another watchmaker, Henri Berney, who kept up the old tradition. In 2011, the next CEO, Philippe Belais, a man with long experience in the industry, took charge. He also heads Vaudaux, a maker of high-end boxes and cases in Geneva.

Claude Meylan's products, which show many different aspects of the art of skeletonization, live up to the brand's tagline: "Sculptors of time." The company has four main wristwatch collections, all relating in some way to the region: Lac, for Joux Lake; l'Abbaye, the village where the company has its headquarters; Lionne, the tiny, 1,800-foot-long river with a big name (Lioness, because it sometimes turns into a raging torrent) that flows by the workshops; and, finally, Tortue, whose tonneau case is reminiscent of a turtle. There is also the Montre de Poches (or pocket watch) collection. Lately, the Lionne line has been evolving, with a smaller version to attract female watch fans, and the *sur-mesure* (bespoke) version that lets buyers have initials placed on the watch dial. The Lionne Ondine is a ladies' watch released in 2024. It features a special bracelet made of rings filled with mother-of-pearl. It, too, mirrors that short river, but when it is lingering poetically toward the Lac de Joux. The ladies' Tortue was born in the mind of the company's communication officer, Pia de Chefdebien, who was asked to dream up her own a mechanical watch.

CLAUDE MEYLAN
Route de l'Hôtel de Ville 2
CH-1344 L'Abbaye
Switzerland

TEL.:
+41(0)21 841 14 57

E-MAIL:
info@claudemeylan.ch

WEBSITE:
www.claudemeylan.ch

FOUNDED:
originally mid-18th century; revived in mid-20th century and purchased in 2011

NUMBER OF EMPLOYEES:
7

ANNUAL PRODUCTION:
approx. 2,500 pieces

MOST IMPORTANT COLLECTIONS/PRICE RANGE:
Tortue, Lac, Lionne, Abbaye / $2,000-$10,000

L'Abbaye

Reference number: 3262P
Movement: automatic, ETA 2892/2 caliber; ø 25.6 mm, height 3.60 mm; 21 jewels; 28,800 vph; fully skeletonized movement; 42-hour power reserve
Functions: hours, minutes, sweep seconds
Case: yellow gold-plated stainless steel, ø 38 mm, height 9 mm; sapphire crystal; transparent case back; water-resistant to 5 atm
Band: leather, pin buckle
Price: $5,200

Lionne Ondine

Reference number: 6060
Movement: hand-wound, Peseux 7001; ø 23 mm, height 2.50 mm; 17 jewels; 21,600 vph; fully skeletonized movement; 42-hour power reserve
Functions: hours, minutes
Case: silver, ø 35 mm, height 8 mm; sapphire crystal; transparent case back; water-resistant to 3 atm
Band: silver, clasp
Price: $7,200
Variations: silver or gold plated

Tortue

Reference number: 6091
Movement: automatic, ETA 2892 caliber; ø 25.6 mm, height 5 mm; 21 jewels; 28,800 vph; entirely skeletonized, finely finished movement; 42-hour power reserve
Functions: hours, minutes, sweep seconds
Case: stainless steel, ø 40 mm, height 11 mm; sapphire crystal; transparent case back; water-resistant to 3 atm
Band: leather, pin buckle
Price: $6,300

CORUM

Founded in 1955, Corum celebrated seventy years of unusual, and sometimes even outlandish, case and dial designs in 2025. The brand has had quite a busy history, but still largely remains true to the collections launched by founders Gaston Ries and his nephew René Bannwart: the Admiral's Cup, Bridges, and Heritage. Among Corum's most iconic pieces is the legendary Golden Bridge baguette, or stick, movement, which has received a complete makeover in recent years with the use of modern materials and complicated mechanisms. It is built around the idea of concentrating all parts along a straight axis in the middle of a rectangular dial. The development of these extraordinary movements required great watchmaking craftsmanship.

The Bridges collection has always been an eye-catcher. It was originally the brainchild of the great watchmaker Vincent Calabrese, though these types of movements trace back further in time. Its introduction was a milestone in watchmaking history. The Golden Bridge recently acquired a new highlight in the Golden Bridge Avant-Garde, with all components appearing to float in thin air, with six black indices framing the movement, themselves surrounded by a striking black frame. It's very sleek and modern.

But Corum also has more classical watches. The sporty Admiral's Cup collection is divided into the staid Legend and the more athletic AC-One 45.

In 2013, the Chinese Citychamp Group became a shareholder and added much needed development cash and an extensive distribution network in Hong Kong and China. However, in 2025, Haso Mehmedovic, now CEO, along with a group of investors from Switzerland, triggered a management buy-out. This means that the brand is once again back in Swiss hands.

Corum's vision is expressed in its logo: a key facing the sky, which symbolizes both the mysteries to be discovered as well as openness to the new. For a more popular experience of watch-wearing, the company revived the remarkable Bubble, which earned its moniker from the domed shape of the crystal, allowing room for all sorts of dial decoration.

MONTRES CORUM SÀRL
Rue du Petit-Château 1
Case postale 374
CH-2301 La Chaux-de-Fonds
Switzerland

TEL.:
+41-32-967-0670

E-MAIL:
info@corum.ch

WEBSITE:
www.corum-watches.com

FOUNDED:
1955

NUMBER OF EMPLOYEES:
50 worldwide

ANNUAL PRODUCTION:
5,000 watches

U.S. DISTRIBUTOR:
Montres Corum USA
CWJ BRANDS
1551 Sawgrass Corporate Parkway, Suite 109
Sunrise, FL 33323
954-279-1220
www.corum.ch

MOST IMPORTANT COLLECTIONS/PRICE RANGE:
Admiral's Cup, Golden Bridge, Lab, Bubble, Coin, Heritage, Romvlvs and Artisan / $4,400 to over $1,000,000

Bubble 47 Dragon

Reference number: L082/04508
Movement: automatic, Caliber CO 082; ø 25.6 mm, height 3.6 mm; 25 jewels; 28,800 vph; 42-hour power reserve
Functions: hours, minutes
Case: stainless steel with black PVD, ø 47 mm, height 18.5 mm; sapphire crystal; transparent case back; water-resistant to 10 atm
Band: rubber, pin buckle
Remarks: gold plated dial with the image of a dragon's eye
Price: $7,600

Admiral 42 Automatic

Reference number: A395/04482
Movement: automatic, Caliber CO 395; ø 25.6 mm, height 4.35 mm; 27 jewels; 28,800 vph; 42-hour power reserve
Functions: hours, minutes, subsidiary seconds; date
Case: stainless steel, ø 42 mm, height 10.3 mm; sapphire crystal; transparent case back; water-resistant to 10 atm
Band: stainless steel, triple folding clasp
Remarks: meteorite dial
Price: $9,800
Variations: various cases, straps, and dials

Golden Bridge Classic

Reference number: B113/01042
Movement: hand-winding, Caliber CO 113; 11 mm x 33 mm, height 3 mm; 19 jewels; 28,800 vph; hand engraved baguette movement, hand-engraved gold bridges and mainplate; 40-hour power reserve
Functions: hours, minutes
Case: white gold, 34 mm x 51 mm, height 10.9 mm; sapphire crystal; transparent case back; water-resistant to 3 atm
Band: reptile skin, triple folding clasp
Price: $41,600

CUERVO Y SOBRINOS

Many brands have been going vintage to surf a wave of nostalgia in an age of techno-frigidity. Cuervo y Sobrinos, however, has vintage, nostalgia, romance, and a touch of derring-do as a genome set. The brand originated with Ramón Fernandos Cuervo, who emigrated from Spain to Cuba in 1862 and opened a jewelry business. Twenty years later, he recruited his sister's sons to help out with the booming business (that would be his nephews, the *sobrinos* of the brand name). Don Ramón died in 1907, but the company continued to expand, adding wristwatches made in La Chaux-de-Fonds.

The advent of Communist rule on the island ended the streak of successes. But in 2002, an Italian watch enthusiast, Marzio Villa, resuscitated the brand. The tagline "Latin heritage, Swiss manufacture" says it all. The purchase was well-advised, because vintage, even in an updated form, will always find a fan, and Cuba is filled with iconic images from its past.

The many collections produced by Cuervo y Sobrinos epitomize—or even romanticize—the island's heyday. In these pieces is the faded elegance of the age of steamships and the nostalgia for a past time, mostly the 1930s to the 1950s, when the world's troubles could be ignored by those with enough wherewithal to travel to the island, walk down shop-lined streets with a good cigar, and then lose some cash in the casinos. The lines are elegant and sober, or blatantly vintage with fissured dial effect (like the Historiador collection), or they radiate the ease of those who still have time on their hands, as it were. The color codes recall Cuba's famous products: tobacco, coffee, salmon. In fact, when you purchase a Cuervo y Sobrinos watch, it comes in a humidor. Lately, the brand has focused on these decades of slightly decadent life on the island with a range of models in the Robusto line.

While some collections, like the Buceador, have some more modern models, the Espléndidos and Prominente collections are the ones that really epitomize the brand's DNA, with at times overly long, languorous, elegant, rectangular, thin cases and colors named "rhum," "salmon," or "tobacco."

CYS SA
Via Carlo Maderno 54
CH-6825 Capolago
Switzerland

TEL.:
+41 21-552-18-82

E-MAIL:
contact@cuervoysobrinos.com

WEBSITE:
www.cuervoysobrinos.com

FOUNDED:
1882

ANNUAL PRODUCTION:
3,500 watches

DISTRIBUTOR:
Provenance Gems LLC
ines@provenancegems.com
800-305-3869

MOST IMPORTANT COLLECTIONS/PRICE RANGE:
Esplendidos, Historiador, Pirata, Prominente,
Robusto, Vuelo/ $2,000 to $20,000

Chronograph Aga Blue Classic

Reference number: 3141.1AB
Movement: automatic, Valjoux 7750 caliber; ø 30 mm, height 7.9 mm; 25 jewels; 28,800 vph; oscillating weight with fan decoration; 48-hour power reserve
Functions: hours, minutes, subsidiary seconds; chronograph with tachymeter scale; date
Case: stainless steel, ø 40 mm, height 11.85 mm; sapphire crystal; transparent case back; screw-down crown; water-resistant to 10 atm
Band: stainless steel, folding clasp
Remarks: case back engraved with Aga Blu Classic printed logo
Price: $5,700; limited to 882 pieces
Variations: various dials: silver, blue, and green

Historiador Heritage Limited Edition

Reference number: 3145.1HLE
Movement: automatic, La Joux-Perret L 110 caliber (Execution Premium Top); ø 30 mm, height 7.9 mm, 37 jewels; 28,800 vph; oscillating weight with fan decoration; 60-hour power reserve
Functions: hours, minutes, subsidiary seconds; chronograph with tachymeter scale; date
Case: stainless steel, ø 41 mm, height 15.25 mm; sapphire crystal; screw-mounted transparent case back; water-resistant to 5 atm
Band: calfskin, folding clasp
Price: $6,900; limited to 82 editions

Historic Endurance

Reference number: 3141.1HEP
Movement: automatic, Valjoux 7750 caliber; ø 30 mm, height 7.9 mm, 25 jewels; 28,800 vph; oscillating weight with fan decoration; 48-hour power reserve
Functions: hours, minutes, subsidiary seconds; chronograph with tachymeter scale; date
Case: stainless steel, ø 41 mm, height 15.24 mm; sapphire crystal; screw-mounted transparent case back; water-resistant to 5 atm
Band: calfskin, folding clasp
Price: $5,700; limited to 76 editions

Espléndidos Vitola

Reference number: 2452.1VT
Movement: automatic, La Joux-Perret G120 caliber (Execution Premium Top); ø 25.6 mm, height 5.45 mm; 29 jewels; 28,800 vph; oscillating weight with fan decoration; 68-hour power reserve
Functions: hours, minutes, subsidiary seconds; date
Case: stainless steel, 47 mm x 36 mm, height 13 mm; sapphire crystal; transparent case back; water-resistant to 3 atm
Band: reptile skin, folding clasp
Remarks: dial with printed tobacco leaf
Price: $4,500

Espléndidos Heritage

Reference number: 2452.1HLE
Movement: automatic, La Joux-Perret G120 caliber (Execution Premium Top); ø 25.6 mm, height 5.45 mm; 29 jewels; 28,800 vph; oscillating weight with fan decoration; 68-hour power reserve
Functions: hours, minutes, subsidiary seconds; date
Case: stainless steel, 47 mm x 36 mm, height 13 mm; sapphire crystal; transparent case back; water-resistant to 3 atm
Band: reptile skin, folding clasp
Price: $4,900; limited to 82 pieces

Prominente Clásico

Reference number: 1015.1RB
Movement: automatic, CYS 5103 caliber (Soprod M100 base); ø 25.6 mm, height 3.6 mm; 25 jewels; 28,800 vph; oscillating weight with CyS logo; 42-hour power reserve
Functions: hours, minutes, sweep seconds; date
Case: stainless steel, 43 mm x 32 mm, height 8.6 mm; sapphire crystal; transparent case back; water-resistant to 3 atm
Band: reptile skin, folding clasp
Price: $3,550

Buceador Caribe

Reference number: 2860.1TQ
Movement: automatic, Soprod P024 caliber; ø 26 mm, height 4.6 mm; 25 jewels; 28,800 vph; oscillating weight with côtes de Genève and logo; 38-hour power reserve
Functions: hours, minutes, sweep seconds; date
Case: stainless steel, 43 mm x 43 mm, height 15.8 mm; bezel locking function; sapphire crystal; water-resistant to 20 atm
Band: FKM rubber, pin buckle
Remarks: comes with additional orange rubber strap with green lining
Price: $4,500

Sir Winston

Reference number: 2810.1SWBL
Movement: automatic, Sellita SW240-1 caliber (Execution Premium Top); ø 29 mm, height 5.05 mm; 26 jewels; 28,800 vph; oscillating weight with logo; 38-hour power reserve
Functions: hours, minutes, sweep seconds; date, day
Case: stainless steel with titanium barrel, ø 43 mm, height 12.45 mm; sapphire crystal; transparent case back; water-resistant to 10 atm
Band: reptile skin, folding clasp
Remarks: dial with black clous de Paris guilloché
Price: $4,750; limited to 282 pieces
Variations: with various dial colors; comes with reptile skin strap

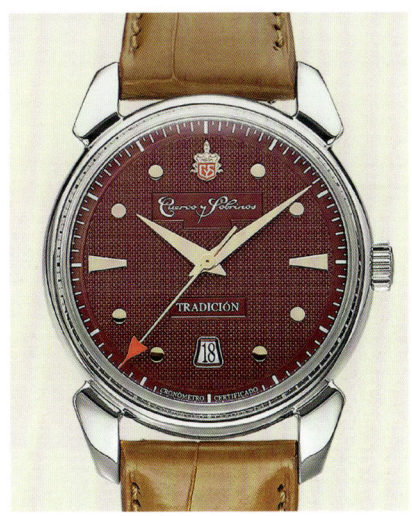

Historiador Tradición

Reference number: 3195.1TBY
Movement: automatic, Soprod Newton caliber (P-092); ø 26 mm, height 4.6 mm; 23 jewels; 28,800 vph; finished oscillating weight with engraving; COSC-certified movement; 44-hour power reserve
Functions: hours, minutes, sweep seconds; date
Case: stainless steel, ø 40 mm, height 12.33 mm; sapphire crystal; water-resistant to 10 atm
Band: reptile skin, folding clasp
Remarks: burgundy dial with traditional "frappage" motif; case back features engraving of former Cuervo y Sobrinos boutique on San Rafael Street in Havana, Cuba
Price: $4,500; limited to 282 pieces
Variations: with champagne or white dial

CURTIS AUSTRALIA

Watches made by independents often possess a special aura. It is rarely about the caliber inside—usually a robust and precise off-the-shelf movement that has been tweaked and decorated. What truly catches the eye is the unique design, the result of countless subtle cues that reflect the craftsperson's skill and the influence of their environment.

Glenn Curtis grew up in Gippsland, Australia, a region in the country's southeast embraced by the Australian Alps to the north and the sea to the south. He descends from a family-run business that dates back to 1890. For the past sixty years in particular, the family has been dedicated to crafting fine writing instruments and jewelry. Curtis added watches to the repertoire after inheriting his watchmaking grandfather's tools.

Curtis Australia's creations draw aesthetic inspiration from Art Deco, infused with a tribute to the local scenery, from tranquil lakes and golden beaches to the region's rich biodiversity. Curtis channels his craftsmanship to weave these influences into all his works, including his watches, of which he produces about 200 per year. "A watch isn't just a tool to mark time," he notes. "It's a companion that holds memories, milestones, and meaning."

A rare feature in the watch world is Curtis's choice of 9-carat gold for certain models—an alloy known for its durability, incorporating a substantial amount of copper, silver, and nickel. The result is a material that retains the warm appearance of gold while being more affordable.

Curtis offers three men's collections, all powered by reliable Sellita SW300-family movements. Each line, however, has its own distinct character. The Motima (a blend of "motion" and "time") is designed for daily wear, featuring a hand-carved coin bezel on either a round (RT) or octagonal (XT) case, with a complex dial showcasing a sun-brushed center and grained outer ring. The Myst and Alpha collections stand out for their richly engraved cases with flowing lines and space for decorative elements, allowing for personalization on request. In early 2026, Curtis introduced the Mechanika 288, a skeletonized tourbillon framed by a titanium openworked dial and housed in a tonneau case.

CURTIS AUSTRALIA
129 Macleod Street
Bairnsdale, Victoria
Australia 3875

TEL.:
+61-35-152-1089

EMAIL:
replyto@curtisaustralia.com

WEBSITE:
www.curtisaustralia.com

FOUNDED:
1890

ANNUAL PRODUCTION:
less than 200 watches

DISTRIBUTION:
Contact Curtis Australia

MOST IMPORTANT COLLECTIONS/PRICE RANGE:
Motima, Myst, Alpha, range of ladies' watches (Colours, Floriale, Fortuna, Grace, Monroe, Myst, Sophia) / $6,800 to $84,000, higher for some set with diamonds

Mechanika 288 Tourbillon Skeleton

Movement: hand-wound, CT 01-5 caliber; 33 mm x 39 mm, height 5.34 mm; 26 Jewels; 28,800 vph; tourbillon with two serial spring barrels; skeletonized movement; 72-hour power reserve
Functions: hours, minutes, seconds on tourbillon cage
Case: stainless steel, 56 mm x 39.5 mm, height 10.4 mm; sapphire crystal crown; sapphire crystal; oval transparent case back aperture; water-resistant to 3 atm
Band: calfskin, folding clasp
Remarks: titanium open worked dial; diamonds at 3, 6, 9 o'clock
Price: $14,600
Variations: azure or titanium royal dials; yellow-gold case ($119,000); yellow gold with diamonds and gold band ($295,000)

Motima Racing RT Perpetual

Movement: automatic, Sellita SW 300-1 caliber; ø 25.6 mm, height 3.6 mm; 25 jewels; 28,800 vph; custom-engraved rotor; 42-hour power reserve
Functions: hours, minutes, sweep seconds; date
Case: stainless steel, ø 46 mm, height 11 mm; with fluted (coin) bezel; sapphire crystal with gem set transparent case back; screw-down crown; water-resistant to 3 atm
Band: stainless steel, folding clasp
Remarks: tachymeter style dial in British racing green
Price: $9,800
Variations: various dial colors; 9ct gold case ($21,800)

Myst Diamond

Movement: automatic, Sellita SW300-1 caliber; ø 25.6mm, height 3.6 mm; 25 jewels; 28,800 vph; custom-engraved rotor; 42-hour power reserve
Functions: hours, minutes, sweep seconds
Case: yellow gold set with 54 brilliant-cut diamonds; 46 mm x 38 mm, height 7.5 mm; sapphire crystal; gold case back; screw-down crown; water-resistant to 3 atm
Band: calfskin, folding clasp
Price: $26,000
Variations: dials in black guilloché, antique white; 9ct gold case ($26,000); 18-ct gold case, gold bracelet with diamonds ($98,800)

CZAPEK

Born in Bohemia (today's Czech Republic) in 1811, watchmaker Franciszek Czapek (in Czech: František Čapek) took part in the failed Polish insurrection of 1832 against Russia before fleeing to Geneva. In 1839, he joined fellow Pole Antoine de Patek in a business venture. When their partnership ended in 1845, Patek teamed up with Jean Philippe, inventor of the keyless watch. Czapek went on to become watchmaker to Emperor Napoleon III and the author of a treatise on watchmaking. Sometime in the late 1860s, however, he closed up shop and ultimately returned to his native Bohemia, where he died.

His "resurrection" is credited to entrepreneur, art specialist, and avid watch collector Harry Guhl, who revived the name in 2015 and assembled a management team including Xavier de Roquemaurel and Sébastien Follonier. They based the reborn brand on Czapek's model No. 3430—an intriguing piece distinguished by elongated Roman numerals, elegant fleur-de-lis hands, and two asymmetrically placed subdials at 7:30 and 4:30: one for small seconds, the other with a double hand indicating both the seven-day power reserve and the days of the week.

Over the years, Czapek has expanded its portfolio with creations such as the Place Vendôme and the Faubourg de Cracovie that hark back to Czapek's life as a Polish exile watchmaker in Geneva and Paris. During the pandemic, the brand gained considerable traction as collectors increasingly turned online, enabling it to build inventory and real manufacturing capacity. The Antarctique collection, in particular, captured the attention of enthusiasts worldwide. Subsequent releases showcased serious complications, such as a split-seconds chronograph paired with elegant skeletonization, tourbillons, and explorations of métiers d'art.

In 2025, Czapek celebrated both its tenth anniversary and the 180th of the original Czapek & Cie. with a remarkable lineup of timepieces, notably a bold and contemporary Time Jumper with a 24-hour digital display, and the Quai des Bergues "Sursum Corda," a homage to the first Quai des Bergues model inspired by the historic No. 3430 pocket watch.

CZAPEK & CIE
18 Rue de la Corraterie
CH-1204 Geneva
Switzerland

TEL.:
+41 22 557 41 41

E-MAIL:
info@czapek.com

WEBSITE:
www.czapek.com

FOUNDED:
2012

U.S. DISTRIBUTOR:
Horology Works
11 Flagg Road
West Hartford, CT 06117
860-986-9676
info@horologyworks.com

MOST IMPORTANT COLLECTIONS/PRICE RANGE:
Promenade, Antarctique, Quai des Bergues men's and ladies' watches, Place Vendôme, Faubourg de Cracovie / $12,000 - $226,000

The Time Jumper

Movement: automatic, 10.01 caliber; ø 30 mm, height 6.3 mm; 44 jewels; 28,800 vph; micro-rotor of recycled platinum, balance wheel with variable inertia with four gold blocks; finely finished movement; 60-hour power reserve
Functions: jumping hours, trailing minutes
Case: yellow gold with guilloché, ø 42.4 mm, height 12.35 mm (including magnifying glass); screw-down crown; sapphire crystal; transparent case back; water-resistant to 3 atm
Band: rubber, folding clasp with micro-adjustment system
Remarks: unique dials with hand-applied varnish
Price: $89,900; limited to 30 pieces
Variations: stainless steel ($58,800)

Quai des Bergues "Sursum Corda"

Movement: automatic, SXH1 caliber; ø 32 mm, height 4.75 mm; 31 jewels; 21,600 vph; 2 barrel springs, balance wheel with variable inertia; finely finished movement with sandblasted bridges and mainplate, perlage; 168-hour power reserve
Functions: hours, minutes, subsidiary seconds; power reserve indicator
Case: rose gold, ø 40.5 mm, height 11.9 mm; screw-down crown; sapphire crystal; transparent case back; water-resistant to 5 atm
Band: reptile skin, folding clasp with micro-adjustment system
Remarks: grand-feu enamel dial with "secret" sentence: "Sursum Corda" (Raise your hearts) at 12, "Czapek" at 7:30, and 10/180 tribute to the double anniversary of the company
Price: $51,500
Variations: without the secret signatures on the dial; with stainless-steel case ($26,900)

Antarctique Plique-à-jour – Polar Blue

Movement: automatic, SXH5 caliber; ø 30 mm, height 4.2 mm; 25 jewels; 28,800 vph; microrotor with recycled platinum mass, balance wheel with variable inertia with four gold blocks; finely finished movement; 60-hour power reserve
Functions: hours, minutes, subsidiary seconds
Case: white gold, ø 40.5 mm, height 10.6 mm; screw-down crown; sapphire crystal; transparent case back; water-resistant to 12 atm
Band: stainless steel, folding clasp with micro-adjustment system
Remarks: white-gold dial with gradient grand-feu enamel
Price: $76,200; limited to 10 pieces

DAMASKO

When it comes to sheer toughness, Damasko has built up quite a track record ever since its founding in 1994, in Germany. But it's not visible at first glance. These unadorned watches with clean, sharp lines are almost archetypical watches. They are robust, indestructible even, and will not need much servicing.

The company's claim to fame lies in its choice of materials, such as polycrystalline silicon hairsprings and components made of a special ice-hardened steel. This special patent involves adding nitrogen and carbon to the molten stainless steel and then cooling it quickly. The resulting material, which has been used in machines like the space shuttle, is extremely hard and does not corrode easily, so these are watches that will keep their look for a long time.

In fact, the research done by this small brand, located near Regensburg in southern Germany, has generated over one hundred patents for the brand, as well as registered samples and designs. The "German" look means well-groomed dials and an immediate view of the time, thanks to contrasting hues.

These watches boast outstanding technical quality, which combines with a very clear stylistic concept. The collection ranges from very classical-functional pilot watches to a line of timeless sportive chronographs, and some very elegant watches for daily use. The latest models in the Damasko watch collection are the DC76/2 and DC86/2 chronographs with manufacture movement C51-6 and the DK36 as a three-hand watch with manufacture caliber A26-3. An innovative feature is the chronograph with a sweep minute totalizer.

Many of the models run on ETA movements, but Damasko also assembles its own caliber, the A35, which allows for a manufacturing depth of ninety percent. Parts made in the small factory include plates, bridges, pinions, balance, spring barrel, and rotors. And the company has its own tough black, scratchproof coating for cases and bracelets called Damest. Despite this, Damasko watches manage to stay in the affordable range.

DAMASKO GMBH
Unterheising 17c
93092 Barbing
Germany

TEL.:
+49-9401-80481

E-MAIL:
sales@damasko-watches.com

WEBSITE:
www.damasko-watches.com

FOUNDED:
1994

NUMBER OF EMPLOYEES:
30

DISTRIBUTION:
U.S. Sales
Island Watch
273 Walt Whitman Road, Suite 217
11746 Huntington Station, NY
631-470-0762
sales@longislandwatch.com

PRICE RANGE:
$1,000 to $6,000

DC 87

Movement: automatic, Damasko Caliber C51-6; ø 30.4 mm, height 7.9 mm; 27 jewels; 28,800 vph; DIN standard shock protection and antimagnetic; 50-hour power reserve
Functions: hours, minutes, subsidiary seconds; additional 24-hour display; chronograph
Case: ice-hardened stainless steel, ø 42 mm, height 14.4 mm; bidirectional bezel, with 0-12 scale; sapphire crystal; screw-down crown; water-resistant to 10 atm
Band: leather, pin buckle
Price: $4,659

DC 96

Movement: automatic, Damasko Caliber C51-6; ø 30.4 mm, height 7.9 mm; 27 jewels; 28,800 vph; DIN standard shock protection and antimagnetic; 50-hour power reserve
Functions: hours, minutes, subsidiary seconds; additional 24-hour display; chronograph; date
Case: stainless steel (austenitic steel), ø 41 mm, height 14.6 mm; sapphire crystal; screw-down crown; water-resistant to 10 atm
Band: leather, pin buckle
Price: $5,375

DC 86/2

Movement: automatic, Damasko Caliber C51-6; ø 30.4 mm, height 7.9 mm; 27 jewels; 28,800 vph; DIN standard shock protection and antimagnetic; 50-hour power reserve
Functions: hours, minutes, subsidiary seconds; additional 24-hour display; chronograph; date
Case: ice-hardened stainless steel, ø 42 mm, height 14.4 mm; bidirectional bezel, with 0-12 scale; sapphire crystal; screw-down crown; water-resistant to 10 atm
Band: stainless steel, folding clasp
Price: $5,650

DF 20 Black

Movement: automatic, Damasko Caliber A26-1; ø 25.6 mm, height 4.6 mm; 20 jewels; 28,800 vph; silicon escape wheel; DIN standard shock protection and antimagnetic; 42-hour power reserve
Functions: hours, minutes, sweep seconds
Case: stainless steel (submarine steel), ø 39 mm, height 9.95 mm; sapphire crystal; transparent case back; water-resistant to 20 atm
Band: leather, pin buckle
Price: $2,075
Variations: the DF 20 Old Radium with a plain or orange seconds hand

DK 26

Movement: automatic, Damasko Caliber A26-1; ø 25.6 mm, height 4.6 mm; 20 jewels; 28,800 vph; silicon escape wheel; DIN standard shock protection and antimagnetic; 42-hour power reserve
Functions: hours, minutes, sweep seconds
Case: stainless steel (submarine steel), ø 39 mm, height 9.95 mm; sapphire crystal; transparent case back; screw-down crown; water-resistant to 20 atm
Band: leather, pin buckle
Price: $1,850

DK 36/2 Old Radium

Movement: automatic, Damasko Caliber A26-3; ø 25.6 mm, height 5.05 mm; 20 jewels; 28,800 vph; silicon escape wheel; DIN standard shock protection and antimagnetic; 42-hour power reserve
Functions: hours, minutes, sweep seconds; date and weekday
Case: ice-hardened stainless steel, ø 40 mm, height 12.3 mm; sapphire crystal; screw-down crown; water-resistant to 10 atm
Band: leather, pin buckle
Price: $1,775

DK 44

Movement: automatic, Damasko Caliber A26-3; ø 25.6 mm, height 5.05 mm; 20 jewels; 28,800 vph; silicon escape wheel; DIN standard shock protection and antimagnetic; 42-hour power reserve
Functions: hours, minutes, sweep seconds; date and weekday
Case: ice-hardened stainless steel, ø 41.9 mm, height 12.4 mm; bezel bidirectional bezel with 0-60 scale; sapphire crystal; screw-down crown; water-resistant to 10 atm
Band: leather, pin buckle
Price: $2,575

DK 46 Black

Movement: automatic, Damasko Caliber A26-3; ø 25.6 mm, height 5.05 mm; 20 jewels; 28,800 vph; silicon escape wheel; DIN standard shock protection and antimagnetic; 42-hour power reserve
Functions: hours, minutes, sweep seconds; date and weekday
Case: ice-hardened stainless steel with Damest coating ø 41.9 mm, height 12.4 mm; bidirectional bezel with 0-12 scale; sapphire crystal; screw-down crown; water-resistant to 10 atm
Band: leather, pin buckle
Price: $2,675

DK 47

Movement: automatic, Damasko Caliber A26-3; ø 25.6 mm, height 5.05 mm; 20 jewels; 28,800 vph; silicon escape wheel; DIN standard shock protection and antimagnetic; 42-hour power reserve
Functions: hours, minutes, sweep seconds; date and weekday
Case: hardened stainless steel, ø 41.9 mm, height 12.4 mm; bidirectional bezel with 0-12 scale; sapphire crystal; screw-down crown; water-resistant to 10 atm
Band: leather, pin buckle
Price: $2,675

DAVOSA

One of the more important brands occupying the lower segment of the market is Davosa, which manufactures a wide range of watches with all the complications one might want but in an affordable segment: pilot watches, quality divers (with helium valve), dress watches, and ladies' watches. The brand has even come out with an apnea training watch that can be removed from its case and stood upright. These timepieces use solid Swiss movements (Sellita and ETA), which are occasionally modified to fit the watches' specific designs. Among these dressy-in-a-sporty-sort-of-way timepieces, one finds a limited-edition automatic chronograph with a moon phase, at under $2,400.

To create a broad portfolio requires experience, and that is something Davosa has in spades. The company was founded in 1891, when farmer Abel Frédéric Hasler from Tramelan, in Switzerland's Jura mountains, spent the winter months making silver pocket watch cases. The following generation of Haslers took up the flame. However, playing the role of unassuming private-label watchmakers, they remained in the background and let their customers in Europe and the United States run away with the show. It wasn't until after World War II that brothers Paul and David Hasler dared produce their own timepieces.

The long experience with watchmaking and watches culminated in 1987 with the brothers developing their own line of watches under the brand name Davosa. The Haslers then signed a partnership with the German distributor Bohle. In Germany, mechanical watches were experiencing a new boom, so the brand was able to evolve quickly. In 2000, Corinna Bohle took over as manager of strategic development. Davosa now reaches well beyond Switzerland's borders and has become an integral part of the world of mechanical watches. It has streamlined its offering, which is now divided into three families: diving, performance, and pilot.

DAVOSA SWISS BOHLE GMBH
Bunsenstrasse 1a
32052 Herford
Germany

TEL.:
+49 (0)5221-9942400

E-MAIL:
info@davosa.com

WEBSITE:
www.davosa.com

FOUNDED:
1881

U.S. DISTRIBUTOR:
Gyrax LTD - Davosa U.S.A,
200 S. Biscayne Blvd
Miami, FL 33131
877-DAVOSA1
info@davosa-usa.com
www.davosa-usa.com

MOST IMPORTANT COLLECTIONS/PRICE RANGE:
Apnea Diver, Argonautic, Classic, Gentleman, Military, Newton, Pilot, Ternos, / $800 to $2,600

Newton Pilot Rally Chronograph Limited Edition

Reference number: 161.536.55
Movement: automatic, Davosa Caliber DAV3052 (base Sellita SW510); ø 30 mm, height 7.9 mm; 27 jewels; 28,800 vph; 62-hour power reserve
Functions: hours, minutes, subsidiary seconds; chronograph; date
Case: stainless steel, ø 42 mm, height 15.5 mm; sapphire crystal; transparent case back; water-resistant to 7 atm
Band: leather, pin buckle
Remarks: limited to 300 pieces
Price: $2,495
Variations: various colors (limited to 300 pieces each)

Ternos Professional Black Rock Limited Edition

Reference number: 161.583.20
Movement: automatic, Davosa Caliber DAV3021 (base Sellita SW200-1); ø 25.6 mm, height 4.6 mm; 26 jewels; 28,800 vph; 41-hour power reserve
Functions: hours, minutes, sweep seconds; date
Case: stainless steel with black DLC, ø 42 mm, height 14.6 mm; unidirectional bezel with ceramic insert, with 0–60 scale; sapphire crystal; screw-down crown; water-resistant to 50 atm
Band: stainless steel with black DLC, folding clasp, with safety lock
Price: $1,250; limited to 500 pieces
Variations: with rubber strap

Ternos Professional 68H Automatic

Reference number: 161.538.50
Movement: automatic, Davosa Caliber DAV3121 (base MLJP G100); ø 25.6 mm, height 4.45 mm; 24 jewels; 28,800 vph; 68-hour power reserve
Functions: hours, minutes, sweep seconds; date
Case: stainless steel, ø 42 mm, height 12.8 mm; unidirectional bezel with ceramic insert and 0–60 scale; sapphire crystal; screw-down crown, helium valve; water-resistant to 30 atm
Band: stainless steel, folding clasp, with safety lock, with extension link
Price: $1,395
Variations: various colors

Newton Lady Diamond Automatic

Reference number: 166.191.10
Movement: automatic, Davosa Caliber DAV3021 (base Sellita SW200-1); ø 25.6 mm, height 4.6 mm; 26 jewels; 28,800 vph; 41-hour power reserve
Functions: hours, minutes, sweep seconds; date
Case: stainless steel, ø 34 mm, height 10.5 mm; bezel set with 56 diamonds; sapphire crystal; transparent case back; water-resistant to 5 atm
Band: stainless steel, folding clasp
Remarks: mother-of-pearl dial
Price: $1,995
Variations: various dial and strap colors

Newton Pilot Automatic

Reference number: 161.530.70
Movement: automatic, Davosa Caliber DAV3021ND (base Sellita SW200-1); ø 25.6 mm, height 4.6 mm; 26 jewels; 28,800 vph; 41-hour power reserve
Functions: hours, minutes, sweep seconds
Case: stainless steel, ø 40 mm, height 11.6 mm; sapphire crystal; transparent case back; water-resistant to 7 atm
Band: stainless steel, folding clasp
Price: $1,100
Variations: various colors and straps

Argonautic Lumis Automatic

Reference number: 161.529.10
Movement: automatic, Davosa Caliber DAV3021 (base Sellita SW200-1); ø 25.6 mm, height 4.6 mm; 26 jewels; 28,800 vph; 41-hour power reserve
Functions: hours, minutes, sweep seconds; date
Case: stainless steel, ø 43 mm, height 13.5 mm; unidirectional bezel, with 0–60 scale; sapphire crystal; screw-down crown, helium valve; water-resistant to 30 atm
Band: stainless steel, folding clasp, with safety lock, with extension link
Remarks: self-luminous tritium gas tubes on hour markers as well as on the hour and minute hands
Price: $1,120
Variations: various colors and straps

Evo 1908 Automatic

Reference number: 161.575.44
Movement: automatic, Davosa Caliber DAV3020 (base Sellita SW260); ø 25.6 mm, height 5.6 mm; 31 jewels; 28,800 vph; 41-hour power reserve
Functions: hours, minutes, subsidiary seconds; date
Case: stainless steel, ø 42 mm, height 12 mm; sapphire crystal; transparent case back; water-resistant to 5 atm
Band: leather, pin buckle
Price: $995
Variations: various colors

Ternos Professional Nebulous

Reference number: 161.535.50
Movement: automatic, Davosa Caliber DAV3021 (base Sellita SW200-1); ø 25.6 mm, height 4.6 mm; 26 jewels; 28,800 vph; 41-hour power reserve
Functions: hours, minutes, sweep seconds; date
Case: stainless steel, ø 42 mm, height 12.8 mm; unidirectional bezel with ceramic insert and 0–60 scale; sapphire crystal; screw-down crown; water-resistant to 30 atm
Band: stainless steel, folding clasp, with fine adjustment
Remarks: transparent dial
Price: $1,195

Argonautic 43 Automatic

Reference number: 161.528.70
Movement: automatic, Davosa Caliber DAV3021 (base Sellita SW200-1); ø 25.6 mm, height 4.6 mm; 26 jewels; 28,800 vph; 41-hour power reserve
Functions: hours, minutes, sweep seconds; date
Case: stainless steel, ø 43 mm, height 13.5 mm; unidirectional bezel with ceramic insert, with 0–60 scale; sapphire crystal; screw-down crown, helium valve; water-resistant to 30 atm
Band: stainless steel, folding clasp, with safety lock, with extension link
Price: $1,080
Variations: various colors and straps

DE BETHUNE

De Bethune is named after an eighteenth-century French navy captain from an esteemed aristocratic family, the Chevalier De Béthune. He conducted extensive research in watch and clockmaking, and his name is associated with a particularly ingenious escapement mechanism. Similarly, Denis Flageollet has attained years of expertise in the research, design, and implementation of prestigious timepieces. In 2002, he and David Zanetta, a well-known consultant for numerous high-end watch brands, founded their own company in what was once the village pub, transforming it into a remarkable factory.

Equipped with cutting-edge CNC machinery and supported by a talented team of watchmakers and research and development specialists, De Bethune rapidly developed prototypes and produced small series of movements with remarkable efficiency. The *manufacture* even crafted its own cases, dials, and hands. In 2021, in a bid to fuel growth, they partnered with the Watchbox trading platform, which is now a majority owner.

De Bethune watches are aesthetically striking, characterized by simple color schemes, mirror-polished titanium, and subtle microlight engraving. Flageollet explains the distinctive "delta" shape on many dials: "The triangle is crucial for securing the gearwheel pivots, so why not transform them into a natural ogival arch?" This modern visual is beautifully contrasted with classic elements that soften the brand's sharpness, exemplified in the innovative two-sided watch, the Kind of Two, released in early 2021.

Engineering excellence is another hallmark of De Bethune. The company has developed a manually wound caliber with a power reserve of up to eight days, a self-regulating double barrel, and a balance wheel crafted from titanium and platinum to achieve an optimal inertia-to-mass ratio. Additionally, it features a patented balance spring with a De Bethune end curve and a triple "parachute" shock-absorbing system. Furthermore, De Bethune is known for producing one of the lightest and fastest silicon/titanium tourbillons available. Recently, the brand has begun to explore the use of warmer colors both on the dial and in the materials chosen. The effect is to enhance the timepieces' trademark cool, technical looks.

DE BETHUNE SA
Chemin des Grangettes 19
CH-1454 L'Auberson
Switzerland

TEL.:
+41 22 310 22 71

E-MAIL:
geneva@debethune.com

WEBSITE:
www.debethune.ch

FOUNDED:
2002

NUMBER OF EMPLOYEES:
40

ANNUAL PRODUCTION:
200

DISTRIBUTION:
For all inquiries from the U.S., please contact the company directly.

DB25XS Starry Varius
Reference number: DB25VxsTiV2
Movement: hand-wound, De Bethune Caliber DB2005; ø 30 mm; 27 jewels; 28,800 vph; twin barrels; titanium balance wheel with white-gold inserts, silicon escape wheel, optimized for temperature fluctuations and air penetration; De Bethune hairspring with flat terminal curve; triple "parachute" shock absorption; 144-hour power reserve
Functions: hours, minutes
Case: rose gold, ø 40.6 mm, height 8.8 mm; sapphire crystal; transparent case back; water-resistant to 3 atm
Band: reptile skin, pin buckle
Remarks: burgundy-colored titanium dial with gold stars and milky way pattern; polished rose-gold hands
Price: $85,000
Variations: titanium case ($80,000)

DB25 Perpetual Sky
Reference number: DB25SQPV2
Movement: hand-wound, De Bethune Caliber DB2005V3; ø 30 mm; 27 jewels; 28,800 vph; self-regulating twin spring barrel, titanium balance wheel with white-gold inserts, balance spring with De Bethune flat terminal, silicon escape wheel, optimized for temperature fluctuations and air penetration; finely finished parts; 120-hour power reserve
Functions: hours, minutes; perpetual calendar with date, month, weekday, spherical moon phase; leap year
Case: polished titanium, ø 40 mm, height 11.3 mm; sapphire crystal; transparent case back; water-resistant to 3 atm
Band: reptile skin (extra-supple), pin buckle
Remarks: blued titanium dial with gold stars and Milky Way
Price: $145,000; limited to 20 pieces

DB28XS Yellow Tones
Reference number: DB28XSY
Movement: hand-wound, De Bethune Caliber DB2115V14; ø 30 mm; height 5.19 mm; 36 jewels; 28,800 vph; twin barrels; titanium balance wheel with white-gold inserts, silicon escape wheel, optimized for temperature fluctuations and air penetration; De Bethune hairspring with flat terminal curve; triple "parachute" shock absorption; 144-hour power reserve
Functions: hours, minutes; power reserve indicator on case back
Case: yellow titanium, ø 38.7 mm, height 8 mm; sapphire crystal; transparent screw-mounted case back; water-resistant to 3 atm
Band: reptile skin (extra-supple), pin buckle
Remarks: yellow-gold hands
Price: $115,000

DETROIT WATCH COMPANY

Patrick Ayoub and Amy Ayoub launched Detroit Watch Company in 2013 with the first and only mechanical timepieces designed and assembled in Detroit, Michigan. Patrick, a car designer, and Amy, an interior designer, share a passion for original design and timepieces and have worked hard to develop their brand, which draws inspiration from, and celebrates, the city of "Détroit."

Detroit means a lot of things to different people. Because the history of the people and places have shaped the city, Detroit's stories are also part of the Detroit Watch Company's collective story. The 1701, for instance, commemorates Antoine de la Mothe Cadillac, Knight of St. Louis, who, with his company of colonists, arrived at Détroit on July 24, 1701. On that day, under the patronage of Louis XIV and protected by the flag of France, the city, then called Fort Pontchartrain, was founded. These watches, while modern and chic, do recall the fairly clear-cut lines of an old church clock (*horloge*).

People phoning Detroit will understand why the company came out with a watch named 313. It's the area code of the city that brought not only cars, but also Motown (*motor + town*) music to the world. Needless to say, the dial looks like an old-fashioned phone dial. And where did Detroit's cars ride and race informally? On Woodward Avenue, the first mile of concrete highway in the USA, where carriages once rolled. It's the name for a collection of sporty chronographs. Finally, the city supplied the war effort against the Axis with many vital vehicles, including the B-24 Liberator bomber. No wonder the brand's line of watches includes an aviator collection.

The Detroit Watch Company timepieces are classically designed and hand-assembled in-house and may be purchased directly through the Detroit Watch Company website. The company also offers a wide range of straps and has a transparent and affordable servicing program.

DETROIT WATCH COMPANY, LLC
P.O. Box 1328
Birmingham, MI 48012
USA

TEL:
248-321-5601

E-MAIL:
dwc@detroitwatchco.com

WEBSITE:
www.detroitwatchco.com

FOUNDED:
2013

NUMBER OF EMPLOYEES:
2

ANNUAL PRODUCTION:
400 watches

DISTRIBUTION:
direct sales only

MOST IMPORTANT COLLECTIONS/PRICE RANGE:
M1 Woodward classic, 1701 Pontchartrain GMT, 1701 Louis XIV; / $1,100 to $2,950

1701 Pontchartrain GMT – Great Lakes Edition

Reference number: DWC-1701GMTGLE-S1
Movement: automatic, ETA Caliber 2893-2, ø 26.6 mm, height 4.1 mm; 21 jewels; 28,800 vph; 42-hour power reserve
Functions: hours, minutes, subsidiary seconds; 2nd time zone, date
Case: stainless steel, ø 43 mm, height 13 mm; sapphire crystal, unidirectional bezel, screw-down crown; helium valve; water resistant to 30 atm
Band: calfskin, buckle
Price: $1,750; limited to 150 numbered pieces
Variations: with blue or black dial and bezel

1701 Pontchartrain GMT Dual Timezone

Reference number: DWC-A-PW
Movement: automatic, ETA Caliber 2893-2, ø 26.6 mm, height 4.1 mm; 21 jewels; 28,800 vph; 42-hour power reserve
Functions: hours, minutes, sweep seconds; 2nd time zone (24-hour scale); date with quick corrector
Case: stainless steel, ø 42 mm, height 11.5 mm; sapphire crystal; transparent case back, screw-down crown; water-resistant to 5 atm
Band: calf leather, folding clasp
Price: $1,695
Variations: with white dial; with full case back ($1,595)

1701 Pontchartrain Power Reserve

Reference number: DWC-1701-PW
Movement: automatic, Sellita SW279-1; ø 25.6 mm, height 5.6 mm, 26 jewels; 28,800 vph; decorated movement with blued screws, perlage, côtes de Genève; 38-hour power reserve
Functions: hours, minutes, subsidiary seconds; power reserve indicator; date with quick corrector
Case: stainless steel, ø 42 mm, height 9.7; mm; sapphire crystal, transparent case back, screw-down crown; water-resistant to 5 atm
Band: calf leather, buckle
Price: $1,550

M1 1805 Edition

Reference number: DWC M1W-EXH
Movement: automatic, Sellita caliber SW 510b; ø 30 mm, height 7.9 mm; 25 jewels; 28,800 vph; custom M1 rotor; 62-hour power reserve
Functions: hours, minutes, subsidiary seconds; chronograph with tachymeter scale
Case: stainless steel, 42 mm height 14.4 mm; screw-down crown, transparent case back, sapphire crystal; water-resistant to 5 atm
Band: calfskin; folding clasp
Price: $2,375
Variations: comes with stainless-steel bracelet; second iteration with hand-wound Sellita caliber

M1 Woodward Chronograph Graphite

Movement: automatic, Valjoux ETA 7750 caliber; ø 30 mm, height 7.9 mm; 25 jewels; 28,800 vph; custom M1 rotor; 48-hour power reserve
Functions: hours, minutes, subsidiary seconds; chronograph with tachymeter scale; day and date
Case: stainless steel, ø 42 mm, height 14.5 mm; sapphire crystal; transparent case back, screw-down crown; water-resistant to 5 atm
Band: calf leather, folding clasp
Price: $2,475
Variations: various straps

Aviator Power Reserve

Reference number: DWC-A-PW
Movement: automatic (or manual wound), Sellita SW279-1; ø 25.6, height 5.6 mm, 26 jewels (manual wound: height 4.35 mm, 24 jewels); 28,800 vph; decorated movement with blued screws, perlage, côtes de Genève; 38-hour power reserve
Functions: hours, minutes, subsidiary seconds; power reserve indicator; date with quick corrector
Case: stainless steel, ø 42 mm, height 9.7 mm; sapphire crystal, transparent case back, screw-in crown; water-resistant to 5 atm
Band: calf leather, pin buckle
Price: $1,550
Variations: graphite dial, green dial

Pontchartrain Watch Co. 1st Edition

Movement: automatic, Caliber ETA 2892-A2, ø 25.6 mm, height 3.6 mm; 21 jewels; 28,800 vph; decorated movement with blued screws, perlage, côtes de Genève; 42-hour power reserve
Functions: hours, minutes, sweep seconds
Case: stainless steel, ø 42 mm, height 9.7 mm; sapphire crystal, transparent case back, screw-down crown; water-resistant to 5 atm
Band: calf leather, buckle
Price: $1,495
Variations: with stainless steel bracelet and folding clasp; black dial

1701 Louis XIV

Reference number: DWC-1701-XIV
Movement: automatic, Sellita caliber SW280-1; ø 25.6 mm, height 5.4 mm; 26 jewels; 28,800 vph; finely finished movement with perlage and côtes de Genève; blued screws; DWC custom rotor; 38-hour power reserve
Functions: hours, minutes, subsidiary seconds; moon phase; date
Case: stainless steel, ø 39 mm, height 11 mm; transparent case back; screw-down crown; water-resistant to 5 atm
Band: calfskin, pin buckle
Price: $1,550
Variations: with hand-wound caliber

1701 Moonphase Chronograph

Reference number: PCT-Moon-Chrono
Movement: automatic, ETA Caliber 7751; ø 30 mm, height 7.9 mm; 25 jewels; 28,800 vph; 48-hour power reserve
Functions: hours, minutes, subsidiary seconds; chronograph; date, day, month; moon phase
Case: stainless steel, ø 42 mm, height 14.5 mm, sapphire crystal with anti-reflective coating, screw-down transparent case back with engraving; water resistant to 5 atm
Band: calfskin, pin buckle
Price: $2,950

DOXA

Watch aficionados who have visited the world-famous museum in Le Locle will know that the little castle in which it is housed once belonged to Georges Ducommun, the founder of Doxa. The *manufacture* was launched as a backyard operation in 1889 and originally produced pocket watches. Quality products and good salesmanship quickly put Doxa on the map, but the company's real game changer came in 1967 with the uncompromising SUB 300, a heavy, bold diver's watch. It featured a unidirectional bezel with the official U.S. dive table engraved on it. The bright orange dial might seem quite ostentatious, but, in fact, it offers the best legibility under water. It also marked the beginning of a trend for colorful dials.

The popularity of Doxa watches was boosted early on by the commercialization of diving in the 1970s. Thriller writer Clive Cussler, chairman and founder of the National Underwater and Marine Agency (NUMA), even chose a Doxa as gear for his action hero Dirk Pitt.

The enduring vintage trend has shaped the recent development of the brand. Focus is on fewer lines with greater variations, with almost every model coming in different colors besides the striking orange: brilliant white, dreamy turquoise, bright yellow, and more.

Doxa has maintained its diving profile and, mostly, the cushion case and avoided too many fancy complications. The watches are usually three-handers with a date. The SUB 200 C-Graph is an automatic chronograph, however, which comes in various colors and a "beads of rice" rubber strap. The SUB 300 Professional is another genuine diver's that also comes in various colors. The SUB 300 Carbon Aqua Lung US Divers is, as the name says, made of a modern material. It's a revived and improved watch created in a collaboration with Aqua Lung, the company that essentially launched scuba diving with the creation of a demand regulator in 1943. In 2023, it received a companion, the β (beta) Sharkhunter, a dark ceramic, elegant, diver's watch conceived for a night out or a day under water. The carbon case is light and robust and a good background for the no-decompression dive table—devised originally by the U.S. Navy—made up of an orange depth scale on the outer bezel and an inner scale for the dive timing.

MONTRES DOXA SA
Rue de Zurich 23A
P.O. Box 6031
2500 Bienne 6,
Switzerland

TEL.:
+41-32-344-42-72

E-MAIL:
contact@doxawatches.com

WEBSITE:
doxawatches.com

FOUNDED:
1889

NUMBER OF EMPLOYEES:
40

DISTRIBUTION:
DOXA USA
520-369-2872
usa@doxawatches.com

MOST IMPORTANT COLLECTION/PRICE RANGE:
DOXA SUB dive watch collection / $950 to $4,900

SUB 300 Professional

Reference number: 821.10.351.10
Movement: automatic, Sellita Caliber SW200-1; ø 25.6 mm, height 4.6 mm; 25 jewels; 28,800 vph; 38-hour power reserve; COSC-certified chronometer
Functions: hours, minutes, sweep seconds; date
Case: stainless steel, ø 42.4 mm, height 13.4 mm; unidirectional bezel, with 0-60 scale and decompression times; sapphire crystal; screw-down crown; water-resistant to 30 atm
Band: stainless steel, folding clasp, with extension link
Price: $2,890
Variations: with FKM-rubber strap ($2,800); various dial colors

SUB 250T Caribbean

Reference number: 855.10.201.32
Movement: automatic, Sellita Caliber SW330-1; ø 25.6 mm, height 4.1 mm; 25 jewels; 28,800 vph; 50-hour power reserve
Functions: hours, minutes, sweep seconds; additional 24-hour display (second time zone); date
Case: stainless steel, ø 40 mm, height 10.85 mm; unidirectional bezel, with 0-60 scale and decompression times; sapphire crystal; screw-down crown; water-resistant to 25 atm
Band: stainless steel, folding clasp, with extension link
Price: $2,790
Variations: with FKM-rubber strap ($2,790)

SUB 750T Searambler

Reference number: 825.10.021.10
Movement: automatic, Sellita Caliber SW300-1; ø 25.6 mm, height 3.6 mm; 25 jewels; 28,800 vph; 56-hour power reserve
Functions: hours, minutes, sweep seconds; date
Case: stainless steel, ø 45 mm, height 11.95 mm; unidirectional bezel, with 0-60 scale and decompression times; sapphire crystal; screw-down crown; water-resistant to 75 atm
Band: stainless steel, folding clasp, with extension link
Price: $2,790
Variations: with FKM-rubber strap ($2,790); various dial colors

EBERHARD & CO.

Chronographs weren't always the main focus of the Eberhard & Co. brand. In 1887, Georges-Emile Eberhard rented a workshop in La Chaux-de-Fonds to produce a small series of pocket watches, but it was the unstoppable advancement of the automotive industry that gave the young company its inevitable direction. By the 1920s, Eberhard was producing timekeepers for the first auto races. In Italy, Eberhard & Co. functioned well into the 1930s as the official timekeeper for all important events relating to motor sports. And the Italian air force later commissioned some split-second chronographs from the company, one of which went for 56,000 euros at auction.

Eberhard & Co. is still doing well, thanks to the late Massimo Monti. In the 1990s, he associated the brand with legendary racer Tazio Nuvolari. The company dedicated a chronograph collection to Nuvolari and sponsored the annual Gran Premio Nuvolari vintage car rally in his hometown of Mantua.

With the launch of its four-counter chronograph, this most Italian of Swiss watchmakers underscored its expertise and ambitions where short time/sports time measurement is concerned. Indeed, Eberhard & Co.'s Chrono 4 chronograph, featuring four little counters all in a row, has brought new life to the chronograph in general. CEO Mario Peserico has continued to develop it, putting out versions with new colors and slightly altered looks.

In 2024, Eberhard & Co. presented two chronographs from the 1887 collection, equipped with exclusive calibers from the specialty workshop AMT. And in 2025, the brand presented the Contodat collection at Watches and Wonders in Geneva, a timepiece inspired by a mechanical watch from the 1970s.

Worth noting, too: Eberhard & Co. is also known for its active presence at prestigious events in various fields, including sailing, historic car racing, photography, and art.

EBERHARD & CO.
73, Ave. Léopold-Robert
CH-2300 La Chaux-de-Fonds
Switzerland

TEL.:
+41 32 342 51 41

E-MAIL:
info@eberhard-co-watches.ch

WEBSITE:
www.eberhard-co-watches.ch

FOUNDED:
1887

DISTRIBUTION:
Contact main office for information
Astor Time Ltd
Riva Paradiso, 12
CH-6900 Lugano
+41 91 993 26 01

MOST IMPORTANT COLLECTIONS:
Chrono 4, 8 Jours, Tazio Nuvolari, Extra-fort, Gilda, Scafograf, Scientigraf

Contodat Chronographe
Reference number: 31156.01
Movement: automatic, Sellita Caliber SW510 BH; ø 30 mm, height 7.9 mm; 25 jewels; 28,800 vph; 48-hour power reserve
Functions: hours, minutes, small seconds; chronograph; date
Case: stainless steel, ø 39 mm, height 13.9 mm; sapphire crystal; screw-down crown; water-resistant to 10 atm
Band: stainless steel, folding clasp
Price: $5,500

Contodat Automatic
Reference number: 41156.02
Movement: automatic, Sellita Caliber SW290-1; ø 25.6 mm, height 4.6 mm; 26 jewels; 28,800 vph; 38-hour power reserve
Functions: hours, minutes, small seconds; date
Case: stainless steel, ø 39 mm, height 11.3 mm; sapphire crystal; screw-down crown; water-resistant to 10 atm
Band: stainless steel, folding clasp
Price: $4,000

Chronographe 1887 Édition Limitée
Reference number: 31081.01 CP
Movement: hand-wound, Eberhard Caliber EB 280 (Sellita AMT 5100 base); ø 30 mm, height 7 mm; 23 jewels; 28,800 vph; column-wheel control of chronograph functions; 58-hour power reserve
Functions: hours, minutes, small seconds; flyback chronograph
Case: stainless steel, ø 41.5 mm, height 13.9 mm; sapphire crystal; transparent case back; water-resistant to 5 atm
Band: reptile skin, pin buckle
Remarks: limited to 250 pieces
Price: $9,750

Chronographe 1887 Automatique

Reference number: 31082.03 CP
Movement: automatic, Eberhard Caliber EB 380 (Sellita AMT 5100 base); ø 30 mm, height 7.9 mm; 23 jewels; 28,800 vph; column-wheel control of chronograph functions; 55-hour power reserve
Functions: hours, minutes, small seconds; flyback chronograph
Case: stainless steel, ø 41.5 mm, height 14.4 mm; sapphire crystal; transparent case back; water-resistant to 5 atm
Band: reptile skin, pin buckle
Price: $8,230
Variations: with white dial

8 Jours Grande Taille

Reference number: 21027.7 CP
Movement: hand-wound, Eberhard caliber EB 896 (Peseux 7001 base) ø 23.3 mm, height 2.5 mm; 17 jewels; 28,800 vph; with special Eberhard 8-day power reserve module
Functions: hours, minutes, small seconds; power reserve indicator
Case: stainless steel, ø 41 mm, height 10.85 mm; sapphire crystal; screw-down crown; window on caseback with view of skeleton bridge over the main barrel; water-resistant to 3 atm
Band: reptile skin, pin buckle
Price: $6,080

Scientigraf

Reference number: 41043.02 CAPS
Movement: automatic, Sellita Caliber SW300-1; ø 25.6 mm, height 3.6 mm; 25 jewels; 28,800 vph; 42-hour power reserve
Functions: hours, minutes, sweep seconds
Case: stainless steel, ø 41 mm, height 11.2 mm; sapphire crystal; screw-down crown; water-resistant to 10 atm
Band: stainless steel, folding clasp
Remarks: soft-iron inner cage as magnetic shield
Price: $4,040

Extra-fort Roue à Colonnes Retour En Vol

Reference number: 31957.02 CP
Movement: automatic, Sellita AMT 5100; ø 30 mm, height 7.9 mm; 23 jewels; 28,800 vph; column-wheel control of chronograph functions; 50-hour power reserve
Functions: hours, minutes, small seconds; flyback chronograph; date
Case: stainless steel, ø 41 mm, height 14.2 mm; sapphire crystal; transparent case back; screw-down crown; water-resistant to 5 atm
Band: reptile skin, pin buckle
Price: $6,400

Chrono 4 "21-42"

Reference number: 31073.05/CN CU
Movement: automatic, Eberhard Caliber EB 251-12 1/2 (ETA 2894-2 base); ø 33 mm, height 7.5 mm; 53 jewels; 28,800 vph; 4 counters in a line; 42-hour power reserve
Functions: hours, minutes, small seconds; additional 24-hour display; chronograph; date
Case: stainless steel, ø 42 mm, height 13.3 mm; ceramic bezel; sapphire crystal; screw-down crown; water-resistant to 5 atm
Band: rubber, pin buckle
Remarks: the collection's name "21-42" stands for the launch year 2021 of the anniversary edition (20 years of Chrono 4) and the 42-mm case
Price: $7,930

Scafograf 300 MCMLIX

Reference number: 41034.10/VS CA2C
Movement: automatic, Sellita Caliber SW200-1; ø 25.6 mm, height 4.6 mm; 26 jewels; 28,800 vph; 38-hour power reserve
Functions: hours, minutes, sweep seconds; date
Case: stainless steel, ø 43 mm, height 12.6 mm; unidirectional bezel with ceramic insert and 0-60 scale; sapphire crystal; screw-down crown; helium valve; water-resistant to 30 atm
Band: stainless steel, folding clasp
Remarks: the diving watch model refers to a template/design from the year 1959
Price: $4,900

EDOUARD KOEHN

Long before Germany became a federal republic, it consisted of a large collection of states—both small and large—ruled by a mix of nobles and high clergymen. One particularly wealthy state was the Grand Duchy of Saxe-Weimar-Eisenach, located in what is today the German state of Thuringia. As with all royal courts, it granted warrants to suppliers of exceptional goods and services. Among these recipients was the clockmaker Karl Köhn.

In 1859, his son Edouard Koehn—who later Gallicized his name—set off to Geneva to study watchmaking at the leading school of the time. By 1861, he had joined Patek Philippe and soon began promoting the brand as far away as the United States, eventually becoming a partner in the firm.

Koehn was both an outstanding salesman and a fine watchmaker, notably skilled in crafting ultra-thin pocket watches. He even patented an improvement on a Breguet retrograde mechanism. In 1891, he acquired the company of the Swedish watchmaker Henri-Robert Ekegren and began producing highly complicated pocket watches under his own name.

After lying dormant since the 1930s, the company was revived in 2018 and, in 2020, launched the Tempus collection—a modern line that pays tribute to the brand's rich heritage without compromising on contemporary technology. The sporty tricompax chronograph, featuring a brushed ceramic bezel, is also available in a skeletonized version with an elegant clous-de-Paris dial. The Tempus II is a bicompax chronograph operated by a single pusher, while the Tempus III, crafted from lightweight titanium, measures 41 millimeters in diameter.

The World Heritage collection features a central 24-hour, 24-city display surrounded by a refined wave guilloché pattern. Travelers will appreciate the inclusion of an alarm function, an invaluable companion for power naps on the move. The Legacy Rattrapante, a split-seconds chronograph, reproduces an original Koehn pocket watch within a comfortably proportioned 40-millimeter case. In 2025, the Legacy line was expanded to include a moon phase model, also inspired by a vintage Koehn pocket watch.

EDOUARD KOEHN
Edouard Koehn Master Watchmaker Sàrl
Rue des 22-Cantons 36
2300 La Chaux-de-Fonds
Switzerland

TEL.:
+41 (0)79-137-60-29

WEBSITE:
www.edouardkoehn.com

FOUNDED:
2018

US DISTRIBUTION:
Totally Worth It Inc.
76 Division Ave
Summit, NJ 07901
+1 724-263-2286
info@totallyworthit.com

ANNUAL PRODUCTION:
approx. 300 pieces

MOST IMPORTANT COLLECTIONS/PRICE RANGE:
World Heritage ($9,950), Tempus I ($7,950), Tempus II ($9,950), Tempus III ($8,950), Legacy Rattrapante ($16,800), Legacy Moonphase ($19,900)

Legacy Moonphase

Reference number: EK-CHR12SS-SN-ASBEI
Movement: automatic, Caliber EK-CHR MVT04 (modified Concepto base); ø 30.4 mm, height 8.4 mm, 25 jewels; 28,800 vph; 60-hour power reserve
Functions: hours, minutes, subsidiary seconds; date; moon phase; chronograph
Case: stainless steel, ø 40 mm, height 14.1 mm; ceramic bezel; sapphire "glass box" crystal; transparent case back; water-resistant to 5 atm
Band: reptile skin, pin buckle
Remarks: skeleton dial
Price: $14,800; limited to 50 pieces
Variations: comes in blue; limited to 50 pieces

Legacy Rattrapante

Reference number: EK-CHR11SS-SL-WEEL-ASBK
Movement: automatic, Caliber EK-MVT-CHR03 (modified Concepto base); ø 30.4 mm, height 8.4 mm; 31 jewels; 28,800 vph; oscillating mass with côtes de Genève; 48-hour power reserve
Functions: hours, minutes, subsidiary seconds; split-seconds chronograph with 60-minute totalizer at 12 o'clock
Case: stainless steel, ø 40 mm, height 13.1 mm (without sapphire crystal); sapphire; transparent case back; water-resistant to 5 atm
Remarks: grand-feu enamel dial
Band: reptile skin, folding clasp
Price: $19,900; limited to 50 pieces
Variations: in rose-gold case (price on request); limited to 25 pieces

World Heritage II Ice Blue

Reference number: EK-WTA05IBASBK
Movement: automatic, Caliber EK-MVT-WTA01 (modified Concepto base); ø 30.4 mm, height 7.6 mm; 31 jewels; 28,800 vph; double barrel for time and alarm mechanism; 48-hour power reserve
Functions: hours, minutes, sweep seconds, 24-hour display (world time, with 24 reference cities); day/night indicator; alarm (around 12 seconds)
Case: titanium, ø 42 mm, height 14.5 mm; sapphire; transparent case back; water-resistant to 5 atm
Remarks: wave-pattern guilloché on the dial
Band: reptile skin, folding clasp
Price: $10,950
Variations: comes with different color dials

ELKA WATCH

The old saying "Many are called, few are chosen" could be the motto for any start-up watch brand facing off high start-up costs, stiff competition, and a fickle market. It is not enough to look for a niche to fill—you need to get into the fray with confidence and long-term planning.

The story of Elka seems to reveal almost mystical forces at play. Founder Hakim El Kadiri was born in Casablanca, Morocco. His mother, a photographer, was Swiss, and his father, a forest and water engineer, was Moroccan. The family moved to Neuchâtel, a hub of Swiss watchmaking, where young Hakim studied precision engineering and ultimately went to work for a big watch brand as a designer. But he dreamt of developing his own brand: "I wanted above all to have a story, truth and credibility," he says. "I was particularly inspired by the products and aesthetics of the 60s." He had the technical knowledge to ensure quality, and he had name: Elka, an old defunct brand and, curiously, a portmanteau nickname from his youth that derived from his surname, El Kadiri.

The original Elka had existed in the early 70s and was founded by a Dutchman named Eduard Louis Kiek. It had worked closely with other big names in the business, including Ulysse Nardin, Heuer, Rolex, and Minerva. The Fates, he felt, were favorable, and in 2022, El Kadiri launched "his" Elka. To celebrate the Dutch connection, Elka partnered in 2025 with Ace Jewelers in Amsterdam for a watch that celebrates the great—and alas inimical—cultures of the Middle East.

Currently, there are three main collections plus some special editions, all run on "you-can't-go-wrong" La Joux-Perret calibers. The X series is inspired from an airplane gauge (and a Heuer dial). The D series is a minimalistic dress watch with sun-brushed dial and slim hands and markers. The Arinis model, named for a prehistoric village that once stood on the banks of Lake Neuchâtel, is a solid diver's watch. As a "local hero," it is tested in the neighboring lake. 2025 also saw the launch of a 36-millimeter case that reinforces El Kadiri's devotion to the 1960s.

ELKA WATCH CO. SARL
Rue du Musée 4,
CH-2000 Neuchâtel
Switzerland

TEL.:
+41-79-500-9113

E-MAIL:
info@elkawatch.com

WEBSITE:
www.elkawatch.com

FOUNDED:
2022

NUMBER OF EMPLOYEES:
1

ANNUAL PRODUCTION:
230 watches

DISTRIBUTION:
direct sales only, with retailers in Switzerland, Austria, Netherland, Germany, UK, Canada, France , USA

MOST IMPORTANT COLLECTIONS/PRICE RANGE:
X, S, D series, Arinis, special editions / $1,760-$2,300

Elka x Ace Jewelers
Reference number: MN04
Movement: automatic, La Joux-Perret G101; ø 26.6 mm, height 4.45 mm; 24 jewels; 28,800 vph; 68-hour power reserve
Functions: hours, minutes, sweep seconds
Case: stainless steel, ø 36 mm, height 10.05 mm; "chevé" sapphire crystal; water-resistant to 20 atm
Band: rubber (FKM), pin buckle
Remarks: a celebration of the 50th anniversary of Ace Jewelers in Amsterdam
Price: $2,100; limited to 50 pieces
Variations: as MN03, green dial with Eastern Arabic numerals ($2,100; limited to 50 pieces)

Arinis
Reference number: AF03w-1002
Movement: automatic, La Joux-Perret G100; ø 25.60 mm, height 4.45 mm; 24 jewels; 28,800 vph; 68-hour power reserve
Functions: hours, minutes, sweep seconds; date or not
Case: stainless steel, ø 41 mm, height 11.85 mm; unidirectional rotating bezel with ceramic insert with SuperLumiNova; "chevé" sapphire crystal; stamped case back with 3 fishes resembling ancient artifacts; water-resistant to 20 atm
Band: stainless-steel rice-grain, folding clasp
Remarks: Arinis is the prehistoric name of St. Blaise, the stamped case back with 3 fishes resembling ancient artefacts
Price: $2,215
Variations: blue or black dials colors; with leather strap ($2,175)

NS Series
Reference number: S01-0811
Movement: automatic, La Joux-Perret G101; ø 25.60 mm, height 4.45 mm; 25 jewels; 28,800 vph; with côtes de Genève; grey NAC coating on bridges; the rhodium-plated gold oscillator; COSC-certified; 68-hour power reserve
Functions: hours, minutes, sweep seconds
Case: stainless steel, ø 36 mm, height 10.5 mm; "chevé" sapphire crystal; water-resistant to 5 atm
Band: NATO Nylon strap, pin buckle
Remarks: inspired by 1930s field watches
Price: $1,990

FAVRE LEUBA

Favre Leuba was founded in 1737 in Le Locle, Switzerland, making it the second oldest continuously existing Swiss watch brand. Through the centuries, the name became associated with technical ingenuity and a very practical approach to watchmaking, with luxury timepieces that were also tool-watches. In the 1960s, for example, Favre Leuba created genuine professional instruments: the Bivouac, the first mechanical wristwatch with an aneroid barometer capable of displaying altitude and air pressure; and the Bathy, the first mechanical wristwatch able to indicate the depth of a dive. These were not concept pieces: they were actually used in expeditions—on high-altitude climbs, polar crossings, and deep-water dives—and they defined the brand as a companion to human ambition and to the limits of what people could physically reach.

Favre Leuba remained in family hands until the late 1980s, after which it was handed around to various investors who had no clear idea what to do with such a venerable brand. After all, in the 1960s, it had been one of Switzerland's leaders, even collaborating with Patek Philippe.

It finally found a home with Silver City Brands, which engineered a relaunch in 2024. The comeback is not nostalgic. Focus is on the clear and functional design codes of the 1960s, the recognizable geometry and the bold cases, and on rebuilding them with modern Swiss engineering. The company taps into excellent technical material, collaborating with companies like Chronode or La Joux-Perret for its calibers. Today's flagship collections—the Deep Raider revival, the Chief chronograph, and the Sea Sky revival—are not replicas but contemporary watches that carry the pioneering idea into a new cycle. The brand is headquartered in Grenchen and led by Patrik Hoffmann as CEO. It continues to build robust mechanical watches, reliable companions for the real world, drawing on nearly three centuries of continuous watchmaking history.

FAVRE LEUBA
SilverCity Brands AG
CH-2540 Grenchen
Switzerland

TEL.:
+41 32 652 1925

E-MAIL:
info@favreleuba.com

WEBSITE:
www.favreleuba.com

FOUNDED:
1737; relaunched 2024

DISTRIBUTION:
Exquisite Timepieces
4380 Gulfshore Blvd, N. Suite 800
Naples, FL 34103
239-227-2932
team@exquisitetimepieces.com

MOST IMPORTANT COLLECTIONS/PRICE RANGE
Sea Sky Revival, Chief, Deep Raider / $1,800-$6,000

Deep Raider Revival
Reference number: 00.20307.100.06.200
Movement: automatic, Favre Leuba caliber FLD01 (on MLJP G100 base); ø 26 mm, height 4.45 mm; 24 jewels; 28,800 vph; 68-hour power reserve
Functions: hours, minutes, sweep seconds; date
Case: stainless steel; ø 39 mm, height 12.75 mm; unidirectional bezel with luminous marker, 60-minute scale; sapphire crystal; water-resistant to 30 atm
Band: stainless steel, double folding clasp
Price: $2,900

Chief Chronograph
Reference number: 00.20101.113.04.200
Movement: automatic, Favre Leuba caliber FLC02 (on MLJP L100 base); ø 30.4 mm, height 7.9 mm; 26 jewels; 28,800 vph; column-wheel control; 60-hour power reserve
Functions: hours, minutes, subsidiary seconds; chronograph
Case: stainless steel; ø 41 mm, height 14 mm; sapphire crystal; transparent caseback; water-resistant to 10 atm
Band: stainless steel, double folding clasp
Price: $5,800
Variations: various straps and dials

Sea Sky Revival
Reference number: 00.20212.112.01.101
Movement: automatic, Favre Leuba caliber FLC01 (on MLJP base caliber L100); ø 30.4 mm, height 7.9 mm; 26 jewels; 28,800 vph; column-wheel control; 60-hour power reserve
Functions: hours, minutes, subsidiary seconds; chronograph
Case: stainless steel; ø 40 mm, height 15.23 mm; unidirectional bezel with 0-60 scale and ceramic insert; sapphire crystal; transparent caseback; water-resistant to 10 atm
Band: leather, pin buckle
Price: $4,950

FERDINAND BERTHOUD

The old saying "nomen est omen" could be the slogan for many brands in the watch industry, whose strategy and style is all in the name they choose. Karl-Friedrich Scheufele, himself vice president of a brand named after a Swiss watchmaker, Louis-Ulysse Chopard, stumbled upon another historical personality when he founded his factory in the Jura in 1996. Ferdinand Berthoud (1727-1807) was one of the most important watchmakers of his era, a contemporary of Abraham-Louis Breguet and Thomas Mudge, a master watchmaker at the French court and supplier to the Royal Navy. He was also the author of numerous books and writings on the theory of watchmaking. Finally, he was not French, but Swiss, born in Val-de-Travers near Fleurier.

Reviving that eighteenth-century DNA seemed worthwhile. In 2015, the first Berthoud watch of the modern era was presented in Paris, a chronometer, of course. The movement of the FB 1 was equipped with a constant force mechanism using a traditional chain and fusee. It also features an unusual power reserve display (53 hours) and a rather large tourbillon under a filigree one-armed cock.

The FB 1R model presented in 2016 had a special regulator dial with a discreet time display, and the FB 1L iteration that followed a little later shows the moon phase and moon age in an unconventional manner. In 2020, Ferdinand Berthoud launched a completely new collection with the FB 2RE, which is conspicuously inspired by Berthoud's marine chronometer No. 6 and has a sophisticated mechanism chain and fusee constant force escapement (*remontoir d'égalité*) and a jumping seconds.

The FB 3 chronometer was unveiled in 2022. Powered by a mechanical movement with a cylindrical balance-spring, it is the only timepiece of its kind to be awarded a COSC chronometer certificate. The elegance of its 42 mm case, inspired by nineteenth century pocket watches, reveals the movement and provides a stage for the regulating organ.

Only a few dozen of these exquisite timepieces are produced each year. They are all developed, manufactured, decorated, adjusted, and tested by hand in the workshops of Chronométrie Ferdinand Berthoud in Fleurier (Switzerland).

CHRONOMÉTRIE FERDINAND BERTHOUD SA
20, rue des Moulins
CH-2114 Fleurier
Switzerland

E-MAIL:
contact@ferdinandberthoud.ch

WEBSITE:
www.ferdinandberthoud.ch

FOUNDED:
2013

DISTRIBUTOR:
Cellini Jewelers
430 Park Avenue at 56th Street
New-York 10022
212-888-0505
www.cellinijewelers.com

COLLECTIONS / PRICE RANGE:
Exclusively built chronometers: $150,000 to $260,000

Chronomètre FB 3

Reference number: FB 3SPC.3
Movement: hand-wound, Ferdinand Berthoud caliber FB-SPC; ø 34 mm, height 6.84 mm; 47 jewels; 21,600 vph; balance wheel with variable inertia with 4 regulating and 8 weighted screws; mainplate and bridges in gilded nickel silver; 72-hour power reserve; COSC-certified chronometer
Functions: hours, minutes, subsidiary seconds; power reserve indicator
Case: platinum, ø 42.3 mm, height 9.43 mm; sapphire crystal; transparent case back; water-resistant to 3 atm
Band: reptile skin, pin buckle
Remarks: limited to 20 pieces
Price: on request

Chronomètre FB 3 (movement side)

Reference number: FB 3SPC.3
The FB 3 mechanical movement is based on a cylindrical balance spring, a rare horological specialty that was familiar to Ferdinand Berthoud. At 9 o'clock, the three key components of the escapement – balance wheel, anchor, and escape wheel – are clearly visible. The ample space dedicated to the regulating organ allows its workings to be observed at leisure—the cylindrical balance spring looks as if it is "breathing" during the entire three-day power reserve—not only from above but also from the side through a transparent case porthole in the case band.

Chronomètre FB RSM

Reference number: FB 2RSM.1
Movement: hand-wound, Ferdinand Berthoud caliber FB-T.FC.RSM; ø 37.3 mm, height 9.89 mm; 60 jewels; 21,600 vph; one-minute tourbillon; jumping seconds display ("seconde morte") with balance stop; fusée-and-chain constant force mechanism; 53-hour power reserve; COSC-certified chronometer
Functions: hours (disc display, off-center), minutes (off-center), sweep seconds (jumping); power reserve indicator (on the back)
Case: white gold, ø 44 mm, height 14.3 mm; sapphire crystal; transparent case back; crown with torque-limiting mechanism; water-resistant to 3 atm
Band: reptile skin, pin buckle
Price: on request

FORTIS

Fortis has been an independent, owner-managed, and fairly unconventional brand since 1912. From the outset, its mission was to build what are considered "tools for life," meaning robust timepieces that could withstand rugged treatment. The name Fortis derives from the Latin for "strong" and reflects a longstanding reputation for reliability and consistency, expressed through striking, sturdily engineered watches.

A major milestone in the company's history came in 1926, when Fortis, working with British watchmaker John Harwood, launched the world's first automatic wristwatch produced in series. This pioneering spirit continued through the 1990s, with an alarm watch built in the 1950s and collaborations with the space program in the USA. In 1987, the Flieger cemented Fortis's standing in the world of pilot's watches, and in 1994 the Official Cosmonauts Chronograph flew into orbit aboard the space station Mir.

The close collaboration with aeronautics and space specialist, including the European space program, has continued in the past years and has shaped a new generation of space-ready chronographs. These instruments, approved for use on Mir and later aboard the International Space Station, channel their technical rigor back into Fortis's pilot's watches, which have long served as benchmarks for modern cockpit timepieces. It is hardly surprising that many international squadrons choose Fortis on the wrist.

This commitment to performance has not diminished the brand's appetite for creativity. Alongside its high-performance, space-traveling instruments, Fortis regularly develops limited art and design editions in collaboration with contemporary artists. Recent years have seen a dynamic expansion of the collection: in 2023, the Novonaut, a modern reinterpretation of the legendary Cosmonauts watches, was launched and quickly became a bestseller. In 2024, the Vagabond Collection followed, inspired by the idea of feeling at home in a world in constant motion. In 2025, Fortis added another milestone with the new WERK 7, a manufacture caliber distinguished by sophisticated technology and finely tuned rate performance, further proof that the brand's concept of "robust luxury" is still guiding the company.

FORTIS WATCHES AG
John Harwood-Stasse 13
CH-2540 Grenchen
Switzerland

TEL:
+41 32 653 33 61

E-MAIL:
info@fortis-swiss.com

WEBSITE:
www.fortis-swiss.com

FOUNDED:
1912

EMPLOYEES:
20

ANNUAL PRODUCTION:
Around 2,500

DISTRIBUTION:
retail, webshop

MOST IMPORTANT COLLECTIONS
Flieger, Stratoliner, Novonaut

Stratoliner S-41 Gravity Black

Reference number: F2340018
Movement: automatic, Fortis caliber WERK 17 (based on MLJP); ø 30 mm, height 7.9 mm; 25 jewels; 28,800 vph; column-wheel control of the chronograph functions; 60-hour power reserve
Functions: hours, minutes, subsidiary seconds; chronograph; date and weekday
Case: recycled stainless steel with black DLC, ø 41 mm, height 14.5 mm; sapphire crystal; case back with sapphire display window; screw-down crown; water-resistant to 20 atm
Band: textile and rubber strap with pin buckle
Price: $5,670

Stratoliner S-41 Reentry Edition

Reference number: F2340019
Movement: automatic, Fortis caliber WERK 17 (based on MLJP); ø 30 mm, height 7.9 mm; 25 jewels; 28,800 vph; column-wheel control of the chronograph functions; 60-hour power reserve
Functions: hours, minutes, subsidiary seconds; chronograph; date and weekday
Case: recycled stainless steel, ø 41 mm, height 14.5 mm; sapphire crystal; transparent case back; screw-down crown; water-resistant to 20 atm
Band: recycled stainless-steel bracelet with folding clasp and fine adjustment
Remarks: hand-flamed titanium dial (unique piece)
Price: $5,450

Flieger F-41

Reference number: F4220030
Movement: automatic, Fortis caliber WERK 7 (based on MLJP); ø 25.6 mm, height 4.45 mm; 24 jewels; 28,800 vph; balance with variable inertia; 60-hour power reserve
Functions: hours, minutes, sweep seconds; date
Case: recycled stainless steel with black DLC, ø 41 mm, height 12.5 mm; bidirectional bezel with 0–12 scale; sapphire crystal; transparent case back; screw-down crown; water-resistant to 20 atm.
Band: textile and rubber strap with pin buckle
Price: $4,510

Novonaut N-42 Titanium Legacy

Reference number: F2040017
Movement: automatic, Fortis caliber WERK 17 (based on MLJP); ø 30 mm, height 7.9 mm; 25 jewels; 28,800 vph; column-wheel control of the chronograph functions; 60-hour power reserve
Functions: hours, minutes, subsidiary seconds; chronograph; date and weekday
Case: titanium, ø 42 mm, height 15 mm; bidirectional bezel with ceramic insert and 60-minute scale; sapphire crystal; screw-down crown; water-resistant to 20 atm
Band: titanium bracelet with folding clasp and fine adjustment.
Price: $5,230
Variations: with FKM rubber strap

Novonaut N-42 Legacy Edition

Reference number: F2040008
Movement: automatic, Fortis caliber WERK 17 (based on MLJP); ø 30 mm, height 7.9 mm; 25 jewels; 28,800 vph; column-wheel control of the chronograph functions; 60-hour power reserve
Functions: hours, minutes, subsidiary seconds; chronograph; date and weekday
Case: recycled stainless steel, ø 42 mm, height 15.5 mm; bidirectional bezel with ceramic insert and 0–60 scale; sapphire crystal; screw-down crown; water-resistant to 20 atm
Band: stainless-steel bracelet with folding clasp and fine adjustment
Price: $5,230
Variations: with FKM rubber strap ($5,230)

Vagabond V-40 Stormy Gray

Reference number: F6660000
Movement: automatic, Fortis caliber WERK 13 GMT (based on Kenissi); ø 31.8 mm, height 7.52 mm; 28 jewels; 28,800 vph; 70-hour power reserve; COSC-certified chronometer
Functions: hours (stepwise adjustable via the crown), minutes, sweep seconds; additional 24-hour display (second time zone); date
Case: titanium, 40 x 40 mm, height 13.9 mm; sapphire crystal; transparent case back; water-resistant to 20 atm
Band: titanium bracelet with folding clasp and fine adjustment
Remarks: GMT chapter ring in white gold
Price: $7,480

Marinemaster M-44 Amber Orange

Reference number: F8120013
Movement: automatic, Fortis caliber WERK 11 (based on Kenissi); ø 31.8 mm, height 7.52 mm; 28 jewels; 28,800 vph; 70-hour power reserve; COSC-certified chronometer
Functions: hours, minutes, sweep seconds; date
Case: recycled stainless steel, ø 44 mm, height 14 mm; bidirectional bezel with 0–60 scale and anti-rotation safety; sapphire crystal; screw-down crown; water-resistant to 50 atm
Band: rubber strap with pin buckle
Price: $5,120

Marinemaster M-40 Amber Orange

Reference number: F8120024
Movement: automatic, Fortis caliber UW-30 (based on Sellita SW300-1); ø 25.6 mm, height 3.6 mm; 25 jewels; 28,800 vph; 38-hour power reserve
Functions: hours, minutes, sweep seconds; date
Case: recycled stainless steel, ø 40 mm, height 12 mm; unidirectional bezel with 0–60 scale; sapphire crystal; screw-down crown; water-resistant to 30 atm
Band: rubber strap with pin buckle
Price: $3,520

Flieger F-43 Bicompax Original

Reference number: F4240004
Movement: automatic, Fortis caliber UW-51 (based on Sellita SW510 BH); ø 30 mm, height 7.9 mm; 25 jewels; 28,800 vph; adjusted to chronometer standards; 48-hour power reserve
Functions: hours, minutes, subsidiary seconds; chronograph; date
Case: recycled stainless steel, ø 43 mm, height 15.5 mm; bidirectional bezel with 0–12 scale; sapphire crystal; screw-down crown; water-resistant to 20 atm
Band: recycled stainless-steel bracelet with folding clasp and fine adjustment
Price: $4,180

F.P.JOURNE

In the pantheon of exceptional watchmakers, François-Paul Journe holds a special place. Born in Marseilles, he decided early on to attend a watchmaking school in Paris and then went to work for his uncle. By the age of twenty, he had made his first tourbillon and was soon producing watches for very high-flying connoisseurs of the art.

He moved to Switzerland and continued cultivating his rarified clientele while at the same time developing the most creative and complicated timekeepers for other brands. Then he took the plunge and founded his own brand in the heart of Geneva. He conceived and produced these timepieces basically single-handedly and certainly single-mindedly, hence his tagline *invenit et fecit*, invented and made. They are of such extreme complexity that it is no wonder they leave his workshop in relatively small quantities. Journe has won numerous top awards, some several times over. He particularly values the Prix de la Fondation de la Vocation Bleustein-Blanchet, since it came from his peers.

The family of Journe watches is divided into several collections: the automatic Octa collection, with classic complications based on a very powerful caliber, the 1300.3, which offers 120 hours of power; the lineSport, focusing on contemporary sportive aesthetics; the Souverain (or Souveraine, depending of the preceding noun's gender), with a range of complications, such as a minute repeater, a constant force tourbillon with dead-beat seconds, and a unique Chronomètre à Résonance with two escapements beating in resonance and providing chronometer precise timekeeping, especially in its most recent version, where it is equipped with a remontoire system to even out the mainspring's torque. In 2025, the company came out with the Chronomètre Furtif to add to the lineSport collection. It is a simple three-hand watch on the front, but that hides a moon phase and power reserve on the back. Adding to the furtiveness of the watch is the tungsten carbide case, a material that is sintered and is twice as hard as steel. It promises to be quite scratch resistant and shockproof. Some elements on the dial are of tantalum.

F.P. Journe's timepieces are mostly sold in dedicated boutiques.

MONTRES JOURNE SA
17 rue de l'Arquebuse
CH-1204 Geneva
Switzerland

TEL.:
+41-22-322-09-09

E-MAIL:
info@fpjourne.com

WEBSITE:
www.fpjourne.com

FOUNDED:
1999

NUMBER OF EMPLOYEES:
135

ANNUAL PRODUCTION:
850–900 watches

U.S. DISTRIBUTOR:
305-572-9802
america@fpjourne.com

MOST IMPORTANT COLLECTIONS:
Souveraine, Octa, LineSport, Elégante, Classique
(Prices all on request)

Chronometre Souverain

Reference number: CS
Movement: manual-wound, F.P.Journe Caliber 1304; ø 30.4 mm, height 4 mm; 22 jewels; 21,600 vph; rose-gold movement; 2 parallel barrel springs; free-sprung balance; finely finished movement; 56-hour power reserve
Functions: hours, minutes, subsidiary seconds; power reserve indicator
Case: platinum, ø 40 mm, height 8 mm; sapphire crystal; transparent case back; water-resistant to 3 atm
Band: leather, pin buckle
Remarks: blue guilloche on silver, white-gold or 5N pink-gold applique numerals
Price: on request
Variations: comes with 6N gold

LineSport Chronomètre Furtif

Reference number: CF
Movement: manual-wound, F.P.Journe Caliber 1522; ø 33.5 mm, height 5.9 mm; 21 jewels; 21,600 vph; rose-gold mainplate and bridges balance with 4 inertia weights; 56-hour power reserve
Functions: hours, minutes, sweep seconds; moon phase and power reserve indicator on the back
Case: tungsten carbide and tantalum, ø 42 mm, height 9.3 mm; sapphire crystal; transparent case back; water-resistant to 3 atm
Band: tungsten carbide, folding clasp
Remarks: anthracite grey grand-feu enamel on white gold
Price: on request

Tourbillon Souverain

Reference number: TV
Movement: manually wound, F.P.Journe Caliber 1519; ø 34.6 mm, height 10 mm; 32 jewels; 21,600 vph; rose-gold mainplate and bridges; vertical tourbillon with constant force; balance with 4 inertia weights; 80-hour power reserve
Functions: hours, minutes, subsidiary dead-beat seconds; power reserve indicator
Case: rose gold, ø 42 mm, height 13.6 mm; sapphire crystal; transparent case back; water-resistant to 3 atm
Band: calfskin, buckle
Remarks: rose-gold clous de Paris guilloché dial formed from gold bridges with small grand-feu enamel dial on white gold
Price: on request

FRÉDÉRIQUE CONSTANT

Peter and Aletta Stas, the Dutch couple who founded Frédérique Constant, have always sought to make high-end watches for consumers without deep pockets. So high-end, in fact, that in 2004 they went public with their first movement produced entirely in-house and equipped with silicon components.

The brand was founded in 1988 and named for Aletta's great-grandmother Frédérique Schreiner and Peter's great-grandfather Constant Stas. The couple parlayed affordable watches with very classic—i.e., not boat-rocking—design into a modern factory in Geneva's industrial Plan-les-Ouates.

Following the sale of the company to the Japanese Citizen Group (2016), Dutchman Niels Eggerding was named CEO of the Frédérique Constant brand. The factory in Geneva was expanded in 2019 to almost double its original size. This permitted a production projection of 250,000 watches per year by 2025. In 2021, Frédérique Constant achieved a mechanical breakthrough, with a compact silicon escapement rather than a normal escapement with balance. The oscillator vibrates at a frequency of 288,000 vibrations per hour. The Slimline Monolithic Manufacture ticks ten times faster than most mechanical watches and appears to achieve far better chronometric results as well. The new escapement—a genuine horological innovation—can be viewed through an opening at 6 o'clock.

To date, Frédérique Constant has developed 30 mechanical in-house calibers, with major complications such as a tourbillon or perpetual calendar, but also with practical "minor" complications such as a flyback chronograph or a classic automatic movement with date and moon phase display.

The future looks bright for this relatively young brand. In addition to its main collections, by which it aims to bring high-quality, affordable watchmaking to the market, the company has at the same time gradually expanded its product range to include more exclusive pieces for discerning collectors. The tourbillon is undoubtedly one of the most popular high complications, and now Frédérique Constant has one at a reasonable price.

FREDERIQUE CONSTANT SA
Chemin du Champ-des-Filles 32
CH-1228 Plan-les-Ouates (Geneva)
Switzerland

TEL.:
+41 22 860 04 40

E-MAIL:
info@frederique-constant.com

WEBSITE:
us.frederiqueconstant.com

FOUNDED:
1988

NUMBER OF EMPLOYEES:
150

U.S. DISTRIBUTOR:
Alpina Frédérique Constant USA
350 5th Avenue, 29th Floor
New York, NY 10118
646-438-8124
customercare@usa.frederiqueconstant.com

MOST IMPORTANT COLLECTIONS/PRICE RANGE:
Manufacture collection / from approx. $3,195 to $44,995; Highlife collection / from approx. $2,295 to $48,995; Classics collection / from approx. $1,095 to $2,850

Classic Perpetual Calendar Manufacture

Reference number: FC-776SAL3H6
Movement: automatic, Caliber FC-776; ø 30.5 mm, height 6.67 mm; 26 jewels; 28,800 vph; finely finished movement; 72-hour power reserve
Functions: hours, minutes; perpetual calendar with date, weekday, month, moon phase, leap year
Case: stainless steel, ø 40 mm, height 12.1 mm; sapphire crystal; transparent case back; water-resistant to 5 atm
Band: reptile skin, folding clasp
Price: $9,995

Classic Tourbillon Manufacture

Reference number: FC-980GR3H6
Movement: automatic, Caliber FC-980-4; ø 30 mm; 33 jewels; 28,800 vph; 1-minute tourbillon; silicon escape wheel and anchor; finely finished movement; 42-hour power reserve
Functions: hours, minutes, small seconds (on the tourbillon cage)
Case: stainless steel, ø 39 mm, height 10.99 mm; sapphire crystal; transparent case back; water-resistant to 5 atm
Band: reptile skin, folding clasp
Remarks: limited to 150 pieces
Price: $15,995

Worldtimer Manufacture

Reference number: FC-718KWM4H6
Movement: automatic, Caliber FC-718; ø 30 mm, height 6.2 mm; 26 jewels; 28,800 vph; finely finished movement; 38-hour power reserve
Functions: hours, minutes, sweep seconds; world timer (second time zone); date
Case: stainless steel, ø 42 mm, height 12.1 mm; crown-activated ring with reference cities; sapphire crystal; transparent case back; water-resistant to 5 atm
Band: reptile skin, folding clasp
Remarks: limited to 718 pieces
Price: $4,795
Variations: in rose gold ($19,595)

Classics Carrée Small Seconds

Reference number: FC-235S2C6B
Movement: quartz
Functions: hours, minutes, small seconds
Case: stainless steel, 25.2 x 36 mm, height 5.85 mm; sapphire crystal; transparent case back; water-resistant to 3 atm
Band: stainless steel, folding clasp
Price: $1,195

Classics Vintage Rally Healey Chronograph Automatic

Reference number: FC-397HLBN5B6
Movement: automatic, Caliber FC-397 (base Sellita SW500); ø 30 mm, height 7.9 mm; 27 jewels; 28,800 vph; 62-hour power reserve
Functions: hours, minutes, small seconds; chronograph
Case: stainless steel, ø 42 mm, height 14.45 mm; sapphire crystal; transparent case back; water-resistant to 5 atm
Band: leather, pin buckle
Remarks: limited to 1888 pieces
Price: $3,395

Classics Vintage Rally Healey Automatic

Reference number: FC-301HGRS5B26
Movement: automatic, Caliber FC-301 (base La Joux-Perret G100); ø 25.6 mm, height 4.45 mm; 24 jewels; 28,800 vph; 68-hour power reserve
Functions: hours, minutes, sweep seconds
Case: stainless steel, ø 40 mm, height 10.16 mm; sapphire crystal; transparent case back; water-resistant to 5 atm
Band: leather, pin buckle
Price: $1,895

Classics Moneta Moonphase

Reference number: FC-206B3S6
Movement: quartz
Functions: hours, minutes; moon phase
Case: stainless steel, ø 37 mm, height 7.65 mm; sapphire crystal; water-resistant to 5 atm
Band: leather, pin buckle
Price: $1,295

Classics Manchette

Reference number: FC-200MA1MC6B
Movement: quartz
Functions: hours, minutes
Case: stainless steel, 20 x 25.7 mm, height 6.45 mm; sapphire crystal; water-resistant to 3 atm
Band: stainless steel, folding clasp
Remarks: malachite dial
Price: $1,895
Variations: various dials

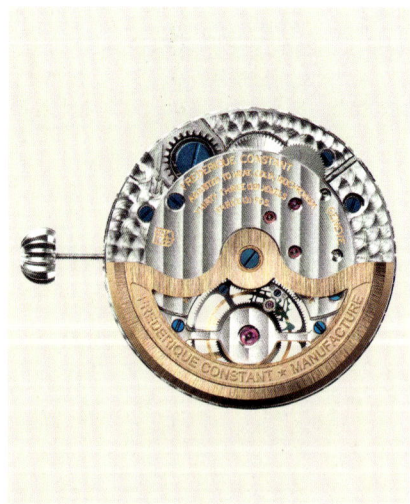

Caliber FC-980

Automatic; 1-minute tourbillon; silicon anchor and escape wheel; single spring barrel, 38-hour power reserve
Functions: hours, minutes, small seconds
Diameter: 30 mm
Height: 5.7 mm
Jewels: 33
Balance: silicon
Frequency: 28,800 vph
Hairspring: flat hairspring
Shock absorber: Incabloc
Remarks: perlage on mainplate, bridges with côtes de Genève, gold-plated rotor; 188 parts

GARRICK WATCHMAKERS

Britain has contributed enormously to the development of watchmaking, so it's hardly astonishing to find that the country is home to a growing number of brands vying on the international markets. Garrick Watchmakers is one of them. It was founded in 2013 in Devon by David Brailsford together with Simon Michlmayr, one of the top English watchmakers. The aim of these two men was to revive the old tradition of English watchmaking and to achieve the greatest possible vertical integration in the construction of their watches.

Wherever possible, Garrick either manufactures in its own workshop in Norwich, Norfolk or purchases from English suppliers. The company goes so far as to make its own hands, which is rare in the industry, since hands are very time-consuming to manufacture. The elaborately designed dials, too, are also entirely made in-house. Even cases are produced in England.

In the beginning Garrick had to delve deep into the history of English watchmaking and precision mechanics to gain the necessary knowledge to realize their vision. While the first models were still based on a Unitas caliber, the Portsmouth was presented in 2016, the first of what are now six of the company's own *manufacture* calibers. The same year saw the appearance of the Regulator, which uses its 42-millimeter case for three subdials and an opening on the free-sprung balance designed and built by the company. The so-called Trinity balance is made of a nonmagnetic alloy, Sircumet. To adjust the rate, the balance wheel is equipped with rim screws. The hairspring's position can be changed as well. In addition to genuine enamel dials, Garrick specializes in guilloché and finely engraved dials that appear in several of the S series, which have been released recently in 38-millimeter cases.

Garrick Watchmakers build no more than seventy watches every year. Thanks to its vertical manufacturing and the fact that each Garrick is made to order, customers are free to get some parts customized and create unique pieces. When ordering, make sure you check lead-time, though, because these are handmade pieces.

GARRICK WATCHMAKERS
Unit 2, Fletcher Way, Norwich, Norfolk
NR3 3ST
England

TEL.:
+44 (0)1603 327272

E-MAIL:
info@garrick.co.uk

WEBSITE:
www.garrick.co.uk

FOUNDED:
2013

EMPLOYEES:
9

ANNUAL PRODUCTION:
70 watches maximum

DISTRIBUTION:
direct sales

MOST IMPORTANT COLLECTIONS/PRICE RANGE:
Regulator and S series / £2,500 to £30,000; Prices only in pounds sterling

S7

Movement: hand wound, Garrick caliber BF-04 (modified Unitas 6425); ø 29.4 mm, height 4.6 mm; 19 jewels; 21,600 vph; finely finished movement with black polishing; hand-polished and screw-mounted chatons; 47-hour power reserve
Functions: hours, minutes, subsidiary seconds
Case: stainless steel, ø 38 mm, height 9 mm; sapphire crystal; transparent case back; water-resistant to 10 atm
Band: reptile skin, pin buckle
Remarks: heat-blued hands; hand-made guilloché
Price: £9,500
Variations: engine turned dials in various colors

Regulator MK II

Movement: manual wound, Garrick Caliber UT-G02; 19 jewels; 18,000 vph; Trinity free-sprung balance; screw-mounted, hand-polished chatons; 45-hour power reserve
Functions: hours, minutes, subsidiary seconds
Case: stainless steel, ø 42 mm, height 10 mm; sapphire crystal; transparent case back; water-resistant to 10 atm
Band: reptile skin or calfskin; pin buckle
Remarks: guilloche dial; options for personalization
Price: £14,000
Variations: various colors

S3 Deadbeat Seconds Power Reserve

Movement: hand wound, Garrick DB-G07 caliber; ø 36 mm, height 4.5 mm; 21 jewels; 18,000 vph; frosted plates, German-silver chapter ring; Trinity free-sprung balance; 45-hour power reserve
Functions: hours, minutes, sweep seconds; power reserve indicator
Case: stainless steel, ø 42 mm, height 11 mm; sapphire crystal; water-resistant to 3 atm
Band: reptile skin (or leather), pin buckle
Remarks: openworked dial with blued hands
Price: £40,000
Variations: comes in gold (£47,000)

GIRARD-PERREGAUX

This venerable watch *manufacture* headquartered in La Chaux-de-Fonds is one of few in Switzerland with a long and verifiable history. The company was founded in 1791 in Geneva, Switzerland, but really hit its stride in the second half of the nineteenth century, 1867 to be precise, with the aesthetically and technically sophisticated "Tourbillon with three golden bridges." Girard-Perregaux maintained its position at the forefront of Swiss watchmaking in the twentieth century with one of the first wrist-worn men's watches, as well as several other pioneering achievements in mechanical watchmaking. One of the latest came in 2013 with the installation of a constant force mechanism made with an integrated blade that collects the energy and "snaps" it in even bursts into the escapement.

Beginning in 1992, Italian entrepreneur Luigi "Gino" Macaluso revitalized the brand by returning focus to mechanical watches. Following his death in 2011, the company joined the Kering Group for a brief while before regaining independence under CEO Patrick Pruniaux in 2022.

The tourbillon—in increasingly modern guises—remains the brand's focus, but along with the vintage trend and, no doubt, some nostalgia for the rational, elegant watches of older days, Girard-Perregaux decided to modernize the Laureato a few years ago, a collection that was first introduced in 1975. It is considered one of the icons of the 1970s thanks to its sporty, striking aesthetics, octagonal bezel over a round base, and metal bracelet seamlessly integrated into the case.

The recently rebuilt and modernized *manufacture* in La Chaux-de-Fonds quickly produced several remarkable creations based on the distinctive sports watch. Girard-Perregaux has also released a number of special editions to pay tribute to the brand's long-term partnership with the British sports car manufacturer Aston Martin and the Formula 1 team, such as the Neo Bridges Aston Martin Edition, a skeletonized watch with sporty, green NAC-coated bridges, the British racing team's color.

GIRARD-PERREGAUX
1, Place Girardet
CH-2300 La Chaux-de-Fonds
Switzerland

TEL.:
+41-32-911-3333

WEBSITE:
www.girard-perregaux.com

FOUNDED:
1791

U.S. DISTRIBUTOR:
Girard-Perregaux
Tradema of America, Inc.
7900 Glades Road, Suite 200
Boca Raton, FL 33434
833-GPWATCH
www.girard-perregaux.com

MOST IMPORTANT COLLECTIONS/PRICE RANGE:
Laureato / Vintage 1945 / Neo / approx. $7,500 to $625,000; ww.tc / $12,300 to $23,800; GP 1966 / $7,500 to $291,000

Tourbillon Three Flying Bridges

Reference number: 99296-52-3434-5CC
Movement: automatic, GP Caliber 09400-1273; ø 42 mm, height 9.45 mm; 27 jewels; 21,600 vph; 1-minute tourbillon under three titanium bridges; white-gold micro-rotor; balance with variable inertia and golden regulating screws, hairspring with Phillips end curve; fully skeletonized movement; 60-hour power reserve
Functions: hours, minutes
Case: rose gold, ø 44 mm, height 15.35 mm; sapphire crystal; transparent case back; water-resistant to 3 atm
Band: textile, triple folding clasp
Price: $171,000

La Esmeralda Tourbillon "à secret" Eternity Edition

Reference number: 99274-52-3423-5CC
Movement: automatic, GP Caliber 09400–0004; ø 32 mm, height 7.68 mm; 31 jewels; 21,600 vph; 1-minute tourbillon under three gold bridges; gold micro-rotor; balance with variable inertia and regulating screws, hairspring with Phillips end curve; 50-hour power reserve
Functions: hours, minutes
Case: rose gold (hand-engraved and enameled), ø 43 mm, height 15.1 mm; sapphire crystal; transparent case back; water-resistant to 3 atm
Band: leather, triple folding clasp
Remarks: hand-guilloché enamel dial; case back with hinged cover
Price: $447,000; limited to 18 pieces

Neo Constant Escapement

Reference number: 93510-21-1930-5CX
Movement: hand-wound, GP Caliber 09200; ø 39.5 mm, height 7.4 mm; 29 jewels; 21,600 vph; patented constant force escapement with two escape wheels and impulse silicon leaf spring, 2 barrels with 4 mainsprings; 168-hour power reserve; COSC-certified chronometer
Functions: hours, minutes, sweep seconds; linear power reserve indicator
Case: titanium, ø 45 mm, height 14.8 mm; sapphire crystal; transparent case back; water-resistant to 3 atm
Band: rubber, triple folding clasp
Price: $99,600

Laureato 42mm Skeleton

Reference number: 81015_52_002_52A
Movement: automatic, GP Caliber 01800-0006;
ø 30 mm, height 4.16 mm; 25 jewels; 28,800 vph;
escapement with variable momentum, rose gold rotor,
fully skeletonized movement; 54-hour power reserve
Functions: hours, minutes, subsidiary seconds
Case: rose gold, ø 42 mm, height 10.68 mm; sapphire
crystal; transparent case back; water-resistant to 5 atm
Band: rose gold, triple folding clasp
Remarks: skeletonized dial
Price: $84,800

Laureato Chronograph 42mm

Reference number: 81020-52-432-52A
Movement: automatic, GP Caliber 03300-
0137/0138/0141; ø 25.95 mm, height 6.5 mm; 63 jewels;
28,800 vph; 46-hour power reserve
Functions: hours, minutes, subsidiary seconds;
chronograph; date
Case: rose gold, ø 42 mm, height 12.01 mm; sapphire
crystal; water-resistant to 5 atm
Band: rose gold, triple folding clasp
Price: $61,000

Laureato Chronograph 42mm

Reference number: 81020-11-131-11A
Movement: automatic, GP Caliber 03300-
0137/0138/0141; ø 25.95 mm, height 6.5 mm; 63 jewels;
28,800 vph; 46-hour power reserve
Functions: hours, minutes, subsidiary seconds;
chronograph; date
Case: stainless steel, ø 42 mm, height 12.01 mm;
sapphire crystal; water-resistant to 10 atm
Band: stainless steel, double folding clasp
Price: $18,600

Laureato 42mm Automatic

Reference number: 81010-11-431-11A
Movement: automatic, GP Caliber 01800-0013;
ø 30 mm, height 3.97 mm; 28 jewels; 28,800 vph;
54-hour power reserve
Functions: hours, minutes, sweep seconds; date
Case: stainless steel, ø 42 mm, height 10.68 mm;
sapphire crystal; transparent case back; water-resistant
to 10 atm
Band: stainless steel, double folding clasp
Price: $14,300

Laureato 38mm Blue Sapphire

Reference number: 81005_11S3464_1CM
Movement: automatic, GP Caliber 03300-2564;
ø 25.95 mm, height 3.36 mm; 27 jewels; 28,800 vph;
46-hour power reserve
Functions: hours, minutes, sweep seconds; date
Case: stainless steel, ø 38 mm, height 10 mm; bezel
with 56 sapphires and brilliant-cut diamonds; sapphire
crystal; transparent case back; water-resistant to
10 atm
Band: stainless steel, triple folding clasp
Price: $20,100

Deep Diver

Reference number: 39500-21-3266-6CX
Movement: automatic, GP Caliber 03300; ø 25.95 mm,
height 3.36 mm; 27 jewels; 28,800 vph; 46-hour power
reserve
Functions: hours, minutes, sweep seconds; date
Case: titanium, 38 mm x 40.3 mm, height 13.91 mm;
crown-adjusted sale ring with 0-60 scale; sapphire
crystal; water-resistant to 20 atm
Band: rubber, pin buckle
Remarks: Homage to a historic model from 1969
Price: $18,200; limited to 350 pieces

GLASHÜTTE ORIGINAL

A little nostalgia seems to be creeping into the designers at Glashütte Original. The retro touches that started appearing again a few years ago with the Sixties Square Tourbillon are still in vogue as the company delves into its own past for inspiration, such as the use of a special silver treatment on dials.

Glashütte Original *manufacture* roots go back to the mid-nineteenth century, though the name itself came later. The company, which had a sterling reputation for precision watches, became subsumed in the VEB Glashütter Uhrenbetriebe, a group of Glashütte watchmakers and suppliers who were collectivized as part of the former East German system. After reunification, the company took up its old moniker of Glashütte Original, and in 1995, the *manufacture* released an entirely new collection. Later, it purchased Union Glashütte. In 2000, the Swiss Swatch Group acquired the whole company and invested in expanding the production space at Glashütte Original headquarters. The company decided to separate out Union Glashütte, whose models are not distributed in the USA, by the way.

Manufacturing depth has reached 95 percent. All movements are designed by a team of experienced in-house engineers and the components—plates, screws, pinions, wheels, levers, spring barrels, balance wheels, and tourbillon cages—are manufactured in-house.

Among the highlights of the portfolio is the Senator Chronometer, which boasts second and minute hands that automatically jump to zero when the crown is pulled, allowing for extremely accurate time setting. Recently, the Senator Chronometer Tourbillon was released featuring some virtuoso watchmaking, including a positional error compensation of the flying going train, and the balance wheel and tourbillon cage can be stopped by a pull on the crown. Another sustained pull sets the tip of the seconds index on the tourbillon cage to zero, i.e., pointing vertically upwards.

In 2025, Glashütte Original celebrated the 180th anniversary of watchmaking in Glashütte and the highlights of famous watchmakers like Ferdinand Adolph Lange and Alfred Helwig. These inventions made the town in the valley of the Müglitz the most important center of watchmaking in Germany. As a commitment to the region, the brand opened a new dial factory in Glashütte.

GLASHÜTTER UHRENBETRIEB GMBH
Altenberger Strasse 1
D-01768 Glashütte
Germany

TEL.:
+49-350-53-46-0

E-MAIL:
info@glashuette-original.com

WEBSITE:
www.glashuette-original.com

FOUNDED:
1951 foundation as VEB Glashütter Uhrenbetriebe
1990 privatization and registration as Glashütter Uhrenbetrieb GmbH

U.S. DISTRIBUTOR:
Glashütte Original
The Swatch Group (U.S.), Inc.
1200 Harbor Boulevard
Weehawken, NJ 07087
201-271-1400

MOST IMPORTANT COLLECTIONS/PRICE RANGE:
Senator, Pano, Spezialist, SeaQ, Senator, Vintage, Ladies / $4,900 to $152,300

Senator Chronometer Tourbillon

Reference number: 1-58-06-01-03-61
Movement: hand-wound, Glashütte Original caliber 58-06; ø 36.6 mm, height 8.99 mm; 85 jewels; 21,600 vph; flying 1-minute tourbillon with flyback switch and exact indexing of the minute hand; silicon hairspring; 70-hour power reserve; DIN-tested chronometer
Functions: hours and minutes (off-center), subsidiary seconds (on the tourbillon cage); day/night indication, power reserve indicator
Case: platinum, ø 42 mm, height 12.6 mm; sapphire crystal; transparent case back; water-resistant to 5 atm
Band: reptile skin, double folding clasp
Remarks: limited to 50 pieces
Price: $187,300

PanoLunarInverse

Reference number: 1-91-04-01-03-62
Movement: automatic, Glashütte Original Caliber 91-04; ø 38.2 mm, height 7.3 mm; 53 jewels; 28,800 vph; duplex swan-neck fine regulator; inverted movement construction, hand-engraved balance bridge, skeletonized rotor with gold oscillating mass, finely finished movement; 45-hour power reserve
Functions: hours and minutes (off-center), subsidiary seconds; panorama date, moon phase
Case: platinum, ø 42 mm, height 12.46 mm; sapphire crystal; transparent case back; water-resistant to 5 atm
Band: reptile skin, folding clasp
Remarks: limited to 200 pieces
Price: $45,500

PanoMaticCalendar

Reference number: 1-92-09-02-05-62
Movement: automatic, Glashütte Original caliber 92-09; ø 34.8 mm, height 7.65 mm; 53 jewels; 28,800 vph; screw balance with 4 gold regulating screws, indexless adjustment, hand-engraved balance bridge, Glashütte three-quarter plate with ribbing, skeletonized rotor with gold oscillating mass; 100-hour power reserve
Functions: hours and minutes (off-center), subsidiary seconds; annual calendar with panorama date, month (retrograde), moon phase
Case: red gold, ø 42 mm, height 12.4 mm; sapphire crystal; transparent case back; water-resistant to 5 atm
Band: reptile skin, double folding clasp
Price: $36,000
Variations: in platinum (limited to 150 pieces, $43,800)

PanoMaticLunar

Reference number: 1-90-02-23-35-61
Movement: automatic, Glashütte Original caliber 90-02; ø 32.6 mm, height 7 mm; 47 jewels; 28,800 vph; screw balance with 18 weight screws, duplex swan-neck fine regulator, hand-engraved balance cock, Glashütte three-quarter plate with ribbing, blued screws, skeletonized rotor with gold oscillating mass, finely finished movement; 42-hour power reserve
Functions: hours and minutes (off-center), subsidiary seconds; panorama date, moon phase
Case: red gold, ø 40 mm, height 12.7 mm; sapphire crystal; transparent case back; water-resistant to 5 atm
Band: reptile skin, folding clasp
Price: $26,500
Variations: in stainless steel ($13,400)

PanoMaticInverse

Reference number: 1-91-02-01-05-62
Movement: automatic, Glashütte Original caliber 91-02; ø 38.2 mm, height 7.1 mm; 49 jewels; 28,800 vph; Glashütte three-quarter plate with ribbing, screw balance with 18 weight screws, duplex swan-neck fine regulator; inverted movement architecture, hand-engraved balance cock, skeletonized rotor with gold oscillating mass, finely finished movement; 42-hour power reserve
Functions: hours and minutes (off-center), subsidiary seconds; panorama date
Case: red gold, ø 42 mm, height 12.3 mm; sapphire crystal; transparent case back; water-resistant to 5 atm
Band: reptile skin, folding clasp
Price: $32,400
Variations: in stainless steel ($15,700)

Senator Chronometer

Reference number: 1-58-08-01-04-61
Movement: hand-wound, Glashütte Original caliber 58-08; ø 35 mm, height 6.47 mm; 58 jewels; 28,800 vph; grey galvanic Glashütte three-quarter plate, crown-controlled second-hand reset with exact indexing of the minute hand, screw balance with 18 weight screws, swan-neck fine regulator; hand-engraved balance cock, finely finished movement; 44-hour power reserve; DIN-certified chronometer
Functions: hours, minutes, subsidiary seconds; day/night indication, power reserve indicator; panorama date
Case: white gold, ø 42 mm, height 11.4 mm; sapphire crystal; transparent case back; water-resistant to 5 atm
Band: reptile skin, folding clasp
Price: $39,200

Senator Excellence Perpetual Calendar

Reference number: 1-36-12-02-05-62
Movement: automatic, Glashütte Original caliber 36-12; ø 32.2 mm, height 7.35 mm; 49 jewels; 28,800 vph; silicon hairspring, screw balance with 4 regulating screws, swan-neck fine regulator, Glashütte three-quarter plate with ribbing, blued screws, skeletonized gold rotor, finely finished movement; 100-hour power reserve
Functions: hours, minutes, sweep seconds; perpetual calendar with panorama date, weekday, month, moon phase, leap year
Case: red gold, ø 42 mm, height 12.8 mm; sapphire crystal; transparent case back; water-resistant to 5 atm
Band: reptile skin, folding clasp
Price: $51,500
Variations: in stainless steel ($26,100)

Senator Excellence Panorama Date Moon Phase

Reference number: 1-36-24-04-02-61
Movement: automatic, Glashütte Original caliber 36-24; ø 32.2 mm, height 6.7 mm; 43 jewels; 28,800 vph; silicon hairspring, screw balance with 4 regulating screws, swan-neck fine regulator, Glashütte three-quarter plate with ribbing, blued screws, skeletonized rotor with gold oscillating mass, finely finished movement; 100-hour power reserve
Functions: hours, minutes, sweep seconds; panorama date, moon phase
Case: stainless steel, ø 40 mm, height 12.2 mm; sapphire crystal; transparent case back; water-resistant to 5 atm
Band: reptile skin, folding clasp
Price: $13,100
Variations: in red gold ($26,700)

Senator Chronograph Panorama Date

Reference number: 1-37-01-05-02-36
Movement: automatic, Glashütte Original caliber 37-01; ø 31.6 mm, height 8 mm; 65 jewels; 28,800 vph; screw balance with 4 regulating screws, swan-neck spring to regulate beat; mainplate with ribbing, blued screws, skeletonized er gold rotor, finely finished movement; 70-hour power reserve
Functions: hours, minutes, subsidiary seconds; power reserve indicator; flyback chronograph; panorama date
Case: stainless steel, ø 42 mm, height 14.6 mm; sapphire crystal; transparent case back; water-resistant to 10 atm
Band: textile, folding clasp
Price: $15,900
Variations: with leather strap; with stainless-steel bracelet ($17,100)

Senator Cosmopolite

Reference number: 1-89-02-05-02-64
Movement: automatic, Glashütte Original caliber 89-02; ø 39.2 mm, height 8 mm; 63 jewels; 28,800 vph; Glashütte three-quarter plate, screw balance with 4 regulating screws, swan-neck spring to regulate rate, hand-engraved balance bridge; 72-hour power reserve
Functions: hours, minutes, subsidiary seconds; additional 12-hour display (second time zone), world time display with 35 time zones, day/night indicator for home time and local time, power reserve indicator; panorama date
Case: stainless steel, ø 44 mm, height 14 mm; sapphire crystal; transparent case back; water-resistant to 5 atm
Band: textile, folding clasp
Price: $24,700
Variations: with reptile skin strap ($24,300); in red gold ($44,100)

Seventies Chronograph Panorama Date

Reference number: 1-37-02-09-02-63
Movement: automatic, Glashütte Original Caliber 37-02; ø 31.6 mm, height 8 mm; 65 jewels; 28,800 vph; screw balance with 4 regulating screws, swan-neck fine regulator; mainplate with ribbing, blued screws, skeletonized rotor with gold oscillating mass, finely finished movement; 70-hour power reserve
Functions: hours, minutes, subsidiary seconds; power reserve indicator; flyback chronograph; panorama date
Case: stainless steel, 40 mm x 40 mm, height 14.1 mm; sapphire crystal; transparent case back; screw-down crown; water-resistant to 10 atm
Band: rubber, folding clasp
Price: $15,600

Sixties Subsidiary Seconds

Reference number: 1-39-60-01-01-04
Movement: automatic, Glashütte Original Caliber 39-60; ø 26.2 mm, height 5.9 mm; 30 jewels; 28,800 vph; swan-neck fine regulator, Glashütte three-quarter plate with stripe finish, skeletonized rotor with gold oscillating mass, finely finished movement; 40-hour power reserve Functions: hours, minutes, subsidiary seconds
Case: rose gold, ø 42 mm, height 12.4 mm; sapphire crystal; transparent case back; water-resistant to 3 atm
Band: reptile skin, pin buckle
Price: $19,500

Sixties Chronograph Annual Edition

Reference number: 1-39-34-06-22-04
Movement: automatic, Glashütte Original Caliber 39-34; ø 30.04 mm, height 7.2 mm; 51 jewels; 28,800 vph; swan-neck fine regulator, skeletonized rotor with gold oscillating mass, finely finished movement; 40-hour power reserve
Functions: hours, minutes, subsidiary seconds; chronograph
Case: stainless steel, ø 42 mm, height 12.4 mm; sapphire crystal; transparent case back; water-resistant to 3 atm
Band: textile, pin buckle
Price: $10,000

Serenade Luna

Reference number: 1-35-14-05-15-04
Movement: automatic, Glashütte Original Caliber 35-14; ø 26 mm, height 3.8 mm; 32 jewels; 28,800 vph; Swan-neck fine regulator, silicon hairspring, Glashütte three-quarter plate with stripe finish; finely finished movement; 60-hour power reserve
Functions: hours, minutes, sweep seconds; moon phase
Case: red gold, ø 32.5 mm, height 8.9 mm; bezel in rose gold, with 48 diamonds; sapphire crystal; transparent case back; crown with diamond; water-resistant to 3 atm
Band: reptile skin, folding clasp
Remarks: dial with 20 brilliant-cut diamonds; mother-of-pearl moon phase
Price: $24,800

Serenade Luna

Reference number: 1-35-14-02-12-04
Movement: automatic, Glashütte Original Caliber 35-14; ø 26 mm, height 3.8 mm; 32 jewels; 28,800 vph; swan-neck fine regulation, silicon hairspring, Glashütte three-quarter plate with stripe finish; finely finished movement; 60-hour power reserve
Functions: hours, minutes, sweep seconds; moon phase
Case: stainless steel, ø 32.5 mm, height 8.9 mm; bezel with 48 diamonds; sapphire crystal; transparent case back; crown with diamond; water-resistant to 3 atm
Band: reptile skin, folding clasp
Remarks: mother-of-pearl dial set with 20 brilliant-cut diamonds; mother-of-pearl moon phase
Price: $15,100
Variations: with stainless-steel bracelet

SeaQ Chronograph

Reference number: 1-37-23-03-80-33
Movement: automatic, Glashütte Original Caliber 37-23; ø 34.2 mm, height 8 mm; 47 jewels; 28,800 vph; screw balance with 4 regulating screws, swan-neck fine regulation; skeletonized gold-rotor, finely finished movement; 70-hour power reserve
Functions: hours, minutes, subsidiary seconds; flyback chronograph; panorama date
Case: stainless steel, ø 43.2 mm, height 16.95 mm; unidirectional bezel with ceramic insert and 0-60 scale; sapphire crystal; transparent case back; screw-down crown; water-resistant to 30 atm
Band: rubber, pin buckle
Price: $16,100
Variations: with blue dial

SeaQ Panorama Date

Reference number: 1-36-13-04-91-34
Movement: automatic, Glashütte Original caliber 36-13; ø 32.2 mm, height 6.7 mm; 39 jewels; 28,800 vph; silicon hairspring, screw balance with 4 regulating screws, indexless regulating system, Glashütte three-quarter plate with stripe, blued screws, skeletonized gold rotor, finely finished movement; 100-hour power reserve
Functions: hours, minutes, sweep seconds; panorama date
Case: stainless steel, ø 43.2 mm, height 15.65 mm; unidirectional bezel in red gold with ceramic insert and 0-60 scale; sapphire crystal; transparent case back; screw-down red-gold crown; water-resistant to 30 atm
Band: textile, folding clasp
Price: $17,600
Variations: with rubber strap ($17,600); with rubber strap and pin buckle ($17,300)

SeaQ

Reference number: 1-39-11-13-83-37
Movement: automatic, Glashütte Original Caliber 39-11; ø 26 mm, height 4.3 mm; 25 jewels; 28,800 vph; swan-neck fine regulator, Glashütte three-quarter plate with stripe finish, skeletonized rotor with heavy-metal oscillating mass, finely finished movement; 40-hour power reserve
Functions: hours, minutes, sweep seconds; date
Case: stainless steel, ø 39.5 mm, height 12.15 mm; unidirectional bezel with ceramic insert, with 0-60 scale; sapphire crystal; screw-down crown; water-resistant to 20 atm
Band: rubber, folding clasp
Price: $10,600
Variations: in red gold ($27,200); in stainless steel/red gold ($17,300)

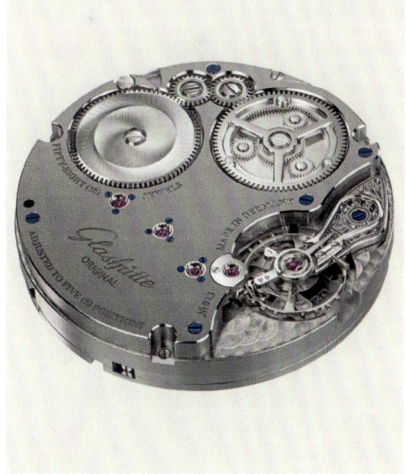

Caliber 37

Automatic; single spring barrel, 70-hour power reserve
Functions: hours, minutes, subsidiary seconds; power reserve indicator; flyback chronograph; panorama date
Diameter: 31.6 mm
Height: 8 mm
Jewels: 65
Balance: screw balance with 4 regulating screws
Frequency: 28,800 vph
Hairspring: flat hairspring, swan-neck fine adjustment
Remarks: finely finished movement, chamfered edges, polished steel parts, blued screws, mainplate with Glashütte ribbing, skeletonized rotor with gold oscillating mass

Caliber 58-06

Hand-wound; flying 1-minute tourbillon with balance stop and indexed reset; single mainspring barrel, 70-hour power reserve
Functions: hours and minutes (off-center), subsidiary seconds (on the tourbillon cage); day/night indicator, power reserve indicator
Diameter: 36.6 mm
Height: 8.99 mm
Jewels: 85
Balance: screw balance screw balance
Frequency: 21,600 vph
Hairspring: silicon
Remarks: three-quarter plate with Glashütte ribbing, blued screws, stop wheel with double sunburst ribbing, hand-engraved structural parts; 572 parts

Caliber 58-08

Hand-wound; swan-neck fine adjustment; balance stop and indexed reset; single spring barrel, 44-hour power reserve
Functions: hours, minutes, subsidiary seconds; day/night indication, power reserve indicator; panorama date
Diameter: 35 mm
Height: 6.47 mm
Jewels: 58
Balance: screw balance with 18 weight screws
Frequency: 28,800 vph
Hairspring: Anachron
Shock protection: Incabloc
Remarks: silver-plated mainplate, galvanic grey, planetary, double sunburst on winding wheel, screw-mounted white-gold chatons; 572 parts

Caliber 35-14

Automatic; swan-neck fine adjustment; single mainspring barrel, 60-hour power reserve
Functions: hours, minutes, sweep seconds; moon phase
Diameter: 26 mm
Height: 3.8 mm
Jewels: 32
Frequency: 28,800 vph
Hairspring: silicon
Remarks: Glashütte three-quarter plate with ribbing; finely finished movement

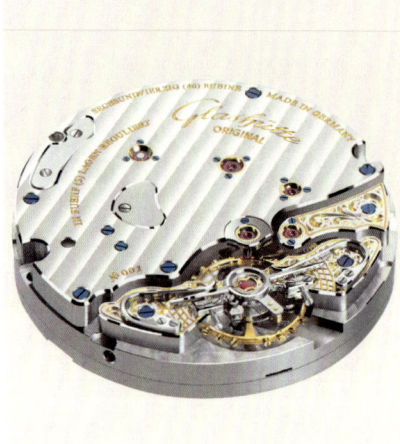

Caliber 65

hand-wound; second-stop system; single mainspring barrel, 42-hour power reserve
Functions: hours and minutes (off-center), subsidiary seconds; power reserve indicator; panorama date
Diameter: 32.2 mm
Height: 6.1 mm
Jewels: 48
Balance: screw balance with 18 weight screws
Frequency: 28,800 vph
Hairspring: flat hairspring, duplex swan-neck fine adjustment for rate and beat
Shock protection: Incabloc
Remarks: screw-mounted gold chatons, winding gears with double sunburst, three-quarter plate with Glashütte ribbing, hand-engraved balance cock

Caliber 89-02

Automatic; second-stop system; single mainspring barrel, 72-hour power reserve
Functions: hours, minutes, subsidiary seconds; second time zone, world time display with 35 time zones, day/night indicator, power reserve indicator; panorama date
Diameter: 39.2 mm
Height: 8 mm
Jewels: 63
Balance: screw balance with 4 regulating screws
Frequency: 28,800 vph
Hairspring: flat hairspring, duplex swan-neck fine adjustment for rate and beat
Shock protection: Incabloc
Remarks: very finely finished movement, screw-mounted gold chatons, hand-engraved balance cock

Caliber 90

Automatic; second-stop system; single mainspring barrel, 42-hour power reserve
Functions: hours and minutes (off-center), subsidiary seconds; panorama date, moon phase Diameter: 32.6 mm
Height: 5.4 mm
Jewels: 28
Balance: screw balance with 18 weight screws
Frequency: 28,800 vph
Hairspring: flat hairspring, duplex swan-neck fine adjustment for beat and rate
Shock protection: Incabloc
Remarks: very finely finished movement, three-quarter plate; with Glashütte ribbing, off-center skeletonized rotor, with 21ct gold oscillating mass

Caliber 91-04

Automatic; inverted movement construction with dial-side rate regulator; single spring barrel, 45-hour power reserve
Functions: hours and minutes (off-center), subsidiary seconds; panorama date, moon phase
Diameter: 38.2 mm
Height: 7.3 mm
Jewels: 53
Balance: screw balance with 18 weight screws
Frequency: 28,800 vph
Hairspring: flat hairspring, duplex-swan-neck fine regulator for beat and rate
Shock protection: Incabloc
Remarks: skeletonized rotor with 21-ct gold oscillating mass, hand-engraved balance bridge

Caliber 93-02

Automatic; flying tourbillon; single mainspring barrel, 48-hour power reserve
Functions: hours and minutes (off-center), subsidiary seconds (on the tourbillon cage); panorama date, moon phase
Diameter: 32.2 mm
Height: 7.65 mm
Jewels: 48, plus two diamond capstones
Balance: screw balance with 18 weight screws in the cage
Frequency: 21,600 vph
Hairspring: flat hairspring
Remarks: very finely finished movement, mainplate with Glashütte ribbing, off-center skeletonized rotor with 21ct gold oscillating mass

GRAHAM

In the mid-1990s, unusual creations gave an old English name in watchmaking a brand-new life. In the eighteenth century, George Graham perfected the cylinder escapement and the dead-beat escapement with a temperature compensated pendulum, and he built an orrery, a mechanical model of the solar system. Graham certainly earned the right to be considered one of the big wheels in watchmaking history.

Despite his merits in the development of precision timekeeping, it was the mechanism he invented to measure short times on clocks (a kind of chronograph) that became the trademark of his wristwatch company. It consisted of a second set of hands that could be engaged to or disengaged from the constant flow of energy of the movement. Not surprisingly, the current Graham collection includes quite a few fascinating chronograph variations.

In 2000, the company released the Chronofighter, with its striking thumb-controlled lever mechanism—a modern twist on a function designed for World War II British fighter pilots, who couldn't activate the crown button of their flight chronographs while wearing their thick gloves. The company has also started a special series to "give back," as it were. Made of a special carbon, this U.S. Navy SEAL Chronofighter also features a special camo look designed to help hide soldiers from satellite cameras. A part of the sales of these watches will go to the nonprofit Navy SEAL Foundation.

And as was to be expected, the carbon Chronofighters, which are much lighter than the stainless-steel versions, are now available as a separate line. And in 2024, the company reached way back into a pre-Graham past to design a Chronofighter pulsometer watch inspired from the 1920s.

The Fortress line has also been designed in the same military look but without the prominent lever on the side. Instead, the chronograph functions are selected by a single pusher that is on the left-hand side of the watch, housed in a large onion-shaped crown.

GRAHAM
Boulevard des Eplatures 38
CH-2300 La Chaux-de-Fonds
Switzerland

TEL.:
+41-32-910-9888

E-MAIL:
info@graham1695.com

WEBSITE:
www.graham1695.com

FOUNDED:
1995

NUMBER OF EMPLOYEES:
approx. 30

ANNUAL PRODUCTION:
5,000–7,000 watches

U.S. DISTRIBUTOR:
Graham Watchmakers
305-890-6409
m.leemon@graham1695.com

MOST IMPORTANT COLLECTIONS:
Chronofighter, Fortress, Geo.Graham, Silverstone, Swordfish

Chronofighter Vintage Bronze & Blue

Reference number: 2CVAK.U01A
Movement: automatic, Graham Caliber G1747; ø 30 mm, height 8 mm; 25 jewels; 28,800 vph; 48-hour power reserve
Functions: hours, minutes, subsidiary seconds; chronograph; date and weekday
Case: bronze, ø 44 mm, height 12 mm; sapphire crystal; transparent case back; crown with trigger on the left side; water-resistant to 10 atm
Band: leather, pin buckle
Price: $7,950
Variations: various straps and dial versions

Fortress City GMT

Reference number: 2FOBC.R01A
Movement: automatic, Graham Caliber G1725; ø 25.6 mm, height 3.8 mm; 26 jewels; 28,800 vph; 42-hour power reserve
Functions: hours, minutes, sweep seconds; additional 24-hour display (second time zone)
Case: stainless steel, ø 44 mm; unidirectional rotating bezel with ceramic insert and reference city names; sapphire crystal; transparent case back; crown with integrated pusher for adjustment of the GMT hand; water-resistant to 10 atm
Band: leather, pin buckle
Price: $6,450; limited to 50 pieces
Variations: various dial colors

Chronofighter Vintage Pulsometer Silver

Reference number: 2CVCS.S01A
Movement: automatic, Graham Caliber G1718; ø 30 mm, height 8 mm; 25 jewels; 28,800 vph; 48-hour power reserve
Functions: hours, minutes, subsidiary seconds; chronograph; date and weekday
Case: stainless steel, ø 44 mm; sapphire crystal; transparent case back; crown and pushers with trigger on the left side; water-resistant to 10 atm
Band: leather, pin buckle
Remarks: pulsometer scale on the dial
Price: $6,450; limited to 250 pieces
Variations: various straps and dial versions

GRAND SEIKO

In 2017, Shinji Hattori, president of the Seiko Watch Company, announced that the Grand Seiko line had become a separate *manufacture* brand with a very clear identity.

For the brand's fiftieth anniversary in 2010, the Grand Seiko collection was given a host of new models and started being sold in the European market.

What makes the Grand Seiko collection special is the "Spring Drive" technology invented by a Seiko engineer. It took twenty-eight years to perfect. It's mostly mechanical but with a small, crucial electronic regulating element to tame the energy from the mainspring. The caliber has been continuously improved over time, notably with the use of a special alloy called SPRON, used for the mainspring and the hairspring.

Recent models based on that platform include the Spring Drive Chronograph with the automatic caliber 9R86 with ratchet wheel control and vertical chronograph clutch. The caliber 9S86 Hi-Beat vibrates at 36,000 vph.

It's no surprise, then, that classic watch fans have welcomed the Grand Seikos into their midst. The look is just retro enough to hint at the company's original watches of the 1960s, and the innovations are vigorous enough to keep the brand in the public eye. In 2022, the high-end skeletonized constant-force tourbillon named "Kodo," which means "heartbeat" in Japanese, drew a lot of welcome attention. Indeed, its carefully tuned escapement sounds like a beating heart.

The Evolution 9 collection features an innovative design that is entirely in keeping with the Grand Seiko style of 1967. Next, there is the new 9SA4 hand-wound caliber running at 36,000 vph. The new caliber with 47 jewels features a power reserve indicator on the movement side and the in-house double impulse escapement, also used in the 9SA5 with automatic winding.

In 2025, this horological legacy reached a new pinnacle with the introduction of the Spring Drive Caliber 9RB2. It bears the designation U.F.A., or "Ultra Fine Accuracy," which is precision defined by accuracy over an entire year: ±20 seconds.

SEIKO HOLDINGS
Ginza, Chuo, Tokyo
Japan

WEBSITE:
www.grand-seiko.com

FOUNDED:
1960

NUMBER OF EMPLOYEES:
90,000 (for the entire holding)

U.S. DISTRIBUTOR:
Grand Seiko Corporation of America
2 Park Way Suite 2A
Upper Saddle River, NJ 07458
800-334-0962
info@grand-seiko.us.com
www.grand-seiko.us.com

MOST IMPORTANT COLLECTIONS/PRICE RANGE:
Elegance, Sport, Heritage / approx. $5,000 to $59,000

Evolution 9 Collection

"Tentagraph"
Reference number: SLGC007
Movement: automatic, Grand Seiko Caliber 9SC5; ø 33 mm, height 8 mm; 60 jewels; 36,000 vph; column-wheel control of chronograph functions; two spring barrels; antimagnetic to 4,800 A/m; 72-hour power reserve
Functions: hours, minutes, small seconds; chronograph; date
Case: titanium, ø 43.2 mm, height 15.3 mm; ceramic bezel; sapphire crystal; transparent case back; screw-down crown; water-resistant to 10 atm
Band: titanium, folding clasp, with safety lock
Price: $14,000

Heritage Collection

Mechanical Hi-Beat 36000
Reference number: SBGH368
Movement: automatic, Grand Seiko Caliber 9S85; ø 31.6 mm, height 5.18 mm; 37 jewels; 36,000 vph; antimagnetic to 4,800 A/m; 55-hour power reserve
Functions: hours, minutes, sweep seconds; date
Case: rose gold, ø 38 mm, height 12.9 mm; sapphire crystal; transparent case back; screw-down crown; water-resistant to 10 atm
Band: reptile skin, pin buckle
Price: $32,800

Evolution 9 Collection

Spring Drive "U.F.A."
Reference number: SLGB003
Movement: automatic, Grand Seiko Caliber 9RB2; ø 30 mm, height 5.02 mm; 34 jewels; electromagnetic "tri-synchro regulator" escapement with sliding wheel; antimagnetic to 4,800 A/m; 72-hour power reserve
Functions: hours, minutes, sweep seconds; date
Case: titanium, ø 37 mm, height 11.4 mm; sapphire crystal; transparent case back; screw-down crown; water-resistant to 10 atm
Band: titanium, folding clasp, with fine adjustment
Price: $10,900

Heritage Collection

62GS Mechanical Hi-Beat 36000
Reference number: SBGH343
Movement: automatic, Grand Seiko Caliber 9S85; ø 31.6 mm, height 5.18 mm; 37 jewels; 36,000 vph; antimagnetic to 4,800 A/m; 55-hour power reserve
Functions: hours, minutes, sweep seconds; date
Case: titanium, ø 38 mm, height 12.9 mm; sapphire crystal; transparent case back; screw-down crown; water-resistant to 10 atm
Band: titanium, folding clasp, with safety lock
Price: $7,900

Heritage Collection

62GS Mechanical Hi-Beat 36000
Reference number: SBGH341
Movement: automatic, Grand Seiko Caliber 9S85; ø 31.6 mm, height 5.18 mm; 37 jewels; 36,000 vph; antimagnetic to 4,800 A/m; 55-hour power reserve
Functions: hours, minutes, sweep seconds; date
Case: titanium, ø 38 mm, height 12.9 mm; sapphire crystal; transparent case back; screw-down crown; water-resistant to 10 atm
Band: titanium, folding clasp, with safety lock
Price: $7,900

Heritage Collection

Manual-winding Mechanical
Reference number: SBGW323
Movement: hand-wound, Grand Seiko Caliber 9S64; ø 28.4 mm; 24 jewels; 28,800 vph; antimagnetic to 4,800 A/m; 72-hour power reserve
Functions: hours, minutes, sweep seconds
Case: stainless steel, ø 36.5 mm, height 11.6 mm; sapphire crystal; water-resistant to 10 atm
Band: stainless steel, triple folding clasp
Price: $5,900

Heritage Collection

62GS Mechanical Hi-Beat 36000 "Rikka"
Reference number: SBGH351
Movement: automatic, Grand Seiko Caliber 9S85; ø 31.6 mm, height 5.18 mm; 37 jewels; 36,000 vph; antimagnetic to 4,800 A/m; 55-hour power reserve
Functions: hours, minutes, sweep seconds; date
Case: stainless steel, ø 40 mm, height 12.9 mm; sapphire crystal; transparent case back; screw-down crown; water-resistant to 10 atm
Band: stainless steel, triple folding clasp
Price: $7,500

Heritage Collection

62GS Mechanical Hi-Beat 36000 "Shūbun"
Reference number: SBGH353
Movement: automatic, Grand Seiko Caliber 9S85; ø 31.6 mm, height 5.18 mm; 37 jewels; 36,000 vph; antimagnetic to 4,800 A/m; 55-hour power reserve
Functions: hours, minutes, sweep seconds; date
Case: stainless steel, ø 40 mm, height 12.9 mm; sapphire crystal; transparent case back; screw-down crown; water-resistant to 10 atm
Band: stainless steel, triple folding clasp
Price: $7,500

Elegance Collection

Automatic GMT
Reference number: SBGM221
Movement: automatic, Grand Seiko Caliber 9S66; ø 28.4 mm; 35 jewels; 36,000 vph; antimagnetic to 4,800 A/m; 72-hour power reserve
Functions: hours, minutes, sweep seconds; additional 24-hour display (second time zone); date
Case: stainless steel, ø 39.5 mm, height 13.7 mm; sapphire crystal; transparent case back; water-resistant to 3 atm
Band: reptile skin, folding clasp
Price: $5,400

HABRING²

The name Habring² stands for Maria Kristina Habring and her husband, Richard. This very gifted, fun, and creative couple have been manufacturing fine mechanical works of art in a small workshop in Austria's Völkermarkt "You get two for one," Richard jokes with the ease of someone whose name, when uttered, triggers sage nodding. Before setting off on his own, he had a very distinguished career at IWC developing a split-seconds chronograph.

The couple's first watch labeled with their own name came out in 2004: a simple three-handed watch based on a refined and unostentatiously decorated ETA pocket watch movement, the Unitas 6498-1. The exceptional quality visible in every detail made Habring2 an instant success among connoisseurs.

Since then, they have worked on a wide range of products, notably their movements, like the Caliber A09, which is available in both a manual and a bidirectionally wound automatic version, or the versatile A11, which appears in numerous models with a few iterations. All the little details that differentiate this caliber are either especially commissioned or are made in-house. Its sporty version drives a pilot's watch.

Also more or less in-house are the components of Habring²'s Seconde Foudroyante, with the foudroyante mechanism fed by a separate spring barrel. For the twentieth anniversary of the IWC double chronograph, Habring² built a limited, improved edition. The movement, based on the ETA 7750 "Valjoux," was conceived in 1991/1992 with an additional module between the chronograph and automatic winder.

Suffice to say, the five-member team's technical sophistication is remarkable. They do not shy away from modern materials like silicon, or technologies, or ion etching. And if they can offer clever complications at a reasonable price, they will. The latest is a red dot in the "9" of the Chrono-Felix Top Second that flashes every five seconds.

HABRING UHRENTECHNIK OG
Konrad-Weg 1 / Top 12
A-8430 Leibnitz
Austria

TEL.:
+43 3452 86300

E-MAIL:
info@habring.com

WEBSITE:
www.habring2.com

FOUNDED:
1997

NUMBER OF EMPLOYEES:
7

ANNUAL PRODUCTION:
300 watches

U.S. RETAILERS:
Martin Pulli (USA-East)
877-897-8554
www.martinpulli.com

Brandon Skinner (USA-West)
760-815-1659
www.horologybythesea.com

MOST IMPORTANT COLLECTIONS/PRICE RANGE:
Felix / from $5,800; Erwin / from $7,200;
Doppel Felix / from $9,800; COS Felix / from $8,900

Oskar Pointer Date and Moon
Reference number: Oskar Pointer Date and Moon
Movement: hand-wound, Habring Caliber A11Ups; ø 30 mm, height 5.5 mm; 18 jewels; 28,800 vph; tangential screws for fine adjustment; antimagnetic escapement; finely finished movement; 48-hour power reserve
Functions: hours, minutes, small seconds; date, moon phase
Case: stainless steel, ø 38.5 mm, height 9 mm; sapphire crystal; transparent case back; water-resistant to 3 atm
Band: stainless steel, folding clasp
Price: $8,200

Oskar Moon
Reference number: Oskar Moon
Movement: hand-wound, Habring Caliber A11Ups; ø 30 mm, height 5.5 mm; 18 jewels; 28,800 vph; tangential screws for fine adjustment; antimagnetic escapement; finely finished movement; 48-hour power reserve
Functions: hours, minutes, small seconds; moon phase
Case: stainless steel, ø 38.5 mm, height 9 mm; sapphire crystal; transparent case back; water-resistant to 3 atm
Band: leather, pin buckle
Price: $7,150

Josef
Reference number: Josef
Movement: hand-wound, Habring Caliber A11GSP; ø 30 mm, height 6.25 mm; 21 jewels; 28,800 vph; tangential screws for fine adjustment; antimagnetic escapement; finely finished movement; 48-hour power reserve
Functions: hours (off-center), minutes, small seconds (jumping); power reserve indicator
Case: stainless steel, ø 38.5 mm, height 8.4 mm; sapphire crystal; transparent case back; water-resistant to 3 atm
Band: leather, pin buckle
Price: $8,800

Felix

Reference number: Felix
Movement: hand-wound, Habring Caliber A11B;
ø 30 mm, height 4.2 mm; 18 jewels; 28,800 vph; Triovis
fine regulation, finely finished movement; 48-hour
power reserve
Functions: hours, minutes, small seconds
Case: stainless steel, ø 38.5 mm, height 7 mm; sapphire
crystal; transparent case back; water-resistant to 3 atm
Band: leather, pin buckle
Price: $5,850

Erwin

Reference number: Erwin
Movement: hand-wound, Habring Caliber A11S;
ø 30 mm, height 5.7 mm; 21 jewels; 28,800 vph;
antimagnetic escapement with Carl-Haas hairspring,
finely finished movement; 48-hour power reserve
Functions: hours, minutes, sweep seconds (jumping)
Case: stainless steel, ø 38.5 mm, height 9 mm; sapphire
crystal; transparent case back; water-resistant to 3 atm
Band: leather, pin buckle
Price: $7,150
Variations: various dials

Chrono-Felix

Reference number: Chrono-Felix
Movement: automatic, Habring Caliber A11C-H1;
ø 30 mm, height 6.5 mm; 25 jewels; 28,800 vph;
tangential screws for fine adjustment; antimagnetic
escapement; monopusher control of chronograph
functions; 48-hour power reserve
Functions: hours, minutes, small seconds; chronograph
Case: stainless steel, ø 42 mm, height 11 mm; sapphire
crystal; transparent case back; water-resistant to 5 atm
Band: leather, pin buckle
Price: $8,350
Variations: various dials

Chrono-Felix Top Second

Reference number: Chrono-Felix Top Second
Movement: hand-wound, Habring Caliber A11C-H1;
ø 30 mm, height 7 mm; 25 jewels; 28,800 vph;
tangential screws for fine adjustment; antimagnetic
escapement; monopusher control of chronograph
functions; 48-hour power reserve
Functions: hours, minutes, rate display (blinking second
dot); chronograph
Case: stainless steel, ø 38.5 mm, height 11 mm;
sapphire crystal; transparent case back; water-resistant
to 3 atm
Band: textile, pin buckle
Price: $9,500

Doppel 38

Reference number: Doppel38
Movement: hand-wound, Habring Caliber A11R_
H1; ø 30 mm, height 7 mm; 27 jewels; 28,800 vph;
tangential screws for fine adjustment; antimagnetic
escapement; monopusher control of chronograph
functions; 48-hour power reserve
Functions: hours, minutes, small seconds; split-
seconds chronograph
Case: stainless steel, ø 38.5 mm, height 11.5 mm;
sapphire crystal; transparent case back; water-resistant
to 3 atm
Band: leather, pin buckle
Price: $10,915
Variations: various dials

Chrono-Felix Perpetual

Reference number: Chrono-Felix Perpetual
Movement: automatic, Habring Caliber A11CP;
ø 30 mm, height 7.3 mm; 25 jewels; 28,800 vph;
tangential screws for fine adjustment; antimagnetic
escapement; monopusher control of chronograph
functions; 48-hour power reserve
Functions: hours, minutes; chronograph; perpetual
calendar with date, weekday, month, moon phase, leap
year
Case: stainless steel, ø 38.5 mm, height 12 mm;
sapphire crystal; transparent case back; water-resistant
to 3 atm
Band: leather, pin buckle
Price: $27,750
Variations: with black dial and strap

HAGER

Keeping it simple is the best way to get things going. Hager, owned and operated by American service veteran Pierre "Pete" Brown, is simply named after Hagerstown where the company was started in 2009. The business model was equally streamlined: create high-quality and affordable automatic watches accessible to those who have never experienced the joy of owning a mechanical watch. The look: rugged and refined, for individuals with a sense of adventure in their bones.

It began with sports watches, classic divers. They were designed by Brown and his small team in Hagerstown. All the cues are there for the watch connoisseur, the brushed and polished cases with beveled edges, two-tiered stadium dial, with brass markers and hands outlined in black and coated with Super-LumiNova. The domed sapphire crystal, 120-click ceramic bezel and 24 click GMT ceramic bezels are also enhanced with Super-LumiNova. The cases are rated at 20 atm, meaning they are good for more than just washing the dishes. Inside them beats one of a variety of automatic winding Swiss and Japanese mechanical movements that are both encased and regulated in the USA. Lately, Hager has started making its own movements by using trusty ETA calibers as a basis.

Since its modest beginnings, Hager has expanded its line of watches and styles without, however, abandoning the sportive touch. It is why a number of models run on a convenient quart mechanism, like the new U2 Chronograph equipped with a Seiko Meca-Quartz caliber, which has a mechanical feel. For the elegant, yet casual dresser needing an everyday time-telling tool, there is the Pheon (an arrowhead), with a sandwich dial, or the square Interceptor, which was commissioned by a friend, Tom Wotring, whose father had flown an interceptor aircraft for a record number of hours. Affordable luxury, one might say. "We aren't just selling watches," he says, "we are selling the experience of owning a luxury timepiece."

HAGER WATCHES
36 South Potomac Street
Suite 204
Hagerstown, MD 21740

TEL.:
240-232-2172

E-MAIL:
info@hagerwatches.com

WEBSITE:
www.hagerwatches.com

FOUNDED:
2009

NUMBER OF EMPLOYEES:
2

ANNUAL PRODUCTION:
1,000 to 1,500 watches

MOST IMPORTANT COLLECTIONS/PRICE RANGE:
Commando, GMT Aquamariner, U2, Interceptor, Pheon / $550 to $3,000

Diplomat Freemason Edition
Reference Number: 21007
Movement: automatic, caliber MD7082 (base ETA 2895 clone stamped and assembled USA); ø 25.6 mm, height 4.35 mm; 28,800 vph; 27 jewels; 42-hour power reserve
Functions: hours, minutes, subsidiary seconds
Case: stainless steel with rose gold PVD; ø 40 mm, height 9.3 mm; screw-in crown; sapphire crystal; transparent case back; water-resistant to 5 atm
Band: leather, pin buckle
Price: $895
Variations: multiple color convex sunburst patterned dials

Hager National Security Agency (NSA) Echelon Limited Edition
Reference Number: 2025LE
Movement: quartz, GA2100 caliber digital
Functions: hours, minutes, seconds; date; world timer, stop watch, 5 daily alarm; LED light, hand shift feature (hands move out of the way to show digital display contents)
Case: stainless steel; ø 43.5 mm x 51 mm, height 12 mm; custom NSA case back; water resistant to 3 atm
Band: stainless steel with 2-button clasp and 2-button slidelock extension quick release system
Price: $650
Variations: blue/black ceramic insert with blue fumé dial; red/blue ceramic insert with blue fumé dial; black/sand ceramic insert with green fumé dial

Aquamariner SSN
Reference number: 6203N
Movement: automatic, Miyota 8215 caliber; ø 26 mm, height 5.67 mm; 21 jewels; 21,600 vph; 40 hours power reserve
Functions: hours, minutes, sweep seconds; date
Case: stainless steel ø 41 mm, height 13 mm; screw-in crown; unilateral bezel with blue ceramic insert; sapphire crystal; screwed-down case back; water-resistant to 30 atm
Band: stainless steel, folding clasp with slide lock extension
Price: $650
Variations: blue dial and blue ceramic insert; gilt dial and ceramic gilt insert

HAMILTON

Hamilton Watch Co. was founded in 1892 in Lancaster, Pennsylvania, and, within a very brief period, grew into one of the world's largest *manufactures*. Around the turn of the twentieth century, every second railway employee in the United States was carrying a Hamilton watch in his pocket. This ensured that not only were they able to make sure the trains were running punctually, but also they could assist in coordinating them and organizing schedules. And during World War II, the American army officers' kits included a service Hamilton.

Hamilton is the sole survivor of the large U.S. watchmakers—though only as a brand within the Swiss Swatch Group. At one time, Hamilton had itself owned a piece of the Swiss watchmaking industry in the form of the Büren brand in the 1960s and 1970s. As part of a joint venture with Heuer-Leonidas, Breitling, and Dubois Dépraz, Hamilton-Büren also made a significant contribution to the development of the automatic chronograph.

Just prior in its history, the tuning fork watch pioneer was all the rage when it took the new movement technology and housed it in a modern case created by renowned industrial designer Richard Arbib. The triangular Ventura took the watch world by storm in 1957, in what was truly a frenzy of innovation that benefited the brand especially in the U.S. market. The American spirit of freedom and belief in progress evoked by this model, ideals reflected in Hamilton's current marketing, are taken quite seriously by its designers—even those working in Biel/Bienne, Switzerland. Today's collections are more focused on ostentatious "adventure" and aviator watches. But the brand also continues to create revamped versions of its classics, like the aforementioned Ventura and the digital PSR.

HAMILTON INTERNATIONAL LTD.
Mattenstrasse 149
CH- 2503 Biel/Bienne
Switzerland

TEL.:
+41-32-343-4004

E-MAIL:
info@hamiltonwatch.com

WEBSITE:
www.hamiltonwatch.com
shop.hamiltonwatch.com

FOUNDED:
1892

U.S. DISTRIBUTOR:
Hamilton
Swatch Group (US), Inc.
800 Waterford Way, Suite 1000
Miami, FL 33126
800-234-8463
Hamilton.US@swatchgroup.com

PRICE RANGE:
between approx. $500 and $2,800

Khaki Field Murph 38mm
Reference number: H70405130
Movement: automatic, Hamilton Caliber H-10 (base ETA C07.611); ø 25.6 mm, height 4.6 mm; 25 jewels; 21,600 vph; 80-hour power reserve
Functions: hours, minutes, sweep seconds
Case: stainless steel; ø 38 mm; height 11.1 mm; sapphire crystal; water-resistant to 10 atm
Band: stainless steel, folding clasp
Price: $1,045

Khaki Field Automatic
Reference number: H70605160
Movement: automatic, Hamilton Caliber H-10 (base ETA C07.611); ø 25.6 mm, height 4.6 mm; 25 jewels; 21,600 vph; 80-hour power reserve
Functions: hours, minutes, sweep seconds; date
Case: stainless steel; ø 42 mm; height 11 mm; sapphire crystal; water-resistant to 10 atm
Band: stainless steel, folding clasp
Price: $845
Variations: with blue dial; with leather strap $795)

Khaki Field Quartz
Reference number: H69301960
Movement: quartz
Functions: hours, minutes, sweep seconds
Case: stainless steel; ø 33 mm, height 7.55 mm; sapphire crystal; water-resistant to 5 atm
Band: textile, pin buckle
Price: $445
Variations: with black, blue, or white dial; with stainless-steel bracelet

Jazzmaster Performer Auto Chrono

Reference number: H36646780
Movement: automatic, Hamilton Caliber H-31 (base ETA 7753); ø 30 mm, height 7.9 mm; 27 jewels; 28,800 vph; 60-hour power reserve
Functions: hours, minutes, subsidiary seconds; chronograph; date
Case: stainless steel with black PVD coating; ø 42 mm; height 15.2 mm; sapphire crystal; water-resistant to 10 atm
Band: leather, folding clasp
Price: $2,695

Jazzmaster Open Heart Auto 42mm

Reference number: H32705140
Movement: automatic, Hamilton Caliber H-10 (base ETA C07.611); ø 25.6 mm, height 4.6 mm; 25 jewels; 21,600 vph; 80-hour power reserve
Functions: hours, minutes, sweep seconds
Case: stainless steel; ø 42 mm; height 11.5 mm; sapphire crystal; transparent case back; water-resistant to 5 atm
Band: stainless steel, folding clasp
Remarks: partially skeletonized dial
Price: $1,295
Variations: with green dial; with leather strap ($1,245)

American Classic Intra-Matic Auto Chrono

Reference number: H38446731
Movement: automatic, Hamilton Caliber H-31 (base ETA A05.231); ø 30 mm, height 7.9 mm; 27 jewels; 28,800 vph; 60-hour power reserve
Functions: hours, minutes, subsidiary seconds; chronograph; date
Case: stainless steel with black PVD coating; ø 40 mm; height 14.45 mm; sapphire crystal; screw-down crown; water-resistant to 10 atm
Band: leather, pin buckle
Price: $2,625
Variations: with white or orange tachymeter scale

Khaki Navi Scuba GMT

Reference number: H82565930
Movement: automatic, Hamilton Caliber H-14 (base ETA C07.661); ø 25.6 mm, height 4.6 mm; 23 jewels; 21,600 vph; 80-hour power reserve
Functions: hours, minutes, sweep seconds; additional 24-hour display (second time zone); date
Case: bronze; ø 43 mm; height 13.9 mm; bezel with ceramic insert, unidirectionally rotatable, with 24-hour scale; sapphire crystal; screw-down crown; water-resistant to 30 atm
Band: textile, pin buckle
Price: $1,675
Variations: in stainless steel with stainless-steel bracelet ($1,525)

Khaki Aviation Pilot Pioneer

Reference number: H76709510
Movement: hand-wound, ETA Caliber 6498-1 ("Unitas"); ø 36.6 mm, height 4.5 mm; 17 jewels; 18,000 vph; 46-hour power reserve
Functions: hours, minutes, subsidiary seconds
Case: bronze; ø 43 mm; height 13 mm; unidirectionally rotatable bezel with 0–60 scale; sapphire crystal; water-resistant to 10 atm
Band: leather, pin buckle
Price: $1,795
Variations: in stainless steel with 38-mm case ($1,495)

Khaki Aviation X-Wind Auto Chrono

Reference number: H77506540
Movement: automatic, Hamilton Caliber H-21 (base ETA A05.H21); ø 30 mm, height 7.9 mm; 25 jewels; 28,800 vph; 60-hour power reserve; COSC-certified chronometer
Functions: hours, minutes, subsidiary seconds; chronograph; date and weekday
Case: stainless steel; ø 44 mm; height 15.6 mm; crown-adjusted scale ring with slide rule for calculating drift angle in crosswinds; sapphire crystal; transparent case back; screw-down crown; water-resistant to 10 atm
Band: leather, pin buckle
Price: $2,095
Variations: with green dial

HANHART

The reputation of this rather special company goes all the way back to 1920, when one Wilhelm Hanhart noticed that chronographs were not easy to come by. That meant a market niche, and he aimed to step into it. And so, in 1924, he founded a company to manufacture affordable and robust stopwatches, pocket watches, and chronograph wristwatches. These core instruments were exactly what fans of functional tool watches wanted, and enthusiasm grew when the company gradually left behind its quartz experiments of the 1980s and refocused on its rich and honorable heritage. A new collection was taking shape, raising expectations for what was to come. Backing from the Gaydoul Group provided the financial foundation to restart momentum.

Hanhart rebuilt its name with one foot in Switzerland and the other in Gütenbach in southern Germany, but the brand began to drift after the 2009 recession. Following bankruptcy, the company reorganized under the name Hanhart 1822 GmbH and consolidated all operations in its German hometown. It also returned to its stylistic roots: the signature red start/stop pusher once again defines the collections, including the bi-compax chronographs of the Racemaster line, which feature a smooth bezel.

Pilots' chronographs have never lost their appeal, and Hanhart was already producing them in the 1930s—most notably the Caliber 41 and the Tachy Tele, both with asymmetrical pushers and the characteristic red pusher. These timepieces were built to withstand extreme conditions, from shocks to severe temperature fluctuations. Hanhart's long tradition and expertise in aviation chronographs resonated with the Austrian Army, which commissioned a special edition of the Primus series certified by the military and featuring the coat of arms of the Austrian Air Force on the dial. The 417 ES series continues this military lineage; it served as a chronograph for the German Air Force around the time of its postwar reconstruction.

HANHART 1882 GMBH
Hauptstrasse 33
D-78148 Gütenbach
Germany

TEL.:
+49-7723-93-44-0

FAX:
+49-7723-93-44-40

E-MAIL:
info@hanhart.com

WEBSITE:
www.hanhart.com

FOUNDED:
1882 in Diessenhofen, Switzerland; in Germany since 1902

NUMBER OF EMPLOYEES:
22

ANNUAL PRODUCTION:
approx. 1,000 chronographs and 30,000 stopwatches

U.S. DISTRIBUTOR:
WatchBuys
888-333-4895
www.watchbuys.com

MOST IMPORTANT COLLECTIONS/PRICE RANGE:
Mechanical stopwatches / from approx. $600;
Pioneer / from approx. $1,070; Primus / from approx. $2,400

Preventor HD12

Reference number: 792.870-6429
Movement: automatic, Sellita Caliber SW200-1; ø 25.6 mm, height 4.6 mm; 26 jewels; 28,800 vph; 38-hour power reserve
Functions: hours, minutes, sweep seconds
Case: hardened stainless steel, ø 39 mm, height 10.5 mm; sapphire crystal; water-resistant to 15 atm
Band: stainless steel with transparent PVD coating, folding clasp
Price: $1,660

415 ES Pure Chronograph

Reference number: H703.215-8010
Movement: hand-wound, Sellita Caliber SW510 M; ø 30 mm, height 7.9 mm; 23 jewels; 28,800 vph; antimagnetic to 16,000 A/m; 58-hour power reserve
Functions: hours, minutes, subsidiary seconds; chronograph
Case: stainless steel, ø 39 mm, height 13.5 mm; bidirectional bezel with 0–60 scale; sapphire crystal; water-resistant to 10 atm
Band: leather, pin buckle
Price: $3,180

Aquasphere FreeFall Blue

Reference number: 772.270-6428
Movement: automatic, Sellita Caliber SW200-1; ø 25.6 mm, height 4.6 mm; 26 jewels; 28,800 vph; 38-hour power reserve
Functions: hours, minutes, sweep seconds
Case: stainless steel, ø 42 mm, height 12.95 mm; unidirectional ceramic bezel with 0–60 scale; sapphire crystal; water-resistant to 30 atm
Band: stainless steel, folding clasp
Price: $2,170
Variations: on blue strap ($1,870)

HAUTLENCE

Time can be read in so many ways. Back in 2004, after spending years in the Swiss watch industry, Guillaume Tetu and Renaud de Retz decided that their idea for tracking it was new and unique. They were not watchmakers, but they knew whom to bring on board for the genesis of Hautlence, an anagram of Neuchâtel, the town where their small company made its debut. And soon, the first HL model was produced: a large, rectangular timepiece with the ratios of a television set and a lively and visible mechanical life, with connecting rods between a retrograde minute and an hour chain, and other mechanical oddities.

But the road to finding that ideal balance between intricate engineering and design and public perception is often rocky. Fast forward to the 2020s… Hautlence is now a (founding) member of MELB Holding, headed by two men steeped in the watch business, Georges-Henri Meylan (formerly of Audemars Piguet) and former Breguet CFO Bill Muirhead. The industrial look with the "television" proportions has become the only Hautlence shape, though it has been given a more distinctive shape, with rounded edges. The use of blue rubber straps has also given the company a clear profile. More importantly, engineering has evolved and become more subtle, though no less complicated.

This all led to the "Sphere," a ball shaped, jumping hour display and retrograde minutes.

At the 2023 Grand Prix d'Horlogerie in Geneva, the watch captured the Innovation Prize. In the meantime, the Series 2 has been released. The dial is a granular rose gold covering, looking like a sandy backdrop to the blue minute numerals.

Two other collections, the Linear Series 1 and the Vagabonde, allow the company to experiment with other complications, like tourbillons, or with designs and finishing that can fit on the space afforded by the "television set." The most recent of the series has a spiderweb-like design in Super-LumiNova on the dial. In 2025, the Linear came out with an homage to the former motorcyclist Giacomo "Ago" Agostini.

HAUTLENCE
Rundbuckstrasse 10
CH - 8212 Neuhausen am Rheinfall
Switzerland

TEL.
+41-32-924-00-60

E-MAIL:
info@hautlence.com

WEBSITE:
www.hautlence.com

FOUNDED:
2004

NUMBER OF EMPLOYEES:
10

ANNUAL PRODUCTION:
150–200 watches

U.S. DISTRIBUTOR:
Westime
8569 Westime Sunset Boulevard
West Hollywood, CA 90069
310-289-0808
info@westime.com
www.westime.com

MOST IMPORTANT COLLECTIONS:
Concepts d'Exception, Vagabonde Series 4, Linear Series 1

The Linear – Giacomo Agostini
Reference number: AD50-ST04
Movement: automatic, in-house D50; 32.8 mm x 37.4 mm x 8.7 mm; 39 jewels; 21,600 vph; double hairspring tourbillon with bidirectional pawl winding system; 72-hour power reserve
Functions: linear retrograde jumping hours, 1 minute flying tourbillon
Case: stainless steel, 50.8 mm × 43 mm, height 12.2 mm; polished and engraved steel crown with rubber ring; transparent case back; water-resistant to 10 atm
Band: red rubber, steel pin buckle
Remark: tribute to motorbike speed rider Giacomo Agostini; large 15 on minutes track for Agostini's racing number and 15 victories
Price: $77,500; limited to 28 pieces

The Vagabonde Tourbillon Series 5
Reference number: AD30-ST03
Movement: automatic, in-house D30 caliber; ø 32.6 mm, height 8.25 mm; 39 jewels; 21,600 vph; double hairspring tourbillon with bidirectional pawl winding system; decorated and finished by hand; 72-hour power reserve
Functions: wandering hours and minutes, 1 minute flying tourbillon
Case: stainless steel with blue PVD; 50.8 mm × 43 mm x 12.2 mm; polished and engraved steel crown with rubber ring; beveled sapphire crystal; transparent case back; water-resistant to 10 atm
Band: white rubber, steel pin buckle with blue PVD coating
Remarks: base dial with blue PVD structure and white SuperLumiNova
Price: $69,900; limited to 28 pieces

The Helix Series 1
Reference number: CD51-TI00
Movement: automatic, in-house D51 caliber; 30.6 mm x 39.6 mm x 12.5 mm; 21,600 vph; 36 jewels; microrotor, openworked dial, central tourbillon with cylindrical hairspring; 65-hour power reserve
Functions: hours and minutes (both retrograde)
Case: titanium; 45.10 mm x 37 mm x 16.7 mm; polished and engraved titanium crown with rubber ring; domed sapphire crystal; water-resistant to 10 atm
Band: grey rubber with fabric inserts, titanium pin buckle
Remarks: blued openworked hands
Price: $82,500; limited to 28 pieces

HEDONE WATCH

In the many and often endless deliberations by professional and amateur thinkers, the branch of philosophy known as hedonism often gets a bad name. This is partly due to the fact that it seems to fly in the face of a capitalist work ethic that demands suffering. Yet, there is something to say about taking pleasure in life itself. After all, what would be the point of living otherwise?

The question is: Does the name Hedone mean anything special in Chinese? No, says Jacky Wong, it's a reference to hedonism, having a positive attitude, and doing things with good humor and fun.

By the same token, one of the brand's most noticeable—or iconic—models is the Philosophe, which borrows the famous yin-yang symbol from Daoism for the design of the dial. On the one side is the yin principle, the receptive, passive principle, third dimensional existence, perhaps. The oscillating balance, which appears on the dial as well is the active principle, the yang, the spiritual. The day/night indicator is also a reminder of this duality.

Hedone founder and CEO Jacky Wong literally grew up with watches, spending summer vacations with his father at his watch factory. His dream was to follow in the paternal footsteps, so for the past twenty years, he has been involved in watches. "End users often buy into a brand, or follow a designer label, and the actual aesthetics and function of the timepieces often becomes the secondary concern," he said in an interview. "I want to correct that, and bring back affordable, beautiful watches that are truly a joy to own."

Armed with a team that can rework and assemble movements and watches in-house, Wong has explored several aesthetic avenues. The Architect line features a sober dial with a clever day and month date appearing on two parallel slits on the dial. The Sculpteur collection is a classic skeleton watch, a kind of complication the brand has extended to the ladies' watches, which feature a bridge shaped like a rose. Finally, Wong has a line of hand-painted dials celebrating the Hong Kong movie scene, which has made a number of cult movies already.

HEDONE COMPANY
Flat A-6, 9th Floor,
Block A, Mai Hing Industrial Building,
16-18 Hing Yip Street,
Kwun Tong, Kowloon,
Hong Kong

TEL.:
+852-234-184-36

EMAIL:
info@hedone-watch.com

WEBSITE:
www.hedone-watch.com

NUMBER OF EMPLOYEES:
8

DISTRIBUTION:
Online sales and through the company website

MOST IMPORTANT COLLECTIONS AND PRICES:
Philosophe, Sculpteur, Architect, La Rose / $485 to $1,200

Hong Kong Watch

Movement: automatic, Ronda R150 caliber, ø 26.00 mm, height 4.40 mm; 25 jewels; 28,800 vph; 40-hour power reserve
Functions: hours, minutes, sweep seconds; day/date on two arched apertures
Case: stainless steel; ø 42 mm, height 10.8 mm; sapphire crystal; transparent case back; water-resistant to 5 atm
Band: calfskin, pin buckle
Remarks: dial with hand-painted scenes from Hong Kong movies
Price: on request
Variations: various color schemes

Philosophe

Reference number: H1001.0001
Movement: automatic, HM8202 caliber, ø 31.00 mm, height 5.75 mm; 20 jewels; 21,600 vph; rotor decorated with côtes de Genève; escapement on the dial; 36 hours power reserve
Functions: hours, minutes; day/night indicator
Case: stainless steel; ø 44 mm, height 12.5 mm; sapphire crystal; transparent case back; water-resistant to 3 atm
Band: calfskin, pin buckle
Price: $485
Variations: various color schemes

Sculpteur

Reference number: H4102.0006
Movement: hand-wound, HM7130; ø 36.60 mm, height 4.23 mm, 17 jewels; 21,600 vph; skeletonized movement, with blue PVD on bridges; 42-hour power reserve
Functions: hours, minutes
Case: stainless steel, ø 42 mm, height 10.8 mm; sapphire glass, transparent case back, water-resistant to 5 atm
Band: calfskin, pin buckle
Price: $1,160
Variations: with various colored bridges ($1,250)

HERMÈS

Thierry Hermès's timing was perfect. When he founded his saddlery in Paris in 1837, France's middle class was rising, spending money on beautiful goods and activities like horseback riding. Hermès quickly became a household name and a symbol of good taste—not too flashy, not trendy, but practical and timeless. The advent of the automobile sparked demand for luggage, bags, and headgear. Hermès, still family-owned today, diversified its product range over time—foulards, fashion, porcelain, glass, perfume, and gold jewelry now form integral parts of its portfolio.

Watches were a natural extension, particularly with the rise of the wristwatch before World War I. Hermès even produced a timepiece that could be worn on a belt. However, it wasn't until later that the company fully embraced "real" watchmaking. In 1978, La Montre Hermès opened its watch manufactory in Biel/Bienne.

Hermès went all-in to acquire genuine expertise in watchmaking. "Our philosophy is all about the quality of time," says CEO Laurent Dordet. "It's about imagination; we want people to dream." The path to this vision was through "poetic" complications, allowing Hermès to navigate between elegant yet simple watches and more intricate timepieces filled with complications. These are sometimes crafted in collaboration with external designers and movement makers. One recent example is the Arceau Le Temps Voyageur (time as traveler), a collaboration with Chronode in Le Locle.

Hermès watches feature unique hand movements with varying speeds, hands that can be stopped, captivating moon phase and time zone displays, as well as charming countdown functions.

In 2023, the brand introduced the modern H08 chronograph, made from a unique combination of materials: a carbon case paired with a titanium crown. A year later, a completely new sports watch joined the collection in a medium-sized format. This model stylistically departs from established norms, with a sharply geometric circle for the bezel, contrasting with the soft roundness of the case. The brushed stainless-steel case contrasts with the polished surfaces on the sides, highlighting the meticulous, handcrafted finish. The perfectly proportioned 36 mm watch is equipped with the first-class Hermès Manufacture caliber H1912 with automatic winding.

LA MONTRE HERMÈS SA
Erlenstrasse 31A
CH-2555 Brügg
Switzerland

TEL.:
+41-32-545-0400

E-MAIL:
lmh.reception@hermes.com

WEBSITE:
www.hermes.com

FOUNDED:
1978

NUMBER OF EMPLOYEES:
344

U.S. DISTRIBUTOR:
CHEK AVEC LINDSEY – Attente retour JEA
Hermès of Paris, Inc.
55 East 59th Street
New York, NY 10022
800-441-4488
www.hermes.com

MOST IMPORTANT COLLECTIONS/PRICE RANGE:
Arceau, Cape Cod, Faubourg, Galop d'Hermès, Heure H, H08, Cut, Klikti, Kelly, Medor, Slim d'Hermès /
$2,800 to $600,000
All prices subject to change

Arceau "Le Temps Suspendu"

Reference number: 408234WW00
Movement: automatic, Hermès Caliber H1837; ø 26 mm, height 3.7 mm; 28 jewels; 28,800 vph; time display can be interrupted by a pusher (the hands can be "parked" and then "returned" to the right time); 45-hour power reserve
Functions: hours, minutes; "Time suspended" mode; date (retrograde)
Case: white gold, ø 42 mm; sapphire crystal; transparent case back; water-resistant to 3 atm
Band: reptile skin, folding clasp
Remarks: skeletonized dial
Price: $48,100
Variations: with red "saddler" dial and strap ($48,100); in rose gold ($44,900)

Cut "Le Temps Suspendu"

Reference number: 408060WW00
Movement: automatic, Hermès Caliber H1912; ø 23.9 mm, height 3.7 mm; 28 jewels; 28,800 vph; time display can be interrupted by a pusher (the hands can be "parked" and then "returned" to the right time); finely finished movement; 50-hour power reserve
Functions: hours, minutes, subsidiary seconds
Case: rose gold, ø 39 mm; sapphire crystal; transparent case back; water-resistant to 10 atm
Band: rose gold, folding clasp
Price: $54,420
Variations: with white dial ($58,525); with white dial and rubber strap ($38,100); with white dial and diamond bezel ($65,325)

Arceau "Le Temps Voyageur"

Reference number: 404995WW00
Movement: automatic, Hermès Caliber H1837 (with "Le Temps Voyageur" module) ø 26 mm, height 3.7 mm; 28 jewels; 28,800 vph; 45-hour power reserve
Functions: hours and minutes (off-center, peripheral rotation); dual time display with city indications (second time zone)
Case: white gold, ø 41 mm; pusher-activated satellite dial rotating around a ring dial with reference city names; sapphire crystal; transparent case back; water-resistant to 3 atm
Band: reptile skin, pin buckle
Remarks: the "continents" on the world map on the dial are fictitious and named after equestrian terms echoing the world of Hermès
Price: $46,825

Arceau 18.3.7

Reference number: 407913WW00
Movement: automatic, Hermès Caliber H1837;
ø 26 mm, height 3.7 mm; 28 jewels; 28,800 vph; finely
finished movement; 50-hour power reserve
Functions: hours, minutes
Case: white gold, ø 41 mm; sapphire crystal; transparent
case back; water-resistant to 3 atm
Band: calfskin, pin buckle
Remarks: the model name is a reference to the year
of Hermès' founding, 1837; dial with leather inserts, a
motive by Geoff McFetridge
Price: $45,000

Arceau Rocabar de Rire

Reference number: 408274WW00
Movement: automatic, Hermès Caliber H1837;
ø 26 mm, height 3.7 mm; 28 jewels; 28,800 vph; finely
finished movement; 50-hour power reserve
Functions: hours, minutes
Case: white gold, ø 41 mm; sapphire crystal; transparent
case back; water-resistant to 3 atm
Band: reptile skin pin buckle
Remarks: dial crafted with horsehair marquetry,
adorned with an engraved and hand-painted
horse head-shaped appliqué, designed by Dimitri
Rybaltchenko; horse head sticks its tongue out on
pressing a pusher; limited to 12 pieces
Price: $162,600

Slim d'Hermès Cheval brossé

Reference number: 407968WW00
Movement: automatic, Hermès Caliber H1950;
ø 30 mm, height 2.6 mm; 29 jewels; 21,600 vph; micro-
rotor; 48-hour power reserve
Functions: hours, minutes
Case: white gold, ø 39.5 mm, height 8.11 mm; sapphire
crystal; transparent case back; water-resistant to 3 atm
Band: reptile skin, pin buckle
Remarks: enameled dial, horse made by tampography;
limited to 24 pieces
Price: $47,800

Arceau Petite Lune

Reference number: 403957WW00
Movement: automatic, Hermès Caliber H1837 (base
with "Petite Lune" module); ø 26 mm, height 3.7 mm;
28 jewels; 28,800 vph; finely finished movement;
42-hour power reserve Functions: hours, minutes; moon
phase
Case: stainless steel, ø 38 mm; bezel set with
99 diamonds; sapphire crystal; transparent case back;
crown with diamond cabochon; water-resistant to 3 atm
Band: reptile skin, pin buckle
Remarks: dial with 15 diamonds
Price: $19,875
Variations: various cases, straps, and dials

Maillon Libre Brooch

Reference number: 408281WW00
Movement: quartz
Functions: hours, minutes
Case: white gold, ø 35 mm; bezel set with 65 diamonds;
sapphire crystal
Remarks: watch can be used as a brooch; with
diamonds, a tourmaline, and two baguette-cut
diamonds
Price: $72,600

Maillon Libre Wristwatch

Reference number: 408209WW00
Movement: quartz
Functions: hours, minutes
Case: white gold, ø 28 mm; bezel set with 38 diamonds;
sapphire crystal
Band: white gold with diamonds, folding clasp
Price: From $258,100

H. MOSER & CIE.

H. Moser & Cie has been making a name for itself in the industry as a serious watchmaker, though not averse to flashes of humor, like the Swiss Mad (sic) Watch made of Vacherin cheese it presented in 2017 (the cheese for the case is mixed with a hardening resin). And there's the Swiss Alp watch, made to look like an Apple Watch, but with all the essential Moser codes: streamlined design, top-notch technical implementation.

The company was originally founded in Le Locle in 1825 by one Heinrich Moser (1805–1874), from Schaffhausen, at the tender age of twenty-one. Soon after, he moved to Saint Petersburg, Russia, where ambitious watchmakers were enjoying a good market. In 1828, H. Moser & Cie. was brought to life—a brand resuscitated in modern times by a group of investors and watch experts together with Moser's great-grandson, Roger Nicholas Balsiger.

With the support of a host of Swiss and German specialists, the company returned to quality fundamentals. Its claim to fame is movements that contain a separate, removable escapement module supporting the pallet lever, escape wheel, and balance. The latter is fitted with the Straumann spring, made by Precision Engineering, another one of the Moser Group companies.

This small company has considerable technical know-how, which is probably what attracted MELB Holding, owners of Hautlence, as an investor. Under a new CEO, the brand redefined its style: understatement, soft tones, humor, and subtle technicity. A buy-in to the Genevan movement maker Agenhor will no doubt extend the company's technical abilities.

Moser & Cie.'s three core collections—Endeavour, Venturer, and Pioneer—feature "clean" dials in solid colors, including the blackest black, called Vantablack. The month hand on the Endeavour is a mere arrowhead in the center of the dial that points to the hours, which double as the months. The minimalism extends to watches that would otherwise clamor for more complexity. The Streamliner collection celebrated its fifth anniversary in 2025 with a successful modernization and a collaboration with the top-tier watchmakers Agenhor. To consolidate this alliance, MELB Holdings has even invested in the company, which is promising for the future.

H. MOSER & CIE
Rundbuckstrasse 10
CH-8212 Neuhausen am Rheinfall
Switzerland

TEL.:
+41-52-674-0050

E-MAIL:
info@h-moser.com

WEBSITE:
www.h-moser.com

FOUNDED:
1828

NUMBER OF EMPLOYEES:
80+

ANNUAL PRODUCTION:
approx. 2,000 watches

U.S. DISTRIBUTOR:
Melb Americas
info@melb-americas.com

MOST IMPORTANT COLLECTIONS/PRICE RANGE:
Endeavour / approx. $17,500 to $352,000; Pioneer / approx. $14,200 to $86,900; Streamliner / approx. $21,900 to $175,000; Heritage / approx. $15,300 to $290,000; concept watches

Streamliner Alpine Drivers Edition

Reference number: 6700-1200
Movement: automatic, Moser Caliber HMC 700; ø 34.4 mm, height 7.3 mm; 55 jewels; 21,600 vph; escapement with Straumann hairspring, bridges and mainplate coated anthracite rhodium, dial-side rotor with skeletonized tungsten oscillating mass; 72-hour power reserve
Functions: hours, minutes; flyback chronograph
Case: stainless steel with blue PVD, ø 42.3 mm, height 14.2 mm; sapphire crystal; transparent case back; screw-down crown; water-resistant to 12 atm
Band: rubber, pin buckle
Remarks: skeletonized mainplate and dial
Price: $74,400

Streamliner Flyback Chronograph Automatic "Frozen"

Reference number: 6907-1205
Movement: automatic, Moser Caliber HMC 907; ø 34.4 mm, height 7.3 mm; 55 jewels; 21,600 vph; escapement with Straumann hairspring, bridges and mainplate coated anthracite rhodium; 72-hour power reserve
Functions: hours, minutes; flyback chronograph
Case: stainless steel, ø 42.3 mm, height 14.2 mm; sapphire crystal; transparent case back; screw-down crown; water-resistant to 12 atm
Band: stainless steel, folding clasp
Price: $59,300
Variations: with blue dial; with rubber strap

Endeavour Centre Seconds Concept Purple Enamel

Reference number: 1201-1200
Movement: automatic, Moser Caliber HMC 201; ø 32 mm, height 5.5 mm; 27 jewels; 21,600 vph; escapement with Straumann hairspring, skeletonized bridges; 72-hour power reserve
Functions: hours, minutes, sweep seconds
Case: stainless steel, ø 40 mm, height 11.2 mm; sapphire crystal; transparent case back; water-resistant to 3 atm
Band: kudu leather, pin buckle
Remarks: structured enamel dial
Price: $34,100

Endeavour Tourbillon Concept Turquoise Enamel

Reference number: 1805-0400
Movement: automatic, Moser Caliber HMC 805; ø 32 mm, height 5.5 mm; 21,600 vph; flying 1-minute tourbillon, Straumann double hairspring, skeletonized bridges, red-gold oscillating mass; 72-hour power reserve
Functions: hours, minutes
Case: red gold, ø 40 mm, height 11.2 mm; sapphire crystal; transparent case back; screw-down crown; water-resistant to 3 atm
Band: ostrich leather, pin buckle
Remarks: structured enamel dial
Price: $94,500

Endeavour Small Seconds Concept "Pop"

Reference number: 1202-1203
Movement: automatic, Moser Caliber HMC 202; ø 32 mm, height 5.5 mm; 27 jewels; 21,600 vph; escapement with Straumann hairspring, skeletonized bridges, gold oscillating mass; 72-hour power reserve
Functions: hours, minutes, small seconds
Case: stainless steel, ø 38 mm, height 10.4 mm; sapphire crystal; transparent case back; water-resistant to 3 atm
Band: ostrich leather, pin buckle
Remarks: jade and opal dial; limited to 28 pieces
Price: $38,500
Variations: various limited color variations

Pioneer Spiced Aqua

Reference number: 3201-1202
Movement: automatic, Moser Caliber HMC 201; ø 32 mm, height 5.5 mm; 27 jewels; 21,600 vph; flying 1-minute tourbillon, Straumann double hairspring, anthracite finish with double stripe, engraved oscillating mass; 72-hour power reserve
Functions: hours, minutes, sweep seconds (hacking)
Case: stainless steel, ø 40 mm, height 10.6 mm; sapphire crystal; transparent case back; screw-down crown; water-resistant to 12 atm
Band: rubber, pin buckle
Price: $18,300

Pioneer Sunny-Side Up

Reference number: 3201-1200
Movement: automatic, Moser Caliber HMC 201; ø 32 mm, height 5.5 mm; 27 jewels; 21,600 vph; flying 1-minute tourbillon, Straumann double hairspring, anthracite finish with double stripe, engraved oscillating mass; 72-hour power reserve
Functions: hours, minutes, sweep seconds (hacking)
Case: stainless steel, ø 40 mm, height 10.6 mm; sapphire crystal; transparent case back; screw-down crown; water-resistant to 12 atm
Band: rubber, pin buckle
Price: $17,500

Caliber HMC 812

Hand-wound; exchangeable escapement with gold pallet lever and escape wheel; "flash calendar" functions correctable forward and backward; twin 2 spring barrels; 168-hour power reserve
Functions: hours, minutes, sweep seconds; power reserve indicator; perpetual calendar with date, sweep month, leap year indicator on movement side
Diameter: 34 mm
Height: 6.3 mm
Jewels: 33
Balance: glucydur
Frequency: 18,000 vph
Hairspring: Straumann
Shock protection: Incabloc

Caliber HMC 500

Automatic; platinum micro-rotor; double spring barrel, 74-hour power reserve
Functions: hours, minutes, subsidiary seconds
Diameter: 30 mm
Height: 4.5 mm
Jewels: 26
Frequency: 21,600 vph
Hairspring: Straumann
Remarks: finely finished movement

HUBLOT

Ever since Hublot moved into a new, modern, spacious factory building in Nyon, near Geneva, the brand has evolved with stunning speed. The growth has been such that Hublot has even built a second factory, which is even bigger than the first. The ground-breaking ceremony took place on March 3, 2014, and the man holding the spade was then-Hublot chairman Jean-Claude Biver, who now also heads LVMH Group's Watch Division.

Hublot grew and continues to grow thanks to a combination of innovative watchmaking and vigorous communication. It was together with current CEO Ricardo Guadalupe that Biver developed the idea of fusing different and at times incompatible materials in a watch: carbon composite and gold, ceramic and steel, denim and diamonds. In 2011, the brand introduced the first scratchproof precious metal, an alloy of gold and ceramic named "Magic Gold." In 2014, Hublot came out with a watch whose dial is made of osmium, one of the world's rarest metals. Using a new patented process, Hublot has also implemented a unique concept of cutting wafer-thin bits of glass that are set in the open spaces of a skeletonized movement plate.

The "art of fusion" tagline drove the brand into all sorts of technical and scientific partnerships and created a buzz that is ongoing, apparently, regardless of the economic environment. Hublot's concept is based on the idea of "being the first, different and unique." To achieve that goal, it has associated its name with major sports events and brands and has created technoid, martial, exuberant, eye-burning timepieces that holler rather than merely display the time.

The models in the constantly expanding Classic Fusion Original collection look like good old friends. With their clean lines and reduced dimensions, they are very similar to the original Hublot timepieces from the 1980s. *La Montre des Montres* (MDM) is what Hublot inventor Carlo Crocco once called his creation, "the watch of all watches." In any case, the watches, which are also available in classic precious metals, form a stylistic counterpoint to the frenzied, colorful, effusive devices for which the brand is known.

HUBLOT SA
Chemin de la Vuarpillière 33
CH-1260 Nyon
Switzerland

TEL.:
+41-22-990-9000

E-MAIL:
info@hublot.ch

WEBSITE:
www.hublot.com

FOUNDED:
1980

NUMBER OF EMPLOYEES:
over 800 worldwide

ANNUAL PRODUCTION:
approx. 50,000 watches

U.S BRANCH:
Hublot of America Inc
2455 E Sunrise Blvd, #402
Fort Lauderdale, FL 33304
954-568-9400

MOST IMPORTANT COLLECTIONS/PRICE RANGE:
Big Bang / $11,000 to $1,053,000; Classic Fusion / $5,200 to $474,000; Manufacture Piece (MP) / $82,000 to $579,000

Big Bang 20th Anniversary Titanium Ceramic 43mm

Reference number: 431.NM.1337.RX
Movement: automatic, Caliber HUB 1280 "Unico"; ø 30.4 mm, height 6.75 mm; 43 jewels; 28,800 vph; 72-hour power reserve
Functions: hours, minutes, subsidiary seconds; flyback chronograph; date
Case: titanium, ø 43 mm, height 14.5 mm; ceramic bezel, mounted to case back with 6 titanium screws; sapphire crystal; transparent case back; water-resistant to 10 atm
Band: rubber, folding clasp
Price: $21,700
Variations: various cases, bands, and dials

Big Bang 20th Anniversary Red Magic

Reference number: 431.CF.1313.RX
Movement: automatic, Caliber HUB 1280 "Unico"; ø 30.4 mm, height 6.75 mm; 43 jewels; 28,800 vph; 72-hour power reserve
Functions: hours, minutes, subsidiary seconds; flyback chronograph; date
Case: ceramic, ø 43 mm, height 14.5 mm; ceramic bezel, mounted to case back with 6 titanium screws; sapphire crystal; transparent case back; water-resistant to 10 atm
Band: rubber, folding clasp
Price: $33,200
Variations: various cases, bands, and dials

Big Bang Meca-10 Titanium 42mm

Reference number: 444.NX.1170.RX
Movement: hand-wound, Caliber HUB 1205; ø 33.4 mm, height 6.8 mm; 24 jewels; 21,600 vph; silicon escapement, skeletonized movement; 240-hour power reserve
Functions: hours, minutes, subsidiary seconds; power reserve indicator
Case: titanium, ø 42 mm, height 13.9 mm; bezel mounted to case back with 6 titanium screws; sapphire crystal; transparent case back; water-resistant to 10 atm
Band: rubber, folding clasp
Price: $24,000

Big Bang Meca-10 King Gold 42mm

Reference number: 444.OX.1180.RX
Movement: hand-wound, Caliber HUB 1205; ø 33.4 mm, height 6.8 mm; 24 jewels; 21,600 vph; silicon escapement, skeletonized movement; 240-hour power reserve
Functions: hours, minutes, subsidiary seconds; power reserve indicator
Case: rose gold, ø 42 mm, height 13.9 mm; bezel mounted to case back with 6 titanium screws; sapphire crystal; transparent case back; water-resistant to 10 atm
Band: rubber, folding clasp
Price: $44,700

Big Bang Tourbillon Automatic Green Saxem 44mm

Reference number: 429.JG.0110.RT
Movement: automatic, Hublot Caliber 6035; ø 34 mm, height 5.7 mm; 26 jewels; 21,600 vph; flying one-minute tourbillon, micro-rotor, skeletonized movement; 72-hour power reserve
Functions: hours, minutes
Case: synthetic sapphire ("Saxem"), ø 44 mm, height 13.9 mm; bezel mounted to case back with 6 titanium screws; sapphire crystal; transparent case back; water-resistant to 3 atm
Band: rubber, folding clasp
Remarks: sapphire crystal dial
Price: $242,000

Big Bang Unico Petrol Blue Ceramic

Reference number: 441.ES.5121.RX
Movement: automatic, Caliber HUB 1280 "Unico 2"; ø 30.4 mm, height 6.75 mm; 43 jewels; 28,800 vph; 72-hour power reserve
Functions: hours, minutes, subsidiary seconds; flyback chronograph; date
Case: ceramic, ø 42 mm, height 14.5 mm; bezel mounted to case back with 6 titanium screws; sapphire crystal; transparent case back; water-resistant to 10 atm
Band: rubber, folding clasp
Price: $25,200

Big Bang One Click Joyful Steel (Orange Sapphire)

Reference number: 485.SO.2210.RX.1206
Movement: automatic, Hublot Caliber 1120 (base Sellita SW1000-1a); ø 25.6 mm; 18 jewels; 28,800 vph; 40-hour power reserve
Functions: hours, minutes, sweep seconds; date
Case: stainless steel, ø 33 mm, height 10.55 mm; bezel with 36 orange sapphires mounted to back with 6 titanium screws; sapphire crystal; water-resistant to 10 atm
Band: rubber, folding clasp
Remarks: push-button mechanism for quick swapping of the movement; comes with additional rubber strap
Price: $14,800
Variations: various cases, bands, and dials

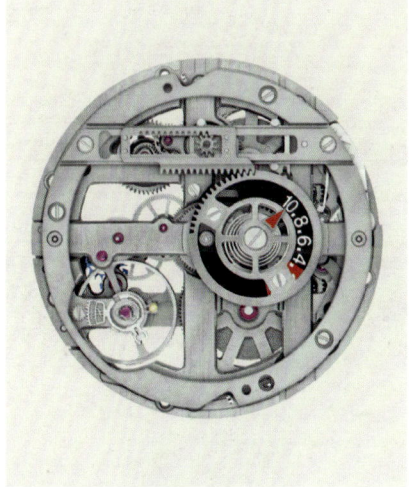

Caliber HUB 1205

Hand-wound; skeletonized movement; silicon anchor and escape wheel; double spring barrel, 240-hour power reserve
Functions: hours, minutes, subsidiary seconds; power reserve indicator; date
Diameter: 33.4 mm
Height: 6.8 mm
Jewels: 29
Balance: CuBe
Frequency: 21,600 vph
Hairspring: flat hairspring with fine regulation
Shock protection: Incabloc
Remarks: 264 parts

Caliber HUB 6035

Automatic; flying one-minute tourbillon; off-center microrotor, skeletonized movement; single spring barrel, 72-hour power reserve
Functions: hours, minutes
Diameter: 34 mm
Height: 5.7 mm
Jewels: 26
Balance: glucydur
Frequency: 21,600 vph
Hairspring: flat hairspring with fine regulation
Shock protection: Incabloc
Remarks: 282 parts

ITAY NOY

Our relationship with precious objects is complex and ultimately reveals as much about our-selves as it does about the objects. Itay Noy's collections, always limited editions, are each unique in their look and feel. No doubt about it: his watches foster conversations both with the outside world and within the wearer. Each piece is a talking point for the public and a touchstone for its owner.

Noy, who hails from and lives in Israel, began his journey into watchmaking around 2000 with the City Squares model, which displays time against the backdrop of a map of the own-er's city of choice. In 2013, he unveiled a square watch powered by a Technotime automatic movement with a face-like dial—well before another famous watchmaker did the same—that changes with the movement of the hands, a tongue-in-cheek reminder of our daily communi-cation with our phones and of the significance of the frame.

Exploring this intimacy between watch and owner remains an endless source of inspiration for Noy, a jeweler by trade who, with time, has begun venturing into the engineer's magic box. He has even collaborated on a bespoke movement with a Swiss firm. An attempt to woo time itself is evident in the Time Tone collection, featuring another "dynamic dial," to use Noy's term. This watch allows the owner to choose a colored disk acting as an hour hand that only they will know, while the minute hand continues its work at the center of the dial.

Not having brand managers breathing down his neck has given Noy the freedom to invent all sorts of ways to display time. For instance, Full Month shows the date or the moon appear-ing through a circle of digits carved into the dial. ReOrder has the hours digitally flashing on a sandwich dial, seemingly at random. Another rearrangement comes with Time Quarters, whose dial is divided into four independent quadrants. As for Part Time, his most recent pro-duction, it takes the most logical approach: dividing the dial into day and night.

ITAY NOY
19 Mazal Arieh,
Old Jaffa
Israel

TEL.:
+972-352-473-80

FAX:
+972-352-473-81

E-MAIL (FOR CUSTOMER QUESTIONS):
studio@itay-noy.com

WEBSITE:
www.itay-noy.com

FOUNDED:
2000

NUMBER OF EMPLOYEES:
4

ANNUAL PRODUCTION:
150

DISTRIBUTION:
Please contact Studio ITAY NOY for information.
www.itay-noy.com

MOST IMPORTANT COLLECTIONS/PRICE RANGE:
Time Quarters, ReOrder, Full Month, Chrono Gears, Part Time and Seven-Day Cycle / $2,800-$16,800

Identity Hebrew
Reference number: ID-HEB.GN
Movement: automatic, IN.S200; ø 25.6 mm, height 4.6 mm; 25 jewels; 28,800 vph; 38-hour power reserve
Functions: hours, minutes, sweep seconds, quick-set date window
Case: stainless steel; ø 42.4 mm, height 10 mm; sapphire crystal; screw-down case back; water-resistant to 10 atm
Band: leather, double folding clasp
Price: $3,200; limited edition of numbered 99 pieces

Hebrew Full Month
Reference number: HEB.FM.BL
Movement: caliber IN.VMF5400, automatic extra-thin micro-rotor; ø 30 mm, height 3 mm; 29 jewels; 21,600 vph; 48-hour power reserve
Functions: hours, minutes, sweep seconds, full date window
Case: stainless steel; 40 × 44 mm, height 6.24 mm (+1.2 mm sapphire crystal box); transparent case back; water-resistant to 10 atm
Band: leather, double folding clasp
Price: $12,800; limited edition of 18 numbered pieces
Variations: black, blue, or brown leather band

Seven-Day Cycle
Reference number: SDC.WT
Movement: automatic, IN.S240; ø 29 mm, height 5.05 mm; 26 jewels; 28,800 vph; 38-hour power reserve
Functions: hours, minutes, sweep seconds, quick-set date, day window
Case: stainless steel; ø 40 mm, height 8.4 mm; sapphire crystal; screw-down case back; water-resistant to 10 atm
Band: leather; double folding clasp
Price: $4,900; limited edition of 77 numbered pieces

Open Mind

Reference number: OM-S.GB
Movement: manually wound skeleton 6497-1; ø 36.6 mm, height 4.5 mm; 17 jewels; 21,600 vph; 38-hour power reserve
Functions: hours, minutes, subsidiary seconds
Case: stainless steel; ø 44 mm, height 12 mm; sapphire crystal; transparent case back; water-resistant to 10 atm
Band: leather, double folding clasp
Price: $4,900; limited edition of 99 numbered pieces
Variations: blue or black dial; black or brown leather band

Part Time

Reference number: PT-DN.BL
Movement: manually wound IN.DD & 6498-1; ø 36.6 mm, height 5.2 mm; 17 jewels; 21,600 vph; 38-hour power reserve
Functions: analog hours 6 am–6 pm and hours 6 pm–6 am, moon disk, sun disk, minutes, subsidiary seconds
Case: stainless steel; ø 41.6 × 44.6 mm, height 10.6 mm; sapphire crystal; transparent case back; water-resistant to 10 atm
Band: leather, double folding clasp
Price: $7,800; limited edition of 24 numbered pieces
Variations: blue or black

Celestial Time

Reference number: CT.W
Movement: manually wound IN.AR; ø 36.6 mm, height 5.5 mm; 20 jewels; 18,000 vph; 46-hour power reserve
Functions: dynamic dial with zodiac hour disc, minutes, seconds
Case: stainless steel; ø 44 mm, height 12 mm; sapphire crystal dome; transparent case back; water-resistant to 10 atm
Band: handmade leather, double folding clasp
Price: $6,600; limited edition of 24 numbered pieces
Variations: Western or Chinese zodiac signs

Chrono Gears

Reference number: CG.BK
Movement: manually wound IN.AR; ø 36.6 mm, height 5.5 mm; 20 jewels; 21,600 vph; 42-hour power reserve
Functions: chronogear hand indicator for am/pm, chronogear hand indicator for 8 time situations, central hours, minutes, and seconds
Case: stainless steel; ø 44 mm, height 12 mm; sapphire crystal; transparent case back; water-resistant to 10 atm
Band: leather, double folding clasp
Price: $7,800; limited edition of 24 numbered pieces
Variations: blue or black

Time Tone

Reference number: TT.BL
Movement: manually wound IN.AR; ø 36.6 mm, height 5.5 mm; 20 jewels; 21,600 vph; 42-hour power reserve
Functions: dynamic dial with tone color hours disc, minutes and sweep seconds
Case: stainless steel; ø 44 mm, height 12 mm; sapphire crystal; transparent case back; water-resistant to 10 atm
Band: leather, double folding clasp
Price: $6,600; limited edition of 24 numbered pieces
Variations: blue, green, or black

Night Flight Jerusalem

Reference number: NF.JERUSALEM
Movement: manually wound skeleton 6497-1; ø 36.6 mm, height 4.5 mm; 17 jewels; 18,000 vph; 46-hour power reserve
Functions: hours, minutes, subsidiary seconds
Case: black PVD stainless steel; ø 44 mm, height 12 mm; sapphire crystal dome; transparent case back; water-resistant to 10 atm
Band: leather, double folding clasp
Remarks: dial made of layers of lacquer-work combined with gold
Price: $16,800; unique piece
Variations: different cities around the world

IWC

It was an American who laid the cornerstone for an industrial watch factory in Schaffhausen—now environmentally state-of-the-art facilities. In 1868, Florentine Ariosto Jones, a watchmaker and engineer from Boston, moved to then low-wage Switzerland to open the International Watch Company Schaffhausen.

Jones was a talented designer, who had a significant influence on the development of watch movements. Soon, he gave IWC its own seal of approval, the *Ingenieursmarke* (Engineer's Brand), a standard it still maintains today. The company has maintained its codes more or less ever since. The portfolio includes the rugged and sportive Pilot and Big Pilot watches, the refined Da Vincis, elegant Portofinos, and complicated Portugieser, which was named for two Portuguese fellows who went to Schaffhausen to commission a super-precise watch.

IWC movements include the Jones caliber, named for the IWC founder, and the pocket watch caliber 89, introduced in 1946 as the creation of then-technical director Albert Pellaton. Four years later, Pellaton created the first IWC automatic movement. In 2020, IWC decided to equip all the Portuguese models with in-house calibers, including the automatic 52000 and 82000 caliber families, which use Pellaton or double-pawl winding mechanisms.

While pilot's watches play an important role in IWC's portfolio, with the broad Top Gun line including some models in ceramic cases, the flagship model is undoubtedly the Portugieser. The reference 325 from 1939, which was in fact a pocket watch inside a wristwatch case, was inspired by the early observation watches for seafaring.

In 2025, the Ingenieur underwent a complex update. For the first time, the model was combined with the perpetual calendar developed by IWC watchmaker and designer Kurt Klaus. The moon phase of the Ingenieur Perpetual Calendar 41 is also significantly more precise than conventional displays. It only deviates by one day every 577.5 years. In 2024, however, IWC surpassed this with the Portugieser Eternal Calendar and its stunning moon phase accuracy of 45 million years.

INTERNATIONAL WATCH CO.
Baumgartenstrasse 15
CH-8201 Schaffhausen
Switzerland

TEL.:
+41-52-635-6565

E-MAIL:
info@iwc.com

WEBSITE:
www.iwc.com

FOUNDED:
1868

NUMBER OF EMPLOYEES:
approx. 750

U.S. DISTRIBUTOR:
IWC North America
645 Fifth Avenue, 5th Floor
New York, NY 10022
800-432-9330

MOST IMPORTANT COLLECTIONS/PRICE RANGE:
Da Vinci, Pilot's, Portugieser, Ingenieur, Aquatimer, Pallweber / approx. $4,000 to $260,000

Ingenieur Automatic 35

Reference number: IW324903
Movement: automatic, IWC Caliber 47110; ø 26.18 mm, height 3.76 mm; 23 jewels; 28,800 vph; finely finished with côtes de Genève; 42-hour power reserve
Functions: hours, minutes, sweep seconds; date
Case: red gold, ø 35.1 mm, height 9.4 mm; bezel mounted to case back with five visible screws; sapphire crystal; transparent case back; water-resistant to 10 atm
Band: red gold, folding clasp, with fine adjustment
Price: $41,500
Variations: in stainless steel ($10,500)

Ingenieur Automatic 35

Reference number: IW324906
Movement: automatic, IWC Caliber 47110; ø 26.18 mm, height 3.76 mm; 23 jewels; 28,800 vph; finely finished with côtes de Genève; 42-hour power reserve
Functions: hours, minutes, sweep seconds; date
Case: stainless steel, ø 35.1 mm, height 9.4 mm; bezel mounted to case back with five visible screws; sapphire crystal; transparent case back; water-resistant to 10 atm
Band: stainless steel, folding clasp, with fine adjustment
Price: $10,500
Variations: with silver dial; in red gold ($41,500)

Ingenieur Automatic 35

Reference number: IW324901
Movement: automatic, IWC Caliber 47110; ø 26.18 mm, height 3.76 mm; 23 jewels; 28,800 vph; finely finished with côtes de Genève; 42-hour power reserve
Functions: hours, minutes, sweep seconds; date
Case: stainless steel, ø 35.1 mm, height 9.4 mm; bezel mounted to case back with five visible screws; sapphire crystal; transparent case back; water-resistant to 10 atm
Band: stainless steel, folding clasp, with fine adjustment
Price: $10,500
Variations: with black dial; in red gold ($41,500)

Pilot's Watch Performance Chronograph 41

Reference number: IW388309
Movement: automatic, IWC Caliber 69385; ø 30 mm, height 7.9 mm; 33 jewels; 28,800 vph; finely finished with côtes de Genève; 46-hour power reserve
Functions: hours, minutes, subsidiary seconds; chronograph; date and weekday
Case: red gold, ø 41 mm, height 14.7 mm; bezel with ceramic insert; sapphire crystal; transparent case back; screw-down crown; water-resistant to 10 atm
Band: rubber, pin buckle
Price: $27,900

Pilot's Watch Chrono 41 APXGP

Reference number: IW388116
Movement: automatic, IWC Caliber 69385; ø 30 mm, height 7.9 mm; 33 jewels; 28,800 vph; finely finished with côtes de Genève; 46-hour power reserve
Functions: hours, minutes, subsidiary seconds; chronograph; date and weekday
Case: stainless steel, ø 41 mm, height 14.5 mm; sapphire crystal; transparent case back; screw-down crown; water-resistant to 10 atm
Band: rubber, pin buckle
Price: $7,200

Pilot's Watch Chrono 43 APXGP

Reference number: IW378009
Movement: automatic, IWC Caliber 69385; ø 30 mm, height 7.9 mm; 33 jewels; 28,800 vph; finely finished with côtes de Genève; 46-hour power reserve
Functions: hours, minutes, subsidiary seconds; chronograph; date and weekday
Case: stainless steel, ø 43 mm, height 14.8 mm; sapphire crystal; transparent case back; screw-down crown; water-resistant to 10 atm
Band: rubber, pin buckle
Price: $7,400

Pilot's Watch Performance Chrono QP Digital Date-Month

Reference number: IW388801
Movement: automatic, IWC Caliber 89802; ø 30.38 mm, height 9.91 mm; 51 jewels; 28,800 vph; Pellaton winding, blackened bridges and rotor; 68-hour power reserve
Functions: hours, minutes, subsidiary seconds; flyback chronograph; perpetual calendar with date and month (digital disc display), leap year
Case: special titanium-ceramic alloy (Ceratanium), ø 43 mm, height 16.5 mm; bezel with ceramic insert; sapphire crystal; transparent case back; screw-down crown; water-resistant to 10 atm
Band: Ceratanium, folding clasp
Price: $96,400

Big Pilot's Watch Shock Absorber Tourbillon Skeleton XPL

Reference number: IW357701
Movement: automatic, IWC Caliber 82915; ø 32.38 mm, height 6.9 mm; 25 jewels; 28,800 vph; flying 1-minute tourbillon, Pellaton winding, skeletonized movement and rotor; 80-hour power reserve
Functions: hours, minutes
Case: special titanium-ceramic alloy (Ceratanium); shock absorber system with spring and eight arms ("SPRIN-g Protect" system), ø 44 mm, height 13 mm; sapphire crystal; transparent case back; screw-down crown; water-resistant to 10 atm
Band: rubber, pin buckle
Remarks: limited to 100 pieces
Price: on request

Pilot's Watch Mark XX Mercedes-AMG PETRONAS F1

Reference number: IW328210
Movement: automatic, IWC Caliber 32111; ø 28.2 mm, height 3.77 mm; 21 jewels; 28,800 vph; finely finished with côtes de Genève; 120-hour power reserve
Functions: hours, minutes, sweep seconds; date
Case: titanium, ø 40 mm, height 10.6 mm; sapphire crystal; transparent case back; water-resistant to 10 atm
Band: rubber, pin buckle
Price: $6,400

Ingenieur Automatic 40

Reference number: IW328702
Movement: automatic, IWC Caliber 32111; ø 28.2 mm, height 3.77 mm; 21 jewels; 28,800 vph; finely finished with côtes de Genève; 120-hour power reserve
Functions: hours, minutes, sweep seconds; date
Case: red gold, ø 40 mm, height 10.7 mm; bezel mounted to case with five visible screws; sapphire crystal; water-resistant to 10 atm
Band: red gold, folding clasp, with fine adjustment
Remarks: antimagnetic to 40,000 A/m using soft iron core
Price: $48,900
Variations: in stainless steel ($12,300); in titanium ($15,400)

Ingenieur Automatic 42

Reference number: IW338903
Movement: automatic, IWC Caliber 82110; ø 30 mm; 22 jewels; 28,800 vph; 60-hour power reserve
Functions: hours, minutes, sweep seconds; date
Case: ceramic, ø 42 mm, height 11.5 mm; bezel mounted to case with five visible screws; sapphire crystal; transparent case back; screw-down crown; water-resistant to 10 atm
Band: ceramic, folding clasp
Price: $20,600

Ingenieur Perpetual Calendar 41

Reference number: IW344903
Movement: automatic, IWC Caliber 82600; ø 30.38 mm, height 7.76 mm; 46 jewels; 28,800 vph; Pellaton winding; skeletonized rotor; finely finished with côtes de Genève; 60-hour power reserve
Functions: hours, minutes; perpetual calendar with date, weekday, month, moon phase, leap year
Case: stainless steel, ø 41.6 mm, height 13.3 mm; bezel mounted to case with five visible screws; sapphire crystal; transparent case back; water-resistant to 10 atm
Band: stainless steel, folding clasp
Price: $38,900

Ingenieur Automatic 40

Reference number: IW328908
Movement: automatic, IWC Caliber 32111; ø 28.2 mm, height 3.77 mm; 21 jewels; 28,800 vph; finely finished with côtes de Genève; 120-hour power reserve
Functions: hours, minutes, sweep seconds; date
Case: stainless steel, ø 40 mm, height 10.7 mm; bezel mounted to case with five visible screws; sapphire crystal; water-resistant to 10 atm
Band: stainless steel, folding clasp, with fine adjustment
Remarks: antimagnetic to 40,000 A/m using soft iron core
Price: $13,600
Variations: various dial colors; in titanium ($15,400); in red gold ($48,900)

Ingenieur Automatic 40

Reference number: IW328907
Movement: automatic, IWC Caliber 32111; ø 28.2 mm, height 3.77 mm; 21 jewels; 28,800 vph; finely finished with côtes de Genève; 120-hour power reserve
Functions: hours, minutes, sweep seconds; date
Case: stainless steel, ø 40 mm, height 10.7 mm; bezel mounted to case with five visible screws; sapphire crystal; water-resistant to 10 atm
Band: stainless steel, folding clasp, with fine adjustment
Remarks: antimagnetic to 40,000 A/m using soft iron core
Price: $12,300
Variations: various dial colors; in titanium ($15,400); in red gold ($48,900)

Ingenieur Automatic 40

Reference number: IW328904
Movement: automatic, IWC Caliber 32111; ø 28.2 mm, height 3.77 mm; 21 jewels; 28,800 vph; finely finished with côtes de Genève; 120-hour power reserve
Functions: hours, minutes, sweep seconds; date
Case: titanium, ø 40 mm, height 10.7 mm; bezel mounted to case with five visible screws; sapphire crystal; water-resistant to 10 atm
Band: titanium, folding clasp, with fine adjustment
Remarks: antimagnetic to 40,000 A/m using soft iron core
Price: $15,400
Variations: in stainless steel ($12,300); in red gold ($48,900)

Caliber 32111

Automatic; second-stop system; single mainspring barrel, 120-hour power reserve
Functions: hours, minutes, sweep seconds; date
Diameter: 28.2 mm
Height: 3.77 mm
Jewels: 21
Frequency: 28,800 vph
Remarks: finely finished with côtes de Genève; 163 parts

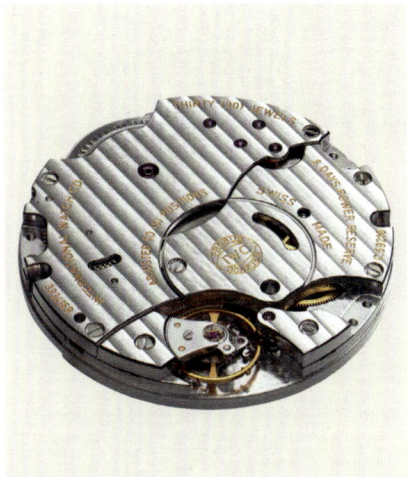

Caliber 59210

Hand-wound; single mainspring barrel, 192-hour power reserve
Functions: hours, minutes, subsidiary seconds; power reserve indicator; date
Diameter: 37.8 mm
Height: 5.8 mm
Jewels: 30
Balance: glucydur with variable inertia
Frequency: 28,800 vph
Hairspring: Breguet
Shock protection: Incabloc

Caliber 82200

Automatic; double-pawl winding (Pellaton system); single mainspring barrel, 60-hour power reserve
Functions: hours, minutes, subsidiary seconds
Diameter: 30 mm
Height: 6.6 mm
Jewels: 31
Frequency: 28,800 vph
Hairspring: flat hairspring
Remarks: finely finished movement with perlage and côtes de Genève

Caliber 69355

Automatic; column-wheel control of the chronograph functions; single mainspring barrel, 46-hour power reserve
Functions: hours, minutes, subsidiary seconds; chronograph
Diameter: 30 mm
Height: 7.9 mm
Jewels: 27
Balance: glucydur
Frequency: 28,800 vph
Hairspring: flat hairspring
Remarks: finely finished movement with perlage and côtes de Genève

Caliber 52615

Automatic; double-pawl winding (Pellaton system) with ceramic wheels; two spring barrels, 168-hour power reserve
Functions: hours, minutes, subsidiary seconds; power reserve indicator; perpetual calendar with month, weekday, date, double moon phase (for northern and southern hemispheres), year display (four digits)
Diameter: 37.8 mm
Height: 9 mm
Jewels: 54
Balance: with variable inertia
Frequency: 28,800 vph
Hairspring: Breguet
Shock protection: Incabloc

Caliber 89361

Automatic; double-pawl winding (Pellaton system), column-wheel control of chronograph functions; single spring barrel, 68-hour power reserve
Base caliber: 89000
Functions: hours, minutes, subsidiary seconds; flyback chronograph; date
Diameter: 30 mm
Height: 7.46 mm
Jewels: 38
Balance: glucydur with variable inertia
Frequency: 28,800 vph
Hairspring: flat hairspring
Shock protection: Incabloc
Remarks: concentric chronograph totalizer for minutes and hours

JAEGER-LECOULTRE

The Jaeger-LeCoultre *manufacture* has had a long and tumultuous history. In 1833, Antoine LeCoultre opened his own workshop for the production of gearwheels. Having made his fortune, he then did what many other artisans did; in 1866, he brought together all the crafts-people needed to produce timepieces, from the watchmakers to the turners and polishers. He outfitted his workshop with the most modern machinery of the day, all powered by a steam engine. "La Grande Maison" was the first watch *manufacture* in the Vallée de Joux.

At the start of the twentieth century, the grandson of the company founder, Jacques-David LeCoultre, built slender, complicated watches for the Paris manufacturer Edmond Jaeger. The Frenchman was so impressed with these that, after a few years of fruitful cooperation, he engineered a merger of the two companies.

Thanks to its inclusion in the Richemont stable, Jaeger-LeCoultre continued to grow. A vast array of calibers (around 1,400), including minute repeaters, tourbillons, and other *grandes complications*, a lubricant-free movement, and more than 400 patents, tell their own story. Today, it is the largest employer in the Vallée de Joux—just as it was back in the 1860s.

The Reverso is one of Jaeger-LeCoultre's most enduring achievements. Created in 1931 as a sports watch, the rectangular reversible design has remained remarkably unchanged over the past 94 years, though it has continuously evolved in quality and technical sophistication. The Reverso collection now spans everything from complicated pieces featuring minute repeaters and world clocks with oversized date displays to elegant jewelry watches and classic time-only models. The standout model for 2025 is the Reverso Tribute Monoface Small Seconds, with a new Milanese bracelet in rose gold. The entire watch embraces a sophisticated "tone-on-tone" aesthetic, with the case, matte grained dial, and bracelet all executed in rose gold. This mono-chromatic approach represents a refined departure from mixed-metal designs.

Jaeger-LeCoultre also boasts other iconic collections, like the Master, the Polaris, and the Atmos. They further showcase the brand's technical wizardry with a very fine sense of aes-thetics, expressed via the application of many *métiers d'art* from the watch world.

MANUFACTURE JAEGER-LECOULTRE
Rue de la Golisse, 8
CH-1347 Le Sentier
Switzerland

TEL.:
+41-21-852-0202

E-MAIL:
info@jaeger-lecoultre.com
client.relations.us@jaeger-lecoultre.com

WEBSITE:
www.jaeger-lecoultre.com

FOUNDED:
1833

NUMBER OF EMPLOYEES:
Around 1,400

ANNUAL PRODUCTION:
approx. 75,000 watches

U.S. DISTRIBUTOR:
Jaeger-LeCoultre
701 Madison Ave
New York, NY 10065
877-552-1833
www.jaeger-lecoultre.com

MOST IMPORTANT COLLECTIONS/PRICE RANGE:
Atmos / starting at $7,100; Duomètre / starting at $41,700; Master / starting at $7,250; Polaris / starting at $7,250; Rendez-Vous / starting at $7,850; Reverso / starting at $4,750

Duometre Heliotourbillon Perpetual

Reference number: Q6202420
Movement: hand-wound, JLC caliber 388; ø 34.3 mm, height 11.15 mm; 89 jewels; 28,800 vph; triple-axis tourbillon with different rotation times (2x30, 1x60 seconds), two separate gear trains for time display and complications, each with its own spring barrel; 46-hour power reserve
Functions: hours and minutes (off-center); power reserve indicator (for each spring barrel); perpetual calendar with large date, weekday, month, moon phase, year display (four digits)
Case: red gold, ø 44 mm, height 14.7 mm; sapphire crystal; transparent case back; water-resistant to 3 atm
Band: reptile skin, pin buckle
Price: $438,000; limited to 20 pieces

Duometre Chronograph Moon

Reference number: Q622656J
Movement: hand-wound, JLC caliber 391; ø 34.3 mm, height 8.24 mm; 54 jewels; 21,600 vph; two separate gear train for time and complications, each with its own spring barrel; 50-hour power reserve
Functions: hours and minutes (off-center); "flashing" sixth of a second; day/night indicator; power reserve indicator (for each spring barrel); chronograph; moon phase display
Case: platinum, ø 42.5 mm, height 14.2 mm; sapphire crystal
Band: reptile skin, pin buckle
Price: $70,000

Master Ultra Thin Perpetual Calendar

Reference number: Q114258J
Movement: automatic, JLC caliber 868AA; ø 26 mm, height 4.72 mm; 54 jewels; 28,800 vph; 70-hour power reserve
Functions: hours, minutes, sweep seconds; perpetual calendar with date, weekday, month, moon phase, year display (four digits)
Case: red gold, ø 39 mm, height 9.2 mm; sapphire crystal; transparent case back; water-resistant to 5 atm
Band: reptile skin, pin buckle
Price: $42,400

Master Ultra Thin Perpetual Calendar

Reference number: Q114842J
Movement: automatic, JLC caliber 868AA; ø 26 mm, height 4.72 mm; 54 jewels; 28,800 vph; 70-hour power reserve
Functions: hours, minutes, sweep seconds; perpetual calendar with date, weekday, month, moon phase, year display (four digits)
Case: stainless steel, ø 39 mm, height 9.2 mm; sapphire crystal; transparent case back; water-resistant to 5 atm
Band: reptile skin, double folding clasp
Price: $29,700
Variations: red gold; red gold with bezel set with diamonds

Polaris Geographic

Reference number: Q9078640
Movement: automatic, JLC caliber 939; ø 26 mm, height 4.9 mm; 34 jewels; 28,800 vph; 70-hour power reserve
Functions: hours, minutes, sweep seconds; additional 12-hour display (second time zone); world time display; day/night indicator; power reserve indicator
Case: stainless steel, ø 42 mm, height 11.54 mm; crown-activated ring with reference cities; sapphire crystal; water-resistant to 10 atm
Band: textile, double folding clasp
Remarks: comes with extra rubber strap
Price: $16,800

Polaris Chronograph

Reference number: Q9028651
Movement: automatic, JLC caliber 761; ø 25.6 mm, height 5.76 mm; 35 jewels; 28,800 vph; two spring barrels; skeletonized rotor; 65-hour power reserve
Functions: hours, minutes; chronograph
Case: stainless steel, ø 42 mm, height 13.39 mm; sapphire crystal; transparent case back; water-resistant to 10 atm
Band: textile, pin buckle
Remarks: comes with additional rubber strap
Price: $15,900

Reverso Tribute Minute Repeater

Reference number: Q7122480
Movement: hand-wound, JLC caliber 953; 17.2 mm × 22 mm, height 6.65 mm; 38 jewels; 28,800 vph; 72-hour power reserve
Functions: hours, minutes; minute repeater
Case: pink gold, 31 mm × 51.1 mm, height 12.6 mm; sapphire crystal; transparent case back; water-resistant to 3 atm
Band: reptile skin, pin buckle
Remarks: case turns and swivels 180°; comes with additional leather strap; enamel dial; limited to 30 pieces
Price: $299,000

Reverso Hybris Artistica Calibre 179

Reference number: Q39424E1
Movement: hand-wound, JLC caliber 179; 26.2 mm × 41 mm, height 6.85 mm; 52 jewels; 21,600 vph; spherical double-axis tourbillon with different rotational speeds (60 and 12.6 secs.), Gyrolab escapement with hemispheric hairspring; 40-hour power reserve
Functions: hours, minutes, subsidiary seconds (on the tourbillon cage); additional 24-hour display
Case: pink gold, 31 mm × 51.2 mm, height 13.63 mm; sapphire crystal; water-resistant to 3 atm
Band: reptile skin, double folding clasp
Remarks: case turns and swivels 180°; limited to 10 pieces
Price: $565,000

Reverso Tribute Nonantième "Enamel"

Reference number: Q71125E1
Movement: hand-wound, JLC caliber 826; 17.2 mm × 22 mm, height 6.38 mm; 19 jewels; 21,600 vph; 42-hour power reserve
Functions: hours, minutes, subsidiary seconds; large date; moon phase
Case: red gold, 29.9 mm × 49.4 mm, height 11.7 mm; sapphire crystal; water-resistant to 3 atm
Band: reptile skin, pin buckle
Remarks: case turns and swivels 180°
Price: $74,000

Reverso Tribute Small Seconds

Reference number: Q713216J
Movement: hand-wound, JLC caliber 822;
17.2 mm × 22 mm, height 2.94 mm; 19 jewels;
21,600 vph; 42-hour power reserve
Functions: hours, minutes, subsidiary seconds
Case: pink gold, 27.4 mm × 45.6 mm, height 7.56 mm;
sapphire crystal; water-resistant to 3 atm
Band: pink gold Milanese, double folding clasp
Price: $74,000

Reverso Tribute Geographic

Reference number: Q714256J
Movement: hand-wound, JLC caliber 834;
17.2 mm × 22 mm, height 6.07 mm; 18 jewels;
21,600 vph; 42-hour power reserve
Functions: hours, minutes, subsidiary seconds; large
date; world time display (on the rear)
Case: pink gold, 29.9 mm × 49.4 mm, height 11.14 mm;
sapphire crystal; transparent case back; water-resistant
to 3 atm
Band: leather, pin buckle
Remarks: case turns and swivels 180°; comes with
additional reptile skin strap
Price: $34,900
Variations: stainless steel ($21,200)

Reverso Tribute Geographic

Reference number: Q714845J
Movement: hand-wound, JLC caliber 834;
17.2 mm × 22 mm, height 6.07 mm; 18 jewels;
21,600 vph; 42-hour power reserve
Functions: hours, minutes, subsidiary seconds; large
date; world time display (on the rear)
Case: stainless steel, 29.9 mm × 49.4 mm, height
11.14 mm; sapphire crystal; transparent case back;
water-resistant to 3 atm
Band: leather, pin buckle
Remarks: case turns and swivels 180°; comes with
additional reptile skin strap
Price: $21,200
Variations: pink gold ($34,900)

Reverso Tribute Duoface Small Seconds

Reference number: Q3988481
Movement: hand-wound, JLC caliber 854A/2;
17.2 mm × 22 mm, height 3.8 mm; 19 jewels; 21,600 vph;
42-hour power reserve
Functions: hours, minutes, subsidiary seconds;
additional time display (second time zone) on the rear
Case: stainless steel, 28.3 mm × 47 mm, height
10.34 mm; sapphire crystal; transparent case back;
water-resistant to 3 atm
Band: leather, pin buckle
Remarks: case turns and swivels 180°; comes with
additional leather strap
Price: $13,700
Variations: black dial and strap

Reverso Tribute Duoface Small Seconds

Reference number: Q398847J
Movement: hand-wound, JLC caliber 854A/2;
17.2 mm × 22 mm, height 3.8 mm; 19 jewels; 21,600 vph;
42-hour power reserve
Functions: hours, minutes, subsidiary seconds;
additional time display (second time zone) on the rear
Case: stainless steel, 28.3 mm × 47 mm, height
10.34 mm; sapphire crystal; transparent case back;
water-resistant to 3 atm
Band: leather, pin buckle
Remarks: case turns and swivels 180°; comes with
additional leather strap
Price: $13,700
Variations: blue dial and strap

Reverso Tribute Enamel "Shahnameh" 1

Reference number: Q39334S1
Movement: hand-wound, JLC caliber 822A/2;
17.2 mm × 22 mm, height 2.94 mm; 19 jewels;
21,600 vph; 42-hour power reserve
Functions: hours, minutes
Case: white gold, 27.4 mm × 45.6 mm, height 9.73 mm;
sapphire crystal; water-resistant to 3 atm
Band: reptile skin, pin buckle
Remarks: miniature painting on the rear with motive
from the Shahnameh (Persian for Book of Kings); case
turns and swivels 180°
Price: $142,000; limited to 10 pieces
Variations: three further models with various motives

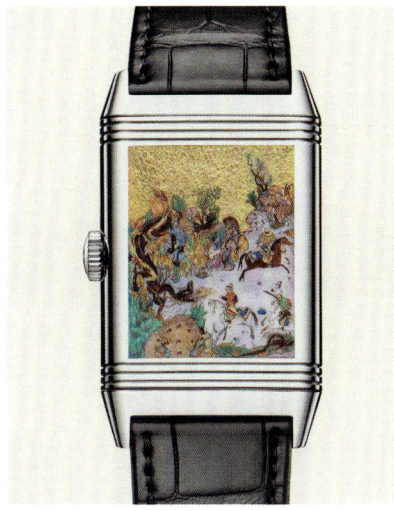

Reverso Tribute Enamel "Shahnameh" 2

Reference number: Q39334S2
Movement: hand-wound, JLC caliber 822A/2; 17.2 mm × 22 mm, height 2.94 mm; 19 jewels; 21,600 vph; 42-hour power reserve
Functions: hours, minutes
Case: white gold, 27.4 mm × 45.6 mm, height 9.73 mm; sapphire crystal; water-resistant to 3 atm
Band: reptile skin, pin buckle
Remarks: miniature painting on the rear with motive from the Shahnameh; case turns and swivels 180°
Price: $142,000; limited to 10 pieces

Reverso Tribute Enamel "Shahnameh" 3

Reference number: Q39334S3
Movement: hand-wound, JLC caliber 822A/2; 17.2 mm × 22 mm, height 2.94 mm; 19 jewels; 21,600 vph; 42-hour power reserve
Functions: hours, minutes
Case: white gold, 27.4 mm × 45.6 mm, height 9.73 mm; sapphire crystal; water-resistant to 3 atm
Band: reptile skin, pin buckle
Remarks: miniature painting on the rear with motive from the Shahnameh; case turns and swivels 180°
Price: $142,000; limited to 10 pieces

Reverso Tribute Enamel "Shahnameh" 4

Reference number: Q39334S4
Movement: hand-wound, JLC caliber 822A/2; 17.2 mm × 22 mm, height 2.94 mm; 19 jewels; 21,600 vph; 42-hour power reserve
Functions: hours, minutes
Case: white gold, 27.4 mm × 45.6 mm, height 9.73 mm; sapphire crystal; water-resistant to 3 atm
Band: reptile skin, pin buckle
Remarks: miniature painting on the rear with motive from the Shahnameh; case turns and swivels 180°
Price: $142,000; limited to 10 pieces

Master Grande Tradition Calibre 985

Reference number: Q5242461
Movement: automatic, JLC caliber 985; ø 30 mm, height 8.25 mm; 49 jewels; 28,800 vph; cylindrical 1-minute tourbillon; 45-hour power reserve
Functions: hours, minutes, subsidiary seconds (on the tourbillon cage); perpetual calendar with date, weekday, month, moon phase, year display (four digits)
Case: red gold, ø 42 mm, height 13.05 mm; sapphire crystal; transparent case back; water-resistant to 5 atm
Band: reptile skin, double folding clasp
Price: on request

Master Grande Tradition Calibre 985

Reference number: Q5246580
Movement: automatic, JLC caliber 985; ø 30 mm, height 8.25 mm; 49 jewels; 28,800 vph; cylindrical 1-minute tourbillon; 45-hour power reserve
Functions: hours, minutes, subsidiary seconds (on the tourbillon cage); perpetual calendar with date, weekday, month, moon phase, year display (four digits)
Case: platinum, ø 42 mm, height 13.27 mm; sapphire crystal; transparent case back; water-resistant to 5 atm
Band: reptile skin, double folding clasp
Price: on request

Master Grande Tradition Calibre 985

Reference number: Q5246508
Movement: automatic, JLC caliber 985; ø 30 mm, height 8.25 mm; 49 jewels; 28,800 vph; cylindrical 1-minute tourbillon; 45-hour power reserve
Functions: hours, minutes, subsidiary seconds (on the tourbillon cage); perpetual calendar with date, weekday, month, moon phase, year display (four digits)
Case: platinum, ø 42 mm, height 13.27 mm; bezel set with diamonds; sapphire crystal; transparent case back; water-resistant to 5 atm
Band: reptile skin, double folding clasp
Price: on request

Caliber 860

Hand-wound; column-wheel control chronograph functions; single mainspring barrel, 52-hour power reserve

Functions: hours, minutes; additional 12-hour display (second time zone, on the rear); chronograph with retrograde minutes totalizer (on the rear)
Dimensions: 17.2 mm x 22 mm
Height: 5.5 mm
Jewels: 38
Balance: glucydur
Frequency: 28,800 vph
Remarks: skeletonized movement; 300 parts

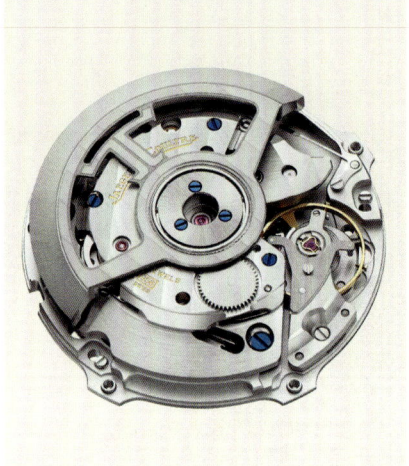

Caliber 956AA

Automatic; automatic movement for the watch and alarm function; single mainspring barrel, 44-hour power reserve

Functions: hours, minutes, sweep seconds; alarm; date
Diameter: 28 mm
Height: 7.47 mm
Jewels: 24
Balance: glucydur
Frequency: 28,800 vph
Hairspring: flat hairspring
Remarks: perlage on mainplate, bridges with côtes de Genève, fixture for a resonance case back; 271 parts

Caliber 899AC

Automatic; silicon escapement; gold rotor; single mainspring barrel, 70-hour power reserve

Functions: hours, minutes, sweep seconds; date
Diameter: 26 mm
Height: 3.7 mm
Jewels: 32
Frequency: 28,800 vph
Remarks: perlage on mainplate, bridges with côtes de Genève; 218 parts

Caliber 866AA

Automatic; silicon escapement; gold rotor; single mainspring barrel, 70-hour power reserve

Functions: hours, minutes, subsidiary seconds; full calendar with date, weekday, month, moon phase
Diameter: 26 mm
Height: 5.65 mm
Jewels: 34
Balance: glucydur
Frequency: 28,800 vph
Remarks: perlage on mainplate, bridges with côtes de Genève

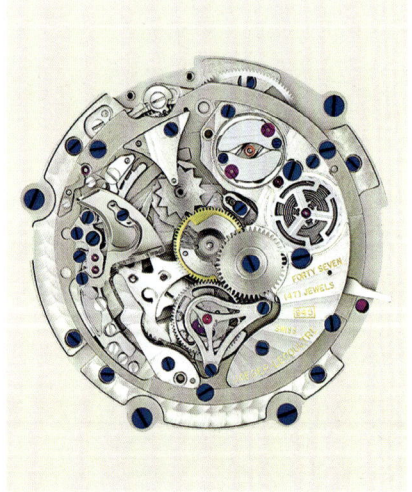

Caliber 945

Hand-wound; silicon anchor with integrated pallets, flying tourbillon rotates with dial in 56 minutes (sidereal time, star time); single spring barrel, 48-hour power reserve

Functions: hours, minutes, hours, quarter hour and minute repeater; perpetual calendar with, date, month, celestial map with zodiac signs
Diameter: 34.7 mm
Height: 12.62 mm
Jewels: 49
Balance: screw balance
Frequency: 28,800 vph
Hairspring: flat hairspring
Remarks: repetition with "trebuchet" hammers to strengthen the impulses; 527 parts

Caliber 925AA

Automatic; single mainspring barrel, 70-hour power reserve

Functions: hours, minutes, sweep seconds; date, moon phase
Diameter: 26 mm
Height: 4.9 mm
Jewels: 30
Frequency: 28,800 vph
Remarks: 245 parts

Caliber 751

Automatic; column-wheel control of the chronograph functions; two spring barrels, 65-hour power reserve
Functions: hours, minutes, subsidiary seconds; chronograph
Diameter: 26.2 mm
Height: 5.7 mm
Jewels: 37
Balance: screw balance with 4 weights
Frequency: 28,800 vph
Hairspring: flat hairspring
Shock protection: Kif
Remarks: 262 parts

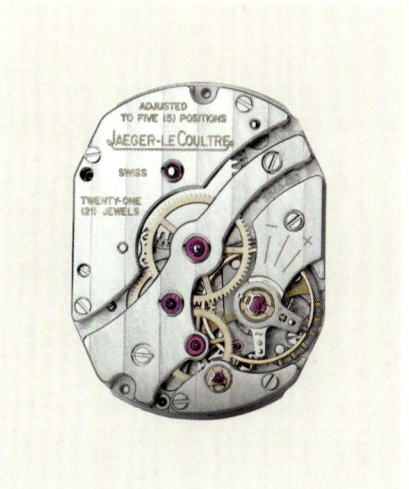

Caliber 822/2

Hand-wound; single mainspring barrel, 42-hour power reserve
Functions: hours, minutes, subsidiary seconds
Dimensions: 17.2 mm x 22 mm
Height: 2.94 mm
Jewels: 19
Balance: screw balance
Frequency: 21,600 vph
Hairspring: flat hairspring

Caliber 925/2

Automatic; single mainspring barrel, 70-hour power reserve
Functions: hours, minutes, sweep seconds; date, moon phase
Diameter: 26 mm
Height: 4.9 mm
Jewels: 30
Frequency: 28,800 vph
Remarks: 245 parts

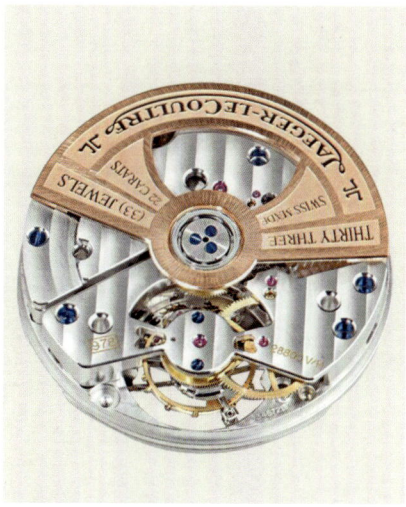

Caliber 978F

Automatic; 1-minute tourbillon; gold rotor; single mainspring barrel, 45-hour power reserve
Functions: hours, minutes, subsidiary seconds (on the tourbillon cage); date hand (jumping hand from the 15th to the 16th of the month)
Diameter: 30 mm
Height: 7.2 mm
Jewels: 33
Balance: glucydur screw balance
Frequency: 28,800 vph
Hairspring: Breguet hairspring
Shock protection: Kif
Remarks: perlage on mainplate, bridges with côtes de Genève; 302 parts

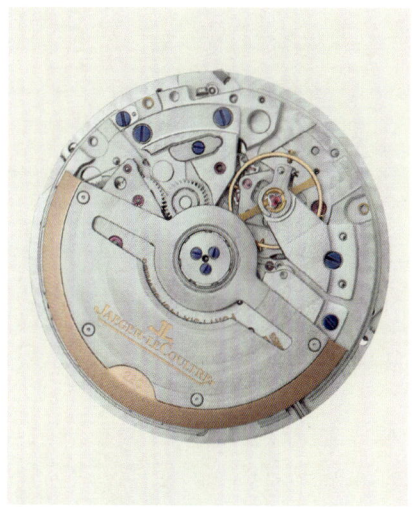

Caliber 868/A2

Automatic; single mainspring barrel, 70-hour power reserve
Functions: hours, minutes, sweep seconds; perpetual calendar with date, weekday, month, moon phase, year display (four digits)
Diameter: 26 mm
Height: 4.72 mm
Jewels: 46
Balance: glucydur
Frequency: 28,800 vph
Remarks: 332 parts

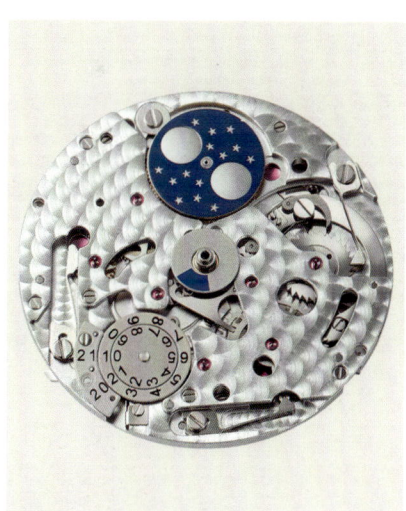

Caliber 868/1

Automatic; single mainspring barrel, 38-hour power reserve
Functions: hours, minutes, sweep seconds; perpetual calendar with date, weekday, month, moon phase, year display (four digits)
Diameter: 27.8 mm
Height: 4.72 mm
Jewels: 46
Balance: glucydur
Frequency: 28,800 vph
Remarks: 336 parts

JS WATCH CO.

When they weren't pillaging Europe and terrorizing populations from the British Isles to Russia, the Vikings were in fact a very hardworking and talented bunch. And when not roaming about, they tended their fields, herds, and houses, and—as a number of exhibitions in recent decades have shown—they made jewelry. Their work in this field was remarkable and fed their commercial supply chains, to use a modern term.

Iceland is where many descendants of the Norsemen live—a rugged and stark landscape, with over three hundred volcanoes and long winter nights. The ability to design and create fine jewelry lives on, and since 2003, the tiny country with a population of over 387,000 has been producing watches as well, thanks to three friends: designer Grimkell Sigurþórsson and watchmakers Sigurður Gilbertsson and Gilbert Guðjónsson.

Their first launch in 2005 of one hundred watches sold out within half a year, and so they persisted, using Swiss or German parts and movements, but creating watches with some unique features paying tribute to their small but very intriguing country. The "execution top" movements provide solid chronometric performance and standard decoration, meaning lower prices but good quality. The timepieces are often inspired and named after an event, place, or year in Iceland or Icelandic history. The Sif N.A.R.T., for instance, was named for the first helicopter of Iceland's Coast Guard rescue teams. The 101 20 Limited Edition is a classic watch to fit many tastes and aspirations without being too extroverted, even if it is celebrating the twentieth anniversary of the company's debut.

The Gilbert collection pays tribute to the company's own watchmaker, Gilbert Guðjónsson, with sober, almost self-effacing timepieces. In the Vinland collection, one finds a wide range of chronographs, some with a tachymeter scale or series that pay tribute to the country's nature—hints of lava—or its special culture—Norse engravings on the mainplate visible through the back. Though small and in a recondite corner of the earth, JS Watch is beginning to make a name for itself.

JS WATCH CO. REYKJAVIK
Laugavegur 62
101 Reykjavik
Iceland

TEL.:
+354-551-05-00

E-MAIL:
info@jswatch.com

WEBSITE:
www.jswatch.com

FOUNDED:
2003

NUMBER OF EMPLOYEES:
5

ANNUAL PRODUCTION:
500 pieces

DISTRIBUTION:
Retail and direct sales
info@jswatch.com
+354-551-4100

PRICE RANGE:
$1,978 to $14,147

101 20 Year Edition

Movement: automatic, Soprod Caliber M100; ø 25.60 mm, height 3.60 mm; 25 jewels; 28,800 vph; "Assortment Chronometer" fine-tuning for near COSC rating; 42-hour power reserve.
Functions: hours, minutes, sweep seconds; date
Case: stainless steel, ø 38.5 mm, height 10 mm; sapphire crystal; transparent case back; water-resistant to 5 atm
Band: ostrich, pin buckle
Price: $2,998

Vinland Chronograph Classic

Movement: automatic, Sellita Caliber SW510; ø 30.40 mm, height 7.90 mm; 27 jewels; 28,800 vph; "Assortment Chronometer" fine tuning for high accuracy; chronograph; 62-hour power reserve.
Functions: hours, minutes, subsidiary seconds; chronograph; 30 minute totalizer; 12 hour totalizer
Case: stainless steel, ø 42 mm, height 14.2 mm; sapphire crystal; transparent case back; water-resistant to 10 atm
Band: ostrich, pin buckle
Price: $7,620

Frisland 1941

Movement: automatic, Soprod Caliber M100; ø 25.60 mm, height 3.60 mm; 25 jewels; 28,800 vph; "Assortment Chronometer" fine-tuning for near COSC rating; 42-hour power reserve.
Functions: hours, minutes, sweep seconds; date
Case: stainless steel, ø 42 mm, height 12 mm; sapphire crystal; transparent case back; water-resistant to 5 atm
Band: calfskin, pin buckle
Price: $3,180

JUNGHANS

The town of Glashütte in Saxony was already a watchmaking name to be reckoned with when Erhard Junghans (b. 1823) founded his factory in 1861 in Schramberg, a small town in the Black Forest. His son Arthur then developed it into a large-scale production site on the American industrial model. At the height of its success, the factory employed nearly three thousand men and women making nine thousand wall clocks and alarm clocks daily.

In the boom years after World War II, the company produced mainly wristwatches. It went on to ring in modern times with its own solar and radio-controlled watches. Junghans was twice the official timekeeper at the Olympic Games.

In 2009, Dr. Hans-Jochem Steim, a successful entrepreneur and political figure from Schramberg, purchased Junghans and brought fresh cash for a new production and distribution schedule. He also initiated the total renovation of the company's spectacular terraced building, a monument of industrial architecture. The work was completed in 2018 for its 100th anniversary and is now open to visitors as a watch and clock museum.

The famous "Terassenbau" is also where Junghans designs, constructs, and manufactures an extensive collection of high-quality wristwatches, ranging from genuine icons of design to major classics, all the way to sporty chronographs. Current collections include Meister, Junghans Form, the 1972 line with reminiscences of 1970s design, and Junghans Max Bill. The watches are all in a sober Bauhaus idiom.

In 2018, to satisfy a broad market and to attach itself to one of its older icons, the company also came out with a brand new radio-controlled movement, the Caliber J101, designed to mix high-tech with a classic look. A brand new time signal enabled rapid synchronization with a smartphone thanks to a specially developed app. In 2025, a limited edition of the Mega Futura was presented. It features digital, radio-controlled time and date display in an asymmetrical case.

UHRENFABRIK JUNGHANS GMBH & CO. KG
Geisshaldenstrasse 49
D-78713 Schramberg
Germany

TEL.:
+49-742-218-0

E-MAIL:
info@junghans.de

WEBSITE:
www.junghans.de

FOUNDED:
1861

NUMBER OF EMPLOYEES:
127

ANNUAL PRODUCTION:
approx. 60,000 watches

U.S. DISTRIBUTOR:
DKSH Luxury & Lifestyle North America Inc.
350 Clark Drive, Suite 325
Mount Olive, NJ 07828
609-750-8800

MOST IMPORTANT COLLECTIONS/PRICE RANGE:
Meister; Max Bill by Junghans; MEGA; 1972
Competition; Form / from approx. $395 to $2,500;
special pieces up to $17,000

Telemeter Edition
Reference number: 27/5588.02
Movement: automatic, Caliber J880.3 (base ETA 2892-A2 with Dubois Dépraz module); ø 30 mm, height 7.6 mm; 49 jewels; 28,800 vph; movement rhodium-plated, blued screws, rotor with stripe finish; 42-hour power reserve
Functions: hours, minutes, subsidiary seconds; chronograph
Case: stainless steel with yellow gold PVD, ø 40.8 mm, height 12.6 mm; sapphire crystal; transparent case back; water-resistant to 5 atm
Band: leather with alligator embossing, pin buckle
Remarks: limited to 150 pieces
Price: $3,180

Telemeter Edition
Reference number: 27/3587.02
Movement: automatic, Caliber J880.3 (base ETA 2892-A2 with Dubois Dépraz module); ø 30 mm, height 7.6 mm; 49 jewels; 28,800 vph; movement rhodium-plated, blued screws, rotor with stripe finish; 42-hour power reserve
Functions: hours, minutes, subsidiary seconds; chronograph
Case: stainless steel, ø 40.8 mm, height 12.6 mm; sapphire crystal; transparent case back; water-resistant to 5 atm
Band: leather, pin buckle
Remarks: limited to 150 pieces
Price: $3,000

Pilot Chronoscope
Reference number: 27/3493.00
Movement: automatic, Caliber J880.4 (base ETA 2892-A2 with Dubois Dépraz module); ø 30 mm, height 7.6 mm; 49 jewels; 28,800 vph; movement rhodium-plated, blued screws, rotor with stripe finish; 42-hour power reserve
Functions: hours, minutes, subsidiary seconds; chronograph
Case: stainless steel, ø 43.3 mm, height 14.4 mm; bidirectional bezel with 0–60 scale; sapphire crystal; water-resistant to 10 atm
Band: leather, pin buckle
Price: $3,220

Meister Chronoscope

Reference number: 27/4224.02
Movement: automatic, Caliber J880.1 (base Sellita SW500); ø 30 mm, height 7.9 mm; 25 jewels; 28,800 vph; movement rhodium-plated, blued screws, rotor with stripe finish; 48-hour power reserve
Functions: hours, minutes, subsidiary seconds; chronograph; date and weekday
Case: stainless steel, ø 40.7 mm, height 13.9 mm; sapphire crystal; transparent case back; water-resistant to 5 atm
Band: ostrich leather, pin buckle
Price: $2,780

Meister Worldtimer

Reference number: 27/3010.02
Movement: automatic, Junghans Caliber J820.5 (base Sellita SW330-2); 28,800 vph; movement rhodium-plated, blued screws, rotor with stripe finish; 42-hour power reserve
Functions: hours, minutes, sweep seconds; world time display (second time zone)
Case: stainless steel, ø 40.4 mm, height 10.5 mm; sapphire crystal; transparent case back; water-resistant to 5 atm
Band: leather, pin buckle
Price: $2,450

Meister Automatic

Reference number: 27/4417.46
Movement: automatic, Caliber J800.1 (base Sellita SW200-1); ø 25.6 mm, height 4.6 mm; 26 jewels; 28,800 vph; movement rhodium-plated, blued screws, rotor with stripe finish; 38-hour power reserve
Functions: hours, minutes, sweep seconds; date
Case: stainless steel, ø 40.4 mm, height 10.9 mm; sapphire crystal; transparent case back; water-resistant to 5 atm
Band: stainless steel, folding clasp
Price: $1,850
Variations: with ostrich leather strap and light gray dial ($1,790)

Pilot Automatic

Reference number: 27/4490.00
Movement: automatic, Caliber J800.1.6 (base Sellita SW261); ø 25.6 mm, height 4.6 mm; 26 jewels; 28,800 vph; movement rhodium-plated, blued screws, rotor with stripe finish; 38-hour power reserve
Functions: hours, minutes, subsidiary seconds; date
Case: stainless steel, ø 43.3 mm, height 12.5 mm; bidirectional bezel with 0–60 scale; sapphire crystal; water-resistant to 10 atm
Band: leather, pin buckle
Price: $2,510
Variations: with dark green dial; with black DLC ($2,620)

Meister S Automatic

Reference number: 27/4518.44
Movement: automatic, Caliber J800.4 (base ETA 2836-2); ø 25.6 mm, height 3.8 mm; 25 jewels; 28,800 vph; movement rhodium-plated, blued screws, rotor with engraved logo; 38-hour power reserve
Functions: hours, minutes, sweep seconds; date, weekday
Case: stainless steel, ø 40.5 mm, height 13 mm; sapphire crystal; screw-down crown; water-resistant to 20 atm
Band: stainless steel, folding clasp
Price: $2,450

Meister S Automatic

Reference number: 27/4411.44
Movement: automatic, Caliber J800.4 (base ETA 2836-2); ø 25.6 mm, height 3.8 mm; 25 jewels; 28,800 vph; movement rhodium-plated, blued screws, rotor with engraved logo; 38-hour power reserve
Functions: hours, minutes, sweep seconds; date, weekday
Case: stainless steel, ø 40.5 mm, height 13 mm; sapphire crystal; screw-down crown; water-resistant to 20 atm
Band: stainless steel, folding clasp
Price: $2,450

1972 Competition

Reference number: 27/4504.00
Movement: automatic, Caliber J880.5 (base Sellita SW500); ø 30 mm, height 7.9 mm; 25 jewels; 28,800 vph; 48-hour power reserve
Functions: hours, minutes, subsidiary seconds; chronograph; date
Case: stainless steel, ø 45.5 mm, height 14.5 mm; sapphire crystal; screw-down crown; water-resistant to 10 atm
Band: leather, folding clasp
Price: $3,110

1972 Competition

Reference number: 27/4509.00
Movement: automatic, Caliber J880.5 (base Sellita SW500); ø 30 mm, height 7.9 mm; 25 jewels; 28,800 vph; 48-hour power reserve
Functions: hours, minutes, subsidiary seconds; chronograph; date
Case: stainless steel, ø 45.5 mm, height 14.5 mm; sapphire crystal; screw-down crown; water-resistant to 10 atm
Band: leather, folding clasp
Price: $3,110

Form A Chronoscope

Reference number: 27/4371.00
Movement: automatic, Caliber J880.1 (base Sellita SW500); ø 30 mm, height 7.9 mm; 25 jewels; 28,800 vph; 48-hour power reserve
Functions: hours, minutes, subsidiary seconds; chronograph; date, weekday
Case: stainless steel with black PVD coating, ø 42 mm, height 13.7 mm; sapphire crystal; transparent case back; water-resistant to 5 atm
Band: leather, pin buckle
Price: $2,510
Variations: various index and strap colors

Max Bill Chronoscope Bauhaus

Reference number: 27/4409.02
Movement: automatic, Caliber J880.2 (base Sellita SW500); ø 30 mm, height 7.9 mm; 25 jewels; 28,800 vph; 48-hour power reserve
Functions: hours, minutes; chronograph; date
Case: stainless steel with black PVD coating, ø 40 mm, height 14.4 mm; sapphire crystal; transparent case back; water-resistant to 5 atm
Band: leather, pin buckle
Price: $3,020

Max Bill Automatic Bauhaus

Reference number: 27/4009.02
Movement: automatic, Caliber J800.1 (base Sellita SW200-1); ø 25.6 mm, height 4.6 mm; 26 jewels; 28,800 vph; 38-hour power reserve
Functions: hours, minutes, sweep seconds; date
Case: stainless steel, ø 38 mm, height 10 mm; sapphire crystal; transparent case back; water-resistant to 5 atm
Band: leather, pin buckle
Price: $1,740
Variations: with black PVD coating ($1,820)

Form A Bauhaus

Reference number: 27/4533.44
Movement: automatic, Caliber J800.2 (base Sellita SW200-1); ø 25.6 mm, height 4.6 mm; 26 jewels; 28,800 vph; 38-hour power reserve
Functions: hours, minutes, sweep seconds; date
Case: stainless steel with black PVD coating, ø 39.3 mm, height 9.5 mm; sapphire crystal; transparent case back; water-resistant to 5 atm
Band: leather, folding clasp
Price: $1,490; limited to 1000 pieces

KLEYNOD

Watches were a common gift in the former Soviet Union, so it may not come as a great surprise that millions of timepieces of all types were manufactured during that period. Today, many can be found for sale online. They are appreciated for their rugged looks, the identifiable symbols (like the red star), and their robust construction. Several big names dominate, of course: Vostok, Sturmanskie, Raketa, among others. Most are still with us these days as new brands appear using the old tools.

Among the more recent enterprises is the Kyiv Watch Factory, founded in 1997 in the Ukrainian capital. It was the manufacturing hub for the Russian brand Poljot, among others. Perhaps more famous, in Ukraine at least, was the making of a watch for Ukrainian astronaut Leonid Kadeniuk, who was on the international STS-87 mission that was carried out by the space shuttle Columbia. In 2002, the company decided to create a distinct brand of its own. They chose the name Kleynod, which derives from the German *Kleinod*, or Polish *klejnot*, an old word for "gem."

The output is divided into six main collections—and still going strong in spite of blackouts and bombing scares due to the ongoing war. For the sake of affordability, the movements used are mostly quartz, but a fair number of the watches do come equipped with Swiss-made mechanical movements by Ronda or Sellita. Still, they are all under the $1,000-dollar mark.

Perhaps more interestingly though are the motifs on the dials that reflect a pride in the country's long history. The 3, 6, 9, and 12 appearing on the Kleynods of Independence collection may hardly be recognizable at first because they have been stylized to look like the *tryzub*, the distinctive Ukrainian trident, on a guilloché background. This heraldic element originates back in the mists of the nation's history. The numerals of the Classic model also mirror the style of the *tryzub*, though the dial is far simpler. And on the ladies' watches, one finds hints of the nation's famous embroidery, with patterns that change depending which part of the country is producing them.

KLEYNOD UKRAINIAN WATCHES
Kyrylivska Street 69
Kyiv, 04080
Ukraine

TEL.:
+38 067-223-1085

E-MAIL:
trade@kleynod.ua

WEBSITE:
www.us.kleynodwatches.com

FOUNDED:
2002

NUMBER OF EMPLOYEES:
100

ANNUAL PRODUCTION:
approx. 90,000 watches

U. S. DISTRIBUTOR:
V2Com Commerce LLC
775 Bloomfield Ave, Suite 1B
Clifton, NJ 07012
862-367-2925
kleynodusa@gmail.com

MOST IMPORTANT COLLECTIONS/PRICE RANGE
Mechanical and quartz: Antonov (quartz), Classic, Embroidery, Kleynods of Independence, Football Collection, Kleynod Forces / up to $890

Kleynods of Independence
Reference number: K 30-536
Movement: automatic, Sellita caliber SW-200-1; ø 25.6 mm, height 4.6 mm; 26 jewels; 28,800 vph; 41-hour power reserve
Functions: hours, minutes, sweep seconds; date
Case: stainless steel, ø 44 mm, height 12 mm; sapphire crystal; water-resistant to 5 atm
Band: leather, folding clasp
Remarks: guilloché on dial with Ukrainian trident coat of arms in the center
Price: $855; limited to 300 pieces
Variations: in stainless steel with IP-gold and bi-color case

Classic Collection
Reference number: K 348-523
Movement: automatic, Sellita caliber SW-200-1; ø 25.6 mm, height 4.6 mm; 26 jewels; 28,800 vph; 41-hour power reserve
Functions: hours, minutes, sweep seconds; date
Case: stainless steel, ø 42 mm, height 11,2 mm; sapphire crystal; water-resistant to 5 atm
Band: leather, folding clasp
Remarks: guilloché on dial
Price: $660
Variations: in stainless steel with IP-gold, blue and black dials

Embroidery Collection
Reference number: K 308-611W
Movement: automatic, Sellita caliber SW-200-1; ø 25.6 mm, height 4.6 mm; 26 jewels; 28,800 vph; 41-hour power reserve
Functions: hours, minutes, sweep seconds; date
Case: stainless steel with gold IPG plating, ø 37 mm, height 10 mm; sapphire crystal; water-resistant to 5 atm
Band: leather, regular clasp
Remarks: print on dial
Price: $660
Variations: in stainless steel case with black strap

KOBOLD

Like many others in the field, Michael Kobold had already developed an interest in the watch industry in childhood. As a young man, he found a mentor in Chronoswiss founder Gerd-Rüdiger Lang, who encouraged him to start his own brand. This happened in 1998 when Kobold was nineteen years of age and still a student at Carnegie Mellon University.

Today, after twenty-five years, Kobold Watch Company is paying homage to mentor Lang with a re-imagined version of master watchmaker Gerd-R. Lang's iconic Kairos, which had its debut in 1986. It is not surprising for a company whose motto is "Embrace Adventure" that explorers such as Sir Ranulph Fiennes, whom Guinness Book of World Records describes as "the world's greatest living explorer," and mountaineers such as Reinhold Messner and David Breashears wear these mechanical instruments as well.

The brand's centerpiece is the Soarway collection and the fabled Soarway case, which was originally created in 1999 by Sir Ranulph, Gerd-R. Lang, and company founder Kobold, himself an avid mountain climber.

Kobold's love of the Himalayas has driven his commitment to the people of Nepal. In 2015, he launched the Soarway Foundation/Engage Nepal, which today is run by the former U.S. ambassador to Nepal. His love of that country is also behind the Fire Truck Expedition as a way to supply the mountain-clad country with key firefighting equipment.

Kobold has contributed to the renaissance of American watchmaking with in-house CNC machining of the cases and in-house assembly. At one point there was even talk of an in-house movement. After Gerd-R. Lang passed away, however, Kobold acquired over 15,000 of the late watchmaker's movements. "By combining Rüdiger's vintage movements with watchcases he designed such as the Kairos and Convertible, we now have a perfect solution while at the same time paying tribute to my late friend and mentor," says Kobold.

KOBOLD TIME GMBH
Willibald-Alexis-Strasse 18
D-10965 Berlin
Germany

TEL.:
+49-151-105-500-10
1-412-596-1585

E-MAIL:
info@koboldwatch.com

WEBSITE:
www.koboldwatch.com

FOUNDED:
1998

NUMBER OF EMPLOYEES:
8

ANNUAL PRODUCTION:
maximum 2,500 watches

DISTRIBUTION:
factory-direct, select retailers
1-412-596-1585

MOST IMPORTANT COLLECTION/PRICE RANGE:
Soarway, Phantom, SMG / $2,650 to $48,000

Gerd-R. Lang Chronograph

Reference number: KD 7523
Movement: automatic, ETA 7750; ø 25.6 mm, height 7.9 mm; 25 jewels; 28,800 vph; with côtes de Genève and perlage; engraved and skeletonized gold-plated rotor; 46-hour power reserve
Functions: hours, minutes, subsidiary seconds; date; chronograph
Case: stainless steel, ø 38 mm, height 15 mm; sapphire crystal; transparent case back; water-resistant to 3 atm
Band: reptile skin, screw-locked buckle
Remarks: fully skeletonized movement available on request
Price: $3,250

Rattrapante Stirling Moss

Reference number: KD 7322
Movement: automatic, ETA 7750; ø 25.6 mm, height 7.9 mm; 25 jewels; 28,800 vph; côtes de Genève, perlage, engraved and skeletonized gold-plated rotor; 46-hour power reserve
Functions: hours, minutes, subsidiary seconds; chronograph
Case: stainless steel, ø 38 mm, height 15 mm; sapphire crystal; transparent case back; water-resistant to 3 atm
Band: reptile skin, screw-locked buckle
Remarks: fully skeletonized movement available on request
Price: $4,500

Cabriolet

Reference number: KD 2803
Movement: automatic, ETA 2670; ø 17.5 mm, height 4.8 mm; 17 jewels; 28,800 vph; with côtes de Genève, perlage, engraved and skeletonized gold-plated rotor; 39-hour power reserve
Functions: hours, minutes, sweep seconds
Case: stainless, 43 mm x 27 mm, height 9 mm; screw-locked lug bars; sapphire crystal; screwed-down case back; water-resistant to 3 atm
Band: calfskin, screw-locked buckle
Remarks: reversible case
Price: $6,450

Jolly Jumper

Reference number: KD 1423
Movement: automatic, Enicar 165 ø 28.6 mm, height 6.9 mm; 32 jewels; 21,600 vph; 42-hour power reserve
Functions: jump hours, retrograde minutes, subsidiary seconds
Case: stainless steel, 19 components, ø 38 mm, height 11 mm; sapphire crystal; screwed-down exhibition case back; screw-down crown; screw-locked lug bars, water-resistant to 10 atm
Band: canvas, screw-locked buckle
Price: $5,750

Seal Ceramic James Gandolfini Meteorite dial

Reference number: KD 842121C
Movement: automatic, ETA 2892-A2; ø 36 mm, height 3.6 mm; 21 jewels; 28,800 vph; 42-hour power reserve
Functions: hours, minutes, sweep seconds
Case: ceramic, ø 44 mm, height 17.0 mm; unidirectional rotating bezel with 60-minute divisions; antireflective sapphire crystal; screwed-in crown; screw-mounted case back; water-resistant to 100 atm
Band: rubber, signed buckle
Price: $8,500; limited to 51 pieces
Variations: varied dials, including Mount Everest summit rock, malachite, turquoise

Limits Safari

Reference number: KD 5546142
Movement: automatic, Caliber ETA 2824-A2; ø 26.2 mm, height 4.6 mm; 25 jewels; 28,800 vph; **40-hour power reserve**
Functions: hours, minutes, sweep seconds
Case: stainless steel, ø 43 mm, height 12.75 mm; unidirectional bezel with 0-60 scale; sapphire crystal; screw-mounted case back; screw-down crown; water-resistant to 20 atm
Band: rubber, pin buckle
Price: $2,550

Timemaster Chronograph

Reference number: KD 7634
Movement: automatic, ETA 7750; ø 25.6 mm, height 7.9 mm; 25 jewels; 28,800 vph; côtes de Genève, perlage, engraved and skeletonized gold-plated rotor; 46-hour power reserve
Functions: hours, minutes, subsidiary seconds; date; chronograph
Case: titanium, ø 42.5 mm, height 15 mm; bezel with tachymeter scale (blank bezel optional); screwed-in crown; sapphire crystal; screw-mounted back; water-resistant to 20 atm
Band: reptile skin, pin buckle
Price: $3,650

Professional Chronograph

Reference number: KD 824531
Movement: automatic, ETA 7750; ø 25.6 mm, height 7.9 mm; 25 jewels; 28,800 vph; with côtes de Genève, Perlage; engraved and skeletonized gold-plated rotor; 46-hour power reserve
Functions: hours, minutes, subsidiary seconds; chronograph
Case: stainless steel, ø 40.5 mm, height 17 mm; bezel with tachymeter scale (blank bezel optional); screw-down crown; sapphire crystal; screw-mounted back; water-resistant to 20 atm
Band: reptile skin, pin buckle
Price: $1,650

Soarway Diver

Reference number: KD 1113145
Movement: automatic, ETA 2892; ø 25.6 mm, height 3.6 mm; 25 jewels; 28,800 vph; côtes de Genève, perlage, engraved and skeletonized gold-plated rotor; 42-hour power reserve
Functions: hours, minutes, sweep seconds; date (optional)
Case: stainless steel with black DLC, ø 40.5 mm, height 10 mm; unidirectional bezel with 60-minute divisions; screwed-down crown; sapphire crystal; screw-mounted back; water-resistant to 30 atm
Band: canvas, pin buckle
Price: $5,950

KUDOKE

Stefan Kudoke, a watchmaker from Frankfurt an der Oder, has earned a reputation as an exceptionally skilled and imaginative creator of timepieces. He apprenticed with two seasoned watchmakers and graduated as the top trainee in the state of Brandenburg, earning him a scholarship from a federal program for gifted individuals. He then moved to one of the major *manufactures* in Glashütte, where he refined his abilities in the workshop for complications and prototyping. At just twenty-two, master's diploma in hand, he decided to pursue an MBA and then devote himself to building his own company.

His guiding principle is individuality—something he believes cannot be achieved with a purely serial product. Kudoke therefore began producing one-of-a-kind creations. By realizing each client's specific wishes, he manages to reflect the personality of the wearer in each watch. The results include remarkable pieces such as ExCentro 1 and 2, and more recently a watch featuring an octopus seemingly climbing out of the case. Even his more minimalist works, like the KUDOKE 1 and 2, are carefully considered. They use deliberately restrained colors, such as anthracite, that interact subtly with the forms.

Kudoke organizes his output into two clear categories: HANDwerk, meaning crafts and referring to classic watchmaking such as the KUDOKE 3; and KUNSTwerk, meaning artwork, which encompasses his sculptural engravings. The latter allows him to explore his specialties, like engraving and goldsmithing, where edges can become elegant contours and plate fragments can be transformed into figures or ornamental motifs. His creativity has earned him major recognition, including the Grand Prix d'Horlogerie de Genève (GPHG) in the Petite Aiguille category in 2019, and again in 2024 for his KUDOKE 3 Salmon.

For Kudoke, preserving and passing on traditional watchmaking is a central mission, which puts him in perfect alignment with the values of the AHCI (Académie Horlogère des Créateurs Indépendants). As a member of this distinguished association of leading independent watchmakers, he represents a blend of artisanal excellence, artistic freedom, and authenticity.

KUDOKE UHREN
Tannenweg 5
D-15236 Frankfurt (Oder)
Germany

TEL.:
+49-335-280-0409

E-MAIL:
info@kudoke.eu

WEBSITE:
www.kudoke.eu

FOUNDED:
2007

NUMBER OF EMPLOYEES:
4

ANNUAL PRODUCTION:
150 watches

DISTRIBUTION:
Contact the brand directly for information

PRICE RANGE:
between approx. $4,500 and $32,000

Kudoke 5

Movement: hand-wound, Kudoke caliber 1 Version 24H-L; ø 30 mm, height 4.3 mm; 18 jewels; 28,800 vph; hand-engraved and finished movement; 46-hour power reserve
Functions: 24-hour display (disc display, each line representing 15 minutes)
Case: stainless steel; ø 38 mm, height 12 mm; sapphire crystal; transparent case back; water-resistant to 5 atm
Band: leather strap with pin buckle
Remarks: hand-engraved celestial disk, galvanically treated in three colors
Price: $22,240

Kudoke 3 "Flakes"

Movement: hand-wound, Kudoke caliber 1; ø 30 mm, height 4.3 mm; 18 jewels; 28,800 vph; hand-engraved and finished movement; 46-hour power reserve
Functions: hours (incremental display), minutes
Case: stainless steel; ø 38 mm, height 10.3 mm; sapphire crystal; transparent case back; water-resistant to 5 atm
Band: leather strap with pin buckle
Remarks: hand-engraved upper plate
Price: $17,760

Kudoke 1

Movement: hand-wound, Kudoke caliber 1; ø 30 mm, height 4.3 mm; 18 jewels; 28,800 vph; hand-engraved and finished movement; 46-hour power reserve
Functions: hours, minutes, subsidiary seconds
Case: stainless steel; ø 38 mm, height 9.5 mm; sapphire crystal; transparent case back; water-resistant to 5 atm
Band: leather strap with pin buckle
Price: $10,730

LAURENT FERRIER

A rock rolling along a riverbed or being buffeted by coastal surf will, over time, achieve a kind of perfect shape, streamlined, flowing, smooth. It will usually become a comfortable touchstone for the human hand—a fine pebble, or *galet* in French. And that is the name given to the first watches made by Laurent Ferrier in Geneva, Switzerland. The name refers to the special look and feel of the cases, which are just one hallmark of this very unusual, yet classical, watch brand.

Laurent Ferrier is a real person, the offspring of a watchmaking family from the Canton of Neuchâtel, and a trained watchmaker. As a young man he had a passion for cars, too, and even raced seven times at the 24 Hours of Le Mans. In 2009, after thirty-five years of employment at Patek Philippe working on new movements, Ferrier decided he had been shaped enough by his industry. He gathered up his deep experience and founded his own enterprise. He was joined by his son, Christian Ferrier, a watchmaker in his own right, and fellow former race driver François Sérvanin.

In 2023, the Grand Sport Tourbillon Pursuit picked up the Tourbillon Prize at the Geneva "grand prix," the GPHG. Like other models in the collection, this one uses a natural escapement with a double hairspring, ensuring greater accuracy (a technical idea going back to Breguet). The tourbillon is once again concealed on the movement side, keeping the dial free of clutter.

The flagship Galet keeps evolving and being used to house different complications, like a second time zone. The Classic Auto Sandstone keeps the *galet* shape with a copper-hued dial that whispers "vintage." And after the 2023 prize for the Tourbillon Pursuit, Laurent Ferrier picked up a second prize in 2024 for the Classic Moon Silver in red gold, this time in the Calendar and Astronomy category. For all of its deep roots in traditional watchmaking, Laurent Ferrier celebrated its fifteenth anniversary in 2025 with a look back to its past and the original "Atelier" series of timekeepers. Grand Feu enamel, tourbillons on the rear of the watch, bright colors, and always sophisticated understatement.

LAURENT FERRIER
Route de Saint Julien 150
CH-1228 Plan-les-Ouates
Switzerland

TEL.:
+41-22-716-3388

E-MAIL:
info@laurentferrier.ch

WEBSITE:
www.laurentferrier.ch

FOUNDED:
2010

NUMBER OF EMPLOYEES:
12

ANNUAL PRODUCTION:
135

U.S. DISTRIBUTOR:
Cellini Jewelers
430 Park Avenue at 56th Street
New York, NY 10022
212.888.0505
800.CELLINI
Contact@CelliniJewelers.com

MOST IMPORTANT COLLECTIONS/PRICE RANGE:
Variations of the Galet / from $40,000 to $345,000

Classic Traveller Globe Night Blue

Reference number: LCF012.G1.NGE10
Movement: automatic, Laurent Ferrier Caliber LF 230.02; ø 31.6 mm, height 5.80 mm; 21,600 vph; 44 jewels; gold off-center micro-rotor; natural lever escapement with double escape wheel; silicon pallet lever; finely decorated bridges and mainplate with côtes de Genève; 72-hour power reserve
Functions: hours, minutes, subsidiary seconds; second time zone at 9 o'clock aperture; date
Case: white gold, ø 41 mm, height 12.64 mm; ball-shaped crown; sapphire crystal, transparent screwed-down case back; water-resistant to 3 atm
Band: calfskin (nubuck), pin buckle
Price: $110,000

Classic Origin Beige

Reference number: LCF036.R5.BR5
Movement: hand-wound, Laurent Ferrier Caliber LF116.01; ø 31.60, height 4.35 mm; 21,600 vph; 21 jewels; Swiss lever escapement; screw balance with variable inertia; 80-hour power reserve
Functions: hours, minutes, subsidiary seconds
Case: red gold, ø 40 mm, height 10.70 mm; domed and tinted sapphire crystal; transparent case back; ball-shaped crown; water-resistant to 10 atm
Band: leather, gold pin buckle
Remarks: the tourbillon is on the movement side in traditional style; beige opaline dial
Price: $49,500

Classic Auto Horizon

Reference number: LCF012.G1.NGE10
Movement: automatic, Laurent Ferrier Caliber LF270.01; ø 31.60 mm, height 4.85 mm; 28,800 vph; 31 jewels; silicon escapement; finely decorated bridges and mainplate with côtes de Genève; micro-rotor, platinum oscillating weight; 72-hour power reserve
Functions: hours, minutes, subsidiary seconds; date
Case: stainless steel, ø 40 mm, height 11.94 mm; ball-shaped crown; sapphire crystal, transparent case back; water-resistant to 3 atm
Band: goat leather, pin buckle
Price: $56,000

LEICA

Alongside fine watchmaking, the manufacture of cameras has long been considered one of the highest disciplines of precision engineering. Leica Camera AG's decision to develop its own wristwatch collection was therefore a natural step. After all, the Leica M series still inspires admiration among connoisseurs of fine cameras. Compact, silent, extremely precise, and robust, these cameras have always set a benchmark. Applying the same standards of quality to a wristwatch was simply a matter of time.

In 2023, Leica launched its first two wristwatches designed and built entirely from scratch. This came after several tentative starts around 2018, when the L1 and L2 models appeared only briefly on the market. Discreetly concealed within the winding crown of the ZM 1 and ZM 2 timepieces is Leica's signature red dot—a detail that, on cameras, would normally carry the company's name.

Following their warm reception, Leica released a second series: the ZM 11, followed by the ZM 12. Compared to its predecessors, the ZM 11 is simpler and more traditional, yet no less refined. Its titanium or stainless-steel case features a flawless surface finish of exceptional quality. The movement was developed by Swiss manufacturer Chronode in Le Locle, a firm renowned for powering the success of many other prestigious brands. A standout feature, inspired by the lens-locking mechanism of Leica cameras, is the rapid strap-changing system, which allows wearers to switch effortlessly between straps. By pressing the red Leica dot under the lug, one can swap the sporty vulcanized rubber or textile strap for an elegant titanium or stainless-steel bracelet, thus rapidly transforming the watch's character.

Design cues from Leica cameras appear throughout the watches. The shutter-inspired dial shifts color depending on the angle of light. Finely crafted hands and indexes, the nuanced shape of the steel case, and the unique crown fluting (echoing the shutter release button) all pay homage to Leica's design language. The domed sapphire crystal recalls the curvature of the company's legendary lenses.

Leica operates a dedicated watchmaking atelier at its historic Wetzlar site, where timepieces undergo final preparation and servicing. Distribution is managed through Leica's global network of specialized camera boutiques.

ERNST LEITZ WERKSTÄTTEN GMBH
Am Leitz-Park 4
D-35578 Wetzlar
Germany

TEL.:
+49 6441-899-330

E-MAIL:
pr@ernst-leitz-werkstaetten.com

WEBSITE:
www.ernst-leitz-werkstaetten.com

FOUNDED:
2022

NUMBER OF EMPLOYEES:
7

DISTRIBUTION
Retail, direct sales
Leica Store LA
424-777-0341
leicastore.la@leica-camera.com
Leica Store
202-787-5900
leicastore.dc@leica-camera.com

MOST IMPORTANT COLLECTIONS/PRICE RANGE:
ZM 1 and ZM 2 /monochrome versions / ZM 11 and ZM 12 / $10,000 to $15,500

ZM 1

Movement: hand-wound, Leica Caliber ZM 1; ø 35.75 mm, height 6.35 mm; 26 jewels; 28,800 vph; automatic seconds zero reset; 60-hour power reserve
Functions: hours, minutes, subsidiary seconds; power-reserve indicator; date
Case: stainless steel, ø 41 mm, height 14.5 mm; sapphire crystal; transparent case back; patented crown with pusher that switches between winding and time-setting with a switch indicator; water-resistant to 5 atm
Band: calfskin, pin buckle
Price: $10,850

ZM 11

Movement: automatic, Leica caliber LA-3001 (Chronode C102 base); ø 30.4 mm, height 4.15 mm; 35 jewels; 28,800 vph; automatic seconds zero reset; 60-hour power reserve
Functions: hours, minutes, sweep seconds; date
Case: titanium, ø 41 mm, height 13 mm; sapphire crystal; transparent case back; water-resistant to 10 atm
Band: titanium; folding clasp
Remarks: rapid strap changing system activated by a red button (like the lens locking mechanism on Leica cameras)
Price: $8,725
Variations: textile, pin buckle ($7,840); in stainless steel with bracelet ($7,975); in stainless steel with rubber or textile strap ($7,250)

ZM 12

Movement: automatic, Leica Caliber LA-3002 (base Chronode C102); ø 30.4 mm, height 4.15 mm; 38 jewels; 28,800 vph; 60-hour power reserve
Functions: hours, minutes, subsidiary seconds
Case: stainless steel, ø 39 mm, height 13 mm; sapphire crystal; transparent case back; water-resistant to 10 atm
Band: rubber and special textile, pin buckle
Remarks: rapid strap changing system activated by a red button on the case rear
Price: $7,440
Variations: in titanium with textile or bracelet

LONGINES

The Longines winged hourglass logo is the world's oldest trademark, according to the World Intellectual Property Organization (WIPO). Since its founding in 1832, the brand has manufactured somewhere in the region of 35 million watches, making it one of the genuine heavyweights of the Swiss watch world. In 1983, Nicolas G. Hayek merged the two major Swiss watch manufacturing groups ASUAG and SSIH into what would later become the Swatch Group. Longines, the leading ASUAG brand, barely missed capturing the same position in the new concern; that honor went to Omega, the SIHH frontrunner. However, from a historical and technical point of view, this brand has what it takes to be at the helm of any group. Was it not Longines that equipped polar explorer Roald Amundsen and air pioneer Charles Lindbergh with their watches? It has also been the timekeeper at many Olympic Games and is a major sponsor at many other sports events, from riding to archery.

Longines now has an impressive portfolio of in-house calibers, from simple manual winders to complicated chronographs. Thanks to this, it can supply Swatch Group with anything from low-cost, thin quartz watches to heavy gold chronographs and calendars with quadruple retrograde displays. In addition to elegant ladies' watches and modern sports watches such as the HydroConquest and Spirit collections, the company has made a point of remaking models from its own history through the Heritage collection. For example, the Ultra-Chron, with its high-speed oscillating movement, has been reissued exclusively for Longines with modern technology. There is also a detailed replica of a pilot's watch from the 1930s, whose special feature is an internal reference time index that can be adjusted via the rotating bezel.

In 2025, Longines celebrated the 100th anniversary of the first wristwatch with a second time zone on the dial and introduced a special model in the Spirit Zulu Time line. The design of the dial, the typography, the proportions of the case—all of this corresponds to the predecessors in the Spirit Zulu Time line. This also applies to the functionality and the mechanics.

LONGINES WATCH CO.
Rue des Longines 8
CH-2610 St-Imier
Switzerland

TEL.:
+41-32-942-5425

E-MAIL:
info@longines.com

WEBSITE:
www.longines.com

FOUNDED:
1832

NUMBER OF EMPLOYEES:
worldwide approx. 2000

U.S. DISTRIBUTOR:
Longines
The Swatch Group (U.S.), Inc.
Longines Division
800 Waterford Way, Ste. 1000
Miami, FL 33126
786-725-5394
www.longines.com

MOST IMPORTANT COLLECTIONS/PRICE RANGE:
The Longines Master Collection, Longines DolceVita, HydroConquest, Heritage Collection / from approx. $1,000 to $10,000

Spirit Zulu Time 1925
Reference number: L3.803.5.53.6
Movement: automatic, Longines Caliber L844.4 (base ETA A31.411); ø 25.6 mm, height 3.85 mm; 21 jewels; 25,200 vph; silicon hairspring, antimagnetic escapement; 72-hour power reserve; COSC-certified chronometer
Functions: hours (crown adjusted), minutes, sweep seconds; additional 24-hour display (second time zone); date
Case: stainless steel, ø 39 mm, height 13,5 mm; bidirectional bezel with rose-gold insert with 0-24 scale; sapphire crystal; transparent case back; screw-down crown; water-resistant to 10 atm
Band: stainless steel, folding clasp
Remarks: special edition for 100 years of the Zulu Time
Price: $4,700

Conquest Chrono Ski Edition
Reference number: L3.836.4.52.9
Movement: automatic, Longines Caliber L898 (base ETA A31. L21); ø 28 mm, height 6.35 mm; 37 jewels; 25,200 vph; silicon hairspring; 72-hour power reserve
Functions: hours, minutes, subsidiary seconds; chronograph
Case: stainless steel, ø 42 mm, height 14.3 mm; bezel with ceramic insert; sapphire crystal; transparent case back; water-resistant to 10 atm
Band: stainless steel, double folding clasp, with fine adjustment
Remarks: special FIS Alpine World Ski Championship edition, limited to 2025 pieces; additional comes with additional rubber strap
Price: $4,850

Ultra-Chron Carbon
Reference number: L2.839.4.52.2
Movement: automatic, Longines Caliber L836 (base ETA C07. L11); ø 25.6 mm, height 4.6 mm; 25 jewels; 36,000 vph; silicon-hairspring, escape wheel and anchor made of antimagnetic nickel-phosphorous (LIGA technology); Timelab-certified chronometer; 52-hour power reserve Functions: hours, minutes, sweep seconds
Case: carbon fiber, ø 43 mm, height 14.2 mm; unidirectional titanium bezel with aluminum insert and 0-60 scale; sapphire crystal; screw-down crown; water-resistant to 30 atm
Band: textile, pin buckle
Price: $5,550

Conquest Heritage Central Power Reserve

Reference number: L1.648.4.78.2
Movement: automatic, Longines Caliber L896.5 (base ETA A31.321); ø 25.6 mm; 21 jewels; 25,200 vph; silicon hairspring, antimagnetic escapement (LIGA technology); 72-hour power reserve
Functions: hours, minutes, sweep seconds; power reserve indicator; date
Case: stainless steel, ø 38 mm, height 12.3 mm; sapphire crystal; water-resistant to 5 atm
Band: reptile skin, pin buckle
Price: $4,300

Conquest

Reference number: L3.720.4.92.9
Movement: automatic, Longines Caliber L888 (base ETA A31. L11); ø 25.6 mm, height 3.85 mm; 21 jewels; 25,200 vph; silicon hairspring; 72-hour power reserve
Functions: hours, minutes, sweep seconds; date
Case: stainless steel, ø 38 mm, height 10.9 mm; sapphire crystal; transparent case back; water-resistant to 10 atm
Band: rubber, double folding clasp, with fine adjustment
Price: $2,200

Conquest

Reference number: L3.830.4.02.6
Movement: automatic, Longines Caliber L888 (base ETA A31. L01); ø 25.6 mm, height 3.85 mm; 21 jewels; 25,200 vph; silicon hairspring; 72-hour power reserve
Functions: hours, minutes, sweep seconds; date
Case: stainless steel, ø 41 mm, height 12 mm; sapphire crystal; transparent case back; water-resistant to 10 atm
Band: stainless steel, triple folding clasp
Price: $2,400

Conquest

Reference number: L3.430.4.92.6
Movement: automatic, Longines Caliber L888 (base ETA A31. L01); ø 25.6 mm, height 3.85 mm; 21 jewels; 25,200 vph; silicon hairspring; 72-hour power reserve
Functions: hours, minutes, sweep seconds; date
Case: stainless steel, ø 34 mm, height 10.9 mm; sapphire crystal; transparent case back; water-resistant to 10 atm
Band: stainless steel, triple folding clasp
Price: $2,400

Conquest Heritage

Reference number: L1.650.4.92.6
Movement: automatic, Longines Caliber L888 (base ETA A31. L11); ø 25.6 mm, height 3.85 mm; 21 jewels; 25,200 vph; silicon hairspring; 72-hour power reserve; COSC-certified chronometer
Functions: hours, minutes, sweep seconds
Case: stainless steel, ø 40 mm, height 12 mm; sapphire crystal; water-resistant to 5 atm
Band: stainless steel, double folding clasp, with fine adjustment
Price: $3,400

Conquest Heritage

Reference number: L1.649.4.62.2
Movement: automatic, Longines Caliber L888 (base ETA A31. L11); ø 25.6 mm, height 3.85 mm; 21 jewels; 25,200 vph; silicon hairspring; 72-hour power reserve; COSC-certified chronometer
Functions: hours, minutes, sweep seconds
Case: stainless steel, ø 38 mm, height 12 mm; sapphire crystal; water-resistant to 5 atm
Band: reptile skin, pin buckle
Price: $3,300

Legend Diver

Reference number: L3.764.4.16.6
Movement: automatic, Longines Caliber L888.6 (base ETA A31.411); ø 25.6 mm, height 3.85 mm; 21 jewels; 25,200 vph; silicon hairspring, antimagnetic escapement (LIGA technology); Timelab-certified chronometer; 72-hour power reserve
Functions: hours, minutes, sweep seconds
Case: stainless steel, ø 39 mm, height 12.7 mm; crown-activated inner ring with 0-60 scale; sapphire crystal; screw-down crown; water-resistant to 30 atm
Band: stainless steel, double folding clasp, with fine adjustment
Price: $3,850

HydroConquest GMT

Reference number: L3.890.4.56.6
Movement: automatic, Longines Caliber L844 (base ETA A31.411); ø 25.6 mm, height 3.85 mm; 21 jewels; 25,200 vph; silicon hairspring, antimagnetic escapement (LIGA technology); 72-hour power reserve
Functions: hours, minutes, sweep seconds (incremental setting of hour hand); additional 24-hour display (second time zone); date
Case: stainless steel, ø 43 mm, height 12.9 mm; unidirectional bezel with ceramic insert, with 0-60 scale; sapphire crystal; screw-down crown; water-resistant to 30 atm
Band: stainless steel, double folding clasp
Price: $3,350

Primaluna Moonphase

Reference number: L8.126.4.71.6
Movement: automatic, Longines Caliber L899 (base ETA A31.L91); ø 25.6 mm, height 3.85 mm; 21 jewels; 25,200 vph; silicon hairspring; 72-hour power reserve
Functions: hours, minutes, sweep seconds; date, moon phase
Case: stainless steel, ø 34 mm, height 8.9 mm; sapphire crystal; transparent case back; water-resistant to 3 atm
Band: stainless steel, triple folding clasp
Price: $3,000

Primaluna Moonphase

Reference number: L8.126.5.79.7
Movement: automatic, Longines Caliber L899 (base ETA A31.L91); ø 25.6 mm, height 3.85 mm; 21 jewels; 25,200 vph; silicon hairspring; 72-hour power reserve
Functions: hours, minutes, sweep seconds; date, moon phase
Case: stainless steel, ø 34 mm, height 8.9 mm; yellow gold bezel; sapphire crystal; transparent case back; water-resistant to 3 atm
Band: stainless steel with yellow-gold middle links, triple folding clasp
Price: $6,350

Primaluna Moonphase

Reference number: L8.126.0.797.2
Movement: automatic, Longines Caliber L899 (base ETA A31.L91); ø 25.6 mm, height 3.85 mm; 21 jewels; 25,200 vph; silicon hairspring; 72-hour power reserve
Functions: hours, minutes, sweep seconds; date, moon phase
Case: stainless steel, ø 34 mm, height 8.9 mm; bezel set with 48 sapphires; sapphire crystal; transparent case back; water-resistant to 3 atm
Band: reptile skin, double folding clasp
Remarks: mother-of-pearl dial set with 14 diamonds
Price: $6,700

Mini Dolcevita

Reference number: L5.200.7.71.6
Movement: quartz
Functions: hours, minutes, subsidiary seconds
Case: yellow gold, set with 38 diamonds, 21.5 mm x 29 mm; sapphire crystal; water-resistant to 3 atm
Band: yellow gold, folding clasp
Price: $27,500

LOUIS ERARD

Once upon a time in the watchmaking workshops, there was a large clock that gave the minutes as the main time increment and the hours on a separate dial. This allowed the watchmakers to set and test the accuracy of the piece they were assembling. Over time, so-called regulator dials became popular with the public. It is said that train conductors preferred them because they needed accuracy to the minute.

Among the rare brands that have made regulator watches an important part of their output is Louis Erard. The company namesake (1893–1964), a watchmaker by trade, founded a watchmaking school in his native La Chaux-de-Fonds, and later a casing business for the thriving industry, and then a watchmaking company under his own name.

Erard's business acumen was as good as his technical skill. In the 1930s, he worked on the legendary Valjoux 72 chronograph movement, and in 1956, his company received the coveted right to manufacture movements. In fact, Louis Erard, the company, managed to weather the quartz crisis thanks to a careful modernization program in the 1970s launched by Erard's grandson.

In 1992, Louis Erard moved to Le Noirmont in the Jura Mountains. It had some trouble maintaining a profile, until Manuel Emch of Jaquet Droz and Romain Jérôme stepped in. The new directive was "make collecting affordable," mainly through daring collaborations with the likes of Alain Silberstein, Konstantin Chaykin, Massena Lab, Vianney Halter, and more. Collections are limited, and most watches are under $5,000 dollars, an exception being the Chaykin tourbillon released in 2025.

As part of the simplification process, all collections were renamed a few years ago. The 2300 series is for chronographs, Noirmont for regular watches, Noirmont X for collaborations, and Noirmont métiers d'art is a platform for the many decorative handcrafts that are deployed in decorating watches. And the recipe for Louis Erard appears to be working. The brand has woken up from a long sleep and become something of a household name thanks to bold products that still depend on solid watchmaking. Those who keep a close eye on the industry are always curious to see what the little company up in the Jura will be producing next.

LOUIS ERARD SA
Ouest 2
CH-2340 Le Noirmont
Switzerland

TEL.:
+41-32-957-65-30

E-MAIL:
info@louiserard.com

WEBSITE:
www.louiserard.com

FOUNDED:
1929

NUMBER OF EMPLOYEES:
15

DISTRIBUTION/SALES:
Contact the company in Switzerland.

In the USA:
Exquisite Timepieces
4380 Gulfshore Blvd., N. Suite 800
Naples, FL 34103
239-227-2932
exquisitetimepieces.com

Cellini Jewelers
430 Park Ave
New York, NY 10022
212-888-0505
cellinijewelers.com

MOST IMPORTANT COLLECTIONS/PRICE RANGE:
2300, Noirmont, Noirmont X, Noirmont métiers d'art
/ $1,000 to $ 6,500

Gravée Main

Reference number: 34237GA82.BVAG170
Movement: automatic, Sellita Caliber SW261-1; ø 25.6 mm, height 5.6 mm; 31 jewels; 28,800 vph; personalized winding rotor; 38-hour power reserve
Functions: hours, minutes, subsidiary seconds
Case: stainless steel, ø 42 mm, height 12.25 mm; bezel and case fully hand-engraved; sapphire crystal; transparent case back; water-resistant to 5 atm
Band: leather, pin buckle
Price: $6,780; limited to 99 pieces

Le Régulateur Tourbillon × Konstantin Chaykin

Reference number: 89241AA90.BGA088
Movement: hand-wound, BCP Caliber T02; ø 31.8 mm, height 6.5 mm; 19 jewels; 21,600 vph; one-minute tourbillon; movement decorated with circular graining; 100-hour power reserve
Functions: hours (off-center), minutes, subsidiary seconds
Case: stainless steel, ø 42 mm, height 12.65 mm; sapphire crystal; transparent case back; water-resistant to 3 atm
Band: leather, pin buckle
Remarks: collaboration with master watchmaker Konstantin Chaykin
Price: $34,900; limited to 78 pieces

Le Régulateur × Vianney Halter

Reference number: 85246AA01.BVA180
Movement: automatic, Sellita Caliber SW266-1; ø 25.6 mm, height 5.6 mm; 31 jewels; 28,800 vph; personalized winding rotor; 38-hour power reserve
Functions: hours (off-center), minutes, subsidiary seconds
Case: stainless steel, ø 43 mm, height 10.95 mm; bezel with twelve golden rivets; sapphire crystal; transparent case back; crown with gold-tone rivet; water-resistant to 3 atm
Band: leather, pin buckle
Remarks: collaboration with watchmaker Vianney Halter
Price: $7,290; limited to 178 pieces

LOUIS MOINET

There's always something happening at Louis Moinet, but what really boosted the brand was a rather special historic discovery: in the race to be the first to invent something new, Louis Moinet (1768–1853), it seems, emerged as the first maker of a chronograph. His *Compteur de tierces*, dating to 1816, was revealed to the public in 2013. This special chronograph counted one-sixtieth of a second with a frequency of 216,000 vph. It was built to make more accurate astronomical calculations.

The original Louis Moinet was a professor at the Academy of Fine Arts in Paris and president of the Société Chronométrique and was without a doubt one of the most inventive, multitalented men of his time. He worked with such eminent watchmakers as Breguet, Berthoud, Winnerl, Janvier, and Perrelet. Among his accomplishments is an extensive two-volume treatise on horology.

Following in such footsteps is hardly an easy task, but Jean-Marie Schaller and Micaela Bertolucci decided that their idiosyncratic creations were indeed imbued with the spirit of the great Frenchman. They work with a team of independent designers, watchmakers, movement specialists, and other suppliers to produce the most unusual wristwatches filled with clever functions and surprising details. The Jules Verne chronographs have hinged levers, for example, and the second hand on the Tempograph changes direction every ten seconds.

Increasingly, this independent-minded brand is exploring the worlds of astronomy, space travel, and science fiction, and it has been attracting a lot of attention. The Cosmopolis won a Guinness world record for being the watch "with the most meteorite inserts." The Black Moon and Moon Tech use rare lunar meteorites to depict the astronomical moon traveling on a central dome surrounded by a dial made from a microelectronic wafer.

The year 2025 saw a release of two "updated" watches. The 1816 Chronograph is inspired by Louis Moinet's *Compteur de tierces*, but with a state-of-the-art caliber inside. The 1806 recalls the year Louis Moinet completed a clock for Napoleon I, then already the emperor of France.

LES ATELIERS LOUIS MOINET SA
Rue du Temple 1
CH-2072 Saint-Blaise
Switzerland

TEL.:
+41-32-753-6814

E-MAIL:
info@louismoinet.com

WEBSITE:
www.louismoinet.com

FOUNDED:
2005

U.S. DISTRIBUTOR:
Fitzhenry Consulting
1029 Peachtree Parkway, #346
Peachtree City, GA 30269
561-212-6812
Don@fitzhenry.com

MOST IMPORTANT COLLECTIONS:
Memoris, Sideralis, Tempograph Chrome, Spacewalker, Ultravox; numerous unique pieces

1816 Chronograph

Reference number: LM-150.20.60
Movement: hand-wound, Louis Moinet Caliber LM1816; ø 30.40 mm, height 7.9 mm; 34 jewels; 28,800 vph; column-wheel chronograph, instantaneous minute counter, 48-hour power reserve.
Functions: hours, minutes, subsidiary seconds, chronograph with 30-minute and 12-hour counters
Case: grade 5 titanium, ø 40.6 mm, height 14.7 mm; transparent case back; water-resistant to 5 atm
Band: titanium, folding clasp
Price: $42,500

Impulsion Titanium Green

Reference number: LM-114.20.DB
Movement: hand-wound, Louis Moinet Caliber LM114; ø 32 mm, height 7.55 mm; 36 jewels; 28,800 vph; 1-minute off-center flying tourbillon; column-wheel monopusher chronograph, with two superimposed barrel springs arranged head to tail ("volte-face") to discharge energy simultaneously, 96-hour power reserve
Functions: hours, minutes, subsidiary seconds; chronograph with 30-minute counter
Case: red gold, ø 42.5 mm, height 14.75 mm; transparent case back; water-resistant to 3 atm
Band: reptile skin, folding clasp
Price: $139,900; limited to 12 pieces

Tourbillon Puzzle Fire Horse

Reference number: LM-135.50.FH
Movement: hand-wound; Caliber LM35; ø 32 mm, height 4.70 mm; 26 jewels; 28,800 vph; 1-minute off-center flying tourbillon; two superimposed barrel springs arranged head to tail ("volte-face") to discharge energy simultaneously; 96-hour power reserve.
Functions: hours, minutes, subsidiary seconds (on the tourbillon)
Case: rose gold satin polished, ø 40.7 mm, height 15.12 mm; concave sapphire crystal; water-resistant to 3 atm
Band: reptile skin, folding clasp
Remarks: puzzle dial made of 81 pieces each individually painted and arranged on four layers
Price: $175,000, unique piece

MAURICE LACROIX

The roots of the brand Maurice Lacroix run deep, all the way to the late nineteenth century, in fact. The name Maurice Lacroix, however, was chosen in 1975 and carried the brand to respectable international success. In 2011, DKSH (Diethelm Keller & SiberHegner), a Swiss holding company that specializes in international market expansions, became the majority shareholder. This has ensured Maurice Lacroix a strong position in all major markets, with flagship stores and its own boutiques.

Nevertheless, the heart of the company remains the production facilities in the highlands of the Jura, in Saignelégier and Montfaucon, where the brand built La Manufacture des Franches-Montagnes SA (MFM) outfitted with state-of-the-art technology to produce very specific individual parts and movement components.

Since 1990, the *manufacture* has redesigned the complete collection, banning every lick of Breguet-like bliss from its watch designs. In 2006, it introduced its first in-house caliber, Le Chronographe. This was followed by the development of further *manufacture* movements, which continue to be used in the Aikon and Masterpiece collections. In the upper segment, *manufacture* models such as the chronograph and the retrograde variations on Unitas calibers set the tone. In the lower segment, modern "little" complications based on ETA and Sellita rule the roost. The brand is still remembered for the hypnotically turning square wheel, the "roue carrée."

The Aikon collection, introduced in 2016, has a back-to-the-roots quality that may be the key to its success: precise timekeeping, high readability, and exceptionally comfortable wear. So, like all other Maurice Lacroix watches, it offers a lot of perceived value. The latest creation in the Aikon family is a collaboration with Tide Ocean SA, a company with the mission of recycling and upcycling plastic collected from the oceans. The AIKON #tide comes in a variety of bright colors. The design is genuinely cool. The new Pontos S Diver has been competing with the Aikon, however. The professionally equipped diver's watch made way for the revived sports watch line in 2016, but now it is coming back—a little less martial than before but more wearable and still a "real diver's watch" from the thick sapphire crystal to the screw-down crown.

MAURICE LACROIX SA
Rue des Rangiers 21
2350 Saignelégier
Switzerland

TEL.:
+41- 43-434-66-66

E-MAIL:
info@mauricelacroix.com

WEBSITE:
www.mauricelacroix.com

FOUNDED:
1975

NUMBER OF EMPLOYEES:
about 150 worldwide

U.S. DISTRIBUTOR:
DKSH Premium Brand Distribution
31 NE 17TH St Suite
Miami, FL 33132
609-750-8800

MOST IMPORTANT COLLECTIONS/PRICE RANGE:
Aikon / $990 to $4,600; Les Classiques / $950 to $4,300; Eliros / $690 to $1,390; Fiaba (ladies') / $1,150 to $2,900; Pontos / $2,090 to $3,750; Masterpiece manufacture models / $6,250 to $14,900

Aikonic Automatic 43 mm

Reference number: AC6008-TTB00-330-2
Movement: automatic, Caliber ML 1000 (base Sellita SW200- 1); ø 25.6 mm, height 4.6 mm; 26 jewels; 28,800 vph; 60-hour power reserve
Functions: hours, minutes, sweep seconds; date
Case: titanium with black DLC, ø 43 mm, height 11 mm; ceramic bezel; sapphire crystal; transparent case back; screw-down crown; water-resistant to10 atm
Band: rubber with textile inlay, pin buckle
Price: $3,700
Variations: in stainless steel ($3,400)

Aikonic Automatic 43 mm

Reference number: AC6008-SSL40-331-4
Movement: automatic, Caliber ML 1000 (base Sellita SW200- 1); ø 25.6 mm, height 4.6 mm; 26 jewels; 28,800 vph; 60-hour power reserve
Functions: hours, minutes, sweep seconds; date
Case: stainless steel, ø 43 mm, height 11 mm; ceramic bezel; sapphire crystal; transparent case back; screw-down crown; water-resistant to 10 atm
Band: rubber with textile inlay, pin buckle
Price: $4,300
Variations: various straps and dials

Aikonic Automatic 43 mm

Reference number: AC6008-SSL70-330-2
Movement: automatic, Caliber ML 1000 (base Sellita SW200- 1); ø 25.6 mm, height 4.6 mm; 26 jewels; 28,800 vph; 60-hour power reserve
Functions: hours, minutes, sweep seconds; date
Case: stainless steel, ø 43 mm, height 11 mm; sapphire crystal; transparent case back; screw-down crown; water-resistant to10 atm
Band: rubber with textile inlay, pin buckle
Price: $3,400
Variations: various straps and dials

1975 Automatic Vagues du Jura

Reference number: 756108-SS001-430-4
Movement: automatic, Caliber ML 155 (base Sellita SW300-1); ø 25.6 mm, height 3.6 mm; 25 jewels; 28,800 vph; 42-hour power reserve
Functions: hours, minutes, sweep seconds; date
Case: stainless steel, ø 40 mm, height 9 mm; sapphire crystal; transparent case back; crown with cabochon; water-resistant to10 atm
Band: leather, pin buckle
Price: $1,600

1975 Automatic GMT Vagues du Jura

Reference number: 756048-SS001-131-2
Movement: automatic, Caliber ML 165 (base Sellita SW330-1); ø 25.6 mm, height 4,1 mm; 25 jewels; 28,800 vph; 56-hour power reserve
Functions: hours, minutes, sweep seconds; additional 24-hour display (second time zone); date
Case: stainless steel, ø 40 mm, height 10 mm; sapphire crystal; crown with cabochon; water-resistant to 5 atm
Band: leather, double folding clasp
Price: $2,250

1975 Automatic 40 mm

Reference number: 756008-SS002-430-1
Movement: automatic, Caliber ML 115 (base Sellita SW200-1); ø 25.6 mm, height 4.6 mm; 26 jewels; 28,800 vph; 38-hour power reserve
Functions: hours, minutes, sweep seconds; date
Case: stainless steel, ø 40 mm, height 10 mm; sapphire crystal; transparent case back; crown with cabochon; water-resistant to10 atm
Band: stainless steel, double folding clasp
Price: $1,500
Variations: with black dial; with leather strap ($1,400)

Aikon Master Grand Date

Reference number: AI6118-DLB0J-430-H
Movement: automatic, Caliber ML 331; ø 37.2 mm; 43 jewels; 18,000 vph; 50-hour power reserve
Functions: hours and minutes (off-center), subsidiary seconds; large date
Case: stainless steel with black DLC, ø 45 mm, height 15 mm; sapphire crystal; transparent case back; screw-down crown; water-resistant to 10 atm
Band: rubber, pin buckle
Remarks: comes with additional black rubber strap
Price: $9,650
Variations: with green, yellow or orange dial and strap

Aikon Automatic Date 39 mm

Reference number: AI6007-SS002-130-1
Movement: automatic, Caliber ML 115 (base Sellita SW200-1); ø 25.6 mm, height 4.6 mm; 26 jewels; 28,800 vph; 38-hour power reserve
Functions: hours, minutes, sweep seconds; date
Case: stainless steel, ø 39 mm, height 11 mm; sapphire crystal; transparent case back; screw-down crown; water-resistant to20 atm
Band: stainless steel, double folding clasp
Price: $2,250
Variations: with rubber strap ($2,150)

Pontos S Diver

Reference number: PT6248-SS002-331-1
Movement: automatic, Caliber ML 115 (base Sellita SW200-1); ø 25.6 mm, height 4.6 mm; 26 jewels; 28,800 vph; 38-hour power reserve
Functions: hours, minutes, sweep seconds; date
Case: stainless steel, ø 42 mm, height 13 mm; crown-adjusted ring with 0-60 scale; sapphire crystal; screw-down crown; water-resistant to 30 atm
Band: stainless steel, double folding clasp
Price: $2,300

MEISTERSINGER

MeisterSinger, headquartered in Münster, Germany, has made minimalism a hallmark of this brand, which was launched in 2001. Founder Manfred Brassler chose a look that, in many ways, returns to the very beginnings of watchmaking. Indeed, watch hands have different functions. The seconds hand is essentially there to tell that the watch is working, and the hour hand is essentially a slower minute hand, so the two can be pressed into service for a single function, thereby making space on the dial for the eye to wander.

MeisterSinger customers are looking for that combination of technical and cultural tradition of early watchmaking with Swiss-made quality and a uniquely purified design, which has earned the brand three dozen awards to date.

Looking at these ultimately simplified dials does tempt one to classify the one-hand watch as an archetype. The single hand simply cannot be reduced any further, and the 144 minutes for 12 hours around the dial do have a normative function of sorts. In other words, the watch does exactly what it's supposed to do. This applies to the looks as well: the unmistakable design elements make each MeisterSinger clearly recognizable, and that is what makes this brand's products so desirable.

By the same token, MeisterSinger also produces watches that deliver other functions without violating any of its codes. The portfolio includes a range of models with day, date, power reserve, and moon phase displays, as well as hour strike. The latest, the Kaenos (Greek for "new"), takes a new approach to one-hand watches. More sportive, the new product family does stand out visually from the rest of the collection. With the new Pangaea Aventurine, MeisterSinger relies on genuine aventurine, a noble material that makes each timepiece a unique one-of-a-kind piece. As for the new Pangaea Day Date 365, it incorporates design features of historical watches that harmonize perfectly with MeisterSinger's philosophy. Exceptional concepts, such as the collaboration with French designer Alain Silberstein, complete the 2025 collection.

MEISTERSINGER GMBH & CO. KG
Hafenweg 46
D-48155 Münster
Germany

TEL.:
+49 251 13 34 86 0

E-MAIL:
info@meistersinger.de

WEBSITE:
www.meistersinger.com

FOUNDED:
2001

NUMBER OF EMPLOYEES:
13

ANNUAL PRODUCTION:
approx. 10,000 watches

U.S. DISTRIBUTOR:
Duber Time
1115 4th Street North, Suite B
St. Petersburg, FL 33701
727-202-3262
damir@dubertime.com

PRICE RANGE:
Kaenos, Lunascope, Neo, N°01 and N°03, Pangaea / from approx. $1,999 to $5,400

Kaenos Open Date
Reference number: KSOD939
Movement: automatic, Sellita Caliber SW200-1; ø 25.6 mm, height 4.6 mm; 26 jewels; 28,800 vph; 38-hour power reserve
Functions: hours (five-minute interval markers); date
Case: stainless steel, ø 40 mm, height 11.2 mm; sapphire crystal; transparent case back; water-resistant to 10 atm
Band: stainless steel, folding clasp
Price: $3,499
Variations: various dial colors

Kaenos Sunburst Ice Blue
Reference number: KS927
Movement: automatic, Sellita Caliber SW400-1; ø 31 mm, height 4.67 mm; 26 jewels; 28,800 vph; antimagnetic; 38-hour power reserve
Functions: hours (five-minute interval markers); date
Case: stainless steel, ø 40 mm, height 11.2 mm; sapphire crystal; transparent case back; water-resistant to 10 atm
Band: stainless steel, folding clasp
Price: $3,149
Variations: various dial colors

MeisterSinger X Alain Silberstein Edition Kaenos Grand Date
Reference number: ED-KSGD-AS2025
Movement: automatic, Sellita Caliber SW400-1; ø 31 mm, height 4.67 mm; 26 jewels; 28,800 vph; antimagnetic; 38-hour power reserve
Functions: hours (five-minute interval markers); date
Case: stainless steel, ø 40 mm, height 11.2 mm; sapphire crystal; transparent case back; water-resistant to 10 atm
Band: stainless steel, folding clasp
Price: $4,799; limited to 225 pieces
Variations: with open date ring

N°03

Reference number: AM903
Movement: automatic, Sellita Caliber SW200-1;
ø 25.6 mm, height 4.6 mm; 26 jewels; 28,800 vph;
38-hour power reserve
Functions: hours (five-minute interval markers)
Case: stainless steel, ø 43 mm, height 12.3 mm;
sapphire crystal; water-resistant to 5 atm
Band: leather, pin buckle
Price: $2,399
Variations: with white or blue dial

Pangaea Aventurine

Reference number: PMN9908AV
Movement: automatic, Sellita Caliber SW200-1;
ø 25.6 mm, height 4.6 mm; 26 jewels; 28,800 vph;
38-hour power reserve
Functions: hours (five-minute interval markers)
Case: stainless steel, ø 40 mm, height 11.7 mm;
sapphire crystal; water-resistant to 5 atm
Band: leather, pin buckle
Remarks: aventurine dial
Price: $3,549

Yaara

Reference number: YA907G
Movement: automatic, Sellita Caliber SW300-1;
ø 25.6 mm, height 3.6 mm; 25 jewels; 28,800 vph;
38-hour power reserve
Functions: hours (five-minute interval markers)
Case: stainless steel, ø 36 mm, height 9 mm; bezel with
yellow-gold PVD; sapphire crystal; water-resistant to
5 atm
Band: stainless steel with yellow-gold-coated middle
link, folding clasp
Price: $3,465
Variations: various dial colors; without PVD

Pangaea Day Date

Reference number: PDD365927
Movement: automatic, Sellita Caliber SW220;
ø 25.6 mm, height 5.1 mm; 26 jewels; 28,800 vph;
38-hour power reserve
Functions: hours (five-minute interval markers); date
and weekday
Case: stainless steel, ø 40 mm, height 11.7 mm;
sapphire crystal; transparent case back; water-resistant
to 5 atm
Band: leather, pin buckle
Price: $2,730
Variations: various dial colors

Lunascope

Reference number: LS908G
Movement: automatic, MeisterSinger Caliber MS Luna
(base Sellita SW220-1); ø 25.6 mm, height 5.1 mm;
26 jewels; 28,800 vph; 38-hour power reserve
Functions: hours (five-minute interval markers); date,
moon phase
Case: stainless steel, ø 40 mm, height 12.4 mm;
sapphire crystal; transparent case back; water-resistant
to 5 atm
Band: leather, folding clasp
Price: $5,099
Variations: with silver moon

Neo Special

Reference number: S-NES921S
Movement: automatic, Sellita Caliber SW200-1;
ø 25.6 mm, height 4.6 mm; 26 jewels; 28,800 vph;
38-hour power reserve
Functions: hours (five-minute interval markers)
Case: stainless steel, ø 36 mm, height 10.5 mm;
sapphire crystal; water-resistant to 5 atm
Band: leather, pin buckle
Price: $2,249
Variations: various dial colors

MIDO

Among the legacies of World War I was the popularization of the wristwatch, which had freed up soldiers' and aviators' hands to fight and steer, respectively, and permitted artillery officers to coordinate barrages. And, not surprisingly, this led to a kind of reindustrialization of the watch industry. Among the earliest companies to appear on the scene was Mido, which was founded on November 11, 1918—Armistice Day—by Georges Schaeren in Solothurn, Switzerland. The name means "I measure" in Spanish.

At first, the brand produced colorful and imaginative watches that were well suited to the Roaring Twenties. But in the 1930s Mido began making more serious, robust, sportive timepieces better suited for everyday use. For the watch fan of today, water resistance and self-winding are normal. Mido, however, was already offering this functionality in the 1930s with the introduction of the Multifort. This Swiss manufacturer also developed a number of practical novelties like the Radiotime model (1939) and the Multicenterchrono (1941), which today have become genuine collectors' items.

In 1971 the Schaeren family sold the company to the General Watch Co. Ltd., a holding company belonging to ASUAG, which, in turn became the SMH and, ultimately, Swatch Group. Mido continues to produce mostly mechanical watches with about one-quarter of its production devoted to quartz movements. In 1998, Mido decided to revive some of its older watches. The Multifort, Commander, Battalion, and Baroncelli collections are each in their own way expressions of that mission. Nothing "in your face," just affordable timepieces with the basic hallmarks of a good Swiss watch, like côtes de Genève on the rotors and, in some cases, even COSC certification. The price-performance ratio is excellent.

The Ocean Star line was first launched in 1944 and has produced many sporty diver's watches, some water-resistant to 300 meters, later even to 600 meters, or featuring multicolored decompression tables on the dial. In the 1980s, Mido promoted these models with slogans such as "King of Waterproof." Today, the Ocean Star line includes a wide variety of models in different sizes, colors, and functions; most recently, a new Worldtimer has been added.

MIDO SA
Chemin des Tourelles 17
CH-2400 Le Locle
Switzerland

TEL.:
+41 32 933 35 11

WEBSITE:
www.midowatches.com

FOUNDED:
1918

NUMBER OF EMPLOYEES:
50 (estimated)

ANNUAL PRODUCTION:
over 100,000

U.S. DISTRIBUTOR:
Mido, division of The Swatch Group (U.S.) Inc.
800 Waterford Way, Suite 1000
Miami, FL 33126
www.midowatches.com

MOST IMPORTANT COLLECTIONS/PRICE RANGES:
Baroncelli / $460 to $1,450; Commander / $710 to $2,000; Multifort / $620 to $2,230; Ocean Star / $890 to $1,900

Multifort 8 Two Crowns
Reference number: M047.507.17.041.00
Movement: automatic, Mido Caliber 72 (base ETA A31.111); ø 25.6 mm, height 3.85 mm; 21 jewels; 25,200 vph; decorated movement; 72-hour power reserve
Functions: hours, minutes, sweep seconds; date
Case: stainless steel, ø 40 mm, height 9.5 mm; crown-adjusted scale ring with 0–60 scale; sapphire crystal; transparent case back; crowns with blue PVD coating; water-resistant to 10 atm
Band: rubber, pin buckle
Price: $1,440

Commander 1959
Reference number: M8429.4.N7.11
Movement: automatic, Mido Caliber 80.611 (base ETA C07.611); ø 25.6 mm, height 4.86 mm; 25 jewels; 21,600 vph; with côtes de Genève; 80-hour power reserve
Functions: hours, minutes, sweep seconds
Case: stainless steel, ø 37 mm, height 10.5 mm; acrylic crystal; transparent case back; water-resistant to 5 atm
Band: stainless-steel Milanese bracelet, folding clasp
Remarks: acrylic-glass dial
Price: $840

Multifort Skeleton Chronograph
Reference number: M038.662.17.040.00
Movement: automatic, Mido Caliber 60 (base ETA A05.231); ø 30 mm, height 7.9 mm; 25 jewels; 21,600 vph; partially skeletonized movement plate; 60-hour power reserve
Functions: hours, minutes, subsidiary seconds; chronograph
Case: stainless steel, ø 43 mm, height 12.15 mm; sapphire crystal; transparent case back; water-resistant to 10 atm
Band: rubber, pin buckle
Remarks: skeletonized dial and movement plate
Price: $2,750

MILUS

Milus is one of those brands that has had quite a journey in recent times. It was founded by Paul William Junod in Biel/Bienne and remained in family hands until the year 2002. A new era began then with the founding of Milus International SA under Jan Edöcs and with investments from the giant Peace Mark Group from Hong Kong.

Within a few years, the brand had made a new name for itself with a triple retrograde seconds module, which was developed together with the specialists at Agenhor in Geneva. And that made all the difference to the Milus image. In the 1970s, the brand had a reputation for jewelry. Now, however, it had become a genuine and respected watchmaker, one producing top-drawer horological complications that could compete quite boldly on a market. The TriRetrograde function is a Milus trademark and could be found in a host of models all named after constellations (Tirion, Merea, Zetios).

After the Peace Mark Group collapsed in 2008, Milus quickly found another investor in the Chow Tai Fook Group owned by Dr. Cheng Yu-tung. In 2011, Cyril Dubois took over at the head of the company. Quietly, but surely, the brand expanded on several fronts with the TriRetrogrades in the lead. Unfortunately, it had no staying power. And in 2017, Luc Tissot and his wife Katia bought the brand and started streamlining the portfolio. The strategy was simple: have three attractive collections on the affordable end of the price scale. Thus we find a robust, functional diver's watch, the Archimèdes with water-resistance to 30 atm. It was also built with a bezel under the sapphire crystal that can be turned using a separate crown and a helium valve. The entry-level LAB 01 features a modern fiberglass dial. And the third, the Snow Star, is all that's left from the old collections. It was originally made in the 1940s and given, so goes the story, to US Navy Pilots in the Pacific (along with other valuables like gold and jewelry) as part of "life barter kits." The model has been rebuilt and modernized. One can imagine that TriRetrograde mechanism will soon show up.

MILUS INTERNATIONAL SA
Rue de Reuchenette 19
CH-2502 Biel/Bienne
Switzerland

TEL.:
+41-32-344-3939

E-MAIL:
info@milus.com

WEBSITE:
www.milus.com

FOUNDED:
1919

DISTRIBUTION:
Contact company in Switzerland

MOST IMPORTANT COLLECTIONS/PRICE RANGE:
Snow Star / from approx. 1,970; Archimèdes by Milus / from approx. $2,200; LAB 01 / from approx. $1,200

Snow Star Midway Edition – Sky Silver

Reference number: KNI.0036.SSILVER
Movement: automatic, ETA 2892-A2; ø 25.6 mm, 9.45 mm (glass included); 21 jewels; 28,800 vph; 42-hours power reserve
Functions: hours, minutes, sweep seconds; date
Case: stainless steel, ø 39 mm; sapphire glass; water-resistant to 10 atm
Band: Calf leather band
Remarks: comes with a hand-polished stainless steel blade, and 11 integrated tools: blades, screwdrivers, corkscrew, and more; with Milus engraving.
Price: $2,840

Archimèdes Aqua Steel – Deep Blue

Reference number: MIH.01.003.DB
Movement: automatic, ETA 2892-A2; ø 25.6 mm, height 11.9 mm, 21 jewels; 28,800 vph; 42-hours power reserve
Functions: hours, minutes, sweep seconds; date
Case: stainless steel, ø 41 mm; sapphire crystal; water-resistant to 30 atm
Band: stainless steel, folding clasp with safe release system
Remarks: bi-directional rotating dial ring, screwed crowns, helium valve
Price: $2,760

LAB 01 – Street Black

Reference number: MIL.01.002
Movement: automatic, Sellita SW200; ø 26 mm, height 9.5mm; 26 jewels; 28,800 vph; 38-hours power reserve
Functions: hours, minutes, sweep seconds
Case: stainless steel, ø 40 mm; sapphire glass; water-resistant to 3 atm
Band: milanese mesh, folding clasp
Remarks: fiberglass dial
Price: $1,350

MINASE

2025 marked the twentieth anniversary of this discrete Japanese brand that is slowly becoming better known. The Minase brand was founded in 2005 by the Kyowa toolmaking enterprise as a way to pay homage to its own skills in working on watch components by launching a watch brand. Its logo, appearing at 12 o'clock on some models, was inspired from a step drill.

Minase Watches was named after a small village some 250 miles north of Tokyo that was absorbed in that same year 2005 into the neighboring city of Yuzawa. Until recently, it produced no more than three hundred watches a year for the Japanese market, but lately it has begun widening its horizons internationally and its focus on a modern design and traditional Japanese decorative techniques has engendered an enthusiastic fan base.

The company's timepieces are all made according to *monozukuri* philosophy, a reference to excellent manufacturing practices. One technique used is *sallaz*, or block polishing, which gives a particularly sparkling polish. The stainless-steel bracelets have been inspired by complex Japanese wooden puzzles.

The brand has three basic collections, each of which expresses the company's dedication to traditional hand-finishing. The Five Windows features multiple sapphire crystals integrated into the cases to reveal each watch's complex case-in-case structure, the intricate dial, and the mechanism inside. The oversized date aperture creates visual space on the dial. A subcollection with two extra openings, the Seven Windows, occasionally becomes a canvas for limited editions decorated by select Japanese artists. The Seven Windows anniversary model features a black dial with a hammered snowflake pattern, known as *yuki-hira*. Another special for 2025 is the *yusai* dial, hand-painted by artist Towa Takaya on a Divido model. *Yu* (悠) signifies flowing of time, and *sai* (彩) the layering of the colors. This technique, which is also applied to the "Garden" version of a Five Windows model, creates an interplay between light and color and animates the dial.

Minase has other dial shapes, too, like the Horizon, which encases movements in a tonneau case under an arched dial and an elegantly curved sapphire crystal.

MINASE
Company representation
H-Development Sarl
Ch. du Long-Champ 99
CH-2504 Biel/Bienne
Switzerland

TEL.:
+41-32-521-06-13

E-MAIL:
info@h-development.ch

WEBSITE:
www.minasewatches.ch
www.h-development.ch

FOUNDED:
2005

DISTRIBUTION:
Contact the representation in Switzerland

ANNUAL PRODUCTION:
approx. 500 pieces

MOST IMPORTANT COLLECTIONS/PRICE RANGE:
Five Windows, Seven Windows, Horizon, Divido, Uruga / $3,800 to $6,000; special editions

Seven Windows Yukihira Black Gradation Dial

Reference number: VM14-RBKURE-SSD
Movement: automatic, KT7002 (base ETA 2892-A2); ø 25.6 mm, height 3.6 mm; 28,800 vph; 21 jewels; bridges with perlage and black-or coating; blued screws; customized Minase rotor; 50-hour power reserve
Functions: hours, minutes, sweep seconds; date
Case: stainless steel, 47 mm x 38 mm, height 13 mm; domed box sapphire crystal (non-reflective coating) on top, see-through sapphire case back and 5 sapphire crystals at 12, 6 and 9 o'clock, and 2 at 3 o'clock; transparent case back; water-resistant to 3 atm
Band: stainless steel, folding clasp
Remarks: dial features yukihira hammering technique
Price: $5,900; limited to 77 pieces
Variations: on leather strap with wavy grain pattern ($4,600)

Yusai

Reference number: VM14-RBKURE-SSD
Movement: automatic, KT7002 (base ETA 2892); ø 25.6 mm, height 3.6 mm; 28,800 vph; 21 jewels; bridges with perlage and black-or coating; blued screws; 50-hour power reserve
Functions: hours, minutes, sweep seconds
Case: stainless steel, ø 40.6 mm, height 11 mm; sapphire crystal, transparent case back; water-resistant to 5 atm
Band: stainless steel, folding clasp
Remarks: each dial hand-painted in layered gradated colors by contemporary artist Towa Takaya
Price: $8,200
Variations: blue, black or grey dial, also available on rubber strap ($6,900)

Five Windows Garden

Reference number: VM15-CBKNGR-KYJ-rg
Movement: automatic, KT8001 (base ETA 2671 or Selitta); ø 17.2 mm, height 4.8 mm; 28,800 vph; 25 jewels; custom black rotor; 38-hour power reserve
Functions: hours, minutes, sweep seconds
Case: stainless steel, 40.3 mm x 32 mm, height 11.6 mm; sapphire crystal on top, transparent case back and sides; water-resistant to 5 atm
Band: calfskin, folding clasp
Remarks: each dial hand-painted by contemporary artist Towa Takaya
Price: $7,750
Variations: on stainless steel bracelet ($9,200); various color dials

MING

It takes a certain courage to launch a new watch brand in a crowded market that is subject to emotional swings. Ming, however, is no ordinary brand. It is a cooperative enterprise made up of six watchmaking enthusiasts from around the world. Leading the team is Ming Thein, a well-known photographer, designer, corporate strategist, and, of course, watch fan, who hails from Malaysia. Combined, the Ming team brings together over eighty years of experience in collecting watches of all kinds—from vintage pieces to avant-garde works of kinetic art, from robust, ground-level timepieces to custom-made creations in the six-figure range.

Each of their purchases always gave them a genuine feeling of value and happiness. The mission of the six brand founders was therefore to reconnect with that emotional excitement that comes from discovering an authentic diamond in the rough. Their strategy was to create a series of watches that are conscientiously finished and distinguished by subtle details in the finishing and design. These are not flashy pieces, but rather subtle seducers by virtue of their refinement—the carefully worked lugs or the modified ETA 7001 caliber, which transforms a fairly standard assembly into a delicate and colorful ballet of gearwheels and bridges.

The company quickly earned widespread admiration, even picking up a coveted prize at the 2024 Grand Prix d'Horlogerie de Genève in the Sports Watch category for the 38-millimeter Bluefin. It reflects Ming's minimalist approach to design, often seen in models that use bright "Polar White" luminescent material against a dark background. This approach, first used for the Minimalist model, reappears on the Lunatic, which features a poetic moon phase display.

Lately, the company has also partnered with Agenhor, a Geneva-based supplier of movements and modules. This collaboration allows the 20.01 Series 5 to forgo subsidiary dials in favor of a highly intricate dial made in cooperation with Femtoprint. It features a borosilicate base with cavities filled with liquid Super-LumiNova, producing an intense, ethereal glow in the dark.

HOROLOGER MING SDN BHD
B-3A-3, Sunway Palazzio
1 Jalan Sri Hartamas 3
50480 Kuala Lumpur
Malaysia

E-MAIL:
hello@ming.watch

WEBSITE:
www.ming.watch

FOUNDED:
August 2017

NUMBER OF EMPLOYEES:
6

ANNUAL PRODUCTION:
3000+ pieces

DISTRIBUTION:
Online, direct to customer

MOST IMPORTANT COLLECTIONS/PRICE RANGE:
20 series, 35 series, 37 series; special projects

37.05 Lunatic
Reference number: 3702M
Movement: automatic, Ming-customized Sellita caliber 288.M1; ø 25.6 mm, height 5.65 mm; 22 jewels; 28,800 vph; skeletonized bridges and customized rotor; hacking seconds; 40-hour power reserve
Functions: hours, minutes; moon phase; date
Case: stainless steel, ø 38 mm, height 11.9 mm; domed sapphire crystal front and rear; water-resistant to 10 atm
Band: FKM rubber, pin buckle
Remarks: metallized dial with Ming's own Polar White luminescent material
Price: $6,500

37.09 Uni
Reference number: 3709B
Movement: automatic, Ming-customized Sellita caliber SW 300.M1; ø 25.6 mm, height 3.6 mm; 22 jewels; 28,800 vph; skeletonized bridges and customized rotor; hacking seconds; 50-hour power reserve
Functions: hours, minutes, sweep seconds, timing dial
Case: stainless steel, ø 38 mm, height 12.8 mm; crown-activated rotating dial with 0-60 scale; sapphire crystal; transparent case back; water-resistant to 60 atm
Band: FKM rubber, pin buckle
Remarks: composite metal and laser-etched sapphire dial with inlaid ceramic SuperLumiNova
Price: $7,200

20.01 Series 3
Reference number: 2001S3
Movement: hand-wound, exclusive AgenGraphe caliber 6361.M1; ø 34 mm, height 5.65 mm; 18 jewels; 28,800 vph; double skeletonized spring barrels; central chronograph; anthracite skeletonized bridges with contrast rhodium circular brushing; 55-hour power reserve
Functions: hours, minutes; chronograph with sweep minute totalizer
Case: stainless steel with DLC-coated titanium core, ø 41.5 mm, height 14.2 mm; water-resistant to 5 atm
Band: alcantara, pin buckle
Remarks: laser-milled titanium dial, two tone finish with blue CVD and silver matte-polished surfaces
Price: $49,000

MK II

If vintage and unserviceable watches had their say, they would probably be naturally attracted to Mk II for the name alone, which is a military designation for the second generation of equipment. The company, which was founded by watch enthusiast and maker Bill Yao in 2002, not only puts retired designs back into service, but also modernizes and customizes them. Before the invention of the screw-down crown, diving watches were not nearly as reliably sealed, for example. And some beautiful old pieces were made with plated brass cases or featured Bakelite components, which are easily damaged or have aged poorly. The company substitutes these materials with modern counterparts and uses more reliable modern manufacturing methods and techniques to ensure a better outcome.

These are material issues that the team at Mk II handles with great care. They will not, metaphorically speaking, airbrush a Model-T. As genuine watch lovers themselves, they make sure that the final design is in the spirit of the watch itself, which still leaves a great deal of leeway for many iterations, given sufficient parts. In the company's output, vintage style and modern functionality are key. The watches are assembled by hand at the company's workshop in Pennsylvania—and subjected to a rigorous regimen of testing. The components are individually inspected, the cases tested at least three times for water resistance, and at the end the whole watch is regulated in six positions.

The ready-to-wear collection is produced in Japan and finished in the United States. These watches are robust, timeless, and—crucially for collectors of modest means—affordable. When appropriate, Yao opts for reliable workhorses such as the Seiko NH series, automatic three-hand movements that drive the company's most recent models.

Looking to the future, Mk II aspires to carry its clean vintage style into the development of what it hopes will be future classics.

MK II CORPORATION
303 W. Lancaster Avenue, #283
Wayne, PA 19087
USA

E-MAIL:
info@mkiiwatches.com

WEBSITES:
www.mkiiwatches.com
https://tornek-rayville.us/

FOUNDED:
2002

NUMBER OF EMPLOYEES:
3

ANNUAL PRODUCTION:
1,200 watches

DISTRIBUTION:
Direct to consumer sales

MOST IMPORTANT COLLECTIONS/PRICE RANGE:
Ready-to-Wear Collection / $500 to $995;
Benchcrafted Collection / $1,000 to $2,000

TR-660

Reference Number: CD02.2-TR660-1201AmK
Movement: automatic (hack setting), TMI caliber NH38; ø 27.40 mm, height 5.32 mm; 24 jewels; 21,600 vph; 41-hour power reserve
Functions: hours, minutes, sweep seconds
Case: stainless steel, ø 40.00 mm, height 14.72 mm; unidirectional bezel with 0-120 scale; high domed sapphire crystal and bezel inlay; screw-down case back and crown; water-resistant to 20 atm
Band: nylon, pin buckle
Price: $995
Variations: rubber strap, aluminium inlay

CISO M38 (SOA collaboration)

Reference Number: CG08-2001S
Movement: automatic (hack setting), custom Seiko TMI caliber NH36; ø 27.40 mm, height 5.32 mm; 24 jewels; 21,600 vph; 41-hour power reserve
Functions: hours, minutes, sweep seconds; day, date
Case: stainless steel; ø 38.0 mm, height 12.45 mm; high domed sapphire box crystal; screw-down case back and crown; water-resistant to 10 atm
Band: stainless steel, folding clasp
Price: $745
Variations: rubber strap, single-pass nylon strap

Hellion-BAKU edition

Reference Number: CG06.1-2101S
Movement: automatic (hack setting), Seiko TMI caliber NH38 (Made in Japan); ø 27.40 mm, height 5.32 mm; 24 jewels; 21,600 vph; 41-hour power reserve
Functions: hours, minutes, sweep seconds
Case: stainless steel, ø 39.00 mm, height 13.55 mm; sapphire crystal; screw-down case back; screw-in crown; water-resistant to 10 atm
Band: single-pass canvas strap; pin buckle
Price: $649

MONTBLANC

Nicolas Rieussec (1781–1866) skillfully used the invention of a special chronograph—the "Time Writer," a device that released droplets of ink onto a rotating sheet of paper—to make a name for himself. Montblanc, once famous only for its exclusive writing implements, borrowed that name on its way to becoming a distinguished watch brand. Within a few years, it had created an impressive range of chronographs driven by in-house calibers: from simple automatic stopwatches to flagship pieces with two independent spring barrels for time and "time-writing."

In 2007, Richemont Group, owner of Montblanc, purchased a little *manufacture* called Minerva, and put it at the disposal of the company. Minerva, which was founded in Villeret in 1858, was already building keyless pocket watches in the 1880s, and went on to produce monopusher chronographs. Today, the Minerva Institute serves as a kind of think tank, a place where young watchmakers can absorb the old traditions and skills, as well as the wealth of experience and mindset of the masters.

Montblanc is maintaining the over 160-year Minerva tradition with four leading collections. The 1858 and the Heritage clearly draw inspiration from the company's past codes, with quotations from the 1920s and 1930s, like those salmon-colored dials. The Star Legacy and the TimeWalker lines allow Montblanc to explore some more complex complications packaged in more modern forms.

Another key focus is the "0 Oxygen" technology. The name says it all: the interior of the case is sealed so tightly that no oxygen can enter. This prevents the watch from fogging up during extreme temperature changes and stops the oxidation of metal parts within the movement. According to Montblanc, this significantly extends the watch's lifespan.

Interestingly, the technology works upward and downward. In other words, it performs just as well at high altitudes on icy mountain peaks as it does when diving into deep waters. Montblanc offers dedicated models for both great depths or lofty heights.

MONTBLANC MONTRE SA
10, chemin des Tourelles
CH-2400 Le Locle
Switzerland

TEL.:
+41-32-933-8888

E-MAIL:
service@montblanc.com

WEBSITE:
www.montblanc.com

FOUNDED:
1997 (1858 Villeret, 1906 in Hamburg)

NUMBER OF EMPLOYEES:
worldwide approx. 3,000 (200 in Le Locle and Villeret)

U.S. DISTRIBUTOR:
Montblanc North America
645 Fifth Avenue, 7th Floor
New York, NY 10022
800-995-4810
www.montblanc.com

MOST IMPORTANT COLLECTIONS:
Heritage Chronométrie, Heritage Spirit, Meisterstück, Minerva, Nicolas Rieussec, 4810, TimeWalker, Collection Villeret, 1858 Collection, Iced Sea

1858 Automatic Zero Oxygen

Reference number: 134339
Movement: automatic, Caliber MB 24.17 (base Sellita SW200); ø 25.6 mm, height 4.6 mm; 26 jewels; 28.800 vph; 38-hour power reserve
Functions: hours, minutes, sweep seconds; date
Case: aluminum-bronze, ø 41 mm, height 11.3 mm; bezel with ceramic insert; sapphire crystal; water-resistant to 10 atm
Band: leather, double folding clasp
Remarks: oxygen-free case
Price: $3,965

1858 Geosphere Zero Oxygen "Monte Rosa"

Reference number: 134018
Movement: automatic, Caliber MB 29.25; ø 29.98 mm, height 9.11 mm; 26 jewels; 28,800 vph; 42-hour power reserve
Functions: hours, minutes; additional 12-hour display (second time zone), synchronously counter-rotating world time indicators for northern and southern hemispheres; date
Case: rose gold, ø 42 mm, height 12.8 mm; bidirectional bezel in stainless steel with ceramic insert, with points of the compass; sapphire crystal; water-resistant to 10 atm
Band: rubber with textile inlay, triple folding clasp
Remarks: oxygen-free case: homage to the Matterhorn pieces
Price: $24,500; limited to 100

1858 Geosphere Zero Oxygen "Mount Vinson"

Reference number: 134019
Movement: automatic, Caliber MB 29.25; ø 29.98 mm, height 9.11 mm; 26 jewels; 28,800 vph; 42-hour power reserve
Functions: hours, minutes; additional 12-hour display (second time zone), synchronously counter-rotating world time indicators for northern and southern hemispheres; date
Case: composite of titanium with bound oxygen, ø 43.5 mm, height 13 mm; bidirectional bezel in stainless steel with aluminum insert, with points of the compass; sapphire crystal; water-resistant to 10 atm
Band: rubber with textile inlay, triple folding clasp
Remarks: oxygen-free case; homage to Mount Vinson
Price: $9,700; limited to 986 pieces

1858 Geosphere Annual Calendar Limited Edition

Reference number: 134026
Movement: hand-wound, Caliber MB M14.58;
ø 31.6 mm, height 9.37 mm; 64 jewels; 18,000 vph;
screw balance; 65-hour power reserve
Functions: hours, minutes, sweep seconds; additional
24-hour display (second time zone), world time display
for the northern hemisphere; annual calendar with large
date, month
Case: stainless steel, ø 42 mm, height 13.3 mm;
sapphire crystal; transparent case back; water-resistant
to 3 atm
Band: leather, triple folding clasp
Price: $45,500; limited to 100 pieces

1858 Geosphere Annual Calendar Limited Edition

Reference number: 134027
Movement: hand-wound, Caliber MB M14.58;
ø 31.6 mm, height 9.37 mm; 64 jewels; 18,000 vph;
screw balance; 65-hour power reserve
Functions: hours, minutes, sweep seconds; additional
24-hour display (second time zone), world time display
for the northern hemisphere; annual calendar with large
date, month
Case: yellow gold, ø 42 mm, height 13.3 mm; sapphire
crystal; transparent case back; water-resistant to 3 atm
Band: leather, triple folding clasp
Price: $59,000; limited to 30 pieces

1858 Split Second Chronograph Limited Edition

Reference number: 134029
Movement: hand-wound, Caliber MB M16.31;
ø 38.4 mm, height 8.13 mm; 25 jewels; 18,000 vph;
two column wheels, sequential control of chronograph
functions via crown pusher, separate pusher for split-
seconds control; 50-hour power reserve
Functions: hours, minutes, small seconds; split-
seconds chronograph
Case: titanium, ø 44 mm, height 15.2 mm; sapphire
crystal; transparent case back; water-resistant to 3 atm
Band: leather, triple folding clasp
Price: $56,500; limited to 100 pieces

The Unveiled Secret Minerva Monopusher Chronograph

Reference number: 134281
Movement: hand-wound, Caliber MB M17.26;
ø 38.4 mm, height 7.7 mm; 26 jewels; 18,000 vph;
inverted movement with dial-side chronograph
mechanism; monopusher column-wheel control; screw
balance, hairspring with Phillips end curve; 50-hour
power reserve
Functions: hours, minutes, small seconds; chronograph
Case: stainless steel, ø 43 mm, height 14.78 mm; bezel
in yellow gold; sapphire crystal; water-resistant to 3 atm
Band: reptile skin, triple folding clasp
Remarks: skeletonized dial
Price: $49,700; limited to 100 pieces

Bohème Automatic Date

Reference number: 133306
Movement: automatic, Caliber MB 24.19 (base Sellita
W300-1); ø 25.6 mm, height 3.6 mm; 25 jewels;
28,800 vph; 38-hour power reserve
Functions: hours, minutes, sweep seconds; date
Case: stainless steel, ø 30 mm, height 9.5 mm; sapphire
crystal; transparent case back; water-resistant to 3 atm
Band: leather, pin buckle
Remarks: dial with 8 diamonds; comes with additional
silver leather strap
Price: $3,510
Variations: with stainless steel bracelet

Bohème Day & Night

Reference number: 133310
Movement: automatic, Caliber MB 24.20 (base Sellita
SW300-1); ø 25.6 mm, height 4.6 mm; 25 jewels;
28,800 vph; 42-hour power reserve
Functions: hours, minutes, sweep seconds; day/night
indication; date
Case: stainless steel, ø 34 mm, height 9.5 mm; sapphire
crystal; transparent case back; water-resistant to 3 atm
Band: stainless steel, folding clasp
Remarks: dial with 8 diamonds
Price: $4,300

Iced Sea Automatic Zero Oxygen

Reference number: 134017
Movement: automatic, Caliber MB 24.17 (base Sellita SW200); ø 25.6 mm, height 4.6 mm; 26 jewels; 28,800 vph; 38-hour power reserve
Functions: hours, minutes, sweep seconds; date
Case: aged stainless steel, ø 38 mm, height 12.3 mm; bidirectional bezel with ceramic insert and 0-60 scale; sapphire crystal; screw-down crown; water-resistant to 30 atm
Band: rubber, double folding clasp
Remarks: oxygen-free case; micro-structured, polished dial
Price: $4,700

Iced Sea Automatic Zero Oxygen

Reference number: 134024
Movement: automatic, Caliber MB 24.17 (base Sellita SW200); ø 25.6 mm, height 4.6 mm; 26 jewels; 28.800 vph; 38-hour power reserve
Functions: hours, minutes, sweep seconds; date
Case: stainless steel, ø 38 mm, height 12.3 mm; bidirectional bezel with aluminum insert and 0-60 scale; sapphire crystal; water-resistant to 30 atm
Band: stainless steel, double folding clasp
Remarks: oxygen-free case; micro-structured, polished dial
Price: $3,965

Star Legacy Full Calendar

Reference number: 134358
Movement: automatic, Montblanc Caliber MB 24.30 (base ETA 7751); ø 30 mm, height 7.9 mm; 25 jewels; 28,800 vph; 50-hour power reserve
Functions: hours, minutes, sweep seconds; full calendar with date, weekday, month, moon phase
Case: stainless steel, ø 42 mm, height 11.38 mm; sapphire crystal; transparent case back; water-resistant to 5 atm
Band: leather, triple folding clasp
Price: $5,100

Star Legacy Nicolas Rieussec

Reference number: 132947
Movement: automatic, Caliber MB R200; ø 31 mm, height 8.46 mm; 40 jewels; 28,800 vph; 2 spring barrels; monopusher column-wheel control of chronograph functions; 72-hour power reserve
Functions: hours, minutes, small seconds; additional 12-hour display (second time zone), day/night indication; chronograph; date
Case: stainless steel, ø 43 mm, height 15.01 mm; sapphire crystal; transparent case back; water-resistant to 5 atm
Band: leather, triple folding clasp
Price: $8,700

1858 Geosphere Zero Oxygen CARBO2

Reference number: 132300
Movement: automatic, Caliber MB 29.27; ø 29.98 mm, height 9.11 mm; 33 jewels; 28.800 vph; 46-hour power reserve
Functions: hours, minutes; additional 12-hour display (second time zone), synchronously counter-rotating world time indicators for northern and southern hemispheres; date
Case: carbon fiber ("CARBO 2"), ø 44 mm, height 17.1 mm; bidirectional bezel in stainless steel with ceramic insert with points of the compass; sapphire crystal; water-resistant to 10 atm
Band: rubber with textile inlay, triple folding clasp
Remarks: oxygen-free case: homage to the 8,000-meter plus Himalayan peaks
Price: $9,400

Iced Sea Zero Oxygen Deep 4810

Reference number: 133268
Movement: automatic, Caliber MB 29.29; ø 25.6 mm, height 4.6 mm; 26 jewels; 28,800 vph; 120-hour power reserve; COSC-certified chronometer
Functions: hours, minutes, sweep seconds; date
Case: titanium, ø 43 mm, height 19.4 mm; unidirectional bezel with ceramic insert with 0-60 scale; sapphire crystal; screw-down crown; water-resistant to 481 atm
Band: rubber, folding clasp
Remarks: oxygen-free case; micro-structured, polished dial
Price: $9,400

Caliber MB M16.29

Hand-wound; column-wheel control of the chronograph functions using separate pushers; single mainspring barrel, 55-hour power reserve
Functions: hours, minutes, subsidiary seconds; chronograph
Diameter: 38.4 mm
Height: 6.3 mm
Jewels: 22
Balance: screw balance
Frequency: 18,000 vph
Hairspring: with Phillips end curve
Remarks: perlage on mainplate, rhodium-plated, bridges with côtes de Genève gold-plated geartrain

Caliber MB M13.21

Hand-wound; column-wheel control of the chronograph functions; single mainspring barrel, 60-hour power reserve
Functions: hours, minutes, subsidiary seconds; chronograph
Diameter: 29.5 mm
Height: 6.4 mm
Jewels: 22
Balance: screw balance with weights
Frequency: 18,000 vph
Hairspring: with Phillips end curve
Shock protection: Incabloc
Remarks: German silver mainplate and bridges, rhodium-plated, partial perlage and hand-chamfered

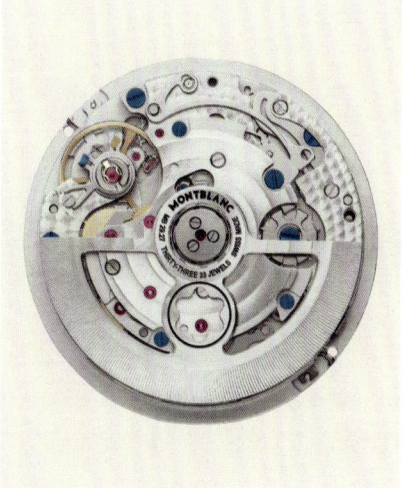

Caliber MB 29.27

Automatic; single spring barrel, 46-hour power reserve
Functions: hours, minutes; second time zone, synchronously counter-rotating world time indicators for northern and southern hemispheres; chronograph; date
Diameter: 29.98 mm
Height: 9.11 mm
Jewels: 33
Frequency: 28,800 vph
Hairspring: flat hairspring
Remarks: perlage on mainplate, rhodium-plated

Caliber MB 29.22

Automatic; single mainspring barrel, 48-hour power reserve
Base caliber: Cartier 1904-PS MC
Functions: hours, minutes; additional 12-hour display (second time zone); perpetual calendar with date, weekday, month, moon phase, leap year
Diameter: 28.2 mm
Height: 4.95 mm
Jewels: 77
Frequency: 28,800 vph
Hairspring: flat hairspring
Remarks: 378 parts

Caliber MB M16.31

Hand-wound; column-wheel control of the chronograph functions over different pushers, swan-neck fine adjustment; single mainspring barrel, 50-hour power reserve
Functions: hours, minutes, subsidiary seconds; stop-seconds chronograph
Diameter: 38.4 mm
Height: 8.13 mm
Jewels: 22
Balance: screw balance with Breguet hairspring
Frequency: 18,000 vph
Hairspring: with Phillips end curve
Remarks: perlage on mainplate, rhodium-plated, bridges with côtes de Genève, gold-plated gear train; 262 parts

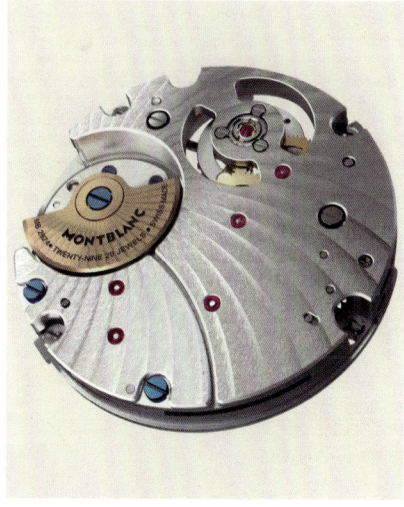

Caliber MB M29.24

Automatic; 1-minute tourbillon with external hairspring; two spring barrels, 48-hour power reserve
Functions: hours, minutes
Diameter: 30.6 mm
Height: 4.5 mm
Jewels: 27
Balance: screw balance with 18 weights
Frequency: 21,600 vph
Hairspring: flat hairspring
Remarks: gold microrotor, bridges with côtes de Genève

MÜHLE GLASHÜTTE

Family-run businesses are notoriously successful, especially as each generation must balance tradition with managing the challenges that time brings. Rob. Mühle & Sohn has been doing this for over 150 years. The company started as a manufacturer of precision measuring instruments and managed to survive the ups and downs of German history. Originally, this was for the local watch industry and the German School of Watchmaking. By the early 1920s, the firm was supplying the automobile industry, making speedometers, automobile clocks, tachometers, and other measurement instruments.

As a supplier for the Wehrmacht, it drew Soviet bombers during World War II and was then nationalized, like most companies in East Germany. After the fall of the Iron Curtain, Hans-Jürgen Mühle took the helm. Responsibility for the brand today lies with three generations: senior Hans-Jürgen Mühle; his son, the current company CEO Thilo Mühle; and Thilo's children Fanny and Dustin Mühle, who joined the company in 2024. As the company has become increasingly international, this multi-generational leadership has helped navigate global markets while maintaining the family's watchmaking heritage.

The wristwatch line was launched as a sideline in mid-1994 but has now overtaken the nautical instruments for which Mühle was famous. Its collection comprises mechanical wristwatches at entry- and mid-level prices. For these, the company uses Swiss base movements that are equipped with such in-house developments as a patented woodpecker-neck regulation system and the Mühle rotor. The modifications are so extensive that they have led to the calibers having their own names. The traditional line named "R. Mühle & Sohn," introduced in 2014, is equipped with the RMK 1 and RMK 2 calibers. And there are other, somewhat less nautically inspired timepieces, like the Lunova series or the 29ers, which are simply elegant in an unspectacular way. While the watches are by and large in the sportive-elegant segment, the company has shown some boldness in the color of the dials and straps.

MÜHLE GLASHÜTTE GMBH
Nautische Instrumente und Feinmechanik
Altenberger Strasse 35
D-01768 Glashütte
Germany

TEL.:
+49-35053-3203-0

E-MAIL:
info@muehle-glashuette.de

WEBSITE:
www.muehle-glashutte.de

FOUNDED:
first founding 1869; second founding 1993

NUMBER OF EMPLOYEES:
47

U.S. DISTRIBUTOR:
Mühle Glashütte USA
1115 4th Street North Unit #B
St Petersburg, FL 33701
727-896-4278
www.muehleglashuetteusa.com

MOST IMPORTANT COLLECTIONS/PRICE RANGE:
mechanical wristwatches / approx. $1,300 to $5,400

Sportivo Active Chronograph
Reference number: M1-52-02-CK
Movement: automatic, Mühle Caliber MU 9419 (base Sellita SW510); ø 30 mm, height 7.9 mm; 25 jewels; 28,800 vph; woodpecker-neck regulator, Glashütte three-quarter plate, Mühle rotor, finely finished with special Mühle finishing; 62-hour power reserve
Functions: hours, minutes, subsidiary seconds; chronograph; date
Case: stainless steel, ø 42.4 mm, height 15.5 mm; bidirectional bezel with ceramic insert and 0–60 scale; sapphire crystal; transparent case back; screw-down crown; water-resistant to 30 atm
Band: rubber with textile overlay, pin buckle
Price: $4,599

S.A.R. Rescue-Timer
Reference number: M1-41-02-KB-II
Movement: automatic, Sellita Caliber SW200-1; ø 25.6 mm, height 4.6 mm; 26 jewels; 28,800 vph; with woodpecker-neck regulator, Mühle rotor, finely finished with special Mühle finishing; 41-hour power reserve
Functions: hours, minutes, sweep seconds; date
Case: stainless steel, ø 42 mm, height 13.5 mm; bezel with rubber ring; sapphire crystal; screw-down crown; water-resistant to 100 atm
Band: rubber, folding clasp with extension link
Price: $2,699
Variations: with stainless-steel bracelet ($2,799)

S.A.R. Mission-Timer Titanium
Reference number: M1-51-03-KB
Movement: automatic, Sellita Caliber SW400-1; ø 31 mm, height 4.67 mm; 26 jewels; 28,800 vph; with woodpecker-neck regulator, Mühle rotor, finely finished with special Mühle finishing; 41-hour power reserve
Functions: hours, minutes, sweep seconds; date
Case: titanium, ø 43 mm, height 13 mm; ceramic bezel; sapphire crystal; screw-down crown; water-resistant to 50 atm
Band: rubber, folding clasp with extension link
Price: $3,599

29er Casual

Reference number: M1-25-78-300-VLB
Movement: automatic, Sellita Caliber SW300-1;
ø 25.6 mm, height 3.6 mm; 25 jewels; 28,800 vph;
woodpecker-neck regulator, Mühle rotor, finely finished
with special Mühle finishing; 56-hour power reserve
Functions: hours, minutes, sweep seconds; date
Case: stainless steel, ø 42.4 mm, height 9.75 mm;
sapphire crystal; transparent case back; screw-down
crown; water-resistant to 10 atm
Band: leather, pin buckle
Price: $2,399

29er Big Small Seconds

Reference number: M1-25-87-CB-V
Movement: automatic, Sellita Caliber SW261-1;
ø 25.6 mm, height 4.6 mm; 26 jewels; 28,800 vph;
woodpecker-neck regulator, Mühle rotor, finely finished
with special Mühle finishing; 41-hour power reserve
Functions: hours, minutes, subsidiary seconds; date
Case: stainless steel, ø 42.4 mm, height 11.3 mm;
sapphire crystal; transparent case back; screw-down
crown; water-resistant to 10 atm
Band: textile, pin buckle
Price: $2,249
Variations: with stainless-steel bracelet ($2,399)

29er Pointer Date

Reference number: M1-25-32-CB
Movement: automatic, Sellita Caliber SW221-1;
ø 25.6 mm, height 5.05 mm; 26 jewels; 28,800 vph;
woodpecker-neck regulator, Mühle rotor, finely finished
with special Mühle finishing; 41-hour power reserve
Functions: hours, minutes, sweep seconds; pointer date
Case: stainless steel, ø 42.4 mm, height 12.2 mm;
sapphire crystal; transparent case back; water-resistant
to 10 atm
Band: textile, pin buckle
Price: $2,199
Variations: with stainless-steel bracelet ($2,349)

Teutonia IV Moon Phase

Reference number: M1-44-05-LB
Movement: automatic, Sellita Caliber SW280-1;
ø 25.6 mm, height 5.4 mm; 26 jewels; 28,800 vph;
woodpecker-neck regulator, Mühle rotor, finely finished
with special Mühle finishing; 41-hour power reserve
Functions: hours, minutes, sweep seconds; date, moon-
phase
Case: stainless steel, ø 41 mm, height 12.6 mm;
sapphire crystal; transparent case back; water-resistant
to 10 atm
Band: leather, double folding clasp
Price: $3,299
Variations: with stainless-steel bracelet ($3,399)

Teutonia Sport II "Racing Green"

Reference number: M1-29-74-LB-B
Movement: automatic, Sellita Caliber SW290-1;
ø 25.6 mm, height 5.6 mm; 31 jewels; 28,800 vph;
woodpecker-neck regulator, Mühle rotor, finely finished
with special Mühle finishing; 38-hour power reserve
Functions: hours, minutes, subsidiary seconds; date
Case: stainless steel, ø 41.6 mm, height 12.8 mm;
sapphire crystal; transparent case back; screw-down
crown; water-resistant to 10 atm
Band: leather, pin buckle
Price: $3,099

Panova Blue

Reference number: M1-40-72-MB
Movement: automatic, Sellita Caliber SW200-1;
ø 25.6 mm, height 4.6 mm; 26 jewels; 28,800 vph;
woodpecker-neck regulator, Mühle rotor, finely finished
with special Mühle finishing; 41-hour power reserve
Functions: hours, minutes, sweep seconds
Case: stainless steel, ø 40 mm, height 10.4 mm;
sapphire crystal; screw-down crown; water-resistant
to 10 atm
Band: Milanese stainless-steel bracelet, folding clasp
Price: $1,599

NIVADA GRENCHEN

Nivada Grenchen is a historic Swiss watch brand with a very complicated history. The birth year is 1979, but the company as such was officially founded in 1926 by Jacob Schneider and two other men in Grenchen, a major hub of industrial watchmaking. Early on, the company built its reputation on robust, functional timepieces, and by 1930 it was among the early manufacturers of automatic watches, positioning itself at the forefront of technical innovation. Distribution in the United States was handled by Croton, so period pieces sometimes bear any number of signatures on the dial, adding an extra layer of intrigue for collectors.

A defining chapter came with the Antarctic, launched in 1950 as Nivada Grenchen's first waterproof automatic watch. Its reliability was proven when members of the U.S. Navy's Deep Freeze I expedition wore it during their journey to the South Pole between 1955 and 1956, cementing the model's reputation for rugged performance in extreme conditions. Around this same era, the brand developed a family of tool watches that would become modern cult classics.

The brand continued producing outstanding watches, such as the Chronomaster in 1961, water-resistant to 200 meters, and the Depthomatic in 1964, notable as the first diver's watch with an integrated depth indicator. The 1965 Depthmaster pushed robustness further with a 100 atm (1,000 meters) rating.

In 2018, Nivada Grenchen was revived from its quartz-crisis-induced hiatus by Guillaume Laidet, a French entrepreneur. He decided that reissuing the brand's old icons was an excellent strategy, notably the Chronomaster Aviator Sea Diver and the Antarctic. The company has also tried out bolder variants such as the so-called "Spider" dials and other creative executions that reinterpret vintage codes for contemporary enthusiasts. In their commitment to all things vintage, they've also taken to refurbishing new old stock, i.e. unused vintage movements, such as the famous Valjoux 23 VZ, a chronograph movement that had a long career from 1916 to 1974. They also rely on TMI (Seiko) Mecaquartz movements that combine accurate quartz timekeeping with a mechanical module for 1/5-second sweeping chronograph functions.

NIVADA GRENCHEN
Via C. Colombara 29
CH-6853 Ligornetto
Switzerland

TEL.:
+41-91-647-2644

E-MAIL:
contact@nivadagrenchenofficial.com

WEBSITE:
www.nivadagrenchenofficial.com

FOUNDED:
1926; 2018

NUMBER OF EMPLOYEES:
25

U.S. DISTRIBUTION:
contact@nivadagrenchenofficial.com

MOST IMPORTANT COLLECTIONS/PRICE RANGE:
Antarctic, Autochron, Chronomaster, Depthmater, F77 / $800 to $5,000

Chronomaster Tropical

Reference number: 85141M01
Movement: hand-wound, Landeron Caliber 72; ø 31.5 mm, height 6 mm; 17 jewels; 18,000 vph; 48-hour power reserve
Functions: hours, minutes, small seconds; chronograph with 30-minute totalizer
Case: stainless steel, ø 41 mm, height 15.85 mm; bidirectional bezel with 0-60 scale; sapphire crystal; water-resistant to 10 atm
Band: leather, folding clasp
Remarks: UV-baked brown dial for vintage look
Price: $2,295
Variations: with various straps and dials

Chronograph Valjoux 23 Broad Arrow

Reference number: 86058M23
Movement: hand-wound, Valjoux 23 VZ; ø 29.5 mm, height 6.95 mm; 25 jewels; 18,000 vph; column-wheel control of chronograph functions; 48-hour power reserve
Functions: hours, minutes, small seconds; chronograph with tachymeter scale
Case: stainless steel, ø 38 mm, height 12.95 mm; bidirectional bezel with 0-60 scale; sapphire crystal; transparent case back; water-resistant to 10 atm
Band: leather racing, folding clasp
Remarks: based on the coveted Valjoux 23 VZ new old stock made from 1916 – 1974.
Price: $2,285 limited to 25 pieces
Variations: with various straps and dials

Chronoking Mecaquartz Racing Carbon

Reference number: 87049Q17
Movement: quartz, TMI Mecaquartz caliber VK63; ø 29.1 mm, height 5.1 mm; 3-year battery reserve
Functions: hours, minutes, small seconds; chronograph with 24-hour totalizer
Case: stainless steel, ø 38 mm, height 13.4 mm; screw-down crown; bezel with tachymeter scale; sapphire crystal; water-resistant to 10 atm
Band: leather, pin buckle
Remarks: carbon fiber dial
Price: $610; limited to 500 numbered pieces
Variations: comes on rubber strap

Antarctic Spider

Reference number: 32023A15
Movement: automatic, Soprod caliber P024; ø 25.6 mm, height 4.6 mm; 25 jewels; 28,800 vph; 38-hour power reserve
Functions: hours, minutes, sweep seconds; date
Case: stainless steel, ø 38 mm, height 11.1 mm; sapphire crystal; screw-down crown; water-resistant to 10 atm
Band: leather, pin buckle
Remarks: reissue of a 1970s watch
Price: $945
Variations: different straps, bracelets, and dial colors

Super Antarctic 3.6.9 Tropical

Reference number: 32031A23
Movement: automatic, Soprod caliber P024; ø 25.6 mm, height 4.6 mm; 25 jewels; 28,800 vph; 38-hour power reserve
Functions: hours, minutes, sweep seconds
Case: stainless steel, ø 38 mm, height 11.1 mm; sapphire crystal; screw-down crown; Antarctica on gold medallion on case back; water-resistant to 10 atm
Band: leather, pin buckle
Remarks: vintage look; 3-6-9 dial
Price: $945
Variations: different straps, bracelets, and dial colors

Antarctic Glacier

Reference number: 35020M01
Movement: hand-wound, Soprod caliber P054; ø 25.6 mm, height 4.6 mm; 25 jewels; 28,800 vph; 42-hour power reserve
Functions: hours, minutes, sweep seconds
Case: stainless steel, ø 35 mm, height 10.1 mm; sapphire crystal; water-resistant to 5 atm
Band: rubber, folding clasp
Remarks: gold penguin engraved on the back
Price: $945

Aquamar Grey

Reference number: 14200A15
Movement: automatic, Soprod caliber P024; ø 25.6 mm, height 4.6 mm; 25 jewels; 28,800 vph; 38-hour power reserve
Functions: hours, minutes, sweep seconds (hacking)
Case: stainless steel, ø 38 mm, height 12.9 mm; helium valve; screw-down crown; unidirectional bezel with 0-120 scale; sapphire crystal; water-resistant to 20 atm
Band: rubber, folding clasp
Remarks: with penguin engraved gold medallion on the back
Price: $1,150
Variations: on stainless steel bracelet ($1,250)

"Pacman" Depthmaster

Reference number: 14200A15
Movement: automatic, Soprod caliber P024; ø 25.6 mm, height 4.6 mm; 25 jewels; 28,800 vph; 38-hour power reserve
Functions: hours, minutes, sweep seconds (hacking)
Case: stainless steel, ø 42 mm, height 14.1 mm; helium valve; screw-down crown; unidirectional bezel with 0-120 scale; sapphire crystal; water-resistant to 100 atm
Band: leather, folding clasp
Remarks: black dial with Pacman indices
Price: $1,050
Variations: stainless steel bracelet ($1,000)

F77 SST Chrono Mecaquartz Blue MK2

Reference number: 68000Q77
Movement: quartz, TMI Mecaquartz caliber VK64; ø 30.8 mm, height 5.1 mm; 3-year battery reserve
Functions: hours, minutes; chronograph with 24-hour totalizer; date
Case: stainless steel, ø 38 mm, height 12.2 mm; screw-down crown; sapphire crystal; water-resistant to 10 atm
Band: stainless steel, folding clasp
Remarks: comes with additional steel bracelet and rubber strap
Price: $945

NOMOS

Who says Germans have no sense of humor? The best of it is subtle enough to be accessible to poets and thinkers (*Dichter und Denker*) with command of the language and its many dialects. At its apex, humor must be self-deprecatory and deadpan. This may be the reason for Nomos's global success. Ever since its founding in 1990 by Roland Schwertner and his associate Uwe Ahrendt, the company's marketing measures have harmonized with the product in a subtly playful and humorous manner.

Nomos Glashütte is now the number one producer of mechanical watches in Germany. It manufactures them in the best tradition of the German Werkbund and Bauhaus—research, design, and production work hand in hand. The emphasis on design meant that the brand needed its own calibers, and these are now wisely distributed throughout the thirteen model families with over one hundred variations that grace the company's portfolio. The one that made a loud splash, however, was the DUW 4401 (Deutsche Uhrenwerke Nomos Glashütte), equipped with the "Swing System," an in-house escapement with a spring "made in Germany." Unveiled in 2014, this caliber has gradually become the core regulating instrument for Nomos watches and been integrated into all the brand's movements. Its great advantage is thinness, which lets the company maintain its USP as it were: very elegant, unobtrusively attractive mechanical watches.

Speaking of design, over 240 people work at Nomos including some who are members of the Berlin-based company Berlinerblau. Others are spread out across the world, from Glashütte to New York, from Hong Kong and Shanghai to Lake Como in Italy. The company's aesthetic-philosophical scrim has produced such genial watch families as the swimmer's watch Ahoi (as in "ship ahoy!"), with an optional synthetic strap like those that carry locker keys at Germany's public swimming pools. The Autobahn is a panegyric to Germany's favorite playground, the highway. Quirky dial colors are also part of the brand's mission. The Tangente watches now come in a slew of colors, each iteration with a special name as well. The recipe has, so far, earned the brand top grades from consumers and over 170 prizes for design and quality.

NOMOS GLASHÜTTE/SA
Roland Schwertner KG
Ferdinand-Adolph-Lange-Platz 2
01768 Glashütte
Germany

TEL.:
+49 35053 4040

E-MAIL:
nomos@glashuette.com

WEBSITE:
nomos-glashuette.com

FOUNDED:
1990

NUMBER OF EMPLOYEES:
over 200

U.S. DISTRIBUTOR:
For the U.S. market, please contact:
NOMOS Glashuette USA Inc.
347 W. 36th St., Suite 600
New York, NY 10018
212-929-2575
contact@nomos-watches.com

MOST IMPORTANT COLLECTIONS/PRICE RANGE:
Ahoi, Autobahn, Club, Club Campus, Club Sport, Ludwig, Lux, Metro, Orion, Tangente, Tangomat, Tetra, Zürich / from $1,440 to $10.920 (for gold models) / Lambda, $18,500

Tangente 2date

Reference number: 135
Movement: hand-wound, Nomos Caliber DUW 4601; ø 34.6 mm, height 2.8 mm; 23 jewels; 21,600 vph; three-quarter plate, finely finished movement; 52-hour power reserve
Functions: hours, minutes, small seconds; date (dual, in aperture and peripheral)
Case: stainless steel, ø 37.5 mm, height 6.8 mm; sapphire crystal; transparent case back; screw-down crown; water-resistant to 5 atm
Band: horse leather, pin buckle
Price: $3,410

Club Sport neomatik World Time

Reference number: 791
Movement: automatic, Nomos Caliber DUW 3202; ø 31 mm, height 4.8 mm; 37 jewels; 21,600 vph; finely finished movement; 42-hour power reserve
Functions: hours, minutes, small seconds; world-time display (second time zone)
Case: stainless steel, ø 40 mm, height 9.9 mm; pusher activated ring with reference names; sapphire crystal; transparent case back; water-resistant to 10 atm
Band: stainless steel, folding clasp
Price: $5,190

Minimatik 39 Date Gold

Reference number: 1251
Movement: hand-wound, Nomos Caliber DUW 4601; ø 34.6 mm, height 2.8 mm; 23 jewels; 21,600 vph; three-quarter plate, finely finished movement; 52-hour power reserve
Functions: hours, minutes, small seconds; date
Case: stainless steel, ø 39.5 mm, height 7.5 mm; sapphire crystal; transparent case back; water-resistant to 5 atm
Band: horse leather, pin buckle
Price: $3,540

Tangente neomatik Doré

Reference number: 192
Movement: automatic, Nomos Caliber DUW 3001;
ø 28.8 mm, height 3.2 mm; 37 jewels; 21,600 vph; three-quarter plate, finely finished movement; 43-hour power reserve
Functions: hours, minutes, small seconds
Case: stainless steel, ø 35 mm, height 6.9 mm; sapphire crystal; transparent case back; water-resistant to 5 atm
Band: horse leather, folding clasp
Price: $4,110

Tangente 2date Blue

Reference number: 136
Movement: hand-wound, Nomos Caliber DUW 4601;
ø 34.6 mm, height 2.8 mm; 23 jewels; 21,600 vph; three-quarter plate, finely finished movement; 52-hour power reserve
Functions: hours, minutes, small seconds; date (dual, in the aperture and peripheral)
Case: stainless steel, ø 37.5 mm, height 6.8 mm; sapphire crystal; transparent case back; screw-down crown; water-resistant to 5 atm
Band: horse leather, pin buckle
Price: $3,410

Ludwig neomatik 39

for "Doctors without Borders"
Reference number: 250.S2
Movement: automatic, Nomos Caliber DUW 3001;
ø 28.8 mm, height 3.2 mm; 37 jewels; 21,600 vph; three-quarter plate, finely finished movement; 43-hour power reserve
Functions: hours, minutes, small seconds
Case: stainless steel, ø 38.5 mm, height 7 mm; sapphire crystal; transparent case back; water-resistant to 5 atm
Band: horse leather, folding clasp
Price: $4,220; limited to 250 pieces

Orion neomatik Doré

Reference number: 397
Movement: automatic, Nomos Caliber DUW 3001;
ø 28.8 mm, height 3.2 mm; 37 jewels; 21,600 vph; three-quarter plate, finely finished movement; 43-hour power reserve
Functions: hours, minutes, small seconds
Case: stainless steel, ø 36.4 mm, height 8.5 mm; sapphire crystal; transparent case back; water-resistant to 5 atm
Band: horse leather, folding clasp
Price: $4,250

Metro Date Power Reserve

Reference number: 1101
Movement: hand-wound, Nomos Caliber DUW 4401;
ø 32.1 mm, height 2.8 mm; 23 jewels; 21,600 vph; three-quarter plate, finely finished movement; 42-hour power reserve
Functions: hours, minutes, small seconds; power reserve indicator; date
Case: stainless steel, ø 37 mm, height 7.7 mm; sapphire crystal; transparent case back; water-resistant to 3 atm
Band: horse leather, pin buckle
Price: $4,420

Club Sport neomatik Worldtimer Blue

Reference number: 790
Movement: automatic, Nomos Caliber DUW 3202;
ø 31 mm, height 4.8 mm; 37 jewels; 21,600 vph; finely finished movement; 42-hour power reserve
Functions: hours, minutes, small seconds; world-time display (second time zone)
Case: stainless steel, ø 40 mm, height 9.9 mm; pusher activated ring with reference cities; sapphire crystal; transparent case back; water-resistant to 10 atm
Band: stainless steel, folding clasp
Price: $5,190

Club Sport neomatik 34 Purple

Reference number: 757.SB
Movement: automatic, Nomos Caliber DUW 3001; ø 28.8 mm, height 3.2 mm; 37 jewels; 21,600 vph; three-quarter plate, finely finished movement; 43-hour power reserve
Functions: hours, minutes, small seconds
Case: stainless steel, ø 34 mm, height 8.2 mm; sapphire crystal; transparent case back; screw-down crown; water-resistant to 20 atm
Band: stainless steel, folding clasp
Price: $3,430

Club Campus 38 Night Sky

Reference number: 722
Movement: hand-wound, Nomos Caliber Alpha; ø 23.3 mm, height 2.6 mm; 17 jewels; 21,600 vph; three-quarter plate, finely finished movement; 43-hour power reserve
Functions: hours, minutes, small seconds
Case: stainless steel, ø 38.5 mm, height 8.5 mm; sapphire crystal; water-resistant to 10 atm
Band: vegan velour leather, pin buckle
Price: $1,960
Variations: various dial colors

Club Campus Starlight

Reference number: 718
Movement: hand-wound, Nomos Caliber Alpha; ø 23.3 mm, height 2.6 mm; 17 jewels; 21,600 vph; three-quarter plate, finely finished movement; 43-hour power reserve
Functions: hours, minutes, small seconds
Case: stainless steel, ø 36 mm, height 8.2 mm; sapphire crystal; water-resistant to 10 atm
Band: vegan velour leather, pin buckle
Price: $1,830
Variations: various dial colors

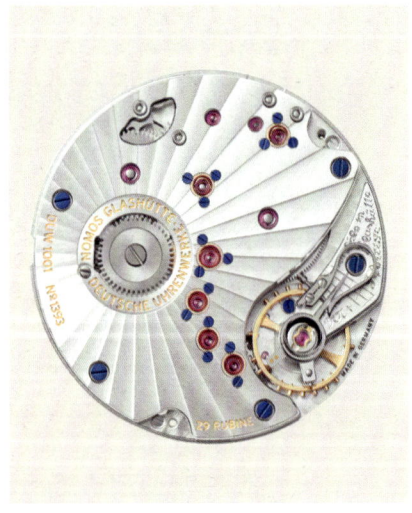

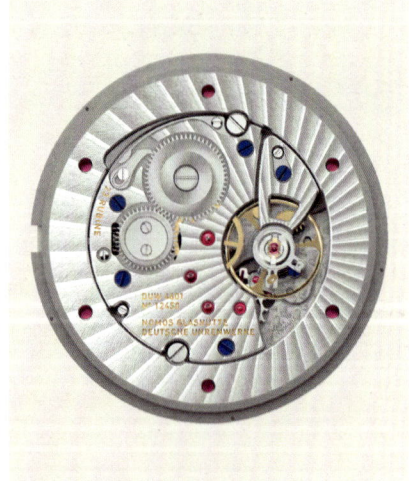

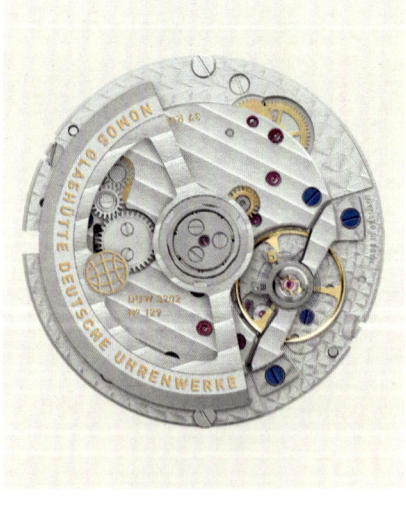

Caliber DUW 1001

Hand-wound; swan-neck fine regulator; twin barrels, 84-hour power reserve
Functions: hours, minutes, small seconds; power reserve indicator
Diameter: 32 mm
Height: 3.6 mm
Jewels: 29, including 5 screw-mounted gold chatons
Balance: screw balance
Frequency: 21,600 vph
Hairspring: Nivarox 1A
Shock protection: Incabloc
Remarks: hand-engraved balance cock, beveled and polished edges, rhodium-plated surfaces with Glashütte sunray finish and perlage

Caliber DUW 4601

Hand-wound; single spring barrel, 52-hour power reserve
Functions: hours, minutes, small seconds; date
Diameter: 34.6 mm
Height: 2.8 mm
Jewels: 23
Balance: in-house manufacture
Frequency: 21,600 vph
Hairspring: in-house, heat-blued
Shock protection: Incabloc
Remarks: three-quarter plate skeletonized balance cock, rhodium-plated surfaces with Glashütte sunray finish and perlage

Caliber DUW 3202

Automatic; single spring barrel, 42-hour power reserve
Functions: hours, minutes, small seconds; second time zone, world-time display
Diameter: 31 mm
Height: 4.75 mm
Jewels: 37
Balance: in-house manufacture
Frequency: 21,600 vph
Hairspring: in-house, heat-blued
Shock protection: Incabloc
Remarks: three-quarter plate skeletonized balance cock, rhodium-plated surfaces with Glashütte sunray finish and perlage

NORQAIN

Norqain was founded in 2018 by CEO Ben Küffer in Nidau near Biel/Bienne, that industrial city at the foot of the Jura Mountains in Switzerland that is home to several watch companies and related enterprises. He invited a number of people as cofounders to form the Board of Directors, notably Ted Schneider, a member of the family that once owned Breitling, and Swiss ice hockey legend Mark Streit, a watch enthusiast and a good ambassador for the new brand. Marc Küffer, Ben's father, was named the Chairman of the Board. He, for his part, had over forty-five years of experience in the manufacturing of Swiss luxury watches and had served on the Board of the Federation of the Swiss Watch Industry for twenty-five years.

The idea was perhaps not terribly original, but in a complicated world with lots of marketing, a clearcut message is often worth a thousand words: affordable quality. The brand's mission statement, as it were, was to be new, open-minded, rebellious, quality time-giving, adventurous, independent, and niche-oriented, which spells Norqain. The logo, a kind of N, is also a stylized mountain peak, expressing the watches' connection to sports and adventure.

The company manufactures mechanical watches only, which are assembled by hand in the production facility in Tavannes, a village in the Jura Mountains. To ensure high quality, Norqain signed a long-term strategic collaboration with Kenissi in Le Locle, a top-notch movement-maker that was founded by Tudor (of Rolex fame) and is twenty percent owned by Chanel.

The first results of this important alliance were two exclusive manufacture movements: the three-hand caliber NN20/1 and the GMT caliber NN20/2, both with a power reserve of seventy hours and chronometer certification.

The design recipe behind the three collections—Adventure, Freedom, and Independence—worked, because Norqain has become a household name amongst connoisseurs. In 2024, Norqain introduced the skeletonized in-house caliber 8K NK24/1 with a flyback chronograph function, developed in cooperation with another company, Manufacture AMT. In 2025, Norqain expanded its three collections with several new releases. Each collection is distinguished by original, bold design elements, notably colors. The brand's portfolio also features special editions and limited series, reflecting Norqain's commitment to innovation as a young and dynamic Swiss watchmaker.

MONTRES NORQAIN SA
Hauptstrasse 7
CH-2560 Nidau
Switzerland

TEL:
+41 32 505 31 55

E-MAIL:
info@norqain.com

WEBSITE:
norqain.com

FOUNDED:
2018

NUMBER OF EMPLOYEES:
40

ANNUAL PRODUCTION:
more than 1,000

DISTRIBUTION:
retailers, own shops

MOST IMPORTANT COLLECTIONS/PRICE RANGE:
Adventure, Freedom, Independence / around $2,000 to $6,000

Independence Wild One Skeleton "Hyper Pink"
Reference number: N3001.07Q04.B03
Movement: automatic, Norqain Caliber N08S (base Sellita SW200-1 Sc); ø 25.6 mm, height 4.6 mm; 26 jewels; 28,800 vph; completely skeletonized movement; 41-hour power reserve; COSC-certified chronometer
Functions: hours, minutes, sweep seconds
Case: composite material (NORTEQ) with titanium movement container with rubber shock absorbers, ø 39 mm, height 11.75 mm; sapphire crystal; transparent case back; screw-down crown, with rubber cover; water-resistant to 20 atm
Band: rubber, pin buckle
Price: $5,990
Variations: also available in sky blue, ice blue or mint

Freedom 60 Chrono "Enjoy Life"
Reference number: N2201.19S01.C01
Movement: automatic, Norqain Caliber N19 (base Sellita SW510a); ø 30.4 mm, height 7.9 mm; 27 jewels; 28,800 vph; 62-hour power reserve
Functions: hours, minutes, small seconds; chronograph; date with "Ice Cream" motif
Case: stainless steel, ø 40 mm, height 14.9 mm; sapphire crystal; transparent case back; screw-down crown; water-resistant to 10 atm
Band: stainless steel, double folding clasp
Price: $5,190
Variations: with white rubber strap ($5,190)

Independence Skeleton Chrono "Jade"
Reference number: N3200.40T02.J01
Movement: automatic, Norqain Caliber 8K (NK24/1); ø 30 mm, height 7.23 mm; 31 jewels; 28,800 vph; column-wheel control of chronograph functions; completely skeletonized movement; 62-hour power reserve; COSC-certified chronometer
Functions: hours, minutes, small seconds; flyback chronograph
Case: titanium with black PVD, ø 42 mm, height 13.9 mm; sapphire crystal; transparent case back; screw-down crown; water-resistant to 10 atm
Band: rubber, pin buckle
Price: $7,890
Variations: available in purple

NOVE

The most popular watch genre is the diver's watch, and for good reason. First, these time-pieces exude an aura of adventure, danger, and fun, mixed with a bit of lizard-brain survival, all wrapped in one. It's part of their history. After all, have they not served on the wrists of extra-tough special commandos in various countries? The other reason is, of course, reliability. As genuine tool watches, they must be built with great care and function extremely well, since the users depend on them to know how long they've been underwater and how much time they have left to perform their tasks.

Any brand wanting to release a new one will face the challenge of innovation and creating a viable USP. Nove, a brand stationed in Hong Kong but with production in Switzerland, came up with the idea of a thin diver's watch, the Trident. This watch clocks in at 6.8 millimeters thickness in quartz. A second diver, the Atlantean, was conceived with a large dose of Super-LumiNova on the dial, hands, and bezel for good visibility even in deep waters. It also features an interior bidirectional bezel that can be locked into place with a special hand lever. The diameter of the Atlantean II, released in 2024, has been reduced to a still-hefty 46 millimeters, down from 50.5!

To cover its market well, Nove also has rather fresh-looking dress watches, including the clever dual-faced Gemini GMT watch, which reverses using a bespoke lever mechanism.

Having fresh ideas might be part of the company DNA, ever since it was founded by Tiffany Meerovitsch in 2015 when she was just nineteen years old and about to go to university to study art and later digital marketing. It was a natural passion for her. She grew up steeped in watchmaking while visiting her father's office at a watchmaking company. "He had me working on the assembly line, where I learned how to assemble a watch," she said in an interview. "Seeing all these beautiful designs got me fascinated with the idea of starting my own label with my own designs."

Nove watches are assembled in Switzerland using Swiss parts. They make use of Ronda and Sellita movements mostly.

NOVE

SWISS OFFICE:
Via ai Boschi 6,
CH-6855 Stabio
Switzerland

HONG KONG OFFICE:
Nove Limited
Unit A, 3/F, Kingsway Industrial Building,
Phase 1, 167-175 Wo Yi Hop Road,
Kwai Chung, N.T., Hong Kong

EMAIL:
mkt@nove.com

WEBSITE:
www.nove.com

FOUNDED:
2015 (incorporated 2018)

NUMBER OF EMPLOYEES:
About 15 employees

DISTRIBUTION:
Webshop (see website)

MOST IMPORTANT COLLECTIONS AND PRICE RANGE:
Atlantean, Atlantean II, Gemini, Trident / $280 - $2,000

Trident 42 Arctic Blue
Reference number: N002-07
Movement: quartz Ronda caliber
Functions: hours, minutes, small seconds
Case: stainless steel, 42 mm, height 6.8 mm; three-lever ratcheting system for the unidirectional bezel; sapphire crystal, transparent case back; water-resistant to 20 atm
Band: stainless steel, safety clasp with micro-adjustment
Remarks: quick-change strap system
Price: $780
Variations: with green or black bezel

Trident Automatic Black
Reference number: G004-02
Movement: automatic, Ronda R150 Caliber; ø 25.6 mm, height 4.4 mm; 25 jewels; 28,800 vph; 40-hour power reserve
Functions: hours, minutes, sweep seconds; date
Case: stainless steel with IP blue coating, ø 46 mm, height 13.05 mm; screw-down crown; sapphire crystal; transparent case back; water-resistant to 20 atm
Band: stainless steel, folding clasp
Remarks: Haitian mother-of-pearl dial
Price: $830
Variations: IP black or rose-gold coating; comes in ultra-slim (6 mm) quartz version ($450)

Marine Automatic
Reference number: M002-07
Movement: automatic, Sellita caliber SW 200; ø 25.6 mm, height 4.6 mm; 25 jewels; 28,800 vph; 41-hour power reserve
Functions: hours, minutes, sweep seconds; date
Case: stainless steel with IP blue coating, ø 41.5 mm, height 13.05 mm; screw-down crown; sapphire crystal; transparent case back; water-resistant to 20 atm
Band: stainless steel, folding clasp
Price: $880
Variations: various colors

OMEGA

As the largest brand in the SSIH Group, Omega played a key role during the quartz crisis that reshaped the Swiss watch industry in the 1970s. Following the merger of the Société Suisse de l'Industrie Horlogère and the Allgemeine Schweizerische Uhrenindustrie AG (ASUAG), the new company became the founding member of what is now the Swatch Group. Within this structure, Omega emerged as the group's flagship brand, leading in design, technology, and functionality.

Innovation in both technology and design has consistently driven Omega's success. The company pioneered the use of new materials such as titanium and ceramic, as well as introducing remarkable complications like the central tourbillon and George Daniels's co-axial escapement.

Today, Omega's 15,000-gauss antimagnetic movement is featured across many models. The brand continues to expand its range of Master Chronometer calibers, which not only meet COSC certification standards but also pass the additional tests set by Switzerland's Federal Institute of Metrology (METAS). Swatch Group subsidiary Nivarox-FAR has perfected production of the system's complex, oil-free components designed by Daniels—although the escapement still retains lubrication, as fully "dry" co-axial movements have proven less reliable over time.

Among Omega's enduring icons, the Seamaster stands unmatched. First introduced in 1948, it evolved into the Seamaster 300 in 1957—a professional diver's watch (or plongeur professionnel, from which the nickname Ploprof originates). A notable highlight came in 1971 with the release of the Seamaster Planet Ocean Ultra Deep, capable of withstanding depths up to 600 atm.

Omega reaffirmed its legacy in precision timekeeping as the official timekeeper of the 2024 Paris Summer Olympics, celebrating the occasion with special models such as the Seamaster 300M in steel with a "Moonshine Gold" bezel and the Speedmaster Chronoscope in stainless steel or gold.

In 2025, Omega paid tribute to a milestone moment from 1965, when NASA selected the Speedmaster as its mission watch, declaring it "fit for all manned space missions." The 60th anniversary of that decision inspired the relaunch of the 2021 Speedmaster Moonwatch with the Co-Axial Master Chronometer movement. Alongside it, the Seamaster collection once again took center stage—continuing to define Omega's vision for innovation and performance.

OMEGA SA
Jakob-Stämpfli-Strasse 96
CH-2502 Biel/Bienne
Switzerland

TEL.:
+41-32-343-9211

E-MAIL:
info@omegawatches.com

WEBSITE:
www.omegawatches.com

FOUNDED:
1848

U.S. DISTRIBUTOR:
Omega
800-766-6342
www.omegawatches.com

MOST IMPORTANT COLLECTIONS / PRICE RANGE:
Constellation, DeVille, Seamaster, Speedmaster / from $3,200

Speedmaster Moonwatch Professional

Reference number: 310.30.42.50.04.001
Movement: hand-wound, Omega Caliber 3861; ø 27 mm, height 6.9 mm; 26 jewels; 21,600 vph; co-axial escapement, silicon hairspring; antimagnetic to 15,000 gauss; METAS-certified chronometer; 50-hour power reserve
Functions: hours, minutes, small seconds; chronograph
Case: stainless steel, ø 42 mm, height 13.2 mm; bezel with aluminum insert; sapphire crystal; water-resistant to 5 atm
Band: stainless steel, folding clasp
Price: $9,100

Speedmaster Super Racing

Reference number: 329.30.44.51.01.003
Movement: automatic, Omega Caliber 9920; ø 32.5 mm, height 7.6 mm; 54 jewels; 28,800 vph; twin barrels, co-axial escapement, silicon hairspring; antimagnetic to 15,000 gauss; METAS-certified chronometer; 60-hour power reserve
Functions: hours, minutes, small seconds; chronograph; date
Case: stainless steel, ø 44.25 mm, height 14.9 mm; bezel with ceramic insert; sapphire crystal; transparent case back; water-resistant to 5 atm
Band: stainless steel, double folding clasp
Price: $13,100

Railmaster

Reference number: 235.10.38.20.06.001
Movement: automatic, Omega Caliber 8806; ø 26 mm, height 4.6 mm; 35 jewels; 25,200 vph; co-axial escapement, silicon balance and hairspring; antimagnetic to 15,000 gauss; METAS-certified chronometer; 55-hour power reserve
Functions: hours, minutes, sweep seconds
Case: stainless steel, ø 38 mm, height 12.36 mm; sapphire crystal; transparent case back; screw-down crown; water-resistant to 15 atm
Band: stainless steel, double folding clasp
Price: $6,200

Seamaster 300

Reference number: 234.92.41.21.10.001
Movement: automatic, Omega Caliber 8912; ø 29 mm, height 5.5 mm; 38 jewels; 25,200 vph; twin barrels, co-axial escapement, silicon hairspring; antimagnetic to 15,000 gauss; METAS-certified chronometer; 60-hour power reserve
Functions: hours, minutes, sweep seconds
Case: bronze-gold alloy, ø 41 mm, height 14.4 mm; unidirectional bezel with ceramic insert, with 0-60 scale; sapphire crystal; transparent case back; screw-down crown; water-resistant to 30 atm
Band: leather, pin buckle
Price: $15,300
Variations: in stainless steel

Seamaster Diver 300M

Reference number: 210.30.42.20.01.001
Movement: automatic, Omega Caliber 8800; ø 26 mm, height 4.6 mm; 35 jewels; 25,200 vph; co-axial escapement, silicon hairspring; antimagnetic to 15,000 gauss; METAS-certified chronometer; 55-hour power reserve
Functions: hours, minutes, sweep seconds; date
Case: stainless steel, ø 42 mm, height 13.56 mm; unidirectional bezel with ceramic insert, with 0-60 scale; sapphire crystal; transparent case back; screw-down crown, helium valve; water-resistant to 30 atm
Band: stainless steel, folding clasp
Price: $6,700
Variations: various cases, bands and dials

Seamaster Diver "Black Black"

Reference number: 210.92.44.20.01.003
Movement: automatic, Omega Caliber 8806; ø 26 mm, height 4.6 mm; 35 jewels; 25,200 vph; co-axial escapement, silicon hairspring; antimagnetic to 15,000 gauss; METAS-certified chronometer; 55-hour power reserve
Functions: hours, minutes, sweep seconds
Case: ceramic, ø 43.5 mm, height 14.5 mm; unidirectional bezel, with 0-60 scale; sapphire crystal; transparent case back; screw-down crown, helium valve; water-resistant to 30 atm
Band: rubber, pin buckle
Price: $10,700

Seamaster Diver 300M

Reference number: 210.30.42.20.03.003
Movement: automatic, Omega Caliber 8800; ø 26 mm, height 4.6 mm; 35 jewels; 25,200 vph; co-axial escapement, silicon hairspring; antimagnetic to 15,000 gauss; METAS-certified chronometer; 55-hour power reserve
Functions: hours, minutes, sweep seconds; date
Case: stainless steel, ø 42 mm, height 13.56 mm; unidirectional bezel with ceramic insert and 0-60 scale; sapphire crystal; transparent case back; screw-down crown, helium valve; water-resistant to 30 atm
Band: stainless steel, folding clasp, with extension link
Price: $7,100
Variations: various cases, bands and dials

Seamaster Aqua Terra 150M Master Chronometer

Reference number: 220.10.41.21.03.006
Movement: automatic, Omega Caliber 8900; ø 29 mm, height 5.5 mm; 39 jewels; 25,200 vph; twin barrels; co-axial escapement, silicon hairspring; antimagnetic to 15,000 gauss; METAS-certified chronometer; 60-hour power reserve
Functions: hours, minutes, sweep seconds; date
Case: stainless steel, ø 41 mm, height 13.26 mm; sapphire crystal; water-resistant to 15 atm
Band: stainless steel, double folding clasp
Price: $7,400

Seamaster Aqua Terra Worldtimer

Reference number: 220.32.43.22.10.001
Movement: automatic, Omega Caliber 8938; ø 29 mm, height 6 mm; 38 jewels; 25,200 vph; co-axial escapement, silicon hairspring; antimagnetic to 15,000 gauss; METAS-certified chronometer; 60-hour power reserve
Functions: hours, minutes, sweep seconds; world-time display (second time zone); date
Case: stainless steel, ø 43 mm, height 14.1 mm; sapphire crystal; transparent case back; screw-down crown; water-resistant to 15 atm
Band: rubber, folding clasp
Price: $12,100
Variations: various cases and dials

Seamaster Planet Ocean Worldtimer 600M

Reference number: 215.92.46.22.01.006
Movement: automatic, Omega Caliber 8938;
ø 29 mm, height 6 mm; 38 jewels; 25,200 vph; co-axial escapement, silicon hairspring; antimagnetic to 15,000 gauss; METAS-certified chronometer; 60-hour power reserve
Functions: hours, minutes, sweep seconds; world-time display (second time zone); date
Case: ceramic, ø 45.5 mm, height 17.38 mm; bidirectional bezel, with 0-60 scale; sapphire crystal; transparent case back; screw-down crown; water-resistant to 60 atm
Band: rubber with textile inlay, folding clasp
Price: $16,700

Seamaster Planet Ocean 600M

Reference number: 215.32.44.21.06.001
Movement: automatic, Omega Caliber 8900; ø 29 mm, height 5.5 mm; 39 jewels; 25,200 vph; twin barrels, co-axial escapement, silicon hairspring; antimagnetic to 15,000 gauss; METAS-certified chronometer; 60-hour power reserve
Functions: hours, minutes, sweep seconds; date
Case: stainless steel, ø 43.5 mm, height 16.2 mm; unidirectional bezel with ceramic insert, with 0-60 scale; sapphire crystal; transparent case back; screw-down crown, helium valve; water-resistant to 60 atm
Band: rubber with textile inlay, folding clasp
Price: $8,000

Seamaster "Ploprof"

Reference number: 227.32.55.21.03.001
Movement: automatic, Omega Caliber 8912; ø 29 mm, height 5.5 mm; 38 jewels; 25,200 vph; twin barrels, co-axial escapement, silicon hairspring; antimagnetic to 15,000 gauss; METAS-certified chronometer; 60-hour power reserve
Functions: hours, minutes, sweep seconds
Case: stainless steel ("O-Megasteel"), 55 mm x 45 mm, height 15.5 mm; unidirectional bezel with ceramic insert, with 0-60 scale; sapphire crystal; screw-down crown, helium valve; water-resistant to 120 atm
Band: rubber, pin buckle
Remarks: the (unofficial) name of the model derives from "Plongeurs Professionnels" (professional divers)
Price: $16,100

Constellation Master Chronometer

Reference number: 131.33.41.21.04.001
Movement: automatic, Omega Caliber 8900; ø 29 mm, height 5.5 mm; 39 jewels; 25,200 vph; twin barrels; co-axial escapement, silicon hairspring, antimagnetic to 15,000 gauss; METAS-certified chronometer; 60-hour power reserve
Functions: hours, minutes, sweep seconds; date
Case: stainless steel, ø 41 mm, height 13.5 mm; sapphire crystal; transparent case back; water-resistant to 5 atm
Band: rubber with reptile skin inlay, folding clasp
Price: $8,000
Variations: various dials

Seamaster Aqua Terra 150M

Reference number: 220.10.30.20.10.002
Movement: automatic, Omega Caliber 8750; ø 20 mm, height 3.98 mm; 35 jewels; 25,200 vph; co-axial escapement, silicon hairspring, antimagnetic to 15,000 gauss; METAS-certified chronometer; 48-hour power reserve
Functions: hours, minutes, sweep seconds; date
Case: stainless steel, ø 30 mm, height 10.55 mm; sapphire crystal; transparent case back; water-resistant to 15 atm
Band: stainless steel, double folding clasp
Price: $7,100

Speedmaster Moonwatch Professional

Reference number: 310.62.42.50.99.001
Movement: hand-wound, Omega Caliber 3861; ø 27 mm, height 6.9 mm; 26 jewels; 21,600 vph; co-axial escapement, silicon hairspring, antimagnetic to 15,000 gauss; METAS-certified chronometer; 50-hour power reserve
Functions: hours, minutes, small seconds; chronograph
Case: yellow gold ("Moonshine Gold"), ø 42 mm, height 13.2 mm; bezel with ceramic insert; sapphire crystal; transparent case back; water-resistant to 5 atm
Band: rubber, folding clasp
Price: $36,500

Speedmaster Dark Side of the Moon "Apollo 8"

Reference number: 310.92.44.50.01.001
Movement: hand-wound, Omega Caliber 3869;
ø 27 mm, height 6.87 mm; 26 jewels; 21,600 vph;
co-axial escapement, silicon hairspring, antimagnetic to
15,000 gauss; mainplate and bridges with black coating
METAS-certified chronometer; 50-hour power reserve
Functions: hours, minutes, small seconds; chronograph
Case: ceramic, ø 44.25 mm, height 13 mm; sapphire
crystal; transparent case back; water-resistant to 5 atm
Band: calfskin, folding clasp
Remarks: mainplate and bridges with carefully designed
structure of the moon's surface
Price: $16,100

Speedmaster Moonwatch Master Chronometer

Reference number: 310.30.42.50.01.001
Movement: hand-wound, Omega Caliber 3861;
ø 27 mm, height 6.9 mm; 26 jewels; 21,600 vph;
co-axial escapement, silicon hairspring, antimagnetic to
15,000 gauss; METAS-certified chronometer; 50-hour
power reserve
Functions: hours, minutes, small seconds; Chronograph
Case: stainless steel, ø 42 mm, height 13.2 mm; Bezel
with aluminum insert; Hesalite glass; water-resistant
to 5 atm
Band: stainless steel, folding clasp
Price: $7,800
Variations: with textile strap ($7,400)

Speedmaster Moonphase

Reference number: 304.33.44.52.03.001
Movement: automatic, Omega Caliber 9904;
ø 32.5 mm, height 8.35 mm; 54 jewels; 28,800 vph;
twin barrels, co-axial escapement, silicon hairspring,
antimagnetic to 15,000 gauss; METAS-certified
chronometer; 60-hour power reserve
Functions: hours, minutes, small seconds;
Chronograph; date, moon phase
Case: stainless steel, ø 44.25 mm, height 16.85 mm;
bezel with ceramic insert; sapphire crystal; water-
resistant to 10 atm
Band: reptile skin, folding clasp
Price: $12,600
Variations: various cases and dials

Seamaster Diver 300M

Reference number: 210.92.42.20.01.003
Movement: automatic, Omega Caliber 8806; ø 26 mm,
height 4.6 mm; 35 jewels; 25,200 vph; co-axial
escapement, silicon hairspring, antimagnetic to
15,000 gauss; mainplate and bridges with black coating;
METAS-certified chronometer; 55-hour power reserve
Functions: hours, minutes, sweep seconds
Case: bronze-gold alloy, ø 42 mm, height
13.8 mm; unidirectional bezel with aluminum insert and
0-60 scale; sapphire crystal; transparent case back;
screw-down crown, helium valve; water-resistant to
30 atm
Band: rubber, pin buckle
Price: $15,700

Seamaster Diver "James Bond"

Reference number: 210.90.42.20.01.001
Movement: automatic, Omega Caliber 8806; ø 26 mm,
height 4.6 mm; 35 jewels; 25,200 vph; co-axial
escapement, silicon hairspring, antimagnetic to
15,000 gauss; mainplate and bridges with black coating;
METAS-certified chronometer; 55-hour power reserve
Functions: hours, minutes, sweep seconds
Case: titanium, ø 42 mm, height 13 mm; unidirectional
bezel with aluminum insert and 0-60 scale; sapphire
crystal; screw-down crown, helium valve; water-
resistant to 30 atm
Band: titanium Milanaise mesh, folding clasp
Price: $11,300
Variations: with textile strap ($10,100)

Speedmaster '57

Reference number: 332.12.41.51.03.001
Movement: hand-wound, Omega Caliber 9906;
ø 32.5 mm, height 6.4 mm; 44 jewels; 28,800 vph;
co-axial escapement, silicon hairspring; column-wheel
control of chronograph functions; METAS-certified
chronometer; 60-hour power reserve
Functions: hours, minutes, small seconds;
Chronograph; date
Case: stainless steel, ø 40.5 mm, height 13 mm;
sapphire crystal; water-resistant to 10 atm
Band: leather, pin buckle
Price: $10,300
Variations: various straps and dials

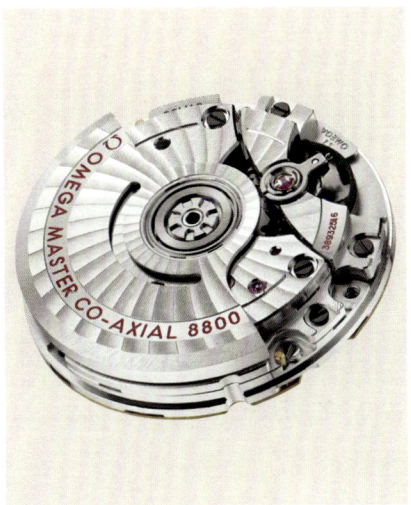

Caliber 8800

Automatic; co-axial escapement; antimagnetic up to 15,000 gauss; METAS-certified chronometer; single spring barrel, 55-hour power reserve

Functions: hours, minutes, sweep seconds; date
Diameter: 26 mm
Height: 4.6 mm
Jewels: 35
Balance: silicon, without regulator
Frequency: 25,200 vph
Balance spring: silicon
Shock protection: Nivachoc
Remarks: blackened screws

Caliber 321B

Hand-wound; Breguet hairspring; column-wheel control of chronograph functions; single spring barrel, 55-hour power reserve

Base caliber: Lémania 2310
Functions: hours, minutes, small seconds; chronograph
Diameter: 27 mm
Height: 6.87 mm
Jewels: 17
Frequency: 18,000 vph
Remarks: re-edition of historic movement used in first Speedmaster models; red-gold plated, finely finished

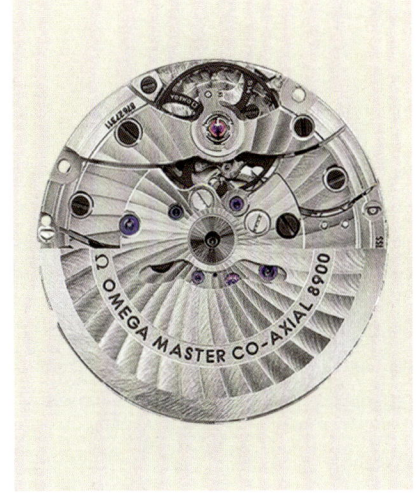

Caliber 8900

Automatic; co-axial escapement; antimagnetic up to 15,000 gauss; METAS-certified chronometer; twin barrels, 60-hour power reserve

Functions: hours, minutes, sweep seconds; date
Diameter: 29 mm
Height: 5.5 mm
Jewels: 39
Balance: silicon, without regulator
Frequency: 25,200 vph
Balance spring: silicon
Shock protection: Nivachoc
Remarks: mainplate, bridges, and rotor with "arabesque" côtes de Genève, rhodium-plated, spring barrels, blackened balance wheel and screws

Caliber 9900

Automatic; co-axial escapement; column-wheel control of chronograph functions; antimagnetic up to 15,000 gauss; METAS-certified chronometer; twin barrels, 60-hour power reserve

Functions: hours, minutes, small seconds; chronograph; date
Diameter: 32.5 mm
Height: 7.6 mm
Jewels: 5.4
Balance: silicon, without regulator
Frequency: 28,800 vph
Balance spring: silicon
Shock protection: Nivachoc
Remarks: mainplate, bridges, and rotor with "arabesque" côtes de Genève

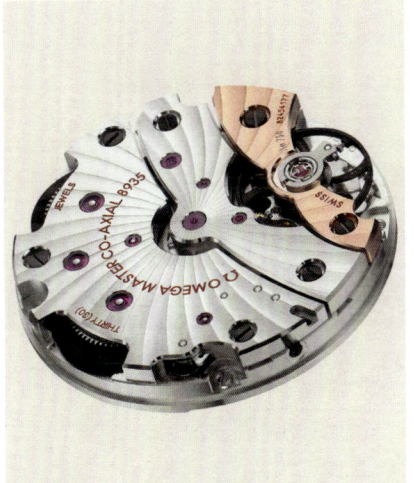

Caliber 8935

Hand-wound; co-axial escapement, antimagnetic to 15,000 gauss; METAS-certified chronometer; twin barrels, 72-hour power reserve

Functions: hours, minutes, small seconds; power reserve display
Diameter: 29 mm
Height: 5.5 mm
Jewels: 30
Balance: silicon, indexless
Frequency: 25,200 vph
Balance: silicon, indexless
Shock protection: Nivachoc
Remarks: mainplate and bridges with côtes de Genève, "Sednagold" balance bridge; blackened spring barrels, balance wheel and screws

Caliber 3861

Hand-wound; co-axial escapement, antimagnetic protection to 15,000 gauss; METAS-certified chronometer; single spring barrel, 50-hour power reserve

Functions: hours, minutes, small seconds; chronograph
Diameter: 27 mm
Height: 6.87 mm
Jewels: 26
Frequency: 21,600 vph
Balance spring: silicon
Remarks: gold-plated movement ("Moonshine Gold"); 240 parts

ORIS

Oris, located near Basel, Switzerland, since its founding in 1904, has stuck to its strategic guns for as long as it has existed: affordable quality. The result has been growing international success, now with a portfolio divided up into four "product worlds," each with its own distinct identity: aviation, motor sports, diving, and culture. In utilizing specific materials—a tungsten bezel for the divers, for example—and functions based on these types, Oris makes certain that each will fit perfectly into the world for which it was designed. Yet the heart of every watch houses a small, high-quality "high-mech" movement identifiable by the brand's standard red rotor.

A bold step came in 2014 with the in-house Caliber 110, a plain, but technically efficient, manually wound movement. It was made together with the engineers from the Technical College of Le Locle and features a 6-foot (1.8-meter) mainspring. Like clockwork, then, Oris produced further calibers, numbered 111, 112 (with GMT function), and 113.

In October 2020, the first wristwatches with the new Caliber 400 were launched. One goal in creating the movement was to eliminate problems even before they occur. COO Beat Fischli and his team spent five years developing a movement with a five-day power reserve, special resistance to magnetic fields, chronometer accuracy, and high serviceability with long maintenance intervals of ten years.

The Caliber 400 family debuted in the Aquis series but has already been used in various editions of the Big Crown and Divers Sixty-Five series. In recent years, the model underwent a complete facelift, with a slimmer case; improved ergonomics; and a lot of visual detail work on the dial, hands, crown, and side protection. The stainless-steel cases are 41.5 and 43.5 mm in diameter. Besides evolving mechanically, Oris watches have been showing boldness in color in recent years. Numerous models come with dials in striking shades for those who need something more expressive on the wrist.

Finally, sustainability is a key concern for Oris, actively reflected in its commitment to ocean and climate protection projects. The company also emphasizes eco-friendly, resource-saving packaging solutions. Since 2021, Oris holds official certification as a CO_2-neutral company.

ORIS SA
Ribigasse 1
CH-4434 Hölstein
Switzerland

TEL.:
+41 61 956 1111

E-MAIL:
MyOris@oris.ch

WEBSITE:
www.oris.ch

FOUNDED:
1904

NUMBER OF EMPLOYEES:
210

U.S. DISTRIBUTOR:
Oris Watches USA
50 Washington Street, Suite 302
Norwalk, CT 06854
203-857-4769

MOST IMPORTANT COLLECTIONS/PRICE RANGE:
Divers Sixty-Five, Big Crown, Artelier, Aquis, ProPilot
/ approx. $1,300 to $10,300

Big Crown Caliber 473

Reference number: 01 473 7786 4065-07 5 19 22FC
Movement: hand-wound, Oris caliber 473; ø 30 mm; 27 jewels; 28,800 vph; 120-hour power reserve
Functions: hours, minutes, small seconds; power reserve indicator (on movement side); date
Case: stainless steel, ø 38 mm, height 11.8 mm; sapphire crystal; transparent case back; water-resistant to 5 atm
Band: deer skin, pin buckle
Price: $5,200

Oris X Cervo Volante

Reference number: 01 754 7779 4065-Set
Movement: automatic, Oris caliber 754 (Sellita SW200-1 base); ø 25.6 mm, height 4.6 mm; 26 jewels; 28,800 vph; 38-hour power reserve
Functions: hours, minutes, sweep seconds; date
Case: stainless steel, ø 38 mm, height 12.8 mm; sapphire crystal; transparent case back; water-resistant to 5 atm
Band: deer skin, pin buckle
Price: $2,600
Variations: with green or grey dial

Big Crown Pointer Date Calibre 403

Reference number: 01 403 7799 4068-07 8 20 06
Movement: automatic, Oris caliber 403; ø 30 mm; 27 jewels; 28,800 vph; 120-hour power reserve
Functions: hours, minutes, small seconds; date
Case: stainless steel, ø 40 mm, height 11.8 mm; sapphire crystal; transparent case back; water-resistant to 5 atm
Band: stainless steel, folding clasp
Price: $4,300

Big Crown Pointer Date

Reference number: 01 754 7798 4069-07 8 20 06
Movement: automatic, Oris caliber 754-1; ø 25.6 mm;
25 jewels; 28,800 vph; 41-hour power reserve
Functions: hours, minutes, sweep seconds; date
Case: stainless steel, ø 40 mm, height 11.8 mm;
sapphire crystal; transparent case back; water-resistant
to 5 atm
Band: stainless steel, folding clasp
Price: $2,400

ProPilot X Calibre 115

Reference number: 01 115 7759 7153-Set7 22 01TLC
Movement: hand-wound, Oris caliber 115; ø 34 mm,
height 6 mm; 38 jewels; 21,600 vph; skeletonized
movement; central, open spring barrel, 240-hour power
reserve
Functions: hours, minutes, small seconds; power
reserve indicator
Case: titanium, ø 44 mm, height 12.5 mm; sapphire
crystal; transparent case back; screw-down crown;
water-resistant to 10 atm
Band: titanium, folding clasp
Remarks: skeletonized dial
Price: $9,400
Variations: with leather strap

ProPilot X Kermit Edition

Reference number: 01 400 7778 7157-Set
Movement: automatic, Oris caliber 400; ø 30 mm,
height 4.75 mm; 21 jewels; 28,800 vph; 120-hour power
reserve
Functions: hours, minutes, sweep seconds; date
Case: titanium, ø 39 mm, height 12 mm; sapphire
crystal; water-resistant to 10 atm
Band: titanium, folding clasp
Remarks: Kermit the Frog appears in the date window
on the first of the month
Price: $5,100

Aquis Date Calibre 400

Reference number: 01 400 7790 4135-07 8 23 02PEB
Movement: automatic, Oris caliber 400; ø 30 mm,
height 4.75 mm; 21 jewels; 28,800 vph; 120-hour power
reserve
Functions: hours, minutes, sweep seconds; date
Case: stainless steel, ø 43.5 mm, height 13.1 mm;
unidirectional bezel with ceramic insert, with 0-60 scale;
sapphire crystal; screw-down crown; water-resistant
to 30 atm
Band: stainless steel, folding clasp, with safety lock,
with extension link
Price: $2,800

Aquis Date Caliber 400

Reference number: 01 400 7790 4157-07 4 23 47EB
Movement: automatic, Oris caliber 400; ø 30 mm,
height 4.75 mm; 21 jewels; 28,800 vph; 120-hour power
reserve
Functions: hours, minutes, sweep seconds; date
Case: stainless steel, ø 43.5 mm, height 13.1 mm;
unidirectional bezel with ceramic insert with 0-60 scale;
sapphire crystal; screw-down crown; water-resistant
to 30 atm
Band: rubber, folding clasp
Price: $2,800

Aquis Date

Reference number: 01 733 7787 4135-07 4 22 35FC
Movement: automatic, Oris caliber 733 (Sellita
SW200-1 base); ø 25.6 mm, height 4.6 mm; 26 jewels;
28,800 vph; 41-hour power reserve
Functions: hours, minutes, sweep seconds; date
Case: stainless steel, ø 41.5 mm, height 12.9 mm;
unidirectional bezel with ceramic insert, with 0-60 scale;
sapphire crystal; transparent case back; screw-down
crown; water-resistant to 30 atm
Band: rubber, pin buckle, with extension link
Price: $2,800

Aquis Date Upcycle

Reference number: 01 733 7787 4150-07 8 22 04PEB
Movement: automatic, Oris caliber 733 (Sellita SW200-1 base); ø 25.6 mm, height 4.6 mm; 26 jewels; 28,800 vph; 41-hour power reserve
Functions: hours, minutes, sweep seconds; date
Case: stainless steel, ø 41.5 mm, height 12.9 mm; unidirectional bezel with ceramic insert, with 0-60 scale; sapphire crystal; transparent case back; screw-down crown; water-resistant to 30 atm
Band: stainless steel, folding clasp, with extension link
Remarks: dial made of recycled PET
Price: $4,400

Aquis Chronograph

Reference number: 01 771 7793 4155-07 8 23 01PEB
Movement: automatic, Oris caliber 771 (Sellita SW500-1 base); ø 30 mm, height 7.9 mm; 27 jewels; 28,800 vph; 62-hour power reserve
Functions: hours, minutes, sweep seconds; chronograph; date
Case: stainless steel, ø 43.5 mm, height 16.2 mm; unidirectional bezel, with 0-60 scale; sapphire crystal; transparent case back; screw-down crown; water-resistant to 30 atm
Band: stainless steel, folding clasp, with extension link
Price: $5,000

Aquis Date Relief

Reference number: 01 733 7789 4153-07 4 23 36FC
Movement: automatic, Oris caliber 733-1 (Sellita SW200-1 base); ø 25.6 mm, height 4.6 mm; 26 jewels; 28,800 vph; 41-hour power reserve
Functions: hours, minutes, sweep seconds; date
Case: stainless steel, ø 43.5 mm, height 12.9 mm; unidirectional bezel with ceramic insert and 0-60 scale; sapphire crystal; transparent case back; screw-down crown; water-resistant to 30 atm
Band: rubber, pin buckle, with extension link
Price: $2,400
Variations: with stainless-steel bracelet ($2,600); with red dial

Divers Sixty-Five Chronograph

Reference number: 01 771 7791 4054-07 8 20 18
Movement: automatic, Oris caliber 771 (Sellita SW500-1 base); ø 30 mm, height 7.9 mm; 27 jewels; 28,800 vph; 62-hour power reserve
Functions: hours, minutes, sweep seconds; chronograph
Case: stainless steel, ø 40 mm, height 15.4 mm; unidirectional bezel, with 0-60 scale; sapphire crystal; transparent case back; screw-down crown; water-resistant to 10 atm
Band: stainless steel, folding clasp, with extension link
Price: $4,700
Variations: with leather strap ($4,500)

Divers Sixty-Five
60th Anniversary Edition

Reference number: 01 733 7772 4034-Set
Movement: automatic, Oris caliber 733-1 (Sellita SW200-1 base); ø 25.6 mm, height 4.6 mm; 26 jewels; 28,800 vph; 41-hour power reserve
Functions: hours, minutes, sweep seconds
Case: stainless steel, ø 40 mm, height 12.8 mm; unidirectional bezel, with 0-60 scale; sapphire crystal; screw-down crown; water-resistant to 10 atm
Band: stainless steel, folding clasp, with extension link
Remarks: comes with additional leather strap
Price: $2,600

Divers Date

Reference number: 01 733 7795 4051-Set
Movement: automatic, Oris caliber 733-1 (Sellita SW200-1 base); ø 25.6 mm, height 4.6 mm; 26 jewels; 28,800 vph; 41-hour power reserve
Functions: hours, minutes, sweep seconds; date
Case: stainless steel, ø 39 mm, height 12.8 mm; unidirectional bezel, with 0-60 scale; sapphire crystal; screw-down crown; water-resistant to 10 atm
Band: stainless steel, folding clasp, with extension link
Price: $2,850
Variations: various colors

PANERAI

Officine Panerai (in English: Panerai Workshops) joined the Richemont Group in 1997. Since then, it has made an unprecedented rise from an insider niche brand to a lifestyle phenomenon. The company, founded in 1860 by Giovanni Panerai, supplied the Italian navy with precision instruments. In the 1930s, the Florentine engineers developed a series of waterproof wristwatches that could be used by commandos under especially extreme and risky conditions. After 1997, under the leadership of Angelo Bonati, the company came out with a collection of oversize wristwatches, both stylistically and technically based on these historical models.

In 2002, Panerai opened a *manufacture* in Neuchâtel, and by 2005 it was already producing its own movements, the caliber family P.2000 and later the P.9000 family. The success of the verticalization of the brand led to the opening of a new *manufacture* in 2014, also in Neuchâtel, to bring development, manufacturing, assembly, and quality control under one roof. Around 250 people work in their respective areas of expertise in this light-filled building. The new environment brings together under one roof all the main processes and technical skills required to produce a watch of the highest quality. By opening the manufacturing process to the public, Panerai offers the opportunity to immerse oneself in a world of innovation and cutting-edge technology.

Parallel to consolidating, the brand has been steadily expanding its portfolio of new calibers.

Besides expanding the Panerai stable of calibers, the company has focused on the new sustainability trend among watch brands.

The technical highlight of 2025 is the Luminor Perpetual Calendar, which sets new standards with its ease of use and excellent readability. Inside is the newly developed Panerai Caliber P.4100, a highly modern design. It features several interesting details, such as a date shock protection system, a low-wear GMT spring, and the calendar display, which can be adjusted forwards and backwards at any time (via the crown) without risk of damaging the movement.

OFFICINE PANERAI
Viale Monza, 259
I-20126 Milan
Italy

TEL.:
+39-02-363-138

WEBSITE:
www.panerai.com

FOUNDED:
1860 in Florence, Italy

NUMBER OF EMPLOYEES:
Around 1,000 employees

U.S. DISTRIBUTOR:
Panerai
645 Fifth Avenue
New York, NY 10022
877-PANERAI
concierge.usa@panerai.com;
www.panerai.com

MOST IMPORTANT COLLECTIONS/PRICE RANGE:
Luminor / $5,000 to $25,000; Luminor / $8,000 to $30,000; Radiomir / $8,000 to $133,000; special editions / $10,000 to $125,000; clocks and instruments / $20,000 to $250,000

Submersible QuarantaQuattro Goldtech OroCarbo

Reference number: PAM02070
Movement: automatic, Panerai caliber P.900; ø 28.19 mm, height 4.2 mm; 23 jewels; 28,800 vph; 72-hour power reserve
Functions: hours, minutes, subsidiary seconds; date
Case: rose gold "Goldtech" alloy, ø 44 mm, height 13.35 mm; unidirectional composite material ("Carbotech") bezel, with 0-60 scale; sapphire crystal; crown with guard and hinged lever; water-resistant to 30 atm
Band: rubber, pin buckle
Price: $33,300

Luminor Submersible Marina Militare Carbotech

Reference number: PAM02979
Movement: automatic, Panerai caliber P.9010; ø 31 mm, height 6 mm; 31 jewels; 28,800 vph; 2 twin barrels, 72-hour power reserve
Functions: hours, minutes, subsidiary seconds; date
Case: composite material ("Carbotech"), ø 47 mm, height 15.45 mm; unidirectional bezel, with 0-60 scale; sapphire crystal; crown with guard and hinged lever; water-resistant to 30 atm
Band: rubber, folding clasp
Price: $20,200

Radiomir Tre Giorni

Reference number: PAM01334
Movement: hand-wound, Panerai caliber P.6000; ø 34.96 mm, height 4.5 mm; 19 jewels; 21,600 vph; 72-hour power reserve
Functions: hours, minutes
Case: stainless steel, ø 45 mm, height 10.5 mm; sapphire crystal; water-resistant to 10 atm
Band: calfskin, pin buckle
Price: $7,100

Radiomir Tre Giorni

Reference number: PAM01350
Movement: hand-wound, Panerai caliber P.6000;
ø 34.96 mm, height 4.5 mm; 19 jewels; 21,600 vph;
72-hour power reserve
Functions: hours, minutes
Case: stainless steel, ø 45 mm, height 10.5 mm;
sapphire crystal; water-resistant to 10 atm
Band: calfskin, pin buckle
Price: $7,100

Luminor Due

Reference number: PAM01248
Movement: automatic, Panerai caliber P.900;
ø 28.19 mm, height 4.2 mm; 23 jewels; 28,800 vph;
72-hour power reserve
Functions: hours, minutes, subsidiary seconds; date
Case: stainless steel, ø 38 mm, height 11.3 mm;
sapphire crystal; crown with guard and hinged lever;
water-resistant to 3 atm
Band: reptile skin, pin buckle
Price: $6,900

Luminor Due Luna Rossa

Reference number: PAM01381
Movement: automatic, Panerai caliber P.900;
ø 28.19 mm, height 4.2 mm; 23 jewels; 28,800 vph;
72-hour power reserve
Functions: hours, minutes, subsidiary seconds; date
Case: stainless steel, ø 42 mm, height 11.3 mm;
sapphire crystal; crown with guard and hinged lever;
water-resistant to 3 atm
Band: rubber with textile overlay, pin buckle
Price: $7,800

Luminor Due

Reference number: PAM01123
Movement: automatic, Panerai caliber P.900;
ø 28.19 mm, height 4.2 mm; 23 jewels; 28,800 vph;
72-hour power reserve
Functions: hours, minutes, subsidiary seconds; date
Case: stainless steel, ø 38 mm, height 11.3 mm;
sapphire crystal; crown with guard and hinged lever;
water-resistant to 3 atm
Band: stainless steel, folding clasp
Price: $7,700

Luminor Base Logo

Reference number: PAM01087
Movement: hand-wound, Panerai caliber P.6000;
ø 34.96 mm, height 4.5 mm; 19 jewels; 21,600 vph;
72-hour power reserve
Functions: hours, minutes
Case: stainless steel, ø 44 mm, height 13 mm; sapphire
crystal; crown with guard and hinged lever; water-
resistant to 10 atm
Band: rubber, pin buckle
Price: $5,600

Luminor Logo

Reference number: PAM01084
Movement: hand-wound, Panerai caliber P.6000;
ø 34.96 mm, height 4.5 mm; 19 jewels; 21,600 vph;
72-hour power reserve
Functions: hours, minutes, subsidiary seconds
Case: stainless steel, ø 44 mm, height 13 mm; sapphire
crystal; crown with guard and hinged lever; water-
resistant to 10 atm
Band: calfskin, pin buckle
Price: $6,100

Luminor Marina

Reference number: PAM01312
Movement: automatic, Panerai caliber P.9010; ø 31 mm, height 6 mm; 31 jewels; 28,800 vph; twin barrels, 72-hour power reserve
Functions: hours, minutes, subsidiary seconds; date
Case: stainless steel, ø 44 mm, height 15.45 mm; sapphire crystal; crown with guard and hinged lever; water-resistant to 30 atm
Band: reptile skin, pin buckle
Price: $8,800

Submersible QuarantaQuattro

Reference number: PAM01229
Movement: automatic, Panerai caliber P.900; ø 28.19 mm, height 4.2 mm; 23 jewels; 28,800 vph; 72-hour power reserve
Functions: hours, minutes, subsidiary seconds; date
Case: stainless steel, ø 44 mm, height 13.35 mm; unidirectional bezel, with 0-60 scale; sapphire crystal; crown with guard and hinged lever; water-resistant to 30 atm
Band: rubber, pin buckle
Price: $9,900

Submersible QuarantaQuattro

Reference number: PAM01226
Movement: automatic, Panerai caliber P.900; ø 28.19 mm, height 4.2 mm; 23 jewels; 28,800 vph; 72-hour power reserve
Functions: hours, minutes, subsidiary seconds; date
Case: stainless steel, ø 44 mm, height 13.35 mm; unidirectional bezel, with 0-60 scale; sapphire crystal; crown with guard and hinged lever; water-resistant to 30 atm
Band: rubber, pin buckle
Price: $9,900

Radiomir Quaranta Goldtech

Reference number: PAM01026
Movement: automatic, Panerai caliber P.900; ø 28.19 mm, height 4.2 mm; 23 jewels; 28,800 vph; 72-hour power reserve
Functions: hours, minutes, subsidiary seconds; date
Case: rose gold, ø 40 mm, height 10.5 mm; sapphire crystal; transparent case back; water-resistant to 5 atm
Band: reptile skin, pin buckle
Price: $18,200

Luminor Chrono

Reference number: PAM01109
Movement: automatic, Panerai caliber P.9200; ø 31 mm, height 6.9 mm; 41 jewels; 28,800 vph; 42-hour power reserve
Functions: hours, minutes, subsidiary seconds; chronograph
Case: stainless steel, ø 44 mm, height 15.65 mm; sapphire crystal; crown with guard and hinged lever; water-resistant to 10 atm
Band: reptile skin, pin buckle
Remarks: comes with extra rubber strap
Price: $10,000

Luminor Due Luna Goldtech

Reference number: PAM01181
Movement: automatic, Panerai caliber P.900/MP; ø 28.19 mm, height 5.9 mm; 23 jewels; 28,800 vph; 72-hour power reserve
Functions: hours, minutes, subsidiary seconds; moon phase
Case: rose gold "Goldtech" alloy, ø 38 mm, height 12.41 mm; sapphire crystal; transparent case back; crown with guard and hinged lever; water-resistant to 5 atm
Band: reptile skin, pin buckle
Remarks: mother-of-pearl dial
Price: $21,500

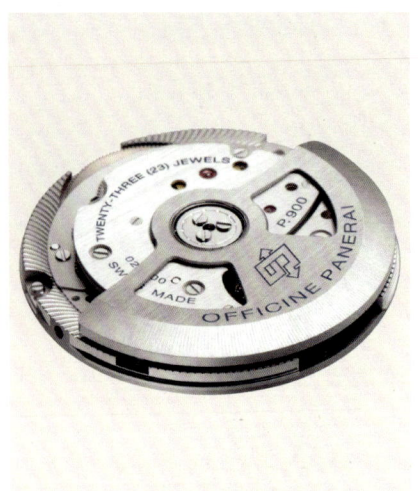

Caliber P.900

Automatic; single barrel, 72-hour power reserve
Functions: hours, minutes, subsidiary seconds; date
Diameter: 28.19 mm
Height: 4.2 mm
Jewels: 23
Balance: glucydur
Frequency: 28,800 vph
Shock protection: Incabloc
Remarks: 171 parts

Caliber P.9010

Automatic; twin barrels arranged serially, 72-hour power reserve
Functions: hours, minutes, subsidiary seconds; date
Diameter: 31 mm
Height: 6 mm
Jewels: 31
Balance: glucydur
Frequency: 28,800 vph
Remarks: 200 parts

Caliber P.9012

Automatic; twin barrels arranged serially, 72-hour power reserve
Functions: hours, minutes, subsidiary seconds; additional 12-hour display (second time zone), power reserve indicator; date
Diameter: 31 mm
Height: 6 mm
Jewels: 31
Balance: glucydur
Frequency: 28,800 vph
Shock protection: Incabloc
Remarks: 231 parts

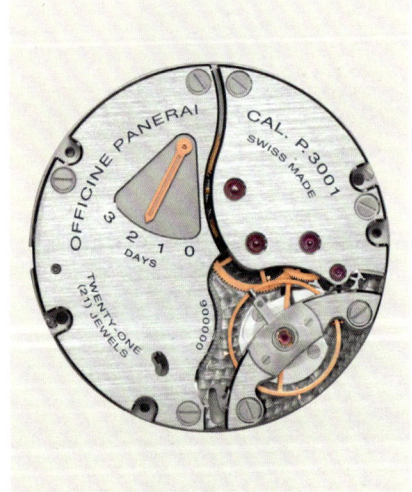

Caliber P.3001

Hand-wound; twin barrels arranged serially, 72-hour power reserve
Functions: hours, minutes, subsidiary seconds; power reserve indicator (on the movement side)
Diameter: 37.2 mm
Height: 6.3 mm
Jewels: 21
Balance: glucydur
Frequency: 21,600 vph
Remarks: 213 parts

Caliber P.6000

Hand-wound; single barrel, 72-hour power reserve
Functions: hours, minutes, subsidiary seconds
Diameter: 34.9 mm
Height: 4.5 mm
Jewels: 19
Balance: glucydur
Frequency: 21,600 vph
Shock protection: Incabloc
Remarks: 110 parts

Caliber P.2005/T

Hand-wound; skeletonized movement; 1-minute tourbillon with rotating axis perpendicular to the balance pivot; triple spring barrel arranged serially, 144-hour power reserve
Functions: hours, minutes, subsidiary seconds; additional 24-hour display (second time zone), day/night indication, power reserve indicator (on movement side)
Diameter: 36.6 mm
Height: 10.05 mm
Jewels: 31
Balance: glucydur
Frequency: 28,800 vph
Remarks: 277 parts

PARMIGIANI FLEURIER

What began as the undertaking of a single man—a gifted watchmaker and reputable restorer of complicated vintage timepieces—in the small town of Fleurier in Switzerland's Val de Travers has now grown into an empire of sorts comprising several factories and more than 400 employees.

Michel Parmigiani is in fact just doing what he has done since 1976, when he began restoring vintage works. His output soon attracted the attention of the Sandoz Family Foundation, an organization established by a member of one of Switzerland's most famous families in 1964. The foundation bought 51 percent of Parmigiani Mesure et Art du Temps SA in 1996, turning what was practically a one-man show into a full-fledged and fully financed watch *manufacture*.

After the merger, Swiss suppliers were acquired by the partners, furthering the quest for horological autonomy. Atokalpa SA in Alle (Canton of Jura) manufactures parts such as pinions, wheels, and micro components. Bruno Affolter SA in La Chaux-de-Fonds produces precious metal cases, dials, and other specialty parts. Les Artisans Boitiers (LAB) and Quadrance et Habillage (Q&H) in La Chaux-de-Fonds manufacture cases out of precious metals and dials as well. Elwin SA in Moutier specializes in turned parts. In 2003, the movement development and production department officially separated from the rest as Vaucher Manufacture, now an autonomous entity with a sterling reputation.

Montre Hermès has also held a stake in Vaucher Manufacture, securing the supply of custom watchmaking technology and leather straps for its ambitious model policy.

Around the time of the firm's 25th anniversary, in 2021, Michel Parmigiani gradually withdrew from day-to-day operations, leaving the executive spot to CEO Guido Terreni. The collections were streamlined; outliers, like the Bugatti, were terminated, and importantly, the Tonda PF collection, for instance, was redesigned and given new complications, including a time zone watch with a split-seconds mechanism for rapidly resetting the second local time. In 2025, Parmigiani Fleurier introduced the Toric Quantième Perpétuel (Perpetual Calendar) with a fascinatingly simple dial.

PARMIGIANI FLEURIER SA
Rue du Temple 11
CH-2114 Fleurier
Switzerland

TEL.:
+41-32-862-6630

E-MAIL:
info@parmigiani.ch

WEBSITE:
www.parmigiani.ch

FOUNDED:
1996

NUMBER OF EMPLOYEES:
425

ANNUAL PRODUCTION:
approx. 6,000 watches

U.S. DISTRIBUTOR:
Parmigiani Fleurier Distribution Americas LLC
2655 S. Le Jeune Road
Penthouse 1G
Coral Gables, FL 33134
305-260-7770; 305-269-7770
americas@parmigiani.com

MOST IMPORTANT COLLECTIONS/PRICE RANGE:
Chronor, Kalpa, Tonda, Toric / approx. $15,000 to $80,000 for core collections, $300,000+ for *haute horlogerie* watches; no limit for unique models

Toric Quantième Perpétuel Platinum Morning Blue

Reference number: PFH952-2010002-300181
Movement: hand-wound, Parmigiani Caliber PF733; ø 31.5 mm, height 5.15 mm; 29 jewels; 28,800 vph; finely finished movement; 60-hour power reserve
Functions: hours, minutes; perpetual calendar with date, weekday, month, leap year
Case: platinum, ø 40.6 mm, height 10.9 mm; sapphire crystal; transparent case back; water-resistant to 3 atm
Band: reptile skin, pin buckle
Remarks: white gold-dial
Price: $104,900; limited to 50 pieces

Toric Chronograph Rattrapante

Reference number: PFH951-2010001-300181
Movement: hand-wound, Parmigiani Caliber PF361; ø 30.6 mm, height 8.45 mm; 35 jewels; 36,000 vph; skeletonized bridges; 65-hour power reserve; COSC-certified chronometer
Functions: hours, minutes, subsidiary seconds; split-seconds chronograph
Case: rose gold, ø 42.4 mm, height 14.4 mm; sapphire crystal; transparent case back; water-resistant to 3 atm
Band: reptile skin, pin buckle
Price: $157,300; limited to 30 pieces

Toric Petite Seconde

Reference number: PFC940-2010001-300181
Movement: hand-wound, Parmigiani Caliber PF780; ø 28.4 mm, height 3.15 mm; 27 jewels; 28,800 vph; finely finished movement; 60-hour power reserve
Functions: hours, minutes, subsidiary seconds
Case: rose gold, ø 40.6 mm, height 8.8 mm; sapphire crystal; transparent case back; water-resistant to 3 atm
Band: reptile skin, pin buckle
Remarks: rose-gold dial
Price: $53,600
Variations: in platinum

Tonda PF Microrotor Platinum

Reference number: PFC914-2020002-200182
Movement: automatic, Parmigiani Caliber PF703;
ø 30 mm, height 3 mm; 29 jewels; 21,600 vph; platinum
micro-rotor; 48-hour power reserve
Functions: hours, minutes; date
Case: platinum, ø 40 mm, height 7.8 mm; sapphire
crystal; transparent case back; water-resistant to
10 atm
Band: platinum, folding clasp
Price: $96,900

Tonda PF Automatic 36mm

Reference number: PFC804-2120002-210182
Movement: automatic, Parmigiani Caliber PF777;
ø 30 mm, height 3.9 mm; 29 jewels; 28,800 vph;
skeletonized rotor in rose gold; 60-hour power reserve
Functions: hours, minutes
Case: rose gold, ø 36 mm, height 8.6 mm; bezel set with
diamonds; sapphire crystal; transparent case back;
water-resistant to 10 atm
Band: rose gold with diamonds, double folding clasp
Remarks: dial with diamond indices (baguette-cut)
Price: $91,200

Tonda PF Flying Tourbillon

Reference number: PFH921-2020002-200182
Movement: automatic, Parmigiani Caliber PF517;
ø 32 mm, height 3.4 mm; 29 jewels; 21,600 vph; flying
1-minute tourbillon; platinum micro-rotor, finely finished
movement; 48-hour power reserve
Functions: hours, minutes, subsidiary seconds (on the
tourbillon cage)
Case: platinum, ø 42 mm, height 8.6 mm; sapphire
crystal; transparent case back; water-resistant to
10 atm
Band: platinum, folding clasp in white gold
Price: $170,900; limited to 25 pieces

Tonda PF Sport Automatic

Reference number: PFC930-1020001-400182
Movement: automatic, Parmigiani Caliber PF770/4100;
ø 25.6 mm, height 3.9 mm; 29 jewels; 28,800 vph;
skeletonized rotor with rose-gold oscillating mass; finely
finished movement; 60-hour power reserve
Functions: hours, minutes, sweep seconds; date
Case: stainless steel, ø 41 mm, height 9.8 mm; sapphire
crystal; transparent case back; water-resistant to
10 atm
Band: rubber, folding clasp
Price: $22,700

Tonda PF Microrotor Platinum Stone Blue

Reference number: PFC914-2020022-200182
Movement: automatic, Parmigiani Caliber PF703;
ø 30 mm, height 3 mm; 29 jewels; 21,600 vph; platinum
micro-rotor; 48-hour power reserve
Functions: hours, minutes
Case: platinum, ø 40 mm, height 7.8 mm; sapphire
crystal; transparent case back; water-resistant to
10 atm
Band: platinum, folding clasp
Remarks: platinum dial
Price: $96,900; limited to 25 pieces

Tonda PF Microrotor No Date

Reference number: PFC914-1020021-100182
Movement: automatic, Parmigiani Caliber PF703;
ø 30 mm, height 3 mm; 29 jewels; 21,600 vph; platinum
micro-rotor; 48-hour power reserve
Functions: hours, minutes
Case: stainless steel, ø 40 mm, height 7.8 mm; sapphire
crystal; transparent case back; water-resistant to
10 atm
Band: stainless steel, folding clasp
Price: $27,100

Tonda PF Sport Chrono No Date Ultra-Cermet

Reference number: PFC931-1020021-400182
Movement: automatic, Parmigiani Caliber PF070/6710; ø 30.6 mm, height 6.95 mm; 42 jewels; 36,000 vph; skeletonized rotor with rose-gold oscillating mass; finely finished movement; 65-hour power reserve; COSC-certified chronometer
Functions: hours, minutes, subsidiary seconds; chronograph
Case: ceramic and metal composite material ("Ultra Cermet"), ø 42.4 mm, height 13.3 mm; sapphire crystal; transparent case back; screw-down crown; water-resistant to 10 atm
Band: rubber, pin buckle
Price: $45,500

Tonda PF Minute Rattrapante

Reference number: PFC904-1020001-100182
Movement: automatic, Parmigiani Caliber PF052; ø 32 mm, height 4.9 mm; 32 jewels; 21,600 vph; rose-gold microrotor, finely finished movement; 48-hour power reserve
Functions: hours, minutes; additional on-demand calibration of minute hand, reset pusher (split-seconds function)
Case: stainless steel, ø 40 mm, height 10.7 mm; sapphire crystal; transparent case back; rose-gold pushers; water-resistant to 6 atm
Band: stainless steel, folding clasp
Price: $33,900

Tonda PF GMT Rattrapante "Verzasca"

Reference number: PFC905-1020002-100182
Movement: automatic, Parmigiani Caliber PF061; ø 32 mm, height 4.9 mm; 31 jewels; 21,600 vph; rose-gold micro-rotor, finely finished movement; 48-hour power reserve
Functions: hours, minutes; additional adjustable hour hand with reset pusher (split-second function)
Case: stainless steel, ø 40 mm, height 10.7 mm; bezel in platinum; sapphire crystal; transparent case back; rose-gold pushers; water-resistant to 6 atm
Band: stainless steel, folding clasp
Remarks: hand-guilloché dial
Price: $32,700

Tonda PF Skeleton Slate Green

Reference number: PFC912-1020002-100182
Movement: automatic, Parmigiani Caliber PF777; ø 30 mm, height 3.9 mm; 29 jewels; 28,800 vph; completely skeletonized movement, skeletonized rotor in rose gold; 60-hour power reserve
Functions: hours, minutes
Case: stainless steel, ø 40 mm, height 8.5 mm; bezel in platinum; sapphire crystal; transparent case back; screw-down crown; water-resistant to 10 atm
Band: stainless steel, folding clasp
Price: $74,100

Tonda PF Hijri Perpetual Calendar

Reference number: PFK999-2020001-200182
Movement: automatic, Parmigiani Caliber PF009; ø 33.8 mm, height 5.7 mm; 32 jewels; 28,800 vph; platinum oscillating mass; finely finished movement; 48-hour power reserve
Functions: hours, minutes, sweep seconds; perpetual calendar with date, weekday, month, moon phase (follows the Islamic calendar)
Case: stainless steel, ø 42 mm, height 11.2 mm; sapphire crystal; transparent case back; water-resistant to 10 atm
Band: stainless steel, folding clasp
Price: $79,400

Tonda PF Chronograph No Date

Reference number: PFC917-1020001-100182
Movement: automatic, Parmigiani Caliber PF070/6710; ø 30.6 mm, height 6.95 mm; 42 jewels; 36,000 vph; skeletonized rotor with rose-gold oscillating mass; finely finished movement; 65-hour power reserve; COSC-certified chronometer
Functions: hours, minutes, subsidiary seconds; chronograph
Case: stainless steel, ø 40 mm, height 12.72 mm; bezel in platinum; sapphire crystal; transparent case back; screw-down crown; water-resistant to 10 atm
Band: stainless steel, folding clasp
Price: $35,900

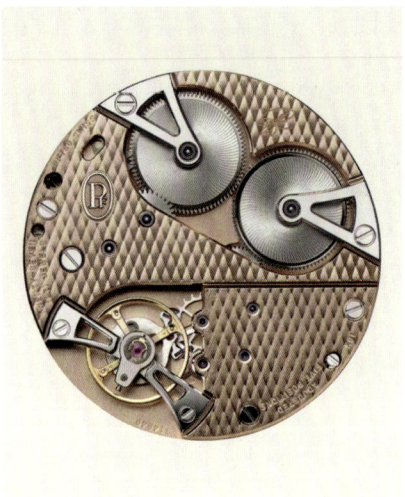

Caliber PF780

Hand-wound; single mainspring barrel, 60-hour power reserve

Functions: hours, minutes, subsidiary seconds
Diameter: 28.4 mm
Height: 3.15 mm
Jewels: 27
Frequency: 28,800 vph
Remarks: finely finished movement; 157 parts

Caliber PF361

Hand-wound; two column wheels; skeletonized movement architecture; rose-gold mainplate and bridges; single mainspring barrel, 65-hour power reserve

Functions: hours, minutes, subsidiary seconds; stop-seconds chronograph
Diameter: 30.6 mm
Height: 8.45 mm
Jewels: 35
Frequency: 36,000 vph
Remarks: 317 parts

Caliber PF070

Automatic; skeletonized bridges, skeletonized rotor in rose gold; single mainspring barrel, 65-hour power reserve; COSC-certified chronometer

Functions: hours, minutes, subsidiary seconds; chronograph; date
Diameter: 30.6 mm
Height: 6.95 mm
Jewels: 42
Frequency: 36,000 vph

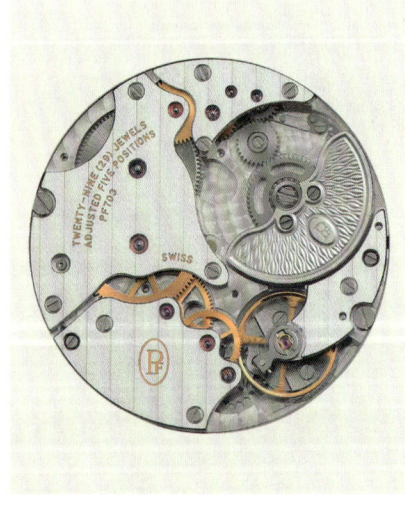

Caliber PF703

Automatic; micro-rotor in platinum; single mainspring barrel, 48-hour power reserve

Functions: hours, minutes; date
Diameter: 30 mm
Height: 3 mm
Jewels: 29
Frequency: 21,600 vph
Remarks: 176 parts

Caliber PF051

Automatic; micro-rotor in rose gold; single mainspring barrel, 48-hour power reserve

Functions: hours, minutes; additional 12-hour display (second time zone) with pusher reset (rattrapante function)
Diameter: 30 mm
Height: 4.9 mm
Jewels: 31
Frequency: 21,600 vph
Remarks: 207 parts

Caliber PF517

Automatic; flying 1-minute tourbillon, micro-rotor in platinum; single mainspring barrel, 48-hour power reserve

Functions: hours, minutes, subsidiary seconds (on the tourbillon cage)
Diameter: 32 mm
Height: 3.4 mm
Jewels: 29
Frequency: 21,600 vph
Remarks: 205 parts

PATEK PHILIPPE

Patek Philippe originated in 1839 with two Polish émigrés to Switzerland, Count Norbert Antoine de Patek and Franciszek Czapek. In 1845, following the natural end of their contract, Patek sought another partner in the master watchmaker Jean Adrien Philippe, who had developed a keyless winding and time-setting mechanism. Ever since, Patek Philippe has had a reputation for creating high-quality mechanical watches, some with extremely sophisticated complications.

In 1932, Charles-Henri Stern took over the *manufacture*. His son Henri and grandson Philippe continued the tradition of solid leadership, carefully navigating through the notorious quartz crisis without ever compromising quality. The next in line, Thierry, heads the enterprise these days.

Producing an impressive 70,000-plus watches yearly demands ultramodern facilities. These were completed in 2019 in Plan-les-Ouates in Geneva, where various manufacturing activities can be performed under a single roof with an optimized workflow. The site is a complement to another industrial hub between La Chaux-de-Fonds and Le Locle, where case components are manufactured, cases are polished, and gem setting is done.

While Patek Philippe's main headquarters remains in Geneva, the *manufacture* no longer really has a need for that city's famed quality seal: all of its mechanical watches now feature the "Patek Philippe Seal," the criteria for which far exceed the requirements of the Poinçon de Genève and include specifications for the entire watch, not just the movement.

For those somewhat disappointed at the discontinuation of the famed Nautilus, the year 2024 brought a surprise—or shock, depending on your expectations. Patek announced a new watch: the Cubitus, a square model, fairly thin, with rounded corners and a vague resemblance to the old Nautilus. The move into the casual-chic world created a lot of buzz online, of course. The first models are equipped with the self-winding Caliber 26-330 S C, which currently powers more than 30 contemporary models from Patek Philippe. The Cubitus 5822P-001 features a large date (a Patek first), weekday display, and moon-phase indication, housed in a platinum case and worn on a casual composite-material strap with a textile pattern. The self-winding Caliber 240 PS CI J LU was developed especially for this model. It demanded six patents.

PATEK PHILIPPE SA
Chemin du pont-du-centenaire 141
CH-1228 Plan-les-Ouates
Switzerland

TEL.:
+41-22-884-20-20

WEBSITE:
www.patek.com

FOUNDED:
1839

NUMBER OF EMPLOYEES:
approx. 2,000 (estimated)

ANNUAL PRODUCTION:
approx. 72,000 watches worldwide

U.S. DISTRIBUTOR:
Patek Philippe USA
45 Rockefeller Center, Suite 401
New York, NY 10111
212-218-1240

MOST IMPORTANT COLLECTIONS:
Aquanaut, Calatrava, Nautilus, Cubitus, complicated watches

Split-Seconds Chronograph

Reference number: 5370R-001
Movement: hand-wound, Patek Philippe Caliber 29-535 PS; ø 29.6 mm, height 7.1 mm; 34 jewels; 28,800 vph; Breguet hairspring; 65-hour power reserve
Functions: hours, minutes, subsidiary seconds; split-seconds chronograph
Case: rose gold, ø 41 mm, height 13.56 mm; sapphire crystal; transparent case back; water-resistant to 3 atm
Band: reptile skin, folding clasp
Remarks: comes with additional rose-gold case back
Price: $348,537

Perpetual Calendar with Retrograde Date

Reference number: 6159G-001
Movement: automatic, Patek Philippe Caliber 26-330 S QR; ø 28 mm, height 5.36 mm; 29 jewels; 28,800 vph; gold rotor; 35-hour power reserve
Functions: hours, minutes, sweep seconds; perpetual calendar with date (retrograde), weekday, month, moon phase, leap year
Case: white gold, ø 39.5 mm, height 11.49 mm; sapphire crystal; transparent case back; water-resistant to 3 atm
Band: textile, triple folding clasp
Price: $142,260

Perpetual Calendar

Reference number: 5320G-011
Movement: automatic, Patek Philippe Caliber 324 S Q; ø 32 mm, height 4.97 mm; 29 jewels; 28,800 vph; silicon Spiromax hairspring; gold rotor; 35-hour power reserve
Functions: hours, minutes, sweep seconds; day/night indication; perpetual calendar with date, weekday, month, moon phase, leap year
Case: white gold, ø 40 mm, height 11.13 mm; sapphire crystal; transparent case back; water-resistant to 3 atm
Band: reptile skin, folding clasp
Remarks: comes with additional white-gold caseback
Price: $125,047

Calatrava 8 Days

Reference number: 5328G-001
Movement: hand-wound, Patek Philippe Caliber 31-505 8J PS IRM CI J; ø 32 mm, height 5.05 mm; 28 jewels; 28,800 vph; silicon Pulsomax-escapement; 192-hour power reserve
Functions: hours, minutes, subsidiary seconds; power reserve indicator; date and weekday
Case: white gold, ø 41 mm, height 10.52 mm; sapphire crystal; transparent case back; water-resistant to 3 atm
Band: leather, triple folding clasp
Remarks: comes with additional taupe leather strap
Price: $XXXXX

Calatrava Pilot Travel Time

Reference number: 5524G-010
Movement: automatic, Patek Philippe Caliber 26-330 S C FUS; ø 31 mm, height 4.82 mm; 29 jewels; 28,800 vph; silicon Spiromax hairspring, gold rotor; 35-hour power reserve
Functions: hours, minutes, sweep seconds; additional 12-hour display (crown-adjusted second time zone); date
Case: white gold, ø 42 mm, height 10.78 mm; sapphire crystal; transparent case back; water-resistant to 3 atm
Band: textile, pin buckle
Price: $73,549

Annual Calendar Moon Phase

Reference number: 4946R-001
Movement: automatic, Patek Philippe Caliber 26-330 S QA LU; ø 30 mm, height 5.32 mm; 34 jewels; 28,800 vph; silicon Spiromax hairspring, gold rotor; 35-hour power reserve
Functions: hours, minutes, sweep seconds; annual calendar with date, weekday, month, moon phase Case: rose gold, ø 38 mm, height 11 mm; sapphire crystal; transparent case back; water-resistant to 3 atm
Band: leather, pin buckle
Price: $66,863

Annual Calendar Moon Phase

Reference number: 5205R-011
Movement: automatic, Patek Philippe Caliber 324 S QA LU 24H; ø 32.6 mm, height 5.78 mm; 34 jewels; 28,800 vph; 35-hour power reserve
Functions: hours, minutes, sweep seconds; additional 24-hour display; annual calendar with date, weekday, month, moon phase
Case: rose gold, ø 40 mm, height 11.36 mm; sapphire crystal; transparent case back; water-resistant to 3 atm
Band: reptile skin, pin buckle
Price: $66,863

World Time Watch with Flyback Chronograph

Reference number: 5935A-001
Movement: automatic, Patek Philippe Caliber CH 28-520 HU; ø 34,5 mm, height 7.97 mm; 38 jewels; 28,800 vph; silicon Spiromax hairspring; gold micro-rotor; 50-hour power reserve
Functions: hours, minutes; world time display (second time zone); flyback chronograph
Case: stainless steel, ø 41 mm, height 12.75 mm; pusher-activated ring with reference cities; sapphire crystal; transparent case back; water-resistant to 3 atm
Band: leather, folding clasp
Remarks: comes with additional leather strap in other colors
Price: $78,386

Calatrava Travel Time

Reference number: 5224R-001
Movement: automatic, Patek Philippe Caliber 31-260 PS FUS 24H; ø 31.74 mm, height 3.7 mm; 44 jewels; 28,800 vph; silicon Spiromax hairspring; off-center platinum micro-rotor; 48-hour power reserve
Functions: hours (24), minutes, subsidiary seconds; additional 24-hour display (crown-adjusted second time zone)
Case: rose gold, ø 42 mm, height 9.85 mm; sapphire crystal; transparent case back; water-resistant to 3 atm
Band: leather, pin buckle
Price: $60,680

The World's Greatest Living Explorer
Designed Our Explorer's Watch

Prototype of the
Kobold Polar Surveyor Chronograph
Soarway case (18 components)
Original Design by Sir Ranulph Fiennes,
Gerd-R. Lang and Michael Kobold.
Tested by Sir Ranulph in Antarctica.

www.koboldwatch.com

Flyback-Chronograph with Annual Calendar

Reference number: 5905R-010
Movement: automatic, Patek Philippe Caliber CH 28-520 QA 24H; ø 33 mm, height 7.68 mm; 37 jewels; 28,800 vph; silicon Spiromax hairspring; gold micro-rotor; 45-hour power reserve
Functions: hours, minutes; flyback chronograph; annual calendar with date, weekday, month
Case: rose gold, ø 42 mm, height 14.03 mm; sapphire crystal; transparent case back; water-resistant to 3 atm
Band: reptile skin, pin buckle
Price: $79,260

Calatrava

Reference number: 6196P-001
Movement: hand-wound, Patek Philippe Caliber 30-255 PS; ø 31 mm, height 2.55 mm; 27 jewels; 28,800 vph; silicon Spiromax hairspring; 65-hour power reserve
Functions: hours, minutes, subsidiary seconds
Case: platinum, ø 38 mm, height 9.33 mm; sapphire crystal; transparent case back; water-resistant to 3 atm
Band: reptile skin, pin buckle
Price: $56,904

Cubitus

Reference number: 7128/1G-001
Movement: automatic, Patek Philippe Caliber 26-330 S C; ø 27 mm, height 3.3 mm; 30 jewels; 28,800 vph; silicon Spiromax hairspring; gold rotor; 35-hour power reserve
Functions: hours, minutes, sweep seconds; date
Case: white gold, 40 mm x 40 mm, height 8.5 mm; sapphire crystal; transparent case back; screw-down crown; water-resistant to 3 atm
Band: white gold, folding clasp
Price: $92,469

Cubitus

Reference number: 5822P-001
Movement: automatic, Patek Philippe Caliber 240 PS CI J LU; ø 31 mm, height 4.76 mm; 52 jewels; 21,600 vph; silicon Spiromax hairspring; gold micro-rotor; 38-hour power reserve
Functions: hours, minutes, subsidiary seconds; large date, weekday, moon phase (each jumping)
Case: platinum, 45 mm x 45 mm, height 9.6 mm; sapphire crystal; transparent case back; screw-down crown
Band: textile, folding clasp in platinum
Price: $106,695

Cubitus

Reference number: 5821/1AR-001
Movement: automatic, Patek Philippe Caliber 26-330 S C; ø 27 mm, height 3.3 mm; 30 jewels; 28,800 vph; silicon Spiromax hairspring; gold rotor; 35-hour power reserve
Functions: hours, minutes, sweep seconds; date
Case: stainless steel, 45 mm x 45 mm, height 8.3 mm; rose-gold bezel and case middle; sapphire crystal; transparent case back; screw-down crown, in rose gold; water-resistant to 3 atm
Band: stainless steel with rose-gold elements, folding clasp
Price: $75,114

Nautilus Flyback Chronograph

Reference number: 5980/60G-001
Movement: automatic, Patek Philippe Caliber CH 28-520 C/522; ø 30 mm, height 6.63 mm; 35 jewels; 28,800 vph; silicon Spiromax hairspring; gold rotor 45-hour power reserve
Functions: hours, minutes, subsidiary seconds; flyback chronograph; date
Case: white gold, ø 40.5 mm, height 12.2 mm; sapphire crystal; transparent case back; screw-down crown; water-resistant to 3 atm
Band: leather, folding clasp
Price: $98,160

Twenty-4 Perpetual Calendar

Reference number: 7340/1R-010
Movement: automatic, Patek Philippe Caliber
240 Q; ø 27.5 mm, height 3.88 mm; 21,600 vph; silicon
Spiromax hairspring; gold micro-rotor; 38-hour power
reserve
Functions: hours, minutes; additional 24 hour display;
perpetual calendar with date, weekday, month, moon
phase, leap year
Case: rose gold, ø 36 mm, height 9.95 mm; sapphire
crystal; transparent case back; water-resistant to 3 atm
Band: rose gold, folding clasp
Price: $145,106

Aquanaut Travel Time

Reference number: 5164G-001
Movement: automatic, Patek Philippe Caliber 26-330 C
FUS; ø 31 mm, height 4.82 mm; 29 jewels; 28,800 vph;
silicon Spiromax hairspring; gold rotor; 35-hour power
reserve
Functions: hours, minutes, sweep seconds; additional
12-hour display (second time zone), day/night indicator;
date
Case: white gold, ø 40.8 mm, height 10.2 mm; sapphire
crystal; transparent case back; screw-down crown;
water-resistant to 3 atm
Band: composite material, folding clasp
Price: $78,386

Aquanaut Travel Time

Reference number: 5269R-001
Movement: quartz
Functions: hours, minutes, sweep seconds; additional
12 hour display (second time zone), day/night indicator
Case: rose gold, ø 38.8 mm, height 8.77 mm; sapphire
crystal; screw-down crown; water-resistant to 3 atm
Band: composite material, folding clasp
Price: $43,959

Caliber 324 S QA LU

Automatic; gold rotor; single spring barrel, 45-hour
power reserve
Functions: hours, minutes, sweep seconds; annual
calendar with date, weekday, month, moon phase
Diameter: 32 mm
Height: 5.32 mm
Jewels: 34
Balance: Gyromax
Frequency: 28,800 vph
Hairspring: silicon Spiromax
Remarks: 319 parts

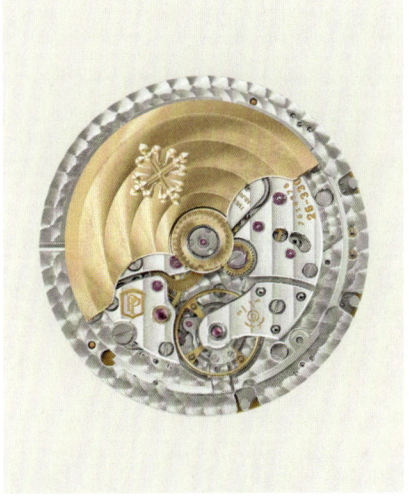

Caliber 26-330 S C FUS

Automatic; Gold rotor; single spring barrel, 35-hour
power reserve
Functions: hours, minutes, sweep seconds; additional
12-hour display (second time zone), day/night indicator;
date
Diameter: 31 mm
Height: 4.82 mm
Jewels: 29
Balance: Gyromax
Frequency: 28,800 vph
Hairspring: silicon Spiromax
Remarks: 290 parts

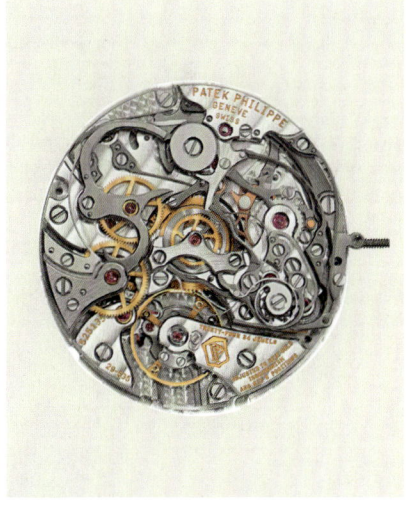

Caliber CH 29-535 PS

Hand-wound; column-wheel control of chronograph
functions, exact jumping 30-minute counter; single
spring barrel, 65-hour power reserve
Functions: hours, minutes, subsidiary seconds; split-
seconds chronograph
Diameter: 29.6 mm
Height: 7.1 mm
Jewels: 34
Balance: Gyromax, 4 arms with 4 regulating weights
Frequency: 28,800 vph
Hairspring: Breguet
Shock protection: Incabloc
Remarks: 312 parts

Caliber CH 28-520 QA 24H

Automatic; gold rotor; single spring barrel, 45-hour power reserve
Functions: hours, minutes; flyback chronograph; annual calendar with date, weekday, month Diameter: 33 mm
Height: 7.68 mm
Jewels: 37
Balance: Gyromax
Frequency: 28,800 vph
Hairspring: silicon Spiromax
Remarks: 402 parts

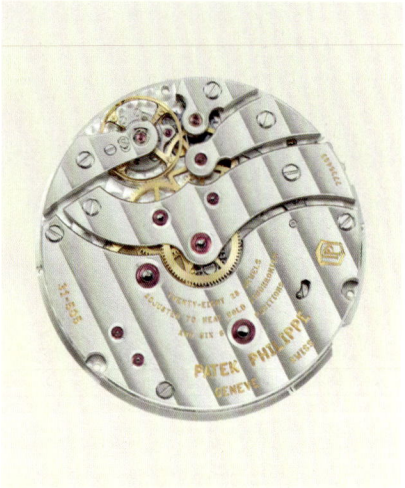

Caliber 31-505 8J PS IRM CI J

Hand-wound; double spring barrel, 192-hour power reserve
Functions: hours, minutes, subsidiary seconds; power reserve indicator; date and weekday (instant change)
Diameter: 32 mm
Height: 5.05 mm
Jewels: 28
Balance: Pulsomax
Frequency: 28,800 vph
Hairspring: silicon Spiromax
Remarks: 256 parts

Caliber 240 PS Ci J LU

Automatic; gold micro-rotor; single spring barrel, 48-hour power reserve
Functions: hours, minutes, subsidiary seconds; large date, moon phase
Diameter: 31 mm
Height: 4.76 mm
Jewels: 52
Balance: Gyromax
Frequency: 21,600 vph
Hairspring: silicon Spiromax
Remarks: 353 parts

Caliber 240 Q

Automatic; gold micro-rotor; single spring barrel, 48-hour power reserve
Functions: hours, minutes; additional 24-hour display (second time zone); perpetual calendar with date, weekday, month, moon phase, leap year
Diameter: 30 mm
Height: 3.75 mm
Jewels: 27
Balance: Gyromax, with 8 "masselotte" regulating weights
Frequency: 21,600 vph
Hairspring: flat hairspring
Shock protection: Kif

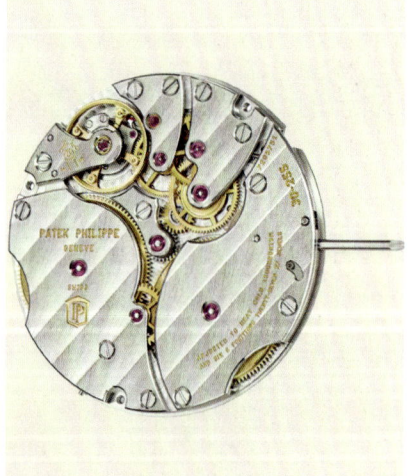

Caliber 30-255 PS

Hand-wound; single spring barrel, 65-hour power reserve
Functions: hours, minutes, subsidiary seconds
Diameter: 31 mm
Height: 2.55 mm
Jewels: 27
Balance: Gyromax
Frequency: 28,800 vph
Hairspring: silicon Spiromax with escapement

Caliber 324 S QA LU 24H-303

Automatic; gold rotor; single spring barrel, 45-hour power reserve
Functions: hours, minutes, sweep seconds; additional 24-hour display (second time zone); annual calendar with date, weekday, month, moon phase
Diameter: 32.6 mm
Height: 5.78 mm
Jewels: 34
Balance: Gyromax
Frequency: 28,800 vph
Hairspring: silicon Spiromax
Remarks: 347 parts

PAUL GERBER

In a world that often values hype more than the real thing, people like watchmaker Paul Gerber tend to get overlooked. And it's a shame because this man, who works out of his home in Zurich, has encyclopedic knowledge and experience of the industry. He has already developed a vast array of mechanisms and complications, including calendar movements, alarms, and tourbillons, for many brands. Gerber is the one who designed the complicated calendar mechanism for the otherwise minimalist MIH watch conceived by Ludwig Oechslin, curator of the International Museum of Horology (MIH) in La Chaux-de-Fonds and himself a watchmaker. To avoid cluttering a dial for a special customer, he recently devised a battery-run moon phase that fits in the watch strap. His work has twice appeared in *Guinness World Records.*

When his daily work for others lets up, Gerber gets around to building watches bearing his own name with such clever and rare complications as a retrograde second hand in an elegant thin case and a synchronously, unidirectional rotor system with miniature oscillating weights for his self-winding Retro Twin model. Gerber's works are usually limited editions.

After designing a tonneau-shaped manually wound wristwatch with a three-dimensional moon phase display, Gerber created a simple three-hand watch with an automatic movement conceived and produced completely in-house. It features a 100-hour power reserve and is wound by three synchronically turning gold rotors. Gerber also offers the triple rotor and large date features in a watch with an ETA movement and lightweight titanium case as a classic pilot watch design or in a version with a more modern dial (the Synchron model). The Model 41 has an optional complication that switches the second hand from sweep to dead-beat motion by way of a pusher at 2 o'clock.

Gerber is allegedly retired. But a watchmaker never really retires. Besides producing outstanding pieces, he also occasionally gives three-day workshops (see page 44) for people wanting to get a real feel for the work.

PAUL GERBER
Uhren-Konstruktionen
Bockhornstrasse 69
CH-8047 Zürich
Switzerland

TEL.:
+41-44-401-4569

E-MAIL:
info@gerber-uhren.ch

WEBSITE:
www.gerber-uhren.ch

FOUNDED:
1976

ANNUAL PRODUCTION:
up to 10 watches

U.S. DISTRIBUTOR:
Intro Swiss—Michel Schmutz
Michel Schmutz
6271 Corinth Rd.
Longmont, CO 80503
303-652-1520
introswiss@gmail.com

MOST IMPORTANT COLLECTIONS/PRICE RANGE:
mechanical watches / from approx. $6,750 to $27,000

Retrograd

Reference number: 152
Movement: manually wound, Gerber Caliber 15 (base ETA 7001); ø 28 mm, 2.9 mm; 21 jewels; twin 21,600 vph; 38-hour power reserve
Functions: hours, minutes, subsidiary seconds (retrograde)
Case: yellow gold, ø 36 mm, height 8.5 mm sapphire crystal; transparent case back; water-resistant to 3 atm
Band: reptile skin, buckle
Remarks: guilloché on the dial
Price: $13,550
Variations: rose gold $13,550

Modell 42

Reference number: 420 DaN pilot
Movement: automatic, Gerber Caliber 42 (base ETA 2824); ø 36 mm, height 6.1 mm; 25 jewels; 28,800 vph; automatic wound with 3 synchronously rotating gold rotors; 38-hour power reserve
Functions: hours, minutes, sweep seconds; large quick set date
Case: titanium, ø 42 mm, height 12 mm; sapphire crystal; transparent case back; screw-in crown; water-resistant to 10 atm
Band: calfskin, buckle
Price: $7,500
Variations: 420 Triple Rotor-1 ($7,050); 420 Triple Rotor-2 ($7,050)

Modell 33 with 3D Moon Phase

Reference number: 42
Movement: automatic, Gerber Caliber 42 (base ETA 2824); ø 36 mm, height 6.1 mm; 20 jewels; 28,800 vph; patented Gerber escapement; côtes de Genève on bridge; 36-hour power reserve
Functions: hours, minutes, subsidiary seconds; moon phase with 3D moon, correct for 128 years
Case: white gold, 40 mm x 34 mm, height 11 mm; sapphire crystal; transparent case back; screw-in crown; water-resistant to 10 atm
Band: calfskin, pin buckle
Remarks: 3D 6-mm moon, half white-gold with 54 brilliant-cut diamonds, and half lapis-lazuli; heat-blued screws
Price: $51,100

PEQUIGNET

The Jura mountains, which saddle Switzerland and France, are not only home to inventive and dogged craftspeople, notably watchmakers, on the Swiss side. In 1973, in Morteau, a small town close to the border, one Emile Pequignet founded a watch and jewelry company producing contemporary pieces that caught the spirit of the age and enjoyed fair success. In 2004, Pequignet himself retired and sold the brand to one Didier Leibundgut. This whole industry was bursting with energy, creating bigger and crazier watches. Pequignet steered a more conservative course and maintained its classic look. But it did develop its own *manufacture* movement, investing millions into the Calibre Royal.

The elaborate automatic movement is subject to eight patents. It can drive various functions, like a full calendar with moon phase or a power reserve indicator to tell the wearer how many of the 100 hours delivered by the large spring barrel have been used up. Since it does not need any modules, the movement is quite thin and can be configured for other functions quite easily. These functions are available in the Royale Sapphire collection.

The Calibre Royal reinvigorated the company, but it also cost inordinate amounts of money. The decade following was spent under the threat of liquidation. Finally, in December 2021, it was announced that a family fund had purchased the brand and the majority shareholder, Hugues Souparis, was now the new CEO. Morteau (pop. around 6,900) breathed a sigh of relief.

Strategic decisions were made smartly, like adding a tourbillon to their portfolio in 2024. Development and manufacture of affordable, high-end movements in the Jura mountains means Pequignet can supply watch brands on both sides of the French-Swiss border with excellent calibers.

In 2025, the Royale Paris line was expanded by a number of watches all equipped with the Calibre Royal. Many feature interchangeable straps for the first time. The highlight is the new Royale Paris 39.5 mm with day, date, and moon display. Its moon phase complication displays both the northern and southern hemispheres.

MONTRES PÉQUIGNET
1, rue du Bief
F-25503 Morteau
France

TEL:
+33 381 67 30 66

E-MAIL:
contact@pequignet.com

WEBSITE:
www.pequignet.com

FOUNDED:
1973

NUMBER OF EMPLOYEES:
50

U.S. DISTRIBUTOR
Grenon's of Newport
210 Bellevue Avenue
Newport, RI 02840
401-846-0598

MOST IMPORTANT COLLECTIONS / PRICE RANGE:
Men's and women's watches from $1,700 to $12,000

Royale Paris
Reference number: 9100173
Movement: hand-wound, Calibre Royal; ø 30 mm; 39 jewels; 21,600 vph; finely finished with beveled edges and perlage; 96-hour power reserve
Functions: hours, minutes, subsidiary seconds; power-reserve indicator
Case: stainless steel, ø 39.5 mm, height 11.5 mm; sapphire crystal; transparent case back; water-resistant to 5 atm
Band: textile, folding clasp
Price: $7,300

Concorde Titanium
Reference number: 9045336
Movement: automatic, Calibre Initial; ø 25.6 mm, height 4.2 mm; 21 jewels; 28,800 vph; skeletonized winding rotor; 65-hour power reserve
Functions: hours, minutes, sweep seconds
Case: titanium, ø 36 mm, height 9.25 mm; sapphire crystal; transparent case back; water-resistant to 10 atm
Band: titanium, folding clasp
Price: $6,600

Royale Paris Moon
Reference number: 9100633
Movement: hand-wound, Calibre Royal; ø 30 mm; 39 jewels; 21,600 vph; finely finished with beveled edges and perlage; 96-hour power reserve
Functions: hours, minutes, subsidiary seconds; power-reserve indicator; large date, weekday, moon phase
Case: stainless steel, ø 39.5 mm, height 11.5 mm; sapphire crystal; transparent case back; water-resistant to 5 atm
Band: reptile skin, folding clasp
Price: $11,000

PERRELET

The story of Perrelet will sound familiar to anyone versed in the history of Swiss watchmaking. Abraham-Louis Perrelet (1729–1826), the son of a middle-class farmer from Le Locle, developed an early fascination with horology. He was the first watchmaker in his region to master cylinder and duplex escapements, and legend has it that one of his repeaters could be heard echoing through the mountain valleys.

Many who would later shape Swiss watchmaking trained in Perrelet's workshop, and some historians have even suggested that Abraham-Louis Breguet was among his apprentices. A tireless innovator, Perrelet is credited with inventing the "perpetual" watch around 1770, a self-winding pocket watch that powered its mechanism using the wearer's motion.

When the modern brand reappeared in 1995, it made headlines with its Double Rotor and the P-181 caliber, a movement that reflected the founder's inventive spirit, with a rotor on the back and front of the dial. The Turbine collections soon followed, featuring a jet-engine-inspired rotor spinning above the dial, a playful and kinetic interpretation of traditional automatic winding that opened endless creative possibilities. Worth noting, however, is the fact that this rotor is strictly decorative, since using it to wind up the watch would slow it down.

Perrelet's audacity caught the attention of the Festina Group, which acquired the brand in 2004. After a period of quiet, Perrelet returned to the forefront with upgraded automatic movements refined to meet COSC-level precision. The P-411 caliber powers the LAB collection, revealing its rotor beneath a transparent dial, while the P-331-MH caliber drives the distinctive Turbine models. Their design versatility allows the brand to explore themes ranging from a skull, or a royal flush, to the intricate beauty of Arabic calligraphy, developed in 2025 in collaboration with Emirati artist Diaa Allam.

In 2025, too, Perrelet revived its emblematic P-181 movement for two assertive women's collections: the Eleonore, a tribute to French sophistication, and the Cleopatra, celebrating the great Egyptian queen.

PERRELET SA
Rue Bubenberg 7
CH-2502 Biel/Bienne
Switzerland

TEL.:
+41-32-346-2626

FAX:
+41-32-346-2627

E-MAIL:
perrelet@perrelet.com

WEBSITE:
www.perrelet.com

FOUNDED:
brand founded in 1777, acquired by Festina Group in 2004

U.S. DISTRIBUTOR:
Perrelet USA
2937 SW 27th Avenue Suite 102
Miami FL 33133
305-588-3628
info@perreletusa.com

MOST IMPORTANT COLLECTIONS:
LAB, Turbine, Joséphone and Cleopatra, Diamond Flower, Weekend

Joséphine

Reference number: A2072/D
Movement: automatic, Perrelet P-181-H caliber; ø 25.6 mm, height 4.9 mm; 26 jewels; 28,800 vph; double-rotor technology; finely finished mainplate and bridges; 42-hour power reserve
Functions: hours, minutes, sweep seconds
Case: stainless steel with black PVD, ø 36.5 mm, height 12.9 mm; sapphire crystal; transparent case back; water-resistant to 5 atm
Band: titanium, folding clasp
Remarks: double rotor, one under and one over the dial; sunray guilloché on dial; diamond hour-marker at 12 o'clock
Price: $7,460
Variations: mother-of-pearl, blue, pink, black guilloché dial; with diamond bezel ($9,500)

Perrelet x Diaa Allam

Reference number: A4067/S8
Movement: automatic, Perrelet Caliber P-331-MH (based on Soprod); ø 26.2 mm, height 3.6 mm; 25 jewels; 28,800 vph; fine finishing on bridges and mainplate, with snailing and perlage; COSC-certified chronometer and Chronofiable certification by Dubois Laboratory in La Chaux-de-Fonds; 42-hour power reserve
Functions: hours, minutes, sweep seconds
Case: titanium with black DLC, ø 41 mm, height 13.9 mm; bezel in stainless steel with black PVD; sapphire crystal; transparent case back; water-resistant to 10 atm
Band: rubber, folding clasp
Remarks: 12-blade aluminum turbine on dial; Arabic numerals inscription on back: "The pulses of the heart do softly chime, life is but seconds—fleeting steps in time"
Price: $5,450

Turbine Poker Royal Flush

Reference number: A4065/S3
Movement: automatic, Perrelet Caliber P-331-MH (based on Soprod); ø 26.2 mm, height 3.6 mm; 25 jewels; 28,800 vph; fine finishing on bridges and mainplate, with snailing and perlage; COSC-certified chronometer and Chronofiable certification by Dubois Laboratory in La Chaux-de-Fonds; 42-hour power reserve
Functions: hours, minutes, sweep seconds
Case: stainless steel with black DLC, ø 45.5 mm, height 14.42 mm; bezel in stainless steel with black PVD; sapphire crystal; transparent case back; water-resistant to 10 atm
Band: leather, folding clasp
Remarks: 12-blade turbine of anodized aluminum on the dial (no winding function), spins with wearer's movements revealing a royal flush motif
Price: $5,995

PIAGET

Piaget began crafting watch movements in the secluded Jura village of La Côte-aux-Fées in 1874. For decades, these movements were supplied to other watch brands, while the Piaget name itself remained curiously in the background. It wasn't until the 1940s that the family began producing complete timepieces under their own name. Even today, though the commercial headquarters have long since moved to Geneva, Piaget still manufactures its movements at its main facility high in the Jura mountains.

This foundational expertise in movement-making paved the way for a defining specialty. In the late 1950s, Piaget began investing in the design and manufacturing of ultrathin movements, establishing the understated elegance that would become the company's hallmark. This pursuit culminated in 1957 with the launch of the first ultrathin men's watch, the Altiplano, powered by the manual caliber 9P at just two millimeters high. Shortly thereafter, Piaget introduced the 12P, an automatic caliber measuring a mere 2.3 millimeters.

For over sixty years, the Altiplano collection has been a faithful testament to this legacy. The movements have continuously evolved, as seen in the caliber 900P, which measures just 3.65 millimeters and features an inverted construction to facilitate repairs.

Piaget's quest for thinness continues into the third millennium. The Altiplano Ultimate Concept, released in 2018 after four years of research and development, briefly held the world record as the thinnest mechanical watch at two millimeters total height. More recently, the brand has shifted some focus to its Polo collection. New developments include delicate skeleton versions and an ultra-thin perpetual calendar with a movement just four millimeters thick. A particular highlight, released in honor of the brand's 150th anniversary, was a faithful reproduction of the original 1979 Polo model, as slim and sporty as ever, and crafted entirely from solid gold.

PIAGET SA
CH-1228 Plan-les-Ouates
Switzerland

TEL.:
+41-32-867-21-21

E-MAIL:
info@piaget.com

WEBSITE:
www.piaget.com

FOUNDED:
1874

NUMBER OF EMPLOYEES:
900

ANNUAL PRODUCTION:
about 15,000 watches

U.S. DISTRIBUTOR:
Piaget North America
645 5th Avenue, 6th Floor
New York, NY 10022
www.piaget.com

MOST IMPORTANT COLLECTIONS:
Altiplano, Polo S, Limelight, Possession

Polo Date

Reference number: G0A50016
Movement: automatic, Piaget Caliber 1110P; ø 25.58 mm, height 4 mm; 25 jewels; 28,800 vph; perlage on mainplate, blued screws, finely finished with côtes de Genève; 50-hour power reserve
Functions: hours, minutes, sweep seconds; date
Case: stainless steel, ø 42.4 mm, height 9.4 mm; sapphire crystal; transparent case back; water-resistant to 10 atm
Band: stainless steel, triple folding clasp
Price: $15,200
Variations: with blue dial; with rubber strap ($13,500); in rose gold ($34,300)

Polo Date

Reference number: G0A50017
Movement: automatic, Piaget Caliber 1110P; ø 25.58 mm, height 4 mm; 25 jewels; 28,800 vph; perlage on mainplate, blued screws, finely finished with côtes de Genève; 50-hour power reserve
Functions: hours, minutes, sweep seconds; date
Case: rose gold, ø 42.4 mm, height 9.4 mm; sapphire crystal; transparent case back; water-resistant to 10 atm
Band: rubber, triple folding clasp
Price: $34,300
Variations: in stainless steel with stainless steel bracelet ($15,200)

Polo Date

Reference number: G0A50022
Movement: automatic, Piaget Caliber 500P1; ø 20.5 mm, height 3.4 mm; 26 jewels; 21,600 vph; finely finished movement; 40-hour power reserve
Functions: hours, minutes, sweep seconds; date
Case: stainless steel, ø 36 mm, height 8.8 mm; bezel set with 60 diamonds; sapphire crystal; transparent case back; water-resistant to 5 atm
Band: stainless steel, folding clasp
Remarks: hour markers set with 36 diamonds
Price: $24,200
Variations: various cases, bands and dials

Altiplano Ultimate Automatic

Reference number: G0A50126
Movement: automatic, Piaget Caliber 910P; ø 41 mm, height 4.3 mm (including case and sapphire crystal); 30 jewels; 21,600 vph; inverted movement construction as a single unit with case, hubless peripheral rotor; 48-hour power reserve
Functions: hours and minutes (off-center)
Case: rose gold, ø 41 mm, height 4.3 mm; sapphire crystal
Band: reptile skin, pin buckle
Price: $29,500
Variations: various cases, bands and dials

Polo Skeleton

Reference number: G0A45004
Movement: automatic, Piaget Caliber 1200S1; ø 29.9 mm, height 2.4 mm; 25 jewels; 21,600 vph; fully skeletonized movement, mainplate and bridges with blue PVD; 44-hour power reserve
Functions: hours, minutes
Case: stainless steel, ø 42 mm, height 6.5 mm; sapphire crystal; transparent case back
Band: stainless steel, folding clasp
Price: $32,200
Variations: with green PVD

Polo Flying Tourbillon Moon Phase

Reference number: G0A49080
Movement: hand-wound, Piaget Caliber 642P; ø 28.8 mm, height 4 mm; 23 jewels; 21,600 vph; flying 1-minute tourbillon, finely finished movement; 37-hour power reserve
Functions: hours, minutes, small seconds (on the tourbillon cage); moon phase
Case: titanium, ø 44 mm, height 12.3 mm; sapphire crystal; transparent case back; water-resistant to 10 atm
Band: rubber, triple folding clasp
Remarks: comes with additional reptile skin strap
Price: $113,000

Polo 79

Reference number: G0A50150
Movement: automatic, Piaget Caliber 1200P1; ø 29.9 mm, height 2.35 mm; 25 jewels; 21,600 vph; gold micro-rotor; finely finished movement; 44-hour power reserve
Functions: hours, minutes
Case: white gold, ø 38 mm, height 7.45 mm; sapphire crystal; transparent case back; water-resistant to 5 atm
Band: white gold, triple folding clasp
Price: $82,500
Variations: in yellow gold ($75,000)

Andy Warhol

Reference number: G0A50240
Movement: automatic, Piaget Caliber 501P1; ø 20.5 mm, height 3.6 mm; 23 jewels; 28,800 vph; finely finished movement; 40-hour power reserve
Functions: hours, minutes
Case: white gold, 45 mm x 43 mm, height 8.08 mm; sapphire crystal; transparent case back; water-resistant to 3 atm
Band: reptile skin, pin buckle
Remarks: tiger-eye dial
Price: $51,000
Variations: various cases, bands and dials

Sixtie

Reference number: G0A50302
Movement: quartz
Functions: hours, minutes
Case: rose gold, ø 29 mm, height 6.5 mm; sapphire crystal; water-resistant to 5 atm
Band: rose gold, triple folding clasp
Price: $32,500
Variations: with diamond bezel ($38,200); in stainless steel ($11,500); in stainless steel with rose gold elements ($13,400)

PILO & CO. GENÈVE

Brimming bank accounts held by mysterious and at times shady characters may no longer be Geneva's best-kept secret in the age of media leaks. Far less known, however, is that Geneva is a veritable hub of artisanship in various fields, including, naturally, watchmaking. Historically, many of these craftspeople were based in the district of St. Gervais, where they were known as Les Cabinotiers. Among them are small, independent watch companies that continue to produce exceptional timepieces, quietly thriving in the shadow of the major brands that also call the city home.

One such independent company, Pilo & Co Genève, will celebrate its twenty-fifth anniversary in 2026. It was founded by Amarildo Pilo, whose story is as Genevan as it is international. His father, an Albanian diplomat, was recalled when the government in his homeland changed in the late 1980s. His two sons remained in Switzerland to continue their studies. Amarildo chose to intern with a watch distributor, an experience that left him captivated by the world of horology. In 2001, feeling equipped with both expertise and ambition, he launched his own brand.

Today, Pilo & Co is represented throughout Switzerland and enjoys a loyal following in Europe and Asia thanks to the combination of affordable prices and good Swiss-made quality. The company operates two boutiques in Geneva and produces a wide range of quartz and mechanical watches. This robust output allows remarkable creative variety in colors, shapes, and dial structures, from classic round cases to daring tonneau designs, with many dials open-worked or fully skeletonized.

The brand's portfolio now includes eleven collections. Highlights include the Extraneō, with its two-level dial and clean, traditional styling; the Corleone Evoluzione Superleggera, a high-end chronograph housed in a rectangular carbon case with a domed and beveled sapphire crystal that enhances dial legibility and a meteor dial with a typical Widmanstätten pattern; and most recently, the Montecristo Monopulsante, an elegant quartz timepiece distinguished by a globe-like central motif. Its dial draws inspiration from the colors of Tuscany, says Pilo, the deep blues of the sea and the earthy tones of the region's rugged landscapes.

PILO & CO GENEVE
11 Faubourg-de-Cruseilles
CH-1227 Carouge
Switzerland

TEL.:
+41-22-328-01-12

E-MAIL:
contact@pilo-watches.com

WEBSITE:
www.pilo-watches.com

FOUNDED:
2001

NUMBER OF EMPLOYEES:
7

DISTRIBUTION:
Contact main office in Geneva
contact@pilo-watches.com

MOST IMPORTANT COLLECTIONS/PRICE RANGE:
Mechanical and quartz watches: Allegra, Corleone, Doppio Orario, Illusione, Invidia, Montecristo, Tempo and Exceptional Pieces /$300 - $5,000

Montecristo Monopulsante
Reference number: P0358CHQS
Movement: quartz, 255.241-ETA caliber
Functions: hours, minutes, subsidiary seconds; monopusher chronograph; date
Case: stainless steel, ø 41 mm, height 10.4 mm; domed scratch-resistant K1 crystal; stainless case back; water resistant to 5 atm
Band: stainless steel; butterfly clasp
Price: $878
Variations: various dial colors

Corleone Superleggera
Reference number: P0559HACF
Movement: automatic, Soprod caliber 7750RM3H; ø 30.40 mm, height 7.9 mm; 25 jewels; 28.800 vph; 42-hour power reserve
Functions: hours, minutes, subsidiary seconds; chronograph; date; power reserve indicator
Case: forged carbon, ø 45 mm x 54 mm, height 15 mm; sapphire crystal domed and beveled; transparent case back; water resistant to 10 atm
Band: sailcloth, pin buckle
Remarks: meteorite dial
Price: $16,000; limited to 25 pieces

Extraneō
Reference number: P0575HAS MB
Movement: automatic, Soprod caliber P024; ø 25.60 mm, height 4.6 mm; 25 jewels; 28,800 vph; 38-hour power reserve
Functions: hours, minutes, sweep seconds
Case: stainless steel, ø 40 mm, height 10.7 mm; sapphire crystal; stainless steel case back; water-resistant to 5 atm
Band: stainless steel, folding clasp
Price: $2,420

PORSCHE DESIGN

In 1972, Professor Ferdinand Alexander Porsche founded his own design studio to create technologically inspired products beyond the realm of automobiles. From the outset, Porsche Design focused on exploring innovative technical possibilities in both watches and accessories. Just like the first Porsche 911, one of the most influential design objects in recent history, the iconic Chronograph 1 was conceived by Professor F. A. Porsche. It marked the first time the design, aesthetics, and functionality of a sports car were faithfully translated into a wristwatch. The Chronograph 1 was also the world's first all-black wristwatch.

Today, Porsche Design engineers draw ongoing inspiration from the automotive industry, particularly in the use of advanced materials and functional innovations. The patented rocker switch, which activates the chronograph in the new Monobloc Actuator, derives from the valve control technology of high-powered race cars. This feature improves usability and reinforces the mechanism's durability.

Collaboration with Porsche Motorsport allows cutting-edge technologies and insights from the world of racing to enhance Porsche Design timepieces. The brand relies on exclusive COSC-certified movements to drive its watches. In partnership with engineers at the Porsche Development Center in Weissach (Germany), Porsche Design has produced technical masterpieces and unique calibers, upholding the high quality associated with the "sports cars on your wrist" philosophy.

These calibers include the 01.200, featuring a sophisticated flyback mechanism; the 04.110, equipped with an innovative GMT switching function; and the 01.100 and 03.100. Among the latest collections is the Chronograph 1 line, a boldly sporty range highlighted by special editions such as the Chronograph 1–All Black Numbered Edition and the Chronograph 1 Utility–Limited Edition.

The revolutionary "Custom-built Timepieces" program brings the principle of vehicle configuration to luxury watchmaking. Countless combinations are offered: cases with unique bezels, dial rings available in over 140 automotive colors, or straps crafted from original vehicle leather with decorative stitching in matching yarns. Even the movement's rotor can be customized to resemble an alloy wheel. Each watch is individually assembled by hand, ensuring every detail reflects its owner's personal aesthetic.

PORSCHE LIFESTYLE GROUP
Groenerstrasse 5
D-71636 Ludwigsburg
Germany

TEL.:
+49-711-911-0

E-MAIL:
contact@porsche-design.us

WEBSITE:
www.porsche-design.com

FOUNDED:
1972

U.S. DISTRIBUTOR:
Porsche Design of America, Inc.
600 Anton Blvd., Suite 1280
Costa Mesa, CA 92626
770-290-7500
timepieces@porsche-design.us

MOST IMPORTANT COLLECTIONS:
Chronograph 1, custom-built timepieces with configurator, 1919 Collection, Chronotimer Flyback

Chronograph 1 – 1975 Limited Edition

Reference number: 6041.8.02.002.10.2
Movement: automatic, Porsche Design Caliber WERK 01.240; ø 30 mm, height 7.9 mm; 25 jewels; 28,800 vph; COSC-certified chronometer; 48-hour power reserve
Functions: hours, minutes, subsidiary seconds; flyback chronograph; date and weekday
Case: titanium, ø 40.8 mm, height 14.15 mm; sapphire crystal; screw-down crown; water-resistant to 10 atm
Band: titanium, folding clasp
Price: $9,650; limited to 350 pieces

Chronograph 1 – 50 Years 911 Turbo

Reference number: 6041.8.01.002.10.2
Movement: automatic, Porsche Design Caliber WERK 01.240; ø 30 mm, height 7.9 mm; 25 jewels; 28,800 vph; COSC-certified chronometer; 48-hour power reserve
Functions: hours, minutes, subsidiary seconds; flyback chronograph; date and weekday
Case: titanium with black titanium carbide coating, ø 40.8 mm, height 15.5 mm; sapphire crystal; transparent case back; screw-down crown; water-resistant to 10 atm
Band: textile, folding clasp
Remarks: comes with additional titanium bracelet
Price: $12,000

Chronograph 1 Utility – Limited Edition

Reference number: 6041.8.41.001.12.2
Movement: automatic, Porsche Design Caliber WERK 01.240 (base Concepto 2000); ø 30 mm, height 7.9 mm; 25 jewels; 28,800 vph; COSC-certified chronometer; 48-hour power reserve
Functions: hours, minutes, subsidiary seconds; flyback chronograph; date and weekday
Case: titanium carbide, ø 42.7 mm, height 15.5 mm; sapphire crystal; transparent case back; screw-down crown; water-resistant to 10 atm
Band: leather, folding clasp
Price: $13,000; limited to 250 pieces

Chronograph 1 – All-Black Numbered Edition

Reference number: 6043.7.01.001.01.5
Movement: automatic, Porsche Design Caliber WERK 01.140 (base Concepto 2000); ø 30 mm, height 7.9 mm; 25 jewels; 28,800 vph; COSC-certified chronometer; 48-hour power reserve
Functions: hours, minutes, subsidiary seconds; chronograph; date and weekday
Case: titanium with black titanium carbide coating, ø 40.8 mm, height 14.15 mm; sapphire crystal; transparent case back; screw-down crown; water-resistant to 10 atm
Band: titanium with black titanium carbide coating, folding clasp
Price: $9,650; limited to 1,000 pieces per year

Custom-built Chronograph

Movement: automatic, Porsche Design caliber WERK 01.100 (ETA 7750 base); ø 30 mm, height 7.9 mm; 25 jewels; 28,800 vph; COSC-certified chronometer; 48-hour power reserve
Functions: hours, minutes; rate control; chronograph; date
Case: titanium, ø 42 mm, height 15.33 mm; bezel with titanium carbide coating; sapphire crystal; transparent case back; screw-down crown; water-resistant to 5 atm
Band: leather, folding clasp
Remarks: watch can be personalized using the online configurator
Price: starting at $6,250

Custom-built Globetimer

Movement: automatic, Porsche Design caliber WERK 04.110; ø 28.5 mm, height 6.94 mm, 26 jewels; 28,800 vph; 38-hour power reserve; COSC-certified chronometer
Functions: hours, minutes, sweep seconds; additional 24-hour display (second time zone), day/night indication; date
Case: titanium, ø 42 mm, height 14.68 mm; bezel set titanium carbide coating; sapphire crystal; screw-down crown; water-resistant to 5 atm
Band: leather, folding clasp
Remarks: watch can be personalized using the online configurator
Price: starting at $6,250

Chronograph 911 Spirit 70

Reference number: WAPA71IND0L141
Movement: automatic, Porsche Design Caliber WERK 01.100 (base ETA 7750); ø 30 mm, height 7.9 mm; 25 jewels; 28,800 vph; rotor design inspired by Porsche 911 Spirit 70 wheel rim; COSC-certified chronometer; 48-hour power reserve
Functions: hours, minutes; rate control; chronograph; date
Case: titanium with black titanium carbide coating, ø 42 mm, height 14.9 mm; sapphire crystal; transparent case back; screw-down crown; water-resistant to 10 atm
Band: leather, double folding clasp
Remarks: exclusively available for owners of the Porsche 911 Sprit 70
Price: starting at $12,553

Chronograph 911 GT3

Reference number: 6004.0.00.062.00.0
Movement: automatic, Porsche Design Caliber WERK 01.200 (base ETA 7750); ø 30 mm, height 7.9 mm; 25 jewels; 28,800 vph; COSC-certified chronometer; 48-hour power reserve
Functions: hours, minutes; rate control; chronograph; date
Case: titanium, ø 42 mm, height 15.33 mm; bezel with titanium carbide coating; sapphire crystal; transparent case back; screw-down crown; water-resistant to 10 atm
Band: leather, double folding clasp
Remarks: exclusively available for owners of the Porsche 911 GT3
Price: starting at $11,135
Variations: with titanium bracelet

Sport Chrono Subsecond 39 Titanium & Blue

Reference number: 6023.3.71.002.07.2
Movement: automatic, Porsche Design Caliber WERK 03.200 (base Sellita SW261); ø 25.6 mm, height 5.6 mm; 31 jewels; 28,800 vph; COSC-certified chronometer; 38-hour power reserve
Functions: hours, minutes, subsidiary seconds; date
Case: titanium, ø 39 mm, height 12.25 mm; sapphire crystal; screw-down crown; water-resistant to 10 atm
Band: leather, folding clasp
Price: $5,350

RAKETA

The city of Saint Petersburg, often called Russia's cultural capital, is relatively young. It was founded in 1703 by Czar Peter I—later known as "the Great"—who sought to modernize his country and turn its gaze toward the West. He envisioned a city built on European models, one that would give the entire country a new, modern look. The project came to fruition, but at a terrible human cost: thousands of serfs perished building on treacherous swampland ravaged by disease. Yet Peter achieved his goal and left behind a city unlike any other in Russia.

A city without an industry would not have been manageable. In 1721, the emperor established a lapidary workshop in his imperial residence at Petrodvorets (Peterhof). Initially devoted to cutting and polishing gemstones for the palace and imperial regalia, the workshop's craftsmanship would ensure its survival through centuries of change. After it sustained heavy damage during a 900-day siege in World War Two, the factory was restored in 1949 and converted to watch production, first under the patriotic names Pobeda (Victory) and Zvezda (Star).

When Yuri Gagarin orbited Earth aboard Vostok 1 in 1961, it marked a new era of Soviet achievement. The following year, the factory launched a brand that captured the spirit of space exploration, Raketa (Rocket). Its sturdy, accessible collections soon became symbols of national pride and modern Soviet identity.

Nearly half a century later, the glow had dimmed. When David Henderson-Stewart, a British entrepreneur, visited the Petrodvorets factory in 2010, he found just a handful of loyal workers keeping the machines running. Although he had little experience in the industry, he recognized the brand's potential. With fresh investments and renewed expertise, Raketa was reborn, producing every component in-house.

Today, the brand continues to embrace its Russian heritage and iconography. Its collections range from the military-inspired 24-hour Russian Code to the science-inspired Copernicus, celebrating the man who finally proved heliocentrism. The Avant-Garde model and the Malevich series pay tribute to the very bold and lively art world.

RAKETA WATCH FACTORY LTD
Sankt-Peterburgskiy prospekt, 60
198516 St. Petersburg, Peterhof
Russia

TEL.:
+7-926-304-0591

E-MAIL:
info@raketa.com

WEBSITE:
www.raketa.com

FOUNDED:
1721 / 1961

DISTRIBUTION:
Contact the company

MOST IMPORTANT COLLECTIONS/PRICE RANGE:
Avant-Garde, Space Launcher, Copernicus, Polar, Russian Code / $800 to $3,750

Russian Code

Reference number: W-12-19-30-0300
Movement: automatic, Raketa Caliber 2615 CR; ø 26 mm, height 6.8 mm; 24 jewels; 18,000 vph; inverted construction to let hands move anticlockwise; bidirectional winding; hand-made Neva waves decoration and nanocoating; 40-hour power reserve
Functions: hours, minutes, sweep seconds
Case: stainless steel, ø 39.5 mm, height 14.9 mm; screw-down crown with synthetic ruby cabochon; sapphire crystal; transparent case back (mineral glass); water-resistant to 5 atm
Band: leather, pin buckle
Remarks: dial center shows constellation over St. Petersburg on April 12, 1961, when Yuri Gagarin became the first man to fly into orbit
Price: $2,460

Malevich Triptych (Black Square)

Reference number: W-13-16-30-0307
Movement: automatic, Raketa caliber 2615; ø 26 mm, height 6.8 mm; 24 jewels; 18,000 vph; bidirectional gold-plated rotor Neva waves decoration and nanocoating; 40-hour power reserve
Functions: hours, minutes
Case: stainless steel, ø 39.5 mm, height 15,78 mm; crown with ruby cabochon; sapphire crystal; transparent case back (mineral glass); water-resistant to 10 atm
Band: leather, folding clasp
Remarks: one of a set of three watches, including the Black Circle and the Black Cross; dial of transparent and tinted agate
Price: $2,110
Variations: various strap colors

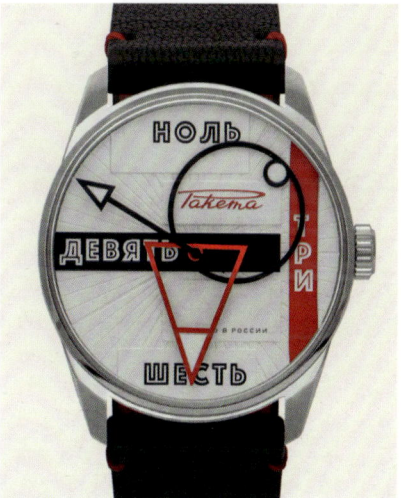

Avant-Garde

Reference number: W-13-16-10-0292
Movement: automatic, Raketa caliber 2615; ø 26 mm, height 6.8; 24 jewels; 18,000 vph; bidirectional rotor with laser-made Neva waves decoration and nanocoating; 40-hour power reserve
Functions: hours, minutes, sweep seconds
Case: stainless steel, ø 39.5 mm, height 15.78 mm; crown with ruby cabochon; sapphire crystal; transparent case back (mineral glass); water-resistant to 5 atm
Band: leather, buckle
Price: $2,110

RAYMOND WEIL

Raymond Weil was more than the founder of a distinguished Geneva watch brand—he was the heart of a family whose deeply held values have been woven into its creations for nearly half a century. As one of a select group of independent, family-led maisons, the brand remains resolutely committed to crafting timepieces of rare elegance and refined sophistication for both women and men.

Founded in 1976 and today steered by Elie Bernheim, the founder's grandson, this quintessentially Genevan brand has, over three generations, become a pillar of the Swiss watchmaking landscape. It has achieved this stature by never straying from its foundation of quality and simplicity. Even when tempted—as in the aftermath of the subprime recession—to alter its course, the company held fast to the principles that had shaped its success. The formula is simple yet enduring: technical mastery combined with grace and timeless style. And nothing too over the top, which is also quite "Swiss."

For Raymond Weil, music and art are not merely sources of inspiration; they are as essential to humanity as thought itself: inexhaustible wellsprings that spark creativity and drive innovation. This enduring family ethos forms more than the cornerstone of the brand's strength. It also defines the character that gives every watch its soul.

This devotion to artistry and creativity continues to guide the brand in forging distinctive partnerships with legendary artists, iconic music companies, celebrated concert venues, arts foundations, and renowned award ceremonies worldwide. Each collaboration adds a new chapter to Raymond Weil's ongoing story as the company looks ahead to its golden fiftieth anniversary in 2026.

The brand's portfolio centers on three main collections, the most emblematic of which is Freelancer. Its name alone lends itself to many interpretations, from the simplicity of a three-hand plus date model to the complexity of GMTs and chronographs. The more feminine Toccata line appeals to those drawn to the discreet elegance of modernized Art Deco rectangles with softened edges, while the Millesime offers a haven of classic design, including a line of chronographs at accessible prices.

RAYMOND WEIL SA
Avenue Eugène-Lance 36-38
CH-1212 Grand-Lancy (Geneva)
Switzerland

EMAIL:
info@raymond-weil.ch

FOUNDED:
1976

WEBSITE:
www.raymond-weil.com

EMPLOYEES:
120

ANNUAL PRODUCTION:
80,000 watches

DISTRIBUTION STRUCTURE:
Specialist retailers, online shop

MAIN COLLECTIONS:
Millesime, Freelancer, Toccata

Freelancer Complete Calendar
Reference number: 2766-ST-50001
Movement: automatic, Caliber RW3281 (on SW381 base); ø 25.6 mm, height 4.85 mm; 26 jewels; 28,800 vph; 56-hour power reserve
Functions: hours, minutes, sweep seconds; calendar with date, weekday, month; moon phase
Case: stainless steel, ø 40 mm, height 10.15 mm; sapphire crystal; water-resistant to 10 atm
Band: stainless steel, double folding clasp
Price: $4,195
Variations: with leather strap

Millesime Chronograph
Reference number: 7765-PC5-20631
Movement: automatic, Caliber RW5030 (on Sellita SW500 base); ø 30 mm, height 7.9 mm; 25 jewels; 28,800 vph; 62-hour power reserve
Functions: hours, minutes, subsidiary seconds; chronograph
Case: stainless steel with gold PVD, ø 39 mm, height 12.9 mm; sapphire crystal; water-resistant to 5 atm
Band: leather, pin buckle
Price: $4,375

Toccata Heritage Manual Winding
Reference number: 2280-STC-64001
Movement: hand-wound, Caliber RW4100 (on Sellita SW210 base); ø 25.6 mm, height 3.35 mm; 18 jewels; 28,800 vph; 45-hour power reserve
Functions: hours, minutes
Case: stainless steel, 33 mm × 38 mm, height 6.9 mm; sapphire crystal; water-resistant to 5 atm
Band: leather, pin buckle
Price: $1,675

RESERVOIR

One of the most logical inspirations for watches is the humble gauge, and for good reason. It usually has a similar shape to a watch (round), and it serves to depict a certain event or action using a pointing device and numerals. It must also be legible at a glance. In addition, gauges tend to be found precisely where a mechanical process is taking place, and that excites the imagination of any person who appreciates the mesmerizing synergism of gears, cams, rackets, and other parts.

While gauges and meters are used fairly frequently as elements in watchmaking, only a few brands have actually made them the centerpiece of their design strategy. Reservoir, a French brand founded in 2017 by François Moreau, has taken this object mirroring to the nth degree, one could say. Connoisseurs of vintage British cars will easily spot the resemblance of many models to the odometers in the Mini Morris: a big round dial with a fuel gauge at the lower end.

Since gauges usually have a single pointer, many Reservoir models have a retrograde minute hand with jumping hours in a separate window below the center. This basic dial serves as a visual pattern for three separate lines inspired by air, land, and sea.

Reservoir has collaborated with a number of outside forces to create special editions, like Monza Design. Another collaboration was with the elite tactical French police force "Groupe d'intervention de la Gendarmerie nationale" or, to use the unnerving acronym, GIGN.

The year 2025 was tough for the brand. When one of its main suppliers declared bankruptcy, the company had to rebuild, a process that included finding fresh capital. As 2026 dawns, however, Reservoir is back in business and manufacturing.

For its movements, which require some dexterity to manufacture, Reservoir uses basic ETA La Joux-Perret calibers with special modifications built by Télôs, an exclusive movement and module maker in La Chaux-de-Fonds that specializes in implementing the ideas, no matter how wild, of horological dreamers.

RESERVOIR WATCH SAS
29, rue Guillaume Tell
75017 Paris
France

TEL:
+33 (0)1 42 89 05 91

E-MAIL:
contact@reservoir-watch.com

WEBSITE:
www.reservoir-watch.com

FOUNDED:
2017

NUMBER OF EMPLOYEES:
6

U. S. DISTRIBUTOR:
Online sales
Timeless Distribution
contactUSA@reservoir-watch.com
305-588-3628

MOST IMPORTANT COLLECTIONS/PRICE RANGE
Cars, Aeronautics, Marine, Music, Comics by Reservoir / from $3,800

Monza Design 325y

Reference number: RSV01.MD/138.YL
Movement: automatic, Caliber RSV-240 based on La Joux-Perret LP G100; ø 25.6 mm, height 4.45 mm; 24 jewels; 28,800 vph, 56-hour power reserve
Functions: retrograde minutes, jumping hours; power reserve indicator
Case: stainless steel, ø 43 mm, height 14 mm; sapphire crystal; transparent case back; screw-down crown; water-resistant to 5 atm
Band: stainless steel, pin buckle
Remarks: collaboration with Monza Design of race car fame; comes with extra rubber strap with tire imprint
Price: $5,400
Variations: black dial with red power reserve, white dial and white power reserve

Black Sparrow

Reference number: RSV02.PL/135.BL
Movement: automatic, Caliber RSV-240 based on La Joux-Perret LP G100; ø 25.6 mm, height 4.45 mm; 24 jewels; 28,800 vph, 56-hour power reserve
Functions: retrograde minutes, jumping hours
Case: stainless steel with black PVD, ø 42 mm, height 12 mm; transparent case back; screw-down crown; water-resistant to 5 atm
Band: leather, pin buckle
Remarks: dial design from early fighter cockpits; tribute to Eugene Bullard, the first WWI Afro-American combat pilot who enlisted in the French air army; comes with extra leather black NATO strap.
Price: $4,300
Variations: with black or sand-colored dial ($4,300)

Kanister

Reference number: RSV01.KN/433-BK1
Movement: automatic, Caliber RSV-240 based on La Joux-Perret LP G100; ø 25.6 mm, height 4.45 mm; 24 jewels; 28,800 vph, 56-hour power reserve
Functions: retrograde minutes, jumping hours; power reserve indicator
Case: stainless steel, ø 41.5 mm, height 13 mm; sapphire crystal; transparent case back; screw-down crown; water-resistant to 5 atm
Band: black leather, pin buckle
Price: $5,350

RESSENCE

Belgian designer Benoît Mintiens had the luck of the newcomer at Baselworld 2010. He arrived at the last minute and managed to show a strange watch he had conceived, with what looked like a two-dimensional dial. He returned in 2011 with the Type 1001, which featured a large rotating dial carrying a hand that pointed to a minute track on the bezel. Hours, small seconds, and a day/night indication rotated on dedicated subsidiary dials, mesmerizing everyone who saw it. All fifty models sold immediately.

The mechanics behind Ressence watches—short for "Renaissance of the Essential"—are ingenious in their simplicity. A stripped-down ETA 2824 movement drives all indications through the minute wheel. In a quest for clarity, Mintiens later immersed the dial in oil, creating a crystal-clear display reminiscent of a digital screen. Because the movement had to stay separate from the oil, it was connected through magnets and a superconductive system shielded by a Faraday cage. Baffles compensate for oil expansion and contraction under temperature changes. The Type 3 also abandoned the crown, replacing it with a smooth, intuitive setting and winding mechanism on the case back.

The display itself is based on a continuously rotating dial with three or four "satellites"—small circular subdials—that move at their own speeds depending on their function, such as hours or seconds. These satellites permanently rotate with the main dial, which carries a painted minute hand, completing one full revolution per hour. The trick, and great technical challenge, is that the satellite scales always remain upright to the viewer's eye, allowing instant recognition of the "12" at the top of the hour scale and easy reading of the short hour hand's position.

Ressence watches derive much of their charm from their seamless, softly domed shape, free of a bezel. The curvature of the surface has a radius of 12.5 centimeters—about the same as a bowling ball. The Type 9, released in 2024, continues that pursuit of minimalism: a smaller 39-millimeter case, fixed bezel, and beautifully restrained dial composition, especially when Japanese lacquer artist Ikeda Terumasa is invited to illuminate the dial.

RESSENCE WATCHES
Meirbrug 1
2000 Antwerp
Belgium

TEL.:
+32-3-446-0060

E-MAIL:
hello@ressence.be

WEBSITE:
www.ressencewatches.com

FOUNDED:
2010

U.S. DISTRIBUTOR:
Totally Worth It (TWI2, Inc.)
76 Division Avenue
Summit, NJ 07901-2309
201-894-4710
724-263-2286
info@totallyworthit.com

COLLECTION PRICES:
Type 1: $20,600; Type 2: $48,800; Type 3: $42,200;
Type 5: $35,800; Type 8: 15,000; Type 9: $15,000

Type 9 IKEDA

Reference number: T9 IKE
Movement: automatic, ROCS 9 (module, base ETA 2892-A2); ø 32 mm; 31 jewels; 28,800 vph; gear train with 20 wheels, 4 ball bearings; total 188 components; winding and time-setting via case back; 36-hour power reserve
Functions: hours, minutes (Ressence Orbital Convex System: revolving minute dial with rotating satellite for hours)
Case: titanium with DLC, ø 39 mm, height 11 mm; bezel with engraved hour markers; sapphire crystal; winding and time-setting via case back (no crown)
Band: horse leather, pin buckle
Remarks: dial of lacquer and mother-of-pearl by Japanese artist Ikeda Terumasa
Price: $41,500; limited to 8 pieces

Type 8 Edition Daniel Engelberg

Reference number: T8.1 DE1
Movement: automatic, ROCS 8 (module, base ETA 2892A2); ø 32 mm; 31 jewels; 28,800 vph; gear train with 20 wheels, 4 ball bearings; total 188 components; winding and time-setting via case back; 36-hour power reserve
Functions: hours, minutes (Ressence Orbital Convex System: revolving minute dial with rotating satellite for hours)
Case: titanium, ø 42.9 mm, height 11 mm; sapphire crystal; winding and time-setting via case back (no crown)
Band: silicone, pin buckle
Remarks: collaboration with artist Daniel Engelberg
Price: $24,900; limited to 40 pieces
Variations: Type 8.1 DE.2 in turquoise; limited to 40 pieces

Type 7 Night Blue

Reference number: T7 N
Movement: automatic, ROCS 7 (module, base ETA 2824-2); ø 32 mm; 37 jewels; 28,800 vph; movement and ROCS module in two separate chambers (module chamber and dial chamber oil-filled with compensation reservoir); magnetic transmission of the drives
Functions: minutes; hours and 180-second "Runner" (Ressence Orbital Convex System: revolving minute dial with rotating satellites); additional 24-hour display (second time zone); oil temperature (color indicator)
Case: titanium, ø 41 mm, height 14 mm; unidirectional bezel with 0–60 scale; sapphire crystal; winding and time-setting via case back; water-resistant to 5 atm
Band: titanium, double folding clasp with fine adjustment
Price: $45,200

RGM

The traditional values of hard work and persistence are alive and well in Roland Murphy, founder of RGM, one of the U.S.'s most famous and exclusive watch companies. Murphy, born in Maryland, went through the watchmaker's drill, studying at the Bowman Technical School, then in Switzerland, and finally working with Swatch before launching his own business in 1992 in Pennsylvania, which could be considered a kind of "watch valley."

The secret to his success, however, has always been to stay in touch with fundamental American values and icons. His first watch, the Signature, resurrected vintage pocket watch movements developed by Hamilton. The Railroad series today is run on restored Hamilton movements. His second big project was the Caliber 801, the first "high-grade mechanical movement made in series in America since Hamilton stopped production of the 992 B in 1969," Murphy shares with a grin. This was followed by an all-American-made watch, the Pennsylvania Tourbillon.

The 801 is a mix of nostalgia and innovation. The inspiration comes from the Edward Howard flagship model of the now-defunct Keystone Howard Watch Co. The winding click originated with the "Illini" model of the Illinois Watch Company. This unique American caliber is gradually being used at RGM to drive various watches.

And so, model by model, Murphy continues to expand his "Made in U.S.A." portfolio. "You cannot compare us to the big brands," he said in an interview. "We are small and specialized, the needs are different. We work directly with the customer." This may account for the brand's diversity. There are retro-themed watches, sports-themed watches (honoring baseball or chess), a diver water-resistant to 70 atm, and the series 400 chronograph with a pulsometer and extra-large subdials for visibility. For the true collector, Roland Murphy offers customization options.

And it is not all technical. Murphy has turned to the many crafts associated with watchmaking, notably engine-turned guilloché and various enameling techniques, such as cloisonné, Grand Feu enameling, or hand-painted images on mother of pearl. The Lady RGM is one such timepiece. It comes in a 28-millimeter case with a guilloché on mother-of-pearl dial.

RGM WATCH COMPANY
801 W. Main Street
Mount Joy, PA 17552
USA

TEL.:
717-653-9799

E-MAIL:
sales@rgmwatches.com

WEB:
www.rgmwatches.com

FOUNDED:
1992

NUMBER OF EMPLOYEES:
12

ANNUAL PRODUCTION:
200–300 watches

DISTRIBUTION:
RGM deals directly with customers
sales@rgmwatches.com

MOST IMPORTANT COLLECTION/PRICE RANGE:
Pennsylvania Series (completely made in the U.S.) / range of different models $2,500 to $125,000

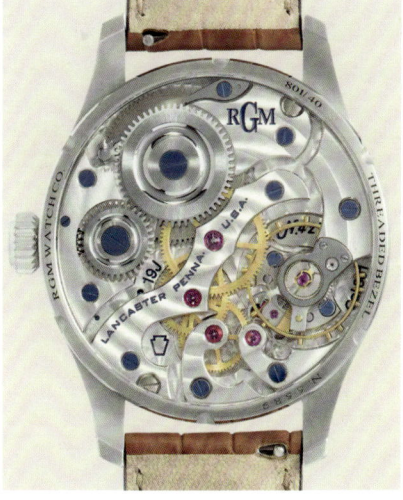

Model 222-RR

Movement: hand-wound, vintage Hamilton (921 or 923) 10-size caliber; ø 37 mm, height 4.6 mm; 21 or 23 jewels; 18,000 vph; rhodium finish with circular decoration côtes de Genève; up to 45-hour power reserve
Functions: hours, minutes, subsidiary seconds
Case: stainless steel, ø 41 mm, height 12 mm; sapphire crystal; transparent case back; water-resistant to 5 atm
Band: leather, pin buckle
Remarks: "Ferguson" dial with glass grand-feu enamel, originally made especially for railway, with inner hour chapter, and outer minute chapter; red hour hand, blued-steel minute hand
Price: $8,950 (921 movement), $9,950 (923 movement)

801/40-CE "Classic Enamel"

Movement: RGM Caliber 801; ø 36.6 mm, height 4.5 mm; 19 jewels; 18,000 vph; screw balance; gold or rhodium finishing, with choice of côtes de Genève, guilloché, or skeletonized parts; 44-hour power reserve
Functions: hours, minutes, subsidiary seconds
Case: stainless steel, ø 40.3 mm, height 10.5 mm; box-style sapphire crystal; transparent case back; water-resistant to 5 atm
Band: calfskin, buckle
Remarks: grand-feu enamel dial
Price: $17,900

Caliber 801

Hand-wound; single mainspring barrel with special winding click originally designed for the Illinois Watch Company's Illini model, 44-hour power reserve
Functions: hours, minutes, sweep seconds
Diameter: 36.6 mm
Height: 4.5 mm
Balance: screw balance
Jewels: 19
Frequency: 18,000 vph
Remarks: comes alternatively with motor-barrel system; finely finished with côtes de Genève and perlage

ROBOT

When brainstorming a name for a new line of watches to be produced by his company, Bohematic, entrepreneur Josef Zajíček turned to the Czech Republic's long, rich literary tradition and chose the name Robot. Few people realize that the word is of Czech origin and originally referred to forced or arduous labor. In that sense, it is related to an older German term denoting burdensome work or drudgery.

For Czechs—and for those familiar with the country's literature—the name inevitably evokes *R.U.R.* (Rossum's Universal Robots), the 1920 science fiction play by Karel Čapek. In it, Čapek describes artificial beings created by humans to serve them, a concept that aligns neatly with the function of mechanical timepieces.

Robot watches are manufactured in Nové Město nad Metují, a small town in northern Czechia with a history of precision engineering and watchmaking. The company was founded in 2018 by Zajíček in collaboration with the design studio Olgoj Chorchoj and a team of experienced watchmakers, designers, and craftsmen. Most of the brand's watches are powered by La Joux-Perret calibers.

The collections draw inspiration from the Czech Republic's industrial heritage. The Aerodynamic line, for example, pays tribute to the Tatra 77, widely regarded as the world's first mass-produced aerodynamic automobile. The Minor series also references motorsport, including a version dedicated to Brazilian racing legend Emerson Fittipaldi, who competed in both Formula One and IndyCar during the 1970s.

The most recent collection honors the L-39 Albatros, a legendary Czech training jet. Launched in 1968, the aircraft was widely used by Warsaw Pact nations and remains in service today in several variants, including among private pilots. Its distinctive profile is echoed on the dial at 9 o'clock.

Robot also produces more restrained, dress-oriented watches, where design takes precedence over explicit thematic references. These include the Ada, created for women, and the Aplos line, designed to be worn by anyone. Among them is a model paying tribute to Franz Kafka, one of Czechia's most internationally recognized writers.

ROBOT WATCH
Bohematic s.r.o.
Maiselova 2
101 00 Prague
Czech Republic

TEL.:
+420-722-977-256

E-MAIL:
info@bohematic.cz

WEBSITE:
www.robot-watch.com

FOUNDED:
2018

NUMBER OF EMPLOYEES:
16

ANNUAL PRODUCTION:
approx. 200 watches

DISTRIBUTION:
Wind Up Watch Shop
540 President St, Suite 1G
Brooklyn, NY 11215
direct sales; online shop; please contact the company directly

COLLECTIONS/PRICE RANGE:
Various models / $4,000 to $10,000

Robotic One

Reference number: 2501ST01
Movement: automatic, Bohematic Caliber R11242 (on MLJP base 8120); ø 30.4 mm, height 7.9 mm; 26 jewels; 28,800 vph; 55-hour power reserve
Functions: hours, minutes, subsidiary seconds; chronograph; date
Case: stainless steel, ø 43.2 mm, height 14.8 mm; sapphire crystal; transparent case back; water-resistant to 10 atm
Band: stainless steel, double folding clasp
Remarks: asymmetrical case, shaped like a stylized robot head; rapid strap-changing system
Price: $9,000

Albatros Blue

Reference number: 2401ST02
Movement: hand-wound, Robot Caliber F150 (on MLJP base 7513); ø 33 mm, height 4.5 mm; 33 jewels; 28,800 vph; 192-hour power reserve
Functions: hours, minutes, subsidiary seconds; power reserve indicator; date
Case: stainless steel, ø 44 mm, height 11.5 mm; sapphire crystal; transparent case back; water-resistant to 10 atm
Band: textile, pin buckle
Price: $6,730

Aplos Franz Kafka

Reference number: 2201LE01
Movement: automatic, Robot (based on La Joux-Perret caliber G100); ø 25.6 mm, height 4.45 mm; 24 jewels; 28,800 vph; 68-hour power reserve
Functions: hours, minutes, sweep seconds; date
Case: stainless steel, ø 39 mm, height 10.3 mm; sapphire crystal; transparent case back; water-resistant to 5 atm
Band: calfskin, pin buckle
Price: $2,500; limited to 100 pieces

ROLEX

The Rolex formula for success has always been simple: "What you see is what you get," and plenty of it. For more than a century, the company has shaped wristwatch history without *grandes complications*, perpetual calendars, tourbillons, or exotic materials. Its output approaches a million watches per year, yet the quality of its timepieces remains legendary.

For as long as anyone can remember, Rolex has topped the COSC's statistics and year after year delivers nearly half of all officially certified mechanical chronometer movements. The brand also pioneered several defining innovations. In the 1920s, founder Hans Wilsdorf introduced the hermetically sealed Oyster case, later adding a screw-down crown and an automatic movement wound by a rotor. Shock protection, water resistance, the antimagnetic Parachrom hairspring, and robust automatic winding are among the qualities that make a Rolex especially durable and reliable in everyday use.

Modern movements continue this spirit of refinement. The automatic Caliber 3255 incorporates nickel-phosphorus components and LIGA-manufactured parts for the Chronergy escapement, along with a barrel spring capable of storing more energy than ever. Rolex also employs "Oystersteel," a highly corrosion-resistant 904L alloy, and fits certain models with the supple five-link-wide "Jubilee" bracelet.

Production is distributed across four locations in Switzerland. Headquarters in Geneva handles final assembly, quality control, and sales. Development, manufacturing, and additional quality testing take place in nearby Plan-les-Ouates. Gem-setting and dial production are located in Geneva's Chêne-Bourg district, while movements are produced in Biel/Bienne.

At Watches and Wonders 2025, Rolex presented the new Land-Dweller, which echoes the angular design of the late-seventies Oysterquartz yet houses a thoroughly modern innovation. The newly developed Caliber 7135 was derived from the slim 1908 movement. It features the Dynapulse escapement, the result of seven years of research. Featuring two escape wheels and an impulse lever, it comes remarkably close to Abraham-Louis Breguet's long-pursued ideal of a frictionless *échappement naturel*. What existed only theoretically two centuries ago has now been made by Rolex engineers using silicon and brought to reliable serial production.

Its benefits are enhanced precision, improved efficiency, and complete resistance to magnetic fields. The Dynapulse escapement will surely play a central role in future Rolex calibers.

ROLEX SA
Rue François-Dussaud 3
CH-1211 Geneva 26
Switzerland

WEBSITE:
www.rolex.com

FOUNDED:
1908

NUMBER OF EMPLOYEES:
over 2,000 (estimated)

ANNUAL PRODUCTION:
approx. 1,000,000 watches (estimated)

U.S. DISTRIBUTOR:
Rolex Watch U.S.A., Inc.
650 Fifth Avenue
New York, NY 10019
212-758-7700
www.rolex.com

Land-Dweller 40

Reference number: 127336
Movement: automatic, Rolex Caliber 7135; ø 28.5 mm, height 4.05 mm; 39 jewels; 36,000 vph; Dynapulse escapement with silicon impulse rocker, escape wheels, and transmission wheel; Syloxi hairspring; ceramic balance staff; COSC-certified chronometer; 66-hour power reserve
Functions: hours, minutes, sweep seconds; date
Case: platinum, ø 40 mm, height 9.7 mm; sapphire crystal; transparent case back; screw-down crown; water-resistant to 10 atm
Band: platinum Jubilee, concealed folding clasp
Remarks: ceramic dial
Price: $64,200

Land-Dweller 40

Reference number: 127334
Movement: automatic, Rolex Caliber 7135; ø 28.5 mm, height 4.05 mm; 39 jewels; 36,000 vph; Dynapulse escapement with silicon impulse rocker, escape wheels, and transmission wheel; Syloxi hairspring; ceramic balance staff; COSC-certified chronometer; 66-hour power reserve
Functions: hours, minutes, sweep seconds; date
Case: stainless steel, ø 40 mm, height 9.7 mm; white-gold bezel; sapphire crystal; transparent case back; screw-down crown; water-resistant to 10 atm
Band: stainless steel Jubilee, concealed folding clasp
Price: $15,350
Variations: in rose gold (Everose, $47,400)

Land-Dweller 36

Reference number: 127285
Movement: automatic, Rolex Caliber 7135; ø 28.5 mm, height 4.05 mm; 39 jewels; 36,000 vph; Dynapulse escapement with silicon impulse rocker, escape wheels, and transmission wheel; Syloxi hairspring; ceramic balance staff; COSC-certified chronometer; 66-hour power reserve
Functions: hours, minutes, sweep seconds; date
Case: rose gold (Everose), ø 36 mm, height 9.7 mm; bezel set with 44 trapezoidal diamonds; sapphire crystal; transparent case back; screw-down crown; water-resistant to 10 atm
Band: rose gold (Everose) Jubilee, concealed folding clasp
Price: $90,850
Variations: without diamonds ($43,300)

GMT-Master II

Reference number: 126710GRNRNR
Movement: automatic, Rolex Caliber 3285; ø 28.5 mm, height 6.4 mm; 31 jewels; 28,800 vph; Chronergy escapement; glucydur balance with Microstella regulating screws; COSC-certified chronometer; 70-hour power reserve
Functions: hours (stepwise adjustment via crown), minutes, sweep seconds; additional 24-hour display (second time zone); date
Case: stainless steel, ø 40 mm, height 13 mm; bezel with ceramic insert, rotatable, with 24-hour scale; sapphire crystal; screw-down crown; water-resistant to 10 atm
Band: Oyster stainless steel, folding clasp with safety lock and extension link
Price: $11,100
Variations: with Jubilee bracelet ($11,300)

GMT-Master II

Reference number: 126729VTNR
Movement: automatic, Rolex Caliber 3285; ø 28.5 mm, height 6.4 mm; 31 jewels; 28,800 vph; Chronergy escapement; glucydur balance with Microstella regulating screws; COSC-certified chronometer; 70-hour power reserve
Functions: hours (stepwise adjustment via crown), minutes, sweep seconds; additional 24-hour display (second time zone); date
Case: white gold, ø 40 mm, height 13 mm; bidirectional bezel with ceramic insert and 0–24 scale; sapphire crystal; screw-down crown; water-resistant to 10 atm
Band: Oyster stainless steel, folding clasp with safety lock and extension link
Remarks: ceramic dial
Price: $48,050

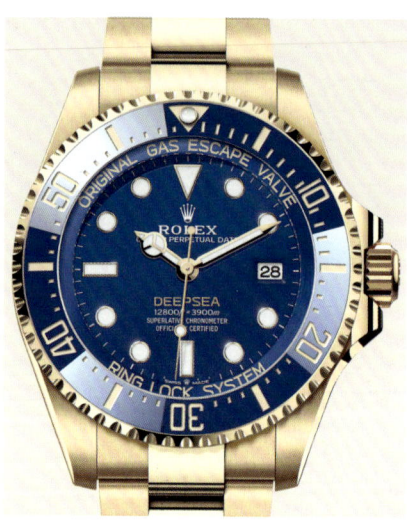

Deepsea

Reference number: 136668LB
Movement: automatic, Rolex Caliber 3235; ø 29.1 mm; 31 jewels; 28,800 vph; Parachrom hairspring; Paraflex shock absorber; Chronergy escapement; glucydur balance with Microstella regulating screws; COSC-certified chronometer; 70-hour power reserve
Functions: hours, minutes, sweep seconds; date
Case: yellow gold, ø 44 mm, 17.7 mm unidirectional bezel with ceramic insert and 0–60 scale; sapphire crystal; screw-down crown; helium valve; water-resistant to 390 atm
Band: Oyster yellow gold, folding clasp with safety lock, extension link, and fine adjustment
Price: $59,700

Sea-Dweller

Reference number: 126603
Movement: automatic, Rolex Caliber 3235; ø 29.1 mm; 31 jewels; 28,800 vph; Chronergy escapement; glucydur balance with Microstella regulating screws; COSC-certified chronometer; 70-hour power reserve
Functions: hours, minutes, sweep seconds; date
Case: stainless steel, ø 43 mm, height 13.8 mm; unidirectional bezel in yellow gold with ceramic insert and 0–60 scale; sapphire crystal; screw-down crown; helium valve; water-resistant to 122 atm
Band: Oyster stainless steel with yellow-gold elements, folding clasp with safety lock, extension link, and fine adjustment
Price: $20,300
Variations: in stainless steel ($13,750)

Submariner Date

Reference number: 126610LV
Movement: automatic, Rolex Caliber 3230; ø 29.1 mm; 31 jewels; 28,800 vph; Parachrom hairspring; Paraflex shock absorber; Chronergy escapement; glucydur balance with Microstella regulating screws; COSC-certified chronometer; 70-hour power reserve
Functions: hours, minutes, sweep seconds; date
Case: stainless steel, ø 41 mm, height 12.5 mm; unidirectional bezel with ceramic insert and 0–60 scale; sapphire crystal; screw-down crown; water-resistant to 30 atm
Band: Oyster stainless steel, folding clasp with extension link
Price: $11,200
Variations: in white gold ($48,000)

Submariner

Reference number: 124060
Movement: automatic, Rolex Caliber 3230; ø 29.1 mm; 31 jewels; 28,800 vph; Parachrom hairspring; Paraflex shock absorber; Chronergy escapement; glucydur balance with Microstella regulating screws; COSC-certified chronometer; 70-hour power reserve
Functions: hours, minutes, sweep seconds
Case: stainless steel, ø 41 mm, height 12.5 mm; unidirectional bezel with ceramic insert and 0–60 scale; sapphire crystal; screw-down crown; water-resistant to 30 atm
Band: Oyster stainless steel, folding clasp with extension link
Price: $9,500

TOURBY
HAGEN IN WESTFALEN

we build your watch

Sport Chrono Orca
40 mm diameter
ETA Valjoux 7753
Price: $4,500

www.tourbywatches.com

Cosmograph Daytona

Reference number: 126518LN
Movement: automatic, Rolex Caliber 4131; ø 30.5 mm, height 6.5 mm; 44 jewels; 28,800 vph; Parachrom hairspring; Paraflex shock absorber; Chronergy escapement; COSC-certified chronometer; 72-hour power reserve
Functions: hours, minutes, subsidiary seconds; chronograph
Case: yellow gold, ø 40 mm, height 12.8 mm; Cerachrom bezel; sapphire crystal; screw-down crown and pushers; water-resistant to 10 atm
Band: rubber Oysterflex, folding clasp with fine adjustment
Price: $37,400

Cosmograph Daytona

Reference number: 126500LN
Movement: automatic, Rolex Caliber 4131; ø 30.5 mm, height 6.5 mm; 44 jewels; 28,800 vph; Parachrom hairspring; Paraflex shock absorber; Chronergy escapement; COSC-certified chronometer; 72-hour power reserve
Functions: hours, minutes, subsidiary seconds; chronograph
Case: stainless steel, ø 40 mm, height 12.8 mm; Cerachrom bezel; sapphire crystal; screw-down crown and pushers; water-resistant to 10 atm
Band: Oyster stainless steel, folding clasp with safety lock and extension link
Price: $16,000
Variations: with black dial

Cosmograph Daytona

Reference number: 126515LN
Movement: automatic, Rolex Caliber 4131; ø 30.5 mm, height 6.5 mm; 44 jewels; 28,800 vph; Parachrom hairspring; Paraflex shock absorber; Chronergy escapement; COSC-certified chronometer; 72-hour power reserve
Functions: hours, minutes, subsidiary seconds; chronograph
Case: rose gold (Everose), ø 40 mm, height 12.8 mm; Cerachrom bezel; sapphire crystal; screw-down crown and pushers; water-resistant to 10 atm
Band: rubber Oysterflex, folding clasp with fine adjustment
Price: $39,300
Variations: in white gold ($37,400)

Explorer II

Reference number: 226570
Movement: automatic, Rolex Caliber 3285; ø 28.5 mm; 31 jewels; 28,800 vph; Parachrom hairspring; Paraflex shock absorbers; Chronergy escapement; glucydur balance with Microstella regulating screws; COSC-certified chronometer; 70-hour power reserve
Functions: hours (stepwise adjustment via crown), minutes, sweep seconds; additional 24-hour display (second time zone); date
Case: stainless steel, ø 42 mm, height 12.5 mm; sapphire crystal; screw-down crown; water-resistant to 10 atm
Band: Oyster stainless steel, folding clasp with extension link
Price: $10,050
Variations: with black dial

Explorer 40

Reference number: 224270
Movement: automatic, Rolex Caliber 3230; ø 29.1 mm; 31 jewels; 28,800 vph; Parachrom hairspring; Paraflex shock absorber; Chronergy escapement; glucydur balance with Microstella regulating screws; COSC-certified chronometer; 70-hour power reserve
Functions: hours, minutes, sweep seconds
Case: stainless steel, ø 40 mm, height 11.6 mm; sapphire crystal; screw-down crown; water-resistant to 10 atm
Band: Oyster stainless steel, folding clasp with extension link
Price: $7,950
Variations: with 36 mm case

Air-King

Reference number: 126900
Movement: automatic, Rolex Caliber 3230; ø 28.5 mm; 31 jewels; 28,800 vph; Parachrom hairspring; Paraflex shock absorber; Chronergy escapement; glucydur balance with Microstella regulating screws; COSC-certified chronometer; 70-hour power reserve
Functions: hours, minutes, sweep seconds
Case: stainless steel, ø 40 mm, height 11.6 mm; sapphire crystal; screw-down crown; water-resistant to 10 atm
Band: Oyster stainless steel, folding clasp with safety lock and extension link
Price: $7,750

Sky-Dweller

Reference number: 336935
Movement: automatic, Rolex Caliber 9002; ø 33 mm, height 8 mm; 40 jewels; 28,800 vph; COSC-certified chronometer; 72-hour power reserve
Functions: hours, minutes, sweep seconds; additional 24-hour display (second time zone); annual calendar with date and month
Case: rose gold (Everose), ø 42 mm, height 14.1 mm; bidirectional bezel to control functions; sapphire crystal; screw-down crown; water-resistant to 10 atm
Band: rose gold (Everose) Jubilee, folding clasp with fine adjustment
Price: $59,500
Variations: with white dial; in yellow gold ($56,200); in stainless steel and white gold ($16,800)

Yacht-Master 42

Reference number: 226627
Movement: automatic, Rolex Caliber 3235; ø 29.1 mm, height 6 mm; 31 jewels; 28,800 vph; Parachrom hairspring; Paraflex shock absorber; Chronergy escapement; 48-hour power reserve; COSC-certified chronometer
Functions: hours, minutes, sweep seconds; date
Case: titanium RLX, ø 42 mm, height 11.9 mm; bidirectional bezel with ceramic insert and 0–60 scale; sapphire crystal; screw-down crown; water-resistant to 10 atm
Band: titanium RLX, folding clasp with fine adjustment
Price: $15,250
Variations: in white gold ($35,000); in yellow gold ($33,500) — both on Oysterflex bracelets

Datejust 41

Reference number: 126333
Movement: automatic, Rolex Caliber 3235; ø 29.1 mm; 31 jewels; 28,800 vph; Parachrom hairspring; Paraflex shock absorber; Chronergy escapement; glucydur balance with Microstella regulating screws; COSC-certified chronometer; 70-hour power reserve
Functions: hours, minutes, sweep seconds; date
Case: stainless steel, ø 41 mm, height 11.6 mm; bezel and crown in yellow gold; sapphire crystal; screw-down crown; water-resistant to 10 atm
Band: Jubilee stainless steel with yellow-gold elements, folding clasp with extension link
Price: $16,100

Day-Date 40

Reference number: 228235
Movement: automatic, Rolex Caliber 3255; ø 29.1 mm, height 5.4 mm; 31 jewels; 28,800 vph; Parachrom hairspring; Paraflex shock absorber; Chronergy escapement; glucydur balance with Microstella regulating screws; COSC-certified chronometer; 70-hour power reserve
Functions: hours, minutes, sweep seconds; date and weekday
Case: rose gold (Everose), ø 40 mm, height 11.6 mm; sapphire crystal; screw-down crown; water-resistant to 10 atm
Band: rose gold (Everose) President, concealed folding clasp
Remarks: "Ombré" dial with gradient colors
Price: $47,500
Variations: in white or yellow gold

Perpetual 1908

Reference number: 52508
Movement: automatic, Rolex Caliber 7140; ø 28.5 mm, height 4.05 mm; 38 jewels; 28,800 vph; Syloxi hairspring; Paraflex shock absorber; Chronergy escapement; 66-hour power reserve; COSC-certified chronometer
Functions: hours, minutes, subsidiary seconds
Case: yellow gold, ø 39 mm, height 9.5 mm; sapphire crystal; transparent case back; water-resistant to 5 atm
Band: yellow gold "Settimo," double folding clasp
Price: $35,900

Perpetual 1908

Reference number: 52506
Movement: automatic, Rolex Caliber 7140; ø 28.5 mm, height 4.05 mm; 38 jewels; 28,800 vph; Syloxi hairspring; Paraflex shock absorber; Chronergy escapement; 66-hour power reserve; COSC-certified chronometer
Functions: hours, minutes, subsidiary seconds
Case: yellow gold, ø 39 mm, height 9.5 mm; sapphire crystal; transparent case back; water-resistant to 5 atm
Band: reptile skin, double folding clasp
Price: $25,250
Variations: with black dial; in white gold ($26,600)

Caliber 3235

Automatic; optimized Chronergy escapement with nickel-phosphorus pallet lever and escape wheel (LIGA process); single mainspring barrel; COSC-certified chronometer; 70-hour power reserve
Functions: hours, minutes, sweep seconds; date
Diameter: 28.5 mm
Height: 6 mm
Jewels: 31
Balance: glucydur with Microstella regulating bolts
Frequency: 28,800 vph
Hairspring: Parachrom Breguet hairspring
Shock protection: Paraflex
Remarks: used in Datejust

Caliber 3255

Automatic; optimized Chronergy escapement with nickel-phosphorus pallet lever and escape wheel (LIGA process); single mainspring barrel; COSC-certified chronometer; 70-hour power reserve
Functions: hours, minutes, sweep seconds; date and weekday
Diameter: 29.1 mm
Height: 5.4 mm
Jewels: 31
Balance: glucydur with Microstella regulating bolts
Frequency: 28,800 vph
Hairspring: Parachrom Breguet hairspring
Shock protection: Paraflex
Remarks: used in Day-Date 40 and Day-Date 36

Caliber 4131

Automatic; optimized Chronergy escapement with nickel-phosphorus pallet lever and escape wheel (LIGA process); single mainspring barrel; COSC-certified chronometer; 72-hour power reserve
Functions: hours, minutes, subsidiary seconds; chronograph
Diameter: 30.5 mm
Height: 6.5 mm
Jewels: 44
Balance: glucydur with Microstella regulating bolts
Frequency: 28,800 vph
Hairspring: Parachrom Breguet hairspring
Shock protection: Paraflex
Remarks: used in Daytona

Caliber 4161

Automatic; single mainspring barrel; COSC-certified chronometer; 72-hour power reserve
Basis: Caliber 4130
Functions: hours, minutes, subsidiary seconds; programmable regatta countdown with memory
Diameter: 31.2 mm
Height: 8.05 mm
Jewels: 42
Balance: glucydur with Microstella regulating bolts
Frequency: 28,800 vph
Hairspring: Parachrom Breguet hairspring
Shock protection: Kif
Remarks: used in Yacht-Master II

Caliber 7135

Automatic; Dynapulse escapement; impulse rocker, silicon escape wheel and transmission wheel; ceramic balance staff; single mainspring barrel; 66-hour power reserve; COSC-certified chronometer
Functions: hours, minutes, sweep seconds; date
Diameter: 28.5 mm
Height: 4.05 mm
Jewels: 39
Balance: brass with Microstella regulating screws
Frequency: 36,000 vph
Hairspring: Syloxi hairspring
Shock protection: Paraflex
Remarks: used in the Land-Dweller

Caliber 9002

Automatic; optimized Chronergy escapement with nickel-phosphorus pallet lever and escape wheel (LIGA process); single mainspring barrel; COSC-certified chronometer; 72-hour power reserve
Functions: hours, minutes, sweep seconds; additional 24-hour display (second time zone); annual calendar with date and month
Diameter: 33 mm
Height: 8 mm
Jewels: 40
Balance: glucydur with Microstella regulating bolts
Frequency: 28,800 vph
Hairspring: Parachrom Breguet hairspring
Shock protection: Kif
Remarks: used in Sky-Dweller

SCHWARZ ETIENNE

Raffaello Radicchi, originally from Perugia, Italy, was a genuine maverick, a lone figure in the somewhat hermetic watch industry. He arrived in Switzerland at the age of eighteen and began working as a mason. Later, he retrained as a carpenter and started buying and renovating houses; before long, he was earning significant money. In the early 2000s, an acquaintance who had acquired a watch brand in La Chaux-de-Fonds suggested that Radicchi purchase the building that came with it. The brand, once a big name and a supplier of movements to companies like Chanel, had originally been founded by Paul Schwarz and Olga Etienne.

By 2008, Radicchi owned the entire operation. Recognizing that independence was essential for survival, Schwarz Etienne set out to produce its own calibers—and by 2015, it had three. These movements now power the brand's watches, including a tourbillon. Classic in appearance yet strikingly modern in engineering, they feature an inverted construction that places the off-centered microrotor on the dial side. Recently, these calibers have also begun appearing in the watches of other independent brands, notably Ming.

The company's collections can be divided between the playfully inventive and the traditional. A youthful sense of creativity—full of daring humor rarely found in watchmaking—animates the Roswell, whose case resembles a comic-book UFO. Meanwhile, despite its classical layout, the Roma collection often features dials with subtly asymmetrical arrangements. The Geometry series, designed by one of the industry's foremost creatives, Eric Giroud, displays a dial divided into four quadrants with contrasting finishes.

Every watchmaker eventually celebrates its origins, and in 2025 Schwarz Etienne did just that with a new collection aptly named the 1902. Elegant and timeless in a 10.9-millimeter case, the model comes either with a seconds subdial at six o'clock or with an added power-reserve indicator at 1:30, a vital reminder to rewind the manual movement, which features twin barrels and a five-day power reserve.

SCHWARZ ETIENNE SA
Boulevard des Éplatures 16
2300 La Chaux-de-Fonds
Switzerland

TEL.:
+41-32-967-9420

E-MAIL:
info@schwarz-etienne.ch

WEBSITE:
www.schwarz-etienne.ch

FOUNDED:
1902

NUMBER OF EMPLOYEES:
22

ANNUAL PRODUCTION:
300 to 500

DISTRIBUTION:
Contact company for information.
Retailers in the USA
Esperluxe – Boston MA
Exquisite Timepieces – Naples FL
Goldsmith Complications – Delray FL
Kaufmann de Suisse – Montreal
Manfredi Jewels – Greenwich CT
Oster Jewelers – Denver CO
Rostovsky Watches – Beverly Hills CA

MOST IMPORTANT COLLECTIONS:
1902, La Chaux-de-Fonds, Fiji, Geometry, Roma, Roswell, special edition

1902 Petite Seconde
Reference number: WCL39PSAS16TICUARD
Movement: automatic, Schwarz Etienne Caliber ASE 300.; ø 30.4 mm, height 5.35 mm; 29 jewels; 21,600 vph; finely finished movement with concentric côtes de Genève, engraved bridges, diamond drops on the micro-rotor; 86-hour power reserve
Functions: hours, minutes, subsidiary seconds (hacking)
Case: titanium, ø 39 mm, height 10.9 mm; sapphire crystal; transparent case back; water-resistant to 5 atm
Band: reptile skin and rubber, pin buckle
Price: $21,900
Variations: various color dials and cases

1902 Réserve de Marche
Reference number: WCL39PSAS16TICUARD
Movement: manual wound, Schwarz Etienne Caliber MSE 311.00; ø 30.4 mm, height 5.35 mm; 35 jewels; 21,600 vph; two spring barrels; finely finished movement with concentric côtes de Genève, engraved bridges, diamond drops on the micro-rotor and ratchet wheels; 120-hour power reserve
Functions: hours, minutes, subsidiary seconds (hacking); power reserve indicator
Case: titanium, ø 39 mm, height 10.9 mm; sapphire crystal; transparent case back; water-resistant to 5 atm
Band: reptile skin and rubber, pin buckle
Price: $21,900
Variations: various color dials and cases

Geometry Black
Reference number: WROGEOMA01SSVEBCLTD
Movement: automatic, Schwarz Etienne Caliber ASE 200.02 with micro-rotor with black PVD; ø 30.4 mm, height 5.35 mm; 33 jewels; 21,600 vph; finely finished movement; mainplate with black PVD; 86-hour power reserve
Functions: hours, minutes, subsidiary seconds
Case: stainless steel, ø 39 mm, height 11 mm; sapphire crystal; water-resistant to 5 atm
Band: leather (aged), folding clasp
Remarks: dial made of gold with black coating with azuré, clous de Paris, fluted, and sandblasted sections
Price: $29,780; limited to 50 pieces
Variations: grey and blue dial

SEIKO

Seiko is among the great enterprises dominating the universe of watches, and it has reached that spot by what business people call innovation, i.e, by keeping a hand on the pulse of the zeitgeist and producing quality. Founder Kintaro Hattori had it right when he distilled his strategy into a single phrase: "Always be one step ahead of the others." Accordingly, Seiko's history is dotted with major milestones. There is the first quartz wristwatch in 1969 and the market launch of the "Spring Drive" technology in 1999. The robust sports watches in the Prospex collection, which Seiko offers in many variations, have always enjoyed great popularity, delighting more than sports fans with their precision and reliability.

Key to the quality is in-house production of everything, from caliber development to the production of parts and the assembly of all components. Seiko diving watches have now been around for almost 60 years and have evolved from the first titanium case for diving to the invention of the "accordion" bracelet and the single-shell construction of the case with shock protection. The company introduced many important innovations and actively contributed to the German Industrial Norm (DIN) standard for diving watches.

Seiko's philosophy mixing traditional craftsmanship with Japan's outstanding industrial expertise in the manufacture of mechanical watches is reflected in the five main collections that have made the company a household name worldwide. The Astron series embodies cutting-edge technology and futuristic design, while Prospex offers robust timepieces built for extreme challenges on water, land, and in the air. With Presage, Seiko expresses the Japanese sense of beauty and craftsmanship, while King Seiko pays homage to precision watchmaking and refined design. The 5 Sports series, meanwhile, appeals to a younger, urban generation and adapts perfectly to today's diverse world with its tagline "Show your Style." Today, over a century after its founding, Seiko remains one of the world's leading watch brands.

SEIKO HOLDINGS
Ginza, Chuo, Tokyo
Japan

WEBSITE:
www.seikowatches.com

FOUNDED:
1881

U.S. DISTRIBUTOR:
Seiko Watch of America LLC
2 Park Way Suite 2A
Upper Saddle River, NJ 07458
201-529-5730
custserv@seikousa.com
www.seikousa.com

MOST IMPORTANT COLLECTIONS/PRICE RANGE:
Astron / approx. $1,850 to $3,400; Presage / approx. $425 to $4,500; Prospex / approx. $395 to $6,000

Prospex 1968 Heritage Automatic GMT Diver's
Reference number: SPB519J1
Movement: automatic, Seiko Caliber 6R54; ø 27.4 mm, height 5.3 mm; 24 jewels; 21,600 vph; 72-hour power reserve
Functions: hours, minutes, sweep seconds; additional 24-hour display (second time zone); date
Case: stainless steel (with hard coating), ø 42 mm, height 13.3 mm; unidirectional bezel with ceramic insert with 0-60 scale; sapphire crystal; screw-down crown; water-resistant to 30 atm
Band: stainless steel (with hard coating), folding clasp, with safety lock, with fine adjustment
Price: $1,700

King Seiko VANAC
Reference number: SLA083J1
Movement: automatic, Seiko Caliber 8L45; ø 28.4 mm, height 6 mm; 35 jewels; 28,800 vph; 72-hour power reserve
Functions: hours, minutes, sweep seconds; date
Case: stainless steel, ø 41 mm, height 14.3 mm; sapphire crystal; transparent case back; water-resistant to 10 atm
Band: stainless steel, double folding clasp
Price: $3,300

Presage Classic
Reference number: SPB524J1
Movement: automatic, Seiko Caliber 6R51; ø 27.4 mm, height 4.95 mm; 24 jewels; 21,600 vph; 72-hour power reserve
Functions: hours, minutes, sweep seconds
Case: stainless steel with yellow-gold PVD, ø 36 mm, height 13 mm; sapphire crystal; transparent case back; water-resistant to 10 atm
Band: stainless steel with yellow-gold PVD, double folding clasp
Price: $1,000

Prospex 1965 Heritage Diver's PADI Special Edition

Reference number: SPB501J1
Movement: automatic, Seiko Caliber 6R55; ø 27.4 mm, height 4.95 mm; 24 jewels; 21,600 vph; 72-hour power reserve
Functions: hours, minutes, sweep seconds; date
Case: stainless steel (with hard coating), ø 40 mm, height 13 mm; unidirectional bezel, with 0-60 scale; sapphire crystal; screw-down crown; water-resistant to 30 atm
Band: stainless steel (with hard coating), folding clasp, with safety lock, with extension link
Price: $1,550

Presage Classic Unglazed Arita Porcelain

Reference number: SPB497J1
Movement: automatic, Seiko Caliber 6R51; ø 27.4 mm, height 4.95 mm; 24 jewels; 21,600 vph; 72-hour power reserve
Functions: hours, minutes, sweep seconds
Case: stainless steel, ø 40.6 mm, height 12.5 mm; sapphire crystal; transparent case back; water-resistant to 10 atm
Band: leather, folding clasp
Remarks: unglazed porcelain dial
Price: $1,850; limited to 1200 pieces

Seiko Prospex Speedtimer Mechanical Chronograph

Reference number: SRQ055J1
Movement: automatic, Seiko Caliber 8R48; ø 28.6 mm, height 7.5 mm; 34 jewels; 28,800 vph; 45-hour power reserve
Functions: hours, minutes, small seconds; chronograph; date
Case: stainless steel (with hard coating), ø 42 mm, height 14.6 mm; sapphire crystal; water-resistant to 10 atm
Band: stainless steel (with hard coating), folding clasp
Price: $2,500
Variations: with white dial

Presage Cocktail Time

Reference number: SRPL64J1
Movement: automatic, Seiko Caliber 4R35; ø 27.4 mm, height 4.67 mm; 24 jewels; 21,600 vph; 41-hour power reserve
Functions: hours, minutes, sweep seconds; date
Case: stainless steel, ø 34 mm, height 10.7 mm; bezel with yellow-gold PVD; acrylic glass; water-resistant to 5 atm
Band: stainless steel with yellow gold-plated middle links, double folding clasp
Remarks: dial set with 4 diamonds
Price: $595

Astron GPS Solar Dual Time Chronograph

Reference number: SSH175J1
Movement: quartz, Seiko Caliber 5X83; self-generated power through solar cell in the dial
Functions: hours, minutes, sweep seconds; second time zone, world time display, flight mode; chronograph; perpetual calendar with date
Case: titanium (hard-coated), diameter 44 mm, height 14.4 mm; bezel with sapphire crystal insert; sapphire crystal; water-resistant to 10 atm
Band: titanium (hard-coated), folding clasp with fine adjustment
Price: $3,100

Seiko 5 Sports SKX Series

Reference number: SRPL85K1
Movement: automatic, Seiko Caliber 4R36; ø 27.4 mm, height 5.32 mm; 24 jewels; 21,600 vph; antimagnetic to 4800 A/m; 41-hour power reserve
Functions: hours, minutes, sweep seconds; date and weekday
Case: stainless steel, ø 42.5 mm, height 13.9 mm; unidirectional bezel, with 0-60 scale; acrylic glass; transparent case back; screw-down crown; water-resistant to 10 atm
Band: stainless steel, folding clasp, with safety lock
Price: $450
Variations: various dial and bezel colors

SHANGHAI WATCH

One of China's most popular brands of watches bears the name of the country's most cosmopolitan-chic city, Shanghai, and is also one of the oldest in the country. The history of Shanghai Watch goes back to 1955.

The People's Republic of China was established in December 1949 after 22 years of war with itself and Japan. Much had changed since the end of the Qing Dynasty in 1911, except for the envisioned necessities of the population, the so-called "Three Great Things," a sewing machine, a bicycle, and a watch. The latter was especially important to run a country efficiently, be that in the military, transportation, or industrial sectors. In 1955, in a bid to end foreign dependence on watches and create a domestic industry, the government launched a competition amongst Chinese cities to start a native watch industry. Teams of watchmakers gathered about and went to work. Tianjin (now Sea-Gull) actually came first, but Shanghai took a little more time and retro-engineered a Swiss movement using Japanese and Soviet parts. Their watch, the A581, went on to become an icon: simple, functional, and quite elegant. It launched production in 1955.

The Shanghai Watch factory, a stylized image of which is used for the logo, is still manufacturing to this day in its original historic building. The design of its first watch has been upgraded to suit more modern tastes, but the functional look is still dominant. Today, they use Swiss or Chinese calibers and have even come out with an in-house movement.

To celebrate its 70th anniversary in 2025, Shanghai Watch has issued a number of special editions celebrating itself and its native city. It released a number of its first horological triumphs, like the A581 and the Commander's Watch, its first diver's built in the 1960s. The Sound of the Bund pays tribute to the clocktower of the famous Customs House in the Bund section of the city along the Huangpu River. And finally, the Artistic collection explores Chinese culture and handcrafts, like Su Xiu embroidery, an ancient technique that uses split silk threads to create images that almost look painted.

SHANGHAI WATCHES COMPANY LTD
201, Yulin Rd.
Yangpu District
Shanghai
China

TEL.:
+86-400-821-6812

E-MAIL:
bd.shby@shwatch.cn

WEBSITE:
https://www.shwatch.cn

DATE FOUNDED:
1955

U.S. DISTRIBUTOR/RETAIL STRUCTURE:
Contact the company for information.

MOST IMPORTANT COLLECTIONS/PRICE RANGE:
Originate, Metropolitan, Artistic / $500 to $14,500

Sound of the Bund
Reference number: S1005.1411.021.08
Movement: automatic, Sellita SW300 caliber; ø 25.6 mm, height 4.6 mm; 25 jewels; 28,800 vph; hacking seconds; 56-hour power reserve
Functions: hours, minutes
Case: stainless steel with gold PVD, ø 40 mm, height 10.45 mm; sapphire crystal; 70th anniversary signature on case back; screw-in crown; water-resistant to 5 atm
Band: reptile skin, pin buckle
Remarks: engraved gold custom house in the Shanghai Bund, with silver boats and with coral flag and black mother-of-pearl for the Huangpu river
Price: $3,300; limited to 700 pieces
Variations: comes with white mother-of-pearl

Commander's Watch –Blue
Reference number: S5200.1807.014.08
Movement: automatic, Sea-Gull caliber ST2130, ø 26 mm, height 4.8 mm; 28 jewels; 28,800 vph; 42-hour power reserve
Functions: hours, minutes, hacking sweep seconds; date
Case: stainless steel, 39 mm, height 10.95 mm; unidirectional bezel with blue ceramic insert and SuperLumiNova; sapphire crystal; screw-down crown; water-resistant to 30 atm
Band: stainless steel, folding clasp,
Remarks: replica of the first Shanghai diver's watch, the Model 114; comes with extra canvas strap
Price: $869
Variations: comes in various colors; bimetal bracelet or rubber strap

Magnolia Embroidery Watch
Reference number: S2600.1643.061.19
Movement: automatic, Sea-Gull caliber ST1812, ø 26.2 mm, height 3.91 mm; 28 jewels; 28,800 vph; 42-hour power reserve
Functions: hours, minutes
Case: stainless steel, 36 mm, height 9.8 mm; bezel set with cubic zirconium; sapphire crystal; transparent; water-resistant to 5 atm
Band: leather, pin buckle
Remarks: "suzho" embroidery for magnolia flowers on silk; pankou (frog) fastening of the strap;
Price: $999
Variations: with red-tinted magnolias; with gold PVD on case ($1,199)

SINN

Pilot and flight instructor Helmut Sinn began manufacturing watches in Frankfurt am Main because he thought the pilot's watches on the market were too expensive. The resulting combination of top quality, functionality, and a good price-performance ratio turned out to be an excellent sales argument. There is hardly another source that offers watch lovers such a sophisticated and reasonable collection of sporty watches, many conceived to survive in extreme conditions by conforming to German DIN industrial norms.

The company remains in Frankfurt (in the Sossenheim district), where its headquarters and manufacturing space are in a two-story building that is the pride of the brand. In 1994, Lothar Schmidt took over leadership, and his product developers began looking for inspiration in other industries and the sciences.

Special Sinn technology includes dehumidifying cases by pumping in an inert gas such as argon. Other Sinn innovations include the Diapal (a lubricant-free lever escapement), the Hydro (an oil-filled diver's watch), and tegiment processing (for hardened steel and titanium surfaces). The latest innovation is a patent-pending alloy of bronze with a sixth of gold mixed in, goldbronze 125.

Having noticed a lack of norms for aviator watches, Schmidt negotiated a partnership with the Aachen Technical University to create the *Technischer Standard Fliegeruhren* (TESTAF, or Technical Standard for Pilot's Watches), which is housed at the Eurocopter headquarters.

Sinn also joined forces with two German watch companies, the Sächsische Uhrentechnologie Glashütte (SUG) and the Uhren-Werke-Dresden (UWD). The latter produced the outstanding UWD 33.1 caliber with Sinn as chaperone.

In recognition of his entrepreneurial responsibility and with the wish to secure his life's work, Lothar Schmidt founded the UWE Foundation in 2024. Its purpose is succession planning in order to preserve the company as a unified whole. Schmidt chose the name "UWE" after his son, who, due to illness, is unable to take over the family legacy. Several of the foundation's objectives also align with those of UNESCO, whose mission is to preserve the world's natural and cultural heritage for future generations.

SINN SPEZIALUHREN GMBH
Wilhelm-Fay-Strasse 21
D-65936 Frankfurt/Main
Germany

TEL.:
+49-69-9784-14-200

E-MAIL:
info@sinn.de

WEBSITE:
www.sinn.de

FOUNDED:
1961

NUMBER OF EMPLOYEES:
approx. 135 (at the Frankfurt location)

ANNUAL PRODUCTION:
approx. 14,000 watches

U.S. DISTRIBUTOR:
WatchBuys
888-333-4895
www.watchbuys.com

MOST IMPORTANT COLLECTIONS/PRICE RANGE:
Financial District, U-Models, Diapal / from approx. $1,500 to $17,000

U16

Reference number: 1026.010
Movement: automatic, Sellita Caliber SW200-1; ø 25.6 mm, height 4.6 mm; 26 jewels; 28,800 vph; antimagnetic according to DIN standard; 42-hour power reserve
Functions: hours, minutes, sweep seconds, date
Case: submarine steel, ø 44 mm, height 14.7 mm; unidirectional bezel with 0–60 scale; sapphire crystal; screw-down crown; water-resistant to 500 atm
Band: stainless steel, folding clasp with fine adjustment
Remarks: submarine steel sourced from the decommissioned German Navy submarine U16
Price: $3,840; limited to 1,000 pieces

T50 Goldbronze B

Reference number: 1052.020
Movement: automatic, Sellita Caliber SW300-1; ø 25.6 mm, height 3.6 mm; 25 jewels; 28,800 vph; antimagnetic according to DIN standard; 42-hour power reserve
Functions: hours, minutes, sweep seconds, date
Case: goldbronze, ø 41 mm, height 12.3 mm; unidirectional bezel in goldbronze with 0–60 scale; sapphire crystal; screw-down crown; water-resistant to 50 atm
Band: textile strap, pin buckle
Remarks: dehumidifying technology (protective gas filling)
Price: $6,380
Variations: in titanium ($4,330); in titanium with bezel in goldbronze ($4,780)

T50

Reference number: 1052.010
Movement: automatic, Sellita Caliber SW300-1; ø 25.6 mm, height 3.6 mm; 25 jewels; 28,800 vph; 42-hour power reserve
Functions: hours, minutes, sweep seconds, date
Case: bead-blasted titanium, ø 41 mm, height 12.3 mm; unidirectional bezel with 0–60 scale; sapphire crystal; screw-down crown; water-resistant to 50 atm
Band: textile strap, pin buckle
Remarks: dehumidifying technology (protective gas filling)
Price: $4,280
Variations: with bezel in goldbronze ($5,260); in goldbronze (€ 4,980)

613 St

Reference number: 613.012
Movement: automatic, Sellita Caliber 515; ø 30 mm, height 7.9 mm; 23 jewels; 28,800 vph; antimagnetic according to DIN standard; 42-hour power reserve
Functions: hours, minutes, subsidiary seconds; chronograph; date, weekday
Case: stainless steel, ø 41 mm, height 15 mm; bidirectional bezel with 0–60 scale; sapphire crystal; screw-down crown; water-resistant to 50 atm
Band: silicone strap, pin buckle
Remarks: dehumidifying technology (protective gas filling)
Price: $3,090
Variations: as 613 St UTC with second time zone ($3,750)

U50 Hydro S

Reference number: 1051.020
Movement: quartz
Functions: hours, minutes, sweep seconds, date
Case: tegimented submarine steel with black hard material finish, ø 41 mm, height 11.8 mm; unidirectional bezel with 0–60 scale; sapphire crystal; screw-down crown; water-resistant to 500 atm
Band: silicone strap, folding clasp with safety lock
Remarks: case completely oil-filled, virtually unlimited pressure resistance; certified according to European diving equipment standard
Price: $4,080
Variations: in submarine steel without black hard material finish ($3,470); in submarine steel with black bezel ($3,250)

156.1

Reference number: 156.030
Movement: automatic, Sinn Caliber SZ01 (base Concepto C99001); ø 30.4 mm, height 7.9 mm; 28 jewels; 28,800 vph; central minute counter; antimagnetic; finely finished movement; 46-hour power reserve
Functions: hours, minutes, subsidiary seconds; chronograph; date
Case: stainless steel, ø 43 mm, height 15.45 mm; bidirectional bezel with black hard material finish and 0–60 scale; sapphire crystal; screw-down crown; water-resistant to 10 atm
Band: leather strap, folding clasp with extension link
Remarks: dehumidifying technology (protective gas filling)
Price: $5,050

356 Flieger Klassik AS E

Reference number: 356.0202
Movement: automatic, Sellita Caliber SW510; ø 30.4 mm, height 7.9 mm; 27 jewels; 28,800 vph; antimagnetic according to DIN standard; 56-hour power reserve
Functions: hours, minutes, subsidiary seconds; chronograph
Case: stainless steel, ø 38.5 mm, height 15.6 mm; acrylic crystal; screw-down crown; water-resistant to 10 atm
Band: leather strap, pin buckle
Price: $3,130
Variations: as Flieger Klassik W with white dial

903 St II

Reference number: 903.090
Movement: automatic, La Joux-Perret Caliber L110; ø 30.4 mm, height 7.9 mm; 26 jewels; 28,800 vph; column-wheel chronograph control; antimagnetic according to DIN standard; 60-hour power reserve
Functions: hours, minutes, subsidiary seconds; chronograph; date
Case: stainless steel, ø 41 mm, height 14.5 mm; bidirectional bezel with integrated slide rule and tachymeter scale; sapphire crystal; transparent case back; screw-down crown; water-resistant to 20 atm
Band: stainless steel, folding clasp
Price: $4,680
Variations: as 903 St B E II with dark blue dial

910 SRS

Reference number: 910.020
Movement: automatic, ETA Caliber 7750 (modified); ø 30 mm, height 8.4 mm; 25 jewels; 28,800 vph; column-wheel chronograph control; antimagnetic according to the German industrial norm (DIN); finely decorated movement; 46-hour power reserve
Functions: hours, minutes, subsidiary seconds; flyback chronograph; date
Case: stainless steel, ø 41.5 mm, height 15.5 mm; sapphire crystal; transparent case back; water-resistant to 10 atm
Band: horse leather, pin buckle
Price: $4,910

3006 Hunting Watch

Reference number: 3006.010
Movement: automatic, Concepto Caliber C99002; ø 30.4 mm, height 7.9 mm; 25 jewels; 28,800 vph; antimagnetic according to the German industrial norm (DIN); 46-hour power reserve
Functions: hours, minutes, subsidiary seconds, 24-hour display; chronograph; date, weekday, month, moon phase
Case: tegimented stainless steel, ø 44 mm, height 15.5 mm; sapphire crystal; transparent case back; screw-down crown; water-resistant to 20 atm
Band: leather, pin buckle
Remarks: dehumidifying technology (protective gas filling)
Price: $6,180

105 St Sa UTC W

Reference number: 105.021
Movement: automatic, Sellita Caliber SW330-2; ø 25.6 mm, height 4.1 mm; 25 jewels; 28,800 vph; antimagnetic according to the German industrial norm (DIN); 42-hour power reserve
Functions: hours, minutes, sweep seconds, 24-hour display (second time zone), date
Case: stainless steel, ø 41 mm, height 11.9 mm; bidirectional bezel with 24-hour scale; sapphire crystal; transparent case back; screw-down crown; water-resistant to 20 atm
Band: leather strap, pin buckle
Price: $2,350
Variations: with black dial

556 A RS

Reference number: 556.0141
Movement: automatic, Sellita Caliber SW200-1; ø 25.6 mm, height 4.6 mm; 26 jewels; 28,800 vph; antimagnetic according to the German industrial norm (DIN); 38-hour power reserve
Functions: hours, minutes, sweep seconds, date
Case: stainless steel, ø 38.5 mm, height 11 mm; sapphire crystal; transparent case back; screw-down crown; water-resistant to 20 atm
Band: stainless steel, folding clasp with safety lock
Price: $1,970
Variations: with index dial ($2,170); with mother-of-pearl dial ($2,260)

1739 Römerberg

Reference number: 1739.015
Movement: automatic, Sellita Caliber SW300-1; ø 25.6 mm, height 3.6 mm; 25 jewels; 28,800 vph; antimagnetic according to the German industrial norm (DIN); 42-hour power reserve
Functions: hours, minutes
Case: stainless steel, ø 39 mm, height 9.1 mm; sapphire crystal; transparent case back; screw-down crown; water-resistant to 10 atm
Band: textile, pin buckle
Price: $2,760; limited to 100 pieces
Variations: various dial versions

6033 B

Reference number: 6033.011
Movement: automatic, Sellita Caliber SW300-1; ø 25.6 mm, height 3.6 mm; 25 jewels; 28,800 vph; antimagnetic according to the German industrial norm (DIN); 50-hour power reserve
Functions: hours, minutes, sweep seconds, date
Case: stainless steel, ø 34 mm, height 10.3 mm; crown-operated rotating scale ring with 0–12 scale; sapphire crystal; transparent case back; screw-down crown
Band: stainless steel, double folding clasp
Remarks: comes with additional leather strap
Price: $3,180

6099 Jubiläum

Reference number: 6099.012
Movement: automatic, Sinn Caliber (base La Joux-Perret L110); ø 30.4 mm, height 7.9 mm; 26 jewels; 28,800 vph; column-wheel chronograph control; antimagnetic according to the German industrial norm (DIN); 60-hour power reserve
Functions: hours, minutes, subsidiary seconds, 12-hour indicator (second time zone); chronograph; date
Case: stainless steel, ø 41.5 mm, height 14.5 mm; crown-operated rotating scale ring with 0–12 scale; sapphire crystal; transparent case back; water-resistant to 10 atm
Band: stainless steel, folding clasp
Remarks: rotor engraving depicting the Frankfurt skyline
Price: $5,980; limited to 250 pieces
Variations: with black dial

SPEAKE MARIN

So many brands these days bear the name of great watchmakers from the distant past. Speake Marin is an exception, because founder Peter Speake-Marin is very much alive but is no longer connected with his company, other than through his name and style.

This dyed-in-the-wool independent from Essex, England moved to Le Locle, Switzerland, in 1996 to work with Renaud et Papi, at which point he set about making his own pieces. A dual-train tourbillon (the Foundation Watch) opened the door to the prestigious A.H.C.I.

Speake-Marin's watches have a strong connection to the industry's traditions. The topping tool logo suggests the expert handicraft that goes into making a watch, rather than hyper-modern CNC machines. He has also had his skilled fingers in a number of iconic timepieces, like the HM1 of MB&F, the Chapter One for Maîtres du Temps, and the Harry Winston Excenter Tourbillon.

The baton was passed to Christelle Rosnoblet in 2012—and then with more finality in 2017 when Peter Speake-Marin decided to step out completely. She had the delicate task of keeping the old fans happy, while letting the brand take on a more distinct identity. The "old bottles," one might say are elements like the small seconds dial at 1:30—which is clearly exhibited on the new Resolute—and which gives space to a retrograde date on the One & Two tourbillon collection. There is, too, the conical crown and the famous Piccadilly case, now remodeled. By the same token, the modernizations are hardly subtle. The company makes sure it is working with experienced partners, like the Cercle des Horlogers platform and industry stars like Eric Giroud. The Ripples dials, with their deep, lacquered engravings, show what happens when a strong wind begins blowing on traditional côtes de Genève.

The Ripples collection has been an excellent canvas for creative iterations. The dial lends itself to colors, some bold like minty greens or a very Mediterranean terracotta. It can also be openworked to show a skeletonized movement.

SPEAKE MARIN
Avenue de Miremont 33C
1206 Geneva
Switzerland

TEL.:
+41 21 695 26 55

E-MAIL:
info@speake-marin.com

WEBSITE:
www.speake-marin.com

FOUNDED:
2002

NUMBER OF EMPLOYEES:
9
Annual production:
400 watches

U.S. SALES
Collective Horology
1070 East Front Street, Suite C
Ventura, California 93001
shop@collectivehorology.com
805-321-8877

MOST IMPORTANT COLLECTIONS:
Piccadilly, Ripples, Haute Horlogerie, Art Series

Resilience Gold
Reference number: 423802000
Movement: automatic, SMA03 Caliber; ø 30 mm, height 3.9 mm; 31 jewels; 28,800 vph; laser-engraved tungsten micro-rotor with; finely finished movement with perlage, côtes de Genève, and gold-plated engraving; 52-hour power reserve
Functions: hours, minutes, subsidiary seconds
Case: gold, ø 38 mm, height 10.05 mm; sapphire crystal; screw-down case back; water-resistant to 3 atm
Band: ostrich leather, pin buckle
Remarks: grand-feu enamel dial and blued-steel hands
Price: $34,990
Variations: in 38- and 42- millimeter titanium case

Openworked Tourbillon Purple Hour
Reference number: 913811570
Movement: automatic, SMA05 Caliber; ø 34 mm, height 7.15 mm; 33 jewels; 21,600 vph; openworked dial; finely decorated bridges and mainplate with côtes de Genève and perlage; laser-engraved tungsten micro-rotor; screw balance; tourbillon; 72-hour power reserve
Functions: hours, minutes, seconds on tourbillon cage at 1:30 o'clock; power reserve indicator at 7:30
Case: titanium, ø 38 mm, height 12.35 mm; sapphire crystal; transparent case back; water-resistant to 3 atm
Band: calfskin with denim pattern, pin buckle
Price: $80,200
Variations: in various color themes; available in 42-millimeter titanium case

Ripples Gold
Reference number: 604020150
Movement: automatic, SMA03-T caliber; ø 30 mm, height 3.9 mm; 31 jewels; 28,800 vph; laser-engraved tungsten micro-rotor with; finely finished movement with perlage, côtes de Genève, and gold-plated engraving; 52-hour power reserve
Functions: hours, minutes, subsidiary seconds at 1:30
Case: rose gold, ø 40.3 mm, height 9.2 mm; sapphire crystal; screw-mounted, transparent case back; screw-down crown; water-resistant to 5 atm
Band: calfskin with denim pattern, folding clasp
Price: $38,750

STOWA

When a watch brand organizes a museum for itself, it is usually with good reason. Stowa may not be the biggest fish in the horological pond, but it has been around since 1927, and its products are excellent illustrations of German watchmaking culture. Stowa was founded by Walter Storz—hence the name—in Pforzheim. After the war, with the premises destroyed, Storz opened a factory in Rheinfelden on the Swiss border. Later the company opened a second production facility in a suburb of Pforzheim, Engelsbrand, and in 2023, finally, moved back to Pforzheim itself.

Stowa is thus one of the few German brands to have operated without interruption since its start, albeit with a new owner as of 1996. It even managed to survive the quartz crisis of the 1970s, during which Europe was flooded with cheap watches from Asia and many traditional German watchmakers were put out of business. Storz managed to keep Stowa going, but even a quality fanatic has to pay a price during times of trouble; with huge input from his son, Werner, Storz restructured the company so that it was able to begin encasing reasonably priced quartz movements rather than being strictly an assembler of mechanical ones.

Another watchmaker, Jörg Schauer, took over the brand in 1996. Spurred on by the success of his own brand, he focused on mechanics from the very beginning. Collaboration with designer Hartmut Esslinger, the founder of Frog Design, resulted in a modern design language that is expressed above all in the Flieger collection. After twenty-five years, Jörg Schauer sold the Stowa watch brand to the Tempus Arte Group, which includes Lang & Heyne Dresden and the affiliated Uhren-Werke-Dresden (UWD) and Leinfelder Uhren in Munich. The group also holds a stake in customization specialist Blaken.

STOWA GMBH & CO. KG
Gewerbepark 16
D-75331 Engelsbrand
Germany

TEL.:
+49-7082-942630

E-MAIL:
info@stowa.com

WEBSITE:
www.stowa.com

FOUNDED:
1927

NUMBER OF EMPLOYEES:
20

ANNUAL PRODUCTION:
around 4,500 watches

DISTRIBUTION:
Direct sales; please contact the company in Germany during business hours
Note: Prices can vary due to fluctuations in the euro/dollar exchange rate

Flieger Original

Reference number: FliegerOriginal
Movement: hand-wound, Stowa Caliber M1 (base ETA 6498-1); ø 37.2 mm, height 5.9 mm; 18 jewels; 18,000 vph; 46-hour power reserve
Functions: hours, minutes, sweep seconds
Case: stainless steel, ø 42 mm, height 13.5 mm; sapphire crystal; transparent case back; water-resistant to 10 atm
Band: leather, pin buckle
Price: $3,450
Variations: with stainless steel Milanese bracelet

Flieger Klassik 40

Reference number: FliegerKlassik40
Movement: automatic, Sellita Caliber SW200-1; ø 25.6 mm, height 4.6 mm; 26 jewels; 28,800 vph; 38-hour power reserve
Functions: hours, minutes, sweep seconds
Case: stainless steel, ø 40 mm, height 10.2 mm; sapphire crystal; transparent case back; water-resistant to 5 atm
Band: leather, pin buckle
Price: $1,450
Variations: with hand-wound movement ($1,475); with date display

Flieger Bronze Vintage Baumuster "B" 40

Reference number: FliegerBronzeVintageBauB40
Movement: automatic, Sellita Caliber SW200-1; ø 25.6 mm, height 4.6 mm; 26 jewels; 28,800 vph; 38-hour power reserve
Functions: hours, minutes, sweep seconds
Case: bronze, ø 40 mm, height 10.2 mm; sapphire crystal; transparent case back; water-resistant to 5 atm
Band: leather, pin buckle
Price: $1,700
Variations: with date display; with hand-wound movement ($1,725)

Flieger Verus Black Forest Lagoon

Reference number: FliegerVerusBFL
Movement: automatic, Sellita Caliber SW200-1; ø 25.6 mm, height 4.6 mm; 26 jewels; 28,800 vph; 38-hour power reserve
Functions: hours, minutes, sweep seconds
Case: stainless steel, ø 40 mm, height 10.2 mm; sapphire crystal; transparent case back; water-resistant to 5 atm
Band: leather, pin buckle
Price: $1,260
Variations: with date display; with decorated movement ($1,420); with hand-wound movement ($1,440)

Marine Klassik 40 Arabic

Reference number: MarineKlassik40arabisch
Movement: automatic, Sellita Caliber SW200-1; ø 25.6 mm, height 4.6 mm; 26 jewels; 28,800 vph; 38-hour power reserve
Functions: hours, minutes, sweep seconds
Case: stainless steel, ø 40 mm, height 10.2 mm; sapphire crystal; transparent case back; water-resistant to 5 atm
Band: leather, pin buckle
Price: $990
Variations: with date display; with movement in "top" quality ($1,010); with hand-wound movement ($1,150)

Marine Original Bronze Vintage Roman

Reference number: MarineOriginalBronzeVintage
Movement: hand-wound, ETA Caliber 6498-1; ø 37.2 mm, height 4.5 mm; 17 jewels; 18,000 vph; screw balance, swan-neck fine regulator, côtes de Genève, blued screws; 46-hour power reserve
Functions: hours, minutes, subsidiary seconds
Case: bronze, ø 41 mm, height 12.1 mm; sapphire crystal; transparent case back; water-resistant to 5 atm
Band: leather, pin buckle
Price: $2,080
Variations: with Arabic numerals

Antea Classic KS

Reference number: AnteaKlassikKS
Movement: hand-wound, ETA Caliber 7001; ø 23.8 mm, height 2.5 mm; 17 jewels; 21,600 vph; 38-hour power reserve
Functions: hours, minutes, subsidiary seconds
Case: stainless steel, ø 35.5 mm, height 6.9 mm; sapphire crystal; transparent case back; water-resistant to 3 atm
Band: leather, pin buckle
Price: $1,400
Variations: with stainless steel Milanese bracelet ($1,475)

Partitio Classic Black

Reference number: PartitioKlassikschwarz
Movement: automatic, Sellita Caliber SW200-1; ø 25.6 mm, height 4.6 mm; 26 jewels; 28,800 vph; 38-hour power reserve
Functions: hours, minutes, sweep seconds
Case: stainless steel, ø 37 mm, height 10.9 mm; sapphire crystal; water-resistant to 5 atm
Band: leather, pin buckle
Price: $1,035
Variations: with hand-wound movement ($1,220)

Prodiver Black Green Ceramic

Movement: automatic, Sellita Caliber SW200-1; ø 25.6 mm, height 4.6 mm; 26 jewels; 28,800 vph; 38-hour power reserve
Functions: hours, minutes, sweep seconds, date
Case: titanium, ø 42 mm, height 15.6 mm; unidirectional bezel with ceramic insert and 0–60 scale; sapphire crystal; screw-down crown; water-resistant to 100 atm
Band: rubber, folding clasp with safety lock
Price: $2,075

TAG HEUER

Measuring speed accurately in ever greater detail was always the goal of TAG Heuer, a company founded in 1860 in St. Imier, Switzerland, by Edouard Heuer. With this in mind, the brand strove for a number of technical milestones, including the first automatic chronograph caliber with a microrotor, created in 1969 with Hamilton-Büren, Breitling, and Dubois Dépraz. That was before Techniques d'Avant Garde (TAG), a high-tech firm, bought the company.

In 1999, TAG Heuer became part of LVMH Group and in addition to producing its own watches also later served as an extended workbench for companion brands Zenith and Hublot.

TAG Heuer has continued to break world speed records for mechanical escapements. For example, the Caliber 360 combined a standard movement with a 360,000-vph (50-Hz) chronograph mechanism able to measure hundredths of a second. And then there is the MikrotourbillonS, which features a separate chronograph escapement driven at a breakneck 360,000 vph.

TAG Heuer, now under CEO Frédéric Arnault, son of LVMH owner Bernard Arnault, is evolving along several lines. One is to re-release Heuer classics in more modern garb. The Heuer 02 manufacture caliber, for example, is a redeveloped chronograph movement. Cooperations with motorsports players are a natural for TAG Heuer, notably in Formula 1 (with Red Bull Racing). It has resulted in a 3,000-piece limited edition of a "Formula 1 Chronograph x Oracle Red Bull Racing" model with black PVD on steel and running on a quartz movement.

In 2023, TAG Heuer redesigned the classic Carrera, adding a high-domed sapphire box crystal and double flange. It was the 60th anniversary of the hit model, which has again become a chronograph trendsetter.

The new Monaco Split-Seconds Chronograph developed in collaboration with movement manufacturer Vaucher in 2023, on the other hand, was a look to the future. Then, 2024 saw the debut of a new Monaco as a category of sports watch, which TAG Heuer intends to expand and cultivate in the coming years. The combination of *haute horlogerie* and sports watches has kept design departments on their toes, meeting a steep rise in customer demands. Head of Movement Development, Carole Forestier-Kasapi, has been working on optimizing her existing movements for some time now and consistently implements the requirements of this "new normal" in all new designs.

TAG HEUER
Branch of LVMH SA
6a, rue L.-J.-Chevrolet
CH-2300 La Chaux-de-Fonds
Switzerland

TEL.:
+41-32-919-8164

E-MAIL:
info@tagheuer.com

WEBSITE:
www.tagheuer.com

FOUNDED:
1860

NUMBER OF EMPLOYEES:
Around 2,000 internationally

ANNUAL PRODUCTION:
Est. 400,000

U.S. DISTRIBUTOR:
TAG Heuer/LVMH Watch & Jewelry USA
966 South Springfield Avenue
Springfield, NJ 07081
973-467-1890

MOST IMPORTANT COLLECTIONS/PRICE RANGE:
TAG Heuer Carrera, Monaco, Aquaracer, Formula 1, Connected, Autovia / from approx. $1,450 to $35,000

Carrera Chronograph
Reference number: CBN201N.FC6620
Movement: automatic, TAG Heuer Caliber TH20-00; ø 31 mm, height 6.9 mm; 33 jewels; 28,800 vph; 80-hour power reserve
Functions: hours, minutes, subsidiary seconds; chronograph; date
Case: stainless steel, ø 42 mm; sapphire crystal; transparent case back; water-resistant to 10 atm
Band: leather, folding clasp
Price: $7,450

Monaco Calibre 11
Reference number: CAW211P.FC6356
Movement: automatic, TAG Heuer Caliber 11 (base Sellita SW300 with Dubois Dépraz module 2006); ø 30 mm, height 7.3 mm; 59 jewels; 28,800 vph
Functions: hours, minutes, subsidiary seconds; chronograph; date
Case: stainless steel, 39 mm × 39 mm, height 14.5 mm; sapphire crystal; transparent case back; water-resistant to 10 atm
Band: leather, folding clasp
Price: $8,300

Monaco Chronograph
Reference number: CBL2180.FC6497
Movement: automatic, TAG Heuer Caliber TH20-00; ø 31 mm, height 6.9 mm; 33 jewels; 28,800 vph; 80-hour power reserve
Functions: hours, minutes, subsidiary seconds; chronograph; date
Case: titanium with black DLC, 39 mm × 39 mm, height 13.8 mm; sapphire crystal; transparent case back; water-resistant to 10 atm
Band: reptile skin, folding clasp
Price: $9,450

Carrera Day-Date

Reference number: WDA2112.BA0043
Movement: automatic, TAG Heuer Caliber TH31-02; 30 jewels; 28,800 vph; 80-hour power reserve
Functions: hours, minutes, sweep seconds; day and date
Case: stainless steel, ø 41 mm, height 12.7 mm; sapphire crystal; transparent case back; water-resistant to 10 atm
Band: stainless steel, folding clasp
Price: $4,300
Variations: various dial colors

Formula 1 Solargraph

Reference number: WBY1161.FT8086
Movement: quartz, TAG Heuer Caliber TH50-00
Functions: hours, minutes, sweep seconds; date
Case: TH-Polylight, ø 38 mm, height 9.9 mm; unidirectional bezel with 0–60 scale; sapphire crystal; stainless steel screw-down crown; water-resistant to 10 atm
Band: rubber, pin buckle
Remarks: powered by solar cell integrated into the dial
Price: $1,850

Aquaracer Professional 300 Date

Reference number: WBP5110.BA0013
Movement: automatic, TAG Heuer Caliber TH31-00 COSC; 30 jewels; 28,800 vph; skeletonized rotor; 80-hour power reserve; COSC-certified chronometer
Functions: hours, minutes, sweep seconds; date
Case: stainless steel, ø 42 mm, height 12 mm; unidirectional bezel with ceramic insert and 0–60 scale; sapphire crystal; screw-down crown; water-resistant to 30 atm
Band: stainless steel, folding clasp with fine adjustment
Price: $4,350

Aquaracer Professional 300 Date

Reference number: WBP5111.BA0013
Movement: automatic, TAG Heuer Caliber TH31-00 COSC; 30 jewels; 28,800 vph; skeletonized rotor; 80-hour power reserve; COSC-certified chronometer
Functions: hours, minutes, sweep seconds; date
Case: stainless steel, ø 42 mm, height 12 mm; unidirectional bezel with ceramic insert and 0–60 scale; sapphire crystal; screw-down crown; water-resistant to 30 atm
Band: stainless steel, folding clasp with fine adjustment
Price: $4,350

Carrera Chronograph

Reference number: CBS2216.BA0048
Movement: automatic, TAG Heuer Caliber TH20-00; ø 31 mm, height 6.9 mm; 33 jewels; 28,800 vph; 80-hour power reserve
Functions: hours, minutes, subsidiary seconds; chronograph; date
Case: stainless steel, ø 39 mm, height 13.9 mm; sapphire crystal; transparent case back; screw-down crown; water-resistant to 10 atm
Band: stainless steel, folding clasp
Price: $7,250

Formula 1 Solargraph

Reference number: WBY1111.BA0042
Movement: quartz, TAG Heuer Caliber TH50-00
Functions: hours, minutes, sweep seconds; date
Case: stainless steel, ø 38 mm, height 9.9 mm; unidirectional TH-Polylight bezel with 0–60 scale; sapphire crystal; screw-down crown; water-resistant to 10 atm
Band: stainless steel, folding clasp
Remarks: powered by solar cell integrated into the dial
Price: $1,950

Formula 1 Chronograph

Reference number: CBZ2085.FT8093
Movement: automatic, TAG Heuer Caliber 16 (base ETA 7750); ø 30.4 mm, height 7.9 mm; 25 jewels; 28,800 vph; 42-hour power reserve
Functions: hours, minutes, subsidiary seconds; chronograph; date
Case: titanium (sandblasted), ø 44 mm, height 14.5 mm; sapphire crystal; screw-down crown; water-resistant to 20 atm
Band: rubber, pin buckle
Price: $5,050
Variations: various dial and strap versions

Carrera Chronograph

Reference number: CBS2214.FC6567
Movement: automatic, TAG Heuer Caliber TH20-00; ø 31 mm, height 6.9 mm; 33 jewels; 28,800 vph; 80-hour power reserve
Functions: hours, minutes, subsidiary seconds; chronograph; date
Case: stainless steel, ø 39 mm, height 13.9 mm; bezel set with 72 diamonds; sapphire crystal; transparent case back; water-resistant to 10 atm
Band: reptile skin, folding clasp
Price: $8,950

Carrera Skipper

Reference number: CBS2213.FN6002
Movement: automatic, TAG Heuer Caliber TH20-06; ø 31 mm, height 6.9 mm; 33 jewels; 28,800 vph; 80-hour power reserve
Functions: hours, minutes, subsidiary seconds; chronograph; date
Case: stainless steel, ø 39 mm, height 13.9 mm; sapphire crystal; screw-down crown; transparent case back; water-resistant to 10 atm
Band: textile, folding clasp
Price: $7,250

Carrera Date

Reference number: WBN2350.BD0000
Movement: automatic, TAG Heuer Caliber 7 (base ETA 2893-2); ø 25.6 mm, height 4.1 mm; 21 jewels; 28,800 vph; 38-hour power reserve
Functions: hours, minutes, sweep seconds; date
Case: stainless steel, ø 36 mm, height 10.2 mm; rose-gold bezel; sapphire crystal; transparent case back; crown in rose gold; water-resistant to 5 atm
Band: stainless steel with rose-gold elements, folding clasp
Price: $7,750
Variations: various cases, bands, and dials

Carrera Date

Reference number: WBN2313.BA0001
Movement: automatic, TAG Heuer Caliber 7 (base ETA 2893-2); ø 25.6 mm, height 4.1 mm; 21 jewels; 28,800 vph; 38-hour power reserve
Functions: hours, minutes, sweep seconds; date
Case: stainless steel, ø 36 mm, height 10.2 mm; sapphire crystal; transparent case back; water-resistant to 5 atm
Band: stainless steel, folding clasp
Price: $3,550
Variations: various cases, bands, and dials

Carrera Date

Reference number: WBN2317.BA0001
Movement: automatic, TAG Heuer Caliber 7 (base ETA 2893-2); ø 25.6 mm, height 4.1 mm; 21 jewels; 28,800 vph; 38-hour power reserve
Functions: hours, minutes, sweep seconds; date
Case: stainless steel, ø 36 mm, height 10.2 mm; sapphire crystal; transparent case back; water-resistant to 5 atm
Band: stainless steel, folding clasp
Remarks: dial with 11 diamonds
Price: $4,600

TISSOT

There is Swiss-made, and then there is the Swiss Watch, as a kind of unobtrusive yet clearly defined icon you will see on many a Swiss wrist. That's a Tissot. The company was founded in 1853 in the town of Le Locle in the Jura mountains. In the century that followed, it gained international recognition for its Savonnette pocket watch. And even when the wristwatch became popular in the early twentieth century, time and again Tissot managed to attract attention to its products. To this day, the Banana Watch of 1916 and its first watches in the art deco style (1919) remain design icons of that epoch. The watchmaker has always been at the top of its technical game as well: the first antimagnetic watch (1930), the first mechanical plastic watch (Astrolon, 1971), and its touchscreen T-Touch (1999) all bear witness to Tissot's remarkable capacity for finding unusual and modern solutions.

Today, Tissot belongs to the Swatch Group and serves as the group's entry-level brand. The brand has been cultivating a sportive image of late, expanding into everything from basketball to superbike racing, from ice hockey to fencing—and water sports, of course. Partnerships with several NBA teams have been signed, notably with the Houston Rockets, Chicago Bulls, and Washington Wizards in October 2018. The chronograph Couturier line is outfitted with the new ETA chronograph caliber C01.211. This caliber features several plastic parts: another step in simplifying, and lowering the cost of, mechanical movements.

The revival of the Tissot PRX from the late seventies was a spectacular success for the brand three years ago. The PRX Powermatic exhibits the lines of the original launched in 1978, which is characterized by the stylistic unity of the watch case and bracelet and adapts them only slightly for the use of automatic movements instead of the then-fashionable (and thinner) quartz movements. The PRX Chronograph became the flagship of the new collection. The latest model (from 2025), the new PRC 100 Solar, was inspired from a 2005 model. The new watch features innovative Lightmaster solar tech from the company itself. The trick was to make microscopic transparent solar cells that can be placed under the sapphire crystal.

TISSOT SA
Chemin des Tourelles, 17
CH-2400 Le Locle
Switzerland

TEL.:
+41-32-933-3111

E-MAIL:
info@tissot.ch

WEBSITE:
www.tissotwatches.com

FOUNDED:
1853

U.S. DISTRIBUTOR:
Tissot
The Swatch Group (U.S.), Inc.
800 Waterford Way, Suite 1000
Miami, FL 33126
www.us.tissotshop.com

MOST IMPORTANT COLLECTION/PRICE RANGE
Ballade / from $925; T-Touch / from $850;
NBA Collection / from $375; PRX Powermatic,
PRC 100 Solar / from $575; Seastar / from $495;
Swissmatic / from $395

PRC 100 Solar Quartz 39 mm

Reference number: T151.422.11.031.00
Movement: quartz, dial with solar cell
Functions: hours, minutes, sweep seconds; date
Case: stainless steel, ø 39 mm, height 9.22 mm; sapphire crystal; water-resistant to 10 atm
Band: stainless steel, double folding clasp
Price: $575
Variations: various cases, bands, and dials

PRC 100 Solar Quartz 39 mm

Reference number: T151.422.11.041.00
Movement: quartz, dial with solar cell
Functions: hours, minutes, sweep seconds; date
Case: stainless steel, ø 39 mm, height 9.22 mm; sapphire crystal; water-resistant to 10 atm
Band: stainless steel, double folding clasp
Price: $575
Variations: various cases, bands, and dials

PRC 100 Solar Quartz 39 mm

Reference number: T151.422.33.051.00
Movement: quartz, dial with solar cell
Functions: hours, minutes, sweep seconds; date
Case: stainless steel with black PVD coating, ø 39 mm, height 9.22 mm; sapphire crystal; water-resistant to 10 atm
Band: stainless steel with black PVD coating, double folding clasp
Price: $625
Variations: various cases, bands, and dials

PRX Powermatic 80 Carbon

Reference number: T137.907.97.201.00
Movement: automatic, ETA caliber Powermatic 80 (base ETA 2824-2); ø 25.6 mm, height 4.74 mm; 23 jewels; 21,600 vph; 80-hour power reserve
Functions: hours, minutes, sweep seconds; date
Case: carbon fiber, ø 40 mm, height 11.23 mm; sapphire crystal; transparent case back; water-resistant to 10 atm
Band: silicone, pin buckle
Price: $1,150
Variations: various cases, bands, and dials

PRX Powermatic 80

Reference number: T137.407.33.041.00
Movement: automatic, ETA caliber Powermatic 80 (base ETA 2824-2); ø 25.6 mm, height 4.74 mm; 23 jewels; 21,600 vph; 80-hour power reserve
Functions: hours, minutes, sweep seconds; date
Case: stainless steel with rose-gold PVD coating, ø 39.5 mm, height 10.93 mm; sapphire crystal; transparent case back; water-resistant to 10 atm
Band: stainless steel with rose-gold PVD, double folding clasp
Price: $950
Variations: various cases, bands, and dials

PRX Automatic Chronograph

Reference number: T137.427.11.011.01
Movement: automatic, ETA caliber A05.231; ø 30 mm, height 7.9 mm; 27 jewels; 28,800 vph; 60-hour power reserve
Functions: hours, minutes, subsidiary seconds; chronograph; date
Case: stainless steel, ø 42 mm, height 14.54 mm; sapphire crystal; transparent case back; water-resistant to 10 atm
Band: stainless steel, double folding clasp
Price: $2,150
Variations: various dial colors

Gentleman Powermatic 80 Silicium

Reference number: T127.407.11.351.00
Movement: automatic, ETA caliber Powermatic 80 (base ETA 2824-2); ø 25.6 mm, height 4.74 mm; 25 jewels; 21,600 vph; silicon balance spring; 80-hour power reserve
Functions: hours, minutes, sweep seconds; date
Case: stainless steel, ø 40 mm, height 11.5 mm; sapphire crystal; transparent case back; water-resistant to 10 atm
Band: stainless steel, double folding clasp
Price: $950

PR516 Powermatic 80

Reference number: T149.407.11.051.00
Movement: automatic, ETA caliber Powermatic 80 (base ETA 2824-2); ø 25.6 mm, height 4.74 mm; 23 jewels; 21,600 vph; 80-hour power reserve
Functions: hours, minutes, sweep seconds; date
Case: stainless steel, ø 38 mm, height 11.18 mm; bezel with mineral glass inlay, unidirectional rotation, 60-minute scale; sapphire crystal; transparent case back; water-resistant to 10 atm
Band: stainless steel, double folding clasp
Price: $825

T-Race MotoGP 2025 Automatic Chronograph

Reference number: T141.462.27.041.00
Movement: automatic, ETA caliber C01.211; ø 30 mm, height 8.44 mm; 15 jewels; 21,600 vph; 68-hour power reserve
Functions: hours, minutes, subsidiary seconds; chronograph
Case: stainless steel, ø 45 mm, height 14.79 mm; bezel with black PVD; sapphire crystal; transparent case back; water-resistant to 10 atm
Band: silicone, pin buckle
Price: $2,175; limited edition of 2,025 pieces

TOURBY WATCHES

In an industry and a world that tries hard to attract attention at times by fairly spectacular means, Tourby Watches has been gathering a solid following and fan club, notably in the U.S.A., by keeping everything simple and elegant. The company, which is headquartered in the town of Wetter in Westphalia, Germany, manufactures mechanical wristwatches whose design is inspired by classic models. Among its famous pieces is a pilot's watch made especially for the dangerous deployments of the Strike Fighters Weapons School Pacific, a U.S. Navy training school for fighter pilots.

The story began when Erdal Yildiz inherited a pocket watch from his grandfather. The Unitas movement inside was in need of serious revision. So, he looked around for a proper watchmaker and was soon enamored with the craft itself. The world of mechanical watches became a genuine passion during his studies. He then contacted several suppliers in Germany and Switzerland, and in 2007 founded his own brand.

The name Tourby has nothing to do with tourbillons, which his company does not manufacture. Rather, it is Yildiz's nickname. It was short and memorable, and the domain name was still available!

All raw materials are purchased from top-notch suppliers in Germany and Switzerland. Some of the parts are ready to use on delivery; others need to be reworked in the company's own workshops in the cities of Bochum and Hagen. The cases are finished by hand, for example, as are the movements—all Swiss ETA calibers—which are extensively decorated, along with the dials, at least in part. The leather straps are stitched by hand. Final assembly, quality control, and after-sales service are all done by the company. Erdal Yildiz ensures that they are adjusted to chronometer precision (top grade).

Tourby Watches produces a wide range of models, from military style vintage to entire series, like the one featuring hand-painted continents. The customer can opt for made-to-order pieces, by choosing the case, dial, hands, strap, and even the movement with a special decoration on request or even skeletonization.

TOURBY WATCHES
Königstrasse 78
D-58300 Wetter an der Ruhr
Hagen in Westfalen
Germany

TEL:
+49 176 83118382

E-MAIL:
info@tourbywatches.com

WEBSITE:
www.tourbywatches.com

FOUNDED:
2007

NUMBER OF EMPLOYEES:
5

ANNUAL PRODUCTION:
500

DISTRIBUTION:
Tourby deals directly with customers

MOST IMPORTANT COLLECTIONS/PRICE RANGE:
America / $12,000; Lawless / from $1,400; Art Deco Classic / from $1,800; Marine / from $1,700; Planetarium / $9,000; special sets

Old Military Vintage

Reference number: 1403
Movement: hand-wound, ETA Caliber 6498-2; ø 37 mm, height 4.5 mm; 17 jewels; 21,600 vph; skeletonized movement, adjusted in 5 positions, côtes de Genève, double sunburst wheels, blued screws, blued swan-neck fine adjustment, 60-hour power reserve
Functions: hours, minutes, subsidiary seconds
Case: stainless steel, 45 mm, height 14.45 mm, sapphire crystal, transparent case back, water-resistant to 5 atm
Band: horse leather, pin buckle
Price: $3,350
Variations: comes in three sizes (40, 43, and 45 mm)

America

Reference number: 7002
Movement: hand-wound, ETA Caliber 6498-2; ø 37 mm, height 4.5 mm;17 jewels; 21,600 vph; skeletonized movement, adjusted in 5 positions, côtes de Genève, blued screws, 60-hour power reserve
Functions: hours, minutes
Case: stainless steel, 40.5 mm, height 10.6 mm, sapphire crystal, transparent case back, water-resistant to 5 atm
Band: reptile skin, pin buckle
Remarks: hand-painted dial
Price: $12,000
Variations: Asia, Australia, Arabia, Europe

Small Pilot Automatic Gradient

Reference number: 1351
Movement: automatic, LJP Caliber G-101; ø 25.6 mm, height 4.5 mm; 24 jewels; 28,800 vph; côtes de Genève, blued screws, 68-hour power reserve
Functions: hours, minutes, sweep seconds
Case: stainless steel, 37 mm, height 11 mm; sapphire crystal, transparent case back, water-resistant to 10 atm
Band: calf leather, pin buckle
Remarks: aged dial
Price: $1,600
Variations: black dial

Marine Automatic Enamel

Reference number: 2005
Movement: automatic, LJP Caliber G-101; ø 25.6 mm, height 4.5 mm; 24 jewels; 28,800 vph; côtes de Genève, blued screws, 68-hour power reserve
Functions: hours, minutes, sweep seconds
Case: stainless steel, 37 mm, height 11 mm; sapphire crystal, transparent case back, water-resistant to 10 atm
Band: calf leather, pin buckle
Price: $1,750
Variations: different dials

Lawless Black 40

Reference number: 6020.1
Movement: automatic, ETA Caliber 2824-2; ø 25.6 mm, height 4.6 mm; 25 jewels; 28,800 vph; chronometer-rated, skeletonized movement, 40-hour power reserve
Functions: hours, minutes, sweep seconds, date
Case: stainless steel, 40 mm, height 11.8 mm; sapphire crystal, water-resistant to 20 atm
Band: stainless steel, folding clasp
Remarks: sapphire-crystal bezel
Price: $4,500
Variations: different case dimensions (40, 43 and 45 mm)

Art Deco Chrono Enamel

Reference number: 2502
Movement: automatic, ETA Caliber 7753, ø 30 mm, height 7.9 mm; 27 jewels; 28,800 vph; adjusted in 5 positions, chronometer-rated; skeletonized movement, 44-hour power reserve
Functions: hours, minutes, small seconds, stop-seconds, stop minutes, stop hours, date
Case: stainless steel, 40 mm, height 14 mm; sapphire crystal, transparent case back, water-resistant to 5 atm
Band: suede, pin buckle
Price: $5,500
Variations: silver and salmon dial

Art Deco Chrono

Reference number: 2501
Movement: automatic, ETA Caliber 7753, ø 30 mm, height 7.9 mm; 27 jewels; 28,800 vph; adjusted in 5 positions, chronometer-rated; skeletonized movement, 44-hour power reserve
Functions: hours, minutes, small seconds, stop-seconds, stop minutes, stop hours, date
Case: stainless steel, 40 mm, height 14 mm; sapphire crystal, transparent case back, water-resistant to 5 atm
Band: reptile skin, pin buckle
Price: $5,500
Variations: enamel and salmon dial

Sport Chrono Orca

Reference number: 2511
Movement: automatic, ETA Caliber 7753, ø 30 mm, height 7.9 mm; 27 jewels; 28,800 vph; adjusted in 5 positions, chronometer-rated; skeletonized movement, 44-hour power reserve
Functions: hours, minutes, small seconds, stop-seconds, stop minutes, stop hours, date
Case: stainless steel, 40 mm, height 14 mm, sapphire crystal, transparent case back, water-resistant to 5 atm
Band: reptile skin, pin buckle
Price: $4,500
Variations: black dial

Planetarium

Reference number: 7000
Movement: hand-wound, ETA Caliber 6498-2; ø 37 mm, height 4.5 mm; 17 jewels; 21,600 vph; skeletonized movement, adjusted in 5 positions, blued screws, 60-hour power reserve
Functions: hours, minutes
Case: stainless steel, 40.5 mm, height 10.6 mm, sapphire crystal, transparent case back, water-resistant to 5 atm
Band: reptile skin, pin buckle
Remarks: hand-engraved dial and movement
Price: $10,000

TOWSON WATCH COMPANY

Spencer Shattuck was thirteen when he wrote an eighth-grade thesis on watchmaking. His key source was a week-long hang-out with George Thomas and Hartwig Balke, two passionate and highly experienced watchmakers. Even though they had been close to retirement, these two men founded Towson Watch Company.

In 2020, while still a student, Shattuck bought the 25% share of Towson that had been owned by Marylander Kevin Plank, founder of the sports apparel company Under Armour. Netflix should pay attention, because this could be material for a series.

Like so many dyed-in-the-wool watchmakers, Thomas and Balke didn't market their achievements loudly. But Thomas's first tourbillon pocket watches are displayed at the National Watch and Clock Museum in Columbia, Pennsylvania. And in 1999, Balke made a chronograph, the STS-99 Mission (now simply the Mission), for a NASA astronaut. The two also restored a venerable clock belonging to Philip Melanchthon, friend and fellow traveler of Martin Luther. In 2009, Thomas was invited to open up a pocket watch belonging to President Lincoln, which revealed a secret message: "Jonathan Dillon April 13 – 1861 Fort Sumpter was attacked by the rebels on the above date. J Dillon."

Towson watches have a clear retro feel. They also pay tribute to local sites, like the Choptank or Potomac rivers, and things like Baltimore's Pride II schooner, with a case shaped like the company logo, and the Martin M-130 flying boat, with a chronograph replicating exactly the standard colors of old pilot watches.

For Spencer Shattuck the challenge has been to refresh the brand without losing its inherent charm and to make it better known to a broader public. The latest models show the way: the Cadet and Recruits connect to Baltimore's importance in naval history. The Choptank has been altered somewhat to make it less bulky, and its characteristic case has been further streamlined into a new line, the Talbot, which is a 10-millimeter thin dress watch with a wavy guilloché dial—excellent choice for a port city—that comes in two colors, a serious blue and a bright, salmon pink.

TOWSON WATCH CO.
502 Dogwood Lane
Towson, MD 21286
USA

TEL.:
410-823-1823

FAX:
410-823-8581

E-MAIL:
towsonwatchco@aol.com

WEBSITE:
www.towsonwatchcompany.com

FOUNDED:
2000

NUMBER OF EMPLOYEES:
4

ANNUAL PRODUCTION:
200 watches

DISTRIBUTION:
Retail

MOST IMPORTANT COLLECTIONS/PRICE RANGE:
Cadet and Recruit, Choptank, Martin, Mission, Pride II, Potomac, Skipjack, Talbot / $1,695 - $9,400

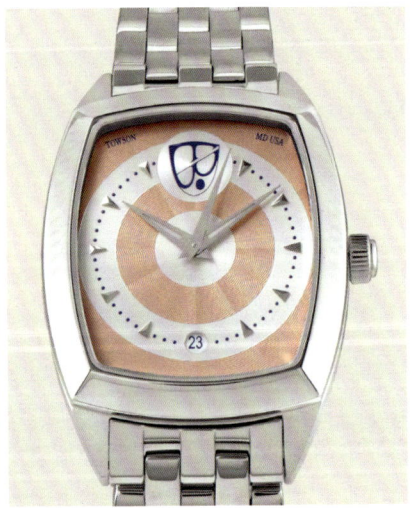

Talbot Pink

Reference number: EP250-C
Movement: automatic; Selitta SW200-1 ("Elaboré" grade); ø 26 mm; height 4.60 mm; 26 jewels; 28,800 vph; finely finished movement with côtes de Genève on rotor, perlage on mainplate, blued screws; 38-hour power reserve
Functions: hours, minutes, sweep seconds (hacking); date
Case: stainless steel; 37 mm x 33 mm; height 10 mm; sapphire crystal; transparent back with sapphire crystal; water-resistant to 5 atm
Band: stainless steel, folding clasp
Price: $3,000; limited to 100 numbered pieces
Variations: with blue dial; various straps and bracelets

Recruit

Reference number: CR250
Movement: automatic, Sellita caliber SW200; ø 26; height 4.60 mm; 21 jewels; 28,800 vph; finely finished with côtes de Genève on rotor, perlage on mainplate, blued screws; 42-hour power reserve
Functions: hours (with inside military time track), minutes, sweep seconds; date
Case: satin-finished stainless steel; ø 41 mm; height 10.5 mm; sapphire crystal; screwed transparent back with sapphire crystal; water-resistant to 5 atm
Band: calf leather, folding clasp.
Price: $1,695; limited to 250 pieces
Variations: as Cadet

Mission

Reference number: M250-2-S
Movement: automatic Valjoux ETA Caliber 7750; ø 30 mm, height 7.6 mm; 25 jewels; 28,800 vph; fine finishing with côtes de Genève, blued screws; 48-hour power reserve
Functions: hours, minutes, subsidiary seconds; chronograph with tachymeter scale, date
Case: stainless steel, 42 mm, height 13 mm, sapphire crystal, screwed down case back with engraving, water resistant to 5 atm
Band: leather, folding clasp.
Price: $3,795; limited to 100 pieces

TRILOBE

Gautier Massonneau, the son of an architect and an interior designer, has a natural attraction to shapes. Still in his twenties and just cutting his teeth in the world of infrastructure financing, he decided to buy himself a watch. The only problem for a finicky person is that he couldn't find one that met his expectations. So he decided to make one.

He stumbled upon a timeless and transcultural form: the trefoil, an arrangement of "leaves" with powerful symbolic value. Indeed, the number three, or the triangle, suggests completion. Do we not live in a world of three dimensions? There is also the past, the present, and the future; religious trinities; and the narrative law that every story must have a beginning, a middle, and an end.

The beating heart of the watch is the off-center seconds disc, an open-worked six-leaved trefoil. The other "leaves" (a minute ring and an hour ring) radiate outward across the dial like ripples on a pond or rays of sunlight. This poetic imagery is echoed in the name as well: Les Matinaux ("the morning people"), a name shared with a collection of poems by René Char.

To realize the module for his first model, Massonneau turned to Jean-François Mojon and his company Chronode in Le Locle, Switzerland. Together, they created the X-Centric caliber, based on an ETA movement.

The broad expanse of the Trilobe dials lends itself beautifully to visual effects. Clients seeking a customized watch can choose a Matinaux model with a favorite constellation of Super-LumiNova stars against a dark blue background. But Massonneau has not run out of ideas since launching his brand. First came the Nuit Fantastique series, inspired by a short story by Austrian author Stefan Zweig about a nobleman's unreal night in Vienna. Then came Une Folle Journée ("a crazy day"), another literary reference—among others to the *Marriage of Figaro*—with the dials of the Matinaux now raised on thin pillars.

The year 2025 saw the company move into offices and workshops at 32 avenue de l'Opéra. It was here that they completed their first in-house movement, appropriately named X-Nihilo, along with the watch it powers, the Trente-Deux, named after their new address.

TRILOBE WATCHES SAS
18 rue Volney
75002, Paris
France

TEL.:
+33-1-4233-5296

E-MAIL:
cercles@trilobewatches.com

WEBSITE:
www.trilobe.com

FOUNDED:
2019

NUMBER OF EMPLOYEES:
8

ANNUAL PRODUCTION:
approx. 700 pieces

U.S. DISTRIBUTOR:
Totally Worth It (TWI2, Inc.)
76 Division Avenue
Summit, NJ 07901-2309
201-894-4710
724-263-2286
info@totallyworthit.com

MOST IMPORTANT COLLECTIONS/PRICE RANGE:
Les Matinaux, La Nuit Fantastique, Une Folle Journée, Trente-Deux / $8,800 to $39,500; jewel versions up to $180,000

Nuit Fantastique Brume Guilloché

Reference number: NF05GB
Movement: automatic, X-Centric caliber; ø 35.2 mm, height 5.78 mm; 33 jewels; micro-rotor, 28,800 vph; 48-hour power reserve
Functions: hours, minutes, subsidiary seconds
Case: titanium, ø 38.5 mm or 40.5 mm, height 9.2 mm; sapphire crystal; transparent case back; water-resistant to 5 atm
Band: reptile skin, pin buckle
Remarks: brown-grey barley-grain guilloche on main dial, clous de Paris on seconds disc
Price: $14,800

Trente-Deux (Sunray Blue)

Reference number: 3201BS
Movement: automatic, X-Nihilo Caliber; ø 35.2 mm, height 7 mm; 34 jewels; 28,800 vph; 42-hour power reserve
Functions: hours, minutes, subsidiary seconds
Case: stainless steel, ø 39.5 mm, height 10.15 mm; sapphire crystal; transparent case back; water-resistant to 5 atm
Band: stainless steel, double folding clasp
Remarks: three off-center concentric and rotating rings for hour, minute and seconds; matte blue sunray on main dial, clous de Paris on seconds disc
Price: $22,400

Une Folle Journée Dune

Reference number: UFJ01GD
Movement: automatic, X-Centric Caliber; ø 35.2 mm, height 5.78 mm; 33 jewels; 28,800 vph; microrotor; dial composed of three off-center concentric circles; 48-hour power reserve
Functions: hours, minutes, subsidiary seconds on rotating discs with a fixed index
Case: titanium, ø 40.5 mm, height 9.2 mm (17.8 mm incl. the domed sapphire crystal); transparent case back; water-resistant to 5 atm
Band: reptile skin, pin buckle
Remarks: time displayed 10 mm above the dial on rotating rings set with 150 diamonds using a special setting technique
Price: $26,500

TUDOR

Rolex founder Hans Wilsdorf started Tudor in 1946 as a second brand to offer the legendary reliability of his watches at a more affordable price. Tudor still benefits from the same industrial platform as Rolex, especially in cases and bracelets, assembly, and quality assurance, not to mention distribution and after-sales. However, the movements themselves are usually delivered by ETA and "Tudorized" according to the company's own aesthetics and technical criteria.

After coming out of the shadows in 2007, the company had an easy time registering with consumers with the Heritage Black Bay, especially considering the trend towards 1970s nostalgia. The first edition of the model with a wine-red bezel was followed by numerous variants with and without a rotating bezel, and with a GMT function. The latter was the second new development by the Rolex sister brand after the three-hand manufacture calibers. In the summer of 2021, Tudor finally presented a brand-new surprise: the Black Bay Ceramic is the first model to feature a ceramic case and a completely magnetic field-resistant movement. As a result, the Black Bay Ceramic even passes the stringent Swiss METAS magnetism test, making Tudor the second brand (after Omega) with a Master Chronometer certificate.

As for movements, the MT-5621 made its debut in the simple North Flag and as the MT-5612 in the Pelagos models. The M5601/5602 calibers, with three hands and a date, were followed by an attractive automatic chronograph using Breitling's B01 Caliber. The Tudor calibers are produced by the movement manufacturer Kenissi, a joint venture with Breitling, among others. The movement of the automatic chronograph, which is basically a Breitling caliber B01, is also "shared" with this brand.

After launching various Black Bay models made of unusual case materials, Tudor invested in the development of the Pelagos special FXD model for professional use with integrated strap bars. Two special editions for various sports, like professional cycling, or Formula One, use this system, and they also boast bezels inlaid with carbon fiber. Price-conscious Tudor fans will be delighted with the Ranger, which is a basic three-hander but done with great attention to detail.

MONTRES TUDOR SA
Rue François-Dussaud 3-5-7
1211 Geneva 26
Switzerland

TEL.:
+41-22-302-2200

WEBSITE:
www.tudorwatch.com

FOUNDED:
1946

U.S. DISTRIBUTOR:
Tudor Watch U.S.A., LLC
665 Fifth Avenue
New York, NY 10022
212-906-0010
www.tudorwatch.com

MOST IMPORTANT COLLECTIONS/PRICE RANGE:
Black Bay, Heritage, Pelagos, Ranger / $2,700 to $7,000

Black Bay Monochrome

Reference number: 7941A1A0NU
Movement: automatic, Tudor caliber MT5602-U; ø 31.8 mm, height 6.5 mm; 25 jewels; 28,800 vph; silicon hairspring, antimagnetic gear train components; Master Chronometer (METAS) certification; COSC-certified chronometer; 70-hour power reserve
Functions: hours, minutes, sweep seconds
Case: stainless steel, ø 41 mm, height 13.6 mm; unidirectional bezel with aluminum numeral disc, with 0-60 scale; sapphire crystal; screw-down crown; water-resistant to 20 atm
Band: five-link stainless steel, folding clasp, with fine adjustment
Price: $4,250
Variations: with three-link bracelet ($4,150); with rubber strap ($3,950)

Black Bay Ceramic Blue

Reference number: 79210CNU
Movement: automatic, Tudor caliber MT5602-1U; ø 31.8 mm, height 6.5 mm; 25 jewels; 28,800 vph; silicon hairspring, antimagnetic gear train components; Master Chronometer (METAS) certification; COSC-certified chronometer; 70-hour power reserve
Functions: hours, minutes, sweep seconds
Case: ceramic, ø 41 mm, height 14.4 mm; unidirectional bezel with ceramic numerals disc, with 0-60 scale; sapphire crystal; screw-down crown; water-resistant to 20 atm
Band: calfskin and rubber, stainless-steel folding clasp with black PVD
Remarks: special edition to support the Visa Cash App RB Formula One Team with the dial in the team color, blue; comes with extra textile strap
Price: $5,150

Black Bay 58 18K

Reference number: 79018V
Movement: automatic, Tudor caliber MT5400; ø 30.3 mm, height 5 mm; 27 jewels; 28,800 vph; silicon hairspring; COSC-certified chronometer; 70-hour power reserve
Functions: hours, minutes, sweep seconds
Case: yellow gold, ø 39 mm; unidirectional bezel with aluminum insert, with 0-60 scale; sapphire crystal; transparent case back; screw-down crown; water-resistant to 20 atm
Band: yellow gold, folding clasp, with fine adjustment
Price: $32,100

Black Bay Pro

Reference number: 79470
Movement: automatic, Tudor caliber MT5652; ø 31.8 mm, height 7.52 mm; 28 jewels; 28,800 vph; silicon hairspring; COSC-certified chronometer; 70-hour power reserve
Functions: hours (crown activated jumping hours), minutes, sweep seconds; additional 24-hour display (second time zone); date
Case: stainless steel, ø 39 mm; with 0-24 scale; sapphire crystal; screw-down crown; water-resistant to 20 atm
Band: stainless steel, folding clasp, with safety lock
Price: $4,225
Variations: with calfskin, rubber, or textile strap ($3,900)

Pelagos LHD

Reference number: 25610TNL
Movement: automatic, Tudor caliber MT5612LHD; ø 31.8 mm, height 6.5 mm; 25 jewels; 28,800 vph; silicon hairspring; COSC-certified chronometer; 70-hour power reserve
Functions: hours, minutes, sweep seconds; date
Case: titanium, ø 42 mm; unidirectional stainless-steel bezel with ceramic numeral disc, with 0-60 scale; sapphire crystal; screw-down crown, helium valve; water-resistant to 50 atm
Band: titanium, folding clasp, with safety lock, with extension link, with fine adjustment
Remarks: comes with rubber strap
Price: $5,025

Pelagos

Reference number: 25600TB
Movement: automatic, Tudor caliber MT5612; ø 31.8 mm, height 6.5 mm; 26 jewels; 28,800 vph; silicon hairspring; COSC-certified chronometer; 70-hour power reserve
Functions: hours, minutes, sweep seconds; date
Case: titanium, ø 42 mm; unidirectional titanium bezel with ceramic numeral disc, insert, with 0-60 scale; sapphire crystal; screw-down crown, helium valve; water-resistant to 50 atm
Band: rubber, pin buckle, with extension link
Remarks: comes with additional titanium link bracelet
Price: $5,025
Variations: with black dial

Pelagos FXD Chrono Cycling Edition

Reference number: 25827KN
Movement: automatic, Tudor caliber MT5813; ø 30.4 mm, height 7.23 mm; 41 jewels; 28,800 vph; silicon hairspring; column wheel control; COSC-certified chronometer; 70-hour power reserve
Functions: hours, minutes, subsidiary seconds; chronograph; date
Case: carbon composite, ø 43 mm; sapphire crystal; screw-down crown; water-resistant to 10 atm
Band: textile, pin buckle
Remarks: fixed lug bars (tear-safe); special edition to support professional cycling
Price: $5,275

Caliber MT5602-U

Automatic; antimagnetic gear train components; Master Chronometer (METAS) certification; single mainspring barrel; COSC-certified chronometer; 70-hour power reserve
Functions: hours, minutes, sweep seconds
Diameter: 31.8 mm
Height: 6.5 mm
Jewels: 25
Balance: glucydur screw balance
Frequency: 28,800 vph
Hairspring: silicon
Related calibers: MT5601/5612 (encasing diameter 33.8/31.8 mm) without antimagnetic components

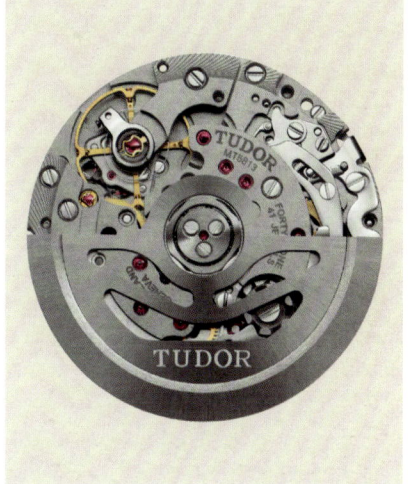

Caliber MT5813

Automatic; single mainspring barrel; COSC-certified chronometer; 70-hour power reserve
Functions: hours, minutes, subsidiary seconds; chronograph; date
Diameter: 30.4 mm
Height: 7.23 mm
Jewels: 41
Balance: glucydur screw balance
Frequency: 28,800 vph
Hairspring: silicon

TUTIMA

The town of Glashütte already had a booming watch industry when World War I, followed by the hyperinflation of the early twenties, shut down the markets. To rebuild the local economy, a conglomerate was founded under the leadership of jurist Dr. Ernst Kurtz, consisting of the movement manufacturer UROFA Glashütte AG and UFAG. The top watches were given the name Tutima, derived from the Latin *tutus*, meaning whole, sound. Among the brand's most famous timepieces was a pilot's watch that set standards in terms of aesthetics and functionality.

A few days before World War II ended, Kurtz left Glashütte and founded Uhrenfabrik Kurtz in southern Germany. A young businessman and former employee of Kurtz by the name of Dieter Delecate is credited with keeping the manufacturing facilities and the name Tutima going even as the company sailed through troubled waters. In founding Tutima Uhrenfabrik GmbH in Ganderkesee, this young, resolute entrepreneur prepared the company's strategy for the coming decades.

Delecate has had the joy of seeing Tutima return to its old home and vertically integrated operations, meaning it is once again a genuine *manufacture*. In 2013, Tutima proudly announced a genuine made-in-Glashütte movement (at least 50 percent must be produced in the town), Caliber 617.

Tutima Glashütte has started reviving the great watchmaking crafts that have made the region world famous. Among these horological treats is the 2011 Hommage, the first German-made minute repeater in a wristwatch, and the three-hand Patria, which comes in a noble steel or gold case with a blue dial. For a genuine vintage feeling, the brand introduced the Tempostopp, a flyback chronograph run on the Caliber 659, a replica of the legendary Urofa Caliber 59 from the 1940s with a few necessary improvements in the details. More contemporary is the Saxon One line with a range of classic complications. And then there are the military-inspired models like the M2 Coastline, made of lightweight titanium but with soft edges that will not ruin a silk shirt cuff. And finally, the pilots' watches—Flieger, Grand Flieger, and Flieger Legacy—which bring Glashütte excellence into the cockpit.

TUTIMA UHRENFABRIK GMBH NDL. GLASHÜTTE
Altenberger Strasse 6
D-01768 Glashütte
Germany

TEL.:
+49-35053-320-20

E-MAIL:
info@tutima.com

WEBSITE:
www.tutima.com

FOUNDED:
1927

NUMBER OF EMPLOYEES:
approx. 40

U.S. DISTRIBUTOR:
Tutima USA, Inc.
P.O. Box 983
Torrance, CA 90508
1-TUTIMA-1927
info@tutimausa.com
www.tutimausa.com

MOST IMPORTANT COLLECTIONS/PRICE RANGE:
Patria, M2, Grand Flieger, Hommage / approx. $1,850 to $47,500

M2 Chronograph

Reference number: 6450-05
Movement: automatic, Tutima caliber 521 (base ETA 7750); ø 30 mm, height 7.9 mm; 25 jewels; 28,800 vph; central minutes counter; rotor with gold seal; 48-hour power reserve
Functions: hours, minutes, chronograph, date
Case: titanium, ø 46 mm, height 15.5 mm; sapphire crystal; screw-down crown; water-resistant to 30 atm
Band: titanium, folding clasp
Price: $6,100

M2 Seven Seas S

Reference number: 6156-23
Movement: automatic, Tutima caliber 330 (base Sellita SW220); ø 25.6 mm, height 5.05 mm; 26 jewels; 28,800 vph; rotor with gold seal; 38-hour power reserve
Functions: hours, minutes, sweep seconds, date
Case: stainless steel, ø 40.2 mm, height 12.5 mm; unidirectional bezel with 0-60 scale; sapphire crystal; screw-down crown; water-resistant to 50 atm
Band: rubber, pin buckle
Price: $2,200

M2 Mara Safari Chronograph

Reference number: 6451-53
Movement: automatic, Tutima caliber 310 (base Sellita SW500); ø 30 mm, height 7.9 mm; 25 jewels; 28,800 vph; rotor with gold seal; 62-hour power reserve
Functions: hours, minutes, subsidiary seconds, chronograph, date
Case: titanium, ø 46.5 mm, height 16 mm; bidirectional bezel with 0-60 scale; sapphire crystal; screw-down crown; water-resistant to 30 atm
Band: rubber, pin buckle
Remarks: limited edition of 250 pieces supporting the Mara Elephant Project within the Serengeti-Maasai Mara ecosystem
Price: $5,500; limited to 250 pieces

Flieger Legacy T5 Chronograph

Reference number: 6405-03
Movement: automatic, Tutima caliber 310 (base Sellita SW500); ø 30 mm, height 7.9 mm; 25 jewels; 28,800 vph; rotor with gold seal; 62-hour power reserve
Functions: hours, minutes, subsidiary seconds, chronograph, date
Case: titanium, ø 41 mm, height 16.1 mm; sapphire crystal; transparent case back; screw-down crown; water-resistant to 10 atm
Band: leather, folding clasp
Price: $4,650

Flieger Legacy T5 Chronograph

Reference number: 6405-02
Movement: automatic, Tutima caliber 310 (base Sellita SW500); ø 30 mm, height 7.9 mm; 25 jewels; 28,800 vph; rotor with gold seal; 62-hour power reserve
Functions: hours, minutes, subsidiary seconds, chronograph, date
Case: titanium, ø 41 mm, height 16.1 mm; sapphire crystal; transparent case back; screw-down crown; water-resistant to 10 atm
Band: titanium, folding clasp
Price: $5,100

Flieger Automatic Bronze

Reference number: 6115-03
Movement: automatic, Tutima caliber 330 (base Sellita SW220); ø 25.6 mm, height 5.05 mm; 26 jewels; 28,800 vph; rotor with gold seal; 38-hour power reserve
Functions: hours, minutes, sweep seconds, date
Case: bronze, ø 41.5 mm, height 12.8 mm; sapphire crystal; transparent case back; screw-down crown; water-resistant to 10 atm
Band: leather, pin buckle
Price: $2,850; limited to 100 pieces

Lady Sky

Reference number: 6705-08
Movement: automatic, Tutima caliber 335 (base Sellita SW200-1); ø 25.6 mm, height 4.6 mm; 25 jewels; 28,800 vph; 41-hour power reserve
Functions: hours, minutes, sweep seconds, date
Case: stainless steel, ø 34 mm, height 10.1 mm; sapphire crystal; transparent case back; screw-down crown; water-resistant to 5 atm
Band: stainless steel, folding clasp
Price: $2,650

Patria

Reference number: 6612-03
Movement: hand-wound, Tutima caliber 617; ø 31 mm, height 4.78 mm; 20 jewels; 21,600 vph; screw balance with gold regulating screws and Breguet hairspring; Glashütte three-quarter plate; winding wheels with bidirectional stopwork; movement gold-plated and finely finished; 65-hour power reserve
Functions: hours, minutes, subsidiary seconds
Case: titanium, ø 41 mm, height 11.2 mm; sapphire crystal; transparent case back; water-resistant to 5 atm
Band: sheepskin leather, pin buckle
Price: $10,400

Tempostopp

Reference number: 6650-01
Movement: hand-wound, Tutima caliber 659; ø 33.7 mm, height 6.6 mm; 28 jewels; 21,600 vph; screw balance with gold regulating screws and Breguet hairspring; winding wheels with bidirectional stopwork; hand-engraved balance cock; movement gold-plated and finely finished; 65-hour power reserve
Functions: hours, minutes, subsidiary seconds, flyback chronograph
Case: rose gold, ø 43 mm, height 12.95 mm; sapphire crystal; transparent case back
Band: reptile skin, rose-gold pin buckle
Remarks: recreation of the legendary Urofa Caliber 59 from the 1940s; limited to 90 pieces
Price: $47,500

ULYSSE NARDIN

Ulysse Nardin celebrated its 175th anniversary in 2021, though the brand was dormant for a few of those years. It was Rolf Schnyder who revived the venerable manufacture after the quartz crisis. The brand had previously built its reputation on marine chronometers and precision timekeeping.

Schnyder had the good fortune to meet the multitalented Dr. Ludwig Oechslin, who developed a host of innovations for Ulysse Nardin, from intelligent calendar complications to novel escapement systems. Under their leadership, Ulysse Nardin was a pioneer in using materials like silicon and synthetic diamonds. In fact, nearly every notable Ulysse Nardin watch is famous for a spectacular technical innovation, be it the Moonstruck with its stunning lunar indication or the outlandish Freak series that more or less does away with the traditional dial.

Following Schnyder's death in 2011, the brand pursued a strategy of partnerships and acquisitions, notably purchasing enameler Donzé Cadrans SA. This acquisition contributed to the creation of the Marine Chronometer Manufacture collection, powered by the in-house Caliber UN-118.

In 2014, the French luxury group Kering, which already owned Sowind (Girard-Perregaux), purchased Ulysse Nardin. As the two companies were neighbors in La Chaux-de-Fonds, Switzerland, the proximity created synergies. Ulysse Nardin continued its innovative streak with developments like a new blade-driven anchor escapement and a regatta countdown watch featuring a seconds hand that runs counterclockwise before switching to a conventional clockwise direction once the race begins.

A joint venture with Sigatec in Sion and its sister company, Mimotec—both specialists in LIGA (lithography, electroplating, and molding) and silicon processing—provided Ulysse Nardin with the advanced manufacturing capabilities to realize its ambitious designs. Specialties such as the Dual Direct Escapement in the Freak model or the Ulysse Anchor Escapement in the tourbillon Caliber 178, with its silicon flying anchor bridge, would not have been feasible otherwise.

The Kering Group ultimately sold Ulysse Nardin and Girard-Perregaux in a management buyout. The two brands are now united under the leadership of CEO Patrick Pruniaux. In a more recent achievement, Ulysse Nardin set a record in 2025 with the Diver AIR. With a skeletonized movement and a total weight of just 52 grams, it became the lightest mechanical diving watch in the world.

ULYSSE NARDIN SA
3, rue du Jardin
CH-2400 Le Locle
Switzerland

TEL.:
+41-32-930-7400

WEBSITE:
www.ulysse-nardin.com

FOUNDED:
1846

U.S. DISTRIBUTOR:
Ulysse Nardin Inc.
7900 Glades Rd., Suite 200
Boca Raton, FL 33434
646-500-8664
usa@ulysse-nardin.com

MOST IMPORTANT COLLECTIONS:
FREAK Collection, Blast Collection, Marine Collection and Diver Collection; Dual Time (also ladies' watches); complications and *métiers d'art* (alarm clocks, perpetual calendar, tourbillons, minute repeaters, jacquemarts, astronomical watches, enamel, micropainting)

Marine Torpilleur
Reference number: 1183-310/43
Movement: automatic, UN-118 caliber; ø 31.6 mm, height 6.45 mm; 50 jewels; 28,800 vph; "DIAMonSIL" escapement, silicon hairspring; 60-hour power reserve; COSC-certified chronometer
Functions: hours, minutes, subsidiary seconds; power reserve indicator; date
Case: stainless steel, ø 42 mm, height 13 mm; sapphire crystal; transparent case back; screw-down crown; water-resistant to 5 atm
Band: reptile skin, folding clasp
Price: $10,400
Variations: with white dial; with rubber or textile strap; with stainless steel Milanese bracelet ($11,400)

Marine Torpilleur Moonphase
Reference number: 1192-310-0A/1A
Movement: automatic, UN-119 caliber; ø 31.6 mm, height 6.2 mm; 45 jewels; 28,800 vph; "DIAMonSIL" escapement, silicon hairspring; 60-hour power reserve; COSC-certified chronometer
Functions: hours, minutes, subsidiary seconds; power reserve indicator; moon phase
Case: rose gold, ø 42 mm, height 13 mm; sapphire crystal; transparent case back; screw-down crown; water-resistant to 5 atm
Band: reptile skin, folding clasp
Price: $25,600

Marine Torpilleur Tourbillon
Reference number: 1283-310-0AE/1A
Movement: automatic, UN-128 caliber; ø 31.6 mm, height 7.4 mm; 36 jewels; 28,800 vph; flying one-minute tourbillon; escapement and hairspring in silicon; 60-hour power reserve
Functions: hours, minutes; power reserve indicator
Case: stainless steel, ø 42 mm, height 11.93 mm; sapphire crystal; transparent case back; screw-down crown; water-resistant to 5 atm
Band: reptile skin, folding clasp
Price: $56,300
Variations: in rose gold with black dial ($67,700)

Marine Torpilleur Dual Time

Reference number: 3343-320-3A/1A
Movement: automatic, UN-24 caliber; ø 25.6 mm, height 5.35 mm; 23 jewels; 28,800 vph
Functions: hours, minutes, subsidiary seconds; additional 24-hour display (second time zone); large date
Case: stainless steel, ø 42 mm, height 13 mm; ceramic bezel; sapphire crystal; transparent case back; screw-down crown; water-resistant to 5 atm
Band: reptile skin, folding clasp
Price: $13,000

Diver 44 mm Hammerhead Shark

Reference number: 1183-170LE-3A-HAMMER/3A
Movement: automatic, UN-118 caliber; ø 31.6 mm, height 6.45 mm; 50 jewels; 28,800 vph; "DIAMonSIL" escapement, silicon hairspring; 60-hour power reserve; COSC-certified chronometer
Functions: hours, minutes, subsidiary seconds; power reserve indicator; date
Case: titanium with blue PVD coating, ø 44 mm, height 14.81 mm; titanium bezel, bidirectional with 0–60 scale; sapphire crystal; screw-down crown; water-resistant to 30 atm
Band: rubber with titanium element, pin buckle
Price: $12,100; limited to 300 pieces
Variations: with textile strap

Diver Net OPS

Reference number: 1183-170-8A/3B
Movement: automatic, UN-118 caliber; ø 31.6 mm, height 6.45 mm; 50 jewels; 28,800 vph; "DIAMonSIL" escapement, silicon hairspring; 60-hour power reserve; COSC-certified chronometer
Functions: hours, minutes, subsidiary seconds; power reserve indicator; date
Case: composite material (recycled fishing nets and carbon fiber), ø 44 mm, height 14.81 mm; bezel in recycled stainless steel with carbon-fiber inlay, bidirectional with 0–60 scale; sapphire crystal; screw-down crown; water-resistant to 30 atm
Band: rubber, folding clasp
Price: $14,700
Variations: with textile strap ($13,300)

Diver AIR

Reference number: 3743-170-2A/0A
Movement: automatic, UN-374 caliber; ø 37 mm, height 5.86 mm; 22 jewels; 21,600 vph; skeletonized movement construction; double spring barrel; escape wheel and hairspring in silicon; 90-hour power reserve
Functions: hours, minutes, sweep seconds
Case: recycled titanium, flanks in composite material (recycled fishing nets/carbon fiber), ø 44 mm, height 14.7 mm; bezel in carbon fiber, unidirectional with 0–60 scale; sapphire crystal; transparent case back; water-resistant to 20 atm
Band: textile, Velcro fastener
Remarks: total weight including strap only 52 grams
Price: $38,000

Diver X Skeleton OPS

Reference number: 3723-170-1A/3A
Movement: automatic, UN-372 caliber; 23 jewels; 21,600 vph; "DIAMonSIL" escapement, silicon hairspring; skeletonized mainplate; 72-hour power reserve
Functions: hours, minutes, sweep seconds
Case: titanium, ø 44 mm, height 15.7 mm; bezel with carbon-fiber inlay, unidirectional with 0–60 scale; sapphire crystal; transparent case back; screw-down crown; water-resistant to 20 atm
Band: rubber, folding clasp
Price: $28,600
Variations: with azure-blue strap and indexes; with textile strap; in stainless steel

Blast Skeleton X

Reference number: 3713-260-3/03
Movement: hand-wound, UN-371 caliber; ø 37 mm, height 5.86 mm; 23 jewels; 18,000 vph; skeletonized movement construction; double spring barrel; escape wheel and hairspring in silicon; 96-hour power reserve
Functions: hours, minutes
Case: titanium, ø 42 mm, height 10.85 mm; bezel with blue PVD; sapphire crystal; transparent case back; water-resistant to 5 atm
Band: rubber, pin buckle
Price: $25,000
Variations: with reptile skin strap; in carbon; in titanium

Blast Tourbillon

Reference number: 1725-400-3A/02
Movement: automatic, UN-172 caliber; ø 36.4 mm, height 6.1 mm; 25 jewels; 18,000 vph; flying one-minute tourbillon; platinum micro-rotor; silicon escapement; fully skeletonized movement; 72-hour power reserve
Functions: hours, minutes
Case: rose gold and DLC-treated titanium, ø 45 mm, height 11 mm; bezel in DLC-treated titanium; sapphire crystal; transparent case back; water-resistant to 5 atm
Band: rubber, folding clasp
Price: $72,100
Variations: with reptile skin strap; with satin strap

Blast Hourstriker

Reference number: 6215-400-3A/02
Movement: automatic, UN-621 caliber; ø 35.5 mm, height 10.8 mm; 46 jewels; 28,800 vph; flying one-minute tourbillon; silicon escapement; platinum micro-rotor (manual winding for the striking mechanism); 60-hour power reserve
Functions: hours, minutes; hour and half-hour strike "au passage" and on demand
Case: rose gold, middle section in DLC-treated titanium, ø 45 mm; sapphire crystal; transparent case back; water-resistant to 3 atm
Band: rubber, folding clasp
Price: $137,300
Variations: with reptile skin strap; with satin strap

Freak X Enamel

Reference number: 2305-270LE-3AE-BLUE/1A
Movement: automatic, UN-230 caliber; ø 34.5 mm, height 10.1 mm; 21 jewels; 28,800 vph; baguette movement mounted on a rotating carousel; silicon balance; movement components serve as hands; conventional winding and setting via crown; 72-hour power reserve
Functions: hours, minutes
Case: rose gold and titanium with PVD, ø 43 mm, height 13.38 mm; sapphire crystal; transparent case back; water-resistant to 5 atm
Band: reptile skin, folding clasp
Price: $48,500; limited to 120 pieces
Remarks: guilloché dial in blue enamel

Freak ONE

Reference number: 2405-500-2A/3D
Movement: automatic, UN-240 caliber; ø 34.5 mm, height 10.1 mm; 21 jewels; 21,600 vph; baguette movement mounted on a rotating carousel; components act as hands; anchor and escape wheel in "DIAMonSIL," balance and hairspring in silicon; 90-hour power reserve
Functions: hours, minutes
Case: titanium with black DLC, ø 44 mm, height 13.3 mm; bezel in rose gold; sapphire crystal; transparent case back
Band: rubber, folding clasp
Price: $76,700

Freak ONE OPS

Reference number: 2403-500-8A/3A
Movement: automatic, UN-240 caliber; ø 34.5 mm, height 10.1 mm; 21 jewels; 21,600 vph; baguette movement mounted on a rotating carousel; components act as hands; anchor and escape wheel in "DIAMonSIL," balance and hairspring in silicon; 90-hour power reserve
Functions: hours, minutes
Case: titanium with black DLC, ø 44 mm, height 13.3 mm; bezel in Carbonium; sapphire crystal; transparent case back; water-resistant to 3 atm
Band: rubber with textile inlay, folding clasp
Price: $72,200
Variations: with two-tone rubber strap

Freak X Crystalium

Reference number: 2303-270-4A/3A
Movement: automatic, UN-230 caliber; ø 34.5 mm, height 10.1 mm; 21 jewels; 28,800 vph; baguette movement mounted on a rotating carousel; silicon balance; movement components serve as hands; conventional winding and setting via crown; 72-hour power reserve
Functions: hours, minutes
Case: titanium with black DLC, ø 43 mm, height 13.38 mm; sapphire crystal; transparent case back; water-resistant to 5 atm
Band: reptile skin, folding clasp
Price: $45,200; limited to 50 pieces
Remarks: dial in rose-gold Crystalium (crystallized and PVD-treated ruthenium)

URWERK

Many watchmakers make unique pieces, but Felix Baumgartner and designer Martin Frei are in and of themselves unique. Their products are immediately recognizable, their ultra-technical style—never losing sight of the visual codes they laid down when they founded their company in 1997—has always been the source of eye-popping mechanisms. It's all in the name, a play on the words *Uhrwerk*, for movement, and *Urwerk*, meaning a sort of primal mechanism. Their specialty is inventing surprising time indicators featuring digital numerals that rotate like satellites and display the time in a relatively linear depiction on a small "dial" at the front of the flattened case, which could almost—but not quite—be described as oval. Their inspiration goes back to the so-called night clock of the eighteenth-century Campanus brothers, but the realization is purely *2001: A Space Odyssey*.

Over the years, Baumgartner and Frei have invented all sorts of new ways of displaying time not always based on the satellite idea. For example, the Black Cobra used cylinders, which also required clever ways to recoup energy for driving the heavy components. With each return to the drawing board, the two men have always managed to push the envelope in one way or another, either by adapting the form, or by exploring high-tech materials, like aluminum titanium nitride (AlTiN), or a gold-silver alloy known as electrum, or finding new functions for the owner to play with.

In 2025, Frei and Baumgartner came up with the Spacemeter, a successor to the 100V Stardust and the LightSpeed, which featured complications that measure distance a human being standing on the Equator travels on rotating Earth and at the same time the journey of Earth around the sun. The Scorpion is also back with a blue dial that enhances the model's sportive look. And finally, Urwerk has joined the collaboration trend and picked Ulysse Nardin as a partner—a good choice since the paired watch is the famous iconoclastic Freak.

URWERK SA
Bourg du Four 5
CH-1204 Geneva
Switzerland

TEL:
+41-22-900-2027

E-MAIL:
info@urwerk.com

WEBSITE:
www.urwerk.com

FOUNDED:
1995

ANNUAL PRODUCTION:
150 watches

U.S. DISTRIBUTOR:
Ildico Inc.
8701 Wilshire Blvd.
Beverly Hills, CA 90211
310-205-5555

UR-10 SpaceMeter

Movement: automatic, Caliber UR 10.01; 44 jewels; 28,800 vph; dual-flow turbines with patented two counter-rotating propellers; baseplates in ARCAP alloy; finely finished movement with circular graining and shot-blasting; 43-hour power reserve.
Functions: hours, minutes; Earth travel distance at the equator on a 10-km scale - dial at 2 o'clock; Earth rotation distance around the sun at 4 o'clock (on a 1,000-km scale); concentric distance counter; 24-hour display and rotation and revolution on case back
Case: titanium with steel case back, 45.4 mm x 44 mm, height 7.13 mm; sapphire crystal; screw-down crown; transparent case back; water-resistant to 3 atm
Band: titanium, folding clasp
Price: $94,000

UR-150 Blue Scorpion

Movement: automatic governed by a double turbine, Caliber UR 50.01; 28,800 vph; 38 jewels; finely finished movement with circular graining and shot-blasting; blue atomic layer deposition (ALD); 43-hour power reserve
Functions: satellite hours (in aluminum) on brass carousel, minutes
Case: stainless steel with anthracite PVD and titanium, 42.5 mm x 51 mm, height 14.8 mm; sapphire crystal; screw-down crown; water-resistant to 5 atm
Band: rubber, folding clasp
Price: $118,000; limited to 50 pieces

UR-Freak

Reference number: 2413-500LE-2A-UR/3B
Movement: automatic, Caliber UN-241; ø 34.5 mm, height 10.1 mm; 25 jewels; 21,600 vph; Grinder Automatic Winding System; flying carousel; components act as hands; anchor and escape wheel in "DIAMonSIL," balance and hairspring in silicon; 90-hour power reserve
Functions: hours, minutes
Case: titanium, ø 44 mm, height 12 mm; bezel in Carbonium; sapphire crystal; transparent case back; water-resistant to 3 atm
Band: rubber, folding clasp
Price: $107,200; limited to 100 pieces

VACHERON CONSTANTIN

The origins of this oldest continuously operating watch *manufacture* can be traced back to 1755 when Jean-Marc Vacheron opened his workshop in Geneva. His highly complex watches were particularly appreciated by clients in Paris. The development of such an important outlet for horological works there had a lot to do with the emergence of a wealthy class around the powerful French court. The Revolution put an end to all the financial excesses of that market, however, and the Vacheron company suffered as well, until the arrival of marketing wizard François Constantin in 1819.

Fast-forward to the late twentieth century: the brand with the Maltese cross logo had evolved into a tradition-conscious keeper of *haute horlogerie* under the aegis, starting in the mid-1990s, of the Vendôme Luxury Group (today's Richemont SA).

Today, most of its basic movements are made in-house at the production facilities and headquarters in Plan-les-Ouates and the workshops in Le Brassus in Switzerland's Jura region. Products range from the world's most complicated watch, like the 57260, to the finely crafted Les Cabinotiers and Traditionnelle collections. For daily use, there are the Overseas models, and the entry-level collection, the Fiftysix, with a basic movement and no Geneva Seal.

When not looking ahead, Vacheron Constantin is looking back to its great feats of the past, which have their own family, Les Collectionneurs. Among the favorites is a revisited American 1921 model, now made from 100-year-old spare parts and components and manufactured with 100-year-old tools. This watchmaking icon with its boldly oblique dial, differs from the current models in the 1921 collection in that the dial and crown are tilted to the left.

Most customers of the brand prefer to remain anonymous, but one spectacular one-off timepiece has now been named after its owner for the first time in a long time. William Robert Berkley, an American insurance entrepreneur, ordered the world's most complicated portable mechanical watch from the company. Among numerous other complications, "The Berkley" pocket watch has a perpetual Chinese calendar, a tricky combination of solar and lunar calendars with countless irregularities. Its movement has a record-breaking number of 2,877 individual parts.

VACHERON CONSTANTIN
Chemin du Tourbillon
CH-1228 Plan-les-Ouates
Switzerland

TEL.:
+41-22-930-2005

E-MAIL:
info@vacheron-constantin.com

WEBSITE:
www.vacheron-constantin.com

FOUNDED:
1755

NUMBER OF EMPLOYEES:
approx. 800

U.S. DISTRIBUTOR:
Vacheron Constantin
645 Fifth Avenue
New York, NY 10022
877-701-1755

MOST IMPORTANT COLLECTIONS:
Patrimony, Traditionnelle, Métiers d'Art, Overseas, Fiftysix, Harmony, Malte, Egérie, Quai de l'Île, Historiques and Égérie. As well as unique and bespoke timepieces from its Les Cabinotiers department

Traditionnelle Perpetual Calendar Retrograde Date Openface

Reference number: 4030T/000P-H054
Movement: automatic, Vacheron Constantin Caliber 2460 QPR31/270; ø 29 mm, height 5.45 mm; 27 jewels; 28,800 vph; 40-hour power reserve; Geneva Seal
Functions: hours, minutes; perpetual calendar with date (retrograde), weekday, month, moon phase, leap year
Case: platinum, ø 41 mm, height 10.94 mm; sapphire crystal; transparent case back; water-resistant to 3 atm
Band: reptile skin, folding clasp
Price: $111,000; limited to 370 pieces

Traditionnelle Tourbillon Retrograde Date Openface

Reference number: 6010T/000P-H055
Movement: automatic, Vacheron Constantin Caliber 2162 R31/270; ø 31 mm, height 6.35 mm; 30 jewels; 18,000 vph; 1-minute tourbillon; hubless peripheral rotor; Geneva Seal; 72-hour power reserve
Functions: hours, minutes, subsidiary seconds (on the tourbillon cage); date (retrograde)
Case: platinum, ø 41 mm, height 11.07 mm; sapphire crystal; transparent case back; water-resistant to 3 atm
Band: reptile skin, folding clasp
Price: on request; limited to 370 pieces

Traditionnelle Hand-Wound

Reference number: 82172/000P-H062
Movement: hand-wound, Vacheron Constantin Caliber 4400 AS/270; ø 28.6 mm, height 2.8 mm; 21 jewels; 28,800 vph; 65-hour power reserve; Geneva Seal
Functions: hours, minutes, subsidiary seconds
Case: platinum, ø 38 mm, height 7.7 mm; sapphire crystal; transparent case back; water-resistant to 3 atm
Band: reptile skin, pin buckle
Price: $37,800; limited to 370 pieces
Variations: in rose gold ($25,800)

Traditionnelle Hand-Wound

Reference number: 82172/000R-H118
Movement: hand-wound, Vacheron Constantin Caliber 4400 AS/270; ø 28.6 mm, height 2.8 mm; 21 jewels; 28,800 vph; 65-hour power reserve; Geneva Seal
Functions: hours, minutes, subsidiary seconds
Case: rose gold, ø 38 mm, height 7.7 mm; sapphire crystal; transparent case back; water-resistant to 3 atm
Band: reptile skin, pin buckle
Price: $25,800; ; Geneva Seal
Variations: in platinum $37,800

Traditionnelle Moon Phase

Reference number: 83570/000R-H060
Movement: hand-wound, Vacheron Constantin Caliber 1410 AS; ø 26 mm, height 4.2 mm; 22 jewels; 28,800 vph; 40-hour power reserve; Geneva Seal
Functions: hours, minutes, subsidiary seconds; power reserve indicator; moon phase
Case: rose gold, ø 36 mm, height 9.1 mm; bezel and lugs set with 81 diamonds; sapphire crystal; transparent case back; crown with diamond; water-resistant to 3 atm
Band: reptile skin, pin buckle
Remarks: mother-of-pearl dial
Price: $50,500

Patrimony Moonphase Retrograde Date

Reference number: 4010U/000G-H057
Movement: automatic, Vacheron Constantin Caliber 2460 R31L; ø 27.2 mm, height 5.4 mm; 27 jewels; 28,800 vph; 40-hour power reserve; Geneva Seal
Functions: hours, minutes; date (retrograde), moon phase
Case: white gold, ø 42.4 mm, height 9.7 mm; sapphire crystal; transparent case back; water-resistant to 3 atm
Band: reptile skin, pin buckle
Price: $55,000

Patrimony Moonphase Retrograde Date

Reference number: 4010U/000R-H117
Movement: automatic, Vacheron Constantin Caliber 2460 R31L; ø 27.2 mm, height 5.4 mm; 27 jewels; 28,800 vph; 40-hour power reserve; Geneva Seal
Functions: hours, minutes; date (retrograde), moon phase
Case: rose gold, ø 42.4 mm, height 9.7 mm; sapphire crystal; transparent case back; water-resistant to 3 atm
Band: reptile skin, pin buckle
Price: $55,000

Patrimony Selfwinding

Reference number: 85180/000G-H035
Movement: automatic, Vacheron Constantin Caliber 2450 Q6/3; ø 25.6 mm, height 3.6 mm; 27 jewels; 28,800 vph; 40-hour power reserve; Geneva Seal
Functions: hours, minutes, sweep seconds; date
Case: white gold, ø 40 mm, height 8.55 mm; sapphire crystal; water-resistant to 3 atm
Band: reptile skin, pin buckle
Price: $36,200

Les Historiques 222

Reference number: 4200H/222A-B934
Movement: automatic, Vacheron Constantin Caliber 2455/2; ø 26.2 mm, height 3.6 mm; 27 jewels; 28,800 vph; 40-hour power reserve; Geneva Seal
Functions: hours, minutes; date
Case: stainless steel, ø 37 mm, height 7.95 mm; sapphire crystal; transparent case back; water-resistant to 5 atm
Band: stainless steel, triple folding clasp
Remarks: modernized re-edition for the 45th anniversary of the "222"
Price: $33,200

Les Historiques American 1921

Reference number: 82035/000R-9359
Movement: hand-wound, Vacheron Constantin Caliber 4400 AS; ø 28.6 mm, height 2.8 mm; 21 jewels; 28,800 vph; 65-hour power reserve; Geneva Seal
Functions: hours, minutes, subsidiary seconds
Case: rose gold, 40 mm x 40 mm, height 8.06 mm; sapphire crystal; transparent case back; water-resistant to 3 atm
Band: reptile skin, pin buckle
Remarks: based on a historic model from 1921
Price: $42,500

Overseas Dual-Time

Reference number: 7920V/210R-B965
Movement: automatic, Vacheron Constantin Caliber 5110 DT; ø 30.6 mm, height 6 mm; 37 jewels; 28,800 vph; 60-hour power reserve; Geneva Seal
Functions: hours, minutes, sweep seconds; additional 12-hour display (second time zone), day/night indicator; date
Case: rose gold, ø 41 mm, height 12 mm; sapphire crystal; transparent case back; screw-down crown; water-resistant to 15 atm
Band: rose gold, triple folding clasp
Remarks: includes an additional rubber and reptile skin strap
Price: $81,000

Overseas Perpetual Calendar Ultra-Thin Skeleton

Reference number: 4300V/220R-B547
Movement: automatic, Vacheron Constantin Caliber 1120/3 QPSQ/1; ø 29.6 mm, height 4.05 mm; 36 jewels; 19,800 vph; 40-hour power reserve; Geneva Seal
Functions: hours, minutes; perpetual calendar with date, weekday, month, moon phase, leap year
Case: rose gold, ø 41.5 mm, height 8.1 mm; sapphire crystal; transparent case back; water-resistant to 5 atm
Band: rose gold, triple folding clasp
Remarks: sapphire crystal dial; includes an additional reptile leather and rubber strap
Price: on request

Overseas Tourbillon Skeleton

Reference number: 6000V/210T-B935
Movement: automatic, Vacheron Constantin Caliber 2160 SQ; ø 31 mm, height 5.65 mm; 30 jewels; 18,000 vph; minute tourbillon; peripheral rotor without central hub; 80-hour power reserve; Geneva Seal
Functions: hours, minutes, subsidiary seconds (on the tourbillon cage)
Case: titanium, ø 42.4 mm, height 10.39 mm; sapphire crystal; transparent case back; water-resistant to 5 atm
Band: titanium, folding clasp
Remarks: sapphire crystal dial
Price: on request

Égérie Moon Phase

Reference number: 8005F/000R-B958
Movement: automatic, Vacheron Constantin Caliber 1088 L; ø 30 mm, height 5.03 mm; 26 jewels; 28,800 vph; 40-hour power reserve
Functions: hours, minutes, sweep seconds; moon phase
Case: rose gold, ø 37 mm, height 9.32 mm; bezel set with 58 diamonds; sapphire crystal; transparent case back; crown with moonstone cabochon; water-resistant to 3 atm
Band: reptile skin, pin buckle
Remarks: dial set with 36 diamonds; includes two additional reptile skin straps
Price: $42,200
Variations: with light-colored dial; in stainless steel

Égérie Automatic

Reference number: 4606F/000G-B649
Movement: automatic, Vacheron Constantin Caliber 1088; ø 20.8 mm, height 3.83 mm; 24 jewels; 28,800 vph; 40-hour power reserve
Functions: hours, minutes, sweep seconds; date
Case: white gold, ø 35 mm, height 9.52 mm; bezel and lugs set with 81 diamonds; sapphire crystal; transparent case back; crown with moonstone cabochon; water-resistant to 3 atm
Band: reptile skin, pin buckle
Remarks: gold dial set with 574 diamonds; includes an additional satin strap
Price: $69,000
Variations: in rose gold ($69,000)

Caliber 2460 R31R7/3

Automatic; single mainspring barrel, 40-hour power reserve; Geneva Seal
Functions: hours, minutes; date and weekday; (retrograde)
Diameter: 27.2 mm
Height: 5.4 mm
Jewels: 27
Balance: glucydur
Frequency: 28,800 vph
Remarks: skeletonized gold rotor; 276 parts

Caliber 2460 QCL/1

Automatic; second stop; single mainspring barrel, 40-hour power reserve; Geneva Seal
Functions: hours, minutes, sweep seconds; full calendar with date, weekday, month
Diameter: 29 mm
Height: 5.4 mm
Jewels: 27
Balance: glucydur
Frequency: 28,800 vph
Remarks: gold rotor; 308 parts

Caliber 2460 R31L/2

Automatic; single mainspring barrel, 40-hour power reserve; Geneva Seal
Functions: hours, minutes; date (retrograde), moon phase
Diameter: 27.2 mm
Height: 5.4 mm
Jewels: 27
Balance: glucydur
Frequency: 28,800 vph
Remarks: gold rotor; 275 parts

Caliber 2162 R31

Automatic; hubless peripheral winding rotor; 1-minute tourbillon; two spring barrels, 72-hour power reserve; Geneva Seal
Functions: hours, minutes, subsidiary seconds (on the tourbillon cage); date (retrograde)
Diameter: 31 mm
Height: 5.65mm
Jewels: 30
Balance: glucydur
Frequency: 18,000 vph
Remarks: gold oscillating mass; 242 parts

Caliber 2455/2

Automatic; gold rotor; single mainspring barrel, 40-hour power reserve; Geneva Seal
Functions: hours, minutes; date
Diameter: 26.2 mm
Height: 3.6 mm
Jewels: 27
Balance: glucydur
Frequency: 28,800 vph
Remarks: 194 parts

Caliber 1120 QP

Automatic; extra thin construction; winding rotor with support ring; single mainspring barrel, 40-hour power reserve; Geneva Seal
Functions: hours, minutes; perpetual calendar with date, weekday, month, moon phase, leap year
Diameter: 29.6 mm
Height: 4.05 mm
Jewels: 36
Balance: glucydur
Frequency: 19,800 vph
Remarks: skeletonized rotor with gold oscillating mass; 276 parts

Caliber 1088 L

Automatic; swan-neck fine adjustment; single mainspring barrel, 40-hour power reserve; Geneva Seal
Functions: hours, minutes, sweep seconds
Diameter: 30 mm
Height: 5.03 mm
Jewels: 26
Balance: glucydur
Frequency: 28,800 vph
Hairspring: flat hairspring
Remarks: skeletonized gold rotor; 172 parts

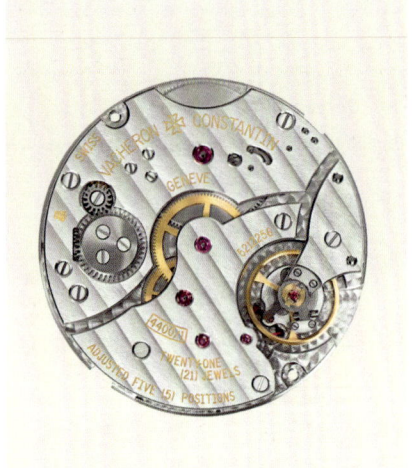

Caliber 4400 AS

Hand-wound; single mainspring barrel, 65-hour power reserve; Geneva Seal
Functions: hours, minutes, subsidiary seconds
Diameter: 28.6 mm
Height: 2.8 mm
Jewels: 21
Balance: glucydur
Frequency: 28,800 vph
Remarks: perlage on mainplate, beveled edges, bridges with côtes de Genève; 127 parts

Caliber 1326

Automatic; two spring barrels, 48-hour power reserve
Functions: hours, minutes, sweep seconds; date
Diameter: 26.2 mm
Height: 4.3 mm
Jewels: 25
Balance: glucydur
Frequency: 28,800 vph
Hairspring: flat hairspring
Remarks: skeletonized er gold rotor; finely finished with côtes de Genève; 142 parts

Caliber 1003

Hand-wound; single spring barrel, 31-hour power reserve; Geneva Seal
Functions: hours, minutes
Diameter: 21.1 mm
Height: 1.64 mm
Jewels: 18
Balance: glucydur
Frequency: 18,000 vph
Remarks: currently the thinnest mechanical movement in production

Caliber 3300

Hand-wound; column wheel control of the chronograph functions, horizontal clutch; single mainspring barrel, 65-hour power reserve; Geneva Seal
Functions: hours, minutes, subsidiary seconds; power reserve indicator; chronograph with crown pusher
Diameter: 32.8 mm
Height: 6.7 mm
Jewels: 35
Balance: glucydur
Frequency: 21,600 vph
Remarks: 252 parts

Caliber 2260

Hand-wound; 1-minute tourbillon; four spring barrels, 336-hour power reserve; Geneva Seal
Functions: hours, minutes, subsidiary seconds (on the tourbillon cage); power reserve indicator
Diameter: 29.1 mm
Height: 6.8 mm
Jewels: 31
Balance: glucydur
Frequency: 18,000 vph
Remarks: 231 parts

VARIO WATCHES

Ivan Chua, who hails from Singapore, found his way to watches in a most unusual fashion. After studying to become an engineer, he started building websites at a time when everyone needed an online presence and web designers were fairly rare. He then decided to expand this ability and went on to study animation, after which he became a motion designer with some major media companies, like MTV, as clients.

Being in business—albeit, a reluctant manager by his own admission— he needed to check the time often, which meant pulling out his phone a lot. One day, he decided to resuscitate his old quartz watches and noticed that the straps were ill-matched, even ugly. So, he started making his own and then selling them. He soon realized that a nice strap should have a nice watch. So, finally, he launched Vario in 2016.

As an engineer with a well-trained eye, Ivan Chu's strategy is to design watches that attract without distracting. Next to a few quartz collections, he began producing series of mechanical, military-themed watches that connect emotionally to dramas of the past with a little touch of humor. The 1918 Trench models resemble timepieces used by soldiers in the trenches, which became very popular following World War One. They sit on a bund strap, the numerals are large, promising good visibility in the dark, as do the broad cathedral hands. World War Two is the inspiration for the 1945 D12 Field Watch, specifically the robust timepieces made for soldiers by Swiss and British watchmakers. To pep up the dial a bit, the Super-LumiNova on the hands and numerals glows in different colors.

For the ИAVI collection (the reverse N is not a typo), Chu turned to the romance of the seafaring life. The dials are clearly inspired by the engine order telegraphs on older ships. And the most recent production—at printing—is a sleek watch called the Futurist. It features guilloche on the cushion dial, comes in bright colors, and is still well under the thousand-dollar mark.

VARIO
Orchard Plaza
150 Orchard Road, #07-05
Singapore 238841

E MAIL:
customer_service@vario.sg

WEBSITE:
www.vario.sg

FOUNDED:
2016

NUMBER OF EMPLOYEES:
1

MOST IMPORTANT COLLECTIONS/ PRICE RANGE:
1918 Trench, Medic, Pilot / approx. $388; 1945 D12 / approx. $368; Empire / approx. $298-$698; Futurist / approx. $698; Versa / approx. $428

1918 Trench
Movement: automatic, Miyota 82s5 caliber; ø 26 mm, height 5.67 mm; 21 jewels; 21,600 vph; 42-hour power reserve
Functions: hours, minutes, subsidiary seconds
Case: stainless steel, ø 40 mm, height 12 mm; sapphire crystal; water-resistant to 10 atm
Band: calfskin, pin buckle
Price: $388
Variations: various dials and straps

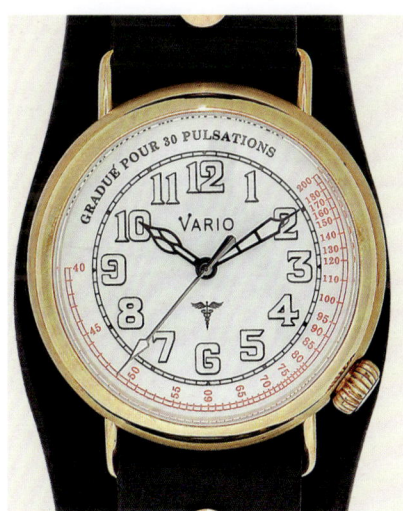

1918 Medic
Movement: automatic, Seiko NH38; ø 27 mm, height 5.32 mm; 24 jewels; 21,600 vph; 42-hour power reserve
Functions: hours, minutes, sweep seconds
Case: stainless steel, ø 40 mm, height 12 mm; sapphire crystal; water-resistant to 10 atm
Band: calfskin, pin buckle
Price: $388
Variations: various dials and straps

Empire Seasons True GMT
Movement: automatic, Miyota 9075 caliber; ø 26 mm, height 4.92 mm; 24 jewels; 28,800 vph; 42-hour power reserve
Functions: hours, minutes, sweep seconds, 24-hour display (second time zone)
Case: stainless steel, ø 38 mm, height 12 mm; sapphire crystal; water-resistant to 5 atm
Band: calfskin, pin buckle
Price: $698
Variations: various dials and straps

VORTIC WATCH COMPANY

The U.S. watch industry produced some very fine timepieces back in the nineteenth century, like Ball, Elgin, Hamilton, and Waltham. So where did the millions of pocket watches go?

Enter R.T. Custer from Pennsylvania. He got wind of companies collecting just the cases of old pocket watches for their gold and silver, and throwing out the movements, dials, hands, and anything deemed worthless to the non-watch fan. So, he took some classes in industrial design, learned all about 3D printing, graduated, and moved out to Colorado. With crowd-funded seed money and a few friends, he started printing simple cases.

This process, known as upcycling, did not please one brand, Hamilton, whose name appears on some of the dials. It decided to use the staggering cash-power of its parent group, Swatch, to stomp out the upstart in Colorado. After five years of litigation, a judge at the Southern District of New York finally ended the absurd battle in Custer's favor, stating clearly that buyers were not about to be confused by the use of the old Hamilton parts in an upcycled watch. Vortic promptly did a victory lap with a Lancaster 065, using a Hamilton dial and caliber from 1930.

Vortic continues to explore the opportunities of modern technology to rebuild old movements. And each year brings new surprises, like the Springfield 069 with a secometer sub-dial in 2024. Even in their modern casings, these watches recall some of the grand old days of American history and business. The difference is subtle at times, but a glance at the Boston (with a Waltham engine) or the Chicago 108, might be enough to see that while both are in "practical" style, the one is just a touch more elegant and might have belonged to the rider rather than the conductor. In 2025, the Springfield 225 was released. It is powered by a 17-jewel Illinois movement manufactured a century before, in 1925. The black DLC treatment of the case and bezel give the watch a very sophisticated aura.

It is worth noting that R.T. Custer has also launched Colorado Watch as a conduit for almost entirely U.S.-made watches.

VORTIC WATCH COMPANY
324 Jefferson St.
Fort Collins, CO 80524
USA

TEL.:
855-285-7884

E-MAIL:
info@vorticwatches.com

WEBSITE:
www.vorticwatches.com

FOUNDED:
2013

NUMBER OF EMPLOYEES:
10

MOST IMPORTANT COLLECTIONS/PRICE RANGE:
American Artisan Series, Railroad Edition, Military Edition, "Convert Your Watch" service / $2,500 to $14,000

The Boston 056

Movement: hand-wound, antique American Waltham Watch Company Riverside (built in 1918, serial number: 22049938); 12 size (39 mm, height 6 mm); 19 jewels; crosshatched côtes de Genéve, concentric scalloping, gold-capped jewels; 36-hour power reserve
Functions: hours, minutes, subsidiary seconds
Case: sandblasted bronze, 45 mm, height 12 mm; sapphire crystal; bronze notched bezel; bronze crown; transparent case back; water-resistant to 5 atm
Band: leather, pin buckle
Price: $4,400

The Chicago 108

Movement: hand-wound, antique Elgin Watch Company movement (built in 1925, serial number: 27464268); 12 size (39 mm, height 6 mm); 17 jewels; overlapping arched engraving and spiral polished wheels, gold-capped jewels; 36-hour power reserve
Functions: hours, minutes, subsidiary seconds
Case: stainless steel, 45 mm, height 12 mm; sapphire crystal; stainless steel bezel; stainless steel crown; transparent case back; water-resistant to 5 atm
Band: leather, pin buckle
Price: $3,700

The Springfield 225

Movement: hand-wound, antique Illinois Watch Company movement (built in 1925, serial number: 4608073), 12 size (39 mm, height 6 mm); 17 jewels; côtes de Genève, gold-capped jewels; 36-hour power reserve
Functions: hours, minutes, subsidiary seconds
Case: titanium with DLC, 46 mm, height 12.5 mm; sapphire crystal; nickel-plated onion style crown; transparent case back; water-resistant to 1 atm
Band: vintage-style leather, pin buckle
Price: $3,700

VOSTOK EUROPE

Vostok Europe is a young brand with old roots. It was established in 2003 in Lithuania—the year the country entered the European Union—by local entrepreneurs who wished to continue the legacy of the original Vostok brand from the USSR. These founders worked on creating an identity rooted in durability and adventure, which is summed up in their tagline: "Watches for going to extremes."

Rather than relying on celebrity endorsements, Vostok Europe draws visibility from the people who actually test the brand's watches in real and rough conditions. These are rally drivers at the famous Dakar Rally, aerobatic pilots, freedivers, a plethora of top athletes, and professionals who work in various rugged industries. Their experiences inform the brand's design philosophy: oversized, robust cases; highly legible dials; and straps engineered to take the strain of a long spelunking expedition, for instance to the bottom of the world in the Krubera Cave.

In 2020 the brand became the official watch of the SSN-571 Alumni Association and a part of the history of the world's first nuclear submarine.

Naturally, Vostok Europe has distinguished itself with practical innovations with regards to technical matters. Many models are water-resistant to professional diving standards (20–30 atm) and feature tritium gas illumination. These are tiny tubes filled with tritium paint that emit light continuously for decades without an external charge. This makes them reliable under conditions where visibility and resilience matter most.

The Vostok Europe portfolio is not just high-tech and muscular. Recent models have become a little more streamlined, and some make references to the Baltic and technological heritage in their design. Commemorative editions have celebrated milestones such as the centenary of engineering achievements and, in 2023, the 700th anniversary of the Lithuanian capital Vilnius. The jubilee collection draws inspiration from the city's founding legend of the Iron Wolf, an emblem of strength and endurance that mirrors the brand's ethos.

KOLIZ VOSTOK CO. LTD.
Vytenio Str. 22
LT-03229 Vilnius
Lithuania

TEL.:
+370-69805460

E-MAIL:
info@vostok-europe.com

WEBSITE:
www.vostok-europe.com

FOUNDED:
2003

NUMBER OF EMPLOYEES:
24

ANNUAL PRODUCTION:
25,000

DISTRIBUTION U.S.:
Vostok Europe USA LLC
848-384-2427
info@vostok-europe.us
www.vostok-europe.us

MOST IMPORTANT COLLECTIONS/PRICE RANGE:
Energia / from $950; Batiscafos / from $850; N1 Rocket / from $350

Batiscafos

Reference number: NH35-511E767
Movement: automatic, TMI NH35 caliber; ø 27.4 mm; height 5.32 mm; 24 jewels; 21,600 vph; 41-hours power reserve
Functions: hours, minutes, sweep seconds; date
Case: stainless steel, ø 49.7 mm, height 17.2 mm; unidirectional bezel with 0-60 scale, hardened K1 mineral glass; screw-down crown; water-resistant to 30 atm
Band: calfskin, pin buckle
Remarks: "Trigalight" constant tritium illumination; changing tool and dry box
Price: $879; limited to 3,000 pieces
Variation: with stainless steel bracelet or silicone strap

Undiné

Reference number: NH38-515A765
Movement: automatic, TMI NH38 caliber; ø 27.4 mm; height 5.32; 24 jewels; 21,600 vph; 41-hour power reserve, open heart
Functions: hours, minutes, sweep seconds
Case: stainless steel, ø 39 mm, height 14.9 mm; unidirectional bezel with 0-60 scale, hardened K1 mineral glass; screw-down crown; water-resistant to 20 atm
Band: suede leather, pin buckle
Price: $549; limited to 3,000 pieces
Variations: with stainless steel Milanese mesh bracelet or silicone strap

Object X

Reference number: NH35-599E776
Movement: automatic, TMI NH35 caliber; ø 27.4 mm; height 5.32 mm; 24 jewels; 21,600 vph; 41-hours power reserve
Functions: hours, minutes, sweep seconds
Case: stainless steel, ø 48 mm, height 16 mm; ceramic bezel; hardened antireflective K1 mineral glass; screw-down crown; water-resistant to 20 atm
Band: luminous silicone strap, pin buckle
Remarks: Rectangle "Trigalight" constant tritium illumination
Price: $779; limited to 1,000 pieces
Variations: with stainless steel bracelet or silicone strap

VULCAIN

For ever so long, watchmakers or companies producing watches kept their names off the face of their products. So, it was not until 1894 that one Maurice Ditisheim put a name to the very fine pocket watches he had been producing in La Chaux-de-Fonds since 1858, the year he opened his little atelier. Among the timepieces in his portfolio were chronographs, a perpetual calendar, and a minute repeater.

Ditisheim understood that the world was bigger than Switzerland, and he extended his networks abroad. His son Ernest-Albert took over in the 1890s and continued not only producing excellent watches but also promoting what was now a brand. He cleverly chose the name Vulcain, or Vulcan, the "patron saint," if you will, of all metal workers. The company became known as Vulcain & Volta in 1911, Vulcain & Studio in the 1950s, and finally, simply and lastly, Vulcain.

The Ditisheims saw the potential of the wristwatch early on and soon began making various models with in-house calibers. The company's major turning point came at the 1947 World's Fair, where it presented its Cricket wristwatch. The aptly named timepiece had an alarm built in that made a loud chirping sound thanks to a double soundboard. The fact that President Truman loved the watch started a tradition: every American president since, except George W. Bush, received a Cricket, even Donald Trump.

After years of ups and downs and changing hands, Vulcain seems to have found its feet again under the able management of Carla Duarte. The collections have been extended beyond the fabled Cricket to include the equally fabled Nautical and Skindiver diving watches. Modern production logistics and digital distribution channels have enabled more competitive pricing. Finally, while the vintage flavor is still present, these watches have a clearly modern look.

VULCAIN
Manufacture des montres Vulcain S.A.
Chemin des Tourelles 4
CH-2400 Le Locle
Switzerland

TEL:
+41-32-930-5370

E-MAIL:
info@vulcain.ch

WEBSITE:
www.vulcain.ch

FOUNDED:
1858

NUMBER OF EMPLOYEES:
8

ANNUAL PRODUCTION:
5,000 watches

RETAIL
Contact the company headquarters

MOST IMPORTANT COLLECTIONS/PRICE RANGE:
Cricket, Chronograph 1970s, Monopusher, Nautical, Salute, Skindiver Nautique / $1,500 to $6,000

Skindiver Nautique GMT
Reference number: 680174B07.BHM286
Movement: automatic, Soprod Caliber C125 GMT; ø 25.6 mm, height 4.1 mm; 25 jewels; 28,800 vph; 42-hour power reserve
Functions: hours, minutes, sweep seconds; additional 24-hour display (second time zone); date
Case: stainless steel, ø 38.3 mm, height 12.2 mm; bezel with ceramic insert, bidirectional, with 24-hour scale; sapphire crystal; screw-down crown; water-resistant to 20 atm
Band: rubber (tropical), pin buckle
Price: $2,080
Variations: with stainless-steel bracelet ($2,370); various fluorescent colors

Skindiver Chronograph Salmon L.E.
Reference number: 590176A87.BAR255
Movement: automatic, ETA Caliber 7753; ø 30.4 mm, height 7.9 mm; 26 jewels; 28,800 vph; 42-hour power reserve
Functions: hours, minutes, subsidiary seconds; chronograph
Case: stainless steel, ø 39.7 mm, height 13 mm; bezel with ceramic insert, 0–60 scale; sapphire crystal; transparent case back; water-resistant to 5 atm
Band: leather, pin buckle
Price: $2,850 limited edition of 100 pieces
Variations: with stainless-steel bracelet ($3,180)

Skindiver Chronograph White
Reference number: 590176A57.BAC201
Movement: automatic, ETA Caliber 7753; ø 30.4 mm, height 7.9 mm; 26 jewels; 28,800 vph; 42-hour power reserve
Functions: hours, minutes, subsidiary seconds; chronograph
Case: stainless steel, ø 39.7 mm, height 13 mm; bezel with ceramic insert, 0–60 scale; sapphire crystal; transparent case back; water-resistant to 5 atm
Band: leather, pin buckle
Price: $2,750
Variations: with stainless-steel bracelet (3,040); various straps and dials

WEMPE GLASHÜTTE

Ever since 2005, the global jewelry chain Gerhard D. Wempe KG has been putting out watches under its own name again. It was probably inevitable: Gerhard D. Wempe, who founded the company in the late nineteenth century in Oldenburg, was himself a watchmaker. And in the 1930s, the company also owned the Hamburg chronometer works that made watches for seafarers and pilots.

Today, while Wempe remains formally in Hamburg, its manufacturing is done in Glashütte. The move to the fully renovated and expanded Urania observatory in the hills above town was engineered by Eva-Kim Wempe, great-granddaughter of the founder. There, the company does all its after-sales service and tests watches using the strict German Industrial Norm (DIN 8319), with official blessings from the Saxon and Thuringian offices for measurement and calibration, and according to international norms paid out by the German Calibration Service. Among other criteria, a chronometer must be tested in the assembled state, which differs from the Swiss COSC certification method. In 2024, the production facility was expanded again so that a total of twenty-four watchmakers can be trained in the future.

The move to Glashütte coincided with a push to verticalize by creating a line of in-house movements reserved for the Chronometerwerke models, like the very retro Power Reserve or the Automatic Moonphase. The calibers, bearing the initials CW, are made in partnership with companies like Nomos in Glashütte or the Swiss workshop MHVJ. The second Wempe line is called Zeitmeister, or Master of Time. This collection uses more standard, but reworked, ETA or Sellita calibers. It meets all the requirements of the high art of watchmaking and, thanks to its accessible pricing, is attractive for budding collectors.

All models are in the middle price range, which the luxury watch industry has long shunned. In 2020, Wempe joined a large community of brands with sportive-elegant timepieces. The Iron Walker series is supposed to be inspired by the workers who built the great skyscrapers of New York in the 1920s. The line is characterized by the elegant bracelet that integrates almost seamlessly into the case. The skyscrapers are hinted at in the shape of the hands.

WEMPE GLASHÜTTE I./SA.
Herbert-Wempe-Platz 1
01768 Glashütte
Germany

TEL.:
+49 35053 312-0

E-MAIL:
info@wempe.de

WEBSITE:
www.wempe.com

FOUNDED:
1878

NUMBER OF EMPLOYEES:
845 worldwide; 78 at Wempe Glashütte I/SA

ANNUAL PRODUCTION:
4,000 watches

U.S. DISTRIBUTOR:
Wempe
700 Fifth Avenue, W 55th St.
New York, NY 10019
212-397-9000
www.wempe.com

MOST IMPORTANT COLLECTIONS/PRICE RANGE:
Wempe Zeitmeister / approx. $1,000 to $4,700;
Wempe Chronometerwerke / approx. $6,000 to
$56,500; Wempe Iron Walker / $1,950 to $5,050

Chronometerwerke Automatic Moon Phase

Reference number: WG 100003
Movement: automatic, Wempe Caliber CW5; ø 32.8 mm, height 6 mm; 35 jewels; 28,800 vph; screw balance with variable inertia; twin spring barrels; three-quarter plate; hand-engraved balance cock; six gold chatons; tungsten microrotor; finely finished with Glashütte stripe decoration; DIN-certified chronometer; 82-hour power reserve
Functions: hours, minutes, sweep seconds; date, moon phase
Case: yellow gold, ø 41 mm, height 11 mm; sapphire crystal; transparent case back; water-resistant to 3 atm
Band: reptile skin, pin buckle
Price: $17,000

Zeitmeister Classic Moon Phase with Complete Calendar

Reference number: WM 350001
Movement: automatic, ETA Caliber 2892-A2 with Dubois Dépraz 5900 module; ø 25.6 mm, height 5.35 mm; 21 jewels; 28,800 vph; ISO 3159-certified chronometer; 42-hour power reserve
Functions: hours, minutes, sweep seconds; complete calendar with date, weekday, month, moon phase
Case: stainless steel, ø 42 mm, height 14.1 mm; sapphire crystal; water-resistant to 5 atm
Band: reptile skin, folding clasp
Price: $3,175

Zeitmeister Classic Automatic

Reference number: WM 140090
Movement: automatic, Sellita Caliber SW300-1a; ø 25.6 mm, height 3.6 mm; 25 jewels; 28,800 vph; certified chronometer (ISO 3159); 56-hour power reserve
Functions: hours, minutes, sweep seconds; date
Case: stainless steel with yellow-gold PVD, ø 38 mm, height 11 mm; sapphire crystal; water-resistant to 5 atm
Band: stainless steel with yellow-gold PVD coating, double folding clasp
Price: $2,880

Iron Walker Automatic GMT

Reference number: WI 250002
Movement: automatic, Sellita Caliber SW330-2;
ø 25.6 mm, height 4.1 mm; 21 jewels; 28,800 vph;
certified chronometer (ISO 3159); 56-hour power
reserve
Functions: hours, minutes, sweep seconds; additional
24-hour display (second time zone); date
Case: stainless steel, ø 42 mm, height 11.7 mm;
bidirectional rotating ring with 24-hour graduation;
sapphire crystal; screw-down crown; water-resistant
to 10 atm
Band: stainless steel, folding clasp with safety lock
Price: $4,440
Variations: with black-and-white bezel

Iron Walker Chronograph 46

Reference number: WI 690013
Movement: automatic, Sellita Caliber SW500-1;
ø 30 mm, height 7.9 mm; 25 jewels; 28,800 vph;
certified chronometer (ISO 3159); 48-hour power
reserve
Functions: hours, minutes, subsidiary seconds;
chronograph; date
Case: carbon fiber, ø 46 mm; bezel, crown, and pushers
with rubber coating; sapphire crystal; water-resistant
to 10 atm
Band: rubber with textile inlay, folding clasp
Price: $8,025

Iron Walker Chronograph 44

Reference number: WI 400001
Movement: automatic, Sellita Caliber SW500-b;
ø 30 mm, height 7.9 mm; 25 jewels; 28,800 vph;
certified chronometer (DIN); 48-hour power reserve
Functions: hours, minutes, subsidiary seconds;
chronograph; date
Case: stainless steel, ø 44 mm; bezel with rubber
coating; sapphire crystal; crown and pushers with
rubber coating; water-resistant to 10 atm
Band: rubber, folding clasp
Price: $5,075

Iron Walker Automatic 40

Reference number: WI 100048
Movement: automatic, Sellita Caliber SW300-1a;
ø 25.6 mm, height 3.6 mm; 25 jewels; 28,800 vph;
certified chronometer (ISO 3159); 56-hour power
reserve
Functions: hours, minutes, sweep seconds; date
Case: stainless steel, ø 40 mm, height 9 mm; sapphire
crystal; water-resistant to 10 atm
Band: stainless steel, folding clasp with safety lock
Price: $3,300
Variations: also available with 36 mm case

Iron Walker Automatic 36

Reference number: WI 100034
Movement: automatic, Sellita Caliber SW300-1a;
ø 25.6 mm, height 3.6 mm; 25 jewels; 28,800 vph;
certified chronometer (ISO 3159); 56-hour power
reserve
Functions: hours, minutes, sweep seconds; date
Case: stainless steel, ø 36 mm, height 9.75 mm; bezel
set with diamonds; sapphire crystal; water-resistant to
10 atm
Band: stainless steel, folding clasp with safety lock
Price: $6,925
Variations: various dial colors

Iron Walker Automatic 36

Reference number: WI 100045
Movement: automatic, Sellita Caliber SW300-1a;
ø 25.6 mm, height 3.6 mm; 25 jewels; 28,800 vph;
certified chronometer (ISO 3159); 56-hour power
reserve
Functions: hours, minutes, sweep seconds; date
Case: stainless steel, ø 36 mm, height 9.75 mm;
sapphire crystal; water-resistant to 10 atm
Band: stainless steel, folding clasp with safety lock
Price: $3,170
Variations: various dial colors

YELLOWSTONE

A French poet and ethnographer once defined culture as "the ensemble of material and immaterial creations through which humankind distinguishes itself from other living species, encompassing language, manners, customs, traditions, and civility." Thanks to its boundless curiosity for the new, the United States has, in just 250 years, become home to a hugely diverse culture that continues to fascinate people around the world.

Through their Detroit Watch Company (see page XXX), Patrick and Amy Ayoub explore the history and identity of their city—shaped by its vibrant car culture and a heritage that stretches back to a time before the United States existed as a political entity. The choice seems natural for two designers immersed in creative industries: Patrick Ayoub previously worked with BMW and Volkswagen, while Amy Ayoub is a designer and architect for Paramount Global and its emblematic brands, including MTV, Nickelodeon, and Comedy Central.

The diverse natural landscape across the fifty states also fuels imaginations worldwide. The Ayoubs decided to launch a second brand that pays tribute to another particularly symbolic place: Yellowstone National Park, whose cultural story began in 1872 as a romantic frontier landscape evoking adventure and poetic grandeur. Its vistas have long inspired explorers, writers, and even presidents. Among the new models is a moon-phase watch showing the lunar cycle over a Yellowstone mountainscape. The Prairie model's dial recalls a wagon wheel, a real emblem of the covered wagons that carried settlers westward.

Another piece, the Gallatin, bears a name deeply woven into American geography and culture: it refers to a river, a mountain range, a national forest, a county in Montana, a town in Tennessee, and even a "Scholars" program at NYU. The historical figure behind the name was one Albert Gallatin (1761–1849), an immigrant from the Republic of Geneva who became a central figure in early American politics, serving as delegate to the 1789 Constitutional Convention, ambassador to France and England, and Secretary of the Treasury under Presidents Thomas Jefferson and James Madison.

YELLOWSTONE WATCH COMPANY, LLC
3596 West Maple Road
Suite 240
Bloomfield Hills, MI 48301
USA

TEL:
406-955-2100

E-MAIL:
ywc@yellowstonewatchcompany.com

WEB:
https://yellowstonewatchcompany.com

FOUNDED:
2024

NUMBER OF EMPLOYEES:
2

ANNUAL PRODUCTION:
Exclusive 300 Timepieces

DISTRIBUTION:
Direct Sales Only

MOST IMPORTANT COLLECTIONS/PRICE RANGE:
1872 Moonphase, La Gallatin, Prairie / $1,350 to $1,695

La Gallatin
Reference number: YWC GTN-EXH
Movement: automatic, Swiss ETA 2824-2; 25 jewels; 28,800 vph; decorated movement with perlage, blued screws, côtes de Genève on rotor; 38-hour power reserve
Functions: hours, minutes, sweep seconds; date
Case: stainless steel, ø 39 mm, height 11 mm; polished and brushed finish; screw-down crown with YWC logo; sapphire crystal, transparent case back; water-resistant to 5 atm
Band: stainless steel, folding clasp
Remarks: named after Albert Gallatin (1761-1849), Swiss immigrant and political figure and early US ethnologist
Price: $1,450

Prairie Gold
Reference number: YWC-P
Movement: automatic, Swiss ETA 2824-2; ø 25.6 mm, height 4.6 mm; 25 jewels; 28,800 vph; decorated movement with perlage, blued screws, côtes de Genève on rotor; 38-hour power reserve
Functions: Hours, minutes, sweep seconds; date
Case: stainless steel with gold PVD, ø 39 mm, height 11 mm; screw-down crown with blue and white YWC logo; sapphire crystal, transparent case back; water-resistant to 5 atm
Band: calf leather, pin buckle
Price: $1,450
Variations: comes with Sellita SW200-1 caliber

1872 Moonphase Arabic Gold
Reference number: YWC MOON-EXH
Movement: automatic, Sellita SW280-1 caliber; ø 25.6 mm, height 5.4 mm; 26 jewels; 28,800 vph; blued screws, perlage, côtes de Genève on plates and bridges; 38-hour power reserve
Functions: hours, minutes, sweep seconds; date; moon phase
Case: stainless steel with gold PVD, ø 39 mm, height 11 mm; screw-down crown with blue and white YWC logo; sapphire crystal, transparent case back; water-resistant to 5 atm
Band: calf leather, pin buckle
Price: $1,695
Variations: comes with manually wound caliber

YEMA

How difficult it is to live in the shadow of a great and geographically close competitor is illustrated by the little town of Morteau, population just under 7,000, in Burgundy, France. But in the world of watchmaking, it has quite a reputation. It lies in *Pays Horloger* (watch country), in a gentle valley traversed by the meandering Doubs River (hence the name, which means dead, or stagnant, water). Watchmaking came to the region and replaced agriculture as a source of income in the mid-1750s. Today, the town's school has an excellent reputation as an institution that supplies extremely talented workers to the entire industry, notably in Switzerland: Le Locle and La Chaux-de-Fonds, global hubs of Swiss watchmaking, are just a few miles away. Not surprisingly, it has two watch brands, one of which is Yema.

Quietly and steadily, Yema has been producing sports watches for divers, motor sports enthusiasts, pilots, and seafarers since 1948. Among its most important achievements was the first watch able to go 200 meters (660 feet) underwater. The Master Elements of the late 1970s let the user calculate speed, flying time, and the amount of fuel left in flight. And the Spationaute was the first French watch to reach space on the wrist of Jean-Loup Chrétien.

In 2009, the company was bought by a local group, Montres Ambre SA, which chose a flight forward strategy. Leveraging the long experience of the employees, it began manufacturing its own calibers, the Yema 2000 and Yema 3000 (GMT), as well as the Morteau 20. French watchmaker Olivier Mory—who achieved brief international fame in 2024 when he turned out to be the fellow behind the Trump tourbillon—specializes in the development and (partial) production of new movements. Mory is a graduate of the famous watchmaking school in Morteau and is therefore very familiar with the aura surrounding the Yema brand. He designed two exclusive automatic calibers for Yema, one with a central rotor (CMM.10) and one with a microrotor (CMM.20). And, as the crown jewel of watchmaking, a tourbillon (CMM.30), which, thanks to optimized and industrialized production, is now more affordable for Yema customers.

YEMA WATCHES
1 rue Fontaine de l'Epine
F-25500 Morteau
France

TEL.:
+33-381-67-67-67

EMAIL:
privilege@yema.com

WEBSITE:
www.yema.com

FOUNDED:
1948

NUMBER OF EMPLOYEES:
60

DISTRIBUTION:
online

MOST IMPORTANT COLLECTIONS:
Superman, Navygraf, Rallygraf, Granvelle

Superman Tourbillon L.E.
Movement: hand-wound, Calibre Manufacture Morteau CMM.31 (base BCP); ø 31 mm; 19 jewels; 21,600 vph; 1-minute tourbillon with free-sprung balance hairspring; 105-hour power reserve
Functions: hours, minutes, subsidiary seconds (on the tourbillon cage)
Case: titanium, ø 43 mm, height 11.7 mm; bidirectional bezel with ceramic insert and 0-60 scale; sapphire crystal; screw-down crown; water-resistant to 20 atm
Band: titanium, double folding clasp
Remarks: limited edition
Price: $13,000

Granvelle CMM.20
Movement: automatic, Calibre Manufacture Morteau CMM.20; ø 25.6 mm, height 3.7 mm; 33 jewels; 28,800 vph; microrotor on ball bearings; 70-hour power reserve
Functions: hours, minutes, subsidiary seconds
Case: stainless steel, ø 39 mm, height 8.6 mm; sapphire crystal; water-resistant to 5 atm
Band: leather, folding clasp
Price: $2,250

Superman Dato
Movement: automatic, Calibre Manufacture Morteau CMM.11; ø 28 mm, height 4.2 mm; 27 jewels; 28,800 vph; 70-hour power reserve
Functions: hours, minutes, sweep seconds; date
Case: stainless steel, ø 39.5 mm, height 11.85 mm; unidirectional bezel with ceramic insert and 0-60 scale; sapphire crystal; screw-down crown; water-resistant to 20 atm
Band: stainless steel with scale-shaped links, double folding clasp
Price: $2,090
Variations: various straps

ZEITWINKEL

The independent brand Zeitwinkel, based in Saint-Imier, one of the hubs of the Swiss watch industry, is anything but a run-of-the-mill enterprise. Its key attributes, ones that many manufacturers claim but few truly embody, is to create timepieces that are "timeless, simple, and sustainable." It may sound banal at first, but Zeitwinkel takes these principles seriously. Because of that "timeless" philosophy, the company feels no pressure to join the frantic race to launch new models like clockwork, preferring instead to wait for genuine inspiration. And since the brand produces largely to order, customers may have to wait a few months before receiving their watch.

The models produced by Zeitwinkel (the name means "time angle") are deceptively classical. The simplest is a two-hand watch; the most complex, the 273°, is a three-hand timepiece with power-reserve display and large date. The most decoration one will find on the dials is a scattering of stylized *W*s, derived from the inverted logo in the brand's proprietary typeface. The cases show a refined interplay of sandblasted and polished surfaces yet remain discreetly elegant in a distinctly "German" way—unsurprising given that Zeitwinkel's founders, Ivica Maksimovic and Peter Nikolaus, hail from Germany. Certain details stand out, notably the extra-large subsidiary seconds dial and the aperture for the patented large date set beside the 11 o'clock marker.

The most valuable aspect of these watches lies in their true *manufacture* movements, with plates and bridges made of German silver, a relatively rare choice in the industry. All components are either made in-house or sourced from long-standing independent suppliers near Zeitwinkel's workshop in Saint-Imier, where every movement and complete watch is assembled and regulated by hand.

Zeitwinkel's workhorse model, the 273°, is available with full-color dials or with a smoky sapphire dial that reveals the movement as if viewed under water. The 082° features a Grand Feu enamel dial, giving it a particularly deep, opaque appearance. A newer model, the 248°, returns to the charm of a guilloché dial center.

In line with the company's ideals, you will not find any alligator leather in Zeitwinkel straps. Options are limited to rubber, calfskin, or calfskin with an alligator-style embossed pattern.

ZEITWINKEL MONTRES SA
Rue Pierre-Jolissaint 35
CH-2610 Saint-Imier
Switzerland

TEL.:
+41-32-940-17-71

E-MAIL:
info@zeitwinkel.ch

WEBSITE:
www.zeitwinkel.ch

FOUNDED:
2006

ANNUAL PRODUCTION:
About 100 watches

U.S. DISTRIBUTOR:
available directly from the manufacture and select partners worldwide; contact manufacture

MOST IMPORTANT COLLECTIONS/PRICE RANGE:
mechanical wristwatches with automatic in-house movements / starting at around CHF 15,000

Prices are listed in Swiss francs subject to daily exchange rates

Zeitwinkel 248° Guilloché Blue-Silver

Reference number: 248-72031-00
Movement: automatic, ZW0102 caliber; ø 30.4 mm, height 5.7 mm; 30 jewels; 28,800 vph; German-silver three-quarter plate with côtes de Genève and perlage; polished screws and edges; "Black Or" coated plates and bridges; 72-hour power reserve,
Functions: hours, minutes, sweep seconds
Case: stainless steel, ø 40.5 mm, height 12.1 mm; sapphire crystal; transparent case back; water-resistant to 10 atm
Band: leather, folding clasp
Remarks: hand-guilloché dial in two-tone blue/silver, dial numerals in Zeitwinkel typeface
Price: CHF 17,900
Variations: silver or anthracite dial

Zeitwinkel 273° Saphir Fumé

Reference number: 273-42018-00
Movement: automatic, ZW0103 caliber; ø 30.4 mm, height 8 mm; 49 jewels; 28,800 vph; German silver three-quarter plate and bridges, côtes de Genève, polished screws and edges; perlage on dial side; 72-hour power reserve
Functions: hours, minutes, subsidiary seconds; power reserve indicator; patented big date mechanism
Case: stainless steel, ø 42.5 mm, height 13.8 mm; sapphire crystal; transparent case back; water-resistant to 5 atm
Band: calfskin, folding clasp
Remarks: smoked sapphire crystal dial
Price: CHF 21,500
Variations: blue sapphire dial; various bands

Zeitwinkel 082° Email Grand Feu

Reference number: 082-46023-00
Movement: automatic, ZW0102 caliber; ø 30.4 mm, height 5.7 mm; 28 jewels; 28,800 vph; German silver three-quarter plate and bridges, with côtes de Genève and perlage, blued screws and polished edges; 72-hour power reserve
Functions: hours, minutes, sweep seconds
Case: stainless steel, ø 39 mm, height 11.6 mm; sapphire crystal; transparent case back; water-resistant to 5 atm
Band: calfskin or natural rubber, folding clasp
Remarks: grand feu enamel dial with blue enamel numerals in Zeitwinkel's own typeface
Price: CHF 17,900

ZENITH

Zenith, still housed in a tall, light-bathed industrial building in Le Locle, Switzerland, was founded in 1865 by Georges Favre-Jacot as a small watch reassembly workshop. It has produced all kinds of watches in its 160-year history, which it celebrated in 2025 with striking blue ceramic Big Pilots.

The company's claim to fame, however, remains the El Primero caliber, the first wristwatch chronograph movement boasting automatic winding and a frequency of 36,000 vph, allowing for measurements of a tenth of a second. It was 1969, and only a few manufacturers had risked such a high oscillation frequency.

LVMH Group bought the brand in 1999, boosting its technical possibilities. Zenith was dusted off and modernized. The historic complex in Le Locle, which was put on UNESCO's World Heritage list in 2009, was thoroughly renovated. Over eighty different crafts are now practiced there, from watchmaking to design, from art to prototyping. Synergies with the Group companions Hublot and TAG Heuer produced the Defy 21, a complex chronograph movement based on the 36,000-vph El Primero. It features two separate gear trains and escapements for time and chronograph functions, respectively. The chronograph movement beats at 360,000 vph, allowing hundredths of a second to be displayed. The other technical feat is the Zero G that keeps the escapement system in the horizontal position.

Re-releasing older models has led the company to promote a circular economy, whereby older models are perfectly restored and remain in circulation. The original El Primero is now the El Primero 3600 caliber, boasting a little more power reserve than the original. Worth noting among the many prize-winning calibers as well is the 135, now with updated technical solutions and materials. It runs in the new G.F.J. collection, named after the founder.

The El Primero 3600 caliber is also used in the latest Chronomaster Sport models, which come in titanium and stainless steel with a green dial and green bezel. The highlight, however, is the comeback of the long-awaited chronograph with triple calendar display. Zenith combines the contemporary performance of the legendary automatic high-frequency chronograph movement with classic complications, like a full calendar and moon phase display—all in a compact, historically inspired, and distinctive Chronomaster design.

ZENITH SA
34, rue des Billodes
CH-2400 Le Locle
Switzerland

TEL.:
+41-32-930-6262

WEBSITE:
www.zenith-watches.com

FOUNDED:
1865

NUMBER OF EMPLOYEES:
over 330 employees worldwide

U.S. DISTRIBUTOR:
Zenith Watches
966 South Springfield Avenue
Springfield, NJ 07081
866-273-3477
contact.zenith@lvmhwatchjewelry.com

MOST IMPORTANT COLLECTIONS/PRICE RANGE:
Chronomaster / from $6,700; Defy / from $5,900; Elite / from $4,700; G.F.J / from $49,000; Pilot / from $5,700

Pilot Big Date Flyback 160th Anniversary Edition

Reference number: 49.4002.3652/51.I009
Movement: automatic, Zenith Caliber 3652 "El Primero"; ø 30 mm, height 7.35 mm; 35 jewels; 36,000 vph; 60-hour power reserve
Functions: hours, minutes, subsidiary seconds; flyback chronograph; large date
Case: ceramic, ø 42.4 mm; sapphire crystal; transparent case back; screw-down crown; water-resistant to 10 atm
Band: rubber with textile inlay, triple folding clasp
Remarks: comes with an additional white rubber strap
Price: $15,900; limited to 160 pieces

Defy Skyline Chronograph 160th Anniversary Edition

Reference number: 49.9502.3600/51.I001
Movement: automatic, Zenith Caliber 3600 "El Primero"; ø 30 mm, height 6.6 mm; 35 jewels; 36,000 vph; 60-hour power reserve
Functions: hours, minutes, subsidiary seconds; chronograph; date
Case: ceramic, ø 42 mm, height 13.6 mm; sapphire crystal; transparent case back; water-resistant to 10 atm
Band: ceramic, folding clasp
Remarks: comes with an additional rubber strap
Price: $23,800; limited to 160 pieces

Chronomaster Sport 160th Anniversary Edition

Reference number: 49.3102.3600/51.M3100
Movement: automatic, Zenith Caliber 3600 "El Primero"; ø 30 mm, height 6.6 mm; 35 jewels; 36,000 vph; 60-hour power reserve
Functions: hours, minutes, subsidiary seconds; chronograph; date
Case: ceramic, ø 41 mm, height 13.6 mm; sapphire crystal; transparent case back; water-resistant to 10 atm
Band: ceramic, folding clasp
Remarks: comes with an additional rubber strap
Price: $22,700; limited to 160 pieces

G.F.J. Caliber 135

Reference number: 40.1865.0135/51.C200
Movement: hand-wound, Zenith Caliber 135; ø 30 mm;
22 jewels; 18,000 vph; 72-hour power reserve; COSC-
certified chronometer
Functions: hours, minutes, subsidiary seconds
Case: platinum, ø 39 mm, height 10.5 mm; sapphire
crystal; transparent case back; water-resistant to 5 atm
Band: reptile skin, pin buckle
Remarks: tribute to company founder Georges Favre-
Jacot
Price: $49,900; limited to 160 pieces

Chronomaster Original

Reference number: 03.3200.3600/52.C910
Movement: automatic, Zenith Caliber
3600 "El Primero"; ø 30 mm, height 6.6 mm; 35 jewels;
36,000 vph; 60-hour power reserve
Functions: hours, minutes, subsidiary seconds;
chronograph; date
Case: stainless steel, ø 38 mm, height 12.6 mm;
sapphire crystal; transparent case back; water-resistant
to 10 atm
Band: leather, pin buckle
Price: $10,700
Variations: also available with stainless-steel bracelet

Chronomaster Sport

Reference number: 03.3100.3600/69.M3100
Movement: automatic, Zenith Caliber
3600 "El Primero"; ø 30 mm, height 6.6 mm; 35 jewels;
36,000 vph; 60-hour power reserve
Functions: hours, minutes, subsidiary seconds;
chronograph; date
Case: stainless steel, ø 41 mm, height 13.6 mm; ceramic
bezel; sapphire crystal; transparent case back; water-
resistant to 10 atm
Band: stainless steel, double folding clasp
Price: $11,800
Variations: various dial colors; also available with
rubber strap ($11,200)

Defy Skyline 36 mm

Reference number: 03.9400.670/51.I001
Movement: automatic, Zenith Caliber 670 "Elite";
ø 25.6 mm, height 3.88 mm; 27 jewels; 28,800 vph;
48-hour power reserve
Functions: hours, minutes, sweep seconds; date
Case: stainless steel, ø 36 mm, height 10.4 mm;
sapphire crystal; transparent case back; screw-down
crown; water-resistant to 10 atm
Band: stainless steel, folding clasp
Price: $9,000
Variations: with green or pink dial; with diamond-set
bezel ($12,800)

Defy Skyline Skeleton

Reference number: 03.9300.3620/78.I001
Movement: automatic, Zenith Caliber 3620 "El
Primero"; ø 30 mm; 26 jewels; 36,000 vph; skeletonized
movement; 60-hour power reserve
Functions: hours, minutes, subsidiary seconds
(10-second rotation)
Case: stainless steel, ø 41 mm, height 11.6 mm; sapphire
crystal; transparent case back; screw-down crown;
water-resistant to 10 atm
Band: stainless steel, folding clasp
Remarks: skeletonized dial; includes an additional
rubber strap
Price: $11,800

Defy Skyline Chronograph

Reference number: 03.9500.3600/51.I001
Movement: automatic, Zenith Caliber
3610 "El Primero"; ø 30 mm, height 7.73 mm; 35 jewels;
36,000 vph; 60-hour power reserve
Functions: hours, minutes, subsidiary seconds;
chronograph; date
Case: stainless steel, ø 42 mm; sapphire crystal;
transparent case back; water-resistant to 10 atm
Band: stainless steel, folding clasp
Remarks: includes an additional rubber strap
Price: $13,900
Variations: with black dial

Defy Skyline Chronograph

Reference number: 03.9500.3600/79.I001
Movement: automatic, Zenith Caliber 3600 SK "El Primero"; ø 30 mm, height 6.6 mm; 30 jewels; 36,000 vph; skeletonized movement; 60-hour power reserve
Functions: hours, minutes, subsidiary seconds; chronograph
Case: stainless steel, ø 42 mm, height 11.6 mm; sapphire crystal; transparent case back; screw-down crown; water-resistant to 10 atm
Band: stainless steel, folding clasp
Remarks: includes an additional rubber strap
Price: $16,100

Defy Revival Shadow

Reference number: 97.A3648.670/21.M3648
Movement: automatic, Zenith Caliber 670 "Elite"; ø 25.6 mm, height 3.88 mm; 27 jewels; 28,800 vph; 48-hour power reserve
Functions: hours, minutes, sweep seconds; date
Case: titanium, ø 37 mm, height 15.5 mm; unidirectional bezel with 0–60 scale; sapphire crystal; water-resistant to 60 atm
Band: titanium, double folding clasp
Remarks: inspired by a historical model from 1969
Price: $8,500

Defy Extreme Diver Shadow

Reference number: 97.9600.3620/21.I300
Movement: automatic, Zenith Caliber 3620 "El Primero"; ø 30 mm; 26 jewels; 36,000 vph; 60-hour power reserve
Functions: hours, minutes, sweep seconds; date
Case: titanium, ø 42.4 mm, height 15.5 mm; ceramic unidirectional bezel with 0–60 scale; sapphire crystal; transparent case back; screw-down crown; helium valve; water-resistant to 60 atm
Band: textile, folding clasp
Price: $12,800
Variations: with rubber strap; with titanium bracelet

Defy Extreme Titanium

Reference number: 95.9100.9004/01.I001
Movement: automatic, Zenith Caliber 9004 "El Primero"; ø 32 mm, height 7.9 mm; 53 jewels; 36,000 vph; independent chronograph mechanism with separate escapement (360,000 vph) and mainspring; certified chronometer (Timelab); 50-hour power reserve
Functions: hours, minutes, subsidiary seconds; power-reserve indicator (for chronograph function); chronograph (hundredths-of-a-second display)
Case: titanium, ø 45 mm, height 15.4 mm; sapphire crystal; transparent case back; water-resistant to 20 atm
Band: titanium, double folding clasp
Price: $19,300

Pilot Automatic Boutique Edition

Reference number: 03.4000.3620/51.I003
Movement: automatic, Zenith Caliber 3620 "El Primero"; ø 30 mm; 26 jewels; 36,000 vph; 60-hour power reserve
Functions: hours, minutes, sweep seconds; date
Case: stainless steel, ø 40 mm; sapphire crystal; transparent case back; screw-down crown; water-resistant to 60 atm
Band: rubber with textile inlay, triple folding clasp
Remarks: includes an additional leather strap; available exclusively in Zenith boutiques
Price: $8,100
Variations: with black dial

Pilot Big Date Flyback

Reference number: 49.4000.3652/21.I001
Movement: automatic, Zenith Caliber 3652 "El Primero"; ø 30 mm; 26 jewels; 36,000 vph; 60-hour power reserve
Functions: hours, minutes, subsidiary seconds; flyback chronograph; large date
Case: ceramic, ø 42.4 mm; sapphire crystal; transparent case back; screw-down crown; water-resistant to 10 atm
Band: rubber with textile inlay, triple folding clasp
Remarks: includes an additional textile strap
Price: $14,500

Caliber 135

Hand-wound; single spring barrel; 72-hour power reserve; COSC-certified chronometer
Functions: hours, minutes, subsidiary seconds
Diameter: 30 mm
Height: 5 mm
Jewels: 22
Balance: glucydur
Frequency: 18,000 vph
Hairspring: Breguet hairspring
Shock protection: Kif
Remarks: modernized reissue of the legendary chronometer movement; 157 components

Caliber 3600 "El Primero"

Automatic; lever escapement with silicon escape wheel; column-wheel control for chronograph functions; single spring barrel; 60-hour power reserve; COSC-certified chronometer
Functions: hours, minutes, subsidiary seconds; chronograph; date
Diameter: 30 mm
Height: 6.6 mm
Jewels: 35
Balance: glucydur
Frequency: 36,000 vph
Hairspring: flat hairspring
Shock protection: Kif

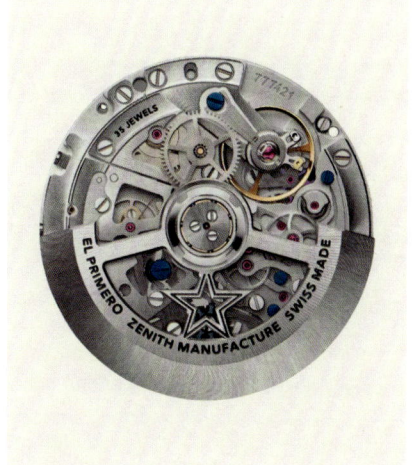

Caliber 3610 "El Primero"

Automatic; lever escapement with silicon escape wheel; column-wheel control for chronograph functions; single spring barrel; 60-hour power reserve; COSC-certified chronometer
Functions: hours, minutes, subsidiary seconds; chronograph; full calendar with date, weekday, month, moon phase
Diameter: 30 mm
Height: 7.73 mm
Jewels: 35
Balance: glucydur
Frequency: 36,000 vph
Hairspring: flat hairspring
Shock protection: Kif
Remarks: 366 components

Caliber 3620 "El Primero"

Automatic; lever escapement with silicon escape wheel; single spring barrel; 60-hour power reserve; COSC-certified chronometer
Functions: hours, minutes, subsidiary seconds; date
Diameter: 30 mm
Jewels: 26
Balance: glucydur
Frequency: 36,000 vph
Hairspring: flat hairspring
Shock protection: Kif

Caliber 9004 "El Primero"

Automatic; independent chronograph mechanism with separate escapement (360,000 vph) and separate power source; twin carbon nanotube hairsprings, unaffected by magnetic fields and temperature variations; certified chronometer (Timelab); single spring barrel; 50-hour power reserve
Functions: hours, minutes, subsidiary seconds; power reserve indicator (for chronograph function); chronograph with hundredth-of-a-second display
Diameter: 32.8 mm
Height: 7.9 mm
Jewels: 53
Balance: glucydur
Frequency: 36,000 vph
Remarks: finely finished; 293 components

Caliber 670 "Elite"

Automatic; skeletonized construction; single spring barrel; 50-hour power reserve
Functions: hours, minutes, sweep seconds; date
Diameter: 25.6 mm
Height: 3.88 mm
Jewels: 27
Balance: glucydur
Frequency: 28,800 vph
Hairspring: flat hairspring
Shock protection: Kif
Remarks: 187 components

ZERO WEST

Time, place, and history are the reference points for Zero West, a company founded in 2015 by Andrew Brabyn and Graham Collins, a leading graphic designer and an aerospace engineer, respectively. The company name itself refers to the coordinates of the Greenwich Royal Observatory. The themes of these watches can be summed up as "great moments and technology in British history," with World War II playing a prominent inspirational role.

Their first watch was a statement; the Longitude L1 paid homage to an icon of British (or even world horology): John Harrison's remarkable H4 maritime clock that managed to keep accurate time on a ship in 1761 and which contributed to the establishment of the Greenwich prime meridian by George Airy in 1851. For the tenth anniversary of its founding, Zero West has released a new edition of the Longitude as a chronograph. It features a world map on the back and a coded date of when London became the "center of the earth," as it were

The company has defined three core collections for its brand: hiOctane, Longitude, and AirSpeed. Its latest aviation model celebrates the S6e. It's made with Merlin engine aluminum from the Spitfire AA810. The pilot was shot down over Norway in 1942 and ended up in Stalag Luft III, the prison camp immortalized by the Hollywood film *The Great Escape* in 1963.

The hiOctane collection is where Zero West's engineering mindset and focus on dial development and production is most visible: preparing and finishing the dial substrate, applying plated or painted surfaces, then laser work and sharp pad printing is all done in-house.

The watches are designed and assembled at the company's workshop and headquarters on the south coast of England. It is where the two founders do their historical research and brainstorm each new watch dial. It is also where Graham Collins makes the straps for the collections. Low volume ensures high quality. Each watch is powered by tried-and-true Swiss calibers, such as the Sellita SW261-1 and the SW500BVc for chronographs.

ZERO WEST LTD
41 Bridgefoot Path
Emsworth, Hampshire
PO10 7EB
United Kingdom

TEL.:
+44 (0)1243-376-676

E-MAIL:
time@zerowest.co.uk

WEBSITE:
www.zerowest.watch

FOUNDED:
2015

NUMBER OF EMPLOYEES:
5

DISTRIBUTION:
Contact the manufacturer directly

MOST IMPORTANT COLLECTIONS:
Airspeed (Spitfire S1/S2/S3), (Hurricane H1), Longitude (Longitude L2), hiOctane (LS-2 Land Speed Bullhead, Flying Scotsman)

Longitude

Reference number: L4
Movement: automatic, Sellita SW500BVc caliber (Top Premium); ø 30 mm, height 7.6 mm; 35 jewels; 28,800 vph; 62-hour power reserve
Functions: hours, minutes, subsidiary seconds; chronograph
Case: stainless steel, ø 42 mm, height 14.2 mm; sapphire crystal, transparent case back; screw-in crown; transparent case back with view of metal disc from a Lancaster ED825 with serial number; water-resistant to 10 atm
Band: stainless steel, folding clasp
Remarks: tribute to John Harrison's H4, with Greenwich reference: date code when London was awarded the Prime Meridian
Price: $4,580; limited to 50 pieces

Spitfire Escape

Reference Number: S6e
Movement: automatic, Sellita SW500BVc caliber (Top Premium); ø 30 mm, height 7.6 mm; 35 jewels; 28,800 vph; 62-hour power reserve
Functions: hours, minutes, subsidiary seconds; chronograph
Case: stainless steel, ø 42 mm, height 14.2 mm; screw-in crown; sapphire crystal; screw-down crown; water-resistant to 10 atm
Band: leather, folding clasp
Remarks: inspired from Spitfire AA810's blueish airspeed gauge; date code on original metal from the Spitfire references the day AA810 was shot down
Price: $5,435; limited to 100 pieces

BWD Heritage Special

Reference Number: HO1
Movement: automatic, Sellita SW500BVc caliber (Top Premium); ø 30 mm, height 7.6 mm; 35 jewels; 28,800 vph; 62-hour power reserve
Functions: hours, minutes, subsidiary seconds; chronograph
Case: stainless steel, ø 42 mm, height 14.2 mm; screw-in crown; water-resistant to 10 atm
Band: leather, folding clasp
Remarks: dial inspired from racing cars; special model for the British Watchmakers' Day
Price: $3,970; limited to 100 pieces

ZEROO TIME CO.

Japan has a few very globally famous brands, like Casio, Citizen, and Seiko. But in their shadow, one finds a number of small brands doing excellent work as well. Zeroo Time, for example, was launched in 2017 by a watch designer named Syuu Kiryou, who prefers to go by the name SYUU, all caps. His experience in the watch industry had left him feeling that watches needed strong design but had to be affordable as well, even if they had serious complications, like tourbillons.

The T8 Orion Full Skeleton Tourbillon, for instance, is fully skeletonized, including an elongated sapphire crystal in the case middle to offer a lateral view into the watch. On the T-6 Quaser, the tourbillon appears in the middle surrounded by a ring, giving it a somewhat extraterrestrial look. The transparent case back reveals a pinwheel côtes de Genève on the mainplate.

Special design involves cost, and Zeroo Time intended to make products that would draw attention and were mechanically reliable but would not financially ruin the buyer. "We want every watch lover to have one of our watches," says SYUU. "We are planning to develop our own movements in the future and create products that are a cross between Swiss and Japanese made."

The way to achieve the delicate cost-quality balance was, first, to crowdfund, and avoid many of the extraneous expenses from distribution and retailing. The second strategy was to source low-cost parts, for instance Sea-Gull movements from China, which are taken apart and rigorously worked over by a team of watchmakers in Japan, where the watches are assembled. In the meantime, these parts are in fact purchased and replicated in China. The company also uses Swiss STP calibers, notably in its M3 Lyra series.

Almost ten years in, Zeroo is making a name for itself. It is present in fifteen countries, including the USA. The designs are also becoming more independent from external inspiration. One of its more recent models, the T9 UFO, comes in a sleek, mellifluous case, like a space vessel. Its clean dial gives stage center (at 6 o'clock) to a simple tourbillon that rotates like a UFO's reactor.

ZEROO TIME CO.
2-1-3, Naganuma-cho, Hachioji-shi,
Tokyo, 192-0907
Japan

TEL.:
+81 50-3656-4608

EMAIL:
hshiba@zerootime.com

WEBSITE:
https://zerootime.com/en-global

FOUNDED:
2017

NUMBER OF EMPLOYEES:
10

ANNUAL PRODUCTION:
approx. 1,000 pieces

U.S. DISTRIBUTOR:
King Jewelers Tennessee
4121 Hillsboro Pike
Nashville, TN 37215
info@kingjewelers.com
KingJewelers.com
615-724-5464

MOST IMPORTANT COLLECTIONS/PRICE RANGE:
T, M, C, DT series / $850 to $5,000

THE ARCHER

Reference number: ZT010PSBK
Movement: automatic, tourbillon caliber ZT08; ø 36 mm x 33.6 mm; 31 jewels; 60-hour power reserve
Functions: hours, minutes
Case: stainless steel, 51 mm x 43 mm; height 14 mm; sapphire crystal; transparent case back (screw-fastened); water-resistant to 3 atm
Band: FKM rubber, pin buckle
Price: $2,805
Variations: with various color straps and cases

T9 UFO Automatic Tourbillon

Reference number: ZT009-02PSWH
Movement: automatic, tourbillon caliber ZT08; ø 34 mm x 34 mm; 31 jewels; 60-hour power reserve
Functions: hours, minutes
Case: stainless steel, 46 mm x 40 mm; height 14.5 mm; sapphire crystal, K9 sapphire case side; screw-mounted transparent case back; water-resistant to 3 atm
Band: FKM rubber, pin buckle
Price: $2,805
Variations: with various color straps and cases

C5 KEIGO Classic

Reference number: ZC005SLG
Movement: automatic caliber 50ZC02 (micro rotor); 40 jewels; 42-hour power reserve
Functions: hours, minutes, subsidiary seconds; date, moon phase, day/night indication
Case: stainless steel, 46 mm x 38 mm; height 12 mm; sapphire crystal; screw-mounted transparent case back; water-resistant to 3 atm
Band: stainless steel, pin buckle
Price: $880
Variations: with various dial colors (light blue, dark blue, light green, white)

CONCEPTO

The Concepto Watch Factory, founded in 2006 in La Chaux-de-Fonds, is the successor to the family-run company Jaquet SA, which changed its name to La Joux-Perret a little while ago and then moved to a different location on the other side of the hub of watchmaking. In 2008, Valérien Jaquet, son of the company founder Pierre Jaquet, began systematically building up a modern movement and watch component factory on an empty floor of the building.

Today, the Concepto Watch Factory employs eighty people in various departments, such as Development/Prototyping, Decoparts (partial manufacturing using lathes, machining, or wire erosion), Artisia (production of movements and complications in large series), as well as Optimo (escapements). In addition to the standard family of calibers, the C2000 (based on the Valjoux) and the vintage chronograph movement C7000 (the evolution of the Venus Caliber), the company's product portfolio includes various tourbillon movements (Caliber C8000) and several modules for adding onto ETA movements (Caliber C1000). A brand-new caliber series, the C3000, features a retrograde calendar and seconds, a power reserve indicator, and a chronograph. The C4000 chronograph caliber with automatic winding is currently in pre-series testing.

One of Concepto's greatest assets is its flexibility. Most of the company's movements are not sold off the shelf, as it were, but rather designed according to the specific requirements of watchmaking companies with regard to form or technical DNA. Some of these cooperations become long-term relationships. Complicated movements are assembled entirely and tested by the company's watchmakers, while others are sold as kits for assembly by the watchmakers. Annual production is somewhere between 30,000 and 40,000 units, with additional hundreds of thousands of components made for contract manufacturing.

1053

Automatic; inverted construction with dial-side escapement; bidirectional off-center winding rotor; single spring barrel; 42-hour power reserve
Functions: hours, minutes, subsidiary seconds (all off-center)
Diameter: 33 mm
Height: 3.75 mm
Jewels: 31
Balance: glucydur
Frequency: 28,800 vph
Balance spring: flat hairspring
Remarks: black finishing on movement

2904 (dial side)

Inverted construction with dial-side escapement; single spring barrel; 48-hour power reserve
Functions: hours, minutes, subsidiary seconds
Diameter: 30.4 mm
Height: 4.6 mm
Jewels: 31
Balance: screw balance
Frequency: 28,800 vph
Balance spring: flat hairspring

3041 Skeleton (dial side)

Hand-wound; skeletonized symmetrical construction; single spring barrel; 48-hour power reserve
Functions: hours, minutes
Diameter: 32.6 mm
Height: 5.5 mm
Jewels: 21
Balance: screw balance
Frequency: 28,800 vph
Balance spring: flat hairspring
Remarks: extensive personalization options for finishing and accessories

2000-RAC

Automatic; column-wheel control of chronograph functions; stop-second system; single spring barrel; 48-hour power reserve
Functions: hours, minutes, subsidiary seconds; chronograph
Diameter: 30.4 mm; Height: 8.4 mm
Jewels: 26; balance: screw balance
Frequency: 28,800 vph
Balance spring: flat hairspring
Shock protection: Incabloc
Remarks: related calibers: 2000 (without control wheel); with two or three totalizers ("tricompax") with or without date; various additional displays (moon phase, retrograde date hand, additional 24-hour sweep hand, power reserve indicator)

8500

Hand-wound; 1-minute tourbillon; column-wheel control of chronograph functions; single spring barrel; 50-hour power reserve
Functions: hours, minutes, subsidiary seconds; split-seconds chronograph
Diameter: 31.3 mm
Height: 7.2 mm
Jewels: 31
Balance: screw balance
Frequency: 21,600 vph
Balance spring: flat hairspring
Remarks: very fine movement finishing

8950-A

Automatic; 1-minute tourbillon; single spring barrel; 60-hour power reserve
Functions: hours, minutes
Diameter: 30.4 mm
Height: 6.7 mm
Jewels: 27
Balance: glucydur
Frequency: 28,800 vph
Balance spring: flat hairspring
Remarks: related caliber: 8950-M (manual winding); extensive personalization options for the finishing, accessories, and functions

8000 (dial side)

Hand-wound; 1-minute tourbillon; single spring barrel; 72-hour power reserve
Functions: hours, minutes
Diameter: 32.6 mm
Height: 5.7 mm
Jewels: 19
Balance: screw balance
Frequency: 21,600 vph
Balance spring: flat hairspring
Remarks: extensive personalization options for the finishing, accessories, and functions

8152

Automatic; 1-minute tourbillon; bridges and plate made of sapphire crystal; off-center, bidirectional rotor; single spring barrel; 72-hour power reserve
Functions: hours, minutes
Diameter: 32.6 mm
Height: 8.5 mm
Jewels: 25
Balance: screw balance
Frequency: 21,600 vph
Balance spring: flat hairspring
Remarks: extensive personalization options for the finishing, accessories, and functions

8600 (dial side)

Hand-wound; 1-minute tourbillon; double spring barrel; 72-hour power reserve
Functions: hours, minutes; minute repeater with carillon (3 gongs)
Diameter: 34.6 mm
Height: 6.45 mm
Jewels: 36
Balance: screw balance
Frequency: 21,600 vph
Hairspring: flat hairspring
Remarks: many customization options for finishing, equipment and functions

ETA

This Swatch Group movement manufacturer ETA produced millions of movements a year. The company offers a broad spectrum of automatic movements in various dimensions with different functions, chronograph mechanisms in varying configurations, pocket watch classics (Calibers 6497 and 98), and hand-wound calibers of days gone by (Calibers 1727 and 7001). Add to that an endless variety of quartz technology from inexpensive three-hand mechanisms to highly complicated multifunctional movements and futuristic ETA quartz mechanisms featuring autonomous energy creation using a rotor and generator.

For a while, the company was selling its products to anyone and everyone. Then, in 2002, ETA's management announced it would discontinue providing half-finished component kits for reassembly and/or embellishment to specialized workshops, and from 2010 they would only offer completely assembled and finished movements for sale. The Swiss Competition Commission known as CoCo, however, studied the issue, and a new deal was struck in 2013, phasing out sales to customers over a period of six years. ETA is already somewhat of a competitor of independent reassemblers such as Soprod, Sellita, La Joux-Perret, Dubois Dépraz, and others thanks to its diversification of available calibers, which has led many brands to counter by creating their own base movements.

The almost stereotypical accusation of ETA being "mass goods" is not justified, however, for it is a real art to manufacture filigreed micromechanical technology in consistently high quality. This is certainly one of the reasons why there have been very few movement factories in Europe that can compete with ETA, or that would want to. Since the success of Swatch—a pure ETA product—millions of Swiss francs have been invested in new development and manufacturing technologies. ETA now only supplies movements to sister companies in the Group, i.e., all Swatch Group brands below Omega. However, these are new generations of movements with, in part, components that are insensitive to magnetic fields (made of silicon or Nivachron).

The internal ETA caliber designations are no longer communicated externally; instead, each Swatch Group brand now assigns its own caliber numbers. The movements presented on these pages represent only a small part of the still huge caliber portfolio —mechanical and quartz— of the Swiss movement giant with production sites Switzerland.

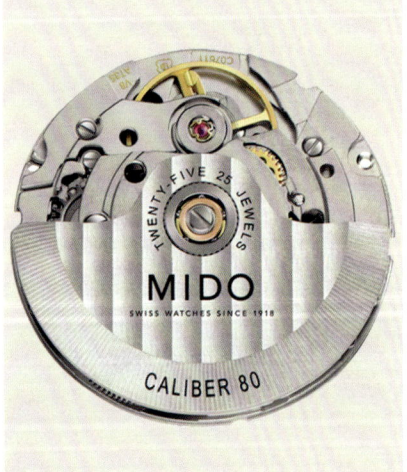

Certina Powermatic 80

Automatic; ball bearing-mounted rotor, hacking seconds, indexless fine adjustment; single mainspring barrel, 80-hour power reserve
Base caliber: ETA C07611
Functions: hours, minutes, sweep seconds; date aperture
Diameter: 26 mm
Height: 4.6 mm
Jewels: 25
Balance: glucydur
Frequency: 21,600 vph
Hairspring: Nivachron
Shock protection: Nivachoc
Remarks: the Powermatic caliber used by many Swatch Group brands is based on the architecture of the reliable ETA 2824-2; also made with a silicon hairspring

Mido Caliber 80

Automatic; ball bearing-mounted rotor, hacking seconds, indexless fine adjustment; single mainspring barrel, 80-hour power reserve
Base caliber: ETA C07611
Functions: hours, minutes, sweep seconds; date aperture
Diameter: 26 mm
Height: 4.6 mm
Jewels: 25
Balance: glucydur
Frequency: 21,600 vph
Hairspring: Nivachron
Shock protection: Novodiac
Remarks: the Powermatic caliber used by many Swatch Group brands is based on the architecture of the reliable ETA 2824-2; also made with a silicon hairspring

Tissot Powermatic 80

Automatic; ball bearing-mounted Rotor, hacking seconds, indexless fine adjustment ; single mainspring barrel, 80-hour power reserve
Base caliber: ETA C07611
Functions: hours, minutes, sweep seconds; date aperture
Diameter: 26 mm
Height: 4.6 mm
Jewels: 25
Balance: glucydur
Frequency: 21,600 vph
Hairspring: Nivachron
Shock protection: Nivachoc
Remarks: the Powermatic caliber used by many Swatch Group brands is based on the architecture of the reliable ETA 2824-2; also made with a silicon hairspring

Hamilton H-31

Automatic; hacking seconds; single mainspring barrel, 60-hour power reserve
Base caliber: ETA 7753
Functions: hours, minutes, subsidiary seconds; chronograph; date aperture with pusher-activated quick-set correction
Diameter: 30.4 mm
Height: 7.9 mm
Jewels: 25
Balance: glucydur
Frequency: 28,800 vph
Hairspring: flat hairspring
Shock protection: Nivachoc
Remarks: improved "Valjoux" chronograph caliber with symmetrical tricompax arrangement of the totalizers

Rado R808 (dial side)

Automatic; skeletonized mainplate and bridges; ball bearing-mounted rotor, hacking seconds, indexless fine adjustment; single mainspring barrel, 80-hour power reserve
Base caliber: ETA C.07611
Functions: hours, minutes, sweep seconds
Diameter: 25.6 mm
Height: 4.74 mm
Jewels: 25
Balance: glucydur
Frequency: 21,600 vph
Hairspring: Nivachron
Shock protection: Nivachoc
Remarks: exclusively used in Rado's True Square Skeleton, DiaStar Original Skeleton and Captain Cook High-Tech Ceramic models; based on the Powermatic caliber

Union Glashütte UNG-56.01

Hand-wound; Glashütte three-quarter plate with ribbing; hacking seconds; ETACHRON index system; single mainspring barrel, 60-hour power reserve
Functions: hours, minutes, subsidiary seconds; power reserve indicator; date
Diameter: 30 mm
Height: 5.4 mm
Jewels: 20
Frequency: 28,800 vph
Hairspring: flat hairspring
Shock protection: Nivachoc
Remarks: ETA construction based on the Valgranges chronograph movement reassembled and finished in Glashütte without hacking seconds and automatic winding; used in the 1893 Johannes Dürrstein jubilee edition

Longines L791.4

Automatic; hacking seconds; single mainspring barrel, 60-hour power reserve
Base caliber: ETA A08.261
Functions: hours, minutes, subsidiary seconds; flyback chronograph; date aperture with pusher-activated quick-set correction
Diameter: 30.4 mm
Height: 7.9 mm
Jewels: 28
Balance: glucydur
Frequency: 28,800 vph
Hairspring: silicon
Shock protection: Nivachoc
Remarks: exclusively used in the Longines Spirit Flyback chronograph

Longines L896.5

Automatic; ball bearing-mounted Rotor, hacking seconds, indexless fine regulation; single mainspring barrel, 72-hour power reserve
Functions: hours, minutes, sweep seconds; power reserve indicator with two central disks; date aperture
Diameter: 26 mm
Jewels: 21
Balance: glucydur
Frequency: 25,200 vph
Hairspring: silicon
Shock protection: Nivachoc
Remarks: exclusively used in Longines' Conquest Heritage Central Power Reserve

Longines L844.5

Automatic; ball bearing-mounted rotor, hacking seconds, indexless fine regulation; single mainspring barrel, 72-hour power reserve
Base caliber: ETA A31.411
Functions: hours (stepwise setting by crown), minutes, sweep seconds; additional 24-hour display (second time zone); date aperture
Diameter: 25.6 mm
Height: 3.85 mm
Jewels: 21
Balance: glucydur
Frequency: 25,200 vph
Hairspring: silicon
Shock protection: Nivachoc
Remarks: exclusively used in the Longines Spirit Zulu Time and Master Collection GMT models

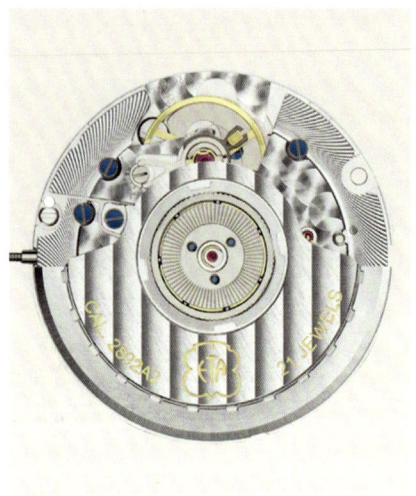

2892-A2

Automatic; ball bearing–mounted rotor; stop-seconds, ETACHRON regulating system; single spring barrel; 42-hour power reserve
Functions: hours, minutes, sweep seconds; quick-set date window
Diameter: 26.2 mm
Height: 3.6 mm
Jewels: 21
Balance: glucydur
Frequency: 28,800 vph
Balance spring: flat hairspring
Shock protection: Incabloc

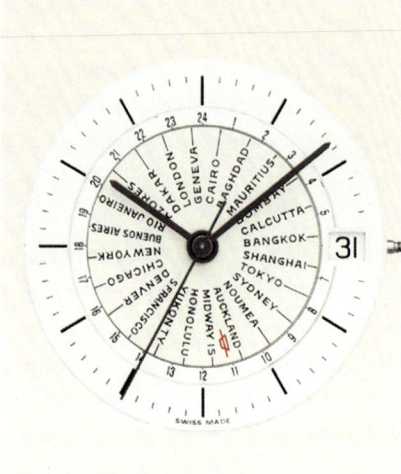

2893-1 (dial side)

Automatic; ball bearing rotor; stop-seconds, ETACHRON regulating system; 42-hour power reserve
Functions: hours, minutes, sweep seconds; quick-set date window at 3 o'clock; world time display via central disk
Diameter: 25.6 mm
Height: 4.1 mm
Jewels: 21
Frequency: 28,800 vph
Related calibers: 2893-2 (24-hour hand; 2nd time zone instead of world time disk); 2893-3 (only world time disk without date window)

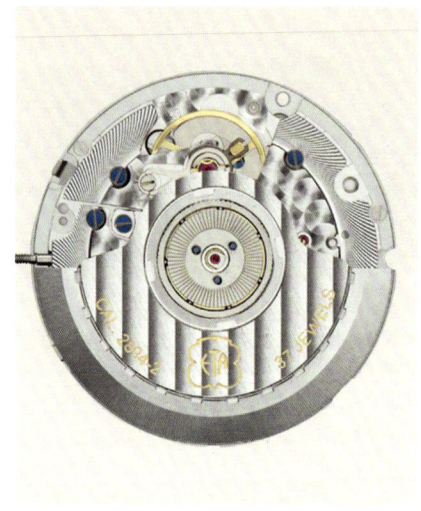

2894-2

Automatic; ball bearing–mounted rotor; stop-seconds, ETACHRON regulating system; single spring barrel; 42-hour power reserve
Functions: hours, minutes, subsidiary seconds; chronograph; quick-set date window
Diameter: 28.6 mm
Height: 6.1 mm
Jewels: 37
Balance: glucydur
Frequency: 28,800 vph
Balance spring: flat hairspring
Shock protection: Incabloc
Related caliber: 2094 (diameter 23.9 mm, height 5.5 mm, 33 jewels)

2895-2 (dial side)

Automatic; ball bearing–mounted rotor; stop-seconds, ETACHRON regulating system; single spring barrel; 42-hour power reserve
Functions: hours, minutes, subsidiary seconds, at 6 o'clock; quick-set date window
Diameter: 26.2 mm
Height: 4.35 mm
Jewels: 27
Balance: glucydur
Frequency: 28,800 vph
Balance spring: flat hairspring
Shock protection: Incabloc

2896 (dial side)

Automatic; ball bearing rotor; stop-seconds, ETACHRON regulating system; 42-hour power reserve
Functions: hours, minutes, sweep seconds; power reserve display at 3 o'clock
Diameter: 25.6 mm
Height: 4.85 mm
Jewels: 21
Frequency: 28,800 vph

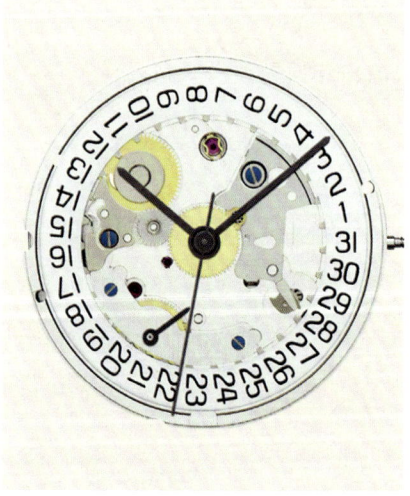

2897 (dial side)

Automatic; ball bearing–mounted rotor; stop-seconds, ETACHRON regulating system; single spring barrel; 42-hour power reserve
Functions: hours, minutes, sweep seconds; power reserve indicator; quick-set date window
Diameter: 26.2 mm
Height: 4.85 mm
Jewels: 21
Balance: glucydur
Frequency: 28,800 vph
Balance spring: flat hairspring
Shock protection: Incabloc

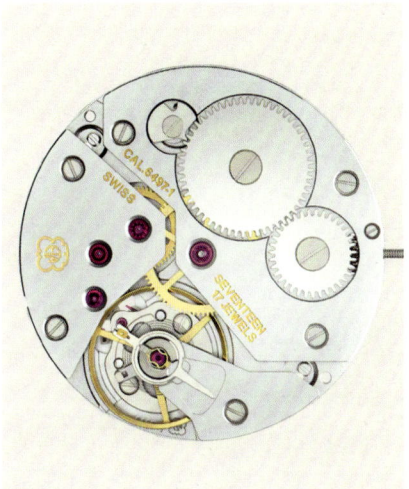

6497-1

Hand-wound; ETACHRON regulating system; single spring barrel; 46-hour power reserve
Functions: hours, minutes, subsidiary seconds
Diameter: 37.2 mm
Height: 4.5 mm
Jewels: 17
Frequency: 18,000 vph
Balance spring: flat hairspring
Remarks: pocket watch movement (Unitas model) in Lépine version with subsidiary seconds extending from the winding stem); as Caliber 6497-2 with 21,600 vph and 53-hour power reserve

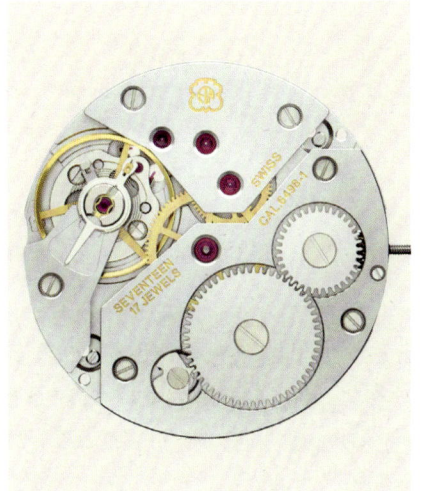

6498-1

Hand-wound; ETACHRON regulating system; single spring barrel; 46-hour power reserve
Functions: hours, minutes, subsidiary seconds
Diameter: 37.2 mm
Height: 4.5 mm
Jewels: 17
Frequency: 18,000 vph
Balance spring: flat hairspring
Remarks: pocket watch movement (Unitas model) in savonette version (subsidiary seconds at right angle to the winding stem); as Caliber 6498-2 with 21,600 vph and 53-hour power reserve

7001

Hand-wound; ultrathin construction; single spring barrel; 42-hour power reserve
Functions: hours, minutes, subsidiary seconds
Diameter: 23.7 mm
Height: 2.5 mm
Jewels: 17
Frequency: 21,600 vph
Balance spring: flat hairspring

7750 (dial side)

Automatic; stop-second system; single spring barrel; 42-hour power reserve
Functions: hours, minutes, subsidiary seconds; chronograph; quick-set date and weekday window
Diameter: 30.4 mm
Height: 7.9 mm
Jewels: 25
Balance: glucydur
Frequency: 28,800 vph
Balance spring: flat hairspring
Shock protection: Incabloc

7751 (dial side)

Automatic; stop-second system; single spring barrel; 42-hour power reserve
Functions: hours, minutes, subsidiary seconds; additional 24-hour display; chronograph; full calendar with date, weekday, month, moon phase
Diameter: 30.4 mm
Height: 7.9 mm
Jewels: 25
Balance: glucydur
Frequency: 28,800 vph
Balance spring: flat hairspring
Shock protection: Incabloc
Remarks: related caliber: 7754 with sweep 24-hour hand (2nd time zone)

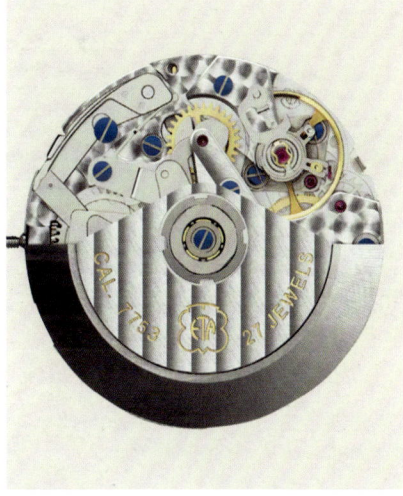

7753

Automatic; stop-second system; single spring barrel; 42-hour power reserve
Functions: hours, minutes, subsidiary seconds; chronograph; quick-set date window with pusher
Diameter: 30.4
Height: 7.9 mm
Jewels: 25
Balance: glucydur
Frequency: 28,800 vph
Balance spring: flat hairspring
Shock protection: Incabloc
Remarks: variation of the Valjoux chronograph caliber with symmetrical "tricompax" layout of the totalizers

FESTINA SOPROD

The name Soprod stands for "Société de Production Horlogère" and refers to a company with a long tradition of movement-building, though, admittedly, mostly in quartz. It was founded in 1966, and later earned a favorable reputation as an external assembly company for ETA movements. Soprod continued enlarging its portfolio, adding customized decorations and finishings as a service and then building complete modules that could be used to enhance base movements.

Around the turn of the millennium, the company finally began to seriously develop its own calibers. The plan received an unexpected boost when ETA (Swatch Group) announced that, in the foreseeable future, they would no longer supply movement kits (*ébauches*) to external assemblers but would only supply end-customers directly. For then Swatch CEO Nicola Hayek, this would boost a reindustrialzation of the industry as larger groups would now be verticalizing their manufacturing. Aspiring watch companies would have to look elsewhere.

In the meantime, Soprod had become a member of the Swiss Festina Group, where it could provide extra capacities in the field of inexpensive quartz movements. But their mechanical division was growing steadily with two caliber lines (M and C) with over fifteen iterations. In 2011, at Baselworld, they presented their Alternance 10, or A10, which had the look and feel of the notoriously robust ETA 2892. As a base movement with a diameter of 25.6 millimeters, it fit inside in many cases, and Soprod already had a wide range of modules on tap to supplement it, like large dates, GMT, power reserves, and moon phases.

Expansion is the name of the game in a fluid market. Soprod continued making quartz movements and working on its mechanical calibers. In 2020 it launched the Newton line aimed at competing with another famous ETA caliber, the 2824-2, and with some of rival Sellita's products. It also ensured its own independence by starting to make its own escapement parts such as anchors, escape wheels, balance wheels, and hairsprings at its founding site in Les Reussilles in the Jura.

M100SQ

Automatic; skeletonized plate and bridges; bidirectional winding rotor, stop-second mechanism; single spring barrel, 42-hour power reserve
Functions: hours, minutes, sweep seconds; date with rapid correction
Diameter: 25.6 mm
Height: 3.6 mm
Jewels: 25
Frequency: 28,800 vph
Shock protection: Incabloc
Related calibers: M100 (standard version without skeletonization); M100 Balancier Visible (with openworked plate under the escapement parts)

M100

Automatic; bidirectional winding rotor, stop-second mechanism; single spring barrel, 42-hour power reserve
Functions: hours, minutes, sweep seconds; date with rapid correction
Diameter: 25.6 mm
Height: 3.6 mm
Jewels: 25
Frequency: 28,800 vph
Shock protection: Incabloc
Remarks: various regulation options (COSC, among others); various finishings (Optimal, Excellence, Manufacture)

Newton

Automatic; in-house escapement and hairspring; unidirectional winding rotor, stop-second mechanism; single spring barrel, 44-hour power reserve
Functions: hours, minutes, sweep seconds; date, with rapid correction
Diameter: 25.6 mm
Height: 4.6 mm
Jewels: 23
Frequency: 28,800 vph
Shock protection: Incabloc
Remarks: with/without côtes de Genève

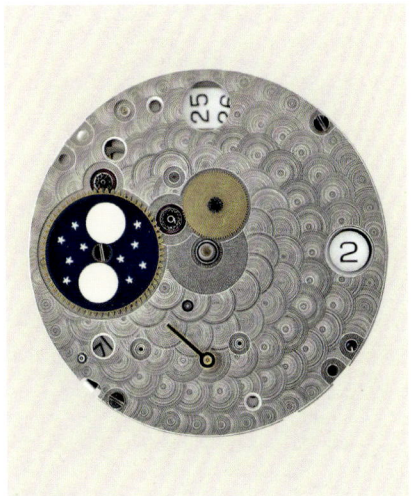

C105

Automatic; bidirectional winding rotor, stop-second mechanism; single spring barrel, 42-hour power reserve
Functions: hours, minutes, subsidiary seconds; date with rapid correction, moon phase Diameter: 25.6 mm
Height: 5.1 mm
Jewels: 33
Frequency: 28,800 vph
Shock protection: Incabloc

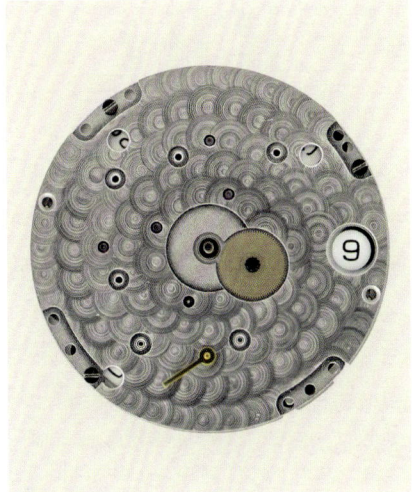

C110

Automatic; bidirectional winding rotor, stop-second mechanism; single spring barrel, 42-hour power reserve
Functions: hours, minutes, subsidiary seconds; date with rapid correction
Diameter: 25.6 mm
Height: 5.1 mm
Jewels: 29
Frequency: 28,800 vph
Shock protection: Incabloc

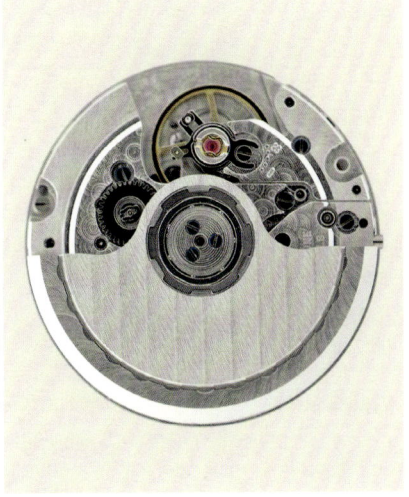

C115

Automatic; bidirectional winding rotor, stop-second mechanism; single spring barrel, 42-hour power reserve
Functions: hours, minutes, sweep seconds; additional 24-hour display (second time zone), power reserve display; date with rapid correction
Diameter: 25.6 mm
Height: 5.1 mm
Jewels: 33
Frequency: 28,800 vph
Shock protection: Incabloc

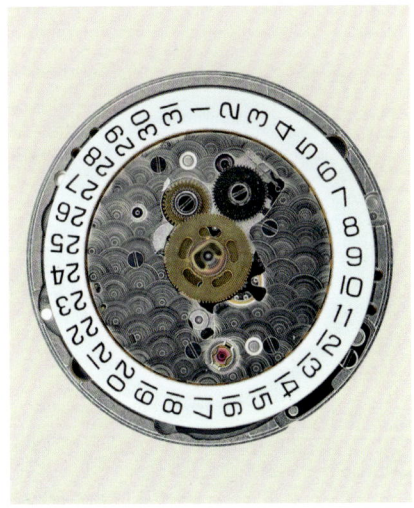

C125

Automatic; bidirectional winding rotor, stop-second mechanism; single spring barrel, 42-hour power reserve
Functions: hours, minutes, sweep seconds; additional 12-hour display (second time zone), day/night indication (with hour and minute at 6 o'clock); large date with rapid correction
Diameter: 25.6 mm
Height: 5.1 mm
Jewels: 25
Frequency: 28,800 vph
Shock protection: Incabloc

C120

Automatic; bidirectional winding rotor, stop-second mechanism; single spring barrel, 42-hour power reserve
Functions: hours, minutes, sweep seconds; additional 24-hour display (sweep second time zone); date, with rapid correction
Diameter: 25.6 mm
Height: 4.1 mm
Jewels: 25
Frequency: 28,800 vph
Shock protection: Incabloc

C130

Automatic; bidirectional winding rotor, stop-second mechanism; single spring barrel, 42-hour power reserve
Functions: hours, minutes, sweep seconds; power reserve display; large date with rapid correction
Diameter: 25.6 mm
Height: 5.1 mm
Jewels: 27
Frequency: 28,800 vph
Shock protection: Incabloc
Related calibers: C135 (with additional sweep 24-hour hand and date aperture); C140 (power reserve display und date aperture)

MANUFACTURE LA JOUX-PERRET

The re-industrialization of the caliber segment in Switzerland, brought about by some very confusing signals from Swatch Group and the Swiss government's Competition Commission, has created a number of opportunities for caliber builders who had until recently been operating in the shadow of ETA. Among them is Manufacture La Joux-Perret (MLJP), known primarily for its bespoke complication calibers for prestigious brands. It has now decided to enter the ready-to-wear caliber market in 2021 with the revised G100 three-hand automatic movement and the L100 automatic chronograph.

Due to their dimensions and specifications, both movements are suitable as replacements for the widely used 2824 and 7750 ("Valjoux") models, which will no longer be available to the watch industry in sufficient quantities after the expiry of the general supply obligation on the part of Swatch Group subsidiary ETA. The two MLJP calibers compete with Sellita's own high-volume movements SW200 and SW500, but they offer a greater amount of power reserve (68 and 60 hours, respectively) and partly better equipment (column-wheel control). Also in the standard portfolio of this caliber specialist is a classic-a hand-wound movement with the caliber number D100, whose architecture is strongly reminiscent of the pocket watch "Unitas" caliber. Its diameter, however, is only 23.3 millimeters.

MLJP has been part of the Citizen Group (Japan) since 2012. The company's headquarters and production facilities are located in La Chaux-de-Fonds, in the heart of watch country.

G100

Automatic; rotor on ball bearing, second stop; single spring barrel, 68-hour power reserve
Functions: hours, minutes, sweep seconds; date aperture
Diameter: 26 mm
Height: 4.45 mm
Jewels: 24
Balance: glucydur
Frequency: 28,800 vph
Hairspring: flat hairspring
Shock protection: Kif
Remarks: functionality and parts compatibility with ETA 2824-2; various display options, many customization options

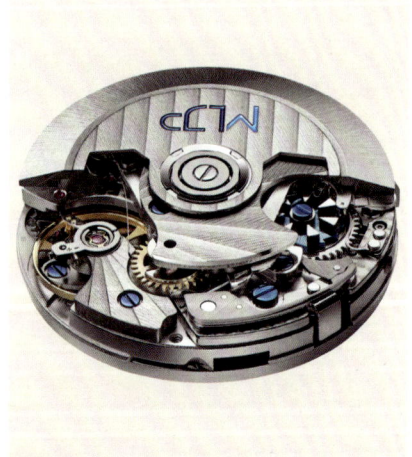

L100

Automatic; column-wheel control of chronograph functions; second stop; single spring barrel, 60-hour power reserve
Functions: hours, minutes, subsidiary seconds; chronograph; date and weekday aperture with rapid correction
Diameter: 30.4 mm
Height: 7.9 mm
Jewels: 26
Balance: Glucydur
Frequency: 28,800 vph
Hairspring: flat hairspring
Shock protection: Incabloc
Remarks: functionality and parts compatibility with ETA 7750; various display options, many customization options

T100

Hand-wound; flying 1-minute tourbillon; skeletonized movement; rhodium-plating; single mainspring barrel, 60-hour power reserve
Base caliber: LJP7814
Functions: hours, minutes
Diameter: 32.8 mm
Height: 4.4 mm
Jewels: 23
Balance: glucydur
Frequency: 28,800 vph
Hairspring: flat hairspring
Shock protection: Triovis

RONDA

Ronda is a Swiss company with a long tradition. It was founded by William Mosset, born in 1909 in the village of Hölstein, a man whose gift for micro-engineering declared itself early on when he invented a way to drill thirty-two holes in a metal plate in one operation and with great accuracy. The company was founded in 1946 in Lausen, a little town in the hinterlands of German-speaking Switzerland near Basel, where the first factory was built.

In the meantime the company has turned into a group with five subsidiaries: There are two production sites in Ticino, one in the Jura mountains, one operation in Thailand, and sales offices in Hong Kong. Overall, Ronda employs around 1,800 people in Switzerland and Asia.

The shareholders of the family enterprise, which is now in its second generation, value the company's absolute independence. This is undoubtedly a key advantage for the customer, since Ronda can continue defining its own strategy and can react decisively to customer needs.

That is why the company, which had already made a name for itself with quartz movements, decided to add a portfolio of automatic mechanical movements. The first product batches arrived on the market in early 2017; in the medium term, the mechanical Ronda Caliber R150 is to be produced in batches of six figures per year.

R150

Automatic; ball bearing–mounted rotor; stop-seconds, index for fine adjustment; single spring barrel; 40-hour power reserve
Functions: hours, minutes, sweep seconds; quick-set date
Diameter: 25.6 mm
Height: 4.4 mm
Jewels: 25
Frequency: 28,800 vph
Balance spring: flat hairspring
Shock protection: Incabloc

5040.B

Quartz; 54-month power reserve; single spring barrel
Functions: hours, minutes, subsidiary seconds; chronograph, with add and split function; large date
Diameter: 28.6 mm
Height: 4.4 mm
Jewels: 13

7004.P

Quartz; 48-month power reserve; single spring barrel
Functions: hours, minutes, subsidiary seconds; large date and weekday (retrograde)
Diameter: 34.6 mm
Height: 5.6 mm
Jewels: 6

WATCH YOUR WATCH

BY GARY GIRDVAINIS

Mechanical watches are not only by and large more expensive and complex than quartzes, they are also a little high-maintenance, as it were. The mechanism within does need servicing occasionally—perhaps a touch of oil and an adjustment. Worse yet, the complexity of all those wheels and pinions engaged in reproducing the galaxy means that a user will occasionally do something perfectly harmless like wind his or her watch up only to find everything grinding to a halt. Here are some tips for dealing with these mechanical beauties for new watch owners and reminders for the old hands.

1. DATE CHANGES

Do not change the date manually (via the crown or pusher) on any mechanical watch—whether manual wind or automatic—when the time indicated on the dial reads between 10 and 2 o'clock. Although some better watches are protected against this horological quirk, most mechanical watches with a date indicator are engaged in the process of automatically changing the date between the hours of 10 p.m. and 2 a.m. Intervening with a forced manual change while the automatic date shift is engaged can damage the movement. Of course, you can make the adjustment between 10 a.m. and 2 p.m. in most cases—but this is just not a good habit to get into. When in doubt, roll the time past 12 o'clock and look for an automatic date change before you set the time and date. The Ulysse Nardin brand is notable, among a very few others, for in-house mechanical movements immune to this effect.

Bovet's barrier to pressing the wrong pusher.

2. CHRONOGRAPH USE

On a simple chronograph, start and stop are almost always the same button. Normally located above the crown, the start/stop actuator can be pressed at will to initiate and end the interval timing. The reset button, normally below the crown, is only used for resetting the chronograph to zero, but only when the chronograph is stopped—never while engaged. Only a "flyback" chronograph allows safe resetting to zero while running. With the chronograph engaged, you simply hit the reset button and all the chronograph indicators (seconds, minutes, and hours) snap back to zero and the chronograph begins to accumulate the interval time once again. In the early days of air travel this was a valuable complication as pilots would reset their chronographs when taking on a new heading—without having to fumble about with a three-step procedure with gloved hands.

Nota bene: Don't actuate or reset your chronograph while your watch is submerged—even if you have one of those that are built for such usage, like Omega, IWC, and a few other brands. Feel free to hit the buttons before submersion and jump in and swim while they run; just don't push anything while in the water.

3. CHANGING TIME BACKWARD

Don't adjust the time on your watch in a counterclockwise direction—especially if the watch has calendar functions. A few watches can tolerate the abuse, but it's better to avoid the possibility of damage altogether. Change the dates as needed (remembering the 10 and 2 rule above).

4. SHOCKS

Almost all modern watches are equipped with some level of shock protection. Best practices for the Swiss brands allow for a three-foot fall onto a hard wood surface. But if your watch is running poorly—or even worse has stopped entirely after an impact—do not shake, wind, or bang it again to get it running; take it to an expert for service as you may do even more damage. Sports like tennis, squash, or golf can have a deleterious effect on your watch, including flattening the pivots, overbanking, or even bending or breaking a pivot.

5. OVERWINDING

Most modern watches are fitted with a mechanism that allows the mainspring to slide inside the barrel—or stops it completely once the spring is fully wound—for protection against overwinding. The best advice here is just don't force it. Over the years, a winding crown may start to get "stickier" and more difficult to turn even when unwound. That's a sure sign it is due for service.

6. JACUZZI TEMPERATURE

Don't jump into the Jacuzzi—or even a steaming hot shower—with your watch on. Better-built watches with a deeper water-resistance rating typically have no problem with this scenario. However, take a 3 or 5 atm water-resistant watch into the Jacuzzi, and there's a chance the different rates of expansion and contraction of the metals and sapphire or mineral crystals may allow moisture into the case.

Panerai makes sure you think before touching the crown.

7. SCREW THAT CROWN DOWN (AND THOSE PUSHERS)!

Always check and double-check to ensure a watch fitted with a screwed-down crown is closed tightly. Screwed-down pushers for a chronograph—or any other functions—deserve the same attention. This one oversight has cost quite a few owners their watches. If a screwed-down crown is not secured, water will likely get into the case and start oxidizing the metal. In time, the problem can destroy the watch.

8. MAGNETISM

If your watch is acting up, running faster or slower, it may have become magnetized. This can happen if you leave your timepiece near a computer, cell phone, or some other electronic device. Many service centers have a so-called degausser to take care of the problem. A number of brands also make watches with a soft iron core to deflect magnetic fields, though this might not work with the stronger ones.

9. TRIBOLOGY

Keeping a mechanical timepiece hidden away in a box for extended lengths of time is not the best way to care for it. Even if you don't wear a watch every day, it is a good idea to run your watch at regular intervals to keep its lubricating oils and greases viscous. Think about a can of house paint: Keep it stirred and it stays liquid almost indefinitely; leave it still for too long and a skin develops. On a smaller level the same thing can happen to the lubricants inside a mechanical watch.

10. SERVICE

Most mechanical watches call for a three- to five-year service cycle for cleaning, oiling, and maintenance. Some mechanical watches can run twice that long and have functioned within acceptable parameters, but if you're not going to have your watch serviced at regular intervals, you do run the risk of having timing issues. Always have your watch serviced by a qualified watchmaker (see box), not at the kiosk in the local mall. The best you can expect there is a quick battery change.

Do it yourself at your own risk.

WATCH REPAIR SERVICE CENTERS

RGM
www.rgmwatches.com/repair

Stoll & Co.
www.americaswatchmaker.com

Swiss Watchmakers & Company
www.swisswatchland.com

Universal Watch Repair
www.universalwatch.net

Watch Repairs USA
www.watchrepairsusa.com

GLOSSARY

ANNUAL CALENDAR

The automatic allowances for the different lengths of each month of a year in the calendar module of a watch. This type of watch usually shows the month and date, and sometimes the day of the week (like this one by Patek Philippe) and the phases of the moon.

ANTIMAGNETIC

Magnetic fields found in common everyday places affect mechanical movements, hence the use of anti- or non-magnetic components in the movement. Some companies encase movements in antimagnetic cores such as Sinn's Model 756, the Duograph, shown here.

ANTIREFLECTION

A film created by steaming the crystal to eliminate light reflection and improve legibility. Antireflection functions best when applied to both sides of the crystal, but because it scratches, some manufacturers prefer to have it only on the interior of the crystal. It is mainly used on synthetic sapphire crystals. Dubey & Schaldenbrand applies antireflection on both sides for all of the company's wristwatches, such as this Aquadyn model.

AUTOMATIC WINDING

A rotating weight set into motion by moving the wrist winds the spring barrel via the gear train of a mechanical watch movement. Automatic winding was invented during the pocket watch era in 1770, but the breakthrough automatic winding movement via rotor began with the ball bearing Eterna-Matic in the late 1940s. Today we speak of unidirectional winding and bidirectionally winding rotors, depending on the type of gear train used. Shown is IWC's automatic Caliber 50611.

BALANCE

The beating heart of a mechanical watch movement is the balance. Fed by the energy of the mainspring, a tirelessly oscillating little wheel, just a few millimeters in diameter and possessing a spiral-shaped balance spring, sets the rhythm for the escape wheel and pallets with its vibration frequency. Today the balance is usually made of one piece of antimagnetic glucydur, an alloy that expands very little when exposed to heat.

BAR OR COCK

A metal plate fastened to the base plate at one point, leaving room for a gear wheel or pinion. The balance is usually attached to a bar called the balance cock. Glashütte tradition dictates that the balance cock be decoratively engraved by hand like this one by Glashütte Original.

BEVELING

To uniformly file down the sharp edges of a plate, bridge, or bar and give it a high polish. The process is also called *anglage*. Edges are usually beveled at a less than 45° angle to reflect light outwards. As the picture shows, this is painstaking work that needs the skilled hands and eyes of an experienced watchmaker or *angleur*.

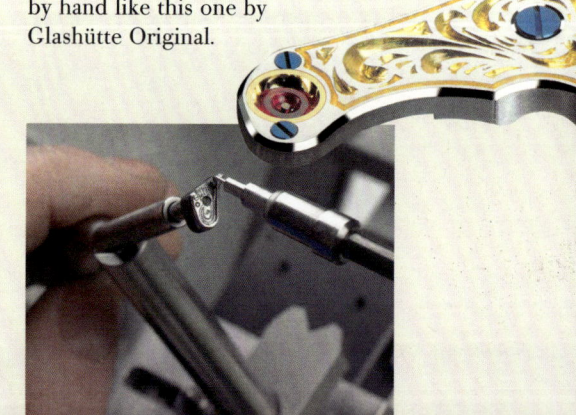

BRIDGE

A metal plate fastened to the base plate at two points leaving room for a gear wheel or pinion. This vintage Favre-Leuba movement illustrates the point with three individual bridges.

CARBON FIBER

A very light, tough composite material, carbon fiber is composed of filaments comprised of several thousand seven-micron carbon fibers held together by resin. The arrangement of the filaments determines the quality of a component, making each unique. Carbon fiber is currently being used for dials, cases, and even movement components.

CALIBER

A term, similar to type or model, that refers to different watch movements. Pictured here is Heuer's Caliber 11, the legendary automatic chronograph caliber from 1969. This movement was a coproduction jointly researched and developed for four years by Heuer-Leonidas, Breitling, and Hamilton-Büren. Each company gave the movement a different name after serial production began.

CHAMPLEVÉ

A dial decoration technique, whereby the metal is engraved, filled with enamel, and baked, as in this cockatoo on a Cartier Tortue, enhanced with mother-of-pearl slivers.

CERAMIC

An inorganic, nonmetallic material formed by the action of heat and practically unscratchable. Pioneered by Rado, ceramic is a high-tech material generally made from aluminum and zirconia oxide. Today, it is used generally for cases and bezels and now comes in many colors.

CHRONOGRAPH

From the Greek *chronos* (time) and *graphein* (to write). Originally a chronograph literally wrote, inscribing the time elapsed on a piece of paper with the help of a pencil attached to a type of hand. Today this term is used for watches that show not only the time of day, but also certain time intervals via independent hands that may be started or stopped at will. Stopwatches differ from chronographs because they do not show the time of day. This exploded illustration shows the complexity of a Breitling chronograph.

CHRONOMETER

Literally, "measurer of time." As the term is used today, a chronometer denotes an especially accurate watch (one with a deviation of no more than 5 seconds a day for mechanical movements). Chronometers are usually supplied with an official certificate from an independent testing office such as the COSC. The largest producer of chronometers in 2008 was Rolex, with 769,850 officially certified movements. Chopard came in sixth with more than 22,000 certified L.U.C mechanisms, like the 4.96 in the Pro One model shown here.

COLUMN WHEEL

The component used to control chronograph functions within a true chronograph movement. The presence of a column wheel indicates that the chronograph is fully integrated into the movement. In the modern era, modules are generally used that are attached to a base caliber movement. This particular column wheel is made of blued steel.

CONSTANT FORCE MECHANISM

Sometimes called a constant force escapement, it isn't really: in most cases this mechanism is "simply" an initial tension spring. It is also known in English by part of its French name, the *remontoir*, which actually means "winding mechanism." This mechanism regulates and portions the energy that is passed on through the escapement, making the rate as even and precise as possible. Shown here is the constant force escapement from A. Lange & Söhne's Lange 31— a mechanism that gets as close to its name as possible.

COSC

The Contrôle Officiel Suisse de Chronomètrage, the official Swiss testing office for chronometers. The COSC is the world's largest issuer of so-called chronometer certificates, which are only otherwise given out individually by certain observatories (such as the one in Neuchâtel, Switzerland). For a fee, the COSC tests the rate of movements that have been adjusted by watchmakers. These are usually mechanical movements, but the office also tests some high-precision quartz movements. Those that meet the specifications for being a chronometer are awarded an official certificate as shown here.

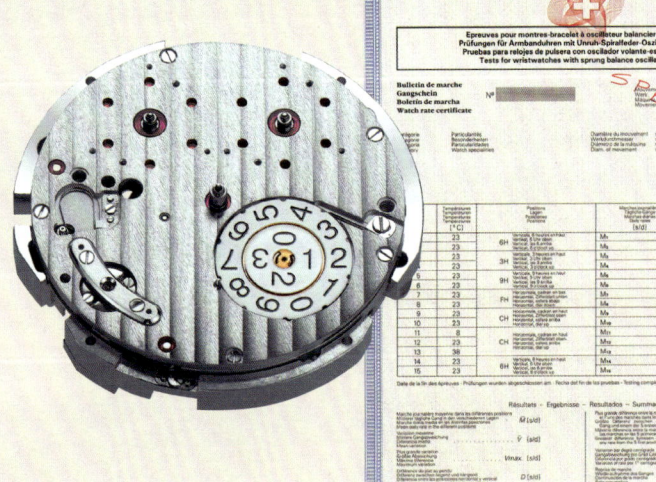

CÔTES DE GENÈVE

Also called *vagues de Genève* and Geneva stripes. This is a traditional Swiss surface decoration comprising an even pattern of parallel stripes, applied to flat movement components with a quickly rotating plastic or wooden peg. Glashütte watchmakers have devised their own version of *côtes de Genève* that is applied at a slightly different angle, called Glashütte ribbing.

CROWN

The crown is used to wind and set a watch. A few simple turns of the crown will get an automatic movement started, while a manually wound watch is completely wound by the crown. The crown is also used for the setting of various functions, almost always including at least the hours, minutes, seconds, and date. A screwed-down crown like the one on the TAG Heuer Aquagraph pictured here can be tightened to prevent water entering the case or any mishaps while performing extreme sports such as diving.

EQUATION OF TIME

The mean time that we use to keep track of the passing of the day (24 hours evenly divided into minutes and seconds) is not equal to true solar time. The equation of time is a complication devised to show the difference between the mean time shown on one's wristwatch and the time the sun dictates. The Équation Marchante by Blancpain very distinctly indicates this difference via the golden sun-tipped hand that also rotates around the dial in a manner known to watch connoisseurs as *marchant.* Other wristwatch models, such as the Boreas by Martin Braun, display the difference on an extra scale on the dial.

ESCAPEMENT

The combination of the balance, balance spring, pallets, and escape wheel, a subgroup which divides the impulses coming from the spring barrel into small, accurately portioned doses. It guarantees that the gear train runs smoothly and efficiently. The pictured escapement is one newly invented by Parmigiani, containing pallet stones of varying colors, though they are generally red synthetic rubies. Here one of them is a colorless sapphire, or corundum, the same geological material that ruby is made of.

FLINQUÉ

A dial decoration in which a guilloché design is given a coat of enamel, softening the pattern and creating special effects, as shown here on a unique Bovet.

GEAR TRAIN

A mechanical watch's gear train transmits energy from the mainspring to the escapement. The gear train comprises the minute wheel, the third wheel, the fourth wheel, and the escape wheel.

GLUCYDUR

Glucydur is a functional alloy of copper, beryllium, and iron that has been used to make balances in watches since the 1930s. Its hardness and stability allow watchmakers to use balances that were assembled at the factory and no longer required adjustment screws.

INDEX

A regulating mechanism found on the balance cock and used by the watchmaker to adjust the movement's rate. The index changes the effective length of the balance spring, thus making it move more quickly or slowly. This is the standard index found on an ETA Valjoux 7750.

JEWEL

To minimize friction, the hardened steel tips of a movement's rotating gear wheels (called pinions) are lodged in synthetic rubies (fashioned as polished stones with a hole) and lubricated with a very thin layer of special oil. These synthetic rubies are produced in exactly the same way as sapphire crystal using the same material. During the pocket watch era, real rubies with hand-drilled holes were still used, but because of the high costs involved, they were only used in movements with especially quickly rotating gears. The jewel shown here on a bridge from A. Lange & Söhne's Double Split is additionally embedded in a gold chaton secured with three blued screws.

FLYBACK CHRONOGRAPH

A chronograph with a special dial train switch that makes the immediate reuse of the chronograph movement possible after resetting the hands. It was developed for special timekeeping duties such as those found in aviation, which require the measurement of time intervals in quick succession. A flyback may also be called a *retour en vol.* An elegant example of this type of chronograph is Corum's Classical Flyback Large Date shown here.

GUILLOCHÉ

A surface decoration usually applied to the dial and the rotor using a grooving tool with a sharp tip, such as a rose engine, to cut an even pattern onto a level surface. The exact adjustment of the tool for each new path is controlled by a device similar to a pantograph, and the movement of the tool can be controlled either manually or mechanically. Real *guillochis* (the correct term used by a master of guilloché) are very intricate and expensive to produce, which is why most dials decorated in this fashion are produced by stamping machines. Yvan Von Kaenel is one of the top guillocheurs still using a hand-controlled tool.

LIGA

The word LIGA is actually a German acronym that stands for lithography (*Lithografie*), electroplating (*Galvanisierung*), and plastic molding (*Abformung*). It is a lithographic process exposed by UV or X-ray light that literally "grows" perfect micro components made of nickel, nickel-phosphorus, or 23.5-karat gold in a plating bath. The components need no finishing or trimming after manufacture.

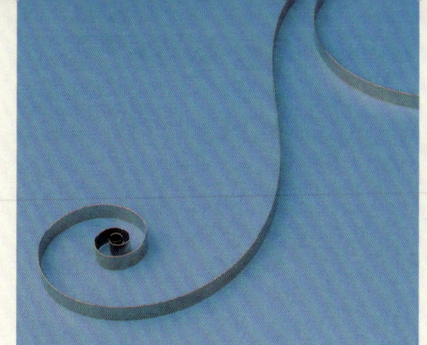

LUMINOUS SUBSTANCE

Tritium paint is a slightly radioactive substance that replaced radium as a luminous coating for hands, numerals, and hour markers on watch dials. Watches bearing tritium must be marked as such, with the letter *T* on the dial near 6 o'clock. It has now for the most part been replaced by nonradioactive materials such as Super-LumiNova. Traser technology (as seen on these Ball timepieces) uses tritium gas enclosed in tiny silicate glass tubes coated on the inside with a phosphorescing substance. The luminescence is constant and will hold around twenty-five years.

MAINSPRING

The mainspring, located in the spring barrel, stores energy when tensioned and passes it on to the escapement via the gear train as the tension relaxes. Today, mainsprings are generally made of Nivaflex, an alloy invented by Swiss engineer Max Straumann at the beginning of the 1950s. This alloy basically comprises iron, nickel, chrome, cobalt, and beryllium.

MINUTE REPEATER

A striking mechanism with hammers and gongs for acoustically signaling the hours, quarter hours, and minutes elapsed since noon or midnight. The wearer pushes a slide, which winds the spring. Normally a repeater uses two different gongs to signal hours (low tone), quarter hours (high and low tones in succession), and minutes (high tone). Some watches have three gongs, called a carillon. The Chronoswiss Répétition à Quarts is a prominent repeating introduction of recent years.

PERPETUAL CALENDAR

The calendar module for this type of timepiece automatically makes allowances for the different lengths of each month as well as leap years until the next secular year, which will occur in 2100. A perpetual calendar usually shows the date, month, and four-year cycle, and may show the day of the week and moon phase as well, as does IWC's Portugieser Eternal Calnedar of 2024, which can indicate leap years until 3999, for example.

PERLAGE

Surface decoration comprising an even pattern of partially overlapping dots, applied with a quickly rotating plastic or wooden peg, as shown here on the plates of Frédérique Constant's *manufacture* Caliber FC 910-1.

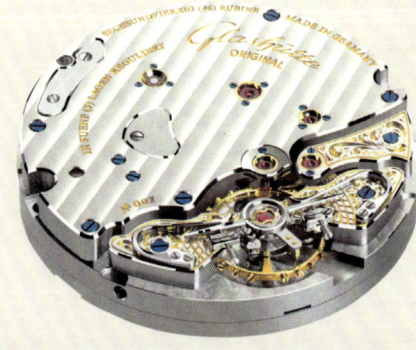

PLATE

A metal platform having several tiers for the gear train. The base plate of a movement usually incorporates the dial and carries the bearings for the primary pinions of the "first floor" of a gear train. The gear wheels are made complete by tightly fitting screwed-in bridges and bars on the back side of the plate. A specialty of the so-called Glashütte school, as opposed to the Swiss school, is the reverse completion of a movement not via different bridges and bars, but rather with a three-quarter plate. Glashütte Original's Caliber 65 (shown) displays a beautifully decorated three-quarter plate.

POWER RESERVE DISPLAY

A mechanical watch contains only a certain amount of power reserve. A fully wound modern automatic watch usually possesses between 36 and 42 hours of energy before it needs to be wound again. The power reserve display keeps the wearer informed about how much energy his or her watch still has in reserve, a function that is especially practical on manually wound watches with several days of possible reserve. The Nomos Tangente Power Reserve pictured here represents an especially creative way to illustrate the state of the mainspring's tension. On some German watches the power reserve is also displayed with the words "auf" and "ab."

PULSOMETER

A scale on the dial, flange, or bezel that, in conjunction with the second hand, may be used to measure a pulse rate. A pulsometer is always marked with a reference number—if it is marked with *gradué pour 15 pulsations*, for example, then the wearer counts fifteen pulse beats. At the last beat, the second hand will show what the pulse rate is in beats per minute on the pulsometer scale. The scale on Sinn's World Time Chronograph (shown) is marked simply with the German world *Puls* (pulse), but the function remains the same.

QUALITÉ FLEURIER

This certification of quality was established by Chopard, Parmigiani Fleurier, Vaucher, and Bovet Fleurier in 2004. Watches bearing the seal must fulfill five criteria, including COSC certification, passing several tests for robustness and precision, top-notch finishing, and being 100 percent Swiss-made (except for the raw materials). The seal appears here on the dial of the Parmigiani Fleurier Tonda 39.

RETROGRADE DISPLAY

A retrograde display shows the time linearly instead of circularly. The hand continues along an arc until it reaches the end of its scale, at which precise moment it jumps back to the beginning instantaneously. This Nienaber model not only shows the minutes in retrograde form, it is also a regulator display.

ROTOR

The rotor is the component that keeps an automatic watch wound. The kinetic motion of this part, which contains a heavy metal weight around its outer edge, winds the mainspring. It can either wind unilaterally or bilaterally (to one or both sides) depending on the caliber. The rotor from this Temption timepiece belongs to an ETA Valjoux 7750.

SCREW BALANCE

Before the invention of the perfectly weighted balance using a smooth ring, balances were fitted with weighted screws to get the exact impetus desired. Today a screw balance is a subtle sign of quality in a movement due to its costly construction and assembly utilizing minuscule weighted screws.

SAPPHIRE CRYSTAL

Synthetic sapphire crystal is known to gemologists as aluminum oxide (Al_2O_3) or corundum. It can be colorless (corundum), red (ruby), blue (sapphire), or green (emerald). It is virtually scratchproof; only a diamond is harder. The innovative Royal Blue Tourbillon by Ulysse Nardin pictured here features not only sapphire crystals on the front and back of the watch, but also actual plates made of both colorless and blue corundum within the movement.

SEAL OF GENEVA

Since 1886 the official seal of this canton has been awarded to Genevan watch *manufactures* who must follow a defined set of high-quality criteria that include the following: polished jewel bed drillings, jewels with olive drillings, polished winding wheels, quality balances and balance springs, steel levers and springs with beveling of 45 degrees and *côtes de Genève* decoration, and polished stems and pinions. The list was updated in 2012 to include the entire watch and newer components. Testing is done on the finished piece. The Seal consists of two, one on the movement, one on the case. The pictured seal was awarded to Vacheron Constantin, a traditional Genevan *manufacture*.

SILICIUM/SILICON

Silicon is an element relatively new to mechanical watches. It is currently being used in the manufacture of precision escapements. Ulysse Nardin's Freak has lubrication-free silicon wheels, and Breguet has successfully used flat silicon balance springs.

SKELETONIZATION

The technique of cutting a movement's components down to their weight-bearing basic substance. This is generally done by hand in painstaking hours of microscopic work with a small handheld saw, though machines can skeletonize parts to a certain degree, such as the version of the Valjoux 7750 that was created for Chronoswiss's Opus and Pathos models. This tourbillon created by Christophe Schaffo is additionally—and masterfully—hand-engraved.

SONNERIE

A variety of minute repeater that—like a tower clock—sounds the time not at the will of the wearer, but rather automatically (*en passant*), every hour (*petite sonnerie*), or quarter hour (*grande sonnerie*). Gérald Genta designed the most complicated sonnerie back in the early nineties. Shown is a recent model from the front and back.

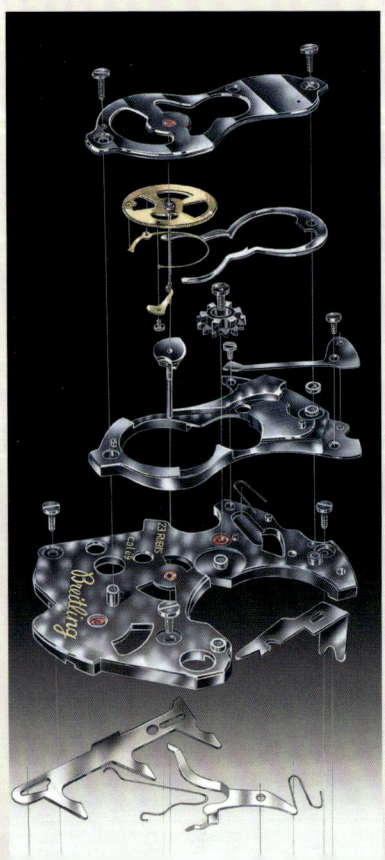

SPLIT-SECONDS CHRONOGRAPH

Also known in the watch industry by its French name, the *rattrapante* (exploded view at left). A watch with two second hands, one of which can be blocked with a special dial train lever to indicate an intermediate time while the other continues to run. When released, the split-seconds hand jumps ahead to the position of the other second hand. The PTC by Porsche Design illustrates this nicely.

SPRING BARREL

The spring barrel contains the mainspring. It turns freely on an arbor, pulled along by the toothed wheel generally doubling as its lid. This wheel interacts with the first pinion of the movement's gear train. Some movements contain two or more spring barrels for added power reserve.

SWAN-NECK FINE ADJUSTMENT

A regulating instrument used by the watchmaker to adjust the movement's rate in place of an index. The swan neck is especially prevalent in fine Swiss and Glashütte watchmaking (here, Lang & Heyne's Moritz model). Mühle Glashütte has varied the theme with its woodpecker's neck.

TACHYMETER

A scale on the dial, flange, or bezel of a chronograph that, in conjunction with the second hand, gives the speed of a moving object. A tachymeter takes a value determined in less than a minute and converts it into miles or kilometers per hour. For example, a wearer could measure the time it takes a car to pass between two mile markers on the highway. When the car passes the marker, the second hand will be pointing to the car's speed in miles per hour on the tachymetric scale.

TOURBILLON

A technical device invented by Abraham-Louis Breguet in 1801 to compensate for the influence of gravity on the balance of a pocket watch. The entire escapement is mounted on an epicyclic train in a "cage" and rotated completely on its axis over regular periods of time. This superb horological highlight is seen as a sign of technological know-how in the modern era. Harry Winston's Histoire de Tourbillon 4 is a spectacular example.

VIBRATION FREQUENCY (VPH)

The spring causes the balance to oscillate at a certain frequency measured in hertz (Hz) or vibrations per hour (vph). Most of today's wristwatches tick at 28,800 vph (4 Hz) or 21,600 vph (3 Hz). Less usual is 18,000 vph (2.5 Hz). Zenith's El Primero (shown) was the first serial movement to beat at 36,000 vph (5 Hz), and the Breguet Type XXII runs at 72,000 vph.

WATER RESISTANCE

Water resistance is an important feature of any timepiece and is usually measured in increments of one atmosphere (atm or bar, equal to 10 meters of water pressure) or meters and is often noted on the dial or case back. Watches resistant to 100 meters are best for swimming and snorkeling. Timepieces resistant to 200 meters are good for scuba diving. To deep-sea dive there are various professional timepieces available for use in depths of 200 meters or more. The Hydromax by Bell & Ross (shown) is water-resistant to a record 11,000 meters.

Copyright © 2026 HEEL Verlag GmbH, Königswinter, Germany

English-language translation copyright © 2026 Abbeville Press,
655 Third Avenue, New York, NY 10017

Editor-in-chief: Peter Braun
Editor: Marton Radkai
Production manager: Louise Kurtz
Copy Editors: Cynthia K. Barton, Stephanie Sarkany
Composition: Erin Morris, Evergreen Design Studio
Project Management: Kourtnay King, Layman Poupard Publishing

For more information about advertising, please contact:
Gary Girdvainis
25 Gay Bower Road, Monroe, CT 06468
203-952-3522, garygeorgeg@gmail.com

ISBN 978-0-7892-1542-0

Twenty-seventh edition
10 9 8 7 6 5 4 3 2 1

Library of Congress Cataloging-in-Publication Data available upon request

For bulk and premium sales and for text adoption procedures, write to Customer Service Manager,
Abbeville Press, 655 Third Avenue, New York, NY 10017, or call 1-800-Artbook.

Visit Abbeville Press online at www.abbeville.com.

ISBN 978-0-7892-1542-0   U.S. $39.95

EAN

9 780789 215420

53995